Landmarks of the Western Heritage

SINCE 1500

LANDMARKS OF THE
Western Heritage
SINCE 1500

Edited by
C. Warren Hollister
University of California, Santa Barbara

JOHN WILEY AND SONS, INC.
New York · London · Sydney

Library of Congress Catalog Card Number: 67-19779
Printed in the United States of America

To Nancy

PREFACE

This book of readings is intended primarily for students in Western Civilization courses. It was prepared in the belief that exposure to a substantial body of original sources provides an essential supplement to the reading of textbooks and modern interpretive studies. Original sources provide a direct encounter with the past that is obtainable in no other way, besides exploring historic sites or examining in museums the cultural products of past ages. Textbooks and lectures enable students to learn about the past; the reading of sources deepens this learning process by enabling students, in some small degree, to *experience* the past. This experience is apt to leave the student with the feeling that history is by no means so neat, simple, and "well-organized" as many textbooks would suggest. The sources raise questions that are yet unsolved or are highly controversial. They illustrate trends and climates of opinion, while at the same time making explicit the exceptions and loose ends that defy the structured categories of the historian. Hence, encounter with the sources is likely to make a Western Civilization course at once more difficult and more authentic.

The selection of sources to be included in a book such as this is necessarily a very difficult process, circumscribed by the limitations of space and dependent on the inclinations and judgments of the individual editor. This book was prepared with certain fundamental ideas in mind. First of all, Western Civilization is far more than a mere sequence of political events. Politics cannot be ignored but must be balanced against social and economic developments and the products of mind and spirit. No proper course in Western Civilization can exclude philosophy or science, economic or political thought, literature or the arts. Painting, sculpture, architecture, and poetry, for example, are almost invariably overlooked in the typical source book, yet they are historical documents of immense significance. Literary and artistic sources will be found here along with the more normal political texts and intellectual treatises, because all are necessary to convey a comprehensive picture of an historical epoch or a cultural milieu.

Finally, in the conviction that a source book should neither substitute for a textbook nor harness the student to the interpretations of the editor, introductory material and editorial comment have been kept to a minimum. By and large, the sources have been left to stand on their own, to challenge the student's judgment and imagination, to supplement lectures in any way that the instructor might devise, and to evoke wide-ranging discussion.

A number of people have given generously of their labors and talents in the preparation of these volumes. I am particularly grateful to Mrs. Barbara Walker and Miss Nancy Unger for their wise and devoted editorial assistance, as well as to Mrs. Betty Iervolino for her patience with detail. Mrs. Mary Ellington and Professor Thomas Reeves contributed their time and perceptive judgment. William L. Gum, editor and friend, shared with me the initial conception of the project and supported it firmly and sympathetically. All of these people made important intellectual contributions to the work. It was, for example, Gum's provocative idea to break with tradition and exclude Woodrow Wilson's often quoted Fourteen Points.

C. Warren Hollister
Santa Barbara, California

ILLUSTRATION CREDITS

SECTION ONE

PART III. A, 1: The Metropolitan Museum of Art, Bequest of Mrs. H. O. Havemeyer, 1929, The H. O. Havemeyer Collection. A, 2: Prado Museum, Madrid.

SECTION TWO

PART II. A, 1: Cliché des Musées Nationaux, Louvre. A, 2: A. G. L.—Art Reference Bureau (*Cathedral, Antwerp*). A, 3: Cliché des Musées Nationaux, Louvre. A, 4: Reproduced by Courtesy of the Trustees, The National Gallery, London. A, 5: National Gallery of Art, Washington, D. C., Widener Collection. A, 6: Reproduced by Courtesy of the Trustees, The National Gallery, London. A, 7: Anderson—Art Reference Bureau. A, 8: Alinari—Art Reference Bureau.

PART III. A, 1: Bulloz—Art Reference Bureau.

SECTION THREE

PART III. A, 1: Marburg—Art Reference Bureau. A, 2: Alinari—Art Reference Bureau (*Vatican Museum*). B, 1: Cliché des Musées Nationaux, Louvre. B, 2: Cliché des Musées Nationaux, Louvre.

SECTION FOUR

PART II. B, 1: Art Reference Bureau (*By kind permission of National Monuments Record*). B, 2: Art Reference Bureau (*By kind permission of National Monuments Record; Copyright Warburg Institute*). C, 1: Cliché des Musées Nationaux, Bordeaux. C, 2: Courtesy, Museum of Fine Arts, Boston, S. A. Denio Collection. C, 3: Courtesy, Museum of Fine Arts, Boston, Henry Lillie Pierce Collection.

PART IV. A, 2: The Bettmann Archive (*Louvre*).

SECTION FIVE

PART II. B, 2: Courtesy of The University of Guadalajara.

SECTION SEVEN

PART II. A, 1: Gamäldegalerie Neue Meister, Dresden. B, 1: Kunsthistorische Museum, Vienna. B, 2: National Gallery of Art, Washington, D. C., Chester Dale Collection. C, 1: Philadelphia Museum of Art, W. P. Wilstach Collection. C, 2: Courtauld Institute Galleries, London (*Lee Collection*). C, 3: Reproduced by Courtesy of the Trustees, The National Gallery, London. C, 4: Collection, The Museum of Modern Art, New York, Acquired through the Lillie P. Bliss Bequest.

SECTION EIGHT

PART I. A, 2: Collection, The Museum of Modern Art, New York, A. Conger Goodyear Fund.

SECTION TEN

PART II. A, 1: Collection, The Museum of Modern Art, New York, Mrs. Simon Guggenheim Fund. A, 2: Collection, The Museum of Modern Art, New York, Mrs. Simon Guggenheim Fund. A, 3: Collection, The Museum of Modern Art, New York. A, 4: Collection of Harry Torczyner, New York; Photo, The Museum of Modern Art, New York. A, 5: Collection, The Museum of Modern Art, New York, Purchase. A, 6: Collection, The Museum of Modern Art, New York, Advisory Committee Fund. B, 1: From the Joseph H. Hirshhorn Collection. B, 2: Collection, The Museum of Modern Art, New York, Van Gogh Purchase Fund. C, 1: Hedrich—Blessing. C, 2: French Government Tourist Office. C, 3: Photograph by Rondal Partridge.

Book design and Section illustrations by Anita L. Duncan.

CONTENTS

The Reformation Era

c. 1500—1600

THE sixteenth century was a revolutionary period in European history, an age of violence and radical change, in which old institutions, old concepts, and old values came under increasing criticism and, in many instances, gave way to new ones. The humanism, antimedievalism, and rigorous scholarship of Renaissance Italy spread northward across the Alps and gave rise to a northern renaissance. The new mood of northern Europe found expression in the rough humor and anticlericalism of Rabelais and the eloquent humanism of Sir Thomas More and Desiderius Erasmus. Both More and Erasmus were critical of the corruption and insensitive complacency of the Church, yet when the crisis came, both numbered themselves among its supporters.

The most spectacular of the sixteenth-century revolutions was the Protestant Reformation. Opposition to the medieval Church, which had been gathering strength for generations, exploded into open religious revolt when Martin Luther posted his ninety-five Theses on the church door at Wittenberg in 1517 and shortly thereafter broke with the papacy. Luther began by opposing abuses such as the selling of indulgences, but very soon came to oppose such fundamental Catholic doctrines as the authority of the living Church, the supremacy of the pope, salvation through good works, and the exclusive sacramental power of the priesthood. To Luther, the Bible was the sole source of Christian revelation, all believers were priests, and salvation was a product of faith alone.

Luther won numerous followers from among the princes and peoples of Germany and Scandinavia. Other Protestant reformers such as Zwingli and John Calvin captured the allegiance of vast numbers of Christians in Switzerland, France, the Netherlands, Scotland, and England. The uncompromising fervor of the Reformation created an atmosphere of intolerance and persecution and gave rise to religious warfare, especially in Germany and France. The English Reformation, although energized by the spread of Calvinism, was very much a product of royal policy, and policy fluctuated wildly as Henry VIII was succeeded by the Protestant Edward VI, the Catholic Mary Tudor, and the moderate pragmatist, Elizabeth I.

By midcentury, the Catholic Church was undergoing a reform of its own, led by the papacy and the new Jesuit Order of St. Ignatius Loyola. The Council of Trent legislated against abuses and tightened and crystalized Catholic doctrine, while Jesuits and Catholic princes sought to reverse the Protestant tide.

The age of the Reformation also witnessed revolutionary developments in European politics. The concept of the sovereign state had prompted several kings and princes to embrace Protestantism and thereby establish unlimited control over the churches of their realms. National sovereignty was manifested by powerful monarchs of the age such as Henry VIII and Elizabeth I of England, Francis I and Henry IV of France, the emperor Charles V, and Philip II of Spain. The sixteenth century was Spain's golden age: her New World empire was unprecedented in extent, her armies dominated the battle-fields of Europe, and her artists and writers achieved a singularly high level of creativity. But Spanish culture was matched by the culture of Elizabethan England—it was the age of Shakespeare, Christopher Marlowe, Ben Jonson, Francis Bacon, and numerous other writers of remarkable ability.

Another revolution, scarcely noticed by most sixteenth-century Europeans, was to have a momentous impact on the evolution of western thought. The Dominican monk Copernicus reversed the order of the universe, by rejecting the age-old geocentric system of the world in favor of a heliocentric system. The earth lost its favored position at the core of the cosmos and became a mere planet. In the very age in which Europe was beginning to assert her mastery over the world, it was discovered that the world was not such an important place after all.

Part I

THE NORTHERN RENAISSANCE

A. The French Humanists

FOUR EXAMPLES ARE INCLUDED to illustrate the development of Renaissance humanism and rationalism in sixteenth-century northern Europe. In all, a common theme is evident: extreme dissatisfaction with contemporary society and a restless yearning for a better and radically different social order. François Rabelais (1490–1553), in his Gargantua and Pantagruel, *satirized in a lusty, exuberant style the medieval ideas and institutions that persisted in the France of his own day. The excerpt given here describes a monastery such as was never seen in medieval Europe—an ideal Renaissance monastery, free of any trace of asceticism—where Castiglione's courtier would have been quite at home.*

1. FRANÇOIS RABELAIS, FROM *GARGANTUA AND PANTAGRUEL*

SOURCE. Samuel Putnam, ed., *The Portable Rabelais,* Samuel Putnam, tr., New York: The Viking Press, 1946, pp. 198–207 and 214–215. Copyright 1946 by The Viking Press, Inc. From *The Complete Works of François Rabelais,* translated by Samuel Putnam. Copyright 1929 by Covici-Friede, Inc. Used by permission of Crown Publishers, Inc.

HOW GARGANTUA HAD THE ABBEY OF THÉLÈME BUILT FOR THE MONK

There remained the monk to provide for. Gargantua wanted to make him Abbot of Seuilly, but the friar refused. He wanted to give him the Abbey of Bourgueil or that of Saint-Florent, whichever might suit him best, or both, if he had a fancy for them. But the monk gave a peremptory reply to the effect that he would not take upon himself any office involving the government of others.

"For how," he demanded, "could I govern others, who cannot even govern myself? If you are of the opinion that I have done you, or may be able to do you in the future, any worthy service, give me leave to found an abbey according to my own plan."

This request pleased Gargantua, and the latter offered his whole province of Thélème, lying along the River Loire, at a distance of two leagues from the great Forest of Port-Huault. The monk then asked that he be permitted to found a convent that should be exactly the opposite of all other institutions of the sort.

"In the first place, then," said Gargantua, "you don't want to build any walls around it; for all the other abbeys have plenty of those."

"Right you are," said the monk, "for where there is a wall (*mur*) in front and behind there is bound to be a lot of *murmur*—ing, jealousy and plotting on the inside."

Moreover, in view of the fact that in certain convents in this world there is a custom, if any woman (by which, I mean any modest or respectable one) enters the place, to clean up thoroughly after her wherever she has been—in view of this fact, a regulation was drawn up to the effect that if any monk or nun should happen to enter this new convent, all the places they had set foot in were to be thoroughly scoured and scrubbed. And since, in other convents, everything is run, ruled, and fixed by hours, it was decreed that in this one there should not be any clock or dial of any sort, but that whatever work there was should be done whenever occasion offered. For, as Gargantua remarked, the greatest loss of time he knew was to watch the hands of the clock. What good came of it? It was the greatest foolishness in the world to regulate one's conduct by the tinkling of a time-piece, instead of by intelligence and good common sense.

Another feature: Since in those days women were not put into convents unless they were blind in one eye, lame, hunchbacked, ugly, misshapen, crazy, silly, deformed, and generally of no account, and since men did not enter a monastery unless they were snotty-nosed, underbred, dunces, and trouble-makers at home—

"Speaking of that," said the monk, "of what use is a woman who is neither good nor good to look at?"

"Put her in a convent," said Gargantua.

"Yes," said the monk, "and set her to making shirts."

And so, it was decided that in this convent they would receive only the pretty ones, the ones with good figures and sunny dispositions, and only the handsome, well set-up, good-natured men.

Item: Since in the convents of women, men never entered, except under-handedly and by stealth, it was provided that, in this one, there should be no women unless there were men also, and no men unless there were also women.

Item: Inasmuch as many men, as well as women, once received into a convent were forced and compelled, after a year of probation, to remain there all the rest of their natural lives—in view of this, it was provided that, here, both men and women should be absolutely free to pick up and leave whenever they happened to feel like it.

Item: Whereas, ordinarily, the religious take three vows, namely, those of chastity, poverty and obedience, it was provided that, in this abbey, one might honorably marry, that each one should be rich, and that all should live in utter freedom.

With regard to the lawful age for entering, the women should be received from the age of ten to fifteen years, the men from the age of twelve to eighteen.

HOW THE ABBEY OF THE THELEMITES WAS BUILT AND ENDOWED

For the building and furnishing of the abbey, Gargantua made a ready-money levy of two-million-seven-hundred-thousand-eight-hundred-thirty-one of the coins known as "big wooly sheep"; and for each year, until everything should be in perfect shape, he turned over, out of the toll-receipts of the Dive River, one-million-six-hundred-sixty-nine-thousand "sunny crowns" and the same number of "seven-chick pieces." For the foundation and support of the abbey, he made a perpetual grant of two-million-three-hundred-sixty-nine-thousand-five-hundred-fourteen "rose nobles," in the form of ground-rent, free and exempt of all encumbrances, and payable every year at the abbey gate, all of this being duly witnessed in the form of letters of conveyance.

As for the building itself, it was in the form of a hexagon, so constructed that at every corner there was a great round tower sixty paces in diameter, all these being of the same size and appearance. The River Loire flowed along the north elevation. Upon the bank of this river stood one of the towers, named Arctic, while, proceeding toward the east, there was another, named Calaer, following it another, named Anatole, then another, named Mesembrine, another after it, named Hesperia, and finally, one named Cryere. Between every two towers, there was a distance of three-hundred-twelve paces. To the building proper, there were six stories in all, counting the underground cellars as one. The second story was vaulted, in the form of a basket-handle. The rest were stuccoed with plaster of Paris, in the manner of lamp-bottoms, the roof being covered over with a fine slate, while the ridge-coping was lead, adorned with little mannikins and animal-figures, well grouped and gilded. The eaves-troughs, which jutted out from the walls, between the mullioned windows, were painted with diagonal gold-and-blue figures, all the way down to the ground, where they ended in huge rain-spouts, all of which led under the house to the river.

This building was a hundred times more magnificent than the one at Bonivet, at Chambord, or at Chantilly; for in it there were nine-thousand-three-hundred-thirty-two rooms, each equipped with a dressing-room, a study, a wardrobe, and a chapel, and each opening into a large hall. Between the towers, in the center of the main building, was a winding-stair, the steps of which were partly of porphyry, partly of Numidian stone, and partly of serpentine marble, each step being twenty-two feet long and three fingers thick, with an even dozen between each pair of landings. On each landing were two fine antique arches, admitting the daylight, while through these arches, one entered a loggia of the width of the stair, the stair itself running all the way to the roof and ending in a pavilion. From this stair one could enter, from either side, a large hall, and from this hall the rooms.

From the tower known as Arctic to the one called Cryere, there were fine large libraries, in Greek, Latin, Hebrew, French, Tuscan, and Spanish, separated from each other according to the different languages. In the middle of the building was another and marvelous stairway, the entrance to which was from outside the house, by way of an arch thirty-six feet wide. This stair was so symmetrical and capacious that six men-at-arms, their lances at rest, could ride up abreast, all the way to the roof. From the tower Anatole to Mesembrine, there were large and splendid galleries, all containing paintings representative of deeds of ancient prowess, along with historical and geographical scenes. In the center of this elevation was still another gateway and stair, like the one on the river-side. Over this gate, there was inscribed, in large old-fashioned letters, the following poem:

INSCRIPTION OVER THE GREAT PORTAL OF THÉLÈME

You hypocrites and two-faced, please stay out:
Grinning old apes, potbellied snivelbeaks,
Stiffnecks and blockheads, worse than Goths, no doubt,
Magogs and Ostrogoths we read about;
You hairshirt whiners and you slippered sneaks;
You fur-lined beggars and you nervy freaks;
You bloated dunces, trouble-makers all;
Go somewhere else to open up your stall.

    Your cursed ways
    Would fill my peaceful days
    With nasty strife;
    With your lying life,
    You'd spoil my roundelays—
    With your cursed ways.

Stay out, you lawyers, with your endless guts,
You clerks and barristers, you public pests,
You Scribes and Pharisees, with your "if's" and "but's,"
You hoary judges (Lord, how each one struts!):
You feed, like dogs, on squabbles and bequests;
You'll find your salary in the hangman's nests;
Go there and bray, for here there is no guile
That you can take to court, to start a trial.

    No trials or jangles
    Or legal wrangles:
    We're here to be amused.
    If your jaws must be used,
    You've bags full of tangles,
    Trials and jangles.

Stay out, you usurers and misers all,
Gluttons for gold, and how you hoard the stuff!
Greedy windjammers, with a world of gall,
Hunchbacked, snubnosed, your money-jars full, you bawl
For more and more; you never have enough;
Your stomachs never turn, for they are tough,
As you heap your piles, each miser-faced poltroon:
I hope Old Death effaces you, right soon!

    That inhuman mug
    Makes us shrug:
    Take it to another shop,
    And please don't stop,
    But elsewhere lug
    That inhuman mug!

Stay out of here, at morning, noon and night,
Jealous old curs, dotards that whine and moan,
All trouble-makers, full of stubborn spite,
Phantom avengers of a Husband's plight,
Whether Greek or Latin, worst wolves ever known;
You syphilitics, mangy to the bone,
Go take your wolfish sores, and let them feed at ease—
Those cakey crusts, signs of a foul disease.

    Honor, praise, delight
    Rule here, day and night;
    We're gay, and we agree;
    We're healthy, bodily;
    And so, we have a right
    To honor, praise, delight.

But welcome here, and very welcome be,
And doubly welcome, all noble gentlemen.
This is the place where taxes all are free,
And incomes plenty, to live merrily,
However fast you come—I shan't "say when":
Then, be my cronies in this charming den;
Be spruce and jolly, gay and always mellow,
Each one of us a very pleasant fellow.

    Companions clean,
    Refined, serene,
    Free from avarice;
    For civilized bliss,
    See, the tools are keen,
    Companions clean.

And enter here, all you who preach and teach
The living Gospel, though the heathen raves:
You'll find a refuge here beyond their reach,
Against the hostile error you impeach,
Which through the world spreads poison, and depraves;
Come in, for here we found a faith that saves;
By voice and letter, let's confound the herd
Of enemies of God's own Holy Word.

    The word of grace
    We'll not efface
    From this holy place;
    Let each embrace,
    And himself enlace
    With the word of grace.

Enter, also, ladies of high degree!
Feel free to enter and be happy here,
Each face with beauty flowering heavenly,
With upright carriage, pleasing modesty:
This is the house where honor's held most dear,
Gift of a noble lord whom we revere,
Our patron, who's established it for you,
And given us his gold, to see it through.

    Gold given by gift
    Gives golden shrift—
    To the giver a gift,
    And very fine thrift,
    A wise man's shift,
    Is gold given by gift. . . .

HOW THE THELEMITES WERE GOVERNED IN THEIR MODE OF LIVING

Their whole life was spent, not in accordance with laws, statutes, or rules, but according to their own will and free judgment. They rose from bed when they felt like it and drank, ate, worked, and slept when the desire came to them. No one woke them, no one forced them to drink or eat or do any other thing. For this was the system that Gargantua had established. In the rule of their order there was but this one clause:

DO WHAT THOU WOULDST

for the reason that those who are free born and well born, well brought up, and used to decent society possess, by nature, a certain instinct and spur, which always impels them to virtuous deeds and restrains them from vice, an instinct which is the thing called honor. These same ones, when, through vile subjection and constraint, they are repressed and held down, proceed to employ that same noble inclination to virtue in throwing off and breaking the yoke of servitude, for we always want to come to forbidden things; and we always desire that which is denied us.

In the enjoyment of their liberty, the Thelemites entered into a laudable emulation in doing, all of them, anything which they thought would be pleasing to one of their number. If anyone, male or female, remarked: "Let us drink," they all drank. If anyone said: "Let us play," they all played. If anyone suggested: "Let us go find some sport in the fields," they all went there. If it was hawking or hunting, the ladies went mounted upon pretty and easy-paced nags or proud-stepping palfreys, each of them bearing upon her daintily gloved wrist a sparrow-hawk, a lanneret, or a merlin. The men carried the other birds.

They were all so nobly educated that there was not, in their whole number, a single one, man or woman, who was not able to read, write, sing, play musical instruments, and speak five or six languages, composing in these languages both poetry and prose.

In short, there never were seen knights so bold, so gallant, so clever on horse and on foot, more vigorous, or more adept at handling all kinds of weapons than were they. There never were seen ladies so well groomed, so pretty, less boring, or more skilled at hand and needlework and in every respectable feminine activity.

THE RENAISSANCE DEVOTION to Classical letters is wittily expressed in "To His Valet" by the French poet Pierre de Ronsard (1524–85).

2. PIERRE DE RONSARD, "TO HIS VALET"

SOURCE. *Songs & Sonnets of Pierre de Ronsard*, Curtis Hidden Page, tr., Boston: Houghton Mifflin Company, 1903.

I want three days to read the Iliad through!
  So, Corydon, close fast my chamber door.
  If anything should bother me before
I've done, I swear you'll have somewhat to rue!

No! not the servant, nor your mate, nor you
  Shall come to make the bed or clean the floor.
  I must have three good quiet days—or four.
Then I'll make merry for a week or two.

Ah! but—if any one should come from HER,
  Admit him quickly! Be no loiterer,
  But come and make me brave for his receiving.

But no one else!—not friends or nearest kin!
  Though an Olympian God should seek me, leaving
  His Heaven, shut fast the door! Don't let him in!

B. More and Erasmus

THE ENGLISH HUMANIST Sir Thomas More criticized the ways of sixteenth-century Europe by describing an ideal, rationally governed island commonwealth, free of ostentation and hypocrisy.

1. SIR THOMAS MORE, FROM *UTOPIA*

SOURCE. Sir Thomas More, *Utopia*, Edward Surtz, S. J., ed., New Haven: Yale University Press, 1964, pp. 67–75, and 77. Copyright 1964 by Yale University Press. Reprinted by permission of Yale University Press.

THE OFFICIALS

Every thirty families choose annually an official whom in their ancient language they call a syphogrant but in their newer a phylarch. Over ten syphogrants with their families is set a person once called a tranibor but now a protophylarch. The whole body of syphogrants, in number two hundred, having sworn to choose the man whom they judge most useful, by secret balloting appoint a governor, specifically one of the four candidates named to them by the people, for one is selected out of each of the four quarters of the city to be commended to the senate.

The governor holds office for life, unless ousted on suspicion of aiming at a tyranny. The tranibors are elected annually but are not changed without good reason. The other officials all hold their posts for one year.

The tranibors enter into consultation with the governor every other day and sometimes, if need arises, oftener. They take counsel about the commonwealth. If there are any disputes between private persons—there are very few—they settle them without loss of time. They always admit to the senate chamber two syphogrants, and different ones every day. It is provided that nothing concerning the commonwealth be ratified if it has not been discussed in the senate three days before the passing of the decree. To take counsel on matters of common interest outside the senate or the popular assembly is considered a capital offense. The object of these measures, they say, is to prevent it from being easy, by a conspiracy between the governor and the tranibors and by tyrannous oppression of the people, to change the order of the commonwealth. Therefore whatever is considered important is laid before the assembly of the syphogrants who, after informing their groups of families, take counsel together and report their decision to the senate. Sometimes the matter is laid before the council of the whole island.

In addition, the senate has the custom of debating nothing on the same day on which it is first proposed but of putting it off till the next meeting. This is their rule lest anyone, after hastily blurting out the first thought that popped into his head, should afterwards give more thought to defending his opinion than to supporting what is for the good of the commonwealth, and should prefer to jeopardize the public welfare rather than to risk his reputation through a wrongheaded and misplaced shame, fearing he might be thought to have shown too little foresight at the first—though he should have been enough foresighted at the first to speak with prudence rather than with haste!

OCCUPATIONS

Agriculture is the one pursuit which is common to all, both men and women, without exception. They are all instructed in it from childhood, partly by principles taught in school, partly by field trips to the farms closer to the city as if for recreation. Here they do not merely look on, but, as opportunity arises for bodily exercise, they do the actual work.

Besides agriculture (which is, as I said, common to all), each is taught one particular craft as his own. This is generally either wool-working or linen-making or masonry or metal-working or carpentry. There is no other pursuit which occupies any number worth mentioning. As for clothes, these are of one and the same pattern throughout the island and down the centuries, though there is a distinction between the sexes and between the single and married. The garments are comely to the eye, convenient for bodily movement, and fit for wear in heat and cold. Each family, I say, does its own tailoring.

Of the other crafts, one is learned by each person, and not the men only, but the women too. The latter as the weaker sex have the lighter occupations and generally work wool and flax. To the men are committed the remaining more laborious crafts. For the most part, each is brought up in his father's craft, for which most have a natural inclination. But if anyone is attracted to another occupation, he is transferred by adoption to a family pursuing that craft for which he has a liking. Care is taken not only by his father but by the authorities, too, that he will be assigned to a grave and honorable householder. Moreover, if anyone after being thoroughly taught one craft desires another also, the same permission is given. Having acquired both, he practices his choice unless the city has more need of the one than the other.

The chief and almost the only function of the syphogrants is to manage and provide that no one sit idle, but that each apply himself industriously to his trade, and yet that he be not wearied like a beast of burden with constant toil from early morning till late at night. Such wretchedness is worse than the lot of slaves, and yet it is almost everywhere the life of workingmen—except for the Utopians. The latter divide the day and night into twenty-four equal hours and assign only six to work. There are three before noon, after which they go to dinner. After dinner, when they have rested for two hours in the afternoon, they again give three to work and finish up with supper. Counting one o'clock as beginning at midday, they go to bed about eight o'clock, and sleep claims eight hours.

The intervals between the hours of work, sleep, and food are left to every man's discretion, not to waste in revelry or idleness, but to devote the time free from work to some other occupation according to taste. These periods are commonly devoted to intellectual pursuits. For it is their custom that public lectures are daily delivered in the hours before daybreak. Attendance is compulsory only for those who have been specially chosen to devote themselves to learning. A great number of all classes, however, both males and females, flock to hear the lectures, some to one and some to another, according to their natural inclination. But if anyone should prefer to devote this time to his trade, as is the case with many minds which do not reach the level for any of the higher intellectual disciplines, he is not hindered; in fact, he is even praised as useful to the commonwealth.

After supper they spend one hour in recreation, in summer in the gardens, in winter in the common halls in which they have their meals. There they either play music or entertain themselves with conversation. Dice and that kind of foolish and ruinous game they are not acquainted with. They do play two games not unlike chess. The first is a battle of numbers in which one number plunders another. The second is a game in which the vices fight a pitched battle with the virtues. In the latter is exhibited very cleverly, to begin with, both the strife of the vices with one another and their concerted opposition to the virtues; then, what vices are opposed to what virtues, by what forces they assail them openly, by what stratagems they attack them indirectly, by what safeguards the virtues check the power of the vices, by what arts they frustrate their designs; and, finally, by what means the one side gains the victory.

But here, lest you be mistaken, there is one point you must examine more closely. Since they devote but six hours to work, you might possibly think the consequence to be some scarcity of necessities. But so far is this from being the case that the aforesaid time is not only enough but more than enough for a supply of all that is requisite for either the necessity or the convenience of living. This phenomenon you too will understand if you consider how large a part of the population in other countries exists without working. First, there are almost all the women, who constitute half the whole; or, where the women are busy, there as a rule the men are snoring in their stead. Besides, how great and how lazy is the crowd of priests and so-called religious! Add to them all the rich, especially the masters of estates, who are commonly termed gentlemen and noblemen. Reckon with them their retainers—I mean, that whole rabble of good-for-nothing swashbucklers. Finally, join in the lusty and sturdy beggars who make some disease an excuse for idleness. You will certainly find far less numerous than you had supposed those whose labor produces all the articles that mortals require for daily use.

Now estimate how few of those who do work are occupied in essential trades. For, in a society where we make money the standard of everything, it is necessary to practice many crafts which are quite vain and superfluous, ministering only to luxury and licentiousness. Suppose the host of those who now toil were distributed over only as few crafts as the few needs and conveniences demanded by nature. In the great abundance of commodities which must then arise, the prices set on them would be too low for the craftsmen to earn their livelihood by their work. But suppose all those fellows who are not busied with unprofitable crafts, as well as all the lazy and idle throng, any one of whom now consumes as much of the fruits of other men's labors as any two of the workingmen, were all set to work and indeed to useful work. You can easily see how small an allowance of time would be enough and to spare for the production of all that is required by necessity or comfort (or even pleasure, provided it be genuine and natural).

The very experience of Utopia makes the latter clear. In the whole city and its neighborhood, exemption from work is granted to hardly five hundred of the total of men and women whose age and strength make them fit for work. Among them the syphogrants, though legally exempted from work, yet take no advantage of this privilege so that by their example they may the more readily attract the others to work. The same exemption is enjoyed by those whom the people, persuaded by the recommendation of the priests, have given perpetual freedom from labor through the secret vote of the syphogrants so that they may learn thoroughly the various branches of knowledge. But if any of these scholars falsifies the hopes entertained of him, he is reduced to the rank of workingman. On the other hand, not seldom does it happen that a craftsman so industriously employs his spare hours on learning and makes such progress by his diligence that he is relieved of his manual labor and advanced into the class of men of learning. It is out of this company of scholars that they choose ambassadors, priests, tranibors, and finally the governor himself, whom they call in their ancient tongue Barzanes but in their more modern language Ademus.

Nearly all the remaining populace being neither idle nor busied with useless occupations, it is easy to calculate how much good work can be produced in a very few hours. . . .

In the matter of clothing, too, see how little toil and labor is needed. First, while at work, they are dressed unpretentiously in leather or hide, which lasts for seven years. When they go out in public, they put on a cape to hide their comparatively rough working clothes. This garment is of one color throughout the island and that the natural color. Consequently not only is much less woolen cloth needed than elsewhere, but what they have is much less expensive. On the other hand, since linen cloth is made with less labor, it is more used. In linen cloth only whiteness, in woolen cloth only cleanliness, is considered. No value is set on fineness of thread. So it comes about that, whereas elsewhere one man is not satisfied with four or five woolen coats of different colors and as many silk shirts, and the more fastidious not even with ten, in Utopia a man is content with a single cape, lasting generally for two years. There is no reason, of course, why he should desire more, for if he had them he would not be better fortified against the cold nor appear better dressed in the least.

Wherefore, seeing that they are all busied with useful trades and are satisfied with fewer products from them, it even happens that when there is an abundance of all commodities, they sometimes take out a countless number of people to repair whatever public roads are in bad order. Often, too, when there is nothing even of this kind of work to be done, they announce publicly that there will be fewer hours of work. For the authorities do not keep the citizens against their will at superfluous labor since the constitution of their commonwealth looks in the first place to this sole object: that for all the citizens, as far as the public needs permit, as much time as possible should be withdrawn from the service of the body and devoted to the freedom and culture of the mind. It is in the latter that they deem the happiness of life to consist.

SOCIAL RELATIONS

But now, it seems, I must explain the behavior of the citizens toward one another, the nature of their social relations, and the method of distribution of goods. Since the city consists of households, households as a rule are made up of those related by blood. Girls, upon reaching womanhood and upon being settled in marriage, go to their husbands' domiciles. On the other hand, male children and then grandchildren remain in the family and are subject to the oldest parent, unless he has become a dotard with old age. In the latter case the next oldest is put in his place. . . .

Every city is divided into four equal districts. In the middle of each quarter is a market of all kinds of commodities. To designated market buildings the products of each family are conveyed. Each kind of goods is arranged separately in storehouses. From the latter any head of a household seeks what he and his require and, without money or any kind of compensation, carries off what he seeks. Why should anything be refused? First, there is a plentiful supply of all things and, secondly, there is no underlying fear that anyone will demand more than he needs. Why should there be any suspicion that someone may demand an excessive amount when he is certain of never being in want? No doubt about it, avarice and greed are aroused in every kind of living creature by the fear of want, but only in man are they motivated by pride alone— pride which counts it a personal glory to excel others by superfluous display of possessions. The latter vice can have no place at all in the Utopian scheme of things.

DESIDERIUS ERASMUS DEDICATED his Praise of Folly *to his friend Sir Thomas More, and in it he attacked directly some of the very things that More, in his* Utopia, *had attacked by implication: the pretense and pomposity of great secular and ecclesiastical leaders—kings and popes, nobles and cardinals who lived like peacocks and neglected the profound responsibilities of their offices.*

2. DESIDERIUS ERASMUS, FROM *THE PRAISE OF FOLLY*

SOURCE. Desiderius Erasmus, *The Praise of Folly,* John Wilson, tr., Ann Arbor: University of Michigan Press, 1958, pp. 110–118. Reprinted by permission of University of Michigan Press.

And now I have a mind to give some small touches of princes and courts, of whom I am had in reverence, aboveboard and, as it becomes gentlemen, frankly. And truly, if they had the least proportion of sound judgment, what life were more unpleasant than theirs, or so much to be avoided? For whoever did but truly weigh with himself how great a burden lies upon his shoulders that would truly discharge the duty of a prince, he would not think it worth his while to make his way to a crown by perjury and parricide. He would consider that he that takes a scepter in his hand should manage the public, not his private, interest; study nothing but the common good; and not in the least go contrary to those laws whereof himself is both the author and exactor: that he is to take an account of the good or evil administration of all his magistrates and subordinate officers; that, though he is but one, all men's eyes are upon him, and in his power it is, either like a good planet to give life and safety to mankind by his harmless influence, or like a fatal comet to send mischief and destruction; that the vices of other men are not alike felt, nor so generally communicated; and that a prince stands in that place that his least deviation from the rule of honesty and honor reaches farther than himself and opens a gap to many men's ruin. Besides, that the fortune of princes has many things attending it that are but too apt to train them out of the way, as pleasure, liberty, flattery, excess; for which cause he should the more diligently endeavor and set a watch over himself, lest perhaps he be led aside and fail in his duty. Lastly, to say nothing of treasons, ill will, and such other mischiefs he's in jeopardy of, that that True King is over his head, who in a short time will call him to account for every the least trespass, and that so much the more severely by how much more mighty was the empire committed to his charge. These and the like if a prince should duly weigh, and weigh it he would if he were wise, he would neither be able to sleep nor take any hearty repast.

But now by my courtesy they leave all this care to the gods and are only taken up with themselves, not admitting anyone to their ear but such as know how to speak pleasant things and not trouble them with business. They believe they have discharged all the duty of a prince if they hunt every day, keep a stable of fine horses, sell dignities and commanderies, and invent new ways of draining the citizens' purses and bringing it into their own exchequer; but under such dainty new-found names that though the thing be most unjust in itself, it carries yet some face of equity; adding to this some little sweet'nings that whatever happens, they may be secure of the common people. And now suppose someone, such as they sometimes are, a man ignorant of laws, little less than an enemy to the public good, and minding nothing but his own, given up to pleasure, a hater of learning, liberty, and justice, studying nothing less than the public safety, but measuring everything by his own will and profit; and then put on him a golden chain that declares the accord of all virtues linked one to another; a crown set with diamonds, that should put him in mind how he ought to excel all others in heroic virtues; besides a scepter, the emblem of justice and an untainted heart; and lastly, a purple robe, a badge of that charity he owes the commonwealth. All which if a prince should compare them with his own life, he would, I believe, be clearly ashamed of his bravery, and be afraid lest some or other gibing expounder turn all this tragical furniture into a ridiculous laughingstock.

And as to the court lords, what should I mention them? than most of whom though there be nothing more indebted, more servile, more witless, more contemptible, yet they would seem as they were the most excellent of all others. And yet in this only thing no men more modest, in that they are contented to wear about them gold, jewels, purple, and those other marks of virtue and wisdom; but for the study of the things themselves, they remit it to others, thinking it happiness enough for them that they can call the king master, have learned the cringe *à la mode*, know when and where to use those titles of Your Grace, My Lord, Your Magnificence; in a word that they are past all shame and can flatter pleasantly. For these are the arts that speak a man truly noble and an exact courtier. But if you look into their manner of life you'll find them mere sots, as debauched as Penelope's wooers; you know the other part of the verse, which the echo will better tell you than I can. They sleep till noon and have their mercenary Levite come to their bedside, where he chops over his matins before they are half up. Then to breakfast, which is scarce done but dinner stays for them. From thence they go to dice, tables, cards, or entertain themselves with jesters, fools, gambols, and horse tricks. In the meantime they have one or two beverages, and then supper, and after that a banquet, and 'twere well, by Jupiter, there were no more than one. And in this manner do their hours, days, months, years, age slide away without the least irksomeness. Nay, I have sometimes gone away many inches fatter, to see them speak big words; while each of the ladies believes herself so much nearer to the gods by how much the longer train she trails after her; while one nobleman edges out another, that he may get the nearer to Jupiter himself; and everyone of them pleases himself the more by how much more massive is the chain he swags on his shoulders, as if he meant to show his strength as well as his wealth.

Nor are princes by themselves in their manner of life, since popes, cardinals, and bishops have so diligently followed their steps that they've almost got the start of them. For if any of them would consider what their Albe should put them in mind of, to wit a blameless life; what is meant by their forked miters, whose each point is held in by the same knot, we'll suppose it a perfect knowledge of the Old and New Testaments; what those gloves on their hands, but a sincere administration of the Sacraments, and free from all touch of worldly business; what their crosier, but a careful looking after the flock committed to their charge; what the cross born before them, but victory over all earthly affections—these, I say, and many of the like kind should anyone truly consider, would he not live a sad and troublesome life? Whereas now they do well enough while they feed themselves only, and for the care of their flock either put it over to Christ or lay it all on their suffragans, as they call them, or some poor vicars. Nor do they so much as remember their name, or what the word bishop signifies, to wit, labor, care, and trouble. But in racking to gather money they truly act the part of bishops, and herein acquit themselves to be no blind seers.

In like manner cardinals, if they thought themselves the successors of the apostles, they would likewise imagine that the same things the other did are required of them, and that they are not lords but dispensers of spiritual things of which they must shortly give an exact account. But if they also would a little philosophize on their habit and think with themselves what's the meaning of their linen rochet, is it not a remarkable and singular integrity of life? What that inner purple; is it not an earnest and fervent love of God? Or what that outward, whose loose plaits and long train fall round his Reverence's mule and are large enough to cover a camel; is it not charity that spreads itself so wide to the succor of all men? that is, to instruct, exhort, comfort, reprehend, admonish, compose wars, resist wicked princes, and willingly expend not only their wealth but their very lives for the flock of Christ: though yet what need at all of wealth to them that supply the room of the poor apostles? These things, I say, did they but duly consider, they would not be so ambitious of that dignity; or, if they were, they would willingly leave it and live a laborious, careful life, such as was that of the ancient apostles.

And for popes, that supply the place of Christ, if they should endeavor to imitate His life, to wit His poverty, labor, doctrine, cross, and contempt of life, or should they consider what the name pope, that is father, or holiness, imports, who would live more disconsolate than themselves? or who would purchase that chair with all his substance? or defend it, so purchased, with swords, poisons, and all force imaginable? so great a profit would the access of wisdom deprive him of—wisdom did I say? nay, the least corn of that salt which Christ speaks of: so much wealth, so much honor, so much riches, so many victories, so many offices, so many dispensations, so much tribute, so many pardons; such horses, such mules, such guards, and so much pleasure would it lose them. You see how much I have comprehended in a little: instead of which it would bring in watchings, fastings, tears, prayers, sermons, good endeavors, sighs, and a thousand the like troublesome exercises. Nor is this least considerable: so many scribes, so many copying clerks, so many notaries, so many advocates, so many promoters, so many secretaries, so many muleteers, so many grooms, so many bankers: in short, that vast multitude of men that overcharge the Roman See—I mistook, I meant honor—might beg their bread.

A most inhuman and economical thing, and more to be execrated, that those great princes of the Church and true lights of the world should be reduced to a staff and a wallet. Whereas now, if there be anything that requires their pains, they leave that to Peter and Paul that have leisure enough; but if there by anything of honor or pleasure, they take that to themselves. By which means it is, yet by my courtesy, that scarce any kind of men live more voluptuously or with less trouble; as believing that Christ will be well enough pleased if in their mystical and almost mimical pontificality, ceremonies, titles of holiness and the like, and blessing and cursing, they play the parts of bishops. To work miracles is old and antiquated, and not in fashion now; to instruct the people, troublesome; to interpret the Scripture, pedantic; to pray, a sign one has little else to do; to shed tears, silly and womanish; to be poor, base; to be vanquished, dishonorable and little becoming him that scarce admits even kings to kiss his slipper; and lastly, to die, uncouth; and to be stretched on a cross, infamous.

Part II

THE REFORMATION

A. Protestant Thought

IT WAS NOT THE HUMANISTS AS SUCH, but the Protestant reformers who transformed Europe; they did so in a way that shocked and alienated men like More and Erasmus, who dreamed of a purified Church rather than a shattered one. Many of Luther's basic doctrines on Church, state, and salvation are presented in our first two selections: the Ninety-Five Theses of 1517, Luther's first formal attack against Catholicism (1), which was a criticism of abuses, rather than a challenge to the basic integrity of the Church; and, excerpts from a subsequent treatise of Luther, On the Babylonish Captivity of the Church (1520), *in which he carries his attack much further and breaks openly with Rome (2).*

1. MARTIN LUTHER, NINETY-FIVE THESES

SOURCE. J. H. Robinson, ed., *Translations and Reprints from the Original Sources of European History*, II, No. 6, Philadelphia: University of Pennsylvania Press, 1894. Reprinted by permission of the University of Pennsylvania Press.

In the desire and with the purpose of elucidating the truth, a disputation will be held on the underwritten propositions at Wittenberg, under the presidency of the Reverend Father Martin Luther, Monk of the Order of St. Augustine, Master of Arts and of Sacred Theology, and ordinary Reader of the same in that place. He therefore asks those who cannot be present and discuss the subject with us orally, to do so by letter in their absence. In the name of our Lord Jesus Christ. Amen.

1. Our Lord and Master Jesus Christ in saying "Repent ye," etc., intended that the whole life of believers should be penitence.

2. This word cannot be understood as sacramental penance, that is, of the confession and satisfaction which are performed under the ministry of priests.

3. It does not, however, refer solely to inward penitence; nay, such

inward penitence is naught, unless it outwardly produces various mortifications of the flesh.

4. The penalty thus continues as long as the hatred of self (that is, true inward penitence); namely, till our entrance into the kingdom of heaven.

5. The pope has neither the will nor the power to remit any penalties except those which he has imposed by his own authority, or by that of the canons.

6. The Pope has no power to remit any guilt, except by declaring and warranting it to have been remitted by God; or at most by remitting cases reserved for himself; in which cases, if his power were despised, guilt would certainly remain.

7. Certainly God remits no man's guilt without at the same time subjecting him, humbled in all things, to the authority of his representative the priest.

8. The penitential canons are imposed only on the living, and no burden ought to be imposed on the dying, according to them.

9. Hence, the Holy Spirit acting in the Pope does well for us in that, in his decrees, he always makes exception of the article of death and of necessity.

10. Those priests act unlearnedly and wrongly who, in the case of the dying, reserve the canonical penances for Purgatory.

11. Those tares about changing the canonical penalty into the penalty of Purgatory seem surely to have been sown while the bishops were asleep.

12. Formerly the canonical penalties were imposed not after but before absolution, as tests of true contrition.

13. The dying pay all penalties by death, and are already dead to the canon laws, and are by right relieved from them.

14. The imperfect vigor or love of a dying person necessarily brings with it great fear, and the less it is, the greater the fear it brings.

15. This fear and horror is sufficient by itself, to say nothing of other things, to constitute the pains of Purgatory, since it is very near to the horror of despair.

16. Hell, Purgatory, and Heaven appear to differ as despair, almost despair, and peace of mind differ.

17. With souls in Purgatory it seems that it must needs be that as horror diminishes so love increases.

18. Nor does it seem to be proved by any reasoning or any Scriptures, that they are outside of the state of merit or of the increase of love.

19. Nor does this appear to be proved, that they are sure and confident of their own blessedness, at least all of them, though we may be very sure of it.

20. Therefore the Pope, when he speaks of the plenary remission of all penalties, does not mean really of all, but only of those imposed by himself.

21. Thus those preachers of indulgences are in error who say that by the indulgences of the Pope a man is freed and saved from all punishment.

22. For in fact he remits to souls in Purgatory no penalty which they would have had to pay in this life according to the canons.

23. If any entire remission of all penalties can be granted to any one it is certain that it is granted to none but the most perfect, that is to very few.

24. Hence, the greater part of the people must needs be deceived by his indiscriminate and high-sounding promise of release from penalties.

25. Such power over Purgatory as the Pope has in general, such has every bishop in his own diocese, and every parish priest in his own parish, in particular.

26. The Pope acts most rightly in granting remission to souls not by the power of the keys (which is of no avail in this case), but by the way of intercession.

27. They preach man who say that the soul flies out of Purgatory as soon as the money thrown into the chest rattles.

28. It is certain that, when the money rattles in the chest, avarice and gain may be increased, but the effect of the intercession of the Church depends on the will of God alone.

29. Who knows whether all the souls in Purgatory desire to be re-deemed from it—witness the story told of Saints Severinus and Paschal?

30. No man is sure of the reality of his own contrition, much less of the attainment of plenary remission.

31. Rare as is a true penitent, so rare is one who truly buys indul-gences—that is to say, most rare.

32. Those who believe that, through letters of pardon, they are made sure of their own salvation will be eternally damned along with their teachers.

33. We must especially beware of those who say that these pardons from the Pope are that inestimable gift of God by which man is recon-ciled to God.

34. For the grace conveyed by these pardons has respect only to the penalties of sacramental satisfaction, which are of human appointment.

35. They preach no Christian doctrine who teach that contrition is not necessary for those who buy souls (out of Purgatory) or buy confes-sional licenses.

36. Every Christian who feels true compunction has of right plenary remission of punishment and guilt even without letters of pardon.

37. Every true Christian, whether living or dead, has a share in all the benefits of Christ and of the Church, given by God, even without letters of pardon.

38. The remission, however, imparted by the Pope is by no means to be despised, since it is, as I have said, a declaration of the divine remission.

39. It is a most difficult thing, even for the most learned theologians, to exalt at the same time in the eyes of the people the ample effect of pardons and the necessity of true contrition.

40. True contrition seeks and loves punishment; while the ampleness of pardons relaxes it, and causes men to hate it, or at least gives occasion for them to do so.

41. Apostolic pardons ought to be proclaimed with caution, lest the people should falsely suppose that they are placed before other good works of charity.

42. Christians should be taught that it is not the wish of the Pope that the buying of pardons should be in any way compared to works of mercy.

43. Christians should be taught that he who gives to a poor man, or lends to a needy man, does better than if he bought pardons.

44. Because by works of charity, charity increases, and the man becomes better; while by means of pardons, he does not become better, but only freer from punishment.

45. Christians should be taught that he who sees any one in need, and, passing him by, gives money for pardons, is not purchasing for himself the indulgences of the Pope but the anger of God.

46. Christians should be taught that, unless they have superfluous wealth, they are bound to keep what is necessary for the use of their own households, and by no means to lavish it on pardons.

47. Christians should be taught that while they are free to buy pardons they are not commanded to do so.

48. Christians should be taught that the Pope, in granting pardons, has both more need and more desire that devout prayer should be made for him than that the money should be readily paid.

49. Christians should be taught that the Pope's pardons are useful if they do not put their trust in them, but most hurtful if through them they lose the fear of God.

50. Christians should be taught that, if the Pope were acquainted with the exactions of the Preachers of pardons, he would prefer that the Basilica of St. Peter should be burnt to ashes rather than that it should be built up with the skin, flesh, and bones of his sheep.

51. Christians should be taught that as it would be the duty so would it be the wish of the Pope even to sell, if necessary, the Basilica of St. Peter, and to give of his own money to very many of those from whom the preachers of pardons extract money.

52. Vain is the hope of salvation through letters of pardon, even if a commissary—nay, the Pope himself—were to pledge his own soul for them.

53. They were enemies of Christ and of the Pope who, in order that the pardons may be preached, condemn the Word of God to utter silence in other churches.

54. Wrong is done to the Word of God when, in the same sermon, an equal or longer time is spent on pardons than on it.

55. The mind of the Pope necessarily is that, if pardons, which are a very small matter, are celebrated with single bells, single processions, and single ceremonies, the Gospel, which is a very great matter, should be preached with a hundred bells, a hundred processions, and a hundred ceremonies.

56. The treasures of the Church, whence the Pope grants indulgences, are neither sufficiently named nor known among the people of Christ.

57. It is clear that they are at least not temporal treasures, for these are not so readily lavished, but only accumulated, by means of the preachers.

58. Nor are they the merits of Christ and of the saints, for these, independently of the Pope, are always working grace to the inner man, and the cross, death, and hell to the outer man.

59. St. Lawrence said that the treasures of the Church are the poor of the Church, but he spoke according to the use of the term in his time.

60. We are not speaking rashly when we say that the keys of the Church, bestowed through the merits of Christ, are that treasure.

61. For it is clear that the power of the Pope is sufficient of itself for the remission of [canonical] penalties and of [reserved] cases.

62. The true treasure of the Church is the Holy Gospel of the glory and grace of God.

63. This treasure, however, is deservedly most hateful, because it makes the first to be last.

64. While the treasure of indulgences is deservedly most acceptable, because it makes the last to be first.

65. Hence the treasures of the Gospel are nets, wherewith of old they fished for the men of riches.

66. The treasures of indulgences are nets, wherewith they now fish for the riches of men.

67. Those indulgences, which the preachers loudly proclaim to be

the greatest graces, are seen to be truly such as regards the promotion of gain.

68. Yet they are in reality most insignificant when compared to the grace of God and the piety of the cross.

69. Bishops and parish priests are bound to receive the commissaries of apostolical pardons with all reverence.

70. But they are still more bound to see to it with all their eyes, and take heed with all their ears, that these men do not preach their own dreams in place of the Pope's commission.

71. He who speaks against the truth of apostolical pardons, let him be anathema and accursed.

72. But he, on the other hand, who exerts himself against the wantonness and license of speech of the preachers of pardons, let him be blessed.

73. As the Pope justly thunders against those who use any kind of contrivance to the injury of the traffic in pardons.

74. Much more is it his intention to thunder against those who, under the pretext of pardons, use contrivances to the injury of holy charity and of truth.

75. To think that the Papal pardons have such power that they could absolve a man even if—by an impossibility—he had violated the Mother of God, is madness.

76. We affirm on the contrary that Papal pardons cannot take away even the least of venial sins, as regards its guilt.

77. The saying that, even if St. Peter were now Pope, he could grant no greater graces, is blasphemy against St. Peter and the Pope.

78. We affirm on the contrary that both he and any other Pope has greater graces to grant, namely, the Gospel, powers, gifts of healing, etc. ("I Cor." XII).

79. To say that the cross set up among the insignia of the Papal arms is of equal power with the cross of Christ, is blasphemy.

80. Those bishops, priests and theologians who allow such discourses to have currency among the people will have to render an account.

81. This license in the preaching of pardons makes it no easy thing, even for learned men, to protect the reverence due to the Pope against the calumnies, or at all events, the keen questioning of the laity.

82. As for instance: Why does not the Pope empty Purgatory for the sake of most holy charity and of the supreme necessity of souls—this being the most just of all reasons—if he redeems an infinite number of souls for the sake of that most fatal thing, money, to be spent on building a basilica—this being a very slight reason?

83. Again; why do funeral masses and anniversary masses for the deceased continue, and why does not the Pope return, or permit the

withdrawal of, the funds bequeathed for this purpose, since it is a wrong to pray for those who are already redeemed?

84. Again; what is this new kindness of God and the Pope, in that, for money's sake, they permit an impious man and an enemy of God to redeem a pious soul which loves God, and yet do not redeem that same pious and beloved soul out of free charity on account of its own need?

85. Again; why is it that the penitential canons, long since abrogated and dead in themselves, in very fact and not only by usage, are yet still redeemed with money, through the granting of indulgences, as if they were full of life?

86. Again; why does not the Pope, whose riches are at this day more ample than those of the wealthiest of the wealthy, build the single Basilica of St. Peter with his own money rather than with that of poor believers?

87. Again; what does the Pope remit or impart to those who through perfect contrition have a right to plenary remission and participation?

88. Again; what greater good could the Church receive than if the Pope, instead of once, as he does now, were to bestow these remissions and participations a hundred times a day on any one of the faithful?

89. Since it is the salvation of souls, rather than money, that the Pope seeks by his pardons, why does he suspend the letters and pardons granted long ago, since they are equally efficacious?

90. To repress these scruples and arguments of the laity by force alone, and not to resolve them by giving reasons, is to expose the Church and the Pope to the ridicule of their enemies, and to make Christian men unhappy.

91. If then pardons were preached according to the spirit and mind of the Pope, all these questions would be resolved with ease; nay, would not exist.

92. Away then with all those prophets who say to the people of Christ: "Peace, peace," and there is no peace.

93. Blessed be all those prophets who say to the people of Christ: "The cross, the cross," and there is no cross.

94. Christians should be exhorted to strive to follow Christ their head through pains, deaths, and hells.

95. And thus trust to enter heaven through many tribulations, rather than in the security of peace.

2. LUTHER, FROM *ON THE BABYLONISH CAPTIVITY OF THE CHURCH*

SOURCE. *First Principles of the Reformation,* H. Wace and C. A. Buchheim, trs., Philadelphia: Lutheran Publication Society, 1885. Reprinted by permission of Fortress Press.

OF ORDERS

Which of the ancient Fathers has asserted that by these words priests were ordained? Whence then this new interpretation? It is because it has been sought by this device to set up a source of implacable discord, by which clergy and laity might be placed farther asunder than heaven and earth, to the incredible injury of baptismal grace and confusion of evangelical communion. Hence has originated that detestable tyranny of the clergy over the laity, in which, trusting to the corporal unction by which their hands are consecrated, to their tonsure, and to their vestments, they not only set themselves above the body of lay Christians, who have been anointed with the Holy Spirit, but almost look upon them as dogs, unworthy to be numbered in the Church along with themselves. Hence it is that they dare to command, exact, threaten, drive, and oppress, at their will. *In fine,* the sacrament of orders has been and is a most admirable engine for the establishment of all those monstrous evils which have hitherto been wrought, and are yet being wrought, in the Church. In this way Christian brotherhood has perished; in this way shepherds have been turned into wolves, servants into tyrants; and ecclesiastics into more than earthly beings.

How if they were compelled to admit that we all, so many as have been baptized, are equally priests? We are so in fact, and it is only a ministry which has been entrusted to them, and that with our consent. They would then know that they have no right to exercise command over us, except so far as we voluntarily allow of it. Thus it is said: "Ye are a chosen generation, a royal priesthood, a holy nation." ("I Pet." ii. 9.) Thus all we who are Christians are priests; those whom we call priests are ministers chosen from among us to do all things in our name; and the priesthood is nothing else than a ministry. . . .

As far then as we are taught from the Scriptures, since what we call the priesthood is a ministry, I do not see at all for what reason a man who has once been made priest cannot become a layman again, since he differs in no wise from a layman, except by his ministerial office. But it is so far from impossible for a man to be set aside from the ministry, that even now this punishment is constantly inflicted on offending priests, who are either suspended for a time, or deprived for ever of their office. For that fiction of an indelible character has long ago become an object of derision. I grant that the Pope may impress this character, though Christ knows nothing of it, and for this very reason the priest thus consecrated is the lifelong servant and bondsman, not of Christ, but of the Pope, as it is at this day. But, unless I deceive myself, if at some future time this sacrament and figment fall to the ground, the Papacy itself will scarcely hold its ground, and we shall recover that joyful liberty in which we shall understand that we are all equal in every right, and shall shake off the yoke of tyranny and know that he who is a Christian has Christ, and he who has Christ has all things that are Christ's, and can do all things.

TURNING NEXT TO CALVIN, we have included excerpts from his fundamental work, The Institutes of the Christian Religion *(1559 edition), which show his characteristic views on original sin, predestination, and the sacraments.*

3. JOHN CALVIN, FROM *THE INSTITUTES OF THE CHRISTIAN RELIGION*

SOURCE. Henry Bettenson, ed., *Documents of the Christian Church*, 2nd ed., London: Oxford University Press, 1963, pp. 298–301. Reprinted by permission of Oxford University Press.

. . . Therefore original sin is seen to be an hereditary depravity and corruption of our nature, diffused into all parts of the soul . . . wherefore those who have defined original sin as the lack of the original righteousness with which we should have been endowed, no doubt include, by implication, the whole fact of the matter, but they have not fully expressed the positive energy of this sin. For our nature is not merely bereft of good, but is so productive of every kind of evil that it cannot be inactive. Those who have called it concupiscence have used a word by no means wide of the mark, if it were added (and this is what many do not concede) that whatever is in man, from intellect to will, from the soul to the flesh, is all defiled and crammed with concupiscence; or, to sum it up briefly, that the whole man is in himself nothing but concupiscence. . . .

No one who wishes to be thought religious dares outright to deny predestination, by which God chooses some for the hope of life, and condemns others to eternal death. But men entangle it with captious quibbles; and especially those who make foreknowledge the ground of it. We indeed attribute to God both predestination and foreknowledge; but we call it absurd to subordinate one to the other. When we attribute foreknowledge to God we mean that all things have ever been, and eternally remain, before his eyes; so that to his knowledge nothing is future or past, but all things are present; and present not in the sense that they are reproduced in imagination (as we are aware of past events which are retained in our memory), but present in the sense that he really sees and observes them placed, as it were, before his eyes. And this foreknowledge extends over the whole universe and over every creature. By predestination we mean the eternal decree of God, by which he has decided in his own mind what he wishes to happen in the case of each individual. For all men are not created on an equal footing, but for some eternal life is pre-ordained, for others eternal damnation. . . .

Concerning Sacraments. . . . It is convenient first of all to notice what a Sacrament is. Now the following seems to me to be a simple and proper definition of a Sacrament. An external symbol by which the Lord attests in our consciences his promises of goodwill towards us to sustain the inferiority of our faith, and we on our part testify to our piety towards him as well in his presence and before the angels as in the sight of men. Another way of putting it, more condensed but equally sound, would be: A testimony of God's grace to us confirmed by an external sign, with our answering witness of piety towards him. . . .

Concerning the Sacred Supper of Christ. . . . That sacred communication of his own flesh and blood by which Christ pours his life into us, just as if he were to penetrate into the marrow of our bones, he witnesses and attests in the Supper. And that he does not by putting before us a vain or empty sign, but offering there the efficacy of his Spirit, by which he fulfils his promise. And in truth he offers and displays the thing there signified to all who share that spiritual feast; though only by the faithful is it perceived and its fruits enjoyed. . . . If it is true that the visible sign is offered to us to attest the granting of the invisible reality, then, on receiving the symbol of the body, we may be confident that the body itself is no less given to us.

B. Protestantism and Politics

TWO DOCUMENTS ILLUSTRATING *the political ramifications of the religious struggle on the Continent are included next: the Peace of Augsburg (1555), which settled the Schmalkaldic War between the Catholic and Lutheran princes of Germany and stipulated that each prince was to be free to choose the religion of his principality (1) and The Edict of Nantes (1598), which came at the end of the French religious wars between Catholics and Calvinist Huguenots (2). France was to remain Catholic, but the Huguenots were to be tolerated. The edict was revoked a little less than a century later by Louis XIV, who drove the remaining Huguenots from France.*

1. THE PEACE OF AUGSBURG, 1555

SOURCE. Henry Bettenson, ed., *Documents of the Christian Church,* 2nd ed., London: Oxford University Press, 1963, pp. 301–302. Translated in Kidd, *Documents of the Continental Reformation.* Reprinted by permission of The Clarendon Press, Oxford.

In order to bring peace into the holy empire of the Germanic Nation, between the Roman Imperial Majesty and the Electors, Princes, and Estates: let neither his Imperial Majesty nor the Electors, Princes, etc., do any violence or harm to any estate of the Empire on account of the Augsburg Confession,[1] but let them enjoy their religious belief, liturgy and ceremonies as well as their estates and other rights and privileges in peace; and complete religious peace shall be obtained only by Christian means of amity, or under threat of the punishment of the imperial ban.

Likewise the Estates espousing the Augsburg Confession shall let all the Estates and Princes who cling to the old religion live in absolute peace and in the enjoyment of all their estates, rights and privileges.

However all such as do not belong to the two above-mentioned religions shall not be included in the present peace but be totally excluded from it.

. . . Where an archbishop, bishop, or prelate or any other priest of our old religion shall abandon the same, his archbishopric, bishopric, prelacy, and other benefices, together with all their income and revenues which he has so far possessed, shall be abandoned by him without

[1] The statement of Lutheran beliefs.

any further objection or delay. The chapters and such as are entitled to it by common law or the custom of the place shall elect a person espousing the old religion, who may enter on the possession and enjoyment of all the rights and incomes of the place without any further hindrance and without prejudging any ultimate amicable settlement of religion. . . .

In case our subjects, whether belonging to the old religion or to the Augsburg Confession, should intend leaving their homes, with their wives and children, in order to settle in another place, they shall neither be hindered in the sale of their estates after due payment of the local taxes nor injured in their honour.

2. THE EDICT OF NANTES, 1598

SOURCE. Henry Bettenson, ed., *Documents of the Christian Church,* 2nd ed., London: Oxford University Press, 1963, pp. 302–303. Reprinted by permission of Oxford University Press.

III. We ordain that the Catholic, Apostolic and Roman faith be restored and re-established in all those districts and places of this our Realm . . . in which its exercise has been interrupted, there to be freely and peaceably exercised. . . .

VI. And to leave no occasion for trouble or difference among our subjects: We permit those of the so-called Reformed Religion to live and abide in all the towns and districts of this our Realm . . . free from inquisition, molestation or compulsion to do anything in the way of Religion, against their conscience . . . provided that they observe the provisions of this Edict. . . .

IX. We also permit those of the aforesaid Religion to practise it in all the towns and districts of our dominion, in which it had been established and publicly observed by them on several distinct occasions during the year 1596 and the year 1597 up to the end of August, all decrees and judgements to the contrary notwithstanding.

XIII. We most expressly forbid to those of this religion the practice thereof, in respect of ministry, organization, discipline or the public instruction of children, or in any respect, in our realm and dominion, save in the places permitted and granted by this edict.

XIV. The practice of this religion is forbidden in our court and suite, in our domains beyond the mountains, in our city of Paris, or within five leagues thereof.

XVIII. We forbid all our subjects, of whatever rank or condition, to take children of this religion, by force or persuasion, to be baptized or confirmed in the Catholic Apostolic and Roman Church; the same being forbidden to those of the so-called Reformed Religion, under penalty of exceptionally severe punishment.

XXI. Books concerning this religion are not to be printed and exposed for sale save in towns and districts where the public practice of the said religion is allowed.

XXII. No distinction is to be made with regard to this religion, in the reception of pupils for education in universities, colleges and schools, nor in the reception of the sick and needy into hospitals almshouses or public charities.

XXVII. Members of this religion are capable of holding any office or position in this Realm.

THE ESSENCE OF HENRY VIII'S religious policy was to free the English Church of papal control, place it under royal authority, and leave it otherwise unchanged. The monarch's leading role in the English Church was proclaimed officially in the Act of Supremacy of 1534 (3), and Henry VIII's fundamental doctrinal and liturgical conservatism are expressed in The Six Articles (1539) (4).

3. THE ACT OF SUPREMACY, 1534

SOURCE. Henry Bettenson, ed., *Documents of the Christian Church*, 2nd ed., London: Oxford University Press, 1963, p. 319. 26 Henry VIII, cap. I: *Statutes of the Realm*, iii. 492. (G. and H. LV.). Reprinted by permission of Oxford University Press.

Albeit the king's majesty justly and rightfully is and ought to be the supreme head of the Church of England, and so is recognized by the clergy of this realm in their Convocations, yet nevertheless for corroboration and confirmation thereof, and for increase of virtue in Christ's religion within this realm of England, and to repress and extirp all errors, heresies, and other enormities and abuses heretofore used in the same; be it enacted by authority of this present Parliament, that the king our sovereign lord, his heirs and successors, kings of this realm, shall be taken, accepted, and reputed the only supreme head in earth of the Church of England, called *Anglicana Ecclesia;* and shall have and enjoy, annexed and united to the imperial crown of this realm, as well the title and style thereof, as all honours, dignities, pre-eminences, jurisdictions, privileges, authorities, immunities, profits, and commodities to the said dignity of supreme head of the same Church belonging and appertaining; and that our said sovereign lord, his heirs and successors, kings of this realm, shall have full power and authority from time to time to visit, repress, redress, reform, order, correct, restrain, and amend all such errors, heresies, abuses, offences, contempts, and enormities, whatsoever they be, which by any manner spiritual authority or jurisdiction ought or may lawfully be reformed, repressed, ordered, redressed, corrected, restrained, or amended, most to the pleasure of Almighty God, the increase of virtue in Christ's religion, and for the conservation of the peace, unity, and tranquillity of this realm; any usage, custom, foreign law, foreign authority, prescription, or any other thing or things to the contrary hereof notwithstanding.

4. THE SIX ARTICLES, 1539

SOURCE. Henry Bettenson, ed., *Documents of the Christian Church,* 2nd ed., London: Oxford University Press, 1963, p. 319. From the Six Articles Act, 31 Henry VIII, cap. 14: *Statutes of the Realm,* iii. 739. (G. and H. LXV.). Reprinted by permission of Oxford University Press.

First, that in the most blessed Sacrament of the altar, by the strength and efficacy of Christ's mighty word (it being spoken by the priest), is present really, under the form of bread and wine, the natural body and blood of our Saviour Jesus Christ, conceived of the Virgin Mary; and that after the consecration there remaineth no substance of bread or wine, nor any other substance, but the substance of Christ, God and man.

Secondly, that communion in both kinds is not necessary *ad salutem,* by the law of God, to all persons; and that it is to be believed, and not doubted of, but that in the flesh, under the form of bread, is the very blood; and with the blood, under the form of wine, is the very flesh; as well apart, as though they were both together.

Thirdly, that priests after the order of priesthood received, as afore, may not marry, by the law of God.

Fourthly, that vows of chastity or widowhood, by man or woman made to God advisedly, ought to be observed by the law of God; and that it exempts them from other liberties of Christian people, which without that they might enjoy.

Fifthly, that it is meet and necessary that private masses be continued and admitted in this the king's English Church and congregation, as whereby good Christian people, ordering themselves accordingly, do receive both godly and goodly consolations and benefits; and it is agreeable also to God's law.

Sixthly, that auricular confession is expedient and necessary to be retained and continued, used and frequented in the Church of God.

THE ENGLISH CALVINISTS quite naturally resented these articles, and, in the reign of Edward VI (1547–53), they succeeded in injecting a great deal of Calvinism into the English Church. Under the Catholic Mary Tudor (1553–58), the English Church was purged of Protestantism and reunited with Rome, and dissenters were burned en masse. At length, under the shrewdly practical Queen Elizabeth I (1558–1603), a religious compromise was reached—a halfway house between Catholicism and extreme Protestantism—which found expression in the Thirty-Nine Articles. These articles were to become the fundamental constitution of the Church of England.

5. THE ELIZABETHAN SETTLEMENT: THE THIRTY-NINE ARTICLES

SOURCE. *The Book of Common Prayer*, London, n.d., pp. 621–633.

Articles of Religion

ARTICLE I. OF FAITH IN THE HOLY TRINITY.

There is but one living and true God, everlasting, without body, parts, or passions; of infinite power, wisdom, and goodness; the Maker, and Preserver of all things both visible and invisible. And in unity of this Godhead there be three Persons, of one substance, power, and eternity; the Father, the Son, and the Holy Ghost. . . .

ART. VI. OF THE SUFFICIENCY OF THE HOLY SCRIPTURES FOR SALVATION.

Holy Scripture containeth all things necessary to salvation: so that whatsoever is not read therein, nor may be proved thereby, is not to be required of any man, that it should be believed as an article of the Faith, or be thought requisite or necessary to salvation. . . .

ART. VII. OF THE OLD TESTAMENT.

The Old Testament is not contrary to the New: for both in the Old and New Testament everlasting life is offered to Mankind by Christ, who is the only Mediator between God and Man, being both God and Man. Wherefore they are not to be heard, which feign that the old

Fathers did look only for transitory promises. Although the Law given from God by Moses, as touching Ceremonies and Rites, do not bind Christian men, nor the Civil precepts thereof ought of necessity to be received in any commonwealth; yet notwithstanding, no Christian man whatsoever is free from the obedience of the Commandments which are called Moral.

ART. VIII. OF THE THREE CREEDS.

The Three Creeds, *Nicene* Creed, *Athanasius's* Creed, and that which is commonly called the *Apostles'* Creed, ought thoroughly to be received and believed: for they may be proved by most certain warrants of Holy Scripture.

ART. IX. OF ORIGINAL OR BIRTH-SIN.

Original Sin standeth not in the following of *Adam* (as the *Pelagians* do vainly talk); but it is the fault and corruption of the Nature of every man, that naturally is engendered of the offspring of *Adam;* whereby man is very far gone from original righteousness, and is of his own nature inclined to evil, so that the flesh lusteth always contrary to the spirit; and therefore in every person born into this world, it deserveth God's wrath and damnation. And this infection of nature doth remain, yea in them that are regenerated; whereby the lust of the flesh, called in Greek, *phronema sarkos,* which some do expound the wisdom, some sensuality, some the affection, some the desire, of the flesh, is not subject to the Law of God. And although there is no condemnation for them that believe and are baptized; yet the Apostle doth confess, that concupiscence and lust hath of itself the nature of sin.

ART. X. OF FREE-WILL.

The condition of Man after the fall of *Adam* is such, that he cannot turn and prepare himself, by his own natural strength and good works, to faith, and calling upon God: Wherefore we have no power to do good works pleasant and acceptable to God, without the grace of God by Christ preventing us, that we may have a good will, and working with us, when we have that good will.

ART. XL. OF THE JUSTIFICATION OF MAN.

We are accounted righteous before God, only for the merit of our Lord and Saviour Jesus Christ by Faith, and not for our own works or deservings. Wherefore, that we are justified by Faith only, is a most wholesome Doctrine, and very full of comfort, as more largely is expressed in the Homily of Justification.

ART. XII. OF GOOD WORKS.

Albeit that Good Works, which are the fruits of Faith, and follow after Justification, cannot put away our sins, and endure the severity of God's Judgment; yet are they pleasing and acceptable to God in Christ, and do spring out necessarily of a true and lively Faith; insomuch that by them a lively Faith may be as evidently known as a tree discerned by the fruit.

ART. XIII. OF WORKS BEFORE JUSTIFICATION.

Works done before the grace of Christ, and the Inspiration of his Spirit, are not pleasant to God, forasmuch as they spring not of faith in Jesus Christ, neither do they make men meet to receive grace, or (as the School-authors say) deserve grace of congruity: yea rather, for that they are not done as God hath willed and commanded them to be done, we doubt not but they have the nature of sin. . . .

ART. XV. OF CHRIST ALONE WITHOUT SIN.

Christ in the truth of our nature was made like unto us in all things, sin only except, from which he was clearly void, both in his flesh, and in his spirit. He came to be the Lamb without spot, who, by sacrifice of himself once made, should take away the sins of the world, and sin, as Saint *John* saith, was not in him. But all we the rest, although baptized, and born again in Christ, yet offend in many things; and if we say we have no sin, we deceive ourselves, and the truth is not in us. . . .

ART. XVII. OF PREDESTINATION AND ELECTION.

Predestination to Life is the everlasting purpose of God, whereby (before the foundations of the world were laid) he hath constantly decreed by his counsel secret to us, to deliver from curse and damnation those whom he hath chosen in Christ out of mankind, and to bring them by Christ to everlasting salvation, as vessels made to honour. Wherefore, they which be endued with so excellent a benefit of God, be called according to God's purpose by his Spirit working in due season: they through Grace obey the calling: they be justified freely: they be made sons of God by adoption: they be made like the image of his only-begotten Son Jesus Christ: they walk religiously in good works, and at length, by God's mercy, they attain to everlasting felicity.

As the godly consideration of Predestination, and our Election in Christ, is full of sweet, pleasant, and unspeakable comfort to godly persons, and such as feel in themselves the working of the Spirit of Christ, mortifying the works of the flesh, and their earthly members, and drawing up their mind to high and heavenly things, as well because it doth greatly establish and confirm their faith of eternal Salvation to be enjoyed through Christ, as because it doth fervently kindle their love towards God: So, for curious and carnal persons, lacking the Spirit of Christ, to have continually before their eyes the sentence of God's Predestination, is a most dangerous downfall, whereby the Devil doth thrust them either into desperation, or into wretchlessness of most unclean living, no less perilous than desperation.

Furthermore, we must receive God's promises in such wise, as they be generally set forth to us in Holy Scripture: and, in our doings, that Will of God is to be followed, which we have expressly declared unto us in the Word of God.

ART. XVIII. OF OBTAINING ETERNAL SALVATION ONLY BY
THE NAME OF CHRIST.

They also are to be had accursed that presume to say, That every man shall be saved by the Law or Sect which he professeth, so that he be diligent to frame his life according to that Law, and the light of Nature. For Holy Scripture doth set out unto us only the Name of Jesus Christ, whereby men must be saved.

ART. XIX. OF THE CHURCH.

The visible Church of Christ is a congregation of faithful men, in the which the pure Word of God is preached, and the Sacraments be duly ministered according to Christ's ordinance, in all those things that of necessity are requisite to the same.

As the Church of *Jerusalem, Alexandria,* and *Antioch,* have erred; so also the Church of *Rome* hath erred, not only in their living and manner of Ceremonies, but also in matters of Faith.

ART. XX. OF THE AUTHORITY OF THE CHURCH.

The Church hath power to decree Rites or Ceremonies, and authority in Controversies of Faith: and yet it is not lawful for the Church to ordain any thing that is contrary to God's Word written, neither may it so expound one place of Scripture, that it be repugnant to another. Wherefore, although the Church be a witness and a keeper of Holy Writ, yet, as it ought not to decree any thing against the same, so besides the same ought it not to enforce any thing to be believed for necessity of Salvation.

ART. XXI. OF THE AUTHORITY OF GENERAL COUNCILS.

General Councils may not be gathered together without the commandment and will of Princes. And when they be gathered together (forasmuch as they be an assembly of men, whereof all be not governed with the Spirit and Word of God), they may err, and sometimes have erred, even in things pertaining unto God. Wherefore things ordained by them as necessary to salvation have neither strength nor authority, unless it may be declared that they be taken out of Holy Scripture.

ART. XXII. OF PURGATORY.

The Romish Doctrine concerning Purgatory, Pardons, Worshipping and Adoration, as well of Images as of Reliques, and also Invocation of Saints, is a fond thing, vainly invented, and grounded upon no warranty of Scripture, but rather repugnant to the Word of God.

ART. XXIII. OF MINISTERING IN THE CONGREGATION.

It is not lawful for any man to take upon him the office of publick preaching, or ministering the Sacraments in the Congregation, before he be lawfully called, and sent to execute the same. And those we ought to judge lawfully called and sent, which be chosen and called to this work by men who have publick authority given unto them in the Congregation, to call and send Ministers into the Lord's vineyard.

ART. XXIV. OF SPEAKING IN THE CONGREGATION IN SUCH A TONGUE AS THE PEOPLE UNDERSTANDETH.

It is a thing plainly repugnant to the Word of God, and the custom of the Primitive Church, to have publick Prayer in the Church, or to minister the Sacraments, in a tongue not understood of the people.

ART. XXV. OF THE SACRAMENTS.

Sacraments ordained of Christ be not only badges or tokens of Christian men's profession, but rather they be certain sure witnesses, and effectual signs of grace, and God's good will towards us, by the which he doth work invisibly in us, and doth not only quicken, but also strengthen and confirm our Faith in him.

There are two Sacraments ordained of Christ our Lord in the Gospel, that is to say, Baptism, and the Supper of the Lord.

Those five commonly called Sacraments, that is to say, Confirmation, Penance, Orders, Matrimony, and Extreme Unction, are not to be counted for Sacraments of the Gospel, being such as have grown partly of the corrupt following of the Apostles, partly are states of life allowed in the Scriptures; but yet have not like nature of Sacraments with Baptism, and the Lord's Supper, for that they have not any visible sign or ceremony ordained of God.

The Sacraments were not ordained of Christ to be gazed upon, or to be carried about, but that we should duly use them. And in such only as worthily receive the same they have a wholesome effect or operation: but they that receive them unworthily, purchase to themselves damnation, as Saint *Paul* saith.

ART. XXVI. OF THE UNWORTHINESS OF THE MINISTERS, WHICH HINDERS NOT THE EFFECT OF THE SACRAMENTS.

Although in the visible Church the evil be ever mingled with the good, and sometimes the evil have chief authority in the Ministration of the Word and Sacraments, yet forasmuch as they do not the same in their own name, but in Christ's, and do minister by his commission and authority, we may use their Ministry, both in hearing the Word of God, and in the receiving of the Sacraments. Neither is the effect of Christ's ordinance taken away by their wickedness, nor the grace of God's gifts diminished from such as by faith and rightly, do receive the Sacraments ministered unto them; which be effectual, because of Christ's institution and promise, although they be ministered by evil men.

Nevertheless, it appertaineth to the discipline of the Church, that enquiry be made of evil Ministers, and that they be accused by those that have knowledge of their offences; and finally, being found guilty, by just judgment be deposed.

ART. XXVII. OF BAPTISM.

Baptism is not only a sign of profession, and mark of difference, whereby Christian men are discerned from others that be not christened, but it is also a sign of Regeneration or newbirth, whereby, as by an instrument, they that receive Baptism rightly are grafted into the Church; the promises of the forgiveness of sin, and of our adoption to be the sons of God by the Holy Ghost, are visibly signed and sealed; Faith is confirmed, and Grace increased by virtue of prayer unto God.

The Baptism of young Children is in any wise to be retained in the Church, as most agreeable with the institution of Christ.

ART. XXVIII. OF THE LORD'S SUPPER.

The Supper of the Lord is not only a sign of love that Christians ought to have among themselves one to another; but rather it is a Sacrament of our Redemption by Christ's death: insomuch that to such as rightly, worthily, and with faith, receive the same, the Bread which we break is a partaking of the Body of Christ; and likewise the Cup of Blessing is a partaking of the Blood of Christ.

Transubstantiation (or the change of the substance of Bread and

Wine) in the Supper of the Lord, cannot be proved by Holy Writ; but is repugnant to the plain words of Scripture, overthroweth the nature of a Sacrament, and hath given occasion to many superstitions.

The Body of Christ is given, taken, and eaten, in the Supper, only after an heavenly and spiritual manner. And the mean whereby the Body of Christ is received and eaten in the Supper, is Faith.

The Sacrament of the Lord's Supper was not by Christ's ordinance reserved, carried about, lifted up, or worshipped.

ART. XXIX. OF THE WICKED WHICH EAT NOT THE BODY OF CHRIST IN USE OF THE LORD'S SUPPER.

The Wicked, and such as be void of a lively faith, although they do carnally and visibly press with their teeth (as Saint *Augustine* saith) the Sacrament of the Body and Blood of Christ; yet in no wise are they partakers of Christ: but rather, to their condemnation, do eat and drink the sign or Sacrament of so great a thing.

ART. XXX. OF BOTH KINDS.

The Cup of the Lord is not to be denied to the Lay-people: for both the parts of the Lord's Sacrament, by Christ's ordinance and commandment, ought to be ministered to all Christian men alike.

ART. XXXI. OF THE ONE OBLATION OF CHRIST FINISHED UPON THE CROSS.

The Offering of Christ once made is that perfect redemption, propitiation, and satisfaction, for all the sins of the whole world, both original and actual; and there is none other satisfaction for sin, but that alone. Wherefore the sacrifices of Masses, in the which it was commonly said, that the Priest did offer Christ for the quick and the dead, to have remission of pain or guilt, were blasphemous fables, and dangerous deceits.

ART. XXXII. OF THE MARRIAGE OF PRIESTS.

Bishops, Priests, and Deacons, are not commanded by God's Law, either to vow the estate of single life, or to abstain from marriage: therefore it is lawful also for them, as for all other Christian men, to marry at their own discretion, as they shall judge the same to serve better to godliness.

ART. XXXIII. OF EXCOMMUNICATE PERSONS, HOW THEY ARE TO BE AVOIDED.

That person which by open denunciation of the Church is rightly cut off from the unity of the Church, and excommunicated, ought to be taken of the whole multitude of the faithful, as an Heathen and Publican, until he be openly reconciled by penance, and received into the Church by a Judge that hath authority thereunto.

ART. XXXIV. OF THE TRADITIONS OF THE CHURCH.

It is not necessary that traditions and ceremonies be in all places one, or utterly like; for at all times they have been divers, and may be changed according to the diversities of countries, times, and men's manners, so that nothing be ordained against God's Word. Whosoever, through his private judgment, willingly and purposely, doth openly break the Traditions and Ceremonies of the Church, which be not repugnant to the Word of God, and be ordained and approved by common authority, ought to be rebuked openly (that others may fear to do the like), as he that offendeth against the common order of the Church, and hurteth the authority of the Magistrate, and woundeth the consciences of the weak brethren.

Every particular or national Church hath authority to ordain, change, and abolish, ceremonies or rites of the Church ordained only by man's authority, so that all things be done to edifying. . . .

ART. XXXVII. OF THE CIVIL MAGISTRATES.

The King's Majesty hath the chief power in this Realm of *England*, and other his Dominions, unto whom the chief Government of all Estates of this Realm, whether they be Ecclesiastical or Civil, in all causes doth appertain, and is not, nor ought to be, subject to any foreign Jurisdiction.

Where we attribute to the King's Majesty the chief government, by which Titles we understand the minds of some slanderous folks to be offended; we give not to our Princes the ministering either of God's Word, or of the Sacraments, the which thing the Injunctions also lately set forth by *Elizabeth* our Queen do most plainly testify; but that only prerogative, which we see to have been given always to all godly Princes in Holy Scriptures by God himself; that is, that they should rule all estates and degrees committed to their charge by God, whether they be Ecclesiastical or Temporal, and restrain with the civil sword the stubborn and evil-doers.

The Bishop of *Rome* hath no jurisdiction in this Realm of *England*.

The Laws of the Realm may punish Christian men with death, for heinous and grievous offences.

It is lawful for Christian men, at the commandment of the Magistrate, to wear weapons, and serve in the wars.

ART. XXXVIII. OF CHRISTIAN MEN'S GOODS WHICH ARE NOT COMMON.

The Riches and Goods of Christians are not common, as touching the right, title, and possession of the same, as certain Anabaptists do falsely boast. Notwithstanding, every man ought, of such things as he possesseth, liberally to give alms to the poor, according to his ability.

ART. XXXIX. OF A CHRISTIAN MAN'S OATH.

As we confess that vain and rash Swearing is forbidden Christian men by our Lord Jesus Christ, and *James* his Apostle, so we judge, that Christian Religion doth not prohibit, but that a man may swear when the Magistrate requireth, in a cause of faith and charity, so it be done according to the Prophet's teaching, in justice, judgment, and truth.

C. The Catholic Reformation

THE CATHOLIC REFORMATION or "Counter-Reformation," drew much of its energy from the new Jesuit order, organized on strict military lines by the Spaniard St. Ignatius Loyola. Loyola's concept of absolute obedience to ecclesiastical authority is clearly expressed in his Spiritual Exercises *(1), and in the excerpt which has been included here from the Jesuit constitutions (2).*

1. IGNATIUS LOYOLA, FROM *SPIRITUAL EXERCISES*

SOURCE. Henry Bettenson, ed., *Documents of the Christian Church*, 2nd ed., London: Oxford University Press, 1963, pp. 364–367. Reprinted by permission of Oxford University Press.

1. Always to be ready to obey with mind and heart, setting aside all judgement of one's own, the true spouse of Jesus Christ, our holy mother, our infallible and orthodox mistress, the Catholic Church, whose authority is exercised over us by the hierarchy.

2. To commend the confession of sins to a priest as it is practised in the Church; the reception of the Holy Eucharist once a year, or better still every week, or at least every month, with the necessary preparation.

3. To commend to the faithful frequent and devout assistance at the holy sacrifice of the Mass, the ecclesiastical hymns, the divine office, and in general the prayers and devotions practised at stated times, whether in public in the churches or in private.

4. To have a great esteem for the religious orders, and to give the preference to celibacy or virginity over the married state.

5. To approve of the religious vows of chastity, poverty, perpetual obedience, as well as the other works of perfection and supererogation. Let us remark in passing, that we must never engage by vow to take a state (such e.g. as marriage) that would be an impediment to one more perfect. . . .

6. To praise relics, the veneration and invocation of Saints: also the stations, and pious pilgrimages, indulgences, jubilees, the custom of lighting candles in the churches, and other such aids to piety and devotion.

7. To praise the use of abstinence and fasts as those of Lent, of Ember Days, of Vigils, of Friday, of Saturday, and of others undertaken out of pure devotion: also voluntary mortifications, which we call penances, not merely interior, but exterior also.

8. To commend moreover the construction of churches, and ornaments; also images, to be venerated with the fullest right, for the sake of what they represent.

9. To uphold especially all the precepts of the Church, and not censure them in any manner; but, on the contrary, to defend them promptly, with reasons drawn from all sources, against those who criticize them.

10. To be eager to commend the decrees, mandates, traditions, rites and customs of the Fathers in the Faith or our superiors. As to their conduct; although there may not always be the uprightness of conduct that there ought to be, yet to attack or revile them in private or in public tends to scandal and disorder. Such attacks set the people against their princes and pastors; we must avoid such reproaches and never attack superiors before inferiors. The best course is to make private approach to those who have power to remedy the evil.

11. To value most highly the sacred teaching, both the Positive and the Scholastic, as they are commonly called. . . .

12. It is a thing to be blamed and avoided to compare men who are still living on the earth (however worthy of praise) with the Saints and Blessed, saying: This man is more learned than St Augustine, etc. . . .

13. That we may be altogether of the same mind and in conformity with the Church herself, if she shall have defined anything to be black which to our eyes appears to be white, we ought in like manner to pronounce it to be black. For we must undoubtingly believe, that the Spirit of our Lord Jesus Christ, and the Spirit of the Orthodox Church His Spouse, by which Spirit we are governed and directed to Salvation, is the same; . . .

14. It must also be borne in mind, that although it be most true, that no one is saved but he that is predestinated, yet we must speak

with circumspection concerning this matter, lest perchance, stressing too much the grace or predestination of God, we should seem to wish to shut out the force of free will and the merits of good works; or on the other hand, attributing to these latter more than belongs to them, we derogate meanwhile from the power of grace.

15. For the like reason we should not speak on the subject of predestination frequently; if by chance we do so speak, we ought so to temper what we say as to give the people who hear no occasion of erring and saying, 'If my salvation or damnation is already decreed, my good or evil actions are predetermined'; whence many are wont to neglect good works, and the means of salvation.

16. It also happens not unfrequently, that from immoderate preaching and praise of faith, without distinction or explanation added, the people seize a pretext for being lazy with regard to any good works, which precede faith, or follow it when it has been formed by the bond of charity.

17. Nor any more must we push to such a point the preaching and inculcating of the grace of God, as that there may creep thence into the minds of the hearers the deadly error of denying our faculty of free will. We must speak of it as the glory of God requires . . . that we may not raise doubts as to liberty and the efficacy of good works.

18. Although it is very praiseworthy and useful to serve God through the motive of pure charity, yet we must also recommend the fear of God; and not only filial fear, but servile fear, which is very useful and often even necessary to raise man from sin. . . . Once risen from the state, and free from the affection of mortal sin, we may then speak of that filial fear which is truly worthy of God, and which gives and preserves the union of pure love.

2. FROM THE CONSTITUTIONS OF THE JESUITS

SOURCE. Henry Bettenson, ed., *Documents of the Christian Church,* 2nd ed., London: Oxford University Press, 1963, p. 367. Reprinted by permission of Oxford University Press.

Let us with the utmost pains strain every nerve of our strength to exhibit this virtue of obedience, firstly to the Highest Pontiff, then to the Superiors of the Society; so that in all things, to which obedience can be extended with charity, we may be most ready to obey his voice, just as if it issued from Christ our Lord . . . , leaving any work, even a letter, that we have begun and have not yet finished; by directing to this goal all our strength an intention in the Lord, that holy obedience may be made perfect in us in every respect, in performance, in will, in intellect; by submitting to whatever may be enjoined on us with great readiness, with spiritual joy and perseverance; by persuading ourselves that all things [commanded] are just; by rejecting with a kind of blind obedience all opposing opinion or judgement of our own, and that in all things which are ordained by the Superior where it cannot be clearly held [*definiri*] that any kind of sin intervenes. And let each one persuade himself that they that live under obedience ought to allow themselves to be borne and ruled by divine providence working through their Superiors exactly as if they were a corpse which suffers itself to be borne and handled in any way whatsoever; or just as an old man's stick which serves him who holds it in his hand wherever and for whatever purpose he wish to use it.

OUR REFORMATION DOCUMENTS conclude with excerpts from the canons of the Council of Trent (1545–63), in which Catholic doctrine is clarified in the light of the Protestant challenge. The time for compromise had passed, and the Church was anxious to assert in unmistakable terms its traditional views on God and man, the sources of divine authority, and the nature of the sacraments.

3. CANONS OF THE COUNCIL OF TRENT

SOURCE. Henry Bettenson, ed., *Documents of the Christian Church*, 2nd ed., London: Oxford University Press, 1963, pp. 368–369, 372–373. Reprinted by permission of Oxford University Press.

On Scripture and Tradition.

SESSION IV, 8 APRIL 1546.

The Holy, Oecumenical and General Synod of Trent . . . having this aim always before its eyes, that errors may be removed and the purity of the Gospel be preserved in the Church, which was before promised through the prophets in the Holy Scriptures and which our Lord Jesus Christ the Son of God first published by his own mouth and then commanded to be preached through his Apostles to every creature as a source of all saving truth and of discipline of conduct; and perceiving that this truth and this discipline are contained in written books and in unwritten traditions, which were received by the Apostles from the lips of Christ himself, or, by the same Apostles, at the dictation of the Holy Spirit, and were handed on and have come down to us; following the example of the orthodox Fathers, this Synod receives and venerates, with equal pious affection and reverence, all the books both of the New and the Old Testaments, since one God is the author of both, together with the said Traditions, as well those pertaining to faith as those pertaining to morals, as having been given either from the lips of Christ or by the dictation of the Holy Spirit and preserved by unbroken succession in the Catholic Church. . . .

On Original Sin.

SESSION V, 17 JUNE 1546.

1. If any one does not confess that the first man Adam, when he had transgressed the command of God in Paradise, straightway lost that holiness and righteousness in which he had been established, and through the offence of this disobedience incurred the wrath and indignation of God, and therefore incurred death, which God had before threatened to him, and, with death, captivity under the power of him who thereafter had the power of death, namely the devil, and that the whole of Adam, through the offence of that disobedience, was changed for the worse in respect of body and soul: let him be anathema.

2. If any one asserts that the disobedience of Adam injured only himself and not his offspring . . . or that . . . only death and the pains of the body were transferred to the whole human race, and not the sin also, which is the death of the soul: let him be anathema [Rom. v. 12].

3. If any one asserts that the sin of Adam—which in origin is one and which has been transmitted to all mankind by propagation, not through imitation, and is in every man and belongs to him—can be removed either by man's natural powers or by any other remedy than the merit of the one mediator our Lord Jesus Christ . . .

4. If any one denies that infants who have just issued from their mother's womb are to be baptized, even if born of baptized parents, or says that they are indeed baptized for the remission of sins but that they are not infected with any original sin from Adam such as would need expiation by the laver of regeneration for the attainment of eternal life; whence it follows that in regard to them the formula of baptism for remission of sins is to be understood not in its true but in a false sense . . .

Canons on the Holy Eucharist.

3. On the Eucharist. If any one denies that in the venerable sacrament of the Eucharist the whole Christ is contained under each species and in each separate part of each species: let him be anathema. . . .

9. If any one denies that each and all of Christ's faithful, of either sex, having come to years of discretion, is bound to communicate at least once a year in Eastertide, in accordance with the precept of Holy Mother Church: let him be anathema.

On Penance; Canons on the Sacrament of Penance.

SESSION XIV, NOVEMBER 1551.

[The following propositions, among others, are anathematized.]

1. That penance is not truly and properly a sacrament in the Catholic Church, instituted for the faithful by Christ our Lord, for their reconciliation to God whenever they fall into sin after baptism.

2. That baptism itself is the sacrament of penance (as if there were not two distinct sacraments) and that therefore it is not right to call penance the "second plank after shipwreck."

3. That the words of our Lord and Saviour, "Whosoever sins," etc. [John xx. 22], are not to be understood of the power of remitting or retaining sins in the sacrament of penance, as the Catholic Church has always, from the first, understood them: but . . . that they refer to the authority to preach the Gospel.

4. That for entire and perfect remission of sins three acts are not required in a penitent, to be as it were the matter of the sacrament, namely contrition, confession and satisfaction.

6. That sacramental confession was neither instituted by divine authority, nor is it necessary to salvation by divine authority; or that the method of private confession to a priest alone, a method always observed from the first down to this day by the Catholic Church, is alien from the institution and command of Christ, and is a human invention.

Part III

NATIONAL POLITICS
AND NATIONAL CULTURES

A. The Golden Age of Spain

SIXTEENTH-CENTURY SPAIN, under Charles V (1516–1556) and Philip II (1556–1598) was the greatest power in Europe. Her explorers and soldiers built a great and lucrative empire in the New World, her saints were widely revered for their austere piety, and her artists, writers, and scholars made significant contributions to the European heritage. Under Philip II, Spain became the power-center of the Counter-Reformation, and Spanish diplomacy supported the Catholic cause throughout Europe.

El Greco (1541–1616), although not a Spaniard by birth, lived and worked in Spain, and in his dramatic paintings caught the somber spirit and uncompromising piety of the Counter-Reformation. His View of Toledo *(1) and* Christ Bearing the Cross *(2) convey a powerful impression of the potent emotionalism of Spanish Catholicism.*

1. EL GRECO, *VIEW OF TOLEDO*, 1600–1614

2. EL GRECO, *CHRIST BEARING THE CROSS*

*THE GREAT SPANISH NOVELIST Miguel de Cervantes (1547–1616),
in his masterpiece,* Don Quixote, *reflected wittily and nostalgically on the
medieval chivalric ideal. The excerpt presented here includes Don Quixote's
famous tilt with the windmills and expresses the madness and grandeur of
his dream of recapturing a dying past.*

3. MIGUEL DE CERVANTES, FROM *DON QUIXOTE*

SOURCE. Miguel de Cervantes Saavedra, *The Ingenious Gentleman, Don Quixote
de la Mancha,* Samuel Putnam, tr., New York: The Viking Press, 1949, I, pp.
62–65. Copyright 1949 by The Viking Press, Inc. Reprinted by permission of The
Viking Press, Inc.

At this point they caught sight of thirty or forty windmills which
were standing on the plain there, and no sooner had Don Quixote laid
eyes upon them than he turned to his squire and said, "Fortune is guiding our affairs better than we could have wished; for you see there
before you, friend Sancho Panza, some thirty or more lawless giants
with whom I mean to do battle. I shall deprive them of their lives,
and with the spoils from this encounter we shall begin to enrich ourselves; for this is righteous warfare, and it is a great service to God
to remove so accursed a breed from the face of the earth."

"What giants?" said Sancho Panza.

"Those that you see there," replied his master, "those with the long
arms some of which are as much as two leagues in length."

"But look, your Grace, those are not giants but windmills, and what
appear to be arms are their wings which, when whirled in the breeze,
cause the millstone to go."

"It is plain to be seen," said Don Quixote, "that you have had little
experience in this matter of adventures. If you are afraid, go off to
one side and say your prayers while I am engaging them in fierce,
unequal combat."

Saying this, he gave spurs to his steed Rocinante, without paying
any heed to Sancho's warning that these were truly windmills and not
giants that he was riding forth to attack. Nor even when he was close
upon them did he perceive what they really were, but shouted at the
top of his lungs, "Do not seek to flee, cowards and vile creatures that
you are, for it is but a single knight with whom you have to deal!"

At that moment a little wind came up and the big wings began
turning.

"Though you flourish as many arms as did the giant Briareus," said

Don Quixote when he perceived this, "you still shall have to answer to me."

He thereupon commended himself with all his heart to his lady Dulcinea, beseeching her to succor him in this peril; and, being well covered with his shield and with his lance at rest, he bore down upon them at a full gallop and fell upon the first mill that stood in his way, giving a thrust at the wing, which was whirling at such a speed that his lance was broken into bits and both horse and horseman went rolling over the plain, very much battered indeed. Sancho upon his donkey came hurrying to his master's assistance as fast as he could, but when he reached the spot, the knight was unable to move, so great was the shock with which he and Rocinante had hit the ground.

"God help us!" exclaimed Sancho, "did I not tell your Grace to look well, that those were nothing but windmills, a fact which no one could fail to see unless he had other mills of the same sort in his head?"

"Be quiet, friend Sancho," said Don Quixote. "Such are the fortunes of war, which more than any other are subject to constant change. What is more, when I come to think of it, I am sure that this must be the work of that magician Frestón, the one who robbed me of my study and my books, and who has thus changed the giants into windmills in order to deprive me of the glory of overcoming them, so great is the enmity that he bears me; but in the end his evil arts shall not prevail against this trusty sword of mine."

"May God's will be done," was Sancho Panza's response. And with the aid of his squire the knight was once more mounted on Rocinante, who stood there with one shoulder half out of joint. And so, speaking of the adventure that had just befallen them, they continued along the Puerto Lápice highway; for there, Don Quixote said, they could not fail to find many and varied adventures, this being a much traveled thoroughfare. The only thing was, the knight was exceedingly downcast over the loss of his lance.

"I remember," he said to his squire, "having read of a Spanish knight by the name of Diego Pérez de Vargas, who, having broken his sword in battle, tore from an oak a heavy bough or branch and with it did such feats of valor that day, and pounded so many Moors, that he came to be known as Machuca, and he and his descendants from that day forth have been called Vargas y Machuca. I tell you this because I too intend to provide myself with just such a bough as the one he wielded, and with it I propose to do such exploits that you shall deem yourself fortunate to have been found worthy to come with me and behold and witness things that are almost beyond belief."

"God's will be done," said Sancho. "I believe everything that your Grace says; but straighten yourself up in the saddle a little, for you seem to be slipping down on one side, owing, no doubt, to the shaking-up that you received in your fall."

"Ah, that is the truth," replied Don Quixote, "and if I do not speak of my sufferings, it is for the reason that it is not permitted knights-errant to complain of any wound whatsoever, even though their bowels may be dropping out."

"If that is the way it is," said Sancho, "I have nothing more to say; but, God knows, it would suit me better if your Grace did complain when something hurts him. I can assure you that I mean to do so, over the least little thing that ails me—that is, unless the same rule applies to squires as well."

Don Quixote laughed long and heartily over Sancho's simplicity, telling him that he might complain as much as he liked and where and when he liked, whether he had good cause or not; for he had read nothing to the contrary in the ordinances of chivalry. Sancho then called his master's attention to the fact that it was time to eat. The knight replied that he himself had no need of food at the moment, but his squire might eat whenever he chose. Having been granted this permission, Sancho seated himself as best he could upon his beast, and, taking out from his saddlebags the provisions that he had stored there, he rode along leisurely behind his master, munching his victuals and taking a good, hearty swig now and then at the leather flask in a manner that might well have caused the biggest-bellied tavernkeeper of Málaga to envy him. Between draughts he gave not so much as a thought to any promise that his master might have made him, nor did he look upon it as any hardship, but rather as good sport, to go in quest of adventures however hazardous they might be.

B. Elizabethan England

THE BUOYANT AGE in which English seafarers conducted daring raids on the Spanish Empire and humbled the Armada, in which Englishmen awoke to a new sense of national identity and pride, and in which Shakespeare and his immensely gifted contemporaries were transforming English literature, cannot be adequately represented in a book such as this. The four brief selections included here provide the merest glimpse at the riches of Eliza-bethan England: a short poem, "On My First Daughter," by the poet-play-wright Ben Jonson (1), a sonnet of Shakespeare (2), an excerpt from Chris-topher Marlowe's play Dr. Faustus (3), and Queen Elizabeth's "Armada

Speech" (1588) (4), *an appeal to the patriotism and personal devotion of her subjects on the eve of the battle of the Spanish Armada.*

1. BEN JONSON, "ON MY FIRST DAUGHTER"

Here lies to each her parents' ruth,
Mary, the daughter of their youth:
Yet, all heaven's gifts, being heaven's due,
It makes the father less to rue.
At six months end, she parted hence
With safety of her innocence;
Whose soule Heaven's Queen (whose name she beares)
In comfort of her mother's teares,
Hath plac'd amongst her Virgin-traine:
Where, while that sever'd doth remaine,
This grave partakes the fleshly birth,
Which cover lightly, gentle earth.

2. WILLIAM SHAKESPEARE, "SONNET XVIII"

Shall I compare thee to a summer's day?
Thou art more lovely and more temperate;
Rough winds do shake the darling buds of May,
And summer's lease hath all too short a date:
Sometime too hot the eye of heaven shines,
And often is his gold complexion dimm'd:
And every fair from fair sometime declines,
By chance, or nature's changing course, untrimm'd.
But thy eternal summer shall not fade,
Nor lose possession of that fair thou owest;
Nor shall Death brag thou wanderest in his shade
When in eternal lines to time thou growest.
   So long as men can breathe, or eyes can see,
   So long lives this, and this gives life to thee.

PERHAPS THE GREATEST LITERARY ACHIEVEMENT of the Eliza-bethans was in the field of drama. The excerpt from Dr. Faustus, in which Faustus commits his soul to the devil in return for twenty-four years of earthly prosperity, is typical of Elizabethan drama in its powerful use of blank verse and its probing into the depths of human emotions.

3. CHRISTOPHER MARLOWE, FROM *DR. FAUSTUS*

SOURCE. Christopher Marlowe, *Dr. Faustus*, from *The Harvard Classics*, Charles W. Eliot, ed., New York: P. F. Collier & Son, 1909, Volume 19, pp. 213–215.

MEPHISTOPHILIS.   I am a servant to great Lucifer,
And may not follow thee without his leave
No more than he commands must we perform.

FAUSTUS.   Did not he charge thee to appear to me?

MEPH.   No, I came hither of mine own accord.

FAUST.   Did not my conjuring speeches raise thee? Speak.

MEPH.   That was the cause, but yet *per accidens;*
For when we hear one rack the name of God,
Abjure the Scriptures and his Saviour Christ,
We fly in hope to get his glorious soul;
Nor will we come, unless he use such means
Whereby he is in danger to be damn'd:
Therefore the shortest cut for conjuring
Is stoutly to abjure the Trinity,
And pray devoutly to the Prince of Hell.

FAUST.   So Faustus hath
Already done; and holds this principle,
There is no chief but only Belzebub,
To whom Faustus doth dedicate himself.
This word "damnation" terrifies not him,
For he confounds hell in Elysium;
His ghost be with the old philosophers!
But, leaving these vain trifles of men's souls,
Tell me what is that Lucifer thy lord?

MEPH.   Arch-regent and commander of all spirits.

FAUST.   Was not that Lucifer an angel once?

MEPH.   Yes, Faustus, and most dearly lov'd of God.

FAUST.   How comes it then that he is Prince of devils?

MEPH.   O, by aspiring pride and insolence;
For which God threw him from the face of Heaven.

FAUST.   And what are you that you live with Lucifer?

MEPH.   Unhappy spirits that fell with Lucifer,
Conspir'd against our God with Lucifer,
And are for ever damn'd with Lucifer.

FAUST.   Where are you damn'd?

MEPH.   In hell.

FAUST.   How comes it then that thou art out of hell?

MEPH.   Why this is hell, nor am I out of it.
Think'st thou that I who saw the face of God,
And tasted the eternal joys of Heaven,
Am not tormented with ten thousand hells,
In being depriv'd of everlasting bliss?
O Faustus! leave these frivolous demands,
Which strike a terror to my fainting soul.

FAUST.   What, is great Mephistophilis so passionate
For being depriv'd of the joys of Heaven?
Learn thou of Faustus manly fortitude,
And scorn those joys thou never shalt possess.
Go bear these tidings to great Lucifer:
Seeing Faustus hath incurr'd eternal death
By desperate thoughts against Jove's deity,
Say he surrenders up to him his soul,
So he will spare him four and twenty years,
Letting him live in all voluptuousness;
Having thee ever to attend on me;
To give me whatsoever I shall ask,
To tell me whatsoever I demand,
To slay mine enemies, and aid my friends,
And always be obedient to my will.
Go and return to mighty Lucifer,
And meet me in my study at midnight,
And then resolve me of thy master's mind.

MEPH.   I will, Faustus.

Exit.

FAUST.   Had I as many souls as there be stars,
I'd give them all for Mephistophilis.
By him I'll be great Emperor of the world,
And make a bridge through the moving air,
To pass the ocean with a band of men:
I'll join the hills that bind the Afric shore,
And make that [country] continent to Spain,
And both contributory to my crown.
The Emperor shall not live but by my leave,
Nor any potentate of Germany.
Now that I have obtain'd what I desire,

I'll live in speculation of this art
Till Mephistophilis return again.

Exit.

Enter MEPHISTOPHILIS

FAUST.   Now tell me, what says Lucifer thy lord?

MEPH.   That I shall wait on Faustus whilst he lives,
So he will buy my service with his soul.

FAUST.   Already Faustus hath hazarded that for thee.

MEPH.   But, Faustus, thou must bequeath it solemnly,
And write a deed of gift with thine own blood,
For that security craves great Lucifer.
If thou deny it, I will back to hell.

FAUST.   Stay, Mephistophilis! and tell me what good
Will my soul do thy lord.

MEPH.   Enlarge his kingdom.

FAUST.   Is that the reason why he tempts us thus?

MEPH.   *Solamen miseris socios habuisse doloris.*[1]

FAUST.   Why, have you any pain that torture others?

MEPH.   As great as have the human souls of men.
But tell me, Faustus, shall I have thy soul?
And I will be thy slave, and wait on thee,
And give thee more than thou hast wit to ask.

FAUST.   Ay, Mephistophilis, I give it thee.

MEPH.   Then, Faustus, stab thine arm courageously.
And bind thy soul that at some certain day
Great Lucifer may claim it as his own;
And then be thou as great as Lucifer.

Stabbing his arm.

FAUST.   Lo, Mephistophilis, for love of thee,
I cut mine arm, and with my proper blood
Assure my soul to be great Lucifer's,
Chief lord and regent of perpetual night!

---

[1] "Misery loves company."

View here the blood that trickles from mine arm.
And let it be propitious for my wish.

MEPH.   But, Faustus, thou must
Write it in manner of a deed of gift.

Writes.

FAUST.   Ay, so I will.
But, Mephistophilis,
My blood congeals, and I can write no more.

MEPH.   I'll fetch thee fire to dissolve it straight.

Exit.

FAUST.   What might the staying of my blood portend?
Is it unwilling I should write this bill?
Why streams it not that I may write afresh?
Faustus gives to thee his soul. Ah, there it stay'd.
Why should'st thou not? Is not thy soul thine own?
Then write again, *Faustus gives to thee his soul.*

Re-enter MEPHISTOPHILIS *with a chafer of coals*

MEPH.   Here's fire. Come, Faustus, set it on.

FAUST.   So now the blood begins to clear again;
Now will I make an end immediately.

Writes.

MEPH.   O what will not I do to obtain his soul.

Aside.

FAUST.   *Consummatum est:*[2] this bill is ended,
And Faustus hath bequeath'd his soul to Lucifer—
But what is this inscription on mine arm?
Homo, fuge![3] Whither should I fly?
If unto God, he'll throw me down to hell.
My senses are deceiv'd; here's nothing writ:—

[2] "It is finished."

[3] "Man, fly!"

> I see it plain; here in this place is writ
> *Homo, fuge!* Yet shall not Faustus fly

MEPH.   I'll fetch him somewhat to delight his mind.

Exit.

Re-enter [MEPHISTOPHILIS] *with* Devils, *giving crowns and rich apparel to* FAUSTUS, *dance, and depart*

FAUST.   Speak, Mephistophilis, what means this show?

MEPH.   Nothing, Faustus, but to delight thy mind withal,
And to show thee what magic can perform.

FAUST.   But may I raise up spirits when I please?

MEPH.   Ay, Faustus, and do greater things than these.

FAUST.   Then there's enough for a thousand souls.
Here, Mephistophilis, receive this scroll,
A deed of gift of body and of soul:
But yet conditionally that thou perform
All articles prescrib'd between us both.

MEPH.   Faustus, I swear by hell and Lucifer
To effect all promises between us made.

FAUST.   Then hear me read them: *On these conditions following. First, that Faustus may be a spirit in form and substance. Secondly, that Mephistophilis shall be his servant, and at his command. Thirdly, that Mephistophilis shall do for him and bring him whatsoever* [*he desires*]. *Fourthly, that he shall be in his chamber or house invisible. Lastly, that he shall appear to the said John Faustus, at all times, and in what form or shape soever he pleases. I, John Faustus, of Wittenberg, Doctor, by these presents do give both body and soul to Lucifer, Prince of the East, and his minister, Mephistophilis; and furthermore grant unto them, that twenty-four years being expired, the articles above written inviolate, full power to fetch or carry the said John Faustus, body and soul, flesh, blood, or goods, into their habitation wheresoever. By me,*
                                        John Faustus.

4. ELIZABETH I, THE ARMADA SPEECH, 1588

SOURCE. Charles W. Colby, ed., *Selections from the Sources of English History,* Harlow: Longmans, Green and Co., 1899, pp. 158–159. Reprinted by permission of Longmans, Green and Co., Ltd.

My loving People,—

We have been persuaded by some that are careful of our safety, to take heed how we commit ourselves to armed multitudes, for fear of treachery; but I assure you, I do not desire to live to distrust my faithful and loving people.

Let tyrants fear; I have always so behaved myself, that, under God, I have placed my chiefest strength and safeguard in the loyal hearts and good will of my subjects, and therefore I am come amongst you, as you see, at this time, not for my recreation and disport, but being resolved in the midst and heat of the battle, to live or die amongst you all, to lay down for my God, and for my kingdoms, and for my people, my honour and my blood, even in the dust.

I know I have the body but of a weak and feeble woman; but I have the heart and stomach of a king, and of a king of England too; and think foul scorn that Parma or Spain, or any prince of Europe should dare to invade the borders of my realm; to which rather than any dishonour shall grow by me, I myself will take up arms, I myself will be your general, judge, and rewarder of every one of your virtues in the field.

I know already for your forwardness you have deserved rewards and crowns; and we do assure you in the word of a prince, they shall be duly paid you. In the meantime my lieutenant-general shall be in my stead, than whom never prince commanded a more noble or worthy subject; no doubting but by your obedience to my general, by your concord in the camp, and your valour in the field, we shall shortly have a famous victory over those enemies of my God, of my kingdoms, and of my people.

Part IV

THE NEW SCIENCE

A. The Copernican Revolution

THE HELIOCENTRIC SYSTEM of Nicolaus Copernicus (1473–1543) was presented to the world in a technical work entitled De Revolutionibus Orbium Coelestium (On the Revolutions of the Heavenly Bodies). *Copernicus had earlier outlined his theory in a letter* ("Commentariolus"), *composed sometime after 1520, excerpts from which are given here.*

1. NICOLAUS COPERNICUS, "*COMMENTARIOLUS*," AFTER 1520

SOURCE. *Three Copernican Treatises*, Edward Rosen, tr., New York: Columbia University Press, 1939, pp. 57–61 and 63. Reprinted by permission of Columbia University Press.

HYPOTHESIS ON HEAVENLY MOTIONS: A PRELIMINARY OUTLINE OF THE THEORY THAT THE EARTH MOVES AROUND THE SUN

Our ancestors assumed, I observe, a large number of celestial spheres for this reason especially, to explain the apparent motion of the planets by the principle of regularity. For they thought it altogether absurd that a heavenly body, which is a perfect sphere, should not always move uniformly. They saw that by connecting and combining regular motions in various ways they could make any body appear to move to any position.

Callippus and Eudoxus, who endeavored to solve the problem by the use of concentric spheres, were unable to account for all the planetary movements; they had to explain not merely the apparent revolutions of the planets but also the fact that these bodies appear to us sometimes to mount higher in the heavens, sometimes to descend; and this fact is incompatible with the principle of concentricity. Therefore it seemed better to employ eccentrics and epicycles, a system which most scholars finally accepted.

Yet the planetary theories of Ptolemy and most other astronomers although consistent with the numerical data, seemed likewise to present no small difficulty. For these theories were not adequate unless certain equants were also conceived; it then appeared that a planet moved with uniform velocity neither on its deferent nor about the center of its epicycle. Hence a system of this sort seemed neither sufficiently absolute nor sufficiently pleasing to the mind.

Having become aware of these defects, I often considered whether there could perhaps be found a more reasonable arrangement of circles, from which every apparent inequality would be derived and in which everything would move uniformly about its proper center, as the rule of absolute motion requires. After I had addressed myself to this very difficult and almost insoluble problem, the suggestion at length came to me how it could be solved with fewer and much simpler constructions than were formerly used, if some assumptions (which are called axioms) were granted me. They follow in this order.

ASSUMPTIONS

1. There is no one center of all the celestial circles or spheres.
2. The center of the earth is not the center of the universe, but only of gravity and of the lunar sphere.
3. All the spheres revolve about the sun as their mid-point, and therefore the sun is the center of the universe.
4. The ratio of the earth's distance from the sun to the height of the firmament is so much smaller than the ratio of the earth's radius to its distance from the sun that the distance from the earth to the sun is imperceptible in comparison with the height of the firmament.
5. Whatever motion appears in the firmament arises not from any motion of the firmament but from the earth's motion. The earth together with its circumjacent elements performs a complete rotation on its fixed poles in a daily motion, while the firmament and highest heaven abide unchanged.
6. What appears to us as motions of the sun arise not from its motion but from the motion of the earth and our sphere, with which we revolve about the sun like any other planet. The earth has, then, more than one motion.
7. The apparent retrograde and direct motion of the planets arises not from their motion but from the earth's. The motion of the earth alone, therefore, suffices to explain so many apparent inequalities in the heavens.

Having set forth these assumptions, I shall endeavor briefly to show how uniformity of the motions can be saved in a systematic way. However, I have thought it well, for the sake of brevity, to omit from this sketch mathematical demonstrations, reserving these for my larger work. But in the explanation of the circles I shall set down here the lengths of the radii; and from these the reader who is not unacquainted with mathematics will readily perceive how closely this arrangement of circles agrees with the numerical data and observations.

Accordingly, let no one suppose that I have gratuitously asserted, with the Pythagoreans, the motion of the earth; strong proof will be found in my exposition of the circles. For the principal arguments by which the natural philosophers attempt to establish the immobility of the earth rest for the most part on the appearances; it is particularly such arguments that collapse here, since I treat the earth's immobility as due to an appearance.

THE ORDER OF THE SPHERES

The celestial spheres are arranged in the following order. The highest is the immovable sphere of the fixed stars, which contains and gives position to all things. Beneath it is Saturn, which Jupiter follows, then Mars. Below Mars is the sphere on which we revolve; then Venus; last is Mercury. The lunar sphere revolves about the center of the earth and moves with the earth like an epicycle. In the same order also one planet surpasses another in speed of revolution, according as they trace greater or smaller circles. Thus Saturn completes its revolution in thirty years, Jupiter in twelve, Mars in two and one half, and the earth in one year, Venus in nine months, Mercury in three.

THE APPARENT MOTIONS OF THE SUN

The earth . . . revolves annually in a great circle about the sun in the order of the signs, always describing equal arcs in equal times; the distance from the center of the circle to the center of the sun is one twenty-fifth of the radius of the circle. The radius is assumed to have a length imperceptible in comparison with the height of the firmament; consequently the sun appears to revolve with this motion, as if the earth lay in the center of the universe. However, this appearance is caused by the motion not of the sun but of the earth, so that, for example, when the earth is in the sign of Capricornus, the sun is seen diametrically opposite in Cancer, and so on. On account of the previously mentioned distance of the sun from the center of the circle, this apparent motion of the sun is not uniform, the maximum inequality being two and one sixth degrees.

The second motion, which is peculiar to the earth, is the daily rotation on the poles in the order of the signs; that is, from west to east. On account of this rotation the entire universe appears to revolve with enormous speed. Thus does the earth rotate together with its circumjacent waters and encircling atmosphere.

The Seventeenth Century

c. 1600–1715

THE seventeenth century was an era of war and unrest, of bitter religious struggles and dynastic conflicts, of brilliant philosophical speculation and notable scientific achievement—a turbulent age whose spirit is reflected in the fluid, grandiose, and sometimes writhing quality of Baroque art.

The first half of the century was dominated by the Thirty Years' War—a grisly affair that produced more than its share of death and suffering in Germany and involved most of the major European states. Beginning as a religious conflict between Catholicism and Protestantism in Germany, it ended as a ruthless dynastic struggle between the Catholic Hapsburgs and the Catholic Bourbons. At the time that it was being settled in the Peace of Westphalia (1648), England was in the midst of a civil struggle between Puritan and Anglican, Crown and Parliament, which resulted in the execution of King Charles I, the rise of Oliver Cromwell, and the eventual restoration of the Stuart monarchy (1660).

The second half of the century revolved around the glittering personality and ambitious policies of Louis XIV (1643–1715). Louis was surrounded by artists and writers devoted to the Classical style. His finance minister Colbert sought to organize the French economy along strict mercantile lines, with a heavy emphasis on royal control and direction; and his war minister Louvois subverted the French economy by pouring money into a series of aggressive but only moderately successful wars.

In the midst of the political turmoil, brilliant and original thinkers were producing the works that would justify the term Age of Genius, which historians have applied to the seventeenth century. Descartes broke sharply with the long-enduring traditions of medieval scholasticism and sought to create a rigorously rational new metaphysics. Hobbes developed the ancient and medieval notions of social contract into tightly reasoned arguments for absolute state sovereignty, and Locke used the same ingredients to justify English constitutionalism. A century of immense scientific advancement was ushered in by Galileo's first telescopic observations of the heavens, and brought to a climax with Newton's *Principia* (1687), which viewed the entire physical universe as a vast machine governed by three laws of motion and the universal law of gravitation. The military and political agonies and brilliant intellectual triumphs of the age laid the foundation for the tolerant cosmopolitanism and confident rationalism of the eighteenth-century Enlightenment.

Part I

POLITICS TO 1660

A. The Continent: the Thirty Years' War

THE TREATY OF WESTPHALIA of 1648, which brought the agonizing Thirty Years' War to an end, was a watershed in European politics, marking the waning of Spanish dominance, the end of the Holy Roman Empire as an effective political force, the rise of Austria and Prussia to political prominence, and the hegemony of France on the European Continent.

1. THE TREATY OF WESTPHALIA, 1648

SOURCE. G. R. Elton, ed., *Renaissance and Reformation, 1300–1648*, New York: The Macmillan Company, 1963, pp. 239–241. Reprinted by permission of The Macmillan Company.

There shall be a Christian, general and lasting peace, and true and genuine amity, between his sacred Imperial Majesty[1] and his sacred Most Christian Majesty,[2] as also between each and all the allies and adherents of the said Imperial Majesty, the House of Austria, its heirs and successors, but chiefly the electors, princes and estates of the empire on the one hand; and each and all the allies and adherents of the said Most Christian Majesty, his heirs and successors, and primarily the most serene queen and the kingdom of Sweden, and the respective electors, princes and estates of the empire, on the other. And this peace shall be so honestly and earnestly preserved and cultivated that each party shall procure the advantage, honor and profit of the other, and that on all sides (both on the part of the whole Roman Empire as against the kingdom of France, and on the part of the kingdom of France towards the Roman Empire) true neighborly relations shall be resumed and the care of peace and amity shall flourish again. . . .

[1] The Holy Roman Emperor.

[2] The king of France.

But to prevent in future any differences arising in political matters, all and every the electors, princes and estates of the Roman Empire shall in this treaty be confirmed and secured in all their rights, prerogatives, liberties, privileges, in the free exercise of territorial rights both in ecclesiastical and in political matters, in their lordships and sovereign rights, and in the possession of all these; so that they never can or ought to be molested therein by anyone under any pretext whatsoever.

They shall enjoy without contradiction the right of suffrage in all deliberations concerning the affairs of the empire, especially when the business in hand touches the making or interpreting of laws, the declaring of war, levying of taxes, raising or maintenance of troops, the erection on imperial behalf of new fortresses or the garrisoning of old in the territories of the states, also the conclusion of peace or of alliances, or similar matters. In these and like concerns nothing is in future to be done or admitted except by the common free choice and consent of all the imperial states. But particularly the individual states shall be for ever at liberty to enjoy the right of making alliances with each other and with other parties for their own support and security; always provided that such alliances shall not be directed against the emperor or empire, nor against the public peace of the empire, nor above all against the present treaty; and in everything without prejudice to the oath which everyone is bound to take to emperor and empire. . . .

. . . The Religious Peace of 1555,[3] as it was later confirmed . . . by various imperial diets, shall, in all its articles entered into and concluded by the unanimous consent of the emperor, electors, princes and estates of both religions, be confirmed and observed fully and without infringement. . . . In all matters there shall be an exact and mutual equality between all the electors, princes and states of either religion, as far as agrees with the constitution of the realm, the imperial decrees, and the present treaty; so that what is right for one side shall also be right for the other; all violence and other contrary proceedings being herewith between the two sides for ever prohibited. . . .

Whereas all immediate states enjoy, together with their territorial rights and sovereignty as hitherto used throughout the empire, also the right of reforming the practice of religion; and whereas in the Religious Peace the privilege of emigration was conceded to the subjects of such states if they dissented from the religion of their territorial lord; and whereas later, for the better preserving of greater concord among the states, it was agreed that no one should seduce another's subjects to his religion, or for that reason make any undertaking of defense or

---

[3] The Religious Peace of Augsburg

protection, or come to their aid for any reason; it is now agreed that all these be fully observed by the states of either religion, and that no state shall be hindered in the rights in matters of religion which belong to it by reason of its territorial independence and sovereignty. . . .

. . . It is agreed by the unanimous consent of His Imperial Majesty and all the estates of the empire that whatever rights and benefits are conferred upon the states and subjects attached to the Catholic and Augsburg[4] faiths, either by the constitutions of the empire, or by the Religious Peace and this public treaty, . . . shall also apply to those who are called reformed[5] . . . Beyond the religions mentioned above, none shall be received or tolerated in the Holy Roman Empire.

B. England: the Civil War

ENGLAND PLAYED NO ROLE in the Thirty Years' War or the Treaty of Westphalia, for she was deeply involved in internal problems arising from parliamentary opposition to Stuart autocracy and from the hostility of the Puritans to Anglican traditionalism. In 1628 Parliament challenged the heavy-handed absolutism of Charles I with the Petition of Right—an assertion of limitations on royal authority.

1. THE PETITION OF RIGHT, 1628

SOURCE. *Journals of the Lords*, III, 526–564.

The petition exhibited to his majesty by the lords spiritual and temporal, and commons in this present parliament assembled, concerning divers rights and liberties of the subjects, with the king's majesty's royal answer thereunto in full parliament.

To the king's most excellent majesty: Humbly show unto our sovereign lord the king the lords spiritual and temporal, and commons in parliament assembled, that, whereas it is declared and enacted by a statute made in the time of the reign of King Edward the First, commonly called *Statutum de Tallagio non Concedendo*, that no tallage or aid

---

[4] Lutheran.

[5] Calvinist.

should be laid or levied by the king or his heirs in this realm without the goodwill and assent of the archbishops, bishops, earls, barons, knights, burgesses, and other the freemen of the commonalty of this realm; and, by authority of parliament holden in the five-and-twentieth year of the reign of King Edward III, it is declared and enacted that from thenceforth no person should be compelled to make any loans to the king against his will, because such loans were against reason and the franchise of the land; and by other laws of this realm it is provided that none should be charged by any charge or imposition, called a benevolence, or by such like charge; by which the statutes before mentioned, and other the good laws and statutes of this realm, your subjects have inherited this freedom, that they should not be compelled to contribute to any tax, tallage, aid, or other like charge not set by common consent in parliament: yet, nevertheless, of late divers commissions directed to sundry commissioners in several counties with instructions have issued, by means whereof your people have been in divers places assembled and required to lend certain sums of money unto your majesty; and many of them, upon their refusal so to do, have had an oath administered unto them, not warrantable by the laws or statutes of this realm, and have been constrained to become bound to make appearance and give attendance before your privy council and in other places; and others of them have been therefor imprisoned, confined, and sundry other ways molested and disquieted; and divers other charges have been laid and levied upon your people in several counties by lord lieutenants, deputy lieutenants, commissioners for musters, justices of peace, and others, by command or direction from your majesty or your privy council, against the laws and free customs of the realm.

And where also, by the statute called the Great Charter of the Liberties of England, it is declared and enacted that no freeman may be taken or imprisoned, or be disseised of his freehold or liberties or his free customs, or be outlawed or exiled or in any manner destroyed, but by the lawful judgment of his peers or by the law of the land; and in the eight-and-twentieth year of the reign of King Edward III it was declared and enacted by authority of parliament that no man, of what estate or condition that he be, should be put out of his land or tenements, nor taken, nor imprisoned, nor disherited, nor put to death, without being brought to answer by due process of law: nevertheless, against the tenor of the said statutes and other the good laws and statutes of your realm to that end provided, divers of your subjects have of late been imprisoned without any cause showed; and when for their deliverance they were brought before your justices by your majesty's writs of *habeas corpus*, there to undergo and receive as the court should order, and their keepers commanded to certify the causes of their detainer, no cause was certified, but that they were detained by your majesty's special command, signified by the lords of your privy council; and yet were returned back to several prisons, without being charged with anything to which they might make answer according to the law.

And whereas of late great companies of soldiers and mariners have been dispersed into divers counties of the realm, and the inhabitants against their wills have been compelled to receive them into their houses, and there to suffer them to sojourn, against the laws and customs of this realm, and to the great grievance and vexation of the people: and whereas also, by authority of parliament in the five-and-twentieth year of the reign of King Edward III, it is declared and enacted that no man should be forejudged of life or limb against the form of the Great Charter and the law of the land; and, by the said Great Charter and other the laws and statutes of this your realm, no man ought to be adjudged to death but by the laws established in this your realm, either by the customs of the same realm or by acts of parliament; and whereas no offender of what kind soever is exempted from the proceedings to be used, and punishments to be inflicted by the laws and statutes of this your realm: nevertheless of late divers commissions under your majesty's great seal have issued forth, by which certain persons have been assigned and appointed commissioners, with power and authority to proceed within the land according to the justice of martial law against such soldiers or mariners, or other dissolute persons joining with them, as should commit any murder, robbery, felony, mutiny, or other outrage or misdemeanour whatsoever, and by such summary course and order as is agreeable to martial law and as is used in armies in time of war, to proceed to the trial and condemnation of such offenders, and them to cause to be executed and put to death according to the law martial; by pretext whereof some of your majesty's subjects have been by some of the said commissioners put to death, when and where, if by the laws and statutes of the land they had deserved death, by the same laws and statutes also they might, and by no other ought to have been, adjudged and executed; and also sundry grievous offenders, by colour thereof claiming an exemption, have escaped the punishments due to them by the laws and statutes of this your realm, by reason that divers of your officers and ministers of justice have unjustly refused or forborne to proceed against such offenders according to the same laws and statutes, upon pretence that the said offenders were punishable only by martial law and by authority of such commissions as aforesaid; which commissions and all other of like nature are wholly and directly contrary to the said laws and statutes of this your realm.

They do therefore humbly pray your most excellent majesty that no man hereafter be compelled to make or yield any gift, loan, benevolence, tax, or such like charge without common consent by act of parliament; and that none be called to make answer, or take such oath, or to give attendance, or be confined, or otherwise molested or disquieted concerning the same, or for refusal thereof; and that no freeman, in any such manner as is before mentioned, be imprisoned or detained; and that your majesty would be pleased to remove the said soldiers and mariners; and that your people may not be so burdened in time to come; and that the foresaid commissions for proceeding by martial law may be revoked and annulled; and that hereafter no commissions of like nature may issue forth to any person or persons whatsoever, to be executed as aforesaid, lest by colour of them any of your majesty's subjects be destroyed or put to death, contrary to the laws and franchise of the land (all of which they most humbly pray of your most excellent majesty as their rights and liberties according to the laws and statutes of this realm); and that your majesty would also vouchsafe and declare that the awards, doings, and proceedings to the prejudice of your people in any of the premises shall not be drawn hereafter into consequence or example; and that your majesty would be also graciously pleased, for the further comfort and safety of your people, to declare your royal will and pleasure that in the things aforesaid all your officers and ministers shall serve you according to the laws and statutes of this realm, as they tender the honour of your majesty and the prosperity of this kingdom.

CHARLES I ACCEPTED THE PETITION OF RIGHT at first, but in 1629 he dissolved Parliament and kept it inactive for the next eleven years. The Civil War that eventually ensued (1642–49) resulted in the defeat and capture of Charles I by the Puritan-Parliamentary forces and in his execution, proclaimed in a sentence by the High Court of Justice in 1649.

2. THE SENTENCE OF THE HIGH COURT OF JUSTICE ON KING CHARLES I, JANUARY 27, 1649

SOURCE. Samuel R. Gardiner, ed., *The Constitutional Documents of The Puritan Revolution,* Oxford: Oxford University Press, 1936, pp. 377–380. Reprinted by permission of The Clarendon Press, Oxford.

Whereas the Commons of England assembled in Parliament, have by their late Act intituled an Act of the Commons of England assembled in Parliament, for erecting an High Court of Justice for the trying and judging of Charles Stuart, King of England, authorised and constituted us an High Court of Justice for the trying and judging of the said Charles Stuart for the crimes and treasons in the said Act mentioned; by virtue whereof the said Charles Stuart hath been three several times convented before this High Court, where the first day, being Saturday, the 20th of January instant, in pursuance of the said Act, a charge of high treason and other high crimes was, in the behalf of the people of England, exhibited against him, and read openly unto him, wherein he was charged, that he, the said Charles Stuart, being admitted King of England, and therein trusted with a limited power to govern by, and according to the law of the land, and not otherwise; and by his trust, oath, and office, being obliged to use the power committed to him for the good and benefit of the people, and for the preservation of their rights and liberties; yet, nevertheless, out of a wicked design to erect and uphold in himself an unlimited and tyrannical power to rule according to his will, and to overthrow the rights and liberties of the people, and to take away and make void the foundations thereof, and of all redress and remedy of misgovernment, which by the fundamental constitutions of this kingdom were reserved on the people's behalf in the right and power of frequent and successive Parliaments, or national meetings in Council; he, the said Charles Stuart, for accomplishment of such his designs, and for the protecting of himself and his adherents in his and their wicked practices, to the same end hath traitorously and maliciously levied war against the present Parliament, and people therein represented, as with the circumstances of time and place is in the said charge more particularly set forth; and that he hath thereby caused and procured many thousands of the free people of this nation to be slain; and by divisions, parties, and insurrections within this land, by invasions from foreign parts, endeavoured and procured by him, and by many other evil ways and means, he, the said Charles Stuart, hath not only maintained and carried on the said war both by sea and land, but also hath renewed, or caused to be renewed, the said war against the Parliament and good people of this nation in this present year 1648, in several counties and places in this kingdom in the charge specified; and that he hath for that purpose given his commission to his son the Prince, and others, whereby, besides multitudes of other persons, many such as were by the Parliament entrusted and employed for the safety of this nation, being by him or his agents corrupted to the betraying of their trust, and revolting from the Parliament, have had entertainment and commission for the continuing and renewing of the war and hostility against the said Parliament and people: and that by the said cruel and unnatural war so levied, continued and renewed, much innocent blood of the free people of this nation hath been split, many families undone, the public treasure wasted, trade obstructed and miserably decayed, vast expense and damage to the nation incurred, and many parts of the land spoiled, some of them even to desolation; and that he still continues his commission to his said son, and other rebels and revolters, both English and foreigners, and to the Earl of Ormond, and to the Irish rebels and revolters associated with him, from whom further invasions of this land are threatened by his procurement and on his behalf; and that all the said wicked designs, wars, and evil practices of him, the said Charles Stuart, were still carried on for the advancement and upholding of the personal interest of will, power, and pretended prerogative to himself and his family, against the public interest, common right, liberty, justice, and peace of the people of this nation; and that he thereby hath been and is the occasioner, author, and continuer of the said unnatural, cruel, and bloody wars, and therein guilty of all the treasons, murders, rapines, burnings, spoils, desolations, damage, and mischief to this nation, acted and committed in the said wars, or occasioned thereby; whereupon the proceedings and judgment of this Court were prayed against him, as a tyrant, traitor, and murderer, and public enemy to the Commonwealth, as by the said charge more fully appeareth. To which charge, being read unto him as aforesaid, he, the said Charles Stuart, was required to give his answer; but he refused so to do, and upon Monday, the 22nd day of January instant, being again brought before this Court, and there required to answer directly to the said charge, he still refused so to do; whereupon his default and contumacy was entered; and the next day, being the third time brought before the Court, judgment was then prayed against him on the behalf of the people of England for his contumacy, and for the matters contained against him in the said charge, as taking the same for confessed, in regard of his refusing to answer thereto: yet notwithstanding this Court (not willing to take advantage of his contempt) did once more require him to answer to the said charge; but he again refused so to do; upon which his several defaults, this Court might justly have proceeded to judgment against him, both for his contumacy and the matters of the charge, taking the same for confessed as aforesaid.

Yet nevertheless this Court, for its own clearer information and further satisfaction, have thought fit to examine witnesses upon oath, and take notice of other evidences, touching the matters contained in the said charge, which accordingly they have done.

Now, therefore, upon serious and mature deliberation of the premises, and consideration had of the notoriety of the matters of fact charged upon him as aforesaid, this Court is in judgment and conscience satisfied that he, the said Charles Stuart, is guilty of levying war against the said Parliament and people, and maintaining and continuing the same; for which in the said charge he stands accused, and by the general course of his government, counsels, and practices, before and since this Parliament began (which have been and are notorious and public, and the effects whereof remain abundantly upon record) this Court is fully satisfied in their judgments and consciences, that he has been and is guilty of the wicked design and endeavours in the said charge set forth; and that the said war hath been levied, maintained, and continued by him as aforesaid, in prosecution, and for accomplishment of the said designs; and that he hath been and is the occasioner, author, and continuer of the said unnatural, cruel, and bloody wars, and therein guilty of high treason, and of the murders, rapines, burnings, spoils, desolations, damage, and mischief to this nation acted and committed in the said war, and occasioned thereby. For all which treasons and crimes this Court doth adjudge that he, the said Charles Stuart, as a tyrant, traitor, murderer, and the public enemy to the good people of this nation, shall be put to death by the severing of his head from his body.

THE DEATH WARRANT OF CHARLES I.

At the High Court of Justice for the trying and judging of Charles Stuart, King of England, Jan. 29, Anno Domini 1648.

Whereas Charles Stuart, King of England, is, and standeth convicted, attained, and condemned of high treason, and other high crimes; and sentence upon Saturday last was pronounced against him by this Court, to be put to death by the severing of his head from his body; of which sentence, execution yet remaineth to be done; these are therefore to will and require you to see the said sentence executed in the open street before Whitehall, upon the morrow, being the thirtieth day of this instant month of January, between the hours of ten in the morning and five in the afternoon of the same day, with full effect. And for so doing this shall be your sufficient warrant. And these are to require all officers, soldiers, and others, the good people of this nation of England, to be assisting unto you in this service.

To Col. Francis Hacker, Col. Huncks, and Lieut.-Col. Phayre, and to every of them.

Given under our hands and seals.

JOHN BRADSHAW.
THOMAS GREY.
OLIVER CROMWELL.
&c. &c.

SOME IMPRESSION OF the Puritans' devotion to the Lord Protector, Oliver Cromwell, and their hope that he would bend every effort to purge England of papish error, is conveyed by the sonnet "To the Lord General Cromwell" by the great Puritan poet, John Milton.

3. JOHN MILTON, "TO THE LORD GENERAL CROMWELL"

TO THE LORD GENERAL CROMWELL, MAY 1652, ON THE PROPOSALS OF CERTAIN MINISTERS AT THE COMMITTEE FOR PROPAGATION OF THE GOSPEL

Cromwell, our chief of men, who through a cloud
 Not of war only, but detractions rude,
 Guided by faith and matchless fortitude,
 To peace and truth thy glorious way hast ploughed,
And on the neck of crowned Fortune proud
 Hast reared God's trophies, and his work pursued,
 While Darwen stream, with blood of Scots imbrued,
 And Dunbar field, resounds thy praises loud,
And Worcester's laureate wreath: yet much remains
 To conquer still; Peace hath her victories
 No less renowned than War: new foes arise,
Threatening to bind our souls with secular chains.
 Help us to save free conscience from the paw
 Of hireling wolves, whose Gospel is their maw.

Part II

THE BAROQUE STYLE

A. Painting, Sculpture and Architecture

THE PAINTER ANTHONY VAN DYCK (1599–1641), in his portrait of Charles I, introduces us not only to the unfortunate Stuart king, but also to the grandiose flair of the Baroque style. Baroque artists based their work on the Classical canons of the Renaissance, but their Classicism was overlaid by an exuberance in the use of color, by a love of ornamentation, and by a feeling for plasticity which one finds in the Renaissance only in the art of the Venetian school and in the later works of Michelangelo. An age of passion and violent emotionalism could not contain itself within the restrained framework of the strict Classical form.

1. ANTHONY VAN DYCK, *CHARLES I,* c. 1635

ALL THE BAROQUE ELEMENTS *are present in the works of the Nether-lands artist Peter Paul Rubens (1577–1640)—the sense of movement, the vivid color, and the rich opulence (2, 3, and 4).*

2. RUBENS, *DESCENT FROM THE CROSS,* c. 1611

3. RUBENS, *COUNTRY FAIR*

4. RUBENS, *JUDGMENT OF PARIS*

IN THE PAINTINGS OF REMBRANDT (1607–1669) *one encounters a more somber quality, a sense of restraint, a mellow warmth, and a love for subject matter from everyday life uncharacteristic of the Baroque style* (5 and 6).

5. REMBRANDT, *THE MILL*

6. REMBRANDT, *WOMAN BATHING*

THE BAROQUE SENSE of massive movement and dramatic contrast of light and shadow emerges clearly in Bernini's Triton Fountain (Rome, c. 1637).

7. GIAN LORENZO BERNINI, *TRITON FOUNTAIN*, c. 1637

THE BREATHTAKING OPULENCE of Baroque architecture is perfectly expressed in the exterior of Pöppelmann's Palace of Dresden (1709–1719).

8. DANIEL PÖPPELMANN, *PALACE OF DRESDEN*, 1709–1719

B. Literature

OUR SELECTIONS CONCLUDE with three short poems from the Baroque age. The first is by the English poet John Donne (1573–1631), whose tightly constructed poems reflect an impassioned yearning for certitude in an age of unrest (1); the next two, by the intense and sensitive English Puritan John Milton (1608–1674), are the sonnets "To the Nightingale" (2) and "On His Blindness" (3).

1. JOHN DONNE, "SONG"

Go and catch a falling star,
   Get with child a mandrake root,
Tell me where all past hours are,
   Or who cleft the Devil's foot;
Teach me to hear mermaids singing,
Or to keep off envy's stinging,
     Or find
     What wind
Serves to advance an honest mind.

If thou be'st born to strange sights,
   Things invisible go see,
Ride ten thousand days and nights,
   Till age snow white hairs on thee.
Thou at thy return wilt tell me
All strange wonders that befell thee,
     And swear,
     Nowhere
Lives a woman true and fair.

If thou find'st one, let me know,
   Such a pilgrimage were sweet;
Yet do not, I would not go,
   Though at next door we should meet.
Though she were true when you met her,
And last till you write your letter,
     Yet she
     Will be
False, ere I come, to two or three.

2. JOHN MILTON, "TO THE NIGHTINGALE"

O nightingale that on yon bloomy spray
  Warblest at eve, when all the woods are still,
  Thou with fresh hope the lover's heart dost fill,
  While the jolly hours lead on propitious May.
Thy liquid notes that close the eye of day,
  First heard before the shallow cuckoo's bill,
  Portend success in love. O, if Jove's will
  Have linked that amorous power to thy soft lay,
Now timely sing, ere the rude bird of hate
  Foretell my hopeless doom, in some grove nigh;
  As thou from year to year hast sung too late
For my relief, yet hadst no reason why.
  Whether the Muse or Love call thee his mate,
  Both them I serve, and of their train am I.

3. JOHN MILTON, "ON HIS BLINDNESS"

When I consider how my light is spent
  Ere half my days in this dark world and wide,
  And that one talent which is death to hide
  Lodged with me useless, though my soul more bent
To serve therewith my Maker, and present
  My true account, lest He returning chide,
  "Doth God exact day-labour, light denied?"
  I fondly ask. But Patience, to prevent
That murmur, soon replies, "God doth not need
  Either man's work or his own gifts. Who best
  Bear his mild yoke, they serve him best. His state
Is kingly: thousands at his bidding speed,
  And post o'er land and ocean without rest;
  They also serve who only stand and wait."

Part III

THE AGE OF LOUIS XIV: 1661–1715

A. France

LOUIS ACCEDED AS A CHILD to the French throne in 1643, but until 1661 he was dominated by his great minister, Cardinal Mazarin. Only after Mazarin's death did the era of Louis XIV's personal rule begin. The Classicism of Louis XIV's age is epitomized in his Palace of Versailles (1669–85) with its simple, imposing lines, its symmetrical structure, its rich ornamentation, and its beautiful and artfully planned formal gardens.

1. THE PALACE OF VERSAILLES, 1669–1685

AN INTIMATE INSIGHT into the monarch himself is provided in the Memoirs of the Count de Saint-Simon (1715).

2. SAINT-SIMON, FROM HIS *MEMOIRS*, 1715

SOURCE. *The Age of Magnificence: The Memoirs of the Duc de Saint-Simon,* Sanche de Gramont, ed. and tr., New York: G. P. Putnam's Sons, 1963, pp. 137–142, 145–147. Copyright 1964 by G. P. Putnam's Sons. Reprinted by permission of G. P. Putnam's Sons.

One can no more refuse this prince a great deal of goodness and even greatness than one can overlook a greater amount of pettiness and meanness. It was impossible to distinguish between what was genuine and what was false. In both cases, nothing is harder to find than writers who knew him well and are capable of writing about him from their own experience, while remaining dispassionate enough to portray him without hate or obsequiousness, being guided in their praise or criticism only by the unadorned truth. As for knowing him, these memoirs may be counted on as reliable; as for objectivity, we can only try to achieve it honestly by suspending all our passions.

We must not speak here of his early years. He was crowned very young, but was stifled by the intrigues of a mother who wanted to govern, and even more by the ambition of a pernicious minister[1] who gambled with the State a thousand times to increase his personal glory. As long as the prime minister lived, the King was bent under his yoke, and we can strike those years from the monarch's reign. However, he learned to free himself. He fell in love; he discovered that idleness is glory's foe by leaning half-heartedly toward one and then the other; he had enough judgment to recognize Mazarin's death as a deliverance, even though he had not had the strength to deliver himself earlier. It was one of the finest moments of his life and eventually bore fruit in this maxim which he has held to implacably: To despise all prime ministers and all clergymen in his Council. At that time, he adopted another maxim, which he was unable to keep as firmly, for he did not always realize it slipped away from him: To govern alone, which was what he most prided himself on, what he was most praised and flattered for, and what he was least capable of.

He was born with a third-rate mind but one capable of improvement, cultivation, and refinement, and ready to borrow from others without imitation or embarrassment. He found infinite profit in being surrounded at court all his life by men and women of different types and ages, and of the highest and most varied wit.

If one must talk like this about a twenty-three-year-old king, one can say that he was fortunate in being surrounded by all kinds of dis-

[1] Anne of Austria, and Mazarin.

tinguished minds as soon as he was introduced to society. His ministers at home and abroad were then the most powerful in Europe, his generals were the most famous, their seconds-in-command were the best and have since become the leading strategists. By unanimous consent, their reputations have survived his reign. The upheaval which had so furiously shaken the State at home and abroad since the death of Louis XIII gave birth to a court made up of a large number of illustrious and capable persons, and refined courtiers. . . .

It must be repeated: The King's mind was less than ordinary but capable of improvement. He loved glory; he aspired to order and discipline. He was born wise, moderate, secretive, and in perfect control of his language and gestures. Will anyone believe it? He was born good and just, and God endowed him with enough qualities to become a good king and perhaps even a great king. All his troubles came from elsewhere. His early education was negligible because no one dared approach him. He often spoke of those days with bitterness, and said he had been neglected to the point that one evening he fell into the pond in the Palais-Royal garden in Paris, where the court was then held. In the years that followed, he became extremely dependent. He barely learned to read and write. He remained so ignorant that he never knew anything about history, events, money, conduct, birth, or laws, which made him prey to the most patent absurdities, sometimes in public. . . .

Soon after he became master, his ministers, his generals, his mistresses and his courtiers noticed that he had a weakness for, rather than a love of, glory. They spoiled him with praise. Commendation and flattery pleased him to such a point that the most obvious compliments were received kindly and the most insidious were relished even more. It was the only way to approach him, and those who won his love knew it well and never tired of praising him. That is why his ministers were so powerful, for they had more opportunities to burn incense before him, attribute every success to him, and vow they had learned everything from him. The only way to please him was submissiveness, baseness, an air of admiring and crawling toadyism, and by giving the impression that he was the only source of wisdom.

Whoever strayed from that path strayed from favor, and that is what finished Louvois. The poison spread. It reached incredible proportions for an experienced and not unintelligent prince. Although he had no voice and no knowledge of music, he would hum to himself the overtures of operas which told of his greatness; you could see him swimming in self-praise, and sometimes at banquets, when violins were playing, you could hear him singing the music between his teeth when it concerned him.

This was the origin of his thirst for glory, which sometimes snatched him from his amorous dalliances. This is why it was so easy for Louvois to start wars in order to overthrow Colbert or to maintain and increase his own power. At the same time Louvois insisted that no one could match the King as a military strategist or a field commander and that he was a better soldier than any of his generals. He convinced the King of this with the help of the generals, who were eager to please. This includes Condé, Turenne, and all those who succeeded them. He took credit for everything with admirable graciousness and complacency, and believed everything he was told. This was the origin of his love of parades, which he pushed to the point where his enemies called him the "parade king." His love of sieges was a cheap way to display his bravery and show off his ability, foresight, vigilance, and endurance. He insisted on staying at his command, and his admirably robust constitution was perfectly suited to protect him from hunger, thirst, cold, heat, rain, and bad weather. As he visited the camps, he enjoyed hearing murmurs of admiration about his splendor, his horsemanship, and his military achievements. His favorite topics of conversation with his mistresses and courtiers were his campaigns and his troops. He was eloquent, chose his words well, and with precision. He could describe an incident and tell a story better than any man alive. His most trivial remarks were never lacking in natural and manifest majesty.

He had a passion for detail. He was interested in everything that touched on his troops: Uniforms, arms, maneuvers, training, discipline, in a word, all sorts of vulgar details. He was just as interested in his construction projects, his household and his kitchens: He was always telling experts what they already knew, and they hung on his words like novices. This waste of time, which the King thought of as meritorious diligence, was the triumph of his ministers, who grew skilled in getting around him. They were delighted to see the King drowning in details, and were able to lead him according to their views and too often according to their interests by making him believe the ideas had originated with him. His increasing vanity and pride were continuously nourished, even by preachers from their pulpits. . . .

We have beheld a king who, as long as he had able ministers and captains, was great, rich, feared and admired as a conqueror and as the arbiter of Europe. Once they were gone, the machine kept rolling for some time on its own. But, inevitably, it came to a halt; faults and errors multiplied; decadence arrived with giant steps, but did not open the eyes of this jealous and despotic master who wanted to command and enact everything himself and who made up for the contempt in which he was held abroad by doubling the terror through which he ruled at home.

He was a fortunate prince in that he was a unique figure of his time, a pillar of strength, with almost uninterrupted good health. The age he lived in was so fertile and liberal in every way that it has been compared to the age of Augustus; he was fortunate also in having adoring subjects who gave their goods, their blood, their talent, sometimes their reputation and honor, and too often their religion and conscience, to serve him or only to please him. . . .

Little by little he reduced everyone to subjection, and brought to his court those very persons he cared least about. Whoever was old enough to serve did not dare demur. It was still another device to ruin the nobles by accustoming them to equality and forcing them to mingle with everyone indiscriminately. The idea was his and Louvois', who wanted to lord it over the nobility and make it dependent on him, so that those born to command found themselves commanding only in theory while removed from real responsibility. Using the pretext that all military service is honorable and that it is reasonable to learn to obey before one learns to command, the King made everyone except the princes of the blood begin as cadets in his guards or in the army, and even serve as simple soldiers, with guardroom duty winter and summer. He switched the scene of this purported basic training to the musketeers, after taking a fancy to that corps. It was no more of a school than the former, and there was nothing at all to be learned there except indolence and how to waste time; one also had to submit to being mixed with all sorts of people of every rank, which is what the King really wanted to obtain through this novitiate. One had to remain for an entire year in the exact observance of this useless and fiddling service. . . .

The court was another instrument of his despotic policy. We have just described the policies that divided, humiliated, and abashed the greatest of men, and the policies that elevated the authority and power of the ministers above everything, even the princes of the blood and people of the best quality, who found themselves diminished. . . .

Louis XIV took great pains to inform himself on what was happening everywhere, in public places, private homes, and even on the international scene. He also wanted to know about family secrets and private relationships. Spies and informers of all kinds were numberless. Some did not know their information would ever reach his ears, while others knew. Some wrote him directly through special channels, and their letters took precedence over all other matters, while others came to see the King secretly in his cabinets. This secret network ruined countless persons of all kinds root and branch, and they never knew how he had found them out. They were often unjustly accused, but the King never went back on a decision, or so rarely that nothing was rarer.

He had another failing which was dangerous for others and often for himself because it deprived him of loyal subjects. Although he had an excellent memory and was able to remember twenty years later a man he had seen once, and did not mix up what he knew, he was incapable of remembering all the countless things he was told daily. If he heard something unfavorable about someone and then forgot what it was, he retained the impression that there was something against the man, and that was enough to exclude him. . . .

But the King's most vicious method of securing information was opening letters. Through their ignorance and imprudence, a great many people continued to provide him with information for years, until the system was exposed. That is why the Pajots and the Rouilles, who were responsible for the postal service, were so respected they could never be removed, or even promoted. The cause long remained a mystery, and they amassed enormous fortunes at the expense of the public and the King. The skill and efficiency of the letter-opening operation defies the imagination. The postmasters and the postmaster general sent the King extracts of all the letters that could interest him, and copies of entire letters when the content or the rank of the sender warranted it. It took so little to condemn someone that those in charge of the postal system, from chiefs to clerks, were able to accuse whomever they wanted. They did not even have to rely on forgeries or prolonged investigations; one word of contempt for the king or his government, one jeer taken out of context and plausibly presented, sufficed to condemn without appeal or inquiry, and this means was always at their fingertips. The number of people who were rightly or wrongly condemned is inconceivable. The King's secret was never discovered, and nothing ever cost him less than to conceal it with profound silence.

THE GOALS AND STRICT REGULATIONS of Louis XIV's mercantile policy are disclosed in a document of his finance minister, Jean-Baptiste Colbert—a letter to the merchants of Marseilles (1664). The French economy was to be centralized, rationalized, and regulated in every detail, on the pattern of the systematically designed gardens at Versailles.

3. JEAN-BAPTISTE COLBERT,
A LETTER TO THE MERCHANTS OF MARSEILLES, 1664

SOURCE. J. H. Robinson, ed., *Readings in European History*, Boston: Ginn & Co., 1906, II, pp. 279–80. Reprinted by permission of Ginn & Co.

Very dear and well beloved:

Considering how advantageous it would be to this realm to reestablish its foreign and domestic commerce. . . we have resolved to establish a council particularly devoted to commerce, to be held every fortnight in our presence, in which all the interests of merchants and the means conducive to the revival of commerce shall be considered and determined upon, as well as all that which concerns manufactures.

We also inform you that we are setting apart, in the expenses of our state, a million livres each year for the encouragement of manufactures and the increase of navigation, to say nothing of the considerable sums which we cause to be raised to supply the companies of the East and West Indies;

That we are working constantly to abolish all the tolls which are collected on the navigable rivers;

That there has already been expended more than a million livres for the repair of the public highways, to which we shall also devote our constant attention;

That we will assist by money from our royal treasury all those who wish to reestablish old manufactures or to undertake new ones;

That we are giving orders to all our ambassadors or residents at the courts of the princes, our allies, to make, in our name, all proper efforts to cause justice to be rendered in all cases involving our merchants, and to assure for them entire commercial freedom.

That we will comfortably lodge at our court each and every merchant who has business during all the time that he shall be obliged to remain there. . . .

That all the merchants and traders by sea who purchase vessels, or who build new ones, for traffic or commerce shall receive from us subsidies for each ton of merchandise which they export or import on the said voyages.

We desire, in this present letter, not only to inform you concerning all these things, but to require you, as soon as you have received it, to cause to be assembled all the merchants and traders of your town of Marseilles, and explain to them very particularly our intentions in all matters mentioned above, in order that, being informed of the favorable treatment which we desire to give them, they may be the more desirous of applying themselves to commerce. Let them understand that for everything that concerns the welfare and advantage of the same they are to address themselves to Sieur Colbert. . . .

B. England

THE ABSOLUTISM OF LOUIS XIV'S MONARCHY stands in sharp contrast to the developing constitutionalism of England in the same period. The English overthrew the Stuart monarchy in the bloodless revolt—the "Glorious Revolution"—of 1688–1689, and installed a new dynasty in the persons of William and Mary. The English Bill of Rights of 1689 is a forthright declaration of Parliamentary authority and limited monarchy.

1. THE ENGLISH BILL OF RIGHTS, 1689

SOURCE. *Statues of the Realm*, VI, 142 f.: William and Mary, st. 2, c.2.

And whereas the said late King James II having abdicated the government, and the throne being thereby vacant, his highness the prince of Orange (whom it hath pleased Almighty God to make the glorious instrument of delivering this kingdom from popery and arbitrary power) did, by the advice of the lords spiritual and temporal and divers principal persons of the commons, cause letters to be written to the lords spiritual and temporal being Protestants, and other letters to the several counties, cities, universities, boroughs, and Cinque Ports for the choosing of such persons to represent them as were of right to be sent to parliament to meet and sit at Westminster . . . , in order to [provide] such an establishment as that their religion, laws, and liberties might not again be in danger of being subverted, upon which letters elections having been accordingly made:

And thereupon the said lords spiritual and temporal and commons, pursuant to their respective letters and elections being now assembled in a full and free representative of this nation, taking into their most serious consideration the best means for attaining the ends aforesaid, do in the first place (as their ancestors in like case have usually done) for the vindicating and asserting their ancient rights and liberties, declare that the pretended power of suspending of laws or the execution of laws by regal authority without consent of parliament is illegal; that the pretended power of dispensing with laws or the execution of laws by regal authority, as it hath been assumed and exercised of late, is illegal; that the commission for erecting the late court of commissioners for ecclesiastical causes and all other commissions and courts of like nature are illegal and pernicious; that levying money for or to the use of the crown by pretence of prerogative without grant of parliament, for longer time or in other manner than the same is or shall be granted, is illegal; that it is the right of the subjects to petition the king, and all commitments and prosecutions for such petitioning are illegal; that the raising or keeping a standing army within the kingdom in time of peace, unless it be with consent of parliament, is against the law; that the subjects which are Protestants may have arms for their defence suitable to their conditions and as allowed by law; that election of members of parliament ought to be free; that the freedom of speech and debates or proceedings in parliament ought not to be impeached or questioned in any court or place out of parliament; that excessive bail ought not to be required, nor excessive fines imposed, nor cruel and unusual punishments inflicted; that jurors ought to be duly impanelled and returned, and jurors which pass upon men in trials for high treason ought to be freeholders; that all grants and promises of fines and forfeitures of particular persons before conviction are illegal and void; and that, for redress of all grievances and for the amending, strengthening, and preserving of the laws, parliaments ought to be held frequently.

And they do claim, demand, and insist upon all and singular the premises as their undoubted rights and liberties, and that no declarations, judgments, doings, or proceedings to the prejudice of the people in any of the said premises ought in any wise to be drawn hereafter into consequence or example. To which demand of their rights they are particularly encouraged by the declaration of his highness the prince of Orange, as being the only means for obtaining a full redress and remedy therein. Having therefore an entire confidence that his said highness the prince of Orange will perfect the deliverance so far advanced by him and will still preserve them from the violation of their rights which they have here asserted and from all other attempts upon their religion, rights, and liberties, the said lords spiritual and temporal and commons assembled at Westminster do resolve that William and Mary, prince and princess of Orange, be and be declared king and queen of England, France, and Ireland, and the dominions thereunto belonging, to hold the crown and royal dignity of the said kingdoms and dominions to them, the said prince and princess, during their lives and the life of the survivor of them; and that the sole and full exercise of the regal power be only in and executed by the said prince of Orange in the names of the said prince and princess during their joint lives, and after their deceases the said crown and royal dignity of the said kingdoms and dominions to be to the heirs of the body of the said princess, and for default of such issue to the princess Anne of Denmark and the heirs of her body and for default of such issue to the heirs of the body of the said prince of Orange.

Part IV

THE SEVENTEENTH-CENTURY MIND

A. Philosophy

THE SEVENTEENTH CENTURY was a time of significant intellectual achievement in philosophy, political theory, and science. The developments of this period were to determine the thinking of those who came afterward, even to the present time. Our excerpt from the Discourse on Method *by René Descartes (1596–1650) includes an explanation of his dissatisfaction with past philosophies, an exposition of his methodological principles, and a discussion of his famous process of systematic doubt, ending with his proof of his own existence and God's.*

1. RENÉ DESCARTES, FROM THE *DISCOURSE ON METHOD*

SOURCE. *The Philosophy of Descartes,* Henry A. P. Torrey, tr., New York: 1892, pp. 37–42, 44–49. "Part Fourth" from *Discourse on Method,* John Veitch, translator, Edinburgh: 1850, pp. 74–82.

PART FIRST

I was brought up to letters from my childhood, and because I was led to believe that by means of them clear and certain knowledge of all that was useful in life might be acquired, I had an extreme desire for learning. But no sooner had I completed the whole course of studies at the end of which it is customary for one to be received into the circle of the learned, than I changed my opinion entirely. For I found myself involved in so many doubts and errors, that it seemed to me that I had derived no other advantage from my endeavors to instruct myself but only to find out more and more how ignorant I was. And yet I was in one of the most celebrated schools in Europe, where I thought there must be learned men if there were any such in the world. I had acquired all that others learned there, and more than that, not being content with the sciences which were taught us, I ran through all the books I could get hold of which treated of matters considered most curious and rare. Moreover, I knew what others thought about me, and I did not perceive that they considered me inferior to my fellow-students, albeit there were among them some who were destined to fill the places of our masters. And finally, our time appeared to me to be flourishing and as prolific of good minds as any preceding time had been. Such considerations emboldened me to judge all others by myself, and served to convince me that there did not exist in the world any such wisdom as I had been led to hope for. However, I did not cease to think well of scholastic pursuits. . . .

Above all I was delighted with the mathematics, on account of the certainty and evidence of their demonstrations, but I had not as yet found out their true use, and although I supposed that they were of service only in the mechanic arts, I was surprised that upon foundations so solid and stable no loftier structure had been raised: while, on the other hand, I compared the writings of the ancient moralists to palaces very proud and very magnificent, but which are built on nothing but sand or mud. . . . I revered our theology, and, as much as anyone, I strove to gain heaven; but when I learned, as an assured fact, that the way is open no less to the most ignorant than to the most learned, and that the revealed truths which conduct us thither lie beyond the reach of our intelligence, I did not presume to submit them to the feebleness of my reasonings. . . .

. . . So soon as I was old enough to be no longer subject to the control of my teachers, I abandoned literary pursuits altogether, and, being resolved to seek no other knowledge than that which I was able to find within myself or in the great book of the world, I spent the remainder of my youth in traveling, in seeing courts and armies, in mingling with people of various dispositions and conditions in life, in collecting a variety of experiences, putting myself to the proof in the crises of fortune, and reflecting on all occasions on whatever might present itself, so as to derive from it what profit I might. For it appeared to me that I might find a great deal more of truth in reasonings such as everyone carries on with reference to the affairs which immediately concern himself, and where the issue will bring speedy punishment if he make a mistake, than in those which a man of letters conducts in his private study with regard to speculations, which have no other effect and are of no further consequence to him than to tickle his vanity the less they are understood by common people, and the more they require wit and skill to make them seem probable. . . .

. . . But after I had spent some years thus in studying in the book of the world, and trying to gain some experience, I formed one day the resolution to study within myself, and to devote all the powers of my mind to choosing the paths which I must thereafter follow; a project attended with much greater success, as I think, than it would have been had I never left my country nor my books. . . .

PART SECOND

As for all the opinions which I had accepted up to that time, I was persuaded that I could do no better than get rid of them at once, in order to replace them afterward with better ones, or perhaps with the same, if I should succeed in making them square with reason. And I firmly believed that in this way I should have much greater success in the conduct of my life than if I should build only on the old foundations, and should rely only on the principles which I had allowed myself to be persuaded of in my youth, without ever having examined whether they were true. . . .

I had studied, in earlier years, of the branches of philosophy, logic, and in mathematics, geometrical analysis and algebra, three arts or sciences which seemed likely to afford some assistance to my design. But on examination of them I observed, in respect to logic, that its syllogisms and the greater part of its processes are of service principally in explaining to another what one already knows himself, or, like the art of Lully, they enable him to talk without judgment on matters in which he is ignorant, rather than help him to acquire knowledge of them; and while it contains in reality many very true and very excellent precepts, there are nevertheless mixed with these many others which are either harmful or superfluous, and which are almost as difficult to separate from the rest as to draw forth a Diana or a Minerva from a block of marble which is not yet rough-hewn. . . . For this reason I thought that some other method should be sought out which, comprising the advantages of these three, should be exempt from their defects. And as a multiplicity of laws often furnishes excuses for vices, so that a state is best governed which has but few and those strictly obeyed; in like manner, in place of the multitude of precepts of which logic is composed, I believed I should find the four following rules quite sufficient, provided I should firmly and steadfastly resolve not to fail of observing them in a single instance.

The first rule was never to receive anything as a truth which I did not clearly know to be such; that is, to avoid haste and prejudice, and not to comprehend anything more in my judgments than that which should present itself so clearly and so distinctly to my mind that I should have no occasion to entertain a doubt of it.

The second rule was to divide every difficulty which I should examine into as many parts as possible, or as might be required for resolving it.

The third rule was to conduct my thoughts in an orderly manner, beginning with objects the most simple and the easiest to understand, in order to ascend as it were by steps to the knowledge of the most composite, assuming some order to exist even in things which did not appear to be naturally connected.

The last rule was to make enumerations so complete, and reviews so comprehensive, that I should be certain of omitting nothing.

Those long chains of reasoning, quite simple and easy, which geometers are wont to employ in the accomplishment of their most difficult demonstrations, led me to think that everything which might fall under the cognizance of the human mind might be connected together in a similar manner, and that, provided only one should take care not to receive anything as true which was not so, and if one were always careful to preserve the order necessary for deducing one truth from another, there would be none so remote at which he might not at last arrive, nor so concealed which he might not discover. . . .

And I am free to say that the exact observance of these few rules which I had laid down gave me such facility in solving all the questions to which these two sciences apply, that in the two or three months which I spent in examining them, having begun with the simplest and most general, and each truth that I discovered being a rule which was of service to me afterward in the discovery of others, not only did I arrive at many which formerly I had considered very difficult, but it seemed to me, toward the end, that I was able to determine even in those matters where I was ignorant by what means and how far it would be possible to resolve them.

PART FOURTH

I had long before remarked that, in relation to practice, it is sometimes necessary to adopt, as if above doubt, opinions which we discern to be highly uncertain, as had been already said; but as I then desired to give my attention solely to the search after truth, I thought that a procedure exactly the opposite was called for, and that I ought to reject as absolutely false all opinions in regard to which I could suppose the least ground for doubt, in order to ascertain whether after that there remained aught in my belief that was wholly indubitable. Accordingly, seeing that our senses sometimes deceive us, I was willing to suppose that there existed nothing really such as they presented to us; and because some men err in reasoning, and fall into paralogisms, even on the simplest matters of Geometry, I, convinced that I was as open to error as any other, rejected as false all the reasonings I had hitherto taken for demonstrations; and finally, when I considered that the very same thoughts [presentations] which we experience when awake may also be experienced when we are asleep, while there is at that time not one of them true, I supposed that all the objects [presentations] that had ever entered into my mind when awake, had in them no more truth than the illusions of my dreams. But immediately upon this I observed that, whilst I thus wished to think that all was false, it was absolutely necessary that I, who thus thought, should be somewhat; and as I observed that this truth, *I think, hence I am,* was so certain and of such evidence, that no ground of doubt, however extravagant, could be alleged by the Sceptics capable of shaking it, I concluded that I might, without scruple, accept it as the first principle of the Philosophy of which I was in search.

In the next place, I attentively examined what I was, and as I observed that I could suppose that I had no body, and that there was no world nor any place in which I might be; but that I could not therefore suppose that I was not; and that, on the contrary, from the very circumstance that I thought to doubt of the truth of other things, it most clearly and certainly followed that I was; while, on the other hand, if I had only ceased to think, although all the other objects which I had ever imagined had been in reality existent, I would have had no reason to believe that I existed; I thence concluded that I was a substance whose whole essence or nature consists only in thinking, and which, that it may exist, has need of no place, nor is dependent on any material thing; so that "I," that is to say, the mind by which I am what I am, is wholly distinct from the body, and is even more easily known than the latter, and is such, that although the latter were not, it would still continue to be all that it is.

After this I inquired in general into what is essential to the truth and certainty of a proposition; for since I had discovered one which I knew to be true, I thought that I must likewise be able to discover the ground of this certitude. And as I observed that in the words *I think, hence I am,* there is nothing at all which gives me assurance of their truth beyond this, that I see very clearly that in order to think it is necessary to exist, I concluded that it might take, as a general rule, the principle, that all the things which we very clearly and distinctly conceive are true, only observing, however, that there is some difficulty in rightly determining the objects which we distinctly conceive.

In the next place, from reflecting on the circumstance that I doubted, and that consequently my being was not wholly perfect, (for I clearly saw that it was a greater perfection to know than to doubt,) I was led to inquire whence I had learned to think of something more perfect than myself; and I clearly recognised that I must hold this notion from some Nature which in reality was more perfect. As for the thoughts of many other objects external to me, as of the sky, the earth, light, heat, and a thousand more, I was less at a loss to know whence these came; for since I remarked in them nothing which seemed to render them superior to myself, I could believe that, if these were true, they were dependencies on my own nature, in so far as it possessed a certain perfection, and, if they were false, that I held them from nothing, that is to say, that they were in me because of a certain imperfection of my nature. But this could not be the case with the idea of a Nature more perfect than myself; for to receive it from nothing was a thing manifestly impossible; and, because it is not less repugnant that the more perfect should be an effect of, and dependence on the less perfect, than that something should proceed from nothing, it was equally impossible that I could hold it from myself: accordingly, it but remained that it had been placed in me by a Nature which was in reality more perfect than mine, and which even possessed within itself all the perfections of which I could form any idea; that is to say, in a single word, which was God. And to this I added that, since I knew some perfections which I did not possess, I was not the only being in existence, (I will here, with your permission, freely use the terms of the schools); but, on the contrary, that there was of necessity some other more perfect Being upon whom I was dependent, and from whom I had received all that I possessed. . . . I perceived that doubt, inconstancy, sadness, and such like, could not be found in God, since I myself would have been happy to be free from them. Besides, I had ideas of many sensible and corporeal things; for although I might suppose that I was dreaming, and that all which I saw or imagined was false, I could not, nevertheless, deny that the ideas were in reality in my thoughts. But, because I had already very clearly recognised in myself that the intelligent nature is distinct from the corporeal, and as I observed that all composition is an evidence of dependency, and that a state of dependency is manifestly a state of imperfection, I therefore determined that it could not be a perfection in God to be compounded of these two natures, and that consequently he was not so compounded; but that if there were any bodies in the world, or even any intelligences, or other natures that were not wholly perfect, their existence depended on his power in such a way that they could not subsist without him for a single moment.

I was disposed straightway to search for other truths; and when I had represented to myself the object of the geometers, which I conceived to be a continuous body, or a space indefinitely extended in length, breadth, and height or depth, divisible into divers parts which admit of different figures and sizes, and of being moved or transposed in all manner of ways, (for all this the geometers suppose to be in the object they contemplate,) I went over some of their simplest demonstrations. And, in the first place, I observed, that the great certitude which by common consent is accorded to these demonstrations, is founded solely upon this, that they are clearly conceived in accordance with the rules I have already laid down. In the next place, I perceived that there was nothing at all in these demonstrations which could assure me of the existence of their object: thus, for example, supposing a triangle to be given, I distinctly perceived that its three angles were necessarily equal to two right angles, but I did not on that account perceive anything which could assure me that any triangle existed: while, on the contrary, recurring to the examination of the idea of a Perfect Being, I found that the existence of the Being was comprised in the idea in the same way that the equality of its three angles to two right angles is comprised in the idea of a triangle, or as in the idea of a sphere, the equidistance of all points on its surface from the centre, or even still more clearly; and that consequently it is at least as certain that God, who is this Perfect Being, is, or exists, as any demonstration of Geometry can be. . . .

Finally, if there be still persons who are not sufficiently persuaded of the existence of God and of the soul, by the reasons I have adduced, I am desirous that they should know that all the other propositions, of the truth of which they deem themselves perhaps more assured, as that we have a body, and that there exist stars and an earth, and such like, are less certain; for, although we have a moral assurance of these things, which is so strong that there is an appearance of extravagance in doubting of their existence, yet at the same time no one, unless his intellect is impaired, can deny, when the question relates to a metaphysical certitude, that there is sufficient reason to exclude entire assurance, in the observation that when asleep we can in the same way imagine ourselves possessed of another body and that we see other stars and another earth, when there is nothing of the kind. For how do we know that the thoughts which occur in dreaming are false rather than those other which we experience when awake, since the former are often not less vivid and distinct than the latter? And though men of the highest genius study this question as long as they please, I do not believe that they will be able to give any reason which can be sufficient to remove this doubt, unless they presuppose the existence of God. For, in the first place, even the principle which I have already taken as a rule, viz., that all the things which we clearly and distinctly conceive are true, is certain only because God is or exists, and because he is a Perfect Being, and because all that we possess is derived from him: whence it follows that our ideas or notions, which to the extent of their clearness

and distinctness are real, and proceed from God, must to that extent
be true. Accordingly, whereas we not unfrequently have ideas or notions
in which some falsity is contained, this can only be the case with such
as are to some extent confused and obscure, and in this proceed from
nothing, that is, exist in us thus confused because we are not wholly
perfect. And it is evident that it is not less repugnant that falsity or
imperfection, in so far as it is imperfection, should proceed from God,
than that truth or perfection should proceed from nothing. But if we
did not know that all which we possess of real and true proceeds from
a Perfect and Infinite Being, however clear and distinct our ideas might
be, we should have no ground on that account for the assurance that
they possessed the perfection of being true.

But after the knowledge of God and of the soul has rendered us
certain of this rule, we can easily understand that the truth of the
thoughts we experience when awake, ought not in the slightest degree
to be called in question on account of the illusions of our dreams. For
if it happened that an individual, even when asleep, had some very
distinct idea, as, for example, if a geometer should discover some new
demonstration, the circumstance of his being asleep would not militate
against its truth. . . . For, in fine, whether awake or asleep, we ought
never to allow ourselves to be persuaded of the truth of anything unless
on the evidence of our Reason. And it must be noted that I say of
our *Reason,* and not of our imagination or of our senses: thus, for example, although we very clearly see the sun, we ought not therefore
to determine that it is only of the size which our sense of sight presents;
and we may very distinctly imagine the head of a lion joined to the
body of a goat, without being therefore shut up to the conclusion that
a chimæra exists; for it is not a dictate of Reason that what we thus
see or imagine is in reality existent; but it plainly tells us that all our
ideas or notions contain in them some truth; for otherwise it could
not be that God, who is wholly perfect and veracious, should have
placed them in us. And because our reasonings are never so clear or
so complete during sleep as when we are awake, although sometimes
the acts of our imagination are then as lively and distinct, if not more
so than in our waking moments, Reason further dictates that, since all
our thoughts cannot be true because of our partial imperfection, those
possessing truth must infallibly be found in the experience of our waking
moments rather than in that of our dreams.

B. Political Theory

WE TURN NEXT to two profound political theorists: Thomas Hobbes (1588–1650) and John Locke (1632–1704). Both began with the notion of an anarchic state of nature which man escaped by voluntarily giving up certain of his liberties through a social contract and thereby forming a state. Hobbes, in his Leviathan, *stresses the brutishness of the original state of nature, the irreversibility of the social contract, and the all but limitless sovereignty of the state (1).*

Locke, on the other hand, in his Second Treatise on Civil Government *(which was written in 1690 immediately following the "Glorious Revolution," in part to justify it), regards the state of nature with less distaste, and stresses the limitations which the social contract places on the arbitrary exercise of state sovereignty. Should the sovereign violate the contract, the people could rightfully rebel and change their sovereign (2).*

1. THOMAS HOBBES, FROM *LEVIATHAN*

SOURCE. Thomas Hobbes, *Leviathan*, New York: E. P. Dutton & Co., 1914, pp. 64–65, 67, 68, 90–96. Everyman's Library edition. Reprinted by permission of E. P. Dutton & Co., Inc. and J. M. Dent & Sons Ltd.

So that in the nature of man, we find three principall causes of quarrell. First, Competition; Secondly, Diffidence; Thirdly, Glory.

The first, maketh men invade for Gain; the second, for Safety; and the third, for Reputation. The first use Violence, to make themselves Masters of other mens persons, wives, children, and cattell; the second, to defend them; the third, for trifles, as a word, a smile, a different opinion, and any other signe of undervalue, either direct in their Persons, or by reflexion in their Kindred, their Friends, their Nation, their Profession, or their Name.

Hereby it is manifest, that during the time men live without a common Power to keep them all in awe, they are in that condition which is called Warre; and such a warre, as is of every man, against every man. For WARRE, consisteth not in Battell onely, or the act of fighting; but in a tract of time, wherein the Will to contend by Battell is sufficiently known: and therefore the notion of *Time,* is to be considered in the nature of Warre; as it is in the nature of Weather. For as the nature of Foule weather, lyeth not in a showre or two of rain; but in an inclination thereto of many dayes together; So the nature of War, consisteth not in actuall fighting; but in the known disposition thereto, during

all the time there is no assurance to the contrary. All other time is
PEACE.

Whatsoever therefore is consequent to a time of Warre, where every
man is Enemy to every man; the same is consequent to the time, wherein
men live without other security, than what their own strength, and their
own invention shall furnish them withall. In such condition, there is
no place for Industry; because the fruit thereof is uncertain: and consequently no Culture of the Earth, no Navigation, nor use of the commodities that may be imported by Sea; no commodious Building; no
Instruments of moving, and removing such things as require much force;
no Knowledge of the face of the Earth; no account of Time; no Arts;
no Letters; no Society; and which is worst of all, continuall feare, and
danger of violent death; And the life of man, solitary, poore, nasty,
brutish, and short.

It may seem strange to some man, that has not well weighed these
things; that Nature should thus dissociate, and render men apt to invade,
and destroy one another: and he may therefore, not trusting to this
Inference, made from the Passions, desire perhaps to have the same
confirmed by Experience. Let him therefore consider with himselfe,
when taking a journey, he armes himselfe, and seeks to go well accompanied; when going to sleep, he locks his dores; when even in his house
he locks his chests; and this when he knowes there bee Lawes, and
publike Officers, armed, to revenge all injuries shall bee done him; what
opinion he has of his fellow subjects, when he rides armed; of his fellow
Citizens, when he locks his dores; and of his children, and servants,
when he locks his chests. Does he not there as much accuse mankind
by his actions, as I do by my words? But neither of us accuse mans
nature in it. The Desires, and other Passions of man, are in themselves
no Sin. No more are the Actions, that proceed from those Passions,
till they know a Law that forbids them: which till Lawes be made
they cannot know: nor can any Law be made, till they have agreed
upon the Person that shall make it.

It may peradventure be thought, there was never such a time, nor
condition of warre as this; and I believe it was never generally so,
over all the world: but there are many places, where they live so now.
For the savage people in many places of *America*, except the government
of small Families, the concord whereof dependeth on naturall lust,
have no government at all; and live at this day in that brutish manner, as
it said before. Howsoever, it may be perceived what manner of life
there would be, where there were no common Power to feare; by the
manner of life, which men that have formerly lived under a peacefull
government, use to degenerate into, in a civill Warre. . . .

And because the condition of Man, (as hath been declared in the precedent Chapter) is a condition of Warre of every one against every one; in which case every one is governed by his own Reason; and there is nothing he can make use of, that may not be a help unto him, in preserving his life against his enemyes; It followeth, that in such a condition, every man has a Right to every thing; even to one anothers body. And therefore, as long as this naturall Right of every man to every thing endureth, there can be no security to any man, (how strong or wise soever he be,) of living out the time, which Nature ordinarily alloweth men to live. And consequently it is a precept, or generall rule of Reason, *That every man, ought to endeavour Peace, as farre as he has hope of obtaining it; and when he cannot obtain it, that he may seek, and use, all helps, and advantages of Warre.* The first branch of which Rule, containeth the first, and Fundamentall Law of Nature; which is, *to seek Peace, and follow it.* The Second, the summe of the Right of Nature; which is, *By all means we can, to defend our selves.*

From this Fundamentall Law of Nature, by which men are commanded to endeavour Peace, is derived this second Law; *That a man be willing, when others are so too, as farre-forth, as for Peace, and defence of himselfe he shall think it necessary, to lay down this right to all things: and be contented with so much liberty against other men, as he would allow other men against himselfe.* For as long as every man holdeth this Right, of doing any thing he liketh; so long are all men in the condition of Warre. But if other men will not lay down their Right, as well as he; then there is no Reason for any one, to devest himselfe of his: For that were to expose himselfe to Prey, (which no man is bound to) rather than to dispose himselfe to Peace. This is that Law of the Gospell; *Whatsoever you require that others should do to you, that do ye to them.* . . .

The mutuall transferring of Right, is that which men call CONTRACT. . . .

A *Common-wealth* is said to be *Instituted,* when a *Multitude* of men do Agree, and *Covenant, every one, with every one,* that to whatsoever *Man,* or *Assembly of Men,* shall be given by the major part, the *Right* to *Present* the Person of them all, (that is to say, to be their *Representative;*) every one, as well he that *Voted for it,* as he that *Voted against it,* shall *Authorise* all the Actions and Judgements, of that Man, or Assembly of men, in the same manner, as if they were his own, to the end, to live peaceably amongst themselves, and be protected against other men.

From this Institution of a Common-wealth are derived all the *Rights,* and *Facultyes* of him, or them, on whom the Soveraigne Power is conferred by the consent of the People assembled.

First, because they Covenant, it is to be understood, they are not obliged by former Covenant to any thing repugnant hereunto. And consequently they that have already Instituted a Common-wealth, being thereby bound by Covenant, to own the Actions, and Judgements of one, cannot lawfully make a new Covenant, amongst themselves, to be obedient to any other, in any thing whatsoever, without his permission. . . .

Secondly, Because the Right of bearing the Person of them all, is given to him they make Soveraigne, by Covenant onely of one to another, and not of him to any of them; there can happen no breach of Covenant on the part of the Soveraigne; and consequently none of his Subjects, by any pretence of forfeiture, can be freed from his Subjection. . . .

Thirdly, because the major part hath by consenting voices declared a Soveraigne; he that dissented must now consent with the rest; that is, be contented to avow all the actions he shall do, or else justly be destroyed by the rest. For if he voluntarily entered into the Congregation of them that were assembled, he sufficiently declared thereby his will (and therefore tacitely covenanted) to stand to what the major part should ordayne: and therefore if he refuse to stand thereto, or make Protestation against any of their Decrees, he does contrary to his Covenant, and therfore unjustly. And whether he be of the Congregation, or not; and whether his consent be asked, or not, he must either submit to their decrees, or be left in the condition of warre he was in before; wherein he might without injustice be destroyed by any man whatsoever.

Fourthly, because every Subject is by this Institution Author of all the Actions, and Judgments of the Soveraigne Instituted; it followes, that whatsoever he doth, it can be no injury to any of his Subjects; nor ought he to be by any of them accused of Injustice. For he that doth any thing by authority from another, doth therein no injury to him by whose authority he acteth: But by this Institution of a Common-wealth, every particular man is Author of all the Soveraigne doth; and consequently he that complaineth of injury from his Soveraigne, complaineth of that whereof he himselfe is Author; and therefore ought not to accuse any man but himselfe; no nor himselfe of injury; because to do injury to ones selfe, is impossible. It is true that they that have Soveraigne power, may commit Iniquite; but not Injustice, or Injury in the proper signification.

Fiftly, and consequently to that which was sayd last, no man that hath Soveraigne power can justly be put to death, or otherwise in any manner by his Subjects punished. For seeing every Subject is Author of the actions of his Soveraigne; he punisheth another, for the actions committed by himselfe.

And because the End of this Institution, is the Peace and Defence of them all; and whosoever has right to the End, has right to the Means; it belongeth of Right, to whatsoever Man, or Assembly that hath the Soveraignty, to be Judge both of the meanes of Peace and Defence; and also of the hindrances, and disturbances of the same; and to do whatsoever he shall think necessary to be done, both before hand, for the preserving of Peace and Security, by prevention of Discord at home, and Hostility from abroad; and, when Peace and Security are lost, for the recovery of the same. And therefore,

Sixtly, it is annexed to the Soveraignty, to be Judge of what Opinions and Doctrines are averse, and what conducing to Peace; and consequently, on what occasions, how farre, and what, men are to be trusted withall, in speaking to Multitudes of people; and who shall examine the Doctrines of all bookes before they be published. For the Actions of men proceed from their Opinions; and in the well governing of Opinions, consisteth the well governing of mens Actions, in order to their Peace, and Concord. . . .

Seventhly, is annexed to the Soveraigntie, the whole power of prescribing the Rules, whereby every man may know, what Goods he may enjoy, and what Actions he may doe, without being molested by any of his fellow Subjects: And this is it men call *Propriety*. . . .

Eightly, is annexed to the Soveraigntie, the Right of Judicature; that is to say, of hearing and deciding all Controversies, which may arise concerning Law, either Civill, or Naturall, or concerning Fact. For without the decision of Controversies, there is no protection of one Subject, against the injuries of another. . . .

Ninthly, is annexed to the Soveraignty, the Right of making Warre, and Peace with other Nations, and Common-wealths; that is to say, of Judging when it is for the publique good, and how great forces are to be assembled, armed, and payd for that end; and to levy mony upon the Subjects, to defray the expences thereof. . . .

Tenthly, is annexed to the Soveraignty, the choosing of all Counsellours, Ministers, Magistrates, and Officers, both in Peace, and War. For seeing the Soveraign is charged with the End, which is the common Peace and Defence; he is understood to have Power to use such Means, as he shall think most fit for his discharge.

Eleventhly, to the Soveraign is committed the Power of Rewarding with riches, or honour; and of Punishing with corporall, or pecuniary punishment, or with ignominy every Subject according to the Law he hath formerly made; or if there be no Law made, according as he shall judge most to conduce to the encouraging of men to serve the Commonwealth, or deterring of them from doing dis-service to the same. . . .

. . . To the Soveraign therefore it belongeth also to give titles of Honour; and to appoint what Order of place, and dignity, each man shall hold; and what signes of respect, in publique or private meetings, they shall give to one another.

These are the Rights, which make the Essence of Soveraignty; and which are the markes, whereby a man may discern in what Man, or Assembly of men, the Soveraign Power is placed, and resideth. . . .

And as the Power, so also the Honour of the Soveraign, ought to be greater, than that of any, or all the Subjects. For in the Soveraignty is the fountain of Honour. The dignities of Lord, Earle, Duke, and Prince are his Creatures. As in the presence of the Master, the Servants are equall, and without any honour at all; So are the Subjects, in the presence of the Soveraign. And though they shine some more, some lesse, when they are out of his sight; yet in his presence, they shine no more than the Starres in presence of the Sun.

2. JOHN LOCKE, FROM *THE SECOND TREATISE ON CIVIL GOVERNMENT*, 1690

SOURCE. John Locke, *Of Civil Government*, London: J. M. Dent, 1924, pp. 117–119, 119–120, 164–166, 228–229, 233, 241–242. Everyman's Library edition. Reprinted by permission of E. P. Dutton & Co., Inc. and J. M. Dent & Sons, Ltd.

Book II   An Essay Concerning the True Original Extent and End of Civil Government

CHAPTER I

1. It having been shown in the foregoing discourse:

Firstly. That Adam had not, either by natural right of fatherhood or by positive donation from God, any such authority over his children, nor dominion over the world, as is pretended.

Secondly. That if he had, his heirs yet had no right to it.

Thirdly. That if his heirs had, there being no law of Nature nor positive law of God that determines which is the right heir in all cases that may arise, the right of succession, and consequently of bearing rule, could not have been certainly determined.

Fourthly. That if even that had been determined, yet the knowledge of which is the eldest line of Adam's posterity being so long since utterly lost, that in the races of mankind and families of the world, there remains not to one above another the least pretence to be the eldest house, and to have the right of inheritance.

All these promises having, as I think, been clearly made out, it is impossible that the rulers now on earth should make any benefit, or derive any the least shadow of authority from that which is held to be the fountain of all power, "Adam's private dominion and paternal jurisdiction"; so that he that will not give just occasion to think that all government in the world is the product only of force and violence, and that men live together by no other rules but that of beasts, where the strongest carries it, and so lay a foundation for perpetual disorder and mischief, tumult, sedition, and rebellion (things that the followers of that hypothesis so loudly cry out against), must of necessity find out another rise of government, another original of political power, and another way of designing and knowing the persons that have it than what Sir Robert Filmer hath taught us.

2. To this purpose, I think it may not be amiss to set down what I take to be political power. That the power of a magistrate over a subject may be distinguished from that of a father over his children, a master over his servant, a husband over his wife, and a lord over his slave. All which distinct powers happening sometimes together in the same man, if he be considered under these different relations, it may help us to distinguish these powers one from another, and show the difference betwixt a ruler of a commonwealth, a father of a family, and a captain of a galley.

3. Political power, then, I take to be a right of making laws, with penalties of death, and consequently all less penalties for the regulating and preserving of property, and of employing the force of the community in the execution of such laws, and in the defence of the commonwealth from foreign injury, and all this only for the public good.

CHAPTER II   OF THE STATE OF NATURE

4. To understand political power aright, and derive it from its original, we must consider what estate all men are naturally in, and that is, a state of perfect freedom to order their actions, and dispose of their possessions and persons as they think fit, within the bounds of the law of Nature, without asking leave or depending upon the will of any other man.

A state also of equality, wherein all the power and jurisdiction is reciprocal, no one having more than another, there being nothing more evident than that creatures of the same species and rank, promiscuously born to all the same advantages of Nature, and the use of the same faculties, should also be equal one amongst another, without subordination or subjection, unless the lord and master of them all should, by any manifest declaration of his will, set one above another, and confer on him, by an evident and clear appointment, an undoubted right to dominion and sovereignty. . . .

6. But though this be a state of liberty, yet it is not a state of licence; though man in that state have an uncontrollable liberty to dispose of his person or possessions, yet he has not liberty to destroy himself, or so much as any creature in his possession, but where some nobler use than its bare preservation calls for it. The state of Nature has a law of Nature to govern it, which obliges every one, and reason, which is that law, teaches all mankind who will but consult it, that being all equal and independent, no one ought to harm another in his life, health, liberty or possessions; for men being all the workmanship of one omnipotent and infinitely wise Maker; all the servants of one sovereign Master, sent into the world by His order and about His business; they are His property, whose workmanship they are made to last during His, not one another's pleasure. And, being furnished with like faculties, sharing all in one community of Nature, there cannot be supposed any such subordination among us that may authorise us to destroy one another, as if we were made for one another's uses, as the inferior ranks of creatures are for ours. Every one as he is bound to preserve himself, and not to quit his station wilfully, so by the like reason, when his own preservation comes not in competition, ought he as much as he can to preserve the rest of mankind, and not unless it be to do justice on an offender, take away or impair the life, or what tends to the preservation of the life, the liberty, health, limb, or goods of another.

7. And that all men may be restrained from invading others' rights, and from doing hurt to one another, and the law of Nature be observed, which willeth the peace and preservation of all mankind, the execution of the law of Nature is in that state put into every man's hands, whereby every one has a right to punish the transgressors of that law to such a degree as may hinder its violation. For the law of Nature would, as all other laws that concern men in this world, be in vain if there were nobody that in the state of Nature had a power to execute that law, and thereby preserve the innocent and restrain offenders; and if any one in the state of Nature may punish another for any evil he has done, every one may do so. For in that state of perfect equality, where naturally there is no superiority or jurisdiction of one over another, what any may do in prosecution of that law, every one must needs have a right to do. . . .

CHAPTER VIII   OF THE BEGINNING OF POLITICAL SOCIETIES

95. Men being, as has been said, by nature all free, equal, and independent, no one can be put out of this estate and subjected to the political power of another without his own consent, which is done by agreeing with other men, to join and unite into a community for their comfortable, safe, and peaceable living, one amongst another, in a secure enjoyment of their properties, and a greater security against any that are not of it. This any number of men may do, because it injures not the freedom of the rest; they are left, as they were, in the liberty of the state of Nature. When any number of men have so consented to make one community or government, they are thereby presently incorporated, and make one body politic, wherein the majority have a right to act and conclude the rest.

96. For, when any number of men have, by the consent of every individual, made a community, they have thereby made that community one body, with a power to act as one body, which is only by the will and determination of the majority. For that which acts any community, being only the consent of the individuals of it, and it being one body, must move one way, it is necessary the body should move that way whither the greater force carries it, which is the consent of the majority, or else it is impossible it should act or continue one body, one community, which the consent of every individual that united into it agreed that it should; and so every one is bound by that consent to be concluded by the majority. And therefore we see that in assemblies empowered to act by positive laws where no number is set by that positive law which empowers them, the act of the majority passes for the act of the whole, and of course determines as having, by the law of Nature and reason, the power of the whole.

97. And thus every man, by consenting with others to make one body politic under one government, puts himself under an obligation to every one of that society to submit to the determination of the majority, and to be concluded by it; or else this original compact, whereby he with others incorporates into one society, would signify nothing, and be no compact if he be left free and under no other ties than he was in before in the state of Nature. For what appearance would there be of any compact? What new engagement if he were no farther tied by any decrees of the society than he himself thought fit and did actually consent to? This would be still as great a liberty as he himself had before his compact, or any one else in the state of Nature, who may submit himself and consent to any acts of it if he thinks fit.

98. For if the consent of the majority shall not in reason be received as the act of the whole, and conclude every individual, nothing but the consent of every individual can make anything to be the act of

the whole, which, considering the infirmities of health and avocations of business, which in a number though much less than that of a commonwealth, will necessarily keep many away from the public assembly; and the variety of opinions and contrariety of interests which unavoidably happen in all collections of men, it is next impossible ever to be had. And, therefore, if coming into society be upon such terms, it will be only like Cato's coming into the theatre, *tantum ut exiret*. Such a constitution as this would make the mighty leviathan of a shorter duration than the feeblest creatures, and not let it outlast the day it was born in, which cannot be supposed till we can think that rational creatures should desire and constitute societies only to be dissolved. For where the majority cannot conclude the rest, there they cannot act as one body, and consequently will be immediately dissolved again.

99. Whosoever, therefore, out of a state of Nature unite into a community, must be understood to give up all the power necessary to the ends for which they unite into society to the majority of the community, unless they expressly agreed in any number greater than the majority. And this is done by barely agreeing to unite into one political society, which is all the compact that is, or needs be, between the individuals that enter into or make up a commonwealth. And thus, that which begins and actually constitutes any political society is nothing but the consent of any number of freemen capable of majority, to unite and incorporate into such a society. And this is that, and that only, which did or could give beginning to any lawful government in the world. . . .

CHAPTER IX   OF THE ENDS OF POLITICAL SOCIETY AND GOVERNMENT

123. If man in the state of Nature be so free as has been said, if he be absolute lord of his own person and possessions, equal to the greatest and subject to nobody, why will he part with his freedom, this empire, and subject himself to the dominion and control of any other power? To which it is obvious to answer, that though in the state of Nature he hath such a right, yet the enjoyment of it is very uncertain and constantly exposed to the invasion of others; for all being kings as much as he, every man his equal, and the greater part no strict observers of equity and justice, the enjoyment of the property he has in this state is very unsafe, very insecure. This makes him willing to quit this condition which, however free, is full of fears and continual dangers; and it is not without reason that he seeks out and is willing to join in society with others who are already united, or have a mind to unite for the mutual preservation of their lives, liberties and estates, which I call by the general name—property.

124. The great and chief end, therefore, of men uniting into common-

wealths, and putting themselves under government, is the preservation of their property; to which in the state of Nature there are many things wanting.

Firstly, there wants an established, settled, known law, received and allowed by common consent to be the standard of right and wrong, and the common measure to decide all controversies between them. For though the law of Nature be plain and intelligible to all rational creatures, yet men, being biased by their interest, as well as ignorant for want of study of it, are not apt to allow of it as a law binding to them in the application of it to their particular cases.

125. Secondly, in the state of Nature there wants a known and indifferent judge, with authority to determine all differences according to the established law. For every one in that state being both judge and executioner of the law of Nature, men being partial to themselves, passion and revenge is very apt to carry them too far, and with too much heat in their own cases, as well as negligence and unconcernedness, make them too remiss in other men's.

126. Thirdly, in the state of Nature there often wants power to back and support the sentence when right, and to give it due execution. They who by any injustice offended will seldom fail where they are able by force to make good their injustice. Such resistance many times makes the punishment dangerous, and frequently destructive to those who attempt it.

127. Thus mankind, notwithstanding all the privileges of the state of Nature, being but in an ill condition while they remain in it are quickly driven into society. Hence it comes to pass, that we seldom find any number of men live any time together in this state. The inconveniences that they are therein exposed to by the irregular and uncertain exercise of the power every man has of punishing the transgressions of others, make them take sanctuary under the established laws of government, and therein seek the preservation of their property. It is this makes them so willingly give up every one his single power of punishing to be exercised by such alone as shall be appointed to it amongst them, and by such rules as the community, or those authorised by them to that purpose, shall agree on. And in this we have the original right and rise of both the legislative and executive power as well as of the governments and societies themselves. . . .

131. But though men when they enter into society give up the equality, liberty, and executive power they had in the state of Nature into the hands of the society, to be so far disposed of by the legislative as the good of the society shall require, yet it being only with an intention in every one the better to preserve himself, his liberty and prop-

erty (for no rational creature can be supposed to change his condition with an intention to be worse), the power of the society or legislative constituted by them can never be supposed to extend farther than the common good, but is obliged to secure every one's property by providing against those three defects above mentioned that made the state of Nature so unsafe and uneasy. And so, whoever has the legislative or supreme power of any commonwealth, is bound to govern by established standing laws, promulgated and known to the people, and not by extemporary decrees, by indifferent and upright judges, who are to decide controversies by those laws; and to employ the force of the community at home only in the execution of such laws, or abroad to prevent or redress foreign injuries and secure the community from inroads and invasion. And all this to be directed to no other end but the peace, safety, and public good of the people.

CHAPTER X   OF THE FORMS OF A COMMONWEALTH

132. The majority having, as has been showed, upon men's first uniting into society, the whole power of the community naturally in them, may employ all that power in making laws for the community from time to time, and executing those laws by officers of their own appointing, and then the form of the government is a perfect democracy; or else may put the power of making laws into the hands of a few select men, and their heirs or successors, and then it is an oligarchy; or else into the hands of one man, and then it is a monarchy; if to him and his heirs, it is a hereditary monarchy; if to him only for life, but upon his death the power only of nominating a successor, to return to them, an elective monarchy. And so accordingly of these make compounded and mixed forms of government, as they think good. And if the legislative power be at first given by the majority to one or more persons only for their lives, or any limited time, and then the supreme power to revert to them again, when it is so reverted the community may dispose of it again anew into what hands they please, and so constitute a new form of government; for the form of government depending upon the placing the supreme power, which is the legislative, it being impossible to conceive that an inferior power should prescribe to a superior, or any but the supreme make laws, according as the power of making laws is placed, such is the form of the commonwealth.

133. By "commonwealth" I must be understood all along to mean not a democracy, or any form of government, but any independent community which the Latins signified by the word *civitas*, to which the word which best answers in our language is "commonwealth," and most

properly expresses such a society of men which "community" does not (for there may be subordinate communities in a government), and "city" much less. And therefore, to avoid ambiguity, I crave leave to use the word "commonwealth" in that sense, in which sense I find the word used by King James himself, which I think to be its genuine signification, which, if anybody dislike, I consent with him to change it for a better. . . .

221. There is, therefore, secondly, another way whereby governments are dissolved, and that is, when the legislative, or the prince, either of them act contrary to their trust.

For the legislative acts against the trust reposed in them when they endeavour to invade the property of the subject, and to make themselves, or any part of the community, masters or arbitrary disposers of the lives, liberties, or fortunes of the people.

222. The reason why men enter into society is the preservation of their property; and the end while they choose and authorise a legislative is that there may be laws made, and rules set, as guards and fences to the properties of all the society, to limit the power and moderate the dominion of every part and member of the society. For since it can never be supposed to be the will of the society that the legislative should have a power to destroy that which every one designs to secure by entering into society, and for which the people submitted themselves to legislators of their own making: whenever the legislators endeavour to take away and destroy the property of the people, or to reduce them to slavery under arbitrary power, they put themselves into a state of war with the people, who are thereupon absolved from any farther obedience, and are left to the common refuge which God hath provided for all men against force and violence. Whensoever, therefore, the legislative shall transgress this fundamental rule of society, and either by ambition, fear, folly, or corruption, endeavour to grasp themselves, or put into the hands of any other, an absolute power over the lives, liberties, and estates of the people, by this breach of trust they forfeit the power the people had put into their hands for quite contrary ends, and it devolves to the people, who have a right to resume their original liberty, and by the establishment of a new legislative (such as they shall think fit), provide for their own safety and security, which is the end for which they are in society. . . .

229. The end of government is the good of mankind; and which is best for mankind, that the people should be always exposed to the boundless will of tyranny, or that the rulers should be sometimes liable to be opposed when they grow exorbitant in the use of their power, and employ it for the destruction, and not the preservation, of the properties of their people?

230. Nor let any one say that mischief can arise from hence as often as it shall please a busy head or turbulent spirit to desire the alteration of the government. It is true such men may stir whenever they please, but it will be only to their own just ruin and perdition. For till the mischief be grown general, and the ill designs of the rulers become visible, or their attempts sensible to the greater part, the people, who are more disposed to suffer than right themselves by resistance, are not apt to stir. . . .

243. To conclude. The power that every individual gave the society when he entered into it can never revert to the individuals again, as long as the society lasts, but will always remain in the community; because without this there can be no community—no commonwealth, which is contrary to the original agreement; so also when the society hath placed the legislative in any assembly of men, to continue in them and their successors, with direction and authority for providing such successors, the legislative can never revert to the people whilst that government lasts; because, having provided a legislative with power to continue for ever, they have given up their political power to the legislative, and cannot resume it. But if they have set limits to the duration of their legislative, and made this supreme power in any person or assembly only temporary; or else when, by the miscarriages of those in authority, it is forfeited; upon the forfeiture of their rulers, or at the determination of the time set, it reverts to the society, and the people have a right to act as supreme, and continue the legislative in themselves or place it in a new form, or new hands, as they think good.

LOCKE'S THOUGHT made a significant impact on the European mind throughout the eighteenth-century Enlightenment. His influence was felt not only in the realm of political theory (where, among other things, it provided a powerful justification for the American Revolution), but also in the area of philosophy, particularly epistemology. He rejected the concept of innate ideas and was rigorously empirical, basing his ideas on the notion of the human mind as a tabula rasa *influenced by experience alone; these ideas encouraged the optimistic eighteenth-century view that new experiences, produced by improved education and a better environment, could result in a new and superior human race.*

3. JOHN LOCKE, FROM *AN ESSAY CONCERNING HUMAN UNDERSTANDING,* 1690

SOURCE. John Locke, *An Essay Concerning Human Understanding,* 13th ed., pp. 53–54 (printed for Thomas Tegg, London, 1846).

OF IDEAS IN GENERAL, AND THEIR ORIGINAL

1. *Idea is the object of thinking.*—Every man being conscious to himself, that he thinks, and that which his mind is applied about, whilst thinking, being the ideas that are there, it is past doubt that men have in their mind several ideas, such as are those expressed by the words, "whiteness, hardness, sweetness, thinking, motion, man, elephant, army, drunkenness," and others. It is in the first place then to be inquired, how he comes by them? I know it is a received doctrine, that men have native ideas and original characters stamped upon their minds in their very first being. . . .

2. *All ideas come from sensation or reflection.*—Let us then suppose the mind to be, as we say, white paper (*tabula rasa*), void of all characters, without any ideas; how comes it to be furnished? Whence comes it by that vast store, which the busy and boundless fancy of man has painted on it with an almost endless variety? Whence has it all the materials of reason and knowledge? To this I answer, in one word, from EXPERIENCE: in that all our knowledge is founded, and from that it ultimately derives itself. Our observation, employed either about external sensible objects, or about the internal operations of our minds, perceived and reflected on by ourselves, is that which supplies our understandings with all the *materials* of thinking. These two are the fountain of knowledge, from whence all the ideas we have, or can naturally have, do spring.

3. *The object of sensation one source of ideas.*—First: Our senses, conversant about particular sensible objects, do convey into the mind several distinct perceptions of things, according to those various ways wherein those objects do affect them; and thus we come by those ideas we have of yellow, white, heat, cold, soft, hard, bitter, sweet, and all those which we call sensible qualities; which when I say the senses convey into the mind, I mean, they from external objects convey into the mind what produces there those perceptions. This great source of most of the ideas we have, depending wholly upon our senses, and derived by them to the understanding, I call "sensation."

4. *The operations of our minds the other source of them.*—Secondly: The other fountain, from which experience furnisheth the understanding with ideas, is the perception of the operations of our own minds within us, as it is employed about the ideas it has got; which operations, when

the soul comes to reflect on and consider, do furnish the understanding with another set of ideas which could not be had from things without; and such are perception, thinking, doubting, believing, reasoning, knowing, willing, and all the different actings of our own minds; which we, being conscious of, and observing in ourselves, do from these receive into our understanding as distinct ideas, as we do from bodies affecting our senses. This source of ideas every man has wholly in himself; and though it be not sense as having nothing to do with external objects, yet it is very like it, and might properly enough be called, "internal sense." But as I call the other "sensation," so I call this "reflection," the ideas it affords being such only as the mind gets by reflecting on its own operations within itself. . . .

5. *All our ideas are of the one or the other of these.*—The understanding seems to me not to have the least glimmering of any ideas which it doth not receive from one of these two. External objects furnish the mind with the ideas of sensible qualities, which are all those different perceptions they produce in us; and the mind furnishes the understanding with ideas of its own operation.

C. Science

GALILEO GALILEI (1564–1642) was an outspoken advocate of Copernican astronomy and a pioneer in the science of mechanics. It was he who first turned a telescope toward the heavens, and his observations, beginning in 1609, opened a new era in the history of astronomy. In his Sidereal Messenger *(1610) he describes some of his initial telescopic discoveries.*

1. GALILEO GALILEI, FROM *THE SIDEREAL MESSENGER*

SOURCE. Translated by Edward Stafford Carlos in 1880.

About ten months ago a report reached my ears that a Dutchman[1] had constructed a telescope, by the aid of which visible objects, although at a great distance from the eye of the observer, were seen distinctly as if near; and some proofs of its most wonderful performances were reported, which some gave credence to, but others contradicted. A few

[1] Hans Lippershey.

days after, I received confirmation of the report in a letter written from Paris by a noble Frenchman, Jacques Badovere, which finally determined me to give myself up first to inquire into the principle of the telescope, and then to consider the means by which I might compass the invention of a similar instrument, which after a little while I succeeded in doing, through deep study of the theory of refraction; and I prepared a tube, at first of lead, in the ends of which I fitted two glass lenses, both plane on one side, but on the other side one spherically convex and the other concave. Then, bringing my eye to the concave lens, I saw objects satisfactorily large and near, for they appeared one third of the distance off and nine times larger than when they are seen with the natural eye alone. I shortly afterward constructed another telescope with more nicety, which magnified objects more than sixty times. At length, by sparing neither labor nor expense, I succeeded in constructing for myself an instrument so superior that objects seen through it appear magnified nearly a thousand times, and more than thirty times nearer than if viewed by the natural powers of sight alone.

It would be altogether a waste of time to enumerate the number and importance of the benefits which this instrument may be expected to confer, when used by land or sea. But without paying attention to its use for terrestrial objects, I betook myself to observations of the heavenly bodies; and first of all I viewed the moon as near as if it was scarcely two semidiameters of the earth distant. After the moon, I frequently observed other heavenly bodies, both fixed stars and planets, with incredible delight; and, when I saw their very great number, I began to consider about a method by which I might be able to measure their distances apart, and at length I found one. And here it is fitting that all who intend to turn their attention to observations of this kind should receive certain cautions. For, in the first place, it is absolutely necessary for them to prepare a most perfect telescope, one which will show very bright objects distinct and free from any mistiness, and will magnify them at least four hundred times, for then it will show them as if only one twentieth of their distance off. For unless the instrument be of such power, it will be in vain to attempt to view all the things which have been seen by me in the heavens, or which will be enumerated hereafter. . . .

Let me first speak of the surface of the moon, which is turned toward us. For the sake of being understood more easily I distinguish two parts in it, which I call respectively the brighter and the darker. The brighter part seems to surround and pervade the whole hemisphere; but the darker part, like a sort of cloud, discolors the moon's surface and makes it appear covered with spots. Now these spots, as they are somewhat dark and of considerable size, are plain to everyone, and every age has seen them, wherefore I shall call them *great* or *ancient* spots, to distinguish them from other spots, smaller in size, but so thickly scattered that they sprinkle the whole surface of the moon, but especially the brighter portion of it. These spots have never been observed by anyone before me; and from my observations of them, often repeated, I have been led to that opinion which I have expressed, namely, that I feel sure that the surface of the moon is not perfectly smooth, free from inequalities, and exactly spherical, as a large school of philosophers considers with regard to the moon and the other heavenly bodies, but that, on the contrary, it is full of inequalities, uneven, full of hollows and protuberances, just like the surface of the earth itself, which is varied everywhere by lofty mountains and deep valleys. . . .

The difference between the appearance of the planets and the fixed stars seems also deserving of notice. The planets present their disks perfectly round, just as if described with a pair of compasses, and appear as so many little moons, completely illuminated and of a globular shape; but the fixed stars do not look to the naked eye bounded by a circular circumference, but rather like blazes of light, shooting out beams on all sides and very sparkling, and with a telescope they appear of the same shape as when they are viewed by simply looking at them, but so much larger that a star of the fifth or sixth magnitude seems to equal Sirius, the largest of all the fixed stars.

But beyond the stars of the sixth magnitude you will behold through the telescope a host of other stars, which escape the unassisted sight, so numerous as to be almost beyond belief. . . .

SCIENCE ADVANCED STEADILY in the seventeenth century. Toward its close, the Principia *(1687) of Isaac Newton (1642–1727) proved that the entire cosmos was governed by simple laws of motion and gravitation. This momentous vision of a vast, rationally ordered, mechanical universe dominated European thought for generations and provided the scientific foundation for the eighteenth-century Enlightenment. Three excerpts have been included from Newton's* Principia: *the preface, a summary of his methodological principles, and an exposition of the three laws of motion that governed the dynamics of the physical universe.*

2. ISAAC NEWTON, SELECTIONS FROM THE *PRINCIPIA,* 1687

PREFACE

Since the ancients (as we are told by *Pappus*), made great account of the science of mechanics in the investigation of natural things; and the moderns, laying aside substantial forms and occult qualities, have endeavoured to subject the phænomena of nature to the laws of mathematics, I have in this treatise cultivated mathematics so far as it regards philosophy. The ancients considered mechanics in a twofold respect; as rational, which proceeds accurately by demonstration; and practical. To practical mechanics all the manual arts belong, from which mechanics took its name. But as artificers do not work with perfect accuracy, it comes to pass that mechanics is so distinguished from geometry, that what is perfectly accurate is called geometrical; what is less so, is called mechanical. But the errors are not in the art, but in the artificers. He that works with less accuracy is an imperfect mechanic; and if any could work with perfect accuracy, he would be the most perfect mechanic of all; for the description of right lines and circles, upon which geometry is founded, belongs to mechanics. Geometry does not teach us to draw these lines, but requires them to be drawn; for it requires that the learner should first be taught to describe these accurately, before he enters upon geometry; then it shows how by these operations problems may be solved. To describe right lines and circles are problems, but not geometrical problems. The solution of these problems is required from mechanics; and by geometry the use of them, when so solved is shown; and it is the glory of geometry that from those few principles, brought from without, it is able to produce so many things. Therefore geometry is founded in mechanical practice, and is nothing but that part of universal mechanics which accurately proposes and demonstrates the art of measuring. But since the manual arts are chiefly conversant in the moving of bodies, it comes to pass that geometry is commonly referred to their magnitudes, and mechanics to their motion. In this sense rational mechanics will be the science of motions resulting from any forces whatsoever, and of the forces required to produce any motions, accurately proposed and demonstrated. This part of mechanics was cultivated by the ancients in the five powers which relate to manual arts, who considered gravity (it not being a manual power), no otherwise than as it moved weights by those powers. Our design not respecting arts, but philosophy, and our subject not manual but natural powers, we consider chiefly those things which relate to gravity, levity, elastic force, the resistance of fluids, and the like forces, whether attractive or impulsive; and therefore we offer this work as the mathematical principles of philosophy; for all the difficulty of philosophy seems to consist in this—from the phænomena of motions to investigate the forces of nature, and then from these forces to demonstrate the other phænomena; and to this end the general propositions in the first and second book are directed. In the third book we give an example of this in the explication of the System of the World; for by the propositions mathematically demonstrated in the former books, we in the third derive from the celestial phænomena the forces of gravity with which bodies tend to the sun and the several planets. Then from these forces, by other propositions which are also mathematical, we deduce the motions of the planets, the comets, the moon, and the sea. I wish we could derive the rest of the phænomena of nature by the same kind of reasoning from mechanical principles; for I am induced by many reasons to suspect that they may all depend upon certain forces by which the particles of bodies, by some causes hitherto unknown, are either mutually impelled towards each other, and cohere in regular figures, or are repelled and recede from each other; which forces being unknown, philosophers have hitherto attempted the search of nature in vain; but I hope the principles here laid down will afford some light either to this or some truer method of philosophy. . . .

RULES OF REASONING IN PHILOSOPHY

Rule I. *We are to admit no more causes of natural things than such as are both true and sufficient to explain their appearances.*

To this purpose the philosophers say that Nature does nothing in vain, and more is in vain when less will serve; for Nature is pleased with simplicity, and affects not the pomp of superfluous causes.

Rule II. *Therefore to the same natural effects we must, as far as possible, assign the same causes.*

As to respiration in a man and in a beast; the descent of stones in Europe and in America; the light of our culinary fire and of the sun; the reflection of light in the earth, and in the planets.

Rule III. *The qualities of bodies, which admit neither intension nor remission of degrees, and which are found to belong to all bodies within the reach of our experiments, are to be esteemed the universal qualities of all bodies whatsoever.*

For since the qualities of bodies are only known to us by experiments, we are to hold for universal all such as universally agree with experiments and such as are not liable to diminution can never be quite taken away. We are certainly not to relinquish the evidence of experiments for the sake of dreams and vain fictions of our own devising; nor are we to recede from the analogy of Nature, which uses to be simple, and always consonant to itself. We no other way know the extension of bodies than by our senses, nor do these reach it in all bodies; but because we perceive extension in all that are sensible, therefore we ascribe it universally to all others also. That abundance of bodies are hard, we learn by experience; and because the hardness of the whole arises from the hardness of the parts, we therefore justly infer the hardness of the undivided particles not only of the bodies we feel but of all others. That all bodies are impenetrable, we gather not from reason, but from sensation. The bodies which we handle we find impenetrable, and thence conclude impenetrability to be an universal property of all bodies whatsoever. That all bodies are moveable, and endowed with certain powers (which we call the *vires inertiæ*) of persevering in their motion, or in their rest, we only infer the like properties observed in the bodies which we have seen. The extension, hardness, impenetrability, mobility, and *vis inertiæ* of the whole, result from the extension, hardness, impenetrability, mobility, and *vires inertiæ* of the parts; and thence we conclude the least particles of all bodies to be also all extended, and hard, and impenetrable, and moveable, and endowed with their proper *vires inertiæ*. And this is the foundation of all philosophy. Moreover, that the divided but contiguous particles of bodies may be separated from one another, is matter of observation; and, in the particles that remain undivided, our minds are able to distinguish yet lesser parts, as is mathematically demonstrated. But whether the parts so distinguished, and not yet divided, may, by the powers of Nature, be actually divided and separated from one another, we cannot certainly determine. Yet, had we the proof of but one experiment that any undivided particle, in breaking a hard and solid body, suffered a division, we might by virtue of this rule conclude that the undivided as well as the divided particles may be divided and actually separated to infinity.

Lastly, if it universally appears, by experiments and astronomical observations, that all bodies about the earth gravitate towards the earth, and that in proportion to the quantity of matter which they severally contain; that the moon likewise, according to the quantity of its matter, gravitates towards the earth; that, on the other hand, our sea gravitates towards the moon; and all the planets mutually one towards another; and the comets in like manner towards the sun; we must, in consequence of this rule, universally allow that all bodies whatsoever are endowed with a principle of mutual gravitation. For the argument from the appearances concludes with more force for the universal gravitation of all bodies than for their impenetrability; of which, among those in the celestial regions, we have no experiments, nor any manner of observation. Not that I affirm gravity to be essential to bodies: by their *vis insita* I mean nothing but their *vis inertiæ*. This is immuntable. Their gravity is diminished as they recede from the earth.

Rule IV. *In experimental philosophy we are to look upon propositions collected by general induction from phænomena as accurately or very nearly true, notwithstanding any contrary hypotheses that may be imagined, till such time as other phænomena occur, by which they may either be made more accurate, or liable to exceptions.*

This rule must follow, that the argument of induction may not be evaded by hypotheses.

THE LAWS OF MOTION

Law I: Every body continues in its state of rest, or of uniform motion, in a right line, unless it is compelled to change that state by forces impressed upon it.

Projectiles continue in their motions, so far as they are not retarded by the resistance of the air, or impelled downwards by the force of gravity. A top, whose parts by their cohesion are continually drawn aside from rectilinear motions, does not cease its rotation, otherwise than as it is retarded by the air. The greater bodies of the planets and comets, meeting with less resistance in freer spaces, preserve their motions both progressive and circular for a much longer time.

Law II: The change of motion is proportional to the motive force impressed; and is made in the direction of the right line in which that force is impressed.

If any force generates a motion, a double force will generate double the motion, a triple force triple the motion, whether that force be impressed altogether and at once or gradually and successively. And this motion (being always directed the same way with the generating force), if the body moved before, is added to or subtracted from the former motion, according as they directly conspire with or are directly contrary to each other; or obliquely joined, when they are oblique, so as to produce a new motion compounded from the determination of both.

Law III: To every action there is always opposed an equal reaction: or, the mutual actions of two bodies upon each other are always equal, and directed to contrary parts.

Whatever draws or presses another is as much drawn or pressed by that other. If you press a stone with your finger, the finger is also pressed by the stone. If a horse draws a stone tied to a rope, the horse (if I may say so) will be equally drawn back towards the stone; for the distended rope, by the same endeavor to relax or unbend itself, will draw the horse as much towards the stone as it does the stone towards the horse, and will obstruct the progress of the one as much as it advances that of the other. If a body impinge upon another, and by its force change the motion of the other, that body also (because of the equality of the mutual pressure) will undergo an equal change, in its own motion, towards the contrary part. The changes made by these actions are equal, not in the velocities but in the motions of the bodies; that is to say, if the bodies are not hindered by any other impediments. For, because the motions are equally changed, the changes of the velocities made toward contrary parts are inversely proportional to the bodies.

SECTION THREE

The Age of Reason

1715–1789

THE seven and a half decades between the death of Louis XIV and the advent of the French Revolution constituted an era of relative peace, security, and optimism. The age was marked by dynastic power politics and wars in both Europe and her New World colonies, but the military struggles were less severe than the wars of the sixteenth and seventeenth centuries or the subsequent French Revolution and the wars of the Napoleonic era. The grandiosity and tortured fluidity of Baroque art gradually gave way to a strict Neo-Classicism—simple, elegant, and restrained. The emotionalism of Baroque poetry was replaced by the balanced verses and optimistic humanism of Alexander Pope and his contemporaries. This was an age of mature, confident synthesis—a new Augustan Age—a relatively peaceful intermission between the religious struggles of the past and the national and social upheavals of the future.

This was, above all, the age of Enlightenment, less original perhaps than the age of genius that preceded it, but imbued with the thought of John Locke and Isaac Newton that nature was orderly and harmonious and that the universe was fundamentally rational. Newton was the patron saint of the Enlightenment, and eighteenth-century thought was beguiled by the vision of the Newtonian world-machine. It was the elusive goal of many Enlightenment thinkers to apply the principles of reason and the harmony of nature to the problems of man and society exactly as Newton had applied them with such spectacular success to the operations of the physical universe. Philosophers such as Voltaire endeavored to rationalize religion, stripping it of superstition and reducing it to its essentials. Voltaire was a deist—he believed in God as the creator of the world-machine but rejected prayer, miracles, holy water, and all the myriad trappings of organized religion. Others, such as David Hume, rejected deism itself as rationally unverifiable, and took a completely skeptical position with regard to God and his works.

The *philosophes* of the Enlightenment sought also to rationalize government and society—to purge the state of inefficient customs and archaic institutions, and to create a rational political order. Voltaire and others endorsed enlightened despotism, giving their blessing to "enlightened" monarchs such as Frederick the Great of Prussia. Enlightenment ideals had at least a superficial effect on the policies of a number of contemporary rulers. Other intellectuals of the day, following Locke, advocated limited, constitutional monarchy and even republicanism, cast within the framework of a carefully ordered constitution. The political ideas of Jean Jacques Rousseau, which transcend in many ways the intellectual categories of the Enlightenment, tended toward a version of popular government based on the rather vague concept of the "general will" which was all-powerful and could not err. Rousseau's state, despite its more-or-less popular basis, was so limitless in its power that some scholars have regarded it as a precursor of modern totalitarianism.

The prevailing concept of natural order and harmony expressed itself in the realm of economic thought in the works of the French Physiocrats and the Englishman Adam Smith. These men were deeply hostile to the widespread policies of government regulation, protective tariffs, state bounties, and navigation laws that constituted the machinery of mercantilism. They argued that economic life was governed by natural laws which were no less orderly, dependable, or beneficent than the laws of physics. The economic system should be left to function without interference; the state should keep its hands off—should follow a policy of strict *laissez-faire*.

In these and other ways, the core concepts of reason and natural order dominated eighteenth-century thought. They were often accompanied by a fundamental optimism with regard to man's future. Reason, many *philosophes* believed, would open the way to a far better world, more prosperous, more peaceful, and more just than anything that Europe had theretofore experienced.

Part I

THE RATIONALIZATION
OF NATURE

A. The Newtonian Background

NEWTON HIMSELF was a devoted Christian, as were many of his follow-ers. The excerpt from Roger Cotes' "Preface" to the second edition of Newton's Principia *(1713) demonstrates how the Newtonian world-machine might be regarded as the handiwork of the Christian God. It also illustrates the profound reverence of eighteenth-century writers toward Newton and his thought. The vision of a mechanical universe may have seemed to some to be consistent with Christianity; to others it drained the cosmos of its mystery and transformed God from a loving, compassionate Father to a remote watchmaker who, in creating the ordered universe, had performed his essential task and was no longer needed.*

1. ROGER COTES, FROM HIS "PREFACE" TO THE SECOND EDITION OF NEWTON'S *PRINCIPIA*, 1713

Without all doubt, this world, so diversified with that variety of forms and motions we find in it, could arise from nothing but the perfectly free will of GoD directing and presiding over all.

From this Fountain it is that those laws, which we call the laws of Nature, have flowed; in which there appear many traces, indeed, of the most wise contrivance, but not the least shadow of necessity. These, therefore, we must not seek from uncertain conjectures, but learn them from observations and experiments. He who thinks to find the true prin-ciples of physics and the laws of natural things by the force alone of his own mind, and the internal light of his reason, must either suppose that the world exists by necessity, and by the same necessity follows the laws proposed; or, if the order of Nature was established by the will of GoD, that himself, a miserable reptile, can tell what was fittest to be done. All sound and true philosophy is founded on the appearances of things, which, if they draw us ever so much against our wills to such principles as most clearly manifest to us the most excellent counsel and supreme dominion of the Allwise and Almighty Being, those principles are not therefore to be laid aside, because some men may perhaps dislike them. They may call them, if they please, miracles or occult qualities; but names maliciously given ought not to be a disadvantage to the things themselves; unless they will say, at last, that all philosophy ought to be founded in atheism. Philosophy must not be corrupted in complaisance to these men; for the order of things will not be changed.

Fair and equal judges will therefore give sentence in favour of this most excellent method of philosophy, which is founded on experiments and observations. To this method it is hardly to be said or imagined what light, what splendor, hath accrued from this admirable work of our illustrious author, whose happy and sublime genius, resolving the most difficult problems, and reaching to discoveries of which the mind of man was thought incapable before, is deservedly admired by all those who are somewhat more than superficially versed in these matters. The gates are now set open; and by his means we may freely enter into the knowledge of the hidden secrets and wonders of natural things. He has so clearly laid open and set before our eyes the most beautiful frame of the System of the World, that, if King Alphonsus were now alive, he would not complain for want of the graces either of simplicity or of harmony in it. Therefore we may now more nearly behold the beauties of Nature, and entertain ourselves with the delightful contemplation; and, which is the best and most valuable fruit of philosophy, be thence incited the more profoundly to reverence and adore the great Maker and Lord of all. He must be blind, who, from the most wise and excellent contrivances of things, cannot see the infinite wisdom and goodness of their Almighty Creator; and he must be mad and senseless who refuses to acknowledge them.

B. Reason and Nature in the Eighteenth Century

REVERENCE FOR REASON and the harmony of nature, which was so basic to the thought of the Enlightenment, expressed itself in countless ways. We have included here two celebrations of the Newtonian natural order: Alexander Pope's Neo-Classical poem "Essay on Man" (1734) (1)—written in the form of four epistles to the English deist Henry St. John, Lord Bolingbroke— and a Prayer to Nature by the physicist Baron d'Holbach who forthrightly rejected the Christian God (2). Holbach's prayer was included in his comprehensive work The System of Nature (1770), Chapter 14.

1. ALEXANDER POPE ON THE HARMONY OF NATURE, FROM "ESSAY ON MAN," 1734

SOURCE. *Poetical Works of Alexander Pope,* Boston: Little, Brown & Co., 1854, II, pp. 36–48.

EPISTLE I

Awake, my St. John! leave all meaner things
To low ambition, and the pride of Kings.
Let us (since Life can little more supply
Than just to look about us and to die)
Expatiate free o'er all this scene of Man;
A mighty maze! but not without a plan;
A Wild, where weeds and flow'rs promiscuous shoot;
Or Garden, tempting with forbidden fruit.
Together let us beat this ample field,
Try what the open, what the covert yield;
The latent tracts, the giddy heights, explore
Of all who blindly creep, or sightless soar;
Eye Nature's walks, shoot Folly as it flies,
And catch the Manners living as they rise;
Laugh where we must, be candid where we can;
But vindicate the ways of God to Man.

I. Say first, of God above, or Man below,
What can we reason, but from what we know?
Of Man, what see we but his station here,
From which to reason, or to which refer?
Thro' worlds unnumber'd tho' the God be known,
'T is ours to trace him only in our own.
He, who thro' vast immensity can pierce,
See worlds on worlds compose one universe,
Observe how system into system runs,
What other planets circle other suns,
What vary'd Being peoples ev'ry star,
May tell why Heav'n has made us as we are.
But of this frame the bearings, and the ties,
The strong connexions, nice dependencies,
Gradations just, has thy pervading soul
Look'd thro'? or can a part contain the whole?
Is the great chain, that draws all to agree,
And drawn supports, upheld by God, or thee?

II. Presumptuous Man! the reason wouldst thou find,
Why form'd so weak, so little, and so blind?
First, if thou canst, the harder reason guess,
Why form'd no weaker, blinder, and no less?

Ask of thy mother earth, why oaks are made
Taller or stronger than the weeds they shade?
Or ask of yonder argent fields above,
Why Jove's satellites are less than Jove?
　Of Systems possible, if 't is confest
That Wisdom infinite must form the best,
Where all must full or not coherent be,
And all that rises, rise in due degree;
Then, in the scale of reas'ning life, 't is plain,
There must be, somewhere, such a rank as Man:
And all the question (wrangle e'er so long)
Is only this, if God has plac'd him wrong?
　Respecting Man, whatever wrong we call,
May, must be right, as relative to all.
In human works, tho' labour'd on with pain,
A thousand movements scarce one purpose gain;
In God's, one single can its end produce;
Yet serves to second too some other use.
So Man, who here seems principal alone,
Perhaps acts second to some sphere unknown,
Touches some wheel, or verges to some goal;
'T is but a part we see, and not a whole.
　When the proud steed shall know why Man restrains
His fiery course, or drives him o'er the plains:
When the dull Ox, why now he breaks the clod,
Is now a victim, and now Egypt's God:
Then shall Man's pride and dulness comprehend
His actions', passions', being's, use and end;
Why doing, suff'ring, check'd, impell'd; and why
This hour a slave, the next a deity.
　Then say not Man's imperfect, Heav'n in fault;
Say rather, Man's as perfect as he ought:
His knowledge measur'd to his state and place;
His time a moment, and a point his space.
If to be perfect in a certain sphere,
What matter, soon or late, or here or there?
The blest to-day is as completely so,
As who began a thousand years ago.

　III. Heav'n from all creatures hides the book of Fate,
All but the page prescrib'd, their present state:
From brutes what men, from men what spirits know:
Or who could suffer Being here below?
The lamb thy riot dooms to bleed to-day,
Had he thy Reason, would he skip and play?
Pleas'd to the last, he crops the flow'ry food,
And licks the hand just rais'd to shed his blood.

Oh blindness to the future! kindly giv'n,
That each may fill the circle mark'd by Heav'n:
Who sees with equal eye, as God of all,
A hero perish, or a sparrow fall,
Atoms or systems into ruin hurl'd,
And now a bubble burst, and now a world.
   Hope humbly then; with trembling pinions soar;
Wait the great teacher Death; and God adore.
What future bliss, he gives not thee to know,
But gives that Hope to be thy blessing now.
Hope springs eternal in the human breast:
Man never Is, but always To be blest:
The soul, uneasy and confin'd from home,
Rests and expatiates in a life to come.
   Lo, the poor Indian! whose untutor'd mind
Sees God in clouds, or hears him in the wind:
His soul, proud Science never taught to stray
Far as the solar walk, or milky way;
Yet simple Nature to his hope has giv'n,
Behind the cloud-topt hill, an humbler heav'n;
Some safer world in depth of woods embrac'd,
Some happier island in the wat'ry waste,
Where slaves once more their native land behold,
No fiends torment, no Christians thirst for gold.
To Be, contents his natural desire,
He asks no Angel's wing, no Seraph's fire;
But thinks, admitted to that equal sky,
His faithful dog shall bear him company.

   IV. Go, wiser thou! and, in thy scale of sense,
Weigh thy Opinion against Providence;
Call imperfection what thou fancy'st such,
Say, here he gives too little, there too much:
Destroy all Creatures for thy sport or gust,
Yet cry, If Man's unhappy, God's unjust;
If Man alone engross not Heav'n's high care,
Alone made perfect here, immortal there:
Snatch from his hand the balance and the rod,
Re-judge his justice, be the God of God.
In Pride, in reas'ning Pride, our error lies;
All quit their sphere, and rush into the skies.
Pride still is aiming at the blest abodes,
Men would be Angels, Angels would be Gods.
Aspiring to be Gods, if Angels fell,
Aspiring to be Angels, Men rebel:
And who but wishes to invert the laws
Of Order, sins against th' Eternal Cause.

V. Ask for what end the heav'nly bodies shine,
Earth for whose use? Pride answers, " 'T is for mine:
For me kind Nature wakes her genial Pow'r,
Suckles each herb, and spreads out ev'ry flow'r;
Annual for me, the grape, the rose renew
The juice nectareous, and the balmy dew;
For me, the mine a thousand treasures brings;
For me, health gushes from a thousand springs;
Seas roll to waft me, suns to light me rise;
My foot-stool earth, my canopy the skies."
    But errs not Nature from this gracious end,
From burning suns when livid deaths descend,
When earthquakes swallow, or when tempests sweep
Towns to one grave, whole nations to the deep?
"No, ('t is reply'd) the first Almighty Cause
Acts not by partial, but by gen'ral laws;
Th' exceptions few; some change since all began:
And what created perfect?"—Why then Man?
If the great end be human Happiness,
Then Nature deviates; and can Man do less?
As much that end a constant course requires
Of show'rs and sun-shine, as of Man's desires;
As much eternal springs and cloudless skies,
As Men for ever temp'rate, calm, and wise.
If plagues or earthquakes break not Heav'n's design,
Why then a Borgia, or a Catiline?
Who knows but he, whose hand the lightning forms,
Who heaves old Ocean, and who wings the storms;
Pours fierce Ambition in a Caesar's mind,
Or turns young Ammon loose to scourge mankind?
From pride, from pride, our very reas'ning springs;
Account for moral, as for nat'ral things:
Why charge we Heav'n in those, in these acquit?
In both, to reason right is to submit.
    Better for Us, perhaps, it might appear,
Were there all harmony, all virtue here;
That never air or ocean felt the wind;
That never passion discompos'd the mind.
But all subsists by elemental strife;
And Passions are the elements of Life.
The gen'ral Order, since the whole began,
Is kept in Nature, and is kept in Man.

VI. What would this Man? Now upward will he soar.
And little less than Angel, would be more;
Now looking downwards, just as griev'd appears
To want the strength of bulls, the fur of bears.

Made for his use all creatures if he call,
Say what their use, had he the pow'rs of all?
Nature to these, without profusion, kind,
The proper organs, proper pow'rs assign'd;
Each seeming want compensated of course,
Here with degrees of swiftness, there of force;
All in exact proportion to the state;
Nothing to add, and nothing to abate.
Each beast, each insect, happy in its own:
Is Heav'n unkind to Man, and Man alone?
Shall he alone, whom rational we call,
Be pleas'd with nothing, if not bless'd with all?
   The bliss of Man (could Pride that blessing find)
Is not to act or think beyond mankind;
No pow'rs of body or of soul to share,
But what his nature and his state can bear.
Why has not Man a microscopic eye?
For this plain reason, Man is not a Fly.
Say what the use, were finer optics giv'n,
T' inspect a mite, not comprehend the heav'n?
Or touch, if tremblingly alive all o'er,
To smart and agonize at every pore?
Or quick effluvia darting thro' the brain,
Die of a rose in aromatic pain?
If nature thunder'd in his op'ning ears,
And stunn'd him with the music of the spheres,
How would he wish that Heav'n had left him still
The whisp'ring Zephyr, and the purling rill?
Who finds not Providence all good and wise,
Alike in what it gives, and what denies?

   VII. Far as Creation's ample range extends,
The scale of sensual, mental pow'rs ascends:
Mark how it mounts, to Man's imperial race,
From the green myriads in the peopled grass:
What modes of sight betwixt each wide extreme,
The mole's dim curtain, and the lynx's beam:
Of smell, the headlong lioness between,
And hound sagacious on the tainted green:
Of hearing, from the life that fills the Flood,
To that which warbles thro' the vernal wood:
The spider's touch, how exquisitely fine!
Feels at each thread, and lives along the line:
In the nice bee, what sense so subtly true
From pois'nous herbs extracts the healing dew?
How Instinct varies in the grov'ling swine,
Compar'd, half-reas'ning elephant, with thine!

'Twixt that, and Reason, what a nice barrier,
For ever sep'rate, yet for ever near!
Remembrance and Reflection how ally'd;
What thin partitions Sense from Thought divide:
And Middle natures, how they long to join,
Yet never pass th' insuperable line!
Without this just gradation, could they be
Subjected, these to those, or all to thee?
The pow'rs of all subdu'd by thee alone,
Is not thy Reason all these pow'rs in one?

    VIII. See, thro' this air, this ocean, and this earth,
All matter quick, and bursting into birth.
Above, how high, progressive life may go!
Around, how wide! how deep extend below!
Vast chain of Being! which from God began,
Natures ethereal, human, angel, man,
Beast, bird, fish, insect, what no eye can see,
No glass can reach; from Infinite to thee,
From thee to Nothing.—On superior pow'rs
Were we to press, inferior might on ours:
Or in the full creation leave a void,
Where, one step broken, the great scale's destroy'd:
From Nature's chain whatever link you strike,
Tenth or ten thousandth, breaks the chain alike.
    And, if each system in gradation roll
Alike essential to th' amazing Whole,
The least confusion but in one, not all
That system only, but the Whole must fall.
Let Earth unbalanc'd from her orbit fly,
Planets and Suns run lawless thro' the sky;
Let ruling angels from their spheres be hurl'd,
Being on Being wreck'd, and world on world;
Heav'n's whole foundations to their centre nod,
And Nature tremble to the throne of God.
All this dread Order break—for whom? for thee?
Vile worm!—Oh Madness! Pride! Impiety!

    IX. What if the foot, ordain'd the dust to tread,
Or hand, to toil, aspir'd to be the head?
What if the head, the eye, or ear repin'd
To serve mere engines to the ruling Mind?
Just as absurd for any part to claim
To be another, in this gen'ral frame:
Just as absurd, to mourn the tasks or pains,
The great directing Mind of All ordains.
    All are but parts of one stupendous whole,
Whose body Nature is, and God the soul;

That, chang'd thro' all, and yet in all the same;
Great in the earth, as in th' ethereal frame;
Warms in the sun, refreshes in the breeze,
Glows in the stars, and blossoms in the trees,
Lives thro' all life, extends thro' all extent,
Spreads undivided, operates unspent;
Breathes in our soul, informs our mortal part,
As full, as perfect, in a hair as heart:
As full, as perfect, in vile Man that mourns,
As the rapt Seraph that adores and burns:
To him no high, no low, no great, no small;
He fills, he bounds, connects, and equals all.

　　X. Cease then, nor Order Imperfection name:
Our proper bliss depends on what we blame.
Know thy own point: This kind, this due degree
Of blindness, weakness, Heav'n bestows on thee.
Submit.—In this, or any other sphere,
Secure to be as blest as thou canst bear:
Safe in the hand of one disposing Pow'r,
Or in the natal, or the mortal hour.
All Nature is but Art, unknown to thee;
All Chance, Direction, which thou canst not see;
All Discord, Harmony not understood;
All partial Evil, universal Good:
And, spite of Pride, in erring Reason's spite,
One truth is clear, WHATEVER IS, IS RIGHT.

EPISTLE II

　　I. Know then thyself, presume not God to scan;
The proper study of Mankind is Man.
Plac'd on this isthmus of a middle state,
A Being darkly wise, and rudely great:
With too much knowledge for the Sceptic side,
With too much weakness for the Stoic's pride,
He hangs between; in doubt to act, or rest;
In doubt to deem himself a God, or Beast;
In doubt his Mind or Body to prefer;
Born but to die, and reas'ning but to err;
Alike in ignorance, his reason such,
Whether he thinks too little, or too much:
Chaos of Thought and Passion, all confus'd;
Still by himself abus'd, or disabus'd;
Created half to rise, and half to fall;
Great lord of all things, yet a prey to all;
Sole judge of Truth, in endless Error hurl'd:
The glory, jest, and riddle of the world!

2. BARON D'HOLBACH, PRAYER TO NATURE
FROM *THE SYSTEM OF NATURE*, 1770

SOURCE. John Herman Randall, *The Making of the Modern Mind,* rev. ed., Boston: Houghton Mifflin Co., 1940, p. 279. Reprinted by permission of Houghton Mifflin Co.

O Nature, sovereign of all beings! and ye, her adorable daughters, Virtue, Reason, and Truth! remain forever our revered protectors! it is to you that belong the praises of the human race; to you appertains the homage of the earth. Show us then, O Nature! that which man ought to do, in order to obtain the happiness which thou makest him desire. Virtue! animate him with thy beneficent fire. Reason! conduct his uncertain steps through the paths of life. Truth! let thy torch illumine his intellect, dissipate the darkness of his road. Unite, O assisting deities! your powers, in order to submit the hearts of mankind to your dominion. Banish error from our mind; wickedness from our hearts; confusion from our footsteps; cause knowledge to extend its salubrious reign; goodness to occupy our souls; serenity to occupy our bosoms.

Part II

THE RATIONALIZATION
OF INSTITUTIONS

A. Religious Institutions and Religious Thought

VOLTAIRE'S HOSTILITY to the Church and his advocacy of deism emerge clearly from the five passages included here from his Philosophical Dictionary *(which began to appear in 1764). The first four are witty attacks on organized religion; the fifth—"Theist"—is a statement in support of the deist position. Voltaire treated "deist" and "theist" as synonyms.*

1. VOLTAIRE, FROM THE *PHILOSOPHICAL DICTIONARY*

SOURCE. B. R. Redman, ed., *The Portable Voltaire*, H. I. Wolf, tr., New York: The Viking Press, 1959, pp. 53–54, 88–90, 187–195, 200–202, 207–208. Reprinted by permission of The Viking Press, Inc.

ABBÉ

The word *abbé*, let it be remembered, signifies father. If you become one you render a service to the state; you doubtless perform the best work that a man can perform; you give birth to a thinking being. In this action there is something divine. But if you are *Monsieur l'Abbé* only because you have had your head shaved, wear a clerical collar, and a short cloak, and are waiting for a fat benefice, you do not deserve the name of *abbé*.

The ancient monks gave this name to the superior whom they elected; the *abbé* was their spiritual father. What different things do the same words signify at different times! The spiritual father was a poor man at the head of others equally poor; but the poor spiritual fathers have since had incomes of two hundred or four hundred thousand livres, and there are poor spiritual fathers in Germany who have regiments of guards.

A poor man, making a vow of poverty, and in consequence becoming a sovereign? It has been said before, but it must be said a thousand times: this is intolerable. The laws protest such an abuse; religion is shocked by it, and the really poor, who want food and clothing, appeal to heaven at the door of *Monsieur l'Abbé*.

But I hear the *abbés* of Italy, Germany, Flanders, and Burgundy ask: "Why are not we to accumulate wealth and honors? Why are we not to become princes? The bishops, who were originally poor, are like us; they have enriched and elevated themselves; one of them has become superior even to kings; let us imitate them as far as we are able."

Gentleman, you are right. Invade the land; it belongs to him whose strength or skill obtains possession of it. You have made ample use of the times of ignorance, superstition, and infatuation, to strip us of our inheritances, and trample us under your feet, that you might fatten on the substance of the unfortunate. But tremble for fear that the day of reason will arrive! . . .

BISHOP

Samuel Ornik, a native of Basel, was a very amiable young man, as you know, and one who had his New Testament by heart in both Greek and German. When he was twenty his parents sent him on a journey. He was commissioned to carry some books to the coadjutor of Paris, at the time of the Fronde. When he arrived at the door of the archbishop's residence, the Swiss servant told him that Monseigneur saw nobody. "Comrade," said Ornik, "you are very rude to your compatriots. The apostles let everyone approach them, and Jesus Christ desired that people should suffer all little children to come unto him. I have nothing to ask of your master; on the contrary, I have brought him something."

"Come inside, then," said the Swiss.

He waited for an hour in an outer chamber. As he was very naïve, he began a conversation with a servant who was very fond of telling all he knew of his master. "He must be extremely rich," said Ornik, "to have this crowd of pages and flunkeys whom I see running about the house."

"I don't know what his income is," answered the other, "but I heard it said that he is already two million in debt."

"But who is the lady who has just come out of that room?"

"That is Madame de Pomèreu, one of his mistresses."

"She is really very pretty; but I have not read that the apostles had any such company of a morning in their bedrooms. Ah! I think monsieur is going to give audience."

"Say 'His Highness, Monseigneur.'"

"Willingly." Ornik saluted His Highness, presented his books, and was received with a very gracious smile. The archbishop said four words to him, then climbed into his coach, escorted by fifty horsemen. In climbing, Monseigneur let fall a sheath. Ornik was quite astonished that Monseigneur carried so large an ink-horn in his pocket. "Don't you see that's his dagger?" said the chatterbox. "Everyone carries a dagger when he goes to parliament."

"That's a nice way of officiating," said Ornik; and he went off very astonished.

He traversed France, learning as he went from town to town; and thence passed into Italy. When he was in the Pope's territory, he met one of those bishops whose income runs to a thousand crowns, walking on foot. Ornik was very polite; he offered him a place in his carriage. "You are doubtless on your way to comfort some sick man, Monseigneur?"

"Sir, I am on my way to my master's."

"Your master? I suppose you mean Jesus Christ?"

"Oh no, sir. I mean Cardinal Azolin. I am his almoner. He pays me very poorly, but he has promised to place me in the service of Donna Olimpia, the favorite sister-in-law *di nostro signore.*"

"What! you are in the pay of a cardinal? But don't you know that there were no cardinals in the time of Jesus Christ and St. John?"

"Is it possible?" cried the Italian prelate.

"Nothing could be truer. You have read it in the Gospels."

"I have never read the Gospels," answered the bishop; "all I know is Our Lady's office."

"I tell you there were neither cardinals nor bishops, and when there were bishops, the priests were very nearly their equals; at least according to what Jerome says in several places."

"Holy Virgin," said the Italian. "I knew nothing about it: and the popes?"

"There were not any popes any more than cardinals."

The good bishop crossed himself; he thought he was with an evil spirit, and jumped out of the carriage. . . .

RELIGION

Tonight I was in a meditative mood. I was absorbed in the contemplation of nature; I admired the immensity, the movements, the harmony of those infinite globes which the vulgar do not know how to admire.

I admired still more the intelligence which directs these vast forces. I said to myself: "One must be blind not to be dazzled by this spectacle; one must be stupid not to recognize the author of it; one must be mad not to worship Him. What tribute of worship should I render Him? Should not this tribute be the same in the whole of space, since it is the same supreme power which reigns equally in all space? Should not a thinking being who dwells in a star in the Milky Way offer Him the same homage as the thinking being on this little globe where we are? Light is uniform for the star Sirius and for us; moral philosophy must be uniform. If a sentient, thinking animal in Sirius is born of a tender father and mother who have been occupied with his happiness, he owes them as much love and care as we owe to our parents. If someone in the Milky Way sees a needy cripple, if he can help him, and if he does not do so, he is guilty in the sight of all globes. Everywhere the heart has the same duties: on the steps of the throne of God, if He has a throne; and in the depth of the abyss, if He is an abyss."

I was plunged in these ideas when one of those genii who throng the interplanetary spaces came down to me. I recognized this aerial creature as one who had appeared to me on another occasion, to teach me how different God's judgments were from our own, and how a good action is preferable to an argument.

He transported me into a desert, covered with piles of bones; and between these heaps of dead men there were walks of evergreen trees, and at the end of each walk there was a tall man of august mien, who regarded these sad remains with pity.

"Alas! my archangel," said I, "where have you brought me?"

"To desolation," he answered.

"And who are these fine patriarchs whom I see sad and motionless at the end of these green walks? They seem to be weeping over this countless crowd of dead."

"You shall know, poor human creature," answered the genie from the interplanetary spaces. "But first of all you must weep."

He began with the first pile. "These," he said, "are the twenty-three thousand Jews who danced before a calf, with the twenty-four thousand who were killed while lying with Midianitish women. The number of those massacred for such errors and offenses amounts to nearly three hundred thousand.

"In the other walks are the bones of the Christians slaughtered by each other in metaphysical quarrels. They are divided into several heaps of four centuries each. One heap would have mounted right to the sky, so they had to be divided."

"What!" I cried. "Brothers have treated their brothers like this, and I have the misfortune to be of this brotherhood!"

"Here," said the spirit, "are the twelve million Americans killed in their native land because they had not been baptized."

"My God! why did you not leave these frightful bones to dry in the hemisphere where their bodies were born, and where they were consigned to so many different deaths? Why assemble here all these abominable monuments to barbarism and fanaticism?"

"To instruct you."

"Since you wish to instruct me," I said to the genie, "tell me if there have been peoples other than the Christians and the Jews in whom zeal and religion wretchedly transformed into fanaticism have inspired so many horrible cruelties."

"Yes," he said. "The Mohammedans were sullied with the same inhumanities, but rarely; and when one asked *amman,* pity, of them and offered them tribute, they were merciful. As for the other nations, there has not been a single one, from the beginning of the world, which has ever made a purely religious war. Follow me now." I followed him.

A little beyond these piles of dead men, we found other piles; they were composed of sacks of gold and silver, and each had its label: "Substance of the heretics massacred in the eighteenth century, the seventeenth, and the sixteenth." And so on in going back: "Gold and silver of Americans slaughtered," etc., etc. And all these piles were surmounted with crosses, mitres, croziers, and triple crowns studded with precious stones.

"What, my genie! Do you mean that these dead were piled up for the sake of their wealth?"

"Yes, my son."

I wept. And when, by my grief, I was worthy of being led to the end of the green walks, he led me there.

"Contemplate," he said, "the heroes of humanity who were the world's benefactors, and who were all united in banishing from the world, as far as they were able, violence and rapine. Question them."

I ran to the first of the band. He had a crown on his head, and a little censer in his hand. I humbly asked him his name. "I am Numa Pompilius," he said to me. "I succeeded a brigand, and I had to govern brigands. I taught them virtue and the worship of God, but after me they forgot both more than once. I forbade that there should be any image in the temples, because the Deity which animates nature cannot be represented. During my reign the Romans had neither wars nor seditions, and my religion did nothing but good. All the neighboring peoples came to honor me at my funeral; and a unique honor it was."

I kissed his hand, and I went to the second. He was a fine old man about a hundred years old, clad in a white robe. He put his middle finger on his mouth, and with the other hand he cast some beans behind him. I recognized Pythagoras. He assured me he had never had a golden thigh, and that he had never been a cock; but that he had governed the Crotoniates with as much justice as Numa governed the Romans, almost at the same time; and that this justice was the rarest and most necessary thing in the world. I learned that the Pythagoreans examined their consciences twice a day. The honest people! How far we are from them! But we, who have been nothing but assassins for thirteen hundred years, we call these wise men arrogant.

In order to please Pythagoras, I did not say a word to him, and I passed on to Zoroaster, who was occupied in concentrating the celestial fire in the focus of a concave mirror, in the middle of a hall with a hundred doors which all led to wisdom. (Zoroaster's precepts are called *doors,* and are a hundred in number.) Over the principal door I read these words which are the sum of all moral philosophy, and which cut short all the disputes of the casuists: "When in doubt if an action is good or bad, refrain."

"Certainly," I said to my genie, "the barbarians who immolated all these victims had never read these beautiful words."

We then saw Zaleucus, Thales, Anaximander, and all the sages who had sought truth and practiced virtue.

When we came to Socrates, I recognized him very quickly by his flat nose. "Well," I said to him, "so you are one of the Almighty's confidants! All the inhabitants of Europe, except the Turks and the Tartars of the Crimea, who know nothing, pronounce your name with respect. It is revered, loved, this great name, to the point that people have wanted to know those of your persecutors. Melitus and Anitus are known because of you, just as Ravaillac is known because of Henry IV; but I know only this name of Anitus. I do not know precisely who was the scoundrel who culumniated you, and who succeeded in having you condemned to drink hemlock."

"Since my adventure," replied Socrates, "I have never thought about that man, but seeing that you make me remember it, I pity him. He was a wicked priest who secretly conducted a business in hides, a trade reputed shameful among us. He sent his two children to my school. The other disciples taunted them with having a father who was a currier, and they were obliged to leave. The irritated father did not rest until he had stirred up all the priests and all the sophists against me. They persuaded the council of five hundred that I was an impious fellow who did not believe that the Moon, Mercury, and Mars were gods. Indeed, I used to think, as I think now, that there is only one God, master of all nature. The judges handed me over to the poisoner of the republic. He cut short my life by a few days: I died peacefully at the age of seventy, and since that time I have led a happy life with all these great men whom you see, and of whom I am the least."

After enjoying some time in conversation with Socrates, I went forward with my guide into a grove situated above the thickets where all the sages of antiquity seemed to be tasting sweet repose.

I saw a man of gentle, simple countenance, who seemed to me to be about thirty-five years old. From afar he cast compassionate glances on these piles of whitened bones, across which I had had to pass to reach the sages' abode. I was astonished to find his feet swollen and bleeding, his hands likewise, his side pierced, and his ribs flayed with whip cuts. "Good Heavens!" I said to him, "is it possible for a just man, a sage, to be in this state? I have just seen one who was treated in a very hateful way, but there is no comparison between his torture and yours. Wicked priests and wicked judges poisoned him. Were priests and judges your torturers?"

He answered with much courtesy: "Yes."

"And who were these monsters?"

"They were hypocrites."

"Ah! that says everything. I understand by this single word that they must have condemned you to death. Had you proved to them then, as Socrates did, that the Moon was not a goddess, and that Mercury was not a god?"

"No, these planets were not in question. My compatriots did not know what a planet is; they were all errant ignoramuses. Their superstitions were quite different from those of the Greeks."

"You wanted to teach them a new religion, then?"

"Not at all. I said to them simply: 'Love God with all your heart and your fellow creature as yourself, for that is man's whole duty.' Judge if this precept is not as old as the universe; judge if I brought them a new religion. I did not stop telling them that I had come not to destroy the law but to fulfill it. I observed all their rites; circumcized as they all were, baptized as were the most zealous among them. Like them I paid the Corban; I observed the Passover as they did, eating, standing up, a lamb cooked with lettuce. I and my friends went to pray in the temple; my friends even frequented this temple after my death. In a word, I fulfilled all their laws without a single exception."

"What! these wretches could not even reproach you with swerving from their laws?"

"Not, not possibly."

"Why then did they reduce you to the condition in which I now see you?"

"What do you expect me to say! They were very arrogant and selfish. They saw that I knew them for what they were; they knew that I was making the citizens acquainted with them; they were the stronger; they took away my life: and people like them will always do as much, if they can, to anyone who does them too much justice."

"But did you say nothing, do nothing that could serve them as a pretext?"

"To the wicked everything serves as pretext."

"Did you not say once that you were come not to bring peace, but a sword?"

"It is a copyist's error. I told them that I brought peace and not a sword. I never wrote anything; what I said may have been changed without evil intention."

"You therefore contributed in no way by your speeches, badly reported, badly interpreted, to these frightful piles of bones which I saw on my road in coming to consult you?"

"It is with horror only that I have seen those who have made themselves guilty of these murders."

"And these monuments of power and wealth, of pride and avarice, these treasures, these ornaments, these signs of grandeur, which I have seen piled up on the road while I was seeking wisdom, do they come from you?"

"That is impossible. I and my followers lived in poverty and meanness: my grandeur was in virtue only."

I was about to beg him to be so good as to tell me just who he was. My guide warned me to do nothing of the sort. He told me that I was not made to understand these sublime mysteries. But I did implore him to tell me in what true religion consisted.

"Have I not already told you? Love God and your fellow creature as yourself."

"What! If one loves God, one can eat meat on Friday?"

"I always ate what was given me, for I was too poor to give anyone food."

"In loving God, in being just, should one not be rather cautious not to confide all the adventures of one's life to an unknown being?"

"That was always my practice."

"Can I not, by doing good, dispense with making a pilgrimage to St. James of Compostella?"

"I have never been in that region."

"Is it necessary for me to imprison myself in a retreat with fools?"

"As for me, I was always making little journeys from town to town."

"Is it necessary for me to take sides either for the Greek Church or the Latin?"

"When I was in the world, I never differentiated between the Jew and the Samaritan."

"Well, if that is so, I take you for my only master." Then he made me a sign with his head which filled me with consolation. The vision disappeared, and a clear conscience stayed with me. . . .

SOCRATES

One day, two citizens of Athens, returning from the temple of Mercury, perceived Socrates in the public square. One said to the other: "Is not that the rascal who says that one can be virtuous without going every day to offer up sheep and geese?" "Yes," said the other, "that is the sage who has no religion; that is the atheist who says there is only one God." Socrates approached them with his simple air, his daemon, and his irony, which Madame Dacier has so highly extolled. "My friends," said he to them, "one word, if you please: a man who prays to God, who adores Him, who seeks to resemble Him as much as human weakness can do, and who does all the good which lies in his power, what would you call him?" "A very religious soul," said they. "Very well; we may therefore adore the Supreme Being, and have a great deal of religion?" "Granted," said the two Athenians. "But do you believe," pursued Socrates, "that when the Divine Architect of the world arranged all the spheres which revolve above our heads, when He gave motion and life to so many different beings, He made use of the arm of Hercules, the lyre of Apollo, or the flute of Pan?" "It is not probable," said they. "But if it is not probable that He called in the aid of others to construct that which we see, it is not credible that He preserves it through others rather than through Himself. If Neptune were the absolute master of the sea, Juno of the air, Aeolus of the winds, Ceres of harvests—and if one desired a calm, when another wanted wind and rain—you see clearly, that the order of nature could not exist as it is. You will confess, that all depends upon Him who has made all. You attribute four white horses to the sun, and four black ones to the moon; but is it not more likely, that day and night are the effect of the motion given to the stars by their Master, than that they were produced by eight horses?" The two citizens looked at him, but answered nothing. In short, Socrates concluded by proving to them that they might have harvests without giving money to the priests of Ceres; go to the chase without offering little silver statues to the temple of Diana; that Pomona gave not fruits; that Neptune gave not horses; and that they should thank the Sovereign who had made all.

His discourse was most exactly logical. Xenophon, his disciple, a man who knew the world, and who afterwards sacrificed to the wind, during the retreat of the ten thousand, took Socrates by the sleeve, and said to him: "Your discourse is admirable; you have spoken better than an oracle; and you are lost. One of these good people to whom you speak is a butcher, who sells sheep and geese for sacrifices; and the other a goldsmith, who profits by making little gods of silver and brass for women. They will accuse you of being a blasphemer, who would diminish their trade. They will depose against you to Melitus and Anitus, your enemies, who have resolved upon your ruin. Have a care of hemlock; your familiar spirit should have warned you not to say to a butcher and a goldsmith what you should say only to Plato and Xenophon."

Some time after, the enemies of Socrates caused him to be condemned by the council of five hundred. He had two hundred and twenty voices in his favor, by which it may be presumed that there were two hundred and twenty philosophers in this tribunal; but it shows that, in all companies, the number of philosophers is always the minority.

Socrates therefore drank hemlock, for having spoken in favor of the unity of God; and the Athenians afterward consecrated a temple to Socrates—to him who disputed against all temples dedicated to inferior beings. . . .

THEIST

The theist is a man firmly persuaded of the existence of a Supreme Being, as good as He is powerful, who has created all beings that are extensive, vegetative, sentient, and reflective; who perpetuates their species, who punishes crimes without cruelty, and rewards virtuous actions with kindness.

The theist does not know how God punishes, how he protects, how he pardons, for he is not bold enough to flatter himself that he knows how God acts, but he knows that God acts and that He is just. Arguments against Providence do not shake him in his faith, because they are merely great arguments, and not proofs. He submits to this Providence, although he perceives only a few effects and a few signs of this Providence: and—judging of the things he does not see by the things he does see—he considers that this Providence extends to all time and space.

United by this principle with the rest of the universe, he does not embrace any of the sects, all of which contradict one another. His religion is the most ancient and the most widespread, for the simple worship of a God has preceded all the systems of the world. He speaks a language that all peoples understand, while they do not understand one another. He has brothers from Pekin to Cayenne, and he counts all wise men as his brethren. He believes that religion does not consist either in the opinions of an unintelligible metaphysic, or in vain display, but in worship and justice. The doing of good, there is his service; being submissive to God, there is his doctrine. The Mohammedan cries to him: "Have a care if you do not make the pilgrimage to Mecca!" "Woe unto you," says a Recollet, "if you do not make a journey to Our Lady of Loretto!" He laughs at Loretto and at Mecca; but he succors the needy and he defends the oppressed.

DAVID HUME (1711–1776), in his Enquiry Concerning Human Understanding, *undertook a ruthless criticism of the rational verifiability of God. His criticism eroded the logical foundations of Christianity, but Christians had long been willing to base their beliefs on faith. The real victim of Hume's analysis was deism—the "religion of reason"—which was now shown to be itself irrational.*

2. DAVID HUME, FROM *AN ENQUIRY CONCERNING HUMAN UNDERSTANDING*

SOURCE. David Hume, *An Enquiry Concerning Human Understanding*, Chicago (La Salle): The Open Court Publishing Co., 1924, pp. 149–150, 151–155. Reprinted by permission of The Open Court Publishing Co., La Salle, Illinois.

But what must a philosopher think of those vain reasoners, who, instead of regarding the present scene of things as the sole object of their contemplation, so far reverse the whole course of nature, as to render this life merely a passage to something farther; a porch, which leads to a greater, and vastly different building; a prologue, which serves only to introduce the piece, and give it more grace and propriety? Whence, do you think, can such philosophers derive their idea of the gods? From their own conceit and imagination surely. For if they derived it from the present phenomena, it would never point to anything farther, but must be exactly adjusted to them. That the divinity may *possibly* be endowed with attributes, which we have never seen exerted; may be governed by principles of action, which we cannot discover to be satisfied: all this will freely be allowed. But still this is mere *possibility* and hypothesis. We never can have reason to *infer* any attributes, or any principles of action in him, but as far as we know them to have been exerted and satisfied.

Are there any marks of a distributive justice in the world? If you answer in the affirmative, I conclude, that, since justice here exerts itself, it is satisfied. If you reply in the negative, I conclude, that you have then no reason to ascribe justice, in our sense of it, to the gods. If you hold a medium between affirmation and negation, by saying, that the justice of the gods, at present, exerts itself in part, but not in its full extent; I answer, that you have no reason to give it any particular extent, but only so far as you see it, *at present*, exert itself. . . .

If you saw, for instance, a half-finished building, surrounded with heaps of brick and stone and mortar, and all the instruments of masonry; could you not *infer* from the effect, that it was a work of design and contrivance? And could you not return again, from this inferred cause, to infer new additions to the effect, and conclude, that the building would soon be finished, and receive all the further improvements, which art could bestow upon it? If you saw upon the sea-shore the print of one human foot, you would conclude, that a man had passed that way, and that he had also left the traces of the other foot, though effaced by the rolling of the sands or inundation of the waters. Why then do you refuse to admit the same method of reasoning with regard to the order of nature? Consider the world and the present life only as an imperfect building, from which you can infer a superior intelligence; and arguing from that superior intelligence, which can leave nothing imperfect; why may you not infer a more finished scheme or plan, which will receive its completion in some distant point of space or time? Are not these methods of reasoning exactly similar? And under what pretence can you embrace the one, while you reject the other?

The infinite difference of the subjects, replied he, is a sufficient foundation for this difference in my conclusions. In works of *human* art and contrivance, it is allowable to advance from the effect to the cause, and returning back from the cause, to form new inferences concerning the effect, and examine the alterations, which it has probably undergone, or may still undergo. But what is the foundation of this method of reasoning? Plainly this; that man is a being, whom we know by experience, whose motives and designs we are acquainted with, and whose projects and inclinations have a certain connexion and coherence, according to the laws which nature has established for the government of such a creature. When, therefore, we find, that any work has proceeded from the skill and industry of man; as we are otherwise acquainted with the nature of the animal, we can draw a hundred inferences concerning what may be expected from him; and these inferences will all be founded in experience and observation. But did we know man only from the single work or production which we examine, it were impossible for us to argue in this manner; because our knowledge of all the qualities, which we ascribe to him, being in that case derived from the production, it is impossible they could point to anything farther, or be the foundation of any new inference. The print of a foot in the sand can only prove, when considered alone, that there was some figure adapted to it, by which it was produced: but the print of a human foot proves likewise, from our other experience, that there was probably another foot, which also left its impression, though effaced by time or other accidents. Here we mount from the effect to the cause; and descending again from the cause, infer alterations in the effect; but this is not a continuation of the same simple chain of reasoning. We comprehend in this case a hundred other experiences and observations, concerning the *usual* figure and members of that species of animal, without which this method of argument must be considered as fallacious and sophistical.

The case is not the same with our reasonings from the works of nature. The Deity is known to us only by his productions, and is a single being in the universe, not comprehended under any species or genus, from whose experienced attributes or qualities, we can, by analogy, infer any attribute or quality in him. As the universe shews wisdom and goodness, we infer wisdom and goodness. As it shews a particular degree of these perfections, we infer a particular degree of them, precisely adapted to the effect which we examine. But farther attributes or farther degrees of the same attributes, we can never be authorised to infer or suppose, by any rules of just reasoning. Now, without some such licence of supposition, it is impossible for us to argue from the cause, or infer any alteration in the effect, beyond what has immediately fallen under our observation. Greater good produced by this Being must still prove a greater degree of goodness: a more impartial distribution of rewards and punishments must proceed from a greater regard to justice and equity. Every supposed addition to the works of nature makes an addition to the attributes of the Author of nature; and consequently, being entirely unsupported by any reason or argument, can never be admitted but as mere conjecture and hypothesis.[1]

The great source of our mistake in this subject, and of the unbounded licence of conjecture, which we indulge, is, that we tacitly consider ourselves, as in the place of the Supreme Being, and conclude, that he will, on every occasion, observe the same conduct, which we ourselves, in his situation, would have embraced as reasonable and eligible. But, besides that the ordinary course of nature may convince us, that almost everything is regulated by principles and maxims very different from ours; besides this, I say, it must evidently appear contrary to all rules of analogy to reason, from the intentions and projects of men, to those of a Being so different, and so much superior. In human nature, there is a certain experienced coherence of designs and inclinations; so that when, from any fact, we have discovered one intention of any man, it may often be reasonable, from experience, to infer another, and draw a long chain of conclusions concerning his past or future conduct. But this method of reasoning can never have place with regard to a Being, so remote and incomprehensible, who bears much less analogy to any other being in the universe than the sun to a waxen taper, and who discovers himself only

---

[1] In general, it may, I think, be established as a maxim, that where any cause is known only by its particular effects, it must be impossible to infer any new effects from that cause; since the qualities, which are requisite to produce these new effects along with the former, must either be different, or superior, or of more extensive operation, than those which simply produced the effect, whence alone the cause is supposed to be known to us. We can never, therefore, have any reason to suppose the existence of these qualities. To say, that the new effects proceed only from a continuation of the same energy, which is already known from the first effects, will not remove the difficulty. For even granting this to be the case (which can seldom be supposed), the very continuation and exertion of a like energy (for it is impossible it can be absolutely the same), I say, this exertion of a like energy, in a different period of space and time, is a very arbitrary supposition, and what there cannot possibly be any traces of in the effects, from which all our knowledge of the cause is originally derived. Let the *inferred* cause be exactly proportioned (as it should be) to the known effect; and it is impossible that it can possess any qualities, from which new or different effects can be *inferred*.

by some faint traces or outlines, beyond which we have no authority to ascribe to him any attribute or perfection. What we imagine to be a superior perfection, may really be a defect. Or were it ever so much a perfection, the ascribing of it to the Supreme Being, where it appears not to have been really exerted, to the full, in his works, savours more of flattery and panegyric, than of just reasoning and sound philosophy. All the philosophy, therefore, in the world, and all the religion, which is nothing but a species of philosophy, will never be able to carry us beyond the usual course of experience, or give us measures of conduct and behaviour different from those which are furnished by reflections on common life. No new fact can ever be inferred from the religious hypothesis; no event foreseen or foretold; no reward or punishment expected or dreaded, beyond what is already known by practice and observation.

B. Government and Society

CHARLES-LOUIS DE MONTESQUIEU, one of the keenest minds of the French Enlightenment, presented in his Spirit of the Laws *(1748) a rational analysis of society and political institutions. He rejected any single blueprint for political and social organization, arguing that the system best suited to particular human groups depended on their geographical location and natural environment. He believed, nevertheless, that a successful political system should include a division of authority among various branches of government. His notion of checks and balances found expression some decades later in the American Constitution.*

1. CHARLES-LOUIS DE MONTESQUIEU, FROM *THE SPIRIT OF THE LAWS*, 1748

SOURCE. Charles-Louis de Montesquieu, *The Spirit of the Laws*, rev. ed., Thomas Nugent, tr., 1873.

As soon as mankind enter into a state of society they lose the sense of their weakness; equality ceases, and then commences the state of war.

Each particular society begins to feel its strength, whence arises a state of war betwixt different nations. The individuals likewise of each society become sensible of their force; hence the principal advantages of this society they endeavour to convert to their own emolument, which constitutes a state of war betwixt individuals.

These two different kinds of states give rise to human laws. Considered as inhabitants of so great a planet, which necessarily contains a variety of nations, they have laws relative to their mutual intercourse, which is what we call the *law of nations*. As members of a society that must be properly supported, they have laws relative to the governors and the governed, and this we distinguish by the name of *politic law*. They have also another sort of laws, as they stand in relation to each other; by which is understood the *civil law*.

The law of nations is naturally founded on this principle, that different nations ought in time of peace to do one another all the good they can, and in time of war as little injury as possible, without prejudicing their real interests.

The object of war is victory; that of victory is conquest; and that of conquest, preservation. From this and the preceding principle all those rules are derived which constitute the *law of nations*.

All countries have a law of nations, not excepting the Iroquois themselves, though they devour their prisoners; for they send and receive ambassadors, and understand the rights of war and peace. The mischief is, that their law of nations is not founded on true principles.

Besides the law of nations relating to all societies, there is a polity or civil constitution for each particularly considered. No society can subsist without a form of government. "The united strength of individuals," as Gravina well observes, "constitutes what we call the body politic."

The general strength may be in the hands of a single person, or of many. Some think that nature having established paternal authority, the most natural government was that of a single person. But the example of paternal authority proves nothing. For if the power of a father be relative to a single government, that of brothers after the death of a father, and that of cousins german after the decease of brother, refer to a government of many. The political power necessarily comprehends the union of several families.

Better is it to say, that the government most conformable to nature, is that which best agrees with the humour and disposition of the people in whose favour it is established.

The strength of individuals cannot be united without a conjunction of all their wills. "The conjunction of those wills," as Gravina again very justly observes, "is what we call the *civil state*."

Law in general is human reason, inasmuch as it governs all the inhabitants of the earth; the political and civil laws of each nation ought to be only the particular cases in which human reason is applied.

They should be adapted in such a manner to the people for whom they are framed, that it is a great chance if those of one nation suit another.

They should be relative to the nature and principle of each government; whether they form it, as may be said of politic laws; or whether they support it, as in the case of civil institutions.

They should be relative to the climate of each country, to the quality of its soil, to its situation and extent, to the principal occupation of the natives, whether husbandmen, huntsmen, or shepherds; they should have a relation to the degree of liberty which the constitution will bear; to the religion of the inhabitants, to their inclinations, riches, numbers, commerce, manners, and customs. In fine, they have relations to each other, as also to their origin, to the intent of the legislator, and to the order of things on which they are established; in all which different lights they ought to be considered.

This is what I have undertaken to perform in the following work. These relations I shall examine, since all these together constitute what I call the *Spirit of Laws.*

I have not separated the political from the civil institutions: for as I do not pretend to treat of laws, but of their spirit; and as this spirit consists in the various relations which the laws may have to different objects, it is not so much my business to follow the natural order of laws, as that of these relations and objects.

When the body of the people is possessed of the supreme power, this is called a *democracy.* When the supreme power is lodged in the hands of a part of the people, it is then an *aristocracy.*

In a democracy the people are in some respects the sovereign, and in others the subject.

There can be no exercise of sovereignty but by their suffrages, which are their own will; now the sovereign's will is the sovereign himself. The laws therefore which establish the right of suffrage, are fundamental to this government. And indeed it is as important to regulate in a republic, in what manner, by whom, to whom, and concerning what, suffrages are to be given, as it is in a monarchy to know who is the prince, and after what manner he ought to govern.

Libanius says that at "Athens a stranger, who intermeddled in the assemblies of the people, was punished with death." This is because such a man usurped the rights of sovereignty.

It is an essential point to fix the number of citizens who are to form the public assemblies; otherwise it would be uncertain whether the whole, or only a part of the people, had given their votes. At Sparta the number was fixed to ten thousand. But Rome, designed by Providence to rise from the weakest beginnings to the highest pitch of grandeur; Rome, doomed to experience all the vicissitudes of fortune; Rome, who had sometimes all her inhabitants without her walls, and sometimes all Italy and a considerable part of the world within them: Rome, I say, never fixed the number; and this was one of the principal causes of her ruin.

The people, in whom the supreme power resides, ought to have the management of every thing within their reach: what exceeds their abilities, must be conducted by their ministers.

But they can not properly be said to have their ministers, without the power of nominating them: it is, therefore, a fundamental maxim in this government, that the people should choose their ministers, that is, their magistrates.

They have occasion, as well as monarchs, and even more so, to be directed by a council or senate. But to have a proper confidence in these, they should have the choosing of the members; whether the election be made by themselves, as at Athens; or by some magistrate deputed for that purpose, as on certain occasions was customary at Rome.

The people are extremely well qualified for choosing those whom they are to intrust with part of their authority. They have only to be determined by things to which they cannot be strangers, and by facts that are obvious to sense. They can tell when a person has fought many battles, and been crowned with success; they are, therefore, very capable of electing a general. They can tell when a judge is assiduous in his office, gives general satisfaction, and has never been charged with bribery: this is sufficient for choosing a prætor. They are struck with the magnificence or riches of a fellow-citizen; no more is requisite for electing an edile. These are facts of which they can have better information in a public forum, than a monarch in his palace. But are they capable of conducting an intricate affair, of seizing and improving the opportunity and critical amount of action? No; this surpasses their abilities.

Should we doubt of the people's natural capacity, in respect to the discernment of merit, we need only cast an eye on the series of surprising elections made by the Athenians and Romans; which no one surely will attribute to hazard.

We know, that though the people of Rome assumed to themselves the right of raising plebeians to public offices, yet they never would exert this power; and though at Athens the magistrates were allowed, by the law of Aristides, to be elected from all the different classes of inhabitants, there never was a case, says Xenophon, that the common people petitioned for employments which could endanger either their security or their glory.

As most citizens have sufficient abilities to choose, though unqualified to be chosen; so the people, though capable of calling others to an account for their administration, are incapable of conducting the administration themselves.

The public business must be carried on with a certain motion, neither too quick nor too slow. But the motion of the people is always either too remiss or too violent. Sometimes with a hundred thousand arms they overturn all before them; and sometimes with a hundred thousand feet they creep like insects.

In a popular state the inhabitants are divided into certain classes. It is in the manner of making this division that great legislators have signalized themselves; and it is on this the duration and prosperity of democracy have ever depended.

Servius Tullius followed the spirit of aristocracy in the distribution of his classes. We find in Livy and in Dionysius Halicarnassus, in what manner he lodged the right of suffrage in the hands of the principal citizens. He had divided the people of Rome into a hundred and ninety-three centuries, which formed six classes; and ranking the rich, who were in smaller numbers, in the first centuries; and those in middling circumstances, who were more numerous, in the next, he flung the indigent multitude into the last; and as each century had but one vote, it was property rather than numbers that decided the elections.

Solon divided the people of Athens into four classes. In this he was directed by the spirit of democracy, his intention not being to fix those who were to choose, but such as were eligible: therefore, leaving to every citizen the right of election, he made the judges eligible from each of those four classes; but the magistrates he ordered to be chosen only out of the first three, consisting of persons of easy fortunes.

As the division of those who have a right of suffrage is a fundamental law in republics, the manner also of giving this suffrage is another fundamental.

The suffrage by *lot* is natural to democracy, as that by *choice* is to aristocracy.

The suffrage by *lot* is a method of electing that offends no one; but animates each citizen with the pleasing hope of serving his country.

Yet as this method is in itself defective, it has been the endeavour of the most eminent legislators to regulate and amend it.

Solon made a law at Athens, that military employments should be conferred by choice; but that senators and judges should be elected by *lot*.

The same legislator ordained that civil magistrates, attended with great expense, should be given by choice; and the others by lot.

In order, however, to amend the suffrage by lot, he made a rule, that none but those who presented themselves should be elected; that the person elected should be examined by judges, and that every one should have a right to accuse him if he were unworthy of the office: this participated at the same time of the suffrage by lot, and of that by choice. When the time of their magistracy was expired, they were obliged to submit to another judgment in regard to their conduct. Persons utterly unqualified, must have been extremely backward in giving in their names to be drawn by lot.

The law which determines the manner of giving suffrage, is likewise fundamental in a democracy. It is a question of some importance, whether the suffrages ought to be public or secret. Cicero observes, that the laws which rendered them secret towards the close of the republic, were the cause of its decline. But as this is differently practised in different republics, I shall offer here my thoughts concerning this subject.

The people's suffrages ought doubtless to be public; and this should be considered as a fundamental law of democracy. The lower class ought to be directed by those of higher rank, and restrained within bounds by the gravity of eminent personages. Hence, by rendering the suffrages secret in the Roman republic, all was lost; it was no longer possible to direct a populace that sought its own destruction. But when the body of the nobles are to vote in an aristocracy; or in a democracy, the senate; as the business is then only to prevent intrigues, the suffrages cannot be too secret.

Intriguing in a senate is dangerous; dangerous it is also in a body of nobles; but not so in the people, whose nature is to act through passion. In countries where they have no share in the government, we often see them as much inflamed on the account of an actor, as ever they could be for the welfare of the state. The misfortune of a republic is, when intrigues are at an end; which happens when the people are gained by bribery and corruption: in this case they grow indifferent to public affairs, and avarice becomes their predominant passion. Unconcerned about the government, and every thing belonging to it, they quietly wait for their hire.

It is likewise a fundamental law in democracies, that the people should have the sole power to enact laws. And yet there are a thousand occasions on which it is necessary the senate should have a power of decreeing; nay, it is frequently proper to make some trial of a law before it is established. The constitutions of Rome and Athens were excellent. The decrees of the senate had the force of laws for the space of a year; but did not become perpetual till they were ratified by the consent of the people. . . .

THE CONSTITUTION OF ENGLAND

In every government there are three sorts of power: the legislative; the executive, in respect to things dependent on the laws of nations; and the executive, in regard to matters that depend on the civil law.

By virtue of the first, the prince or magistrate enacts temporary or perpetual laws, and amends or abrogates those that have been already enacted. By the second, he makes peace or war, sends or receives embassies, establishes the public security, and provides against invasions. By the third, he punishes criminals, or determines the disputes that arise between individuals. The latter we shall call the judiciary power, and the other simply the executive power of the state.

The political liberty of the subject is a tranquillity of mind arising from the opinion each person has of his safety. In order to have this liberty, it is requisite the government be so constituted as one man needs not be afraid of another.

When the legislative and executive powers are united in the same person, or in the same body of magistrates, there can be no liberty; because apprehensions may arise, lest the same monarch or senate should enact tyrannical laws, to execute them in a tyrannical manner.

Again there is no liberty, if the judiciary power be not separated from the legislative and executive. Were it joined with the legislative, the life and liberty of the subject would be exposed to arbitrary control; for the judge would be then the legislator. Were it joined to the executive power, the judge might behave with violence and oppression.

There would be an end of everything, were the same man, or the same body, whether of the nobles or of the people, to exercise those three powers, that of enacting laws, that of executing the public resolutions, and of trying the causes of individuals.

Most kingdoms in Europe enjoy a moderate government, because the prince who is invested with the two first powers, leaves the third to his subjects. In Turkey, where these three powers are united in the Sultan's person, the subjects groan under the most dreadful oppression.

ENLIGHTENED DESPOTISM was, to a number of contemporary thinkers, a valuable means of rationalizing government. For one thing, an autocratic king could act quickly and, if properly disposed, could institute reforms that would require much time in a parliamentary commonwealth. For another, most Continental states were, in fact, dominated by all-powerful kings and princes, and enlightened despotism was a way of achieving reform without revolution. The letters of Voltaire to King Frederick the Great of Prussia illustrate Voltaire's faith in enlightened despotism together with a somewhat unattractive self-abasement before the majesty of the Prussian throne.

2. TWO LETTERS OF VOLTAIRE TO FREDERICK THE GREAT

SOURCE. B. R. Redman, ed., *The Portable Voltaire*, Richard Aldington, tr., New York: The Viking Press, 1959, pp. 439–444. Reprinted by permission of The Viking Press, Inc. and the Ann Elmo Agency, Inc.

Paris, 26th August, 1736.

MONSEIGNEUR,

I should indeed be insensitive were I not infinitely touched by the letter with which your Royal Highness has been graciously pleased to honor me. My self-love was but too flattered; but that love of the human race which has always existed in my heart and which I dare to say determines my character, gave me a pleasure a thousand times purer when I saw that the world holds a prince who thinks like a man, a philosophical prince who will make men happy.

Suffer me to tell you that there is no man on the earth who should not return thanks for the care you take in cultivating by sane philosophy a soul born to command. Be certain there have been no truly good kings except those who began like you, by educating themselves, by learning to know men, by loving the truth, by detesting persecution and superstition. Any prince who thinks in this way can bring back the golden age to his dominions. Why do so few kings seek out this advantage? You perceive the reason, Monseigneur; it is because almost all of them think more of royalty than of humanity: you do precisely the opposite. If the tumult of affairs and the malignancy of men do not in time alter so divine a character, you will be adored by your people and admired by the whole world. Philosophers worthy of that name will fly to your dominions; and, as celebrated artists crowd to that country where their art is most favored, men who think will press forward to surround your throne.

The illustrious Queen Christina left her kingdom to seek the arts; reign, Monseigneur, and let the arts come to seek you.

May you never be disgusted from the sciences by the quarrels of learned men! From those circumstances which you were graciously pleased to inform me of, Monseigneur, you see that most of them are men like courtiers themselves. They are sometimes as greedy, as intriguing, as treacherous, as cruel; and the only difference between the pests of the court and the pests of the school is that the latter are the more ridiculous.

It is very sad for humanity that those who term themselves the messengers of Heaven's command, the interpreters of the Divinity, in a word theologians, are sometimes the most dangerous of all; that some of them are as pernicious to society as they are obscure in their ideas and that their souls are inflated with bitterness and pride in proportion as they are empty of truths. For the sake of a sophism they would trouble the earth and would persuade all kings to avenge with fire and steel the honor of an argument *in ferio* or *in barbara.*

Every thinking being not of their opinion is an atheist; and every king who does not favor them will be damned. You know, Monseigneur, that the best one can do is to leave to themselves these pretended teachers and real enemies of the human race. Their words, when unheeded, are lost in the air like wind; but if the weight of authority is lent them, this wind acquires a force which sometimes overthrows the throne itself.

I see, Monseigneur, with the joy of a heart filled with love of the public weal, the immense distance you set between men who seek the truth in peace and those who would make war for words they do not understand. I see that Newton, Leibnitz, Bayle, Locke, those elevated minds, so enlightened, so gentle, have nourished your spirit and that you reject other pretended nourishment which you find poisoned or without substance.

I cannot sufficiently thank your Royal Highness for your kindness in sending me the little book about M. Wolff. I look upon his metaphysical ideas as things which do honor to the human mind. They are flashes in the midst of a dark night; and that, I think, is all we can hope of metaphysics. It seems improbable that the first principles of things will ever be thoroughly known. The mice living in a few little holes of an immense building do not know if the building is eternal, who is the architect, or why the architect built it. They try to preserve their lives, to people their holes, and to escape the destructive animals which pursue them. We are the mice; and the divine architect who built this universe has not yet, so far as I know, told His secret to any of us. If any man can pretend to have guessed accurately, it is M. Wolff. He may be combated, but he must be esteemed; his philosophy is far from being pernicious; is there anything more beautiful and more true than to say, as he does, that men should be just even if they were so unfortunate as to be atheists?

The protection you appear to give, Monseigneur, to this learned man, is a proof of the accuracy of your mind and of the humanity of your sentiments.

You have the kindness, Monseigneur, to promise that you will send me the *Treatise on God, the Soul and the World.* What a present, Monseigneur, and what an interchange! The heir of a monarchy designs to send instruction from the heart of his palace to a solitary! Be graciously pleased to send me this present, Monseigneur; my extreme love of truth is the one thing which makes me worthy of it. Most princes fear to listen to the truth, but you will teach it.

As to the verses you speak of—you think as wisely of this art as in everything else. Verses which do not teach men new and moving truths do not deserve to be read. You perceive that there is nothing more contemptible than for a man to spend his life in rhyming worn-out common-places which do not deserve the name of thoughts. If there is anything viler it is to be nothing but a satirical poet and to write only to decry others. Such poets are to Parnassus what those doctors, who know nothing but words and intrigue against those who write things, are to the schools.

If *La Henriade* did not displease your Royal Highness I must thank that love of truth, that horror which my poem inspires for the factious, for persecutors, for the superstitious, for tyrants and for rebels. 'Tis the work of an honest man; and should find grace in the eyes of a philosophic prince.

You command me to send you my other work; I shall obey you, Mon-seigneur; you shall be my judge, you shall stand to me in lieu of the public. I will submit to you what I have attempted in philosophy; your instruction shall be my reward: 'tis a prize which few sovereigns can give. I am certain of your secrecy; your virtue must be equal to your knowl-edge.

I should consider it a most valuable privilege to wait upon your Royal Highness. We go to Rome to see churches, pictures, ruins, and bas-reliefs. A prince like yourself is far more deserving of a journey; 'tis a more mar-velous rarity. But friendship, which holds me in my retreat, does not permit me to leave it. Doubtless you think like Julian, that calumniated great man, who said that friends should always be preferred to kings.

In whatever corner of the world I end my life, be certain, Monseigneur, that I shall constantly wish you well, and in doing so wish the happiness of a nation. My heart will be among your subjects; your fame will ever be dear to me. I shall wish that you may always be like yourself and that other kings may be like you. I am with deep respect, your Royal High-ness's most humble, etc.

Leiden, January, 1737.

MONSEIGNEUR,

I shed tears of joy on reading the letter of the 9th September with which your Royal Highness honored me; in it I recognized a prince who will be certainly beloved by the human race. In every way I am aston-ished: you think like Trajan, you write like Pliny, and you use French like our best writers. What difference there is between men! Louis XIV was a great king, I respect his memory; but he did not speak so humanely as you, Monseigneur, and did not express himself in the same way. I have seen his letters; he could not spell his own language. Under your auspices Berlin will be the Athens of Germany and perhaps of Europe. I am now in a town where two private persons, M. Boerhaave on one

side, and M. s'Gravesande on the other attract four or five hundred foreigners. A prince like yourself will attract many more; and I confess I
shall think myself very unfortunate if I die before I have seen the model
of princes and the marvel of Germany.

I would not flatter you, Monseigneur, it would be a crime. It would
be throwing a poisoned breath upon a flower; I am incapable of it; it is
my very heart which speaks to your Royal Highness.

On arriving at Amsterdam I found they had begun an edition of my
poor works. I shall have the honor to send you the first copy. Meanwhile,
I shall be so bold as to send your Royal Highness a manuscript which I
should only dare to show to one so free from prejudices, so philosophic,
so indulgent as you are, and to a prince who among so many homages
deserves that of a boundless confidence. Some time will be needed to
revise and to copy it and I shall send it by whatever way you desire.

Indispensable occupations and circumstances beyond my control forbid
me to carry myself to your feet that homage I owe you. A time will come
perhaps when I shall be more fortunate.

It seems that your Royal Highness likes every sort of literature. A great
prince takes care of all ranks in his dominions; a great genius enjoys every
sort of study. In my little sphere I have only saluted from afar the frontiers of each science; my time has been shared among a little metaphysics,
a little history, some small amount of physics, and a few verses; though
weak in all these matters, I offer you at least what I have.

Were I not so interested in the happiness of mankind I should be sorry
that you are destined to be a king. I could wish you a private man; I could
wish that my soul might freely approach yours; but my wish must yield
to the public good. Permit me, Monseigneur, to respect you more as a
man than as a prince; permit that, among all your grandeurs, your soul
should receive my first homage; and permit me to tell you once more
what admiration and hope you give me.

I am, etc.

*A LETTER OF the self-conscious "enlightened despot" Emperor Joseph II
(1765–1792) to Cardinal Herzan illustrates some of the policies—particularly
anti-ecclesiastical policies—that enlightened despots pursued.*

3. LETTER OF EMPEROR JOSEPH II
TO CARDINAL HERZAN, 1781

SOURCE. "Letter of Emperor Joseph II to Cardinal Herzan . . . .," *The Pamphleteer*, Vol. XIX, No. 38, London: 1822, pp. 274–275. Reprinted by permission of Oxford University Press.

Monsieur le Cardinal,—Since I have ascended the throne, and wear the first diadem in the world, I have made philosophy the legislator of my empire.

In consequence of its logic, Austria will assume another form, the authority of the Ulemas will be restricted, and the rights of majesty will be restored to their primitive extent. It is necessary I should remove certain things out of the domain of religion which never did belong to it.

As I myself detest superstition and the Sadducean doctrines, I will free my people of them; with this view, I will dismiss the monks, I will suppress their monasteries, and will subject them to the bishops of their diocese.

In Rome they will declare this an infringement of the rights of God: I know they will cry aloud, "the greatness of Israel is fallen"; they will complain, that I take away from the people their tribunes, and that I draw a line of separation between dogma and philosophy; but they will be still more enraged when I undertake all this without the approbation of the servant of the servants of God.

To these things we owe the degradation of the human mind. A servant of the altar will never admit that the state is putting him into his proper place, when it leaves him no other occupation than the gospel, and when by laws it prevents the children of Levi from carrying on a monopoly with the human understanding.

The principles of monachism, from Pachomius up to our time, have been directly opposed to the light of reason; respect for their founders ultimately became adoration itself, so that we behold again the Israelites going up to Bethel, in order to adore golden calves.

These false conceptions of religion were transmitted to the common people; they no longer knew God, and expected every thing from their saints.

The rights of the bishops, which I will re-establish, must assist in reforming the ideas of the people; instead of the monk, I will have the priest to preach, not the romances of the canonised, but the holy gospel and morality.

I shall take care that the edifice, which I have erected for posterity, be durable. The general seminaries are nurseries for my priests; whence, on going out into the world, they will take with them a purified mind, and communicate it to the people by wise instruction.

Thus, after the lapse of centuries, we shall have Christians; thus, when I shall have executed my plan, the people of my empire will better know the duties they owe to God, to the country, and to their fellow-creatures; thus shall we yet be blessed by our posterity, for having delivered them from the overgrown power of Rome; for having brought back the priests within the limits of their duties; and for having subjected their future life to the Lord, and their present life to the country alone.

JOSEPH

Vienna, October, 1781.

JEAN JACQUES ROUSSEAU (1712–1778) was a man of broad but eccentric vision and deep sensitivity who went beyond the Enlightenment to foreshadow the subsequent rise of Romanticism. He was, nevertheless, a devotee of reason who, in his Social Contract, *subjected the problems of political authority to logical analysis. He derived from Locke and his predecessors the notion of the state of nature, the social contract, and the popular basis of political authority, and in his use of the idea of the* general will *he developed a concept of unlimited sovereign power that anticipated the extreme nationalism of later generations.*

4. JEAN JACQUES ROUSSEAU, FROM *THE SOCIAL CONTRACT*

SOURCE. Jean Jacques Rousseau, *The Social Contract,* Sir Ernest Barker, ed., Gerard Hopkins, tr., London: Oxford University Press, 1946, pp. 240, 253–258, 260–262, 274–276, 281–282, and 364. Reprinted by permission of Oxford University Press.

Man is born free, and everywhere he is in chains. Many a man believes himself to be the master of others who is, no less than they, a slave. How did this change take place? I do not know. What can make it legitimate? To this question I hope to be able to furnish an answer.

Were I considering only force and the effects of force, I should say: 'So long as a People is constrained to obey, and does, in fact, obey, it does well. So soon as it can shake off its yoke, and succeeds in doing so, it does better. The fact that it has recovered its liberty by virtue of that same right by which it was stolen, means either that it is entitled to resume it, or that its theft by others was, in the first place, without justification.' But the social order is a sacred right which serves as a foundation for all other rights. This right, however, since it comes not by nature, must have been built upon conventions. To discover what these conventions are is the matter of our inquiry. But, before proceeding further, I must establish the truth of what I have so far advanced. . . .

There will always be a vast difference between subduing a mob and governing a social group. No matter how many isolated individuals may submit to the enforced control of a single conqueror, the resulting relationship will ever be that of Master and Slave, never of People and Ruler. The body of men so controlled may be an agglomeration; it is not an association. It implies neither public welfare nor a body politic. An individual may conquer half the world, but he is still only an individual. His interests, wholly different from those of his subjects, are private to himself. When he dies his empire is left scattered and disintegrated. He is like an oak which crumbles and collapses in ashes so soon as the fire consumes it.

'A People,' says Grotius, 'may give themselves to a king.' His argument implies that the said People were already a People before this act of surrender. The very act of gift was that of a political group and presupposed public deliberation. Before, therefore, we consider the act by which a People chooses their king, it were well if we considered the act by which a People is constituted as such. For it necessarily precedes the other, and is the true foundation on which all Societies rest.

Had there been no original compact, why, unless the choice were unanimous, should the minority ever have agreed to accept the decision of the majority? What right have the hundred who desire a master to vote for the ten who do not? The institution of the franchise is, in itself, a form of compact, and assumes that, at least once in its operation, complete unanimity existed.

I assume, for the sake of argument, that a point was reached in the history of mankind when the obstacles to continuing in a state of Nature were stronger than the forces which each individual could employ to the end of continuing in it. The original state of Nature, therefore, could no longer endure, and the human race would have perished had it not changed its manner of existence.

Now, since men can by no means engender new powers, but can only unite and control those of which they are already possessed, there is no way in which they can maintain themselves save by coming together and pooling their strength in a way that will enable them to withstand any resistance exerted upon them from without. They must develop some sort of central direction and learn to act in concert.

Such a concentration of powers can be brought about only as the consequence of an agreement reached between individuals. But the self-preservation of each single man derives primarily from his own strength and from his own freedom. How, then, can he limit these without, at the same time, doing himself an injury and neglecting that care which it is his duty to devote to his own concerns? This difficulty, in so far as it is relevant to my subject, can be expressed as follows:

'Some form of association must be found as a result of which the whole strength of the community will be enlisted for the protection of the person and property of each constituent member, in such a way that each, when united to his fellows, renders obedience to his own will, and remains as free as he was before.' That is the basic problem of which the Social Contract provides the solution.

The clauses of this Contract are determined by the Act of Association in such a way that the least modification must render them null and void. Even though they may never have been formally enunciated, they must be everywhere the same, and everywhere tacitly admitted and recognized. So completely must this be the case that, should the social compact be violated, each associated individual would at once resume all the rights which once were his, and regain his natural liberty, by the mere fact of losing the agreed liberty for which he renounced it.

It must be clearly understood that the clauses in question can be reduced, in the last analysis, to one only, to wit, the complete alienation by each associate member to the community of *all his rights*. For, in the first place, since each has made surrender of himself without reservation, the resultant conditions are the same for all: and, because they are the same for all, it is in the interest of none to make them onerous to his fellows.

Furthermore, this alienation having been made unreservedly, the union of individuals is as perfect as it well can be, none of the associated members having any claim against the community. For should there be any rights left to individuals, and no common authority be empowered to pronounce as between them and the public, then each, being in some things his own judge, would soon claim to be so in all. Were that so, a state of Nature would still remain in being, the conditions of association becoming either despotic or ineffective.

In short, whoso gives himself to all gives himself to none. And, since there is no member of the social group over whom we do not acquire precisely the same rights as those over ourselves which we have surrendered to him, it follows that we gain the exact equivalent of what we lose, as well as an added power to conserve what we already have.

If, then, we take from the social pact all that is not essential to it, we shall find it to be reduced to the following terms: 'each of us contributes to the group his person and the powers which he wields as a person under the supreme direction of the general will and we receive into the body politic each individual as forming an indivisible part of the whole.'

As soon as the act of association becomes a reality, it substitutes for the person of each of the contracting parties a moral and collective body made up of as many members as the constituting assembly has votes, which body receives from this very act of constitution its unity, its dispersed *self*, and its will. The public person thus formed by the union of individuals was known in the old days as a *City*, but now as the *Republic* or *Body Politic*. This, when it fulfils a passive role, is known by its members as *The State*, when an active one, as *The Sovereign People*, and, in contrast to other similar bodies, as a *Power*. In respect of the constituent associates, it enjoys the collective name of *The People*, the individuals who compose it being known as *Citizens*, in so far as they share in the sovereign authority, as *Subjects* in so far as they owe obedience to the laws of the State. But these different terms frequently overlap, and are used indiscriminately one for the other. It is enough that we should realize the difference between them when they are employed in a precise sense. . . .

. . . the body politic, or Sovereign, in that it derives its being simply and solely from the sanctity of the said Contract, can never bind itself, even in its relations with a foreign Power, by any decision which might derogate from the validity of the original act. It may not, for instance, alienate any portion of itself, nor make submission to any other sovereign. To violate the act by reason of which it exists would be tantamount to destroying itself, and that which is nothing can produce nothing.

As soon as a mob has become united into a body politic, any attack upon one of its members is an attack upon itself. Still more important is the fact that, should any offence be committed against the body politic as a whole, the effect must be felt by each of its members. Both duty and interest, therefore, oblige the two contracting parties to render one another mutual assistance. The same individuals should seek to unite under this double aspect all the advantages which flow from it.

Now, the Sovereign People, having no existence outside that of the individuals who compose it, has, and can have, no interest at variance with theirs. Consequently, the sovereign power need give no guarantee to its subjects, since it is impossible that the body should wish to injure all its members, nor, as we shall see later, can it injure any single individual. The Sovereign, by merely existing, is always what it should be. But the same does not hold true of the relation of subject to sovereign. In spite of common interest, there can be no guarantee that the subject will observe his duty to the sovereign unless means are found to ensure his loyalty.

Each individual, indeed, may, as a man, exercise a will at variance with, or different from, that general will to which, as citizen, he contributes. His personal interest may dictate a line of action quite other than that demanded by the interest of all. The fact that his own existence as an individual has an absolute value, and that he is, by nature, an independent being, may lead him to conclude that what he owes to the common cause is something that he renders of his own free will; and he may decide that by leaving the debt unpaid he does less harm to his fellows than he would to himself should he make the necessary surrender. Regarding the moral entity constituting the State as a rational abstraction because it is not a man, he might enjoy his rights as a citizen without, at the same time, fulfilling his duties as a subject, and the resultant injustice might grow until it brought ruin upon the whole body politic.

In order, then, that the social compact may not be but a vain formula, it must contain, though unexpressed, the single undertaking which can alone give force to the whole, namely, that whoever shall refuse to obey the general will must be constrained by the whole body of his fellow citizens to do so: which is no more than to say that it may be necessary to compel a man to be free—freedom being that condition which, by giving each citizen to his country, guarantees him from all personal dependence and is the foundation upon which the whole political machine rests, and supplies the power which works it. Only the recognition by the individual of the rights of the community can give legal force to undertakings entered into between citizens, which, otherwise, would become absurd, tyrannical, and exposed to vast abuses. . . .

It follows from what has been said above that the general will is always right and ever tends to the public advantage. But it does not follow that the deliberations of the People are always equally beyond question. It is ever the way of men to wish their own good, but they do not at all times see where that good lies. The People are never corrupted though often deceived, and it is only when they are deceived that they appear to will what is evil.

There is often considerable difference between the will of all and the general will. The latter is concerned only with the common interest, the former with interests that are partial, being itself but the sum of individual wills. But take from the expression of these separate wills the pluses and minuses—which cancel out, the sum of the differences is left, and that is the general will.

If the People, engaged in deliberation, were adequately informed, and if no means existed by which the citizens could communicate one with another, from the great number of small differences the general will would result, and the decisions reached would always be good. But when intriguing groups and partial associations are formed to the disadvantage of the whole, then the will of each of such groups is general only in respect of its own members, but partial in respect of the State. When such a situation arises it may be said that there are no longer as many votes as men, but only as many votes as there are groups. Differences of interest are fewer in number, and the result is less general. Finally, when one of these groups becomes so large as to swamp all the others, the result is not the sum of small differences, but one single difference. The general will does not then come into play at all, and the prevailing opinion has no more validity than that of an individual man.

If, then, the general will is to be truly expressed, it is essential that there be no subsidiary groups within the State, and that each citizen voice his own opinion and nothing but his own opinion. It was the magnificent achievement of Lycurgus to have established the only State of this kind ever seen. But where subsidiary groups do exist their numbers should be made as large as possible, and none should be more powerful than its fellows. This precaution was taken by Solon, Numa, and Servius. Only if it is present will it be possible to ascertain the general will, and to make sure that the People are not led into error. . . .

From which it becomes clear that the sovereign power, albeit absolute, sacrosanct, and inviolable, does not, and cannot, trespass beyond the limits laid down by general agreement, and that every man has full title to enjoy whatever of property and freedom is left to him by that agreement. The sovereign is never entitled to lay a heavier burden on any one of its subjects than on others, for, should it do so, the matter would at once become particular rather than general, and, consequently, the sovereign power would no longer be competent to deal with it.

These distinctions once admitted, it becomes abundantly clear that to say that the individual, by entering into the social contract, makes an act of renunciation is utterly false. So far from that being the case, his situation within the contract is definitely preferable to what it was before. Instead of giving anything away, he makes a profitable bargain, exchanging peril and uncertainty for security, natural independence for true liberty, the power of injuring others for his own safety, the strength of his own right arm—which others might always overcome—for a right which corporate solidity renders invincible. The life which he devotes to the State is, by the State continually protected, and, when he offers it in the State's defence, what else is he doing than giving back the very boon which he has received at its hands? What, in such circumstances, does he do that he has not done more often and more perilously in a state of nature when, inevitably involved in mortal combat, he defended at the risk of his life what served him to maintain it? All citizens, it is true, may, should the need arise, have to fight for their country, but no one of them has ever to fight singly for himself. Is it not preferable, in the interest of what makes for our security, to run some part of the risks which we should have to face in our own defence, were the boon of forming one of a society taken from us? . . .

The principle of political life is in the sovereign authority. The Legislative Power is the heart of the State, the Executive is its brain, and gives movement to all its parts. The brain may be struck with paralysis and the patient yet live. A man may be an imbecile and yet not die. But once the heart ceases to function, it is all over with the animal.

It is not by the laws that a State exists, but by the Legislative Power. Yesterday's law has no authority to-day, but silence is held to imply consent, and the sovereign is deemed to confirm all laws that it does not abrogate—the assumption being that it has power to do so. When once it has declared its will on some specific issue, that will is perpetually valid, unless it be revoked.

C. The Natural Economy

THE EIGHTEENTH-CENTURY NATIONALISM ATTACK on mercantilism found its most eloquent and comprehensive expression in The Wealth of Nations *(1776) of the Scottish economist Adam Smith (1723–1790).* The Wealth of Nations *was a learned and systematic appeal to the national states of the day to allow the natural economic processes to function without interference. The economic system, like the Newtonian universe, would operate smoothly and to the advantage of all if left alone.*

1. ADAM SMITH, FROM *THE WEALTH OF NATIONS,* 1776

SOURCE. Adam Smith, *The Wealth of Nations,* Edwin Cannan, ed., New York: Modern Library, 1937, pp. 420–21, 422–24, 625–626. Reprinted by permission of Random House, Inc.

By restraining, either by high duties, or by absolute prohibitions, the importation of such goods from foreign countries as can be produced at home, the monopoly of the home market is more or less secured to the domestic industry employed in producing them. Thus the prohibition of importing either live cattle or salt provisions from foreign countries secures to the graziers of Great Britain the monopoly of the home market for butcher's meat. The high duties upon the importation of corn, which in times of moderate plenty amount to a prohibition, give a like advantage to the growers of that commodity. The prohibition of the importation of foreign woollens is equally favourable to the woollen manufacturers. The silk manufacture, though altogether employed upon foreign materials, has lately obtained the same advantage. The linen manufacture has not yet obtained it, but is making great strides towards it. Many other sorts of manufacturers have, in the same manner, obtained in Great Britain, either altogether, or very nearly a monopoly against their countrymen. The variety of goods of which the importation into Great Britain is prohibited, either absolutely, or under certain circumstances, greatly exceeds what can easily be suspected by those who are not well acquainted with the laws of the customs.

That this monopoly of the home-market frequently gives great encouragement to that particular species of industry which enjoys it, and frequently turns towards that employment a greater share of both the labour and stock of the society than would otherwise have gone to it, cannot be doubted. But whether it tends either to increase the general industry of the society, or to give it the most advantageous direction, is not, perhaps, altogether so evident.

The general industry of the society never can exceed what the capital of the society can employ. As the number of workmen that can be kept in employment by any patricular person must bear a certain proportion to his capital, so the number of those that can be continually employed by all the members of a great society, must bear a certain proportion to the whole capital of that society, and never can exceed that proportion. No regulation of commerce can increase the quantity of industry in any society beyond what its capital can maintain. It can only divert a part of it into a direction into which it might not otherwise have gone; and it is by no means certain that this artificial direction is likely to be more advantageous to the society than that into which it would have gone of its own accord.

Every individual is continually exerting himself to find out the most advantageous employment for whatever capital he can command. It is his own advantage, indeed, and not that of the society, which he has in view. But the study of his own advantage naturally, or rather necessarily leads him to prefer that employment which is most advantageous to the society. . . .

. . . every individual who employs his capital in the support of domestic industry, necessarily endeavours so to direct that industry, that its produce may be of the greatest possible value.

The produce of industry is what it adds to the subject or materials upon which it is employed. In proportion as the value of this produce is great or small, so will likewise be the profits of the employer. But it is only for the sake of profit that any man employs a capital in the support of industry; and he will always, therefore, endeavour to employ it in the support of that industry of which the produce is likely to be of the greatest value, or to exchange for the greatest quantity either of money or of other goods.

But the annual revenue of every society is always precisely equal to the exchangeable value of the whole annual produce of its industry, or rather is precisely the same thing with that exchangeable value. As every individual, therefore, endeavours as much as he can both to employ his capital in the support of domestic industry, and so to direct that industry that its produce may be of the greatest value; every individual necessarily labours to render the annual revenue of the society as great as he can. He generally, indeed, neither intends to promote the public interest, nor knows how much he is promoting it. By preferring the support of domestic to that of foreign industry, he intends only his own security, and by directing that industry in such a manner as its produce may be of the greatest value, he intends only his own gain, and he is in this, as in many other cases, led by an invisible hand to promote an end which was no part of his intention. Nor is it always the worse for the society that it was no part of it. By pursuing his own interest he frequently promotes that of the society more effectually than when he really intends to promote it. I have never known much good done by those who affected to trade for the public good. It is an affectation, indeed, not very common among merchants, and very few words need be employed in dissuading them from it.

What is the species of domestic industry which his capital can employ, and of which the produce is likely to be of the greatest value, every individual, it is evident, can, in his local situation, judge much better than any statesman or lawgiver can do for him. The statesman, who should attempt to direct private people in what manner they ought to employ their capitals, would not only load himself with a most unnecessary attention, but assume an authority which could safely be trusted, not only to no single person, but to council or senate whatever, and which would nowhere be so dangerous as in the hands of a man who had folly and presumption enough to fancy himself fit to exercise it.

To give the monopoly of the home-market to the produce of domestic industry, in any particular art or manufacture, is in some measure to direct private people in what manner they ought to employ their capitals, and must, in almost all cases, be either a useless or a hurtful regulation. If the produce of domestic can be brought there as cheap as that of foreign industry, the regulation is evidently useless. If it cannot, it must generally be hurtful. It is the maxim of every prudent master of a family, never to attempt to make at home what it will cost him more to make than to buy. The taylor does not attempt to make his own shoes, but buys them of the shoemaker. The shoemaker does not attempt to make his own clothes, but employs a taylor. The farmer attempts to make neither the one nor the other, but employs those different artificers. All of them find it for their interest to employ their whole industry in a way in which they have some advantage over their neighbours, and to purchase with a part of its produce, or what is the same thing, with the price of a part of it, whatever else they have occasion for.

What is prudence in the conduct of every private family, can scarce be folly in that of a great kingdom. If a foreign country can supply us with a commodity cheaper than we ourselves can make it, better buy it of them with some part of the produce of our own industry, employed in a way in which we have some advantage. The general industry of the country, being always in proportion to the capital which employs it, will not thereby be diminished, no more than that of the above-mentioned artificers; but only left to find out the way in which it can be employed with the greatest advantage. It is certainly not employed to the greatest advantage, when it is thus directed towards an object which it can buy cheaper than it can make. The value of its annual produce is certainly more or less diminished, when it is thus turned away from producing commodities evidently of more value than the commodity which it is directed to produce. According to the supposition, that commodity could be purchased from foreign countries cheaper than it can be made at home. It could, therefore, have been purchased with a part only of the commodities, or, what is the same thing, with a part only of the price of the commodities, which the industry employed by an equal capital would have produced at home, had it been left to follow its natural course. The industry of the country, therefore, is thus turned away from a more, to a less advantageous employment, and the exchangeable value of its annual produce, instead of being increased, according to the intention of the lawgiver, must necessarily be diminished by every such regulation.

Consumption is the sole end and purpose of all production; and the interest of the producer ought to be attended to, only so far as it may be necessary for promoting that of the consumer. The maxim is so perfectly self-evident, that it would be absurd to attempt to prove it. But in the mercantile system, the interest of the consumer is almost constantly sacrificed to that of the producer; and it seems to consider production, and not consumption, as the ultimate end and object of all industry and commerce.

In the restraints upon the importation of all foreign commodities which can come into competition with those of our own growth, or manufacture, the interest of the home-consumer is evidently sacrificed to that of the producer. It is altogether for the benefit of the latter, that the former is obliged to pay that enhancement of price which this monopoly almost always occasions.

It is altogether for the benefit of the producer that bounties are granted upon the exportation of some of his productions. The home-consumer is obliged to pay, first, the tax which is necessary for paying the bounty, and secondly, the still greater tax which necessarily arises from the enhancement of the price of the commodity in the home market.

By the famous treaty of commerce with Portugal, the consumer is prevented by high duties from purchasing of a neighbouring country, a commodity which our own climate does not produce, but is obliged to purchase it of a distant country, though it is acknowledged, that the commodity of the distant country is of a worse quality than that of the near one. The home-consumer is obliged to submit to this inconveniency, in order that the producer may import into the distant country some of his productions upon more advantageous terms than he would otherwise have been allowed to do. The consumer, too, is obliged to pay, whatever enhancement in the price of those very productions, this forced exportation may occasion in the home market.

But in the system of laws which has been established for the management of our American and West Indian colonies, the interest of the home-consumer has been sacrificed to that of the producer with a more extravagant profusion than in all our other commercial regulations. A great empire has been established for the sole purpose of raising up a nation of customers who should be obliged to buy from the shops of our different producers, all the goods with which these could supply them. For the sake of that little enhancement of price which this monopoly might afford our producers, the home-consumers have been burdened with the whole expence of maintaining and defending that empire. For this purpose, and for this purpose only, in the two last wars, more than two hundred millions have been spent, and a new debt of more than a hundred and seventy millions has been contracted over and above all that had been expended for the same purpose in former wars. The interest of this debt alone is not only greater than the whole extraordinary profit, which, it ever could be pretended, was made by the monopoly of the colony trade, but than the whole value of that trade, or than the whole value of the goods, which at an average have been annually exported to the colonies.

It cannot be very difficult to determine who have been the contrivers of this whole mercantile system; not the consumers, we may believe, whose interest has been entirely neglected; but the producers, who interest has been so carefully attended to; and among this latter class our merchants and manufacturers have been by far the principal architects. In the mercantile regulations, which have been taken notice of in this chapter, the interest of our manufacturers has been most peculiarly attended to; and the interest, not so much of the consumers, as that of some other sets of producers, has been sacrificed to it.

Part III

NEO-CLASSICISM

A. Architecture and Sculpture

THE RATIONALISM of eighteenth-century thought was paralleled by the classical balance and restraint of eighteenth-century art. Architects, sculptors, and painters joined in rejecting the ornate and flowing Baroque style in favor of a purer and more elegant form of expression. In Barthélemy Vignon's La Madeleine in Paris (completed 1824), one encounters an unblemished Classicism purged of Baroque exuberance.

1. BARTHÉLEMY VIGNON, LA MADELEINE, PARIS, COMPLETED 1824

THE PERSEUS (1797) *of the sculptor Antonio Canova, although not entirely successful as a work of art, is an excellent example of Neo-Classical purity and simplicity (compare Bernini's Triton Fountain, p. 86).*

2. ANTONIO CANOVA, *PERSEUS,* 1797

B. Painting

ONE FINDS the same qualities of purity and simplicity in the paintings of artists such as Jacques Louis David (1748–1825) (1) and the late Neo-Classicist Jean-Auguste Ingres (1780–1867) (2). In their works Baroque fluidity gives way to immobility, severity, and understatement.

1. JACQUES LOUIS DAVID, *OATH OF THE HORATII*, 1785

2. JEAN-AUGUSTE INGRES, *MADEMOISELLE RIVIÈRE*

Revolution, Romanticism, and Counter-Revolution

1789–1848

THE course of eighteenth-century European history changed abruptly in 1789 with the outbreak of the French Revolution. Plagued by severe financial problems, King Louis XVI was obliged to summon the French Estates General for the first time in 175 years. Grievances had long been building up against the archaic, privilege-ridden *ancien régime*, which offered nothing to the peasantry and very little to the middle class. To the *philosophes* it appeared as a model of unenlightened despotism. Immediately upon the assembling of the Estates General, the Third Estate (representatives of the people in general and the middle class in particular) demanded a greater voice than the First and Second Estates (clergy and nobility), arguing that its authority should be appropriate to the vast numbers that it represented. Organizing themselves into a "National Assembly," the representatives of the Third Estate invited the delegates of the other estates to join them, and thereupon proceeded to direct the course of the Revolution.

Thenceforth the Revolution followed a progressively leftward course. The delegates to the National Assembly prepared a constitution designed to create a constitutional monarchy, but with the abortive flight and subsequent execution of Louis XVI, France became a republic. The radical Jacobin Party rose to power, the Reign of Terror ensued, and after a period of conservative reaction under the Directory government (1795–1799) Napoleon became the master of of France. His far-ranging armies spread French influence and the Revolutionary ideology across the length and breadth of Europe. The era of the Napoleonic wars came to an end with the Congress of Vienna (1815) at which the victorious great powers—Austria, Prussia, Russia, and Great Britain—reconstructed the political system of Europe on a conservative, royalist basis. France was given a new Bourbon king, Louis XVIII.

Europe responded to the French Revolution in a variety of ways. The two potent Revolutionary concepts of liberalism and nationalism extended across Europe and played a significant role in the politics of the nineteenth century. It was these two concepts, above all, that underlay the revolutions of 1830 and 1848, both of which began in France and quickly expanded to the rest of Europe. To many people, however, the French Revolution was simply a bloody catastrophe. Statesmen such as the Austrian Prince Metternich who dominated the Vienna settlement, and writers such as the Englishman Edmund Burke, were bitter opponents of the Revolutionary ideology. They cautioned against the dangers of overturning the social order and preached a philosophy of conservatism and reverence for the past.

The frame of mind that produced Enlightenment rationalism and Neo-Classical art gave way to the radically different mood of Romanticism. The Romantics protested against the bloodless intellectualism and Classical formalism of the past, replacing them with a new emphasis on personal, emotional values. Their works are sometimes tender, sometimes moody, sometimes imaginatively descriptive, and always infused with rich, exotic imagery. They drew their inspiration not so much from Classical Greece and Rome as from the colorful, mystical ethos of the Middle Ages which they idealized and romanticized. Among Romantics, the passions of the heart took priority over the abstractions of the mind, and form bowed before feeling.

Part I

THE FRENCH REVOLUTION
AND NAPOLEON

A. The Onset of the Revolution

THE CLAIMS OF THE THIRD ESTATE, which resulted in the transformation of the Estates General into the National Assembly, are set forth boldly in Abbé Sieyes' pamphlet "What Is the Third Estate?," which appeared in January, 1789, on the eve of the Revolution, just as the election of delegates was beginning.

1. ABBÉ SIEYES, FROM "WHAT IS THE THIRD ESTATE?"

SOURCE. J. H. Stewart, ed., *A Documentary History of the French Revolution,* New York: Macmillan, 1951, pp. 42–47. Copyright 1951 by The Macmillan Company. Reprinted by permission of The Macmillan Company.

The plan of this pamphlet is very simple. We have three questions to ask:

1st. What is the third estate? Everything.

2nd. What has it been heretofore in the political order? Nothing.

3rd. What does it demand? To become something therein.

We shall see if the answers are correct. Then we shall examine the measures that have been tried and those which must be taken in order that the third estate may in fact become *something*. Thus we shall state:

4th. What the ministers have *attempted*, and what the privileged classes themselves *propose* in its favor.

5th. What *ought* to have been done.

6th. Finally, what *remains* to be done in order that the third estate may take its rightful place.

CHAPTER I   THE THIRD ESTATE IS A COMPLETE NATION

What are the essentials of national existence and prosperity? *Private* enterprise and *public* functions.

Private enterprise may be divided into four classes: 1st. Since earth and water furnish the raw material for man's needs, the first class will comprise all families engaged in agricultural pursuits. 2nd. Between the original sale of materials and their consumption or use, further workmanship, more or less manifold, adds to these materials a second value, more or less compounded. Human industry thus succeeds in perfecting the benefits of nature and in increasing the gross produce twofold, tenfold, one hundredfold in value. Such is the work of the second class. 3rd. Between production and consumption, as well as among the different degrees of production, a group of intermediate agents, useful to producers as well as to consumers, comes into being; these are the dealers and merchants. . . . 4th. In addition to these three classes of industrious and useful citizens concerned with goods for consumption and use, a society needs many private undertakings and endeavors which are *directly* useful or agreeable to the *individual*. This fourth class includes from the most distinguished scientific and liberal professions to the least esteemed domestic services. Such are the labors which sustain society. Who performs them? The third estate.

Public functions likewise under present circumstances may be classified under four well known headings: the Sword, the Robe, the Church, and the Administration. It is unnecessary to discuss them in detail in order to demonstrate that the third estate everywhere constitutes nineteen-twentieths of them, except that it is burdened with all that is really arduous, with all the tasks that the privileged order refuses to perform. Only the lucrative and honorary positions are held by members of the privileged order. . . . nevertheless they have dared lay the order of the third estate under an interdict. They have said to it: "Whatever be your services, whatever your talents, you shall go thus far and no farther. It is not fitting that you be honored." . . .

It suffices here to have revealed that the alleged utility of a privileged order to public service is only a chimera; that without it, all that is arduous in such service is performed by the third estate; that without it, the higher positions would be infinitely better filled; that they naturally ought to be the lot of and reward for talents and recognized services; and that if the privileged classes have succeeded in usurping all the lucrative and honorary positions, it is both an odious injustice to the majority of citizens and a treason to the commonwealth.

Who, then, would dare to say that the third estate has not within itself all that is necessary to constitute a complete nation? It is the strong and robust man whose one arm remains enchained. If the privileged order were abolished, the nation would be not something less but something more. Thus, what is the third estate? Everything; but an everything shackled and oppressed. What would it be without the privileged order? Everything; but an everything free and flourishing. Nothing can progress without it; everything would proceed infinitely better without the others. It is not sufficient to have demonstrated that the privileged classes, far from being useful to the nation, can only enfeeble and injure it; it is necessary, moreover, to prove that the nobility does not belong to the social organization at all; that, indeed, it may be a *burden* upon the nation, but that it would not know how to constitute a part thereof. . . .

What is a nation? a body of associates living under a *common* law and represented by the same *legislature*.

Is it not exceedingly clear that the noble order has privileges, exemptions, even rights separate from the rights of the majority of citizens? Thus it deviates from the common order, from the common law. Thus its civil rights already render it a people apart in a great nation. It is indeed *imperium in imperio.*

Also, it enjoys its political rights separately. It has its own representatives, who are by no means charged with representing the people. Its deputation sits apart; and when it is assembled in the same room with the deputies of ordinary citizens, it is equally true that its representation is essentially distinct and separate; it is foreign to the nation in principle, since its mandate does not emanate from the people, and in aim, since its purpose is to defend not the general but a special interest.

The third estate, then, comprises everything appertaining to the nation; and whatever is not the third estate may not be regarded as being of the nation. What is the third estate? Everything!

CHAPTER II   WHAT HAS THE THIRD ESTATE BEEN HERETOFORE? NOTHING

We shall examine neither the state of servitude in which the people has suffered so long, nor that of constraint and humiliation in which it is still confined. Its civil status has changed; it must change still more; it is indeed impossible that the nation as a whole, or that even any order in particular, may become free if the third estate is not. Freedom is not the consequence of privileges, but of the rights appertaining to all. . . .

. . . the third estate must be understood to mean the mass of the citizens belonging to the common order. Legalized privilege in any form deviates from the common order, constitutes an exception to the common law, and, consequently, does not appertain to the third estate at all. We repeat, a common law and a common representation are what constitutes *one* nation. It is only too true that one is *nothing* in France when one has only the protection of the common law; if one does not possess some privilege, one must resign oneself to enduring contempt, injury, and vexations of every sort. . . .

But here we have to consider the order of the third estate less in its civil status than in its relation with the constitution. Let us examine its position in the Estates General.

Who have been its so-called representatives? The ennobled or those privileged for a period of years. These false deputies have not even been always freely elected by the people. Sometimes in the Estates General, and almost always in the provincial Estates, the representation of the people has been regarded as a perquisite of certain posts or offices. . . .

Add to this appalling truth that, in one manner or another, all branches of the executive power also have fallen to the caste which furnishes the Church, the Robe, and the Sword. A sort of spirit of brotherhood causes the nobles to prefer themselves . . . to the rest of the nation. Usurpation is complete; in truth, they reign.

. . . it is a great error to believe that France is subject to a monarchical régime.

. . . it is the court, and not the monarch, that has reigned. It is the court that makes and unmakes, appoints and discharges ministers, creates and dispenses positions, etc. And what is the court if not the head of this immense aristocracy which overruns all parts of France; which through its members attains all and everywhere does whatever is essential in all parts of the commonwealth? . . .

Let us sum up: the third estate has not heretofore had real representatives in the Estates General. Thus its political rights are null.

CHAPTER III   WHAT DOES THE THIRD ESTATE DEMAND? TO BE SOMETHING

. . . The true petitions of this order may be appreciated only through the authentic claims directed to the government by the large municipalities of the kingdom. What is indicated therein? That the people wishes to be *something*, and, in truth, the very least that is possible. It wishes to have real representatives in the Estates General, that is to say, deputies *drawn from its order*, who are competent to be interpreters of its will and defenders of its interests. But what will it avail it to be present at the Estates General if the predominating interest there is contrary to its own! Its presence would only consecrate the oppression of which it would be the eternal victim. Thus, it is indeed certain that it cannot come to vote at the Estates General unless it is to have in that body *an influence at least equal to that of the privileged classes;* and it demands a number of representatives equal to that of the first two orders together. Finally, this equality of representation would become completely illusory if every chamber voted separately. The third estate demands, then, that votes be taken *by head and not by order*. This is the essence of those claims so alarming to the privileged classes, because they believed that thereby the reform of abuses would become inevitable. The real intention of the third estate is to have an influence in the Estates General equal to that of the privileged classes. I repeat, can it ask less? And is it not clear that if its influence therein is less than equality, it cannot be expected to emerge from its political nullity and become *something*?

But what is indeed unfortunate is that the three articles constituting the demand of the third estate are insufficient to give it this equality of influence which it cannot, in reality, do without. In vain will it obtain an equal number of representatives drawn from its order; the influence of the privileged classes will establish itself and dominate even in the sanctuary of the third estate. . . .

Besides the influence of the aristocracy . . . there is the influence of property. This is natural. I do not proscribe it at all; but one must agree that it is still all to the advantage of the privileged classes. . . .

The more one considers this matter, the more obvious the insufficiency of the three demands of the third estate becomes. But finally, such as they are, they have been vigorously attacked. Let us examine the pretexts for this hostility. . . .

I have only one observation to make. Obviously there are abuses in France; these abuses are profitable to someone; they are scarcely advantageous to the third estate—indeed, they are injurious to it in particular. Now I ask if, in this state of affairs, it is possible to destroy any abuse so long as those who profit therefrom control the *veto*? All justice would be powerless; it would be necessary to rely entirely on the sheer generosity of the privileged classes. Would that be your idea of what constitutes the social order?

THERE FOLLOW two important documents marking the genesis of the National Assembly: the Decree Creating the National Assembly (June 17, 1789) (2), and the Tennis Court Oath (June 20, 1789) in which the members of the Assembly pledged mutual allegiance and undertook never to disband until their work of reforming the government was completed (3).

2. DECREE CREATING THE NATIONAL ASSEMBLY, 1789

SOURCE. F. M. Anderson, ed., *The Constitutions and Other Select Documents Illustrative of the History of France,* Minneapolis: H. W. Wilson Co., 1904, pp. 1–2. Reprinted by permission of Dr. Gaylord W. Anderson.

The Assembly, deliberating after the verification of the powers, recognizes that this assembly is already composed of the representatives sent directly by at least ninety-six per cent of the nation.

Such a body of deputies cannot remain inactive owing to the absence of the deputies of some bailliages and some classes of citizens; for the absentees, who have been summoned, cannot prevent those present from exercising the full extent of their rights, especially when the exercise of these rights is an imperious and pressing duty.

Furthermore, since it belongs only to the verified representatives to participate in the formation of the national opinion, and since all the verified representatives ought to be in this assembly, it is still more indispensable to conclude that the interpretation and presentation of the general will of the nation belong to it, and belong to it alone, and that there cannot exist between the throne and this assembly any *veto*, any negative power.— The Assembly declares then that the common task of the national restoration can and ought to be commenced without delay by the deputies present and that they ought to pursue it without interruption as well as without hindrance.—The denomination of NATIONAL ASSEMBLY is the only one which is suitable for the Assembly in the present condition of things; because the members who compose it are the only representatives lawfully and publicly known and verified; because they are sent directly by almost the totality of the nation; because, lastly, the representation being one and indivisible, none of the deputies, in whatever class or order he may be chosen, has the right to exercise his functions apart from the present assembly.—The Assembly will never lose the hope of uniting within its own body all the deputies absent today; it will not cease to summon them to fulfil the obligation laid upon them to participate in the holding of the States-General. At any moment when the absent deputies present themselves in the course of the session which is about to open, it declares in advance that it will hasten to receive them and to share with them, after the verification of their powers, the results of the great labors which are bound to procure the regeneration of France.—The National Assembly orders that the motives of the present decision be immediately drawn up in order to be presented to the King and the nation.

3. THE TENNIS COURT OATH, 1789

SOURCE. F. M. Anderson, ed., *The Constitutions and Other Select Documents Illustrative of the History of France*, Minneapolis: H. W. Wilson Co., 1904, p. 3. Reprinted by permission of Dr. Gaylord W. Anderson.

The National Assembly, considering that it has been summoned to determine the Constitution of the kingdom, to effect the regeneration of public order, to maintain the true principles of the monarchy; that nothing can prevent it from continuing its deliberations in whatever place it may be forced to establish itself, and lastly, that wherever its members meet together, there is the National Assembly.

Decrees that all the members of this Assembly shall immediately take a solemn oath never to separate, and to reassemble wherever circumstances shall require, until the Constitution of the kingdom shall be established and consolidated upon firm foundations; and that, the said oath being taken, all the members and each of them individually shall ratify by their signatures this stedfast resolution.

B. Acts of the National Assembly

THE NEXT GROUP of documents exemplifies some of the more important acts of the National Assembly. The Fourth of August Decrees, in which the National Assembly, in an outburst of enthusiasm, abolished the vestiges of French feudalism and manorialism, were prompted by the violence in the countryside that followed the storming of the Bastille on July 14. These Decrees were promulgated in slightly revised form on August 11, 1789.

1. THE ABOLITION OF FEUDALISM, AUGUST 4, 1789

SOURCE. F. M. Anderson, ed., *The Constitutions and Other Select Documents Illustrative of the History of France*, Minneapolis: H. W. Wilson Co., 1904, pp. 11–15. Reprinted by permission of Dr. Gaylord W. Anderson.

1. The National Assembly hereby completely abolishes the feudal system. It decrees that, among the existing rights and dues, both feudal and *censuel*, all those originating in or representing real or personal serfdom (*main morte*) or personal servitude, shall be abolished without indemnification. All other dues are declared redeemable, the terms and mode of redemption to be fixed by the National Assembly. Those of the said dues which are not extinguished by this decree shall continue to be collected until indemnification shall take place. . . .

3. The exclusive right to hunt and to maintain unenclosed warrens is likewise abolished, and every land owner shall have the right to kill or to have destroyed on his own land all kinds of game, observing, however, such police regulations as may be established with a view to the safety of the public. . . .

The president of the assembly shall be commissioned to ask of the King the recall of those sent to the galleys or exiled, simply for violations of the hunting regulations, as well as for the release of those at present imprisoned for offences of this kind, and the dismissal of such cases as are now pending.

4. All manorial courts are hereby suppressed without indemnification. But the magistrates of these courts shall continue to perform their functions until such time as the National Assembly shall provide for the establishment of a new judicial system.

5. Tithes of every description, as well as the dues which have been substituted for them, under whatever denomination they are known or collected (even when compounded for), possessed by secular or regular congregations, by holders of benefices, members of corporations (including the Order of Malta and other religious and military orders), as well as those devoted to the maintenance of churches, those impropriated to lay persons and those substituted for the *portion congrue*, are abolished, on condition, however, that some other method be devised to provide for the expenses of divine worship, the support of the officiating clergy, for the assistance of the poor, for repairs and rebuilding of churches and parsonages, and for the maintenance of all institutions, seminaries, schools, academies, asylums, and organizations to which the present funds are devoted. Until such provision shall be made and the former possessors shall enter upon the enjoyment of an income on the new system, the National Assembly decrees that the said tithes shall continue to be collected according to law and in the customary manner.

Other tithes, of whatever nature they may be, shall be redeemable in such manner as the Assembly shall determine. Until such regulation shall be issued, the National Assembly decrees that these, too, shall continue to be collected.

6. All perpetual ground rents, payable either in money or in kind, of whatever nature they may be, whatever their origin and to whomsoever they may be due, as to members of corporations, holders of the domain or appanages or to the Order of Malta, shall be redeemable. *Champarts,* of every kind and under all denominations, shall likewise be redeemable at a rate fixed by the Assembly. No due shall in the future be created which is not redeemable.

7. The sale of judicial and municipal offices shall be suppressed forthwith. Justice shall be dispensed *gratis*. Nevertheless, the magistrates at present holding such offices shall continue to exercise their functions and to receive their emoluments until the Assembly shall have made provision for indemnifying them.

8. The fees of the country priests are abolished, and shall be discontinued so soon as provision shall be made for increasing the minimum salary [*portion congrue*] of the parish priests and the payment to the curates. A regulation shall be drawn up to determine the status of the priests in the towns.

9. Pecuniary privileges, personal or real, in the payment of taxes are abolished forever. Taxes shall be collected from all the citizens, and from all property, in the same manner and in the same form. Plans shall be considered by which the taxes shall be paid proportionally by all, even for the last six months of the current year.

10. Inasmuch as a national constitution and public liberty are of more advantage to the provinces than the privileges which some of these enjoy, and inasmuch as the surrender of such privileges is essential to the intimate union of all parts of the realm [*empire*], it is decreed that all the peculiar privileges, pecuniary or otherwise, of the provinces, principalities, districts [*pays*], cantons, cities and communes, are once for all abolished and are absorbed into the law common to all Frenchmen.

11. All citizens, without distinction of birth, are eligible to any office or dignity, whether ecclesiastical, civil or military; and no profession shall imply any derogation.

12. Hereafter no remittances shall be made for annates or for any other purpose to the court of Rome, the vice-legation at Avignon, or to the nunciature at Lucerne. The clergy of the diocese shall apply to their bishops in regard to the filling of benefices and dispensations, the which shall be granted *gratis* without regard to reservations, expectancies and papal months, all the churches of France enjoying the same freedom.

13. The rights of *deport*, of *cotte-morte, depouilles, vacat, droits censaux*, Peter's pence, and other dues of the same kind, under whatever denomination, established in favor of bishops, archdeacons, archpresbyters, chapters, and regular congregations which formerly exercised priestly functions [*cures primitifs*], are abolished, but appropriate provision shall be made for those benefices of archdeacons and archpresbyters which are not sufficiently endowed.

14. Pluralities shall not be permitted hereafter in cases where the revenue from the benefice or benefices held shall exceed the sum of three thousand *livres*. Nor shall any individual be allowed to enjoy several pensions from benefices, or a pension and a benefice, if the revenue which he already enjoys from such sources exceeds the same sum of three thousand *livres*.

15. The National Assembly shall consider, in conjunction with the King, the report which is to be submitted to it relating to pensions, favors and salaries, with a view to suppressing all such as are not deserved and reducing those which shall prove excessive; and the amount shall be fixed which the King may in the future disburse for this purpose.

16. The National Assembly decrees that a medal shall be struck in memory of the recent grave and important deliberations for the welfare of France, and that a *Te Deum* shall be chanted in gratitude in all the parishes and the churches of France.

17. The National Assembly solemnly proclaims the King, Louis XVI, the *Restorer of French Liberty*.

18. The National Assembly shall present itself in a body before the King, in order to submit to him the decrees which have just been passed, to tender to him the tokens of its most respectful gratitude and to pray him to permit the *Te Deum* to be chanted in his chapel, and to be present himself at this service.

19. The National Assembly shall consider, immediately after the constitution, the drawing up of the laws necessary for the development of the principles which it has laid down in the present decree. The latter shall be transmitted without delay by the deputies to all the provinces, together with the decree of the tenth of this month, in order that it may be printed, published, announced from the parish pulpits, and posted up wherever it shall be deemed necessary.

ON AUGUST 27 the National Assembly issued a general statement of principles, the Declaration of the Rights of Man and Citizen, which reflects some of the political ideas of the Enlightenment and seems to have been modeled on the bills of rights of certain American states.

2. DECLARATION OF THE RIGHTS OF MAN AND CITIZEN, 1789

SOURCE. F. M. Anderson, ed., *The Constitutions and Other Select Documents Illustrative of the History of France*, Minneapolis: H. W. Wilson Co., 1904, pp. 58–60. Reprinted by permission of Dr. Gaylord W. Anderson.

The representatives of the French people, organized in National Assembly, considering that ignorance, forgetfulness or contempt of the rights of man are the sole causes of the public miseries and of the corruption of governments, have resolved to set forth in a solemn declaration the natural, inalienable, and sacred rights of man, in order that this declaration, being ever present to all the members of the social body, may unceasingly remind them of their rights and their duties: in order that the acts of the legislative power and those of the executive power may be each moment compared with the aim of every political institution and thereby may be more respected; and in order that the demands of the citizens, grounded henceforth upon simple and incontestable principles, may always take the direction of maintaining the constitution and the welfare of all.

In consequence, the National Assembly recognizes and declares, in the presence and under the auspices of the Supreme Being, the following rights of man and citizen.

1. Men are born and remain free and equal in rights. Social distinctions can be based only upon public utility.

2. The aim of every political association is the preservation of the natural and imprescriptible rights of man. These rights are liberty, property, security, and resistance to oppression.

3. The source of all sovereignty is essentially in the nation; no body, no individual can exercise authority that does not proceed from it in plain terms.

4. Liberty consists in the power to do anything that does not injure others; accordingly, the exercise of the natural rights of each man has for its only limits those that secure to the other members of society the enjoyment of these same rights. These limits can be determined only by law.

5. The law has the right to forbid only such actions as are injurious to society. Nothing can be forbidden that is not interdicted by the law and no one can be constrained to do that which it does not order.

6. Law is the expression of the general will. All citizens have the right to take part personally or by their representatives in its formation. It must be the same for all, whether it protects or punishes. All citizens being equal in its eyes, are equally eligible to all public dignities, places, and employments, according to their capacities, and without other distinction than that of their virtues and their talents.

7. No man can be accused, arrested, or detained except in the cases determined by the law and according to the forms that it has prescribed. Those who procure, expedite, execute, or cause to be executed arbitrary orders ought to be punished: but every citizen summoned or seized in virtue of the law ought to render instant obedience; he makes himself guilty by resistance.

8. The law ought to establish only penalties that are strictly and obviously necessary and no one can be punished except in virtue of a law established and promulgated prior to the offence and legally applied.

9. Every man being presumed innocent until he has been pronounced guilty, if it is thought indispensable to arrest him, all severity that may not be necessary to secure his person ought to be strictly suppressed by law.

10. No one ought to be disturbed on account of his opinions, even religious, provided their manifestation does not derange the public order established by law.

11. The free communication of ideas and opinions is one of the most precious of the rights of man; every citizen then can freely speak, write, and print, subject to responsibility for the abuse of this freedom in the cases determined by law.

12. The guarantee of the rights of man and citizen requires a public force; this force then is instituted for the advantage of all and not for the personal benefit of those to whom it is entrusted.

13. For the maintenance of the public force and for the expenses of administration a general tax is indispensable; it ought to be equally apportioned among all the citizens according to their means.

14. All the citizens have the right to ascertain, by themselves or by their representatives, the necessity of the public tax, to consent to it freely, to follow the employment of it, and to determine the quota, the assessment, the collection, and the duration of it.

15. Society has the right to call for an account from every public agent of its administration.

16. Any society in which the guarantee of the rights is not secured or the separation of powers not determined has no constitution at all.

17. Property being a sacred and inviolable right, no one can be deprived of it unless a legally established public necessity evidently demands it, under the condition of a just and prior indemnity.

THE CIVIL CONSTITUTION OF THE CLERGY (July 12, 1790) can be regarded as an effort to rationalize the French Church along Enlightenment lines. More specifically, however, it was prompted by the continuing financial crisis and the need to add the vast properties of the Church to the resources of the state. Perhaps the most radical act of the National Assembly, it was condemned by the Papacy and became a crucial factor in alienating the monarchists from the work of the Revolution.

3. THE CIVIL CONSTITUTION OF THE CLERGY, 1790

SOURCE. F. M. Anderson, ed., *The Constitutions and Other Select Documents Illustrative of the History of France*, Minneapolis: H. W. Wilson Co., 1904, pp. 16–22. Reprinted by permission of Dr. Gaylord W. Anderson.

The National Assembly, after having heard the report of the Ecclesiastical Committee, has decreed and does decree the following as constitutional articles:—

TITLE I.

1. Each department shall form a single diocese, and each diocese shall have the same extent and the same limits as the department.

2. The seat of the bishoprics of the eighty-three departments of the kingdom shall be established as follows: That of the Department of the Lower Seine at Rouen; that of the Department of Calvados at Bayeux. . . . [The names of the remaining episcopal sees are here omitted.]

All other bishoprics in the eighty-three departments of the kingdom, which are not included by name in the present article are, and forever shall be, abolished.

The kingdom shall be divided into ten metropolitan districts. . . .

4. No church or parish of France nor any French citizen may acknowledge upon any occasion or upon any pretext whatsoever, the authority of an ordinary bishop or of an archbishop whose see shall be under the supremacy of a foreign power, nor that of their representatives residing in France or elsewhere; without prejudice, however, to the unity of the faith and the intercourse which shall be maintained with the Visible Head of the Universal Church, as hereafter provided.

5. After the bishop of a diocese shall have rendered his decision in his synod upon the matters lying within his competence an appeal may be carried to the archbishop, who shall give his decision in the metropolitan synod.

6. A new arrangement and division of all the parishes of the kingdom shall be undertaken immediately in concert with the Bishop and the District Administration. The number and extent of the parishes shall be determined according to rules which shall be laid down.

7. The cathedral church of each diocese shall be restored to its primitive condition and be hereafter at once the church of the parish and of the diocese. This shall be accomplished by the suppression of parishes and by the redistribution of dwellings which it may be deemed necessary to include in the new parish. . . .

15. There shall be but a single parish in all cities and towns having not more than 6,000 inhabitants. The other parishes shall be abolished or absorbed into that of the Episcopal church.

16. In cities having a population of more than 6,000 inhabitants a parish may include a greater number of parishioners, and as many parishes shall be perpetuated as the needs of the people and localities shall require.

17. The administrative assemblies, in concert with the bishop of the diocese, shall indicate to the next legislative assembly, the country and subordinate urban parishes which ought to be contracted or enlarged, established or abolished, and shall indicate farther the limits of the parishes as the needs of the people, the dignity of religion and the various localities shall require. . . .

TITLE II.

1. Beginning with the day of publication of the present decree there shall be but one mode of choosing bishops and parish priests, namely that of election.

2. All elections shall be by ballot and shall be decided by the absolute majority of the votes.

3. The election of bishops shall take place according to the forms and by the electoral body designated in the decree of December 22, 1789, for the election of members of the Departmental Assembly. . . .

7. In order to be eligible to a bishopric one must have fulfilled for fifteen years at least the duties of the church ministry in the diocese as a parish priest, officiating minister or curate or as superior or as directing vicar of the seminary. . . .

17. The archbishop or senior bishop of the province shall have the right to examine the bishop-elect in the presence of his council upon his belief and his character. If he deems him fit for the position he shall give him the canonical institution. If he believes it his duty to refuse this, the reasons for his refusal shall be recorded in writing and signed by the archbishop and his council, reserving to the parties concerned the right to appeal on the ground of an abuse of power as hereinafter provided.

18. The bishop applied to for institution may not exact of the person elected any form of oath except that he makes profession of the Roman Catholic and Apostolic religion.

19. The new bishop may not apply to the pope for any form of conformation, but shall write to him as the Visible Head of the Universal Church as a testimony to the unity of faith and communion maintained with him. . . .

21. Before the ceremony of consecration begins, the bishop-elect shall take a solemn oath in the presence of the municipal officers, of the people and of the clergy to guard with care the faithful of his diocese who are confided to him, to be loyal to the Nation, the Law and the King and to support with all his power the constitution decreed by the National Assembly and accepted by the King. . . .

25. The election of the parish priests shall take place according to the forms and by the electors designated in the decree of December 22, 1789, for the election of members of the Administrative Assembly of the District. . . .

29. Each elector, before depositing his ballot in the ballot-box, shall take oath to vote only for that person whom he has conscientiously selected in his heart as the most worthy, without having been influenced by any gift, promise, solicitation or threat. The same oath shall be required at the election of the bishops as in the case of the parish priests. . . .

TITLE III.

1. The ministers of religion, performing as they do the first and most important functions of society and forced to live continuously in the place where they discharge the offices to which they have been called by the confidence of the people, shall be supported by the nation.

2. Every bishop, priest and officiating clergyman in a chapel of ease, shall be furnished with a suitable dwelling. . . . Salaries shall be assigned to each, as indicated below.

3. The Bishop of Paris shall receive 50,000 *livres;* the bishops of cities having a population of 50,000 or more, 20,000 *livres;* other bishops, 12,000 *livres.* . . .

12. In view of the salary which is assured to them by the present constitution, the bishops, parish priests and curates shall perform the episcopal and priestly functions *gratis.*

TITLE IV.

1. The law requiring the residence of ecclesiastics in the districts under their charge shall be strictly observed. All vested with an ecclesiastical office or function shall be subject to this without distinction or exception.

2. No bishop shall absent himself from his diocese more than two weeks consecutively during the year, except in case of real necessity and with the consent of the Directory of the Department in which his see is situated.

3. In the same manner the parish priests and the curates may not absent themselves from the place of their duties beyond the term fixed above, except for weighty reasons, and even in such cases the priests must obtain the permission both of their bishop and of the Directory of their district, and the curates that of the parish priest.

THE DECREE UPON THE CLERICAL OATH (November 27, 1790) established that the French clergy had to swear to abide by the Civil Constitution. Many clerics refused flatly to do so.

4. DECREE UPON THE CLERICAL OATH, 1790

SOURCE. F. M. Anderson, ed., *The Constitutions and Other Select Documents Illustrative of the History of France,* Minneapolis: H. W. Wilson Co., 1904, pp. 22–23. Reprinted by permission of Dr. Gaylord W. Anderson.

1. The bishops and former archbishops and the *cures* kept in their positions shall be required, if they have not already done so, to take the oath

for which they are liable . . . concerning the Civil Constitution of the Clergy. In consequence, they shall swear . . . to look with care after the faithful of their diocese or the parish which is intrusted to them, to be faithful to the nation, to the law and to the King, and to maintain with all their power the constitution decreed by the National Assembly and accepted by the King.

2. [The same requirement, except the first clause, is made of "all other ecclesiastical public functionaries."] . . .

5. Those of the said bishops, former archbishops, *cures,* and other ecclesiastical public functionaries, who shall not have taken . . . the oath which is prescribed for them respectively, shall be reputed to have renounced their office and there shall be provision made for their replacement, as in case of vacancy by the resignation. . . .

C. The Downfall of the King

IN JUNE, 1791, King Louis XVI and his family attempted to flee France secretly and join an Austrian army that was gathered on the northeastern frontier. The King left a declaration explaining his actions to be read after he had left Paris.

1. THE KING'S DECLARATION, JUNE 20, 1791

SOURCE. F. M. Anderson, ed., *The Constitutions and Other Select Documents Illustrative of the History of France,* Minneapolis: H. W. Wilson Co., 1904, pp. 45–50. Reprinted by permission of Dr. Gaylord W. Anderson.

As long as the King was able to hope to see order and well-being rise again through the means employed by the National Assembly and by his residence near that Assembly, no sacrifice was too expensive; he would not have even drawn any inference from the lack of liberty, of which he has been deprived since the month of October, 1789; but today when the result of all the operations is to see the monarchy destroyed, property violated, the security of persons compromised, in all parts of the empire a complete anarchy, without any appearance of authority sufficient to arrest it, the King, after having protested against all the acts emanating from him during his captivity, believes that he ought to put before the eyes of the French a representation of his conduct.

In the month of July, 1789, the King, secure in his conscience, did not fear to come among the Parisians. In the month of October of the same year, warned by the movements of the factious, he feared that they would make a pretence of his departure to stir up civil war. Everybody is aware of the impunity with which crimes were then committed. The King, yielding to the view expressed by the army of the Parisians, came to establish himself at the chateau of the Tuileries. Nothing was ready to receive him; and the King, very far from finding the accommodations to which he was accustomed in his other residences, did not even meet with the comforts which persons in easy circumstances procure for themselves.

Despite all the constraints, he believed that he ought from the morrow of his arrival to reassure the provinces about his sojourn at Paris. A more painful sacrifice was reserved for him: he was required to send away his body guards, whose fidelity he had proven. Two had been massacred, several had been wounded in carrying out the order not to fire which they had received. Every art of the factious was employed to cause to be considered in a bad light a faithful wife who was about to fill up the measure of her good conduct: it is likewise evident that all the machinations were directed against the King himself. It was to the soldiers of the French guards and to the Parisian National Guard that the protection of the King was confided, under the orders of the municipality of Paris, from which the commanding general took his place.

The King is thus seen a prisoner in his own dominions, for how could one be called otherwise who saw himself forcibly surrounded by persons whom he suspects; it is not in order to inculpate the Parisian National Guard that I recall these details, but in order to relate the exact truth; on the contrary, I render justice to its attachment when it has not been led astray by the factious. The King ordered the convocation of the States-General, he granted to the Third Estate a double representation; the union of the orders, the sacrifices of the twenty-third of June, all that was his work; but his services have been misunderstood and misconstrued. The moment when the States-General gave itself the name of National Assembly, recalls the maneuvers of the factious in several provinces; it recalls the movements which have been effected in order to nullify the provision of the *cahiers,* which provided that the drawing up of the laws should be done in concert with the King. The Assembly has put the King outside of the constitution, in refusing to him the right to sanction the constitutional acts, in arranging in that class those which it was pleased to arrange there, and in limiting to the third legislature in any case refusal of sanction. They gave him 25,000,000 which are entirely consumed by the expense that the pomp necessary for his household requires. They left to him the use of certain domains with embarrassing restrictions, thus depriving him of the patrimony of his ancestors; they took care not to include in his expenses the services rendered to the King, as if they were not inseparable from those rendered to the State. Let one examine the different points of the administration and he will see that the King is removed from it: he has no part in the making of the laws; he can only pray the Assembly to occupy itself with such and such things. As to the administration of justice, he only causes the decrees of the judges to be forwarded and appoints the commissioners of the King, whose functions are indeed less considerable than those of the former *procureurs-generaux*. The public prosecution has been devolved upon new officers. There remained one last prerogative, the most attractive of all, that of pardon and of commuting penalties; you have taken it away from the King, it is now the jurors who have it, applying according to their will the sense of the law. This diminishes the royal majesty; the people were accustomed to have recourse there as to a common centre of bounty and beneficence. The internal administration within the departments is embarrassed by wheels which clog the movement of the machine; the supervision of the ministers is reduced to nothing.

The societies of the Friends of the Constitution are indeed stronger and render null all other actions. The King has been declared supreme head of the army, nevertheless all the business has been done by the committees of the National Assembly without my participation; they have granted to the King the appointment to certain places, yet the choice which he has made has experienced opposition; he has been obliged to revise the employment of the general officers of the army, because the choices were displeasing to the clubs; it is to these alone that the greater part of the revolts of the regiments ought to be attributed; when the army no longer respects the officers, it is the terror and scourge of the State; the King has always thought that the officers ought to be punished as the soldiers are, and that the doors ought to be open to these latter to obtain promotions, according to their merit. As to foreign affairs, they have conceded to the King the appointment of the ambassadors and the conduct of the negotiations; they have taken away from him the right to make war; nevertheless they could not suspect that he would declare it without announcing its purpose. The right to make peace is of a wholly different kind. The King does not wish to act except at one with the nation, but what power will wish to enter into negotiations, when the right of revision is granted to the National Assembly? Independently of the required secrecy, impossible to preserve in an assembly necessarily deliberating in public, they still like to treat only with a person who can, without any interference, conclude the contract. As to the finances, the King had recognized, prior to the States-General, the right of the nation to grant the subsidies, and in this respect he had granted on the 23rd of June all that had been demanded. On the 1st of February, the King prayed the Assembly to occupy itself with the finances; it did so only slowly; it has not yet the exact list of receipts and expenditures; it has allowed itself to proceed upon hypothetical calculations; the ordinary taxation is in arrears and the resource of twelve hundred millions of *assignats* is almost consumed; it has left to the King, in this matter, only barren appointments; he knows the difficulty of this administration; and if it were possible that this machine could go on without his direct supervision, his majesty would only regret that he could not diminish the imposts which he desired and would have effected but for the American war.

The King has been declared the supreme head of the administration of the kingdom, yet he can change nothing without the decision of the Assembly. The leaders of the dominant party have exhibited such a defiance to the agents of the King, and the penalties inflicted upon the disobedient have given birth to so much uneasiness, that these agents have remained without authority. The form of government is especially vicious for two reasons: the Assembly exceeds the limit of its powers, in occupying itself with the administration of justice and internal administration; it exercises through its investigating committees the most barbarous of all despotisms. There have been established associations known under the name of the Friends of the Constitution, which are corporations infinitely more dangerous than the former ones; they deliberate upon all the concerns of the government, exercise a power so preponderant that all the bodies, not even excepting the National Assembly itself, do nothing except by their order. The King does not think that it would be possible to preserve such a government; the more they see approaching the end of the labors of the Assembly, the more wise men lose of their confidence in it. The new regulations, instead of applying balm to the wounds, on the contrary aggravate the discontent; the thousand newspapers and calumniating pamphlets, which are only the echoes of the clubs, perpetuate the disorder and the Assembly has never dared to remedy it; they tend only to a government metaphysical and impossible in the execution.

Frenchmen, is it this that you designed in sending your representatives? Do you desire that the despotism of the clubs should replace the monarchy under which the kingdom has prospered during fourteen hundred years? The love of Frenchmen for their King is reckoned among their virtues. I have had too many touching tokens of it to be able to forget it: the King would not offer the accompanying picture except to trace for his faithful subjects the spirit of the factious. . . . A proposal was even made to carry him off and to put the Queen in a convent, and this proposal was at the moment applauded.

On the night of the 4th to the 5th [of October], when it was proposed to the Assembly to go to hold its sitting with the King, it replied that to transfer itself there was beneath its dignity; from that moment the scenes of horror were renewed. On the arrival of the King at Paris, an innocent person was massacred almost under his eyes in the very garden of the Tuileries; all those who have spoken against religion and the throne have received triumphal honors. At the federation of the 14th of July, the National Assembly declared that the King was its head; that was to assert that it could, in consequence, appoint another; his family was put in a place apart from himself; nevertheless it was then that he passed the most pleasant moments of his sojourn at Paris.

Afterwards when on account of religion, *Mesdames* [the King's aunts] wished to repair to Rome, this was opposed, despite the Declaration of Rights; they advanced to Bellevue and afterwards to Arnay-le-Duc where the command of the Assembly was required in order to permit them to proceed, those of the King having been treated with contempt. On the occasion of the riot which the factious incited at Vincennes, the persons who united under the King out of love for him were maltreated, and audacity was pushed even to the breaking before the King of the arms of those who made themselves his guardians. Upon recovering from his illness he was disposed to go to St. Cloud; he was stopped from paying the respect which one owes to the religion of his fathers; the club of the Cordeliers even denounced him as a breaker of the law; in vain M. de la Fayette did what he could to protect his departure; the faithful servants who surrounded him were torn away by violence and he was returned to his prison. Afterwards he was obliged to order the sending away of his clergy, to approve the letter of the ministry to the foreign powers, and to go to the mass of the new *cure* of Saint-Germain l'Auxerrois. In consequence of all these considerations and the impossibility of preventing the evil, in which the King is, it is natural that he should have sought to place himself in safety.

Frenchmen, and you who may be called inhabitants of the good city of Paris, distrust the suggestion of the factious, return to your King, he will always be your friend, when your holy religion shall be respected, when the government shall be laid upon a firm footing, and liberty established upon an enduring foundation.

Signed,   Louis.

Paris, June 20, 1791.

CAPTURED AT VARENNES, the royal family was returned to Paris, its prestige decisively compromised. The abortive flight doomed the National Assembly's attempt to establish a constitutional monarchy. Nevertheless, the Assembly's Constitution was completed and promulgated later in the year (it took effect in September, 1791), and elections were held for delegates to the new assembly. This newly elected body, known as the National Convention (1792–1795) was radical and anti-royalist in its composition. It repudiated the Constitution of 1791, declared France a republic, sent the King and Queen to the guillotine, and justified the execution in a dramatic proclamation of January 23, 1793.

2. PROCLAMATION AT THE GUILLOTINING OF LOUIS XVI, 1793

SOURCE. J. H. Stewart, ed., A Documentary History of the French Revolution, New York: Macmillan, 1951, pp. 392–396. Copyright 1951 by The Macmillan Company. Reprinted by permission of The Macmillan Company.

Citizens, the tyrant is no more. For a long time the cries of the victims, whom war and domestic dissensions have spread over France and Europe, loudly protested his existence. He has paid his penalty, and only acclamations for the Republic and for liberty have been heard from the people.

We have had to combat inveterate prejudices, and the superstition of centuries concerning monarchy. Involuntary uncertainties and inevitable disturbances always accompany great changes and revolutions as profound as ours. This political crisis has suddenly surrounded us with contradictions and tumults.

. . . but the cause has ceased, and the motives have disappeared; respect for liberty of opinion must cause these tumultuous scenes to be forgotten; only the good which they have produced through the death of the tyrant and of tyranny now remains, and this judgment belongs in its entirety to each of us, just as it belongs to the entire nation. The National Convention and the French people are now to have only one mind, only one sentiment, that of liberty and civic fraternity.

Now, above all, we need peace in the interior of the Republic, and the most active surveillance of the domestic enemies of liberty. Never did circumstances more urgently require of all citizens the sacrifice of their passions and their personal opinions concerning the act of national justice which has just been effected. Today the French people can have no other passion than that for liberty.

Let us, through our union, avert the shame that domestic discord would bring upon our newborn republic. Let us, through our patriotism, avert those horrible shocks, those anarchical and disorderly movements which would soon overwhelm France with disturbances and grief, if our outside enemies, who are fomenting them, could profit therefrom.

There is no longer time to dispute; we must act. Prompt and effective measures are necessary. The despots of Europe can acquire strength only from our dissensions; they have learned in the Argonne and at Jemappes that one soldier of liberty is worth a hundred slaves.

Finally, may this cloud of royalism, which too long has hung over our heads, disappear; today it would be more fatal to the utilization of our great national resources than even the scourge of a universal war. May peace and obedience to laws reign in our cities and in our rural districts; this firm and calm attitude on the part of free men will make the tyrants turn pale, will increase the nation's forces a hundredfold, and will revive our confidence in the perilous duties which you have entrusted to us. May the agitators of the people see public order more strictly maintained, and laws more cherished when they are more attacked. At this time the City of Paris offers the other parts of the Republic a fine example; it is calm. Nevertheless, crime has not been entirely paralyzed in that immense city. An attack has just been made on the national sovereignty. One of your representatives *has been assassinated for voting the tyrant's death,* and his colleagues are still threatened by the vile henchmen of despotism. The lunatics! In their impious oaths they mistake the calm of the people for the slumber of liberty!

Citizens, it is not one man who has been struck, it is you; it is not *Michel Lepelletier* who has been shamefully assassinated, it is you too; it is not the life of a deputy that has been attacked, it is the life of the nation, it is public liberty, it is the sovereignty of the people.

French people, sensitive and generous despite the calumnies of your enemies, it is in contemplation of grief and indignation that your representatives transmit to you the mournful accents which have just resounded in the temple of liberty. "I am satisfied," said he, expiring, "to have given my life for my country. I hope that it will serve to consolidate liberty and equality, and to cause their enemies to be discovered." . . .

The French will always remember that the defender of liberty died under the murderous sword of a royalist, on the eve of the day when the tyrant was to expiate his forfeit under the blade of the law, and monarchy will be the more firmly abolished. Free men will repeat to their last descendants that, at the time when slaves and superstitious people were expressing regrets for a tyrant, secretly they were rejoicing at the assassination of a representative of the people; and aristocracy will be the more abhorred.

Such are the sentiments which actuate your representatives; they will triumph over all obstacles and all crimes as they have triumphed over so many prejudices. They are concerned with the security of the Republic; they know the causes of the destitution of the armies, and the prompt means of remedying it. The stability of the public wealth is a constant object of their labors. Fidelity to agreements rests on French loyalty; they will strengthen this basis of national credit; since 21 September they have calmly appraised the extent and the importance of the duties which you have assigned to them, and they will never betray them. Public liberty will be maintained at the peril of their lives, and cowardly conspirators will learn to know the courage of the delegates of the people. We have already taken measures for the prompt punishment of the crime of *lèse-nation*; the inexorable law will soon strike the parricide and furnish a new example to the slaves of kings.

We are threatened with a general war; attempts are made to disseminate terror throughout the Republic. Citizens, you have already said: "To bring back monarchical servitude to French territory the entire nation would have to be destroyed; it is necessary to surrender all claims to its conquest or expect to reign over ruins and deserts."

We have no allies in the courts of Europe; but it is up to free nations to save themselves. A war waged slowly and parsimoniously would be uncertain and ruinous. Liberty wages only short and terrible wars, and liberty counts only victories. Stand before an astonished Europe. To sustain your armies and your fleets you have a security, still tremendous, in the national territory; your enemies have only loans and precarious riches. The resources of a great and free nation are inexhaustible; the means of absolute governments are soon exhausted. Let the entire nation arise again, and these colossi used by despotism will soon collapse.

It is all of you, citizens, who have contracted the obligation, for yourselves and for your posterity, to maintain and defend the rights of man. It is for you, for your sacred liberty that your representatives have sacrificed peace, and are braving death every day. Has not the passion of Frenchmen for independence and for laws rendered all our successes easy up to now? Has it not suddenly peopled the land with those national phalanxes, those patriotic legions, which have brought triumphs everywhere from the Alps to the banks of the Rhine, and which victory awaits even in the Pyrenees and on the seas?

Already, at the rumor of hostilities contemplated obscurely by the Spanish and English governments, a generous emulation is manifested everywhere; ports and maritime cities are about to solicit the honor of deserving well of their *Patrie* by offering it the use of their vessels; and all their sailors will be eager to defend the flag of liberty. The greatest examples come from the shores of the Mediterranean and the Ocean; French commerce, which perceives the advantage of an energetic war, awaits you with riches which it has accumulated in prosperous times; and its vessels, recently occupied in the peaceful enterprises of industry, are about to be armed for the terrible operations of war.

Who, then, is the citizen who would not wish to co-operate with us in the defence of the Republic? Here is the cause of all Frenchmen, the cause of mankind.

Attending the funeral of Michel Lepelletier, we all swore on the tomb of that martyr to republican opinion to save the *Patrie*; and the *Patrie* shall be saved. . . . we have just solemnly promised the Republic to give it, within a few days, a constitution founded upon the imprescriptible rights of man, a constitution as free as the people, as equal as justice, as wise as reason, and one which will include all the means of remedying its imperfections through the medium of experience.

No, it is no longer possible to set limits to the prosperity and the great destiny of France, now that anarchy will be suppressed everywhere, now that the enemies of order will be combated everywhere, now that respect for the laws will be maintained by the constituted authorities, now that the patriotism of the armies will be equalled by that of the squadrons, now that the representatives of the people will no longer see in the agreement of their wills anything but fidelity to their mandates.

No, the Republic will never lack defenders; if in Rome a friend of Caesar succeeded in arousing the people by waving before them the bloody robes of a tyrant, what may the National Convention not expect for the defence of the *Patrie* by uncovering before the French people the mortal and bleeding wound of one of its representatives?

Citizens . . . remember the heroic firmness of Michel Lepelletier in his last moment; bear in mind that there is not one of your representatives who is not determined to follow his example.

Signed,   VERGNIAUD, *President.*

BANCAL, GORSAS, SALLE, LESAGE, DUFRICHE-VALAZÉ, *Secretaries.*

D. The Terror and Its Aftermath

THE LEFTWARD DRIFT of the National Convention culminated in the rise of Robespierre and the "Committee of Public Safety" in the summer of 1793 which brought on the Reign of Terror. Threatened by hostile armies on France's frontiers, and fearful of internal conservatism and reaction, the Revolutionary leaders adopted a policy of massive executions in which at least 15,000 people lost their lives. The Terror found support in many quarters, as a contemporary article from a Paris newspaper makes clear.

1. A PARISIAN NEWSPAPER SUPPORTS THE TERROR

SOURCE. E. L. Higgins, ed., *The French Revolution as Told by Contemporaries*, Boston: Houghton Mifflin Co., 1939, pp. 306–307. Reprinted by permission of Houghton Mifflin Co.

Yes, terror is the order of the day, and ought to be for the selfish, for the federalists, for the heartless rich, for dishonest opportunists, for shameless intriguers, for unpatriotic cowards, for all who do not feel the dignity of being free men and pure republicans. Rivers of blood have been shed for the gold of Peru and the diamonds of Golconda. Well! Does not liberty, that inestimable blessing which one would surely not tarnish by comparing it with the vile metals of the Indies, have the same right to sacrifice lives, fortunes, and even, for a time, individual liberties? In the thick of battle is there any foolish wailing over the soldiers fallen from the ranks? They are promptly replaced by others, and with the perfidious aggressor repulsed, one is free to weep over the unfortunate victims mowed down on the field of battle. Is not the French Revolution just such a deadly combat, a war to the death between those who want to be free and those content to be slaves? This is the situation, and the French people have gone too far to retreat with honor and safety. There is no middle ground; France must be entirely free or perish in the attempt, and any means are justifiable in fighting for so fine a cause. But our resources are being exhausted, say some. Well, when the Revolution is finished, they will be replenished by peace. A free people, as long as they have weapons and hands, can fight their enemies and plow their fields. . . .

THE REPRESSIVE political atmosphere of the period is illustrated by the Law of Suspects (September 17, 1793).

2. THE LAW OF SUSPECTS, 1793

SOURCE. E. L. Higgins, ed., *The French Revolution as Told by Contemporaries*, Boston: Houghton Mifflin Co., 1939, pp. 477–479. Reprinted by permission of Houghton Mifflin Co.

1. Immediately after the publication of the present decree, all suspected persons within the territory of the Republic and still at liberty shall be placed in custody.

2. The following are deemed suspected persons: 1st, those who, by their conduct, associations, talk, or writings have shown themselves par-

tisans of tyranny or federalism and enemies of liberty; 2nd, those who are unable to justify, in the manner prescribed by the decree of 21 March last, their means of existence and the performance of their civic, duties; 3rd, those to whom certificates of patriotism have been refused; 4th, public functionaries suspended or dismissed from their positions by the National Convention or by its commissioners, and not reinstated, especially those who have been or are to be dismissed by virtue of the decree of 14 August last; 5th, those former nobles, husbands, wives, fathers, mothers, sons or daughters, brothers or sisters, and agents of the *émigrés*, who have not steadily manfested their devotion to the Revolution; 6th, those who have emigrated during the interval between 1 July, 1789, and the publication of the decree of 30 March—8 April, 1792, even though they may have returned to France within the period established by said decree or prior thereto.

3. The Watch Committees established according to the decree of 21 March last, or those substituted therefor, either by orders of the representatives of the people dispatched to the armies and the departments, or by virtue of particular decrees of the National Convention, are charged with drafting, each in its own *arrondissement*, a list of suspected persons, with issuing warrants of arrest against them, and with having seals placed on their papers. Commanders of the public force to whom such warrants are remitted shall be required to put them into effect immediately, under penalty of dismissal.

4. The members of the committee may order the arrest of any individual only if seven are present, and only by absolute majority of votes.

5. Individuals arrested as suspects shall be taken first to the jails of the place of their detention; in default of jails, they shall be kept under surveillance in their respective dwellings.

6. Within the following week, they shall be transferred to national buildings, which the departmental administrations shall be required to designate and to have prepared for such purpose immediately after the receipt of the present decree.

7. The prisoners may have their absolutely essential belongings brought into said buildings; they shall remain there under guard until the peace.

8. The expenses of custody shall be charged to the prisoners, and shall be divided among them equally: such custody shall be confided preferably to fathers of families and to the relatives of citizens who are at or may go to the frontiers. The salary therefor is established, for each man of the guard, at the value of one and one-half days of labor.

9. The Watch Committees shall dispatch to the Committee of General Security of the National Convention, without delay, the list of persons

whom they have arrested, with the reasons for their arrest and with the papers they have seized in such connection.

10. If there is occasion, the civil and criminal courts may have detained, in custody, and dispatched to the jails above stated, those who are accused of offences with regard to which it has been declared that there was no occasion for indictment or who have been acquitted of charges brought against them.

THE POLITICAL AND RELIGIOUS philosophy of Robespierre and his colleagues is expressed in Robespierre's proposed Declaration of Rights (April 24, 1793) (3), and in the deistic Decree for Establishing the Worship of a Supreme Being (May 7, 1794) (4). Notice in the latter document the frequent allusions to the new Revolutionary calendar.

3. ROBESPIERRE'S PROPOSED DECLARATION OF RIGHTS, 1793

SOURCE. F. M. Anderson, ed., *The Constitutions and Other Select Documents Illustrative of the History of France*, Minneapolis: H. W. Wilson Co., 1904, pp. 160–164. Reprinted by permission of Dr. Gaylord W. Anderson.

The representatives of the French people, met in National Convention, recognizing that human laws which do not flow from the eternal laws of justice and reason are only the outrages of ignorance and despotism upon humanity; convinced that neglect and contempt of the natural rights of man are the sole causes of the crimes and misfortunes of the world; have resolved to set forth in a solemn declaration these sacred and inalienable rights, in order that all citizens, being enabled to compare constantly the acts of the government with the purpose of every social institution, may never permit themselves to be oppressed and disgraced by tyranny; and in order that the people may always have before their eyes the foundations of their liberty and their welfare; the magistrate, the rule of his duties; the legislator, the purpose of his mission.

In consequence, the National Convention proclaims in the face of the world and under the eyes of the Immortal Legislator the following declaration of the rights of man and citizen.

1. The purpose of every political association is the maintenance of the natural and imprescriptible rights of man and the development of all his faculties.

2. The principal rights of man are those of providing for the preservation of his existence and his liberty.

3. These rights belong equally to all men, whatever may be the difference of their physical and mental powers.

4. Equality of rights is established by nature: society, far from impairing it, exists only to guarantee it against the abuse of power which renders it illusory.

5. Liberty is the power which belongs to man to exercise at his will all his faculties; it has justice for rule, the rights of others for limits, nature for principle, and the law for safeguard.

6. The right to assemble peaceably, the right to express one's opinions, either by means of the press or in any other manner, are such necessary consequences of the principle of the liberty of man, that the necessity to enunciate them supposes either the presence or the fresh recollection of despotism.

7. The law can forbid only that which is injurious to society; it can order only that which is useful.

8. Every law which violates the imprescriptible rights of man is essentially unjust and tyrannical; it is not a law.

9. Property is the right which each citizen has, to enjoy and dispose of the portion of goods which the law guarantees to him.

10. The right of property is restricted, as are all the others, by the obligation to respect the possessions of others.

11. It cannot prejudice the security, nor the liberty, nor the existence, nor the property of our fellow creatures.

12. All traffic which violates this principle is essentially illicit and immoral.

13. Society is under obligation to provide for the support of all its members either by procuring work for them or by assuring the means of existence to those who are not in condition to work.

14. The relief indispensable for those who lack the necessities of life is a debt of those who possess a superfluity; it belongs to the law to determine the manner in which this debt must be discharged.

15. The citizens whose incomes do not exceed what is necessary for their subsistence are exempted from contributing to the public expenses; the others shall support them progressively, according to the extent of their fortunes.

16. Society ought to favor with all its power the progress of public reason and to put instruction at the door of all the citizens.

17. Law is the free and solemn expression of the will of the people.

18. The people are the sovereign, the government is their creation, the public functionaries are their agents; the people can, when they please, change their government and recall their mandatories.

19. No portion of the people can exercise the power of the entire people; but the opinion which it expresses shall be respected as the opinion of a portion of the people who ought to participate in the formation of the general will. Each section of the assembled sovereign ought to enjoy the right to express its will with entire liberty; it is essentially independent of all the constituted authorities and is capable of regulating its police and its deliberations.

20. The law ought to be equal for all.

21. All citizens are admissible to all public offices, without any other distinctions than those of their virtues and talents and without any other title than the confidence of the people.

22. All citizens have an equal right to participate in the selection of the mandatories of the people and in the formation of the law.

23. In order that these rights may not be illusory and the equality chimerical, society ought to give salaries to the public functionaries and to provide so that all the citizens who live by their labor can be present in the public assemblies to which the law calls them, without compromising their existence or that of their families.

24. Every citizen ought to obey religiously the magistrates and the agents of the government, when they are the organs or the executors of the law.

25. But every act against the liberty, security, or property of a man, committed by anyone whomsoever, even in the name of the law, outside of the cases determined by it and the forms which it prescribes, is arbitrary and void; respect for the law even forbids submission to it; and if an attempt is made to execute it by violence, it is permissible to repel it by force.

26. The right to present petitions to the depositories of the public authority belongs to every person. Those to whom they are addressed ought to pass upon the points which are the object thereof; but they can never interdict, nor restrain, nor condemn their use.

27. Resistance to oppression is a consequence of the other rights of man and citizen.

28. There is oppression against the social body when one of its members is oppressed. There is oppression against each member of the social body when the social body shall be oppressed.

29. When the government violates the rights of the people, insurrection is for the people and for each portion of the people the most sacred of rights and the most indispensable of duties.

30. When the social guarantee is lacking to a citizen he re-enters into the natural right to defend all his rights himself.

31. In either case, to tie down to legal forms resistance to oppression is the last refinement of tyranny. In every free State the law ought espe-

cially to defend public and personal liberty against the abuse of the authority of those who govern: every institution which is not based upon the assumption that the people are good and the magistrate is corruptible is vicious.

32. The public offices cannot be considered as distinctions, nor as rewards, but only as duties.

33. The offenses of the mandatories of the people ought to be severely and quickly punished. No one has the right to claim for himself more inviolability than other citizens. The people have the right to know all the transactions of their mandatories: these ought to render to them a faithful account of their own administration and to submit to their judgment with respect.

34. Men of all countries are brothers and the different peoples ought to aid one another, according to their power, as if citizens of the same State.

35. The one who oppresses a single nation declares himself the enemy of all.

36. Those who make war on a people in order to arrest the progress of liberty and to destroy the rights of man ought to be pursued by all, not as ordinary enemies, but as assassins and rebellious brigands.

37. Kings, aristocrats and tyrants, whoever they may be, are slaves in rebellion against the sovereign of the earth, which is mankind, and against the legislator of the universe, which is nature.

4. DECREE FOR ESTABLISHING THE WORSHIP OF A SUPREME BEING, 1794

SOURCE. F. M. Anderson, ed., *The Constitutions and Other Select Documents Illustrative of the History of France*, Minneapolis: H. W. Wilson Co., 1904, pp. 137–138. Reprinted by permission of Dr. Gaylord W. Anderson.

1. The French people recognize the existence of the Supreme Being and the immortality of the soul.

2. They recognize that the worship worthy of the Supreme Being is the practice of the duties of man.

3. They place in the first rank of these duties, to detest bad faith and tyranny, to punish tyrants and traitors, to relieve the unfortunate, to respect the weak, to defend the oppressed, to do to others all the good that is possible and not to be unjust to anyone.

4. Festivals shall be instituted to remind man of the thought of the Divinity and of the dignity of his being.

5. They shall take their names from the glorious events of our Revolution, from the virtues most cherished and most useful to man, and from the great gifts of nature.

6. The French Republic shall celebrate every year the festival of July 14, 1789, August 10, 1792, January 21, 1793, and May 31, 1793.

7. It shall celebrate on the days of *decadi* the list of festivals that follows: to the Supreme Being and to Nature; to the Human Race; to the French People; to the Benefactors of Humanity; to the Martyrs of Liberty; to Liberty and Equality; to the Republic; to the Liberty of the World; to the Love of the Fatherland; to the Hatred of Tyrants and of Traitors; to Truth; to Justice; to Modesty; to Glory and Immortality; to Friendship; to Frugality; to Courage; to Good Faith; to Heroism; to Disinterestedness; to Stoicism; to Love; to Conjugal Love; to Paternal Love; to Maternal Tenderness; to Filial Affection; to Childhood; to Youth; to Manhood; to Old Age; to Misfortune; to Agriculture; to Industry; to our Forefathers; to Posterity; to Happiness.

8. The committees of public safety and of public instruction are charged to present a plan of organization for these festivals.

9. The National Convention summons all the talents worthy to serve the cause of humanity to the honor of contributing to their establishment by hymns and patriotic songs, and by all the means which can enhance their beauty and utility.

10. The Committee of Public Safety shall confer distinction upon those works which seem the best adapted to carry out these purposes and shall reward their authors.

11. Liberty of worship is maintained, in conformity with the decree of 18 Frimaire.

12. Every gathering that is aristocratic and contrary to public order shall be suppressed.

13. In case of disturbances of which any worship whatsoever may be the occasion or motive, those who may excite them by fanatical preaching or by counter-revolutionary insinuations, those who may provoke them by unjust and gratuitous violence, shall likewise be punished with all the severity of the law.

14. A special report upon the provisions of detail relative to the present decree shall be made.

15. A festival in honor of the Supreme Being shall be celebrated upon 20 Prairial next.

David is charged to present the plan thereof to the National Convention.

ROBESPIERRE'S FALL on July 27, 1794, which ended the Reign of Terror, was described in detail by a contemporary observer.

5. ROBESPIERRE'S FALL, 1794

SOURCE. E. L. Higgins, ed., *The French Revolution as Told by Contemporaries*, Boston: Houghton Mifflin Co., 1939, pp. 357–359. Reprinted by permission of Houghton Mifflin Co.

Robespierre, whose rage may easily be imagined, rushes to the rostrum, thinking to overawe them with the imperious tone that has always been successful. But the charm has been broken; all have been convinced, and from every side they cry at him, "Down with the tyrant!" Overwhelmed by this terrible word, he drops his head. . . .

The orator, after comparing Robespierre to Catiline, and his followers to Verres, demands that there be no adjournment until the glaive of the law has safeguarded the Revolution by arresting Hanriot. These two propositions are decreed, and acclaimed by the Assembly and the people amidst cries of "Long live the Republic!" . . .

Robespierre once more presents himself at the rostrum, but is met by a unanimous cry of indignation. He persists, acting in a furious fashion. "Down with the tyrant" re-echoes on all sides. He turns around for a moment towards Saint-Just, whose attitude shows his despair at being unmasked, and is little calculated to encourage him; he obstinately persists in his attempt to speak, but all members cry out at him anew, "Down with the tyrant!" . . .

Robespierre, tortured in conscience, becomes greatly agitated and cries out that they are bringing his death. "You deserve a thousand deaths," says a member. The younger Robespierre now joins his brother and asks to share his fate. With eyes that gleam with frenzy, and in despair of dominating by affected calm, they reveal the hidden depths of their souls. They abuse the National Convention; they insult; they menace. A general indignation arises in reply to the cries of these madmen; the turmoil steadily increases; the president covers himself. The elder Robespierre, profiting by the moment of silence which always follows this act, denounces the president and the members of the Assembly in the most abusive terms. There is a violent hubbub of murmurs and the National Convention rises as one man. Members demand the arrest of this man who dares to attack the majesty of the people in the person of its representatives. Another cries out that Robespierre has incontestably been a tyrant, and for that alone should have his arrest decreed. . . .

Robespierre threatens and struggles in vain; he tries various points of the chamber; in vain with furious looks he ascends and descends the steps of the rostrum where he has reigned so long as despot. A violent hatred of tyranny is exhaled from every soul, enveloping him in an atmosphere where he can no longer breathe. He falls gasping upon a seat, and there the indignation of republicans holds him as if enchained. His arrest, and that of his brother, are demanded on all sides. This is finally decreed amid numerous and violent bursts of applause.

"The National Convention decrees the immediate arrest of Maximilien Robespierre, one of its members."

THE NATIONAL CONVENTION soon gave way to a more conservative regime dominated by five executive Directors (1795–1799) and the leftward swing of the Revolution was reversed. The relative conservatism of the Directory government emerges clearly in the Manifesto of the Directors, November 5, 1795.

6. THE MANIFESTO OF THE DIRECTORS, 1795

SOURCE. Leo Gershoy, *Ten Years That Shook the World* (Anvil #22), Princeton: D. Van Nostrand Co., 1947, pp. 176–177. Copyright 1958, D. Van Nostrand Co., Inc., Princeton, N. J.

Frenchmen, the Executive Directory has just been installed.

Resolved to maintain liberty or to perish, we are determined to consolidate the Republic and to govern vigorously and speedily under the provisions of the Constitution.

Republicans, place your trust in it; its destiny will never be separated from yours; inflexible justice and the strictest observance of laws will guide it. To wage active war on royalism, to revive patriotism, to repress all factions vigorously, to destroy all factional spirit, and vanquish all desire for vengeance, to establish concord, to restore peace, to regenerate morals, to reopen the sources of production, to revive commerce and industry, to crush speculation, to give new life to the arts and sciences, to re-establish plenty and the public credit, to restore social order for the chaos which is inseparable from revolutions, in a word, to give the French Republic the happiness and glory which it awaits—such is the task of your legislators and of the Executive Directory. . . .

Wise laws, promptly and vigorously enforced, will soon make us forget our protracted sufferings.

But so many evils cannot be atoned nor so much good accomplished in a day. The French people are just and upright; they will see that . . . we need time, calm, patience, and confidence equal to the efforts we have to make. Such confidence will not be betrayed if the people no longer allow themselves to give heed to the perfidious suggestions of royalists who are renewing their plots, of fanatics who tirelessly inflame the minds of people, and of leeches who do not fail to take advantage of our sad plight.

It will not be betrayed if the people do not blame the new authorities for the disorders caused by six years of revolution, which can be expiated only with time; it will not be betrayed if the people recall that, for more than three years, whenever the enemies of the Republic . . . provoked disturbances, . . . such disturbances served only to further discredit us and to impede production and plenty, which only order and public tranquillity can produce.

Frenchmen, you will not hamper a newborn government . . . ; but you will wisely support the active efforts and the calm progress of the Executive Directory in the prompt establishment of public happiness; and without fail will soon bring about national peace and prosperity.

E. The Era of Napoleon

ON NOVEMBER 9, 1799, Napoleon Bonaparte, one of the most successful of the Revolutionary generals, engineered a coup d'état which had the effect of overthrowing the Directory and establishing in its place a three-man executive Consulate with Napoleon as First Consul. In the first proclamation of the new government (December 15, 1799), Napoleon announced the consummation and end of the Revolution. In 1804, he assumed direct power as Emperor of the French.

1. THE FIRST PROCLAMATION OF THE CONSULS, 1799

SOURCE. J. H. Stewart, ed., A Documentary History of the French Revolution, New York: Macmillan, 1951, p. 780. Copyright 1951 by The Macmillan Company. Reprinted by permission of The Macmillan Company.

Frenchmen!

A Constitution is presented to you.

It terminates the uncertainties which the provisional government introduced into external relations, into the internal and military situation of the Republic.

It places in the institutions which it establishes first magistrates whose devotion has appeared necessary for its success.

The Constitution is founded on the true principles of representative government, on the sacred rights of property, equality, and liberty.

The powers which it institutes will be strong and stable, as they must be in order to guarantee the rights of citizens and the interests of the State.

Citizens, the Revolution is established upon the principles which began it: It is ended.

AFTER NAPOLEON'S FALL from power, during his exile on the Island of St. Helena, he expressed himself freely to the Count de Las Cases on the subject of the Revolution (2) and on his own dreams of transforming Europe (3). It should not be surprising that he interpreted his actions in the best possible light.

2. THE NAPOLEONIC INTERPRETATION
OF THE REVOLUTION, 1816

SOURCE. David L. Dowd, *Napoleon: Was He the Heir of the Revolution?*, New York: Holt, Rinehart and Winston, 1957, p. 14. Copyright 1957 by David L. Dowd. Used by permission of Holt, Rinehart and Winston, Inc. All right reserved. From E. A. D. M. J. Count de Las Cases, *Memorial de Sainte Hélène, Journal of the Private Life and Conversations of the Emperor Napoleon at St. Helena*, London: 1823, II, pp. 270–271.

The Emperor also established special presentations to his person and admission to his Court; but instead of making noble birth the only means of securing these honors, the title for obtaining them was founded solely on the combined bases of fortune, influence, and public service.

Napoleon, moreover, created titles, the qualifications for which gave the last blow to the old feudal system. These titles, however, possessed no real value, and were established for an object purely national. Those which were unaccompanied by any prerogatives or privileges might be enjoyed by persons of any rank or profession, and were bestowed as rewards for all kinds of services. The Emperor observed that abroad they had the useful effect of appearing to be an approximation to the old manners of Europe, while at the same time they served as a toy for amusing the vanities of many individuals at home; "for," said he, "how many really clever men are children oftener than once in their lives!"

The Emperor revived decorations of honor, and distributed crosses and ribbons. But instead of confining them to particular and exclusive classes, he extended them to society in general as rewards for every description of talent and public service. By a happy privilege, perhaps peculiar to

Napoleon, it happened that the value of these honors was enhanced in proportion to the number distributed. He estimated that he had conferred about 25,000 decorations of the Legion of Honor; and the desire to obtain the honor, he said, increased until it became a kind of *mania*.

After the battle of Wagram he sent the decoration of the Legion of Honor to the Archduke Charles, and by a refinement in compliment, peculiar to Napoleon, he sent him merely the silver cross, which was worn by the private soldiers.

The Emperor said that it was only by acting strictly and voluntarily in conformity with the maxims that he had become the real national monarch; and an adherence to the same course would have rendered the [Napoleonic] dynasty, the truly constitutional one. Of these facts, said he, the people of the lowest rank frequently evinced an instinctive knowledge. . . .

The Emperor surrounded himself with great crown officers. He established a numerous household of chamberlains, grooms, etc. He selected persons to fill these offices indiscriminately from among those whom the Revolution had elevated, and from the ancient families which it had ruined. The former considered themselves as standing on an estate which they had acquired; the latter on one which they thought they might recover. The Emperor had in view, by this mixture of persons, the extinction of hatreds and the amalgamation of parties.

3. THE NAPOLEONIC DREAM, 1816

SOURCE. David L. Dowd, *Napoleon: Was He the Heir of the Revolution?*, New York: Holt, Rinehart and Winston, 1957, pp. 15–16. Copyright 1957 by David L. Dowd. Used by permission of Holt, Rinehart and Winston, Inc. All rights reserved. From E. A. D. M. J. Count de Las Cases, *Memorial de Sainte Hélène, Journal of the Private Life and Conversations of the Emperor Napoleon at St. Helena*, London: 1823, V, pp. 265–267.

"Peace, concluded at Moscow, would have fulfilled and wound up my hostile expeditions. It would have been, with respect to the grand cause, the term of casualties and the commencement of security. A new horizon, new undertakings, would have unfolded themselves, adapted, in every respect, to the well-being and prosperity of all. The foundation of the European system would have been laid, and my only remaining task would have been its organization.

"Satisfied on these grand points, and everywhere at peace, I should have also had my [peace] congress and my holy alliance. These are plans which were stolen from me. In that assembly of all the sovereigns, we should have discussed our interest in a family way, and settled our accounts with the people, as a clerk does with his master.

"The cause of the age was victorious, the Revolution accomplished; the only point in question was to reconcile it with what it had not destroyed. . . . I became the arch of the old and new alliance, the natural mediator between the ancient and modern order of things. I maintained the principles and possessed the confidence of the one; I had identified myself with the other. I belonged to them both; I should have acted conscientiously in favor of each:

"My glory would have consisted in my equity."

And, after having enumerated what he would have proposed between sovereign and sovereign, and between sovereigns and their people, he continued: "Powerful as we were, all that we might have conceded would have appeared grand. It would have gained us the gratitude of the people. At present, what they may extort will never seem enough to them, and they will be uniformly distrustful and discontented."

He next took a review of what he would have proposed for the prosperity, the interests, the enjoyments and the well-being of the European confederacy. He wished to establish the same principles, the same system everywhere. A European code; a court of European appeal, with full powers to redress all wrong decisions, as ours redresses at home those of our tribunals. Money of the same value but with different coins; the same weights, the same measures, the same laws, etc.

"Europe would soon in that manner," he said, "have really been but the same people, and everyone who traveled would have everywhere found himself in one common country."

He would have required, that all the rivers should be navigable in common; that the seas should be thrown open; that the great standing armies should, in future, be reduced to the single establishment of a guard for the sovereign, etc.

. . . "On my return to France, in the bosom of my country, at once great, powerful, magnificent, at peace and glorious, I would have proclaimed the immutability of boundaries, all future wars, purely *defensive;* all new aggrandizement, *anti-national.* I would have associated my son with the empire; my dictatorship would have terminated, and his constitutional reign commenced. . . . Paris would have been the capital of the world, and the French the envy of nations! . . . These also, my dear Las Cases, were among my dreams!!!"

NAPOLEON'S ARMIES, as they marched across Europe, spread the doctrines of liberalism and fervent devotion to country which the French Revolution had nourished. King William III of Prussia was obviously playing on this new sense of nationalism when on March 17, 1813, he called his people to arms against Napoleonic France.

4. NATIONALISM SPREADS: WILLIAM III OF PRUSSIA CALLS HIS PEOPLE TO ARMS, MARCH 17, 1813

SOURCE. J. H. Robinson, ed., *Readings in European History,* Boston: Ginn and Co., 1906, II, pp. 522–523.

There is no need of explaining to my loyal subjects, or to any German, the reasons for the war which is about to begin. They lie plainly before the eyes of awakened Europe. We succumbed to the superior force of France. The peace which followed deprived me of my people and, far from bringing us blessings, it inflicted upon us deeper wounds than the war itself, sucking out the very marrow of the country. Our principal fortresses remained in the hand of the enemy, and agriculture, as well as the highly developed industries of our towns, was crippled. The freedom of trade was hampered and thereby the sources of commerce and prosperity cut off. The country was left a prey to the ravages of destitution.

I hoped, by the punctilious fulfillment of the engagements I had entered into, to lighten the burdens of my people, and even to convince the French emperor that it would be to his advantage to leave Prussia her independence. But the purest and best of intentions on my part were of no avail against insolence and faithlessness, and it became only too plain that the emperor's treaties would gradually ruin us even more surely than his wars. The moment is come when we can no longer harbor the slightest illusion as to our situation.

Brandenburgers, Prussians, Silesians, Pomeranians, Lithuanians! You know what you have borne for the past seven years; you know the sad fate that awaits you if we do not bring this war to an honorable end. Think of the times gone by,—of the Great Elector, the great Frederick! Remember the blessings for which your forefathers fought under their leadership and which they paid for with their blood,—freedom of conscience, national honor, independence, commerce, industry, learning. Look at the great example of our powerful allies, the Russians; look at the Spaniards, the Portuguese. For such objects as these even weaker peoples have gone forth against mightier enemies and returned in triumph. Witness the heroic Swiss and the people of the Netherlands.

Great sacrifices will be demanded from every class of the people, for our undertaking is a great one, and the number and resources of our enemies far from insignificant. But would you not rather make these sacrifices for the fatherland and for your own rightful king than for a foreign ruler, who, as he has shown by many examples, will use you and your sons and your uttermost farthing for ends which are nothing to you?

Faith in God, perseverance, and the powerful aid of our allies will bring us victory as the reward of our honest efforts. Whatever sacrifices may be required of us as individuals, they will be outweighed by the sacred rights for which we make them, and for which we must fight to a victorious end unless we are willing to cease to be Prussians or Germans. This is the final, the decisive struggle; upon it depends our independence, our prosperity, our existence. There are no other alternatives but an honorable peace or a heroic end. You would willingly face even the latter for honor's sake, for without honor no Prussian or German could live.

However, we may confidently await the outcome. God and our own firm purpose will bring victory to our cause and with it an assured and glorious peace and the return of happier times.

FREDERICK WILLIAM.

Breslau, March 17, 1813.

OPPOSED BY MOST of the powers of Europe, Napoleon was crushed in 1814 and exiled to the Island of Elba. He returned to France in 1815 while delegates of the great powers were assembled at Vienna to work out a peace settlement. His return provoked widespread alarm, and prompted the powers to issue (on March 13) an uncompromising anti-Napoleonic declaration. With Napoleon's subsequent defeat at Waterloo and exile to remote St. Helena, Europe could devote its full attention once again to the problems of the postwar settlement.

5. DECLARATION OF THE POWERS AGAINST NAPOLEON, 1815

SOURCE. F. M. Anderson, ed., *The Constitutions and Other Select Documents Illustrative of the History of France*, Minneapolis: H. W. Wilson Co., 1904, pp. 468–469. Reprinted by permission of Dr. Gaylord W. Anderson.

The Powers who have signed the Treaty of Paris reassembled in Congress at Vienna, having been informed of the escape of Napoleon Bonaparte and of his entrance into France with an armed force, owe to their dignity and the interest of social order a solemn Declaration of the sentiments which that event has inspired in them.

In thus violating the convention which established him in the Island of Elba, Bonaparte destroyed the only legal title for his existence. By reappearing in France with projects of disorder and destruction, he has cut himself off from the protection of the law and has shown in the face of the world that there can be neither peace nor truce with him.

Accordingly, the Powers declare that Napoleon Bonaparte is excluded from civil and social relations, and, as an Enemy and Disturber of the tranquility of the World, that he has incurred public vengeance.

At the same time, being firmly resolved to preserve intact the Treaty of Paris of May 30, 1814, and the arrangements sanctioned by that treaty, as well as those which have been or shall be arranged hereafter in order to complete and consolidate it, they declare that they will employ all their resources and will unite all their efforts in order that the General Peace, the object of the desires of Europe and the constant aim of their labors, may not be again disturbed, and in order to secure themselves from all attempts which may threaten to plunge the World once more into the disorders and misfortunes of revolutions.

And although fully persuaded that all France, rallying around its legitimate sovereign, will strive unceasingly to bring to naught this last attempt of a criminal and impotent madman, all the Sovereigns of Europe, animated by the same feeling and guided by the same principles, declare that if, contrary to all expectation, there shall result from that event any real danger, they will be ready to give to the King of France and the French Nation or to any government which shall be attacked, as soon as shall be required, all the assistance necessary to re-establish the public tranquility, and to make common cause against all who may attempt to compromise it.

The present Declaration, inserted in the protocol of the Congress assembled at Vienna, March 13, 1815, shall be made public.

Part II

ROMANTICISM

A. Literature

THE ROMANTIC REVOLT against Neo-Classicism and Enlightenment rationalism was in many respects profoundly conservative. Some Romantics rebelled against the facile anticlericalism of the eighteenth century and asserted their devotion to the Church. To the Vicomte de Chateaubriand (1768–1848), the mystery and majesty of Christianity were far more appealing than the antiseptic rationalism of its eighteenth-century critics.

1. VICOMTE DE CHATEAUBRIAND, FROM *THE GENIUS OF CHRISTIANITY*

SOURCE. Vicomte de Chateaubriand, *The Genius of Christianity*, C. I. White, tr., Baltimore: J. Murphy and Co., 1862, pp. 51, 53–54.

There is nothing beautiful, pleasing, or grand in life, but that which is more or less mysterious. The most wonderful sentiments are those which produce impressions difficult to be explained. . . .

We perceive at the first glance, that, in regard to mysteries, the Christian religion has a great advantage over the religions of antiquity. The mysteries of the latter bore no relation to man, and afforded, at the utmost, but a subject of reflection to the philosopher or of song to the poet. Our mysteries, on the contrary, speak directly to the heart; they comprehend the secrets of our existence. The question here is not about a futile arrangement of numbers, but concerning the salvation and felicity of the human race. Is it possible for man, whom daily experience so fully convinces of his ignorance and frailty, to reject the mysteries of Jesus Christ? They are the mysteries of the unfortunate!

The Trinity, which is the first mystery presented by the Christian faith, opens an immense field for philosophic study, whether we consider it in the attributes of God, or examine the vestiges of this dogma, which was formerly diffused throughout the East. It is a pitiful mode of reasoning to reject whatever we cannot comprehend.

There is a God. The plants of the valley and the cedars of the mountain bless his name; the insect hums his praise; the elephant salutes him with the rising day; the bird glorifies him among the foliage; the lightning bespeaks his power, and the ocean declares his immensity. Man alone has said, "There is no God."

Has he then in adversity never raised his eyes toward heaven? has he in prosperity never cast them on the earth? Is Nature so far from him that he has not been able to contemplate its wonders; or does he consider them as the mere result of fortuitous causes? But how could chance have compelled crude and stubborn materials to arrange themselves in such exquisite order?

It might be asserted that man is the *idea of God displayed,* and the universe *his imagination made manifest.* They who have admitted the beauty of nature as a proof of a supreme intelligence, ought to have pointed out a truth which greatly enlarges the sphere of wonders. It is this: motion and rest, darkness and light, the seasons, the revolutions of the heavenly bodies, which give variety to the decorations of the world, are successive only in appearance, and permanent in reality. The scene that fades upon our view is painted in brilliant colors for another people; it is not the spectacle that is changed, but the spectator. Thus God has combined in his work absolute duration and progressive duration. The first is placed in time, the second in space; by means of the former, the beauties of the universe are one, infinite, and invariable; by means of the latter, they are multiplied, finite, and perpetually renewed. Without the one, there would be no grandeur in the creation; without the other, it would exhibit nothing but dull uniformity.

Here time appears to us in a new point of view; the smallest of its fractions becomes a complete whole, which comprehends all things, and in which all things transpire, from the death of an insect to the birth of a world; each minute is in itself a little eternity. Combine, then, at the same moment, in imagination, the most beautiful incidents of nature; represent to yourself at once all the hours of the day and all the seasons of the year, a spring morning and an autumnal morning, a night spangled with stars and a night overcast with clouds, meadows enamelled with flowers, forests stripped by the frosts, and fields glowing with their golden harvests; you will then have a just idea of the prospect of the universe.

IN GENERAL, *the Romantics were deeply attracted to what they conceived to be the spirit of the Middle Ages—violent, colorful, mystical, and otherworldly, its ruined churches mellowed with age and haunted by long-dead dreams. Nature was important to the Romantics, as it had been to the men of the Enlightenment, but the Romantic view of nature was far different from that of the eighteenth century. To most philosophes, "nature" suggested the ordered system of Newton and the formal gardens of Versailles. To the Romantics, nature was wild, mysterious, and virgin. William Wordsworth (1770–1850), in his "Tintern Abbey," celebrates nature's lonely beauty (2), and Percy Bysshe Shelley (1792–1822), in his "Dirge," evokes its dark violence (3). The Romantic view of nature permeates the romantic sonnet "When I Have Fears," by John Keats (1795–1821) (4).*

2. WILLIAM WORDSWORTH, "TINTERN ABBEY"

LINES COMPOSED A FEW MILES ABOVE TINTERN ABBEY,
ON REVISITING THE BANKS OF THE WYE DURING A TOUR.
JULY 13, 1798

Five years have past; five summers, with the length
Of five long winters! and again I hear
These waters, rolling from their mountain-springs
With a soft inland murmur.—Once again
Do I behold these steep and lofty cliffs,
That on a wild, secluded scene impress
Thoughts of more deep seclusion, and connect
The landscape with the quiet of the sky.
The day is come when I again repose
Here, under this dark sycamore, and view
These plots of cottage-ground, these orchard-tufts,
Which at this season, with their unripe fruits,
Are clad in one green hue, and lose themselves
 Mid groves and copses. Once again I see
These hedge-rows, hardly hedge-rows, little lines
Of sportive wood run wild: these pastoral farms,
Green to the very door; and wreaths of smoke
Sent up, in silence, from among the trees!
With some uncertain notice, as might seem
Of vagrant dwellers in the houseless woods,
Or of some Hermit's cave, where by his fire
The Hermit sits alone.

              These beauteous forms,
Through a long absence, have not been to me
As is a landscape to a blind man's eye:

But oft, in lonely rooms, and 'mid the din
Of towns and cities, I have owed to them,
In hours of weariness, sensations sweet,
Felt in the blood, and felt along the heart;
And passing even into my purer mind,
With tranquil restoration:—feelings too
Of unremembered pleasure: such, perhaps,
As have no slight or trivial influence
On that best portion of a good man's life,
His little, nameless, unremembered acts
Of kindness and of love. Nor less, I trust,
To them I may have owed another gift,
Of aspect more sublime: that blessed mood,
In which the burden of the mystery,
In which the heavy and the weary weight
Of all this unintelligible world,
Is lightened:—that serene and blessed mood,
In which the affections gently lead us on,—
Until, the breath of this corporeal frame
And even the motion of our human blood
Almost suspended, we are laid asleep
In body, and become a living soul:
While with an eye made quiet by the power
Of harmony, and the deep power of joy,
We see into the life of things.
                                        If this
Be but a vain belief, yet, oh! how oft—
In darkness and amid the many shapes
Of joyless daylight; when the fretful stir
Unprofitable, and the fever of the world,
Have hung upon the beatings of my heart—
How oft, in spirit, have I turned to thee,
O sylvan Wye! thou wanderer through the woods,
How often has my spirit turned to thee!

    And now, with gleams of half-extinguished thought,
With many recognitions dim and faint,
And somewhat of a sad perplexity,
The picture of the mind revives again:
While here I stand, not only with the sense
Of present pleasure, but with pleasing thoughts
That in this moment there is life and food
For future years. And so I dare to hope,
Though changed, no doubt, from what I was when first
I came among these hills; when like a roe
I bounded o'er the mountains, by the sides
Of the deep rivers, and the lonely streams,

Wherever nature led: more like a man
Flying from something that he dreads, than one
Who sought the thing he loved. For nature then
(The coarser pleasures of my boyish days
And their glad animal movements all gone by)
To me was all in all.—I cannot paint
What then I was. The sounding cataract
Haunted me like a passion: the tall rock,
The mountain, and the deep and gloomy wood,
Their colors and their forms, were then to me
An appetite; a feeling and a love,
That had no need of a remoter charm
By thoughts supplied, nor any interest
Unborrowed from the eye.—That time is past,
And all its aching joys are now no more,
And all its dizzy raptures. Not for this
Faint I, nor mourn nor murmur; other gifts
Have followed; for such loss, I would believe,
Abundant recompense. For I have learned
To look on nature, not as in the hour
Of thoughtless youth; but hearing oftentimes
The still, sad music of humanity,
Nor harsh nor grating, though of ample power
To chasten and subdue. And I have felt
A presence that disturbs me with the joy
Of elevated thoughts; a sense sublime
Of something far more deeply interfused,
Whose dwelling is the light of setting suns,
And the round ocean, and the living air,
And the blue sky, and in the mind of man:
A motion and a spirit, that impels
All thinking things, all objects of all thought,
And rolls through all things. Therefore am I still
A lover of the meadows and the woods,
And mountains; and of all that we behold
From this green earth; of all the mighty world
Of eye, and ear,—both what they half create,
And what perceive; well pleased to recognize
In nature and the language of the sense,
The anchor of my purest thoughts, the nurse,
The guide, the guardian of my heart, and soul
Of all my moral being.
                      Nor perchance,
If I were not thus taught, should I the more
Suffer my genial spirits to decay:
For thou art with me here upon the banks

Of this fair river; thou my dearest Friend,
My dear, dear Friend; and in thy voice I catch
The language of my former heart, and read
My former pleasures in the shooting lights
Of thy wild eyes. O yet a little while
May I behold in thee what I was once,
My dear, dear Sister! and this prayer I make,
Knowing that Nature never did betray
The heart that loved her; 't is her privilege,
Through all the years of this our life, to lead
From joy to joy: for she can so inform
The mind that is within us, so impress
With quietness and beauty, and so feed
With lofty thoughts, that neither evil tongues,
Rash judgments, nor the sneers of selfish men,
Nor greetings where no kindness is, nor all
The dreary intercourse of daily life,
Shall e'er prevail against us, or disturb
Our cheerful faith, that all which we behold
Is full of blessings. Therefore let the moon
Shine on thee in thy solitary walk;
And let the misty mountain-winds be free
To blow against thee: and, in after years,
When these wild ecstasies shall be matured
Into a sober pleasure; when thy mind
Shall be a mansion for all lovely forms,
Thy memory be as a dwelling-place
For all sweet sounds and harmonies; O, then,
If solitude, or fear, or pain, or grief,
Should be thy portion, with what healing thoughts
Of tender joy wilt thou remember me,
And these my exhortations! Nor, perchance,—
If I should be where I no more can hear
Thy voice, nor catch from thy wild eyes these gleams
Of past existence,—wilt thou then forget
That on the banks of this delightful stream
We stood together; and that I, so long
A worshipper of Nature, hither came
Unwearied in that service: rather say
With warmer love,—oh! with far deeper zeal
Of holier love. Nor wilt thou then forget,
That after many wanderings, many years
Of absence, these steep woods and lofty cliffs,
And this green pastoral landscape, were to me
More dear, both for themselves and for thy sake!

3. PERCY BYSSHE SHELLEY, "A DIRGE"

Rough wind, that moanest loud
   Grief too sad for song;
Wild wind, when sullen cloud
   Knells all the night long;

Sad storm, whose tears are vain,
Bare woods, whose branches strain,
Deep caves and dreary main,—
   Wail, for the world's wrong!

4. JOHN KEATS, "WHEN I HAVE FEARS"

When I have fears that I may cease to be
   Before my pen has glean'd my teeming brain,
Before high-piled books, in charactery,
   Hold like rich garners the full ripen'd grain;
When I behold, upon the night's starr'd face,
   Hugh cloudy symbols of a high romance,
And think that I may never live to trace
   Their shadows, with the magic hand of chance;
And when I feel, fair creature of an hour,
   That I shall never look upon thee more,
Never have relish in the faery power
   Of unreflecting love;—then on the shore
Of the wide world I stand alone, and think
Till love and fame to nothingness do sink.

B. Architecture

THE EXUBERANT ANTI-CLASSICISM of some Romantic architects and their willingness to draw inspiration from distant times and places are strikingly exemplified in John Nash's Royal Pavilion at Brighton, England (1815–1818), patterned vaguely after the Indian Taj Mahal.

1. JOHN NASH, THE ROYAL PAVILION, BRIGHTON, 1815–1818

THE REVIVAL OF INTEREST in the Middle Ages resulted in many structures being built in the Neo-Gothic style. The Houses of Parliament (begun 1836), designed by Sir Charles Berry and A. Welby Pugin, are notable examples.

2. SIR CHARLES BERRY AND A. WELBY PUGIN, THE HOUSES OF PARLIAMENT, BEGUN 1836

C. Painting

BRILLIANT COLOR, mysterious shadows, and an indefatigable quest for exotic subject matter mark the Oriental Tiger Hunt *(1) and* Oriental Lion Hunt *(2) by the French Romantic painter Eugène Delacroix (1798–1863).*

1. EUGÈNE DELACROIX, *ORIENTAL TIGER HUNT*

2. EUGÈNE DELACROIX, *ORIENTAL LION HUNT*

THE SLAVE SHIP *of Joseph Mallord William Turner (1775–1851), with its dramatic subject, rich colors, and fantastic details, epitomizes the Romantic movement in a single work of art.*

3. JOSEPH MALLORD WILLIAM TURNER, *THE SLAVE SHIP*, 1839

Part III

THE CONSERVATIVE RESPONSE
TO THE FRENCH REVOLUTION

A. Conservative Thought

THE CONSERVATIVE REACTION that accompanied and followed the French Revolution is illustrated here in three sharply contrasting documents. The first is an extensive excerpt from Edmund Burke's Reflections on the Revolution in France *(1790). Burkean thought constitutes the fountainhead of modern conservatism; many of his fundamental ideas are present in the passages given below.*

1. EDMUND BURKE, FROM *REFLECTIONS ON THE REVOLUTION IN FRANCE*, 1790

SOURCE. *Edmund Burke, Selected Prose,* Sir Philip Magnus, ed., London: Falcon Press, 1948, pp. 60–80.

I cannot stand forward, and give praise or blame to anything which relates to human actions and human concerns on a simple view of the object, as it stands stripped of every relation, in all the nakedness and solitude of metaphysical abstraction. Circumstances (which with some gentlemen pass for nothing) give in reality to every political principle its distinguishing colour and discriminating effect. The circumstances are what render every civil and political scheme beneficial or noxious to mankind. Abstractedly speaking, government, as well as liberty, is good; yet could I, in common sense, ten years ago, have felicitated France on her enjoyment of a government (for she then had a government), without inquiring what the nature of that government was, or how it was administered? Can I now congratulate the same nation upon its freedom? Is it because liberty in the abstract may be classed amongst the blessings of mankind, that I am seriously to felicitate a madman who has escaped from the protecting restraint and wholesome darkness of his cell on his restoration to the enjoyment of light and liberty? Am I to congratulate a highwayman and murderer who has broke prison upon the recovery of his natural rights? This would be to act over again the scene of the criminals condemned to the galleys, and their heroic deliverer, the metaphysic Knight of the Sorrowful Countenance.

When I see the spirit of liberty in action, I see a strong principle at work; and this, for a while, is all I can possibly know of it. The wild gas, the fixed air, is plainly broke loose: but we ought to suspend our judgment until the first effervescence is a little subsided, till the liquor is cleared, and until we see something deeper than the agitation of a troubled and frothy surface. I must be tolerably sure, before I venture publicly to congratulate men upon a blessing, that they have really received one. Flattery corrupts both the receiver and the giver; and adulation is not of more service to the people than to kings. I should therefore suspend my congratulations on the new liberty of France, until I was informed how it had been combined with government, with public force, with the discipline and obedience of armies, with the collection of an effective and well-distributed revenue, with morality and religion, with solidity and property, with peace and order, with civil and social manners. All these (in their way) are good things, too; and, without them, liberty is not a benefit whilst it lasts, and is not likely to continue long. The effect of liberty to individuals is that they may do what they please: we ought to see what it will please them to do before we risk congratulations, which may be soon turned into complaints. Prudence would dictate this in the case of separate, insulated, private men. But liberty, when men act in bodies, is power. Considerate people, before they declare themselves, will observe the use which is made of power—and particularly of so trying a thing as new power in new persons, of whose principles, tempers, and dispositions they have little or no experience, and in situations where those who appear the most stirring in the scene may possibly not be the real movers . . .

You will observe, that, from Magna Charta to the Declaration of Right, it has been the uniform policy of our Constitution to claim and assert our liberties as an entailed inheritance derived to us from our forefathers, and to be transmitted to our posterity—as an estate especially belonging to the people of this Kingdom, without any reference whatever to any other more general or prior right. By this means our Constitution preserves an unity in so great a diversity of its parts. We have an inheritable Crown, an inheritable Peerage, and a House of Commons and a people inheriting privileges, franchises, and liberties from a long line of ancestors.

This policy appears to me to be the result of profound reflection—or rather the happy effect of following Nature, which is wisdom without reflection, and above it. A spirit of innovation is generally the result of a

selfish temper and confined views. People will not look forward to posterity, who never look backward to their ancestors. Besides, the people
of England well know that the idea of inheritance furnishes a sure principle of conservation, and a sure principle of transmission, without at all
excluding a principle of improvement. It leaves acquisition free; but it
secures what it acquires. Whatever advantages are obtained by a state
proceeding on these maxims are locked fast as in a sort of family settlement, grasped as in a kind of mortmain forever. By a constitutional policy
working after the pattern of Nature, we receive, we hold, we transmit
our government and our privileges, in the same manner in which we enjoy
and transmit our property and our lives. The institutions of policy, the
goods of fortune, the gifts of Providence, are handed down to us, and
from us, in the same course and order. Our political system is placed in a
just correspondence and symmetry with the order of the world, and with
the mode of existence decreed to a permanent body composed of transitory parts—wherein, by the disposition of a stupendous wisdom, mould-
ing together the great mysterious incorporation of the human race, the
whole, at one time, is never old or middle-aged or young, but, in a condition of unchangeable constancy, moves on through the varied tenor of
perpetual decay, fall, renovation, and progression. Thus, by preserving
the method of Nature in the conduct of the state, in what we improve
we are never wholly new, in what we retain we are never wholly obsolete.
By adhering in this manner and on those principles to our forefathers, we
are guided, not by the superstition of antiquarians, but by the spirit of
philosophic analogy. In this choice of inheritance we have given to our
frame of policy the image of a relation in blood: binding up the Constitution of our country with our dearest domestic ties; adopting our fundamental laws into the bosom of our family affections; keeping inseparable,
and cherishing with the warmth of all their combined and mutually reflected charities, our state, our hearths, our sepulchres, and our altars.

Through the same plan of a conformity to Nature in our artificial institutions, and by calling in the aid of her unerring and powerful instincts
to fortify the fallible and feeble contrivances of our reason, we have
derived several other, and those no small benefits, from considering our
liberties in the light of an inheritance. Always acting as if in the presence
of canonised forefathers, the spirit of freedom, leading in itself to misrule
and excess, is tempered with an awful gravity. This idea of a liberal
descent inspires us with a sense of habitual native dignity, which prevents
that upstart insolence almost inevitably adhering to and disgracing those
who are the first acquirers of any distinction. By this means our liberty
becomes a noble freedom. It carries an imposing and majestic aspect. It
has a pedigree and illustrating ancestors. It has its gallery of portraits, its

monumental inscriptions, its records, evidences, and titles. We procure reverence to our civil institutions on the principle upon which Nature teaches us to revere individual men: on account of their age, and on account of those from whom they are descended. All you sophisters cannot produce anything better adapted to preserve a rational and manly freedom than the course that we have pursued, who have chosen our nature rather than our speculations, our breasts rather than our inventions, for the great conservatories and magazines of our rights and privileges.

Believe me, Sir, those who attempt to level never equalise. In all societies consisting of various descriptions of citizens, some description must be uppermost. The Levellers, therefore, only change and pervert the natural order of things: they load the edifice of society by setting up in the air what the solidity of the structure requires to be on the ground. The associations of tailors and carpenters, of which the republic (of Paris, for instance) is composed, cannot be equal to the situation into which, by the worst of usurpations, an usurpation on the prerogatives of Nature, you attempt to force them.

The Chancellor of France, at the opening of the States, said, in a tone of oratorial flourish, that all occupations were honourable. If he meant only that no honest employment was disgraceful, he would not have gone beyond the truth. But in asserting that anything is honourable, we imply some distinction in its favour. The occupation of a hair-dresser, or a working tallow-chandler, cannot be a matter of honour to any person—to say nothing of a number of other more servile employments. Such descriptions of men ought not to suffer oppression from the state; but the state suffers oppression if such as they, either individually or collectively, are permitted to rule. In this you think you are combating prejudice, but you are at war with Nature.

I do not, my dear Sir, conceive you to be of that sophistical, captious spirit, or of that uncandid dullness, as to require, for every general observation or sentiment, an explicit detail of the correctives and exceptions which reason will presume to be included in all the general propositions which come from reasonable men. You do not imagine that I wish to confine power, authority, and distinction to blood and names and titles. No, Sir. There is no qualification for government but virtue and wisdom, actual or presumptive. Wherever they are actually found, they have, in whatever state, condition, profession, or trade, the passport of Heaven to human place and honour. Woe to the country which would madly and impiously reject the service of the talents and virtues, civil, military, or religious, that are given to grace and to serve it; and would condemn to obscurity everything formed to diffuse lustre and glory around a state! Woe to that country, too, that, passing into the opposite extreme, considers a low education, a mean, contracted view of things, a sordid, mer-

cenary occupation, as a preferable title to command! Everything ought
to be open—but not indifferently to every man. No rotation, no appointment by lot, no mode of election operating in the spirit of sortition or
rotation, can be generally good in a government conversant in extensive
objects; because they have no tendency, direct or indirect, to select the
man with a view to the duty, or to accommodate the one to the other.
I do not hesitate to say that the road to eminence and power, from obscure condition, ought not to be made too easy, nor a thing too much of
course. If rare merit be the rarest of all rare things, it ought to pass
through some sort of probation. The temple of honour ought to be seated
on an eminence. If it be opened through virtue, let it be remembered, too,
that virtue is never tried but by some difficulty and some struggle . . .

Whilst they are possessed by these notions, it is vain to talk to them of
the practice of their ancestors, the fundamental laws of their country, the
fixed form of a Constitution whose merits are confirmed by the solid test
of long experience and an increasing public strength and national prosperity. They despise experience as the wisdom of unlettered men; and as
for the rest, they have wrought under ground a mine that will blow up,
at one grand explosion, all examples of antiquity, all precedents, charters,
and acts of Parliament. They have 'the rights of men.' Against these there
can be no prescription; against these no argument is binding: these admit no temperament and no compromise: anything withheld from their
full demand is so much of fraud and injustice. Against these their rights
of men let no government look for security in the length of its administration. The objections of these speculatists, if its forms do not quadrate
with their theories, are as valid against such an old and beneficent government as against the most violent tyranny or the greenest usurpation.
They are always at issue with governments, not on a question of abuse,
but a question of competency and a question of title. I have nothing to
say to the clumsy subtilty of their political metaphysics. . . . But let them
not break prison to burst like a Levanter, to sweep the earth with their
hurricane, and to break up the fountains of the great deep to overwhelm
us!

Far am I from denying in theory, full as far is my heart from withhold-
ing in practice (if I were of power to give or to withhold), the *real* rights
of men. In denying their false claims of right, I do not mean to injure
those which are real, and are such as their pretended rights would
totally destroy. If civil society be made for the advantage of man, all the
advantages for which it is made become his right. It is an institution of
beneficence; and law itself is only beneficence acting by a rule. Men have
a right to justice, as between their fellows, whether their fellows are in
politic function or in ordinary occupation. They have a right to the fruits
of their industry, and to the means of making their industry fruitful.

They have a right to the acquisitions of their parents, to the nourishment and improvement of their offspring, to instruction in life and to consolation in death. Whatever each man can separately do, without trespassing upon others, he has a right to do for himself; and he has a right to a fair portion of all which society, with all its combinations of skill and force, can do in his favour. In this partnership all men have equal rights; but not to equal things. He that has but five shillings in the partnership has as good a right to it as he that has five hundred pounds has to his larger proportion; but he has not a right to an equal dividend in the product of the joint stock. And as to the share of power, authority, and direction which each individual ought to have in the management of the state, that I must deny to be amongst the direct original rights of man in civil society; for I have in my contemplation the civil social man, and no other. It is a thing to be settled by convention . . .

Government is not made in virtue of natural rights, which may and do exist in total independence of it—and exist in much greater clearness, and in a much greater degree of abstract perfection: but their abstract perfection is their practical defect. By having a right to everything they want everything. Government is a contrivance of human wisdom to provide for human *wants*. Men have a right that these wants should be provided for by this wisdom. Among these wants is to be reckoned the want, out of civil society, of a sufficient restraint upon their passions. Society requires not only that the passions of individuals should be subjected, but that even in the mass and body, as well as in the individuals, the inclinations of men should frequently be thwarted, their will controlled, and their passions brought into subjection. This can only be done by a power out of themselves, and not, in the exercise of its function, subject to that will and to those passions which it is its office to bridle and subdue. In this sense the restraints on men, as well as their liberties, are to be reckoned among their rights. But as the liberties and the restrictions vary with times and circumstances, and admit of infinite modifications, they cannot be settled upon any abstract rule; and nothing is so foolish as to discuss them upon that principle.

The moment you abate anything from the full rights of men each to govern himself, and suffer any artificial, positive limitation upon those rights, from that moment the whole organisation of government becomes a consideration of convenience. This it is which makes the constitution of a state, and the due distribution of its powers, a matter of the most delicate and complicated skill. It requires a deep knowledge of human nature and human necessities, and of the things which facilitate or obstruct the various ends which are to be pursued by the mechanism of civil institutions. The state is to have recruits to its strength and remedies to its distempers. What is the use of discussing a man's abstract right to food or medicine? The question is upon the method of procuring and administering them. In that deliberation I shall always advise to call in the aid of the farmer and the physician, rather than the professor of metaphysics.

The science of constructing a commonwealth, or renovating it, or reforming it, is like every other experimental science, not to be taught *a priori*. Nor is it a short experience that can instruct us in that practical science; because the real effects of moral causes are not always immediate, but that which, in the first instance, is prejudicial may be excellent in its remoter operation, and its excellence may arise even from the ill effects it produces in the beginning. The reverse also happens; and very plausible schemes, with very pleasing commencements, have often shameful and lamentable conclusions. In states there are often some obscure and almost latent causes, things which appear at first view of little moment, on which a very great part of their prosperity or adversity may most essentially depend. The science of government being, therefore, so practical in itself, and intended for such practical purposes, a matter which requires experience, and even more experience than any person can gain in his whole life, however sagacious and observing he may be, it is with infinite caution that any man ought to venture upon pulling down an edifice which has answered in any tolerable degree for ages the common purposes of society, or on building it up again without having models and patterns of approval utility before his eyes.

These metaphysic rights entering into common life, like rays of light which pierce into a dense medium, are, by the laws of Nature, refracted from their straight line. Indeed, in the gross and complicated mass of human passions and concerns, the primitive rights of men undergo such a variety of refractions and reflections that it becomes absurd to talk of them as if they continued in the simplicity of their original direction. The nature of man is intricate; the objects of society are of the greatest possible complexity: and therefore no simple disposition or direction of power can be suitable either to man's nature or to the quality of his affairs. When I hear the simplicity of contrivance aimed at and boasted of in any new political constitutions, I am at no loss to decide that the artificers are grossly ignorant of their trade or totally negligent of their duty. The simple governments are fundamentally defective, to say no worse of them. If you were to contemplate society in but one point of view, all these simple modes of policy are infinitely captivating. In effect each would answer its single end much more perfectly than the more complex purposes. But it is better that the whole should be imperfectly and anomalously answered than that while some parts are provided for with great exactness, others might be totally neglected, or perhaps materially injured, by the over-care of a favourite member.

The pretended rights of these theorists are all extremes; and in proportion as they are metaphysically true, they are morally and politically false. The rights of men are in a sort of middle, incapable of definition, but not impossible to be discerned. The rights of men in governments are their advantages; and these are often in balances between differences of good—in compromises sometimes between good and evil, and sometimes between evil and evil. Political reason is a computing principle: adding, subtracting, multiplying, and dividing, morally, and not metaphysically or mathematically, true moral denominations . . .

It is now sixteen or seventeen years since I saw the Queen of France, then the Dauphiness, at Versailles; and surely never lighted on this orb, which she hardly seemed to touch, a more delightful vision. I saw her just above the horizon, decorating and cheering the elevated sphere she just began to move in—glittering like the morning-star full of life and splendour and joy. Oh! what a revolution! and what an heart must I have, to contemplate without emotion that elevation and that fall! Little did I dream, when she added titles of veneration to those of enthusiastic, distant, respectful love, that she should ever be obliged to carry the sharp antidote against disgrace concealed in that bosom! Little did I dream that I should have lived to see such disasters fallen upon her in a nation of gallant men, in a nation of men of honour, and of cavaliers! I thought ten thousand swords must have leaped from their scabbards to avenge even a look that threatened her with insult. But the age of chivalry is gone. That of sophisters, economists, and calculators has succeeded; and the glory of Europe is extinguished forever. Never, never more, shall we behold that generous loyalty to rank and sex, that proud submission, that dignified obedience, that subordination of the heart, which kept alive, even in servitude itself, the spirit of an exalted freedom! The unbought grace of life, the cheap defence of nations, the nurse of manly sentiment and heroic enterprise, is done! It is gone, that sensibility of principle, that chastity of honour, which felt a stain like a wound, which inspired courage whilst it mitigated ferocity, which ennobled whatever it touched, and under which vice itself lost half its evil by losing all its grossness! . . .

But now all is to be changed. All the pleasing illusions which made power gentle and obedience liberal, which harmonised the different shades of life, and which by a bland assimilation incorporated into politics the sentiments which beautify and soften private society, are to be dissolved by this new conquering empire of light and reason. All the decent drapery of life is to be rudely torn off. All the superadded ideas, furnished from the wardrobe of a moral imagination, which the heart owns and the understanding ratifies, as necessary to cover the defects of our naked, shivering nature, and to raise it to dignity in our own estimation, are to be exploded, as a ridiculous, absurd, and antiquated fashion.

On this scheme of things, a king is but a man, a queen is but a woman, a woman is but an animal—and an animal not of the highest order. All homage paid to the sex in general as such, and without distinct views, is to be regarded as romance and folly. Regicide, and parricide and sacrilege, are but fictions of superstition, corrupting jurisprudence by destroying its simplicity. The murder of a king, or a queen, or a bishop, or a father are only common homicide—and if the people are by any chance or in any way gainers by it, a sort of homicide much the most pardonable, and into which we ought not to make too severe a scrutiny.

On the scheme of this barbarous philosophy, which is the offspring of cold hearts and muddy understandings, and which is as void of solid wisdom as it is destitute of all taste and elegance, laws are to be supported only by their own terrors, and by the concern which each individual may find in them from his own private speculations, or can spare to them from his own private interests. In the groves of *their* academy, at the end of every vista, you see nothing but the gallows. Nothing is left which engages the affections on the part of the commonwealth. On the principles of this mechanic philosophy, our institutions can never be embodied, if I may use the expression, in persons—so as to create in us love, veneration, admiration, or attachment. But that sort of reason which banishes the affections is incapable of filling their place. These public affections, combined with manners, are required sometimes as supplements, sometimes as correctives, always as aids to law. The precept given by a wise man, as well as a great critic, for the construction of poems, is equally true as to states: 'Non satis est pulchra esse poemata, dulcia sunto.' There ought to be a system of manners in every nation which a well-formed mind would be disposed to relish. To make us love our country, our country ought to be lovely.

But power, of some kind or other, will survive the shock in which manners and opinions perish; and it will find other and worse means for its support. The usurpation, which, in order to subvert ancient institutions, has destroyed ancient principles, will hold power by arts similar to those by which it has acquired it. When the old feudal and chivalrous spirit of *fealty*, which by freeing kings from fear, freed both kings and subjects from the precautions of tyranny, shall be extinct in the minds of men, plots and assassinations will be anticipated by preventive murder and preventive confiscation, and that long roll of grim and bloody maxims which form the political code of all power not standing on its own honour and the honour of those who are to obey it. Kings will be tyrants from policy, when subjects are rebels from principle . . .

To avoid, therefore, the evils of inconstancy and versatility, ten thousand times worse than those of obstinacy and the blindest prejudice, we have consecrated the state, that no man should approach to look into its defects or corruptions but with due caution; that he should never dream of beginning its reformation by its subversion; that he should approach to the faults of the state as to the wounds of a father, with pious awe and trembling solicitude. By this wise prejudice we are taught to look with horror on those children of their country who are prompt rashly to hack that aged parent in pieces and put him into the kettle of magicians, in hopes that by their poisonous weeds and wild incantations they may regenerate the paternal constiution and renovate their father's life.

Society is, indeed, a contract. Subordinate contracts for objects of mere occasional interest may be dissolved at pleasure; but the state ought not to be considered as nothing better than a partnership agreement in a trade of pepper and coffee, calico, or tobacco, or some other such low concern, to be taken up for a little temporary interest, and to be dissolved by the fancy of the parties. It is to be looked on with other reverence; because it is not a partnership in things subservient only to the gross animal existence of a temporary and perishable nature. It is a partnership in all science, a partnership in all art, a partnership in every virtue and in all perfection. As the ends of such a partnership cannot be obtained in many generations, it becomes a partnership not only between those who are living, but between those who are living, those who are dead, and those who are to be born. Each contract of each particular state is but a clause in the great primeval contract of eternal society, linking the lower with the higher natures, connecting the visible and invisible world, according to a fixed compact sanctioned by the inviolable oath which holds all physical and all moral natures each in their appointed place. This law is not subject to the will of those who, by an obligation above them, and infinitely superior, are bound to submit their will to that law. The municipal corporations of that universal kingdom are not morally at liberty, at their pleasure, and on their speculations of a contingent improvement, wholly to separate and tear asunder the bonds of their subordinate community, and to dissolve it into an unsocial, uncivil, unconnected chaos of elementary principles. It is the first and supreme necessity only, a necessity that is not chosen, but chooses, a necessity paramount to deliberation, that admits no discussion and demands no evidence, which alone can justify a resort to anarchy. This necessity is no exception to the rule; because this necessity itself is a part, too, of that moral and physical disposition of things to which man must be obedient by consent or force: but if that which is only submission to necessity should be made the object of choice, the law is broken, Nature is disobeyed, and the rebellious are outlawed, cast forth, and exiled, from this world of reason, and order, and peace, and virtue, and fruitful penitence, into the antagonist world of madness, discord, vice, confusion, and un-availing sorrow . . .

I do not know under what description to class the present ruling authority in France. It affects to be a pure democracy, though I think it in a direct train of becoming shortly a mischievous and ignoble oligarchy. But for the present I admit it to be a contrivance of the nature and effect of what it pretends to. I reprobate no form of government merely upon abstract principles. There may be situations in which the purely demo-cratic form will become necessary. There may be some (very few, and very particularly circumstanced) where it would be clearly desirable. This I do not take to be the case of France, or of any other great country. Until now, we have seen no examples of considerable democracies. The ancients were better acquainted with them. Not being wholly unread in the authors who had seen the most of those constitutions, and who best understood them, I cannot help concurring with their opinion, that an absolute democracy no more than absolute monarchy is to be reckoned among the legitimate forms of government. They think it rather the corruption and degeneracy than the sound constitution of a republic. If I recollect rightly, Aristotle observes that a democracy has many striking points of resemblance with a tyranny. Of this I am certain, that in a democracy the majority of the citizens is capable of exercising the most cruel oppressions upon the minority, whenever strong divisions prevail in that kind of policy, as they often must—and that oppression of the minor-ity will extend to far greater numbers, and will be carried on with much greater fury, than can almost ever be apprehended from the dominion of a single sceptre. In such a popular persecution, individual sufferers are in a much more deplorable condition than in any other. Under a cruel prince they have the balmy compassion of mankind to assuage the smart of their wounds, they have the plaudits of the people to animate their generous constancy under their sufferings: but those who are subjected to wrong under multitudes are deprived of all external consolation: they seem deserted by mankind, overpowered by a conspiracy of their whole species . . .

We do not draw the moral lessons we might from history. On the con-trary, without care it may be used to vitiate our minds and to destroy our happiness. In history a great volume is unrolled for our instruction, draw-ing the materials of future wisdom from the past errors and infirmities of mankind. It may, in the perversion, serve for a magazine, furnishing offensive and defensive weapons for parties in Church and State, and supplying the means of keeping alive or reviving dissensions and animosities, and adding fuel to civil fury. History consists, for the greater part, of the miseries brought upon the world by pride, ambition, avarice, revenge, lust, sedition, hypocrisy, ungoverned zeal, and all the train of disorderly appetites, which shake the public with the same

> *'troublous storms that toss*
> *The private state, and render life unsweet.'*

These vices are the causes of those storms. Religion, morals, laws, prerogatives, privileges, liberties, rights of men, are the pretexts. The pretexts are always found in some specious appearance of a real good. You would not secure men from tyranny and sedition by rooting out of the mind the principles to which these fraudulent pretexts apply. If you did, you would root out everything that is valuable in the human breast. As these are the pretexts, so the ordinary actors and instruments in great public evils are kings, priests, magistrates, senates, parliaments, national assemblies, judges, and captains. You would not cure the evil by resolving that there should be no more monarchs, nor ministers of state, nor of the Gospel—no interpreters of law, no general officers, no public councils. You might change the names: the things in some shape must remain. A certain quantum of power must always exist in the community, in some hands, and under some appellation. Wise men will apply their remedies to vices, not to names—to the causes of evil, which are permanent, not to the occasional organs by which they act, and the transitory modes in which they appear. Otherwise you will be wise historically, a fool in practice. Seldom have two ages the same fashion in their pretexts, and the same modes of mischief. Wickedness is a little more inventive. Whilst you are discussing fashion, the fashion is gone by. The very same vice assumes a new body. The spirit transmigrates; and, far from losing its principle of life by the change of its appearance, it is renovated in its new organs with the fresh vigour of a juvenile activity. It walks abroad, it continues its ravages, whilst you are gibbeting the carcass or demolishing the tomb. You are terrifying yourselves with ghosts and apparitions, whilst your house is the haunt of robbers. It is thus with all those who, attending only to the shell and husk of history, think they are waging war with intolerance, pride, and cruelty, whilst, under colour of abhorring the ill principles of antiquated parties, they are authorising and feeding the same odious vices in different factions, and perhaps in worse . . .

In every prosperous community something more is produced than goes to the immediate support of the producer. This surplus forms the income of the landed capitalist. It will be spent by a proprietor who does not labour. But this idleness is itself the sring of labour, this repose the spur to industry. The only concern for the state is, that the capital taken in rent from the land should be returned again to the industry from whence it came, and that its expenditure should be with the least possible detriment to the morals of those who expend it and to those of the people to whom it is returned.

In all the views of receipt, expenditure, and personal employment, a sober legislator would carefully compare the possessor whom he was recommended to expel with the stranger who was proposed to fill his place. Before the inconveniences are incurred which *must* attend all violent revolutions in property through extensive confiscation, we ought to have some rational assurance that the purchasers of the confiscated property will be in a considerable degree more laborious, more virtuous, more sober, less disposed to extort an unreasonable proportion of the gains of the labourer, or to consume on themselves a larger share than is fit for the measure of an individual—or that they should be qualified to dispense the surplus in a more steady and equal mode, so as to answer the purposes of a politic expenditure, than the old possessors, call those possessors bishops, or canons, or commendatory abbots, or monks, or what you please. The monks are lazy. Be it so. Suppose them no otherwise employed than by singing in the choir. They are as usefully employed as those who neither sing nor pray—as usefully even as those who sing upon the stage. They are as usefully employed as if they worked from dawn to dark in the innumerable servile, degrading, unseemly, unmanly, and often most unwholesome and pestiferous occupations to which, by the social economy, so many wretches are inevitably doomed. If it were not generally pernicious to disturb the natural course of things, and to impede in any degree the great wheel of circulation which is turned by the strangely directed labour of these unhappy people, I should be infinitely more inclined forcibly to rescue them from their miserable industry than violently to disturb the tranquil repose of monastic quietude. Humanity, and perhaps policy, might better justify me in the one than in the other. It is a subject on which I have often reflected, and never reflected without feeling from it. I am sure that no consideration, except the necessity of submitting to the yoke of luxury and the despotism of fancy, which in their own imperious way will distribute the surplus product of the soil, can justify the toleration of such trades and employments in a well-regulated state. But for this purpose of distribution, it seems to me that the idle expenses of monks are quite as well directed as the idle expenses of us lay loiterers.

When the advantages of the possession and of the project are on a par, there is no motive for a change. But in the present case, perhaps, they are not upon a par, and the difference is in favour of the possession. It does not appear to me that the expenses of those whom you are going to expel do in fact take a course so directly and so generally leading to vitiate and degrade and render miserable those through whom they pass as the expenses of those favourites whom you are intruding into their houses.

Why should the expenditure of a great landed property, which is a dispersion of the surplus product of the soil, appear intolerable to you or to me, when it takes its course through the accumulation of vast libraries, which are the history of the force and weakness of the human mind—through great collections of ancient records, medals, and coins, which attest and explain laws and customs—through paintings and statues, that, by imitating Nature, seem to extend the limits of creation—through grand monuments of the dead, which continue the regards and connections of life beyond the grave—through collections of the specimens of Nature, which become a representative assembly of all the classes and families of the world, that by disposition facilitate, and by exciting curiosity open, the avenues to science? If by great permanent establishments all these objects of expense are better secured from the inconstant sport of personal caprice and personal extravagance, are they worse than if the same tastes prevailed in scattered individuals? Does not the sweat of the mason and carpenter, who toil in order to partake the sweat of the peasant, flow as pleasantly and as salubriously in the construction and repair of the majestic edifices of religion as in the painted booths and sordid sties of vice and luxury: as honourably and as profitably in repairing those sacred works which grow hoary with innumerable years as on the momentary receptacles of transient voluptuousness—in opera-houses, and brothels, and gaming-houses, and club-houses, and obelisks in the Champ de Mars? Is the surplus product of the olive and the vine worse employed in the frugal sustenance of persons whom the fictions of a pious imagination raise to dignity by construing in the service of God than in pampering the innumerable multitude of those who are degraded by being made useless domestics, subservient to the pride of man? Are the decorations of temples an expenditure less worthy a wise man than ribbons, and laces, and national cockades, and petit maisons, and petit soupers, and all the innumerable fopperies and follies in which opulence sports away the burden of its superfluity?

We tolerate even these—not from love of them, but for fear of worse. We tolerate them, because property and liberty, to a degree, require that toleration. But why proscribe the other, and surely, in every point of view, the more laudable use of estates? Why, through the violation of all property, through an outrage upon every principle of liberty, forcibly carry them from the better to the worse? . . .

The effects of the incapacity shown by the popular leaders in all the great members of the commonwealth are to be covered with the 'all-atoning name' of Liberty. In some people I see great liberty, indeed; in many, if not in the most, an oppressive, degrading servitude. But what is liberty without wisdom and without virtue? It is the greatest of all

possible evils; for it is folly, vice, and madness, without tuition or restraint. Those who know what virtuous liberty is cannot bear to see it
disgraced by incapable heads, on account of their having high-sounding
words in their mouths. Grand, swelling sentiments of liberty I am sure
I do not despise. They warm the heart; they enlarge and liberalise our
minds; they animate our courage in a time of conflict. Old as I am, I read
the fine raptures of Lucan and Corneille with pleasure. Neither do I
wholly condemn the little arts and devices of popularity. They facilitate
the carrying of many points of moment; they keep the people together;
they refresh the mind in its exertions; and they diffuse occasional gaiety
over the severe brow of moral freedom. Every politician ought to sacrifice
to the Graces, and to join compliance with reason. But in such an undertaking as that in France all these subsidiary sentiments and artifices are
of little avail. To make a government requires no great prudence. Settle
the seat of power, teach obedience, and the work is done. To give freedom is still more easy. It is not necessary to guide; it only requires to let
go the rein. But to form a free government, that is to temper together
these opposite elements of liberty and restraint in one consistent work,
requires much thought, deep reflection, a sagacious, powerful, and combining mind. This I do not find in those who take the lead in the National
Assembly. Perhaps they are not so miserably deficient as they appear. I
rather believe it. It would put them below the common level of human
understanding. But when the leaders choose to make themselves bidders
at an auction of popularity, their talents, in the construction of the state,
will be of no service. They will become flatterers instead of legislators—
the instruments, not the guides of the people. If any of them should
happen to propose a scheme of liberty soberly limited, and defined with
proper qualifications, he will be immediately outbid by his competitors,
who will produce something more splendidly popular. Suspicions will be
raised of his fidelity to his cause. Moderation will be stigmatised as the
virtue of cowards, and compromise as the prudence of traitors—until, in
hopes of preserving the credit which may enable him to temper and
moderate on some occasions, the popular leader is obliged to become
active in propagating doctrines and establishing powers that will afterwards defeat any sober purpose at which he ultimately might have aimed.

But am I so unreasonable as to see nothing at all that deserves commendation in the indefatigable labours of this Assembly? I do not deny,
that, among an infinite number of acts of violence and folly, some good
may have been done. They who destroy everything certainly will remove
some grievance. They who make everything new have a chance that they
may establish something beneficial. To give them credit for what they
have done in virtue of the authority they have usurped, or to excuse

them in the crimes by which that authority has been acquired, it must appear that the same things could not have been accomplished without producing such a revolution. Most assuredly they might; because almost every one of the regulations made by them, when not very equivocal, was either in the cession of the king, voluntarily made at the meeting of the States, or in the concurrent instructions to the Orders. Some usages have been abolished on just grounds; but they were such, that, if they had stood as they were to all eternity, they would little detract from the happiness and prosperity of any state. The improvements of the National Assembly are superficial: their errors fundamental.

Whatever they are, I wish my countrymen rather to recommend to our neighbours the example of the British Constitution than to take models from them for the improvement of our own. In the former they have got an invaluable treasure. They are not, I think, without some causes of apprehension and complaint; but these they do not owe to their own conduct. I think our happy situation owing to our Constitution—but owing to the whole of it, and not to any part singly—owing in a great measure to what we have left standing in our several reviews and reformations, as well as to what we have altered or superadded. Our people will find employment enough for a truly patriotic, free, and independent spirit, in guarding what they possess from violation. I would not exclude alteration neither; but even when I changed, it should be to preserve. I should be led to my remedy by a great grievance. In what I did, I should follow the example of our ancestors. I would make the reparation as nearly as possible in the style of the building. A politic caution, a guarded circumspection, a moral rather than a complexional timidity, were among the ruling principles of our forefathers in their most decided conduct. Not being illuminated with the light of which the gentlemen of France tell us they have got so abundant a share, they acted under a strong impression of the ignorance and fallibility of mankind. He that had made them thus fallible rewarded them for having in their conduct attended to their nature. Let us imitate their caution, if we wish to deserve their fortune or to retain their bequests. Let us add, if we please, but let us be satisfied to admire, rather than attempt to follow in their desperate flights, the aeronauts of France.

I have told you candidly my sentiments. I think they are not likely to alter yours. I do not know that they ought. You are young; you cannot guide, but must follow, the fortune of your country. But hereafter they may be of some use to you, in some future form which your commonwealth may take. In the present it can hardly remain; but before its final settlement, it may be obliged to pass, as one of our poets says, 'through great varieties of untried being,' and in all its transmigrations to be purified by fire and blood.

I have little to recommend my opinions but long observation and much impartiality. They come from one who has been no tool of power, no flatterer of greatness, and who in his last acts does not wish to belie the tenor of his life. They come from one almost the whole of whose public exertion has been a struggle for the liberty of others—from one in whose breast no anger durable or vehement has ever been kindled but by what he considered as tyranny, and who snatches from his share in the endeavours which are used by good men to discredit opulent oppression the hours he has employed on your affairs, and who in so doing persuades himself he has not departed from his usual office. They come from one who desires honours, distinctions, and emoluments but little, and who expects them not at all—who has no contempt for fame, and no fear of obloquy—who shuns contention, though he will hazard an opinion; from one who wishes to preserve consistency, but who would preserve consistency, by varying his means to secure the unity of his end—and, when the equipoise of the vessel in which he sails may be endangered by overloading it upon one side, is desirous of carrying the small weight of his reasons to that which may preserve its equipoise.

B. Conservatism in Post-Napoleonic Politics

CLEMENS METTERNICH (1773–1859), a statesman of great influence at the Congress of Vienna and in the political developments of the following generation, summarized his views in a secret memorandum to Czar Alexander I of Russia (1820). His approach was far more royalist and aristocratic—far more hostile to the middle class—than that of Burke.

1. CLEMENS METTERNICH, FROM HIS SECRET MEMORANDUM TO CZAR ALEXANDER, 1820

SOURCE. Prince Richard Metternich, ed., *Memoirs of Prince Metternich*, Mrs. Alexander Napier, tr., London: R. Bentley & Son, 1880–1882, III, pp. 454–476.

Kings have to calculate the chances of their very existence in the immediate future; passions are let loose, and league together to overthrow everything which society respects as the basis of its existence; religion, public morality, laws, customs, rights, and duties, all are attacked, confounded, overthrown, or called in question. The great mass of the people are tranquil spectators of these attacks and revolutions, and of the absolute want of all means of defence. A few are carried off by the torrent, but the wishes of the immense majority are to maintain a repose which exists no longer, and of which even the first elements seem to be lost.

What is the cause of all these evils? By what methods has this evil established itself, and how is it that it penetrates into every vein of the social body?

Do remedies still exist to arrest the progress of this evil, and what are they?

These are doubtless questions worthy of the solicitude of every good man who is a true friend to order and public peace—two elements inseparable in principle, and which are at once the first needs and the first blessings of humanity.

Has there never been offered to the world an institution really worthy of the name? Has truth been always confounded with error ever since society has believed itself able to distinguish one from the other? Have the experiences bought at the price of so many sacrifices, and repeated at intervals, and in so many different places, been all in error? Will a flood of light be shed upon society at one stroke? Will knowledge come by inspiration? If one could believe in such phenomena it would not be the less necessary, first of all, to assure oneself of their reality. Of all things, nothing is so fatal as error; and it is neither our wish nor our intention ever to give ourselves up to it. Let us examine the matter!

Man's nature is immutable. The first needs of society are and remain the same, and the differences which they seem to offer find their explanation in the diversity of influences, acting on the different races by natural causes, such as the diversity of climate, barrenness or richness of soil, insular or continental position, &c. &c. These local differences no doubt produce effects which extend far beyond purely physical necessities; they create and determine particular needs in a more elevated sphere; finally, they determine the laws, and exercise an influence even on religions.

It is, on the other hand, with institutions as with everything else. Vague in their origin, they pass through periods of development and perfection, to arrive in time at their decadence; and, conforming to the laws of man's nature, they have, like him, their infancy, their youth, their age of strength and reason, and their age of decay.

Two elements alone remain in all their strength, and never cease to exercise their indestructible influence with equal power. These are the precepts of morality, religious as well as social, and the necessities created by locality. From the time that men attempt to swerve from these bases, to become rebels against these sovereign arbiters of their destinies, society suffers from a *malaise* which sooner or later will lead to a state of convulsion. . . .

The progress of the human mind has been extremely rapid in the course of the last three centuries. This progress having been accelerated more rapidly than the growth of wisdom (the only counterpoise to passions and to error); a revolution prepared by the false systems, the fatal errors into which many of the most illustrious sovereigns of the last half of the eighteenth century fell, has at last broken out in a country advanced in knowledge, and enervated by pleasure, in a country inhabited by a people whom one can only regard as frivolous, from the facility with which they comprehend and the difficulty they experience in judging calmly.

Having now thrown a rapid glance over the first causes of the present state of society, it is necessary to point out in a more particular manner the evil which threatens to deprive it, at one blow, of the real blessings, the fruits of genuine civilisation, and to disturb it in the midst of its enjoyments. This evil may be described in one word—presumption; the natural effect of the rapid progression of the human mind towards the perfecting of so many things. This it is which at the present day leads so many individuals astray, for it has become an almost universal sentiment.

Religion, morality, legislation, economy, politics, administration, all have become common and accessible to everyone. Knowledge seems to come by inspiration; experience has no value for the presumptuous man; faith is nothing to him; he substitutes for it a pretended individual conviction, and to arrive at this conviction dispenses with all inquiry and with all study; for these means appear too trivial to a mind which believes itself strong enough to embrace at one glance all questions and all facts. Laws have no value for him, because he has not contributed to make them, and it would be beneath a man of his parts to recognise the limits traced by rude and ignorant generations. Power resides in himself; why should he submit himself to that which was only useful for the man deprived of light and knowledge? . . .

It is principally the middle classes of society which this moral gangrene has affected, and it is only among them that the real heads of the party are found.

For the great mass of the people it has no attraction and can have none. The labours to which this class—the real people—are obliged to devote themselves, are too continuous and too positive to allow them to throw themselves into vague abstractions and ambitions. The people know what is the happiest thing for them: namely, to be able to count on the morrow, for it is the morrow which will repay them for the cares and sorrows of to-day. The laws which afford a just protection to individuals, to families, and to property, are quite simple in their essence. The people dread any movement which injures industry and brings new burdens in its train.

Men in the higher classes of society who join the revolution are either falsely ambitious men or, in the widest acceptation of the word, lost spirits. Their career, moreover, is generally short! They are the first victims of political reforms, and the part played by the small number among them who survive is mostly that of courtiers despised by upstarts, their inferiors, promoted to the first dignities of the State; and of this France, Germany, Italy, and Spain furnish a number of living examples.

We do not believe that fresh disorders with a directly revolutionary end—not even revolutions in the palace and the highest places in the Government—are to be feared at present in France, because of the decided aversion of the people to anything which might disturb the peace they are now enjoying after so many troubles and disasters.

In Germany, as in Spain and Italy, the people ask only for peace and quiet.

In all four countries the agitated classes are principally composed of wealthy men—real cosmopolitans, securing their personal advantage at the expense of any order of things whatever—paid State officials, men of letters, lawyers, and the individuals charged with the public education.

To these classes may be added that of the falsely ambitious, whose number is never considerable among the lower orders, but is larger in the higher ranks of society.

There is besides scarcely any epoch which does not offer a rallying cry to some particular faction. This cry, since 1815, has been *Constitution.* But do not let us deceive ourselves: this word, susceptible of great latitude of interpretation, would be but imperfectly understood if we supposed that the factions attached quite the same meaning to it under the different *régimes.* Such is certainly not the case. In pure monarchies it is qualified by the name of "national representation." In countries which have lately been brought under the representative *régime* it is called "development," and promises charters and fundamental laws. In the only State which possesses an ancient national representation it takes "reform" as its object. Everywhere it means change and trouble. . . .

Europe thus presents itself to the impartial observer under an aspect at the same time deplorable and peculiar. We find everywhere the people praying for the maintenance of peace and tranquillity, faithful to God and their Princes, remaining proof against the efforts and seductions of the factions who call themselves friends of the people and wish to lead them to an agitation which the people themselves do not desire!

The Governments, having lost their balance, are frightened, intimidated, and thrown into confusion by the cries of the intermediary class of society, which, placed between the Kings and their subjects, breaks the sceptre of the monarch, and usurps the cry of the people—that class so often disowned by the people, and nevertheless too much listened to, caressed and feared by those who could with one word reduce it again to nothingness.

We see this intermediary class abandon itself with a blind fury and animosity which proves much more its own fears than any confidence in the success of its enterprises, to all the means which seem proper to assuage its thirst for power, applying itself to the task of persuading Kings that their rights are confined to sitting upon a throne, while those of the people are to govern, and to attack all that centuries have bequeathed as holy and worthy of man's respect—denying, in fact, the value of the past, and declaring themselves the masters of the future. We see this class take all sorts of disguises, uniting and subdividing as occasion offers, helping each other in the hour of danger, and the next day depriving each other of all their conquests. It takes possession of the press, and employs it to promote impiety, disobedience to the laws of religion and the State, and goes so far as to preach murder as a duty for those who desire what is good. . . .

We are convinced that society can no longer be saved without strong and vigorous resolutions on the part of the Governments still free in their opinions and actions.

We are also convinced that this may yet be, if the Governments face the truth, if they free themselves from all illusion, if they join their ranks and take their stand on a line of correct, unambiguous, and frankly announced principles.

By this course the monarchs will fulfil the duties imposed upon them by Him who, by entrusting them with power, has charged them to watch over the maintenance of justice, and the rights of all, to avoid the paths of error, and tread firmly in the way of truth. Placed beyond the passions which agitate society, it is in days of trial chiefly that they are called upon to despoil realities of their false appearances, and to show themselves as they are, fathers invested with the authority belonging by right to the heads of families, to prove that, in days of mourning, they know how to be just, wise, and therefore strong, and that they will not abandon the people whom they ought to govern to be the sport of factions, to error and its consequences, which must involve the loss of society. . . .

The Governments, in establishing the principle of *stability*, will in no wise exclude the development of what is good, for stability is not immobility. But it is for those who are burdened with the heavy task of government to augment the well-being of their people! It is for Governments to regulate it according to necessity and to suit the times. It is not by concessions, which the factions strive to force from legitimate power, and which they have neither the right to claim nor the faculty of keeping within just bounds, that wise reforms can be carried out. That all the good possible should be done is our most ardent wish; but that which is not good must never be confounded with that which is, and even real good should be done only by those who unite to the right of authority the means of enforcing it. Such should be also the sincere wish of the people, who know by sad experience the value of certain phrases and the nature of certain caresses.

Respect for all that is; liberty for every Government to watch over the well-being of its own people; a league between all Governments against factions in all States; contempt for the meaningless words which have become the rallying cry of the factions; respect for the progressive development of institutions in lawful ways; refusal on the part of every monarch to aid or succour partisans under any mask whatever—such are happily the ideas of the great monarchs: the world will be saved if they bring them into action—it is lost if they do not.

Union between the monarchs is the basis of the policy which must now be followed to save society from total ruin. . . .

The first and greatest concern for the immense majority of every nation is the stability of the laws, and their uninterrupted action—never their change. Therefore let the Governments govern, let them maintain the groundwork of their institutions, both ancient and modern; for if it is at all times dangerous to touch them, it certainly would not now, in the general confusion, be wise to do so.

Let them announce this determination to their people, and demonstrate it by facts. Let them reduce the Doctrinaires to silence within their States, and show their contempt for them abroad. Let them not encourage by their attitude or actions the suspicion of being favourable or indifferent to error: let them not allow it to be believed that experience has lost all its rights to make way for experiments which at the least are dangerous. Let them be precise and clear in all their words, and not seek by concessions to gain over those parties who aim at the destruction of all power but their own, whom concessions will never gain over, but only further embolden in their pretensions to power.

Let them in these troublous times be more than usually cautious in attempting real ameliorations, not imperatively claimed by the needs of the moment, to the end that good itself may not turn against them—which is the case whenever a Government measure seems to be inspired by fear.

Let them not confound concessions made to parties with the good they ought to do for their people, in modifying, according to their recognised needs, such branches of the administration as require it.

Let them give minute attention to the financial state of their kingdoms, so that their people may enjoy, by the reduction of public burdens, the real, not imaginary, benefits of a state of peace.

Let them be just, but strong; beneficent, but strict.

Let them maintain religious principles in all their purity, and not allow the faith to be attacked and morality interpreted according to the *social contract* or the visions of foolish sectarians.

Let them suppress Secret Societies, that gangrene of society.

In short, let the great monarchs strengthen their union, and prove to the world that if it exists, it is beneficent, and ensures the political peace of Europe: that it is powerful only for the maintenance of tranquillity at a time when so many attacks are directed against it; that the principles which they profess are paternal and protective, menacing only the disturbers of public tranquillity.

CZAR ALEXANDER HIMSELF was the inspiration behind the Holy Alliance of 1815, a rather visionary outgrowth of the Congress of Vienna, which united Russia, Prussia, and Austria on the principles of royal paternalism, devotion to the Christian religion, and the preservation of the status quo.

2. THE HOLY ALLIANCE, 1815

SOURCE. *Translations and Reprints from the Original Sources of European History,* Series I, Vol. I, No. 3, Philadelphia: University of Pennsylvania Press, 1894, pp. 9–10. Reprinted by permission of the University of Pennsylvania Press.

IN THE NAME OF THE VERY HOLY AND INDIVISIBLE TRINITY

Their majesties, the Emperor of Austria, the King of Prussia and the Emperor of Russia, in view of the great events which the last three years have brought to pass in Europe and in view especially of the benefits which it has pleased Divine Providence to confer upon those states whose governments have placed their confidence and their hope in Him alone, having reached the profound conviction that the policy of the powers, in their mutual relations, ought to be guided by the sublime truths taught by the eternal religion of God our Saviour, solemnly declare that the present act has no other aim than to manifest to the world their unchangeable determination to adopt no other rule of conduct, either in the government of their respective countries or in their political relations with other governments, than the precepts of that holy religion, the precepts of justice, charity and peace. These, far from being applicable exclusively to private life, ought on the contrary directly to control the resolutions of princes and to guide their steps as the sole means of establishing human institutions and of remedying their imperfections. Hence their majesties have agreed upon the following articles:

Article I. Conformably to the words of Holy Scripture which command all men to look upon each other as brothers, the three contracting monarchs will continue united by the bonds of a true and indissoluble fraternity and, regarding themselves as compatriots, they shall lend aid and assistance to each other on all occasions and in all places, viewing themselves, in their relations to their subjects and to their armies, as fathers of families, they shall direct them in the same spirit of fraternity by which they are animated for the protection of religion, peace and justice.

Article II. Hence the sole principle of conduct, be it between the said government or their subjects, shall be that of rendering mutual service, and testifying by unceasing good-will, the mutual affection with which they should be animated. Considering themselves all as members of one great Christian nation, the three allied princes look upon themselves as delegates of Providence called upon to govern three branches of the same family, viz: Austria, Russia and Prussia. They thus confess that the Christian nation, of which they and their people form a part, has in reality no other sovereign than He alone to whom belongs by right the power, for in Him alone are to be found all the treasures of love, of knowledge and of infinite wisdom, that is to say God, our Divine Saviour Jesus Christ, the word of the Most High, the word of life. Their majesties recommend, therefore, to their peoples, as the sole means of enjoying that peace which springs from a good conscience and is alone enduring, to fortify themselves each day in the principles and practice of those duties which the Divine Saviour has taught to men.

Article III. All those powers who wish solemnly to make avowal of the sacred principles which have dictated the present act, and who would recognize how important it is to the happiness of nations, too long agitated, that these truths should hereafter exercise upon human destiny all the influence belonging to them, shall be received into this Holy Alliance with as much cordiality as affection.

Engrossed in three copies and signed at Paris, year of grace, 1815, September 14/26.

FRANCIS

Signed .... FREDERICK   WILLIAM

ALEXANDER

Part IV

THE REVOLUTIONS
OF 1830 AND 1848

A. 1830

THE JULY REVOLUTION of 1830 resulted in the overthrow of the Bourbon monarchy in France, the establishment of a new "liberal" monarchy in the person of the Duke of Orleans, Louis-Philippe (1830–1848), and the upsurge of revolutionary violence throughout Europe. The response in other countries to the July Revolution in France is described enthusiastically by Louis Blanc (1811–1882) in his History of Ten Years, 1830–1840. *Louis Blanc, a devoted revolutionary, was to play a major role in the subsequent Revolution of 1848.*

1. LOUIS BLANC DESCRIBES EUROPE'S REACTION TO THE JULY REVOLUTION, 1830

SOURCE. Louis Blanc, *The History of Ten Years, 1830–1840*, London: Chapman and Hall, 1844, I, p. 251. Reprinted by permission of Chapman & Hall Ltd.

That revolution [in France, of July 1830] sent a universal thrill through the world. The nations that had been enthralled by the treaties of 1815 were aroused. The apparition of the tricolour flag floating over the French consulate in Warsaw made the true hearts of the Poles, our old brethren in arms, beat high with hope. At Brussels, Liege, and Antwerp, men asked themselves at last by what right two millions of Dutchmen commanded four millions of Belgians. The Rhenine provinces, which, though they did not speak our language, wished to retain our laws, desired to belong to us from pride. A formidable fermentation was manifested in the German universities, till then tormented by vague aspirations after liberty. But nothing could compare with the movement that pervaded Italy. Throughout the whole peninsula, including the Roman states, the enthusiasm was boundless. In the streets, the squares, and all public places, the multitude thronged round travellers from France; they made them read aloud the journals of their country; and when they had thus recounted to their eager listeners some of the prodigious events recently enacted on the banks of the Seine, a unanimous burst of applause followed the recital, mingled with cries and sobs. It is almost literally true that for several days the Italians never ceased to look towards the Alps, expecting every hour to see the French descending from them. The revolution of July derived from distance something of a marvellous character; and the people of France sprang up again, in the eyes of wondering Europe, in the gigantic proportions given to it by the Republic, and, after the republic, by the Empire.

THE HIGH HOPES of French liberals in 1830 are expressed artistically in Eugène Delacroix's painting Liberty Leading the People.

2. EUGÈNE DELACROIX, *LIBERTY LEADING THE PEOPLE*

B. 1848

THE SUPERFICIALITY of Louis-Philippe's liberalism and the continued growth of French republican sentiment resulted in the overthrow of the Orleanist monarchy in the February Revolution of 1848. The keen observer Alexis de Tocqueville described in his Recollections *the popular, lower-class basis of the February Revolution.*

1. ALEXIS DE TOCQUEVILLE ON THE FEBRUARY REVOLUTION, 1848

SOURCE. *The Recollections of Alexis de Tocqueville,* J. P. Mayer, ed., Alexander Texeira de Mattos, tr., New York: Columbia University Press, 1949, pp. 73–74. Reprinted by permission of Columbia University Press.

I spent the whole afternoon in walking about Paris. Two things in particular struck me: the first was, I will not say the mainly, but the uniquely and exclusively popular character of the revolution that had just taken place; the omnipotence it had given to the people properly so-called—that is to say, the classes who work with their hands—over all others. The second was the comparative absence of malignant passion, or, as a matter of fact, of any keen passion—an absence which at once made it clear that the lower orders had suddenly become masters of Paris.

Although the working classes had often played the leading part in the events of the First Revolution, they had never been the sole leaders and masters of the State, either *de facto* or *de jure;* it is doubtful whether the Convention contained a single man of the people; it was composed of *bourgeois* and men of letters. The war between the Mountain and the Girondists was conducted on both sides by members of the middle class, and the triumph of the former never brought power down into the hands of the people alone. The Revolution of July was effected by the people, but the middle class had stirred it up and led it, and secured the principal fruits of it. The Revolution of February, on the contrary, seemed to be made entirely outside the *bourgeoisie* and against it.

In this great concussion, the two parties of which the social body in France is mainly composed, had, in a way, been thrown more completely asunder, and the mass of the people, which had stood alone, remained in sole possession of power.

THE HOPES of the working classes were disappointed, however, by the bourgeois policies of the republican government that came into power. Later in the year a new wave of popular violence, known as the "June Days," terrorized Paris until suppressed by the army. Tocqueville describes the turbulence of the June Days in vivid terms.

2. ALEXIS DE TOCQUEVILLE ON THE JUNE DAYS, 1848

SOURCE. *The Recollections of Alexis de Tocqueville*, J. P. Mayer, ed., Alexander Texeira de Mattos, tr., New York: Columbia University Press, 1949, pp. 180–181. Reprinted by permission of Columbia University Press.

In the evening [June 26] I decided to go myself to the Hôtel de Ville, in order to obtain more certain news of the results of the day. The insurrection, after alarming me by its violence, now alarmed me by its long duration. For who could foresee the effect which the sight of so long and uncertain a conflict might produce in some parts of France, and especially in the great manufacturing towns, such as Lyons? As I went along the Quai de la Ferraille, I met some National Guards from my neighbourhood, carrying on litters several of their comrades and two of their officers wounded. I observed, in talking with them, with what terrible rapidity, even in so civilized a century as our own, the most peaceful minds enter, as it were, into the spirit of civil war, and how quick they are, in these unhappy times, to acquire a taste for violence and a contempt for human life. The men with whom I was talking were peaceful, sober artisans, whose gentle and somewhat sluggish natures were still further removed from cruelty than from heroism. Yet they dreamt of nothing but massacre and destruction. They complained that they were not allowed to use bombs or to sap and mine the streets held by the insurgents, and they were determined to show no more quarter; already that morning I had almost seen a poor devil shot before my eyes on the boulevards, who had been arrested without arms in his hands, but whose mouth and hands were blackened by a substance which they supposed to be, and which no doubt was, powder. I did all I could to calm these rabid sheep. I promised them we should take terrible measures the next day. Lamoricière, in fact, had told me that morning that he had sent for shells to hurl behind the barricades; and I knew that a regiment of sappers was expected from Douai, to pierce the walls and blow up the besieged houses with petards. I added that they must not shoot any of their prisoners, but that they should kill then and there anyone who made as though to defend himself. I left my men a little more contented, and, continuing my road, I could not help examining myself and feeling surprised at the nature of the arguments I had used, and the promptness with which, in two days, I had become familiarized with those ideas of inexorable destruction which were naturally so foreign to my character.

AS IN 1830 SO IN 1848 the revolutionary unrest that began in France spread quickly across Europe. Metternich was obliged to flee Vienna in disguise, and barricades were thrown up on the streets of Berlin. In general, however, the 1848 revolutions failed. The Second Republic in France gave way to a revival of the Empire under Napoleon III, and elsewhere the old monarchs managed to retain their lands and dominions. The goals of the revolutionaries in France had been liberalism and social justice, but elsewhere in Europe nationalism was a potent factor in revolutionary sentiment. In Italy and Hungary, for example, the goal was independence from the Austrian monarchy. The Hungarian rebel Louis Kossuth (1802–1894) rose for a brief, glorious moment to the leadership of an independent Hungary. When Austria reasserted her control, Kossuth fled into exile. From Harrisburg, Pennsylvania, in 1852, he appealed for American support in the struggle for national independence in Hungary. Kossuth looked back with considerable optimism on the achievements of 1848, and expressed his faith and confidence in the future of European liberalism.

3. FAILURE AND HOPE: LOUIS KOSSUTH, FROM "THE PRESENT WEAKNESS OF DESPOTISM," 1852

SOURCE. Guy Carleton Lee, ed., *The World's Orators*, New York: G. P. Putnam's Sons, 1900, V, pp. 222, 224–230, 233–236. Reprinted by permission of G. P. Putnam's Sons.

. . . let those imposed upon by the attitude of despotism in 1852, consider how much stronger it was in 1847–8. . . .

Austria had not for centuries, and Prussia never yet has, experienced what sort of a thing a revolution is, and the falling of the vault of the sky would have been considered less improbable than a popular revolution in Berlin or Vienna, where Metternich rules in triumphant, proud security.

The House of Austria was considered as a mighty power on earth; respected, because thought necessary to Europe against the preponderance of Russia. No people under the dominion of this dynasty had a national army, and all were divided by absurd rivalries of language, kept up by Metternich's Machiavelianism. The nations were divided; none of them was conscious of its strength, but all were aware of the united strength of a disciplined and large imperial army, the regiments of which had never yet fought one against another, and never yet had broken the spell of the black and yellow flag by tearing it to pieces with their own hands.

And yet, when Paris stirred and I made a mere speech in the Hungarian Parliament, the House of Austria was presently at the mercy of the people of Vienna; Metternich was driven away, and his absolutism replaced by a promise of constitutional life.

In Galicia the odium connected with the despotic Austrian rule had, by satanic craft, been thrown upon those classes which represent the ancient Polish nationality; and the well deserved hatred of aristocratic oppression, though living only in traditional remembrances, had prevailed in the sentiments of the common people over the hatred against Austria, though despotic and a stranger; so much so, that, to triumph over the ill-advised, untimely movement in 1846, Austria had nothing to do but open the field to murder, by granting a two dollars' reward for every head of a Polish land proprietor.

And in Hungary the people of every race were equally excluded from all political right—from any share of constitutional life. The endeavors of myself and my friends for internal improvement—for emancipation of the peasantry—for the people's restoration to its natural rights in civil, political, social, and religious respects—were cramped by the Hapsburg policy. But the odium of this cramping was thrown by Austria upon our own conservative party: and thus our national force was divided into antagonistic elements.

Besides, the idea of Panslavism and of national rivalries, raised by Russia and fostered by Austria, diverted the excitement of the public mind from the development of common political freedom. And Hungary had no national army. Its regiments were filled with foreign elements and scattered over foreign countries, while our own country was guarded with well disciplined foreign troops. And what was far worse than all this, Hungary, by long illegalities, corrupted in its own character, deprived of its ancient heroic stamp, Germanized in its salons, sapped in its cottages and huts, impressed with the unavoidable fatality of Austrian sovereignty and the knowledge of Austrian power, secluded from the attention of the world, which was scarcely aware of its existence,—Hungary had no hope in its national future, because it had no consciousness of its strength, and was highly monarchical in its inclinations and generous in its allegiance to the King. No man dreamed of the possibility of a revolution there, and he who would have suggested it would only have gained the reputation of a madman.

Such was the condition of Europe in the first half of February, 1848. Never yet seemed the power of despots more steady, more sure. Yet, one month later, every throne on the continent trembled except the Czar's.

The existence of dynasties depended upon the magnanimity of their people, and Europe was all on fire.

And in what condition is Europe today? Every man on earth is aware that things cannot endure as they are. Formerly millions believed that a peaceful development of constitutional monarchy was the only future reserved for Europe. Now nobody on the European continent any longer believes that constitutional monarchy can have a future there. Absolutist reaction goes with all that arrogance which revolts every sentiment and infuriates the very child in its mother's arms. The promise, the word, the oath of a king are become equivalent to a lie and to perjury. Faith in the morality of kings is plucked out, even to the last root, from the people's heart.

The experiment of constitutional concessions was thought dangerous to the dynasties, as soon as they became aware that the people of Europe is no imbecile child, that can be lulled to sleep by mockery, but that it will have reality. Thus the kings on the greater part of the continent, throwing away the mask of liberal affectations, deceived every expectation, broke every oath, and embarked with a full gale upon the open sea of unrestricted despotism. They know that love they can no longer get; so we have been told openly that they will not have love, but money, to maintain large armies, and keep the world in servitude. On the other hand, the nations, assailed in their moral dignity and material welfare, degraded into a flock of sheep kept only to be shorn, equally with the kings detest the mockery of constitutional royalty which has proved so ruinous to them.

Royalty has lost its sacredness in France, Germany, Italy, Austria, and Hungary. Both parties equally recognize that the time has come when the struggle of principles must be decided. Absolutism or republicanism —the Czar or the principles of America—there is no more compromise, no more truce possible. The two antagonist principles must meet upon the narrow bridge of a knife-edge, cast across the deep gulf which is ready to swallow him who falls. It is a struggle for life and death.

That is the condition of the European continent in general. A great, terrible, bloody uprising is unavoidable. That is known and felt by every one. And every sound man knows equally well that the temporary success of Louis Napoleon's usurpation has only made the terrible crisis more unavoidable. . . .

Should we, not meeting here with that support, which your glorious Republic in its public capacity and your generous citizens in their private capacity can afford without jeopardizing your own welfare and your own interest (and assuredly it never came into my mind to desire more)— should we, meeting with no support here, be crushed again, and absolutism consolidate its power upon the ruins of murdered nations, I indeed cannot but believe that it would become a historical reproach of conscience, lying like an incubus upon the breast of the people of the United States from generation to generation. I mean, the idea that had you not withheld that support which you might have afforded consistently with your own interest, Hungary perhaps would be a free, flourishing country, instead of being blotted out from the map, and Europe perhaps free, and absolutist tyranny swept from the earth.

You then would in vain shed a tear of compassion over our sad fate, and mourn over the grave of nations: not only so; but the victory of absolutism could not fail to be felt even here in your mighty and blessed home. You would first feel it in your commercial intercourse, and ere long you would become inevitably entangled; for as soon as the Czar had secured the submission of all Europe, he would not look indifferently upon the development of your power, which is an embodiment of republican principles. . . .

Without money there is no war. Now, the nations, when once engaged in the war, will find means enough for home-support of the war in the rich resources of their own land; whereas the despots lose the disposal of those resources by the outbreak of insurrection, and are reduced entirely to foreign loans, which no emperor of Austria will find again in any new revolution.

And, mark well, gentlemen, every friendly step by which your great Republic and its generous people testifies its lively interest for our just cause, adding to the prospects of success, diminishes the credit of the despots, and by embarrassing their attempts to find loans, may be of decisive weight in the issue.

Though absolutism was much more favorably situated in 1847 than in 1851, it was overtaken by the events of 1848, when, but for the want of unity and concert, the liberal party must have triumphed everywhere. That unity and concert is now attained; why should not absolutism in 1852 be as easily shaken as in 1848?

The liberal cause is stronger everywhere, because conscious of its aim and prepared. Absolutism has no more bayonets now than in 1848. Without the interference of Russia our success is not only probable, but is almost sure.

And as to Russia, remember, that if at such a crisis she thinks of subduing Hungary, she has Poland to occupy, Finland to guard, Turkey to watch, and Circassia to fight.

Herein is the reason why I confidently state if the United States declare that a new intervention of Russia will be considered by your glorious Republic a violation of the law of nations, that declaration will be respected, and Russia will not interfere.

Be pleased to consider the consequence of such renewed interference, after the passive acceptance of the first has proved so fatal to Europe, and so dangerous even to England itself. We can scarcely doubt that, if ever Russia plans a new invasion, England could not forbear to encourage Turkey not to lose again the favorable opportunity to shake off the preponderance of Russia. I have lived in Turkey. I know what enthusiasm exists there for that idea, and how popular such a war would be. Turkey is a match for Russia on the continent. The weak point of Turkey lies in the nearness of Sevastopol, the Russian harbor and arsenal, to Constantinople. Well, an English fleet, or an American fleet, or both joined, stationed at the mouth of the Bosphorus, may easily prevent this danger without one cannon-shot; and if this be prevented, Turkey would not stand alone. The brave Circassians, triumphant through a war of ten years, would send down eighty thousand of their unconquerable horsemen to the plains of Moscow. And Poland would rise, and Sweden would remember Finland and Charles XII. With Hungary in the rear, screened by this very circumstance from her invasion, and Austria fallen to pieces for want of foreign support, Russia must respect your protest in behalf of international law, or else she will fall never to rise again.

Gentlemen, I thank you for the patience with which you have listened to this exposition—long and tedious, because I had no time to be brief. And begging leave to assure you of my lasting gratitude for all the generous favors you have been and will yet be pleased to bestow upon my cause, let me proclaim my fervent wishes in this sentiment:

"Pennsylvania, the Keystone State—May it, by its legitimate influence upon the destinies of this mighty power on earth, and by the substantial generosity of its citizens, soon become the keystone of European independence."

Industrialism
and Its Consequences

THE Industrial Revolution, with its radically new organization of the processes of production, began in England in the later eighteenth century. During the nineteenth century it spread to Belgium, France, Germany, the United States, and elsewhere. At the present time it is still continuing to spread. The development of the factory system, and the dramatic population shift from countryside to city, created severe social problems for nineteenth-century Europe and America and, indeed, transformed the social structure. There now emerged two new and often mutually hostile classes—the factory owners and the factory workers —the "capitalists" and the "proletarians," in Marxist terminology. The profound social dislocation and urban poverty wrought by the Industrial Revolution created severe problems to which the political and intellectual leaders of the nineteenth century reacted in a number of ways. As industrialization continues, these problems, and the reactions to them, remain deeply relevant to our own age.

A number of economists in England remained faithful to the *laissez-faire* philosophy of Adam Smith. But influenced also by the pessimistic Malthusian notion that human fecundity outstripped productivity, they tended to take a more somber view of economic reality than did Smith. Poverty to them was unfortunate but inevitable, and any attempt to mitigate it would be not merely pernicious but useless. The works of these *laissez-faire* economists won for their discipline the name "the dismal science."

The unhappy condition of the proletariat evoked a far different response among the Socialist and Communist thinkers of the nineteenth century. These men undertook a direct attack against the concept of private ownership on which the capitalist system was based, argued that the factory owners were unnecessary social parasites, and insisted that the organs of production should be owned by the workers themselves through a proletarian-dominated state. Socialism tended at first to be visionary and utopian, but with the writings of Karl Marx it took on a more scientific, hard-headed character and became rigorously systematic. The European Communist movement, rooted in Marxist thought, made important gains in the later nineteenth and early twentieth centuries. By no means a monolithic force, it was sharply divided as to the best method of achieving the Communist society. Revisionist Marxists argued that the proletariat could rise to power gradually by winning elections and eventually gaining control of national legislatures. Strict Marxists such as Lenin held to the belief that the transition from capitalism to Communism could only take place by violent revolution. All were agreed, however, that the workers were destined to control society and that the replacement of capitalism by Communism was inevitable.

Part I

THE INDUSTRIAL REVOLUTION

A. The Practical Effects

THE WRETCHED CONDITIONS to be found in the factories of the early Industrial Revolution, and the hesitancy of the British government to impose any but the loosest sorts of restrictions on the exploitation of industrial labor, are suggested in the English Factory Act of 1802.

1. THE ENGLISH FACTORY ACT OF 1802

SOURCE. Statutes at Large, XLIII, 632 f.: 42 George III, c.73.

An act for the preservation of the health and morals of apprentices and others employed in cotton and other mills. . . . Be it enacted that . . . all such mills and factories within Great Britain and Ireland, wherein three or more apprentices or twenty or more other persons shall at any time be employed, shall be subject to the . . . rules and regulations contained in this act . . . :

. . . the rooms and apartments in or belonging to any such mill or factory shall, twice at least in every year, be well and sufficiently washed with quick lime and water over every part of the walls and ceiling thereof; and . . . due care and attention shall be paid by the master and mistress of such mills or factories to provide a sufficient number of windows and openings in such rooms or apartments, to insure a proper supply of fresh air. . . .

. . . every . . . master or mistress shall constantly supply every apprentice . . . with two whole and complete suits of clothing . . . , one new complete suit being delivered to such apprentice once at least in every year. . . .

. . . no apprentice . . . bound to any such master or mistress shall be employed or compelled to work for more than twelve hours in any one day. . . . Provided always that, from and after the first day of June, 1803, no apprentice shall be employed or compelled to work upon any occasion whatever between the hours of nine of the clock at night and six of the clock in the morning. . . .

. . . every apprentice shall be instructed in some part of every working day, for the first four years at least of his or her apprenticeship . . . , in reading, writing, and arithmetic . . . such instruction . . . shall be deemed . . . part . . . of the respective periods . . . during which any such apprentice shall be employed or compelled to work. . . .

. . . the room or apartment in which any male apprentice shall sleep shall be entirely separate and distinct from the room or apartment in which any female apprentice shall sleep, and . . . not more than two apprentices shall in any case sleep in the same bed. . . .

. . . every apprentice . . . shall, for the space of one hour at least every Sunday, be instructed and examined in the principles of the Christian religion . . . ; and such master or mistress shall send all his or her apprentices under the care of some proper person, once in a month at least, to attend during divine service in the church of the parish. . . .

And be it further enacted that the justices of the peace for every county . . . shall . . . appoint two persons, not interested in or in any way connected with any such mills or factories, to be visitors . . . ; and the said visitors, or either of them, shall have full power and authority . . . to enter into and inspect any such mill or factory at any time of the day . . . , and . . . report from time to time in writing to the quarter sessions of the peace the state and condition of such mills and factories.

A GENERATION LATER, the British government, succumbing to reformist pressure, conducted an investigation of factory conditions in which the Sadler Committee heard testimony from workers and other employees of the factory owners. The Sadler Committee was predisposed to reform and sought in its hearings to expose the terrible conditions that existed in the factories.

2. TESTIMONY BEFORE THE SADLER COMMITTEE ON FACTORY CONDITIONS

SOURCE. *Parliamentary Papers, Reports from Committees,* XV, "Labour of Children in Factories, 1831–1832," London, 1832.

ELIZABETH BENTLEY, CALLED IN; AND EXAMINED.

5127. What age are you?—Twenty-three.

5128. Where do you live?—At Leeds.

5129. What time did you begin to work at a factory?—When I was six years old.

5130. At whose factory did you work?—At Mr. Busk's.

5131. What kind of mill is it?—Flax-mill.

5132. What was your business in that mill?—I was a little doffer.

5133. What were your hours of labour in that mill?—From 5 in the morning till 9 at night, when they were thronged.

5134. For how long a time together have you worked that excessive length of time?—For about half a year.

5135. What were your usual hours of labour when you were not so thronged?—From 6 in the morning till 7 at night.

5136. What time was allowed for your meals?—Forty minutes at noon.

5137. Had you any time to get your breakfast or drinking?—No, we got it as we could.

5138. And when your work was bad, you hardly had anytime to eat at all?—No; we were obliged to leave it or take it home, and when we did not take it, the overlooker took it, and gave it to his pigs.

5139. Do you consider doffing a laborious employment?—Yes.

5140. Explain what it is you had to do?—When the frames are full, they have to stop the frames, and take the flyers off, and take the full bobbins off, and carry them to the roller; and then put empty ones on, and set the frame going again.

5141. Does that keep you constantly on your feet?—Yes, there are so many frames, and they run so quick.

5142. Your labour is very excessive?—Yes; you have not time for any thing.

5143. Suppose you flagged a little, or were too late, what would they do?—Strap us.

5144. Are they in the habit of strapping those who are last in doffing?—Yes.

5145. Constantly?—Yes.

5146. Girls as well as boys?—Yes.

5147. Have you ever been strapped?—Yes.

5148. Severely?—Yes.

5149. Is the strap used so as to hurt you excessively?—Yes, it is.

5150. Were you strapped if you were too much fatigued to keep up with the machinery?—Yes; the overlooker I was under was a very severe man, and when we have been fatigued and worn out, and had not baskets to put the bobbins in, we used to put them in the window bottoms, and that broke the panes sometimes, and I broke one one time, and the over-looker strapped me on the arm, and it rose a blister, and I ran home to my mother.

5151. How long did you work at Mr. Busk's?—Three or four years.

5152. Where did you go to then?—Benyon's factory.

5153. That was when you were about 10 years?—Yes.

5154. What were you then?—A weigher in the card-room.

5155. How long did you work there?—From half-past 5 till 8 at night.

5156. Was that the ordinary time?—Till 9 when they were thronged.

5157. What time was allowed for meals at that mill?—Forty minutes at noon.

5158. Any time at breakfast or drinking?—Yes, for the card-rooms, but not for the spinning-rooms, a quarter of an hour to get their breakfast.

5159. And the same for their drinking?—Yes.

5160. So that the spinners in that room worked from half-past 5 till 9 at night?—Yes.

5161. Having only forty minutes' rest?—Yes.

5162. The carding-room is more oppressive than the spinning depart-ment?—Yes, it is so dusty they cannot see each other for dust.

5163. It is on that account they are allowed a relaxation of those few minutes?—Yes; the cards get so soon filled up with waste and dirt, they are obliged to stop them, or they would take fire.

5164. There is a convenience in that stoppage?—Yes, it is as much for their benefit as for the working people.

5165. When it was not necessary no such indulgence was allowed?—No.

5166. Never?—No.

5167. Were the children beat up to their labour there?—Yes.

5168. With what?—A strap; I have seen the overlooker go to the top end of the room, where the little girls hug the can to the backminders; [1] he has taken a strap, and a whistle in his mouth, and sometimes he has got a chain and chained them, and strapped them all down the room.

5169. All the children?—No, only those hugging the cans.

5170. What was his reason for that?—He was angry.

5171. Had the children committed any fault?—They were too slow.

5172. Were the children excessively fatigued at that time?—Yes, it was in the afternoon.

5173. Were the girls so struck as to leave marks upon their skin?—Yes, they have had black marks many times, and their parents dare not come to him about it, they were afraid of losing their work.

5174. If the parents were to complain of this excessive ill-usage, the probable consequence would be the loss of the situation of the child?—Yes.

5175. In what part of the mill did you work?—In the card-room.

5176. It was exceedingly dusty?—Yes.

---

[1] A wooden vehicle that persons were tied to when punishment was administered.

5177. Did it affect your health?—Yes; it was so dusty, the dust got upon my lungs, and the work was so hard; I was middling strong when I went there, but the work was so bad; I got so bad in health, that when I pulled the baskets down, I pulled my bones out of their places.

5178. You dragged the baskets?—Yes; down the rooms to where they are worked.

5179. And as you had been weakened by excessive labour, you could not stand that labour?—No.

5180. It has had the effect of pulling your shoulders out?—Yes; it was a great basket that stood higher than this table a good deal.

5181. How heavy was it?—I cannot say; it was a very large one, that was full of weights up-heaped, and pulling the basket pulled my shoulders out of its place, and my ribs have grown over it.

5182. You continued at that work?—Yes.

5183. You think that work is too much for children?—Yes.

5184. It is woman's work, not fit for children?—Yes.

5185. Is that work generally done by women?—Yes.

5186. How came you to do it?—There was no spinning for me.

5187. Did they give you women's wages?—They gave me 5s. and the women had 6s. 6d.

5188. What wages did you get as a spinner?—Six shillings.

5189. Did you perceive that many other girls were made ill by that long labour?—Yes, a good many of them.

5190. So that you were constantly receiving fresh hands to supply the places of those that could no longer bear their work?—Yes, there were fresh hands every week; they could not keep their hands.

5191. Did they all go away on account of illness?—They were sick and ill with the dust.

5192. Do you know whether any of them died in consequence of it?—No, I cannot speak to that.

5193. You do not know what became of them?—No, we did not know that.

5194. If a person was to take an account of a mill, and the hands in it that were ill, they would know very little of those who had suffered from their labour; they would be elsewhere?—Yes.

5195. But you are sure of this, that they were constantly leaving on account of the excessive labour they had to endure?—Yes.

5196. And the unhealthy nature of their employment?—Yes.

5197. Did you take any means to obviate the bad effects of this dust?—No.

5198. Did it make you very thirsty?—Yes, we drank a deal of water in the room.

5199. Were you heated with your employment at the same time?—No, it was not so very hot as in the summer time; in the winter time they were obliged to have the windows open, it made no matter what the weather was, and sometimes we got very severe colds in frost and snow.

5200. You were constantly exposed to colds, and were made ill by that cause also?—Yes.

5201. Could you eat your food well in that factory?—No, indeed I had not much to eat, and the little I had I could not eat it, my appetite was so poor, and being covered with dust; and it was no use to take it home, I could not eat it, and the overlooker took it, and gave it to the pigs.

5202. You are speaking of the breakfast?—Yes.

5203. How far had you to go for dinner?—We could not go home to dinner.

5204. Where did you dine?—In the mill.

5205. Did you live far from the mill?—Yes, two miles.

5206. Had you a clock?—No, we had not.

5207. Supposing you had not been in time enough in the morning at these mills, what would have been the consequence?—We should have been quartered.

5208. What do you mean by that?—If we were a quarter of an hour too late, they would take off half an hour; we only got a penny an hour, and they would take a halfpenny more.

5209. The fine was much more considerable than the loss of time?—Yes.

5210. Were you also beaten for being late?—No, I was never beaten myself, I have seen the boys beaten for being too late.

5211. Were you generally there in time?—Yes; my mother has been up at 4 o'clock in the morning, and at 2 o'clock in the morning; the colliers used to go to their work about 3 or 4 o'clock, and when she heard them stirring she has got up out of her warm bed, and gone out and asked them the time; and I have sometimes been at Hunslet Car at 2 o'clock in the morning, when it was streaming down with rain, and we have had to stay till the mill was opened.

5212. Supposing your hours of labour had been moderate, could you have awoke regularly?—Yes.

5213. Was it a matter of anxiety and difficulty for you to rouse yourself to be early enough for those hours of labour?—Yes.

5214. You are considerably deformed in your person in consequence of this labour?—Yes, I am.

5215. At what time did it come on?—I was about 13 years old when it began coming, and it has got worse since; it is five years since my mother died, and my mother was never able to get me a pair of good stays to hold me up; and when my mother died I had to do for myself, and got me a pair.

5216. Were you perfectly straight and healthy before you worked at a mill?—Yes, I was as straight as little girl as ever went up and down town.

5217. Were you straight till you were 13?—Yes, I was.

5218. Have you been attended to by any medical gentleman at Leeds or the neighbourhood?—Yes, I have been under Mr. Hares.

5219. To what did he attribute it?—He said it was owing to hard labour, and working in the factories.

5220. He told you that?—Yes.

5221. Did he tell your mother so also?—No, she was not alive; I was coming from Leeds, and he asked a good many questions; he asked me if I had a father and mother; I said "No;" he said if I had no objection he would take me in hand; I said I was much obliged to him; he told me to come to his house that night, and I went to the mill, and told them I was going to stop away; I stopped at home ten weeks, and my cousins, that I was living with, had to maintain me, and they told me they were sure he would not do me any good, and they could not find me with support, and Mr. Hares told me it would be a year before I should be straight again.

5222. You were obliged to return to your work?—Yes.

5223. Did he tell you that this misfortune had come upon you from over-working in the factories?—Yes, he did; he said it was nothing else that brought it on.

5224. Where did you go then?—I went to Mr. Walker's.

5225. How old were you when Mr. Hare saw you?—About 21 years old.

5226. About two years ago?—Yes.

5227. Did the deformity come upon you with much pain and weariness?—Yes; I cannot express the pain I had all the time it was coming.

5228. You went to Fatham and Walker's afterwards?—Yes.

5229. Is that a flax mill?—Yes.

5230. In what situation did you go there?—I went into the spinning-room.

5231. What were the hours of labour there when they were busy?—From half-past 5 in the morning to 8, and half-past 8.

5232. Is it found necessary in that mill to strap the children up to their work?—Yes, the doffers; I have seen them strap them as well as others.

5233. So that as far as you have experience in those factories, these poor children are beaten when so much labour is exacted from them?—There is nothing else for them.

5234. You do not think they could be kept up to their work unless they were so abused?—No, they could not.

5235. In that mill also did they strap the children?—Yes, they did.

5236. Perpetually?—Yes.

5237. What were the hours for refreshment at the mill at the time to which we are alluding?—Forty minutes at noon.

5238. There was no time allowed for drinking or breakfast at that mill? —Yes, they have at present.

5239. Had they before the present measure was in agitation?—No, only forty minutes in winter, and half an hour in summer.

5240. Was that time ever abridged?—Yes.

5241. What time did you work in winter?—From 6 in the morning till 7 or 8, if they were much thronged.

5242. The children in all cases did not have that time allowed them for their dinner?—No.

5243. Was it the general impression among the children that the time allowed them for their noon meal was improperly abridged?—Yes, it was.

5244. What do you call the short hours, or common hours, in the flax business?—From 6 in the morning till 7 at night.

5245. What time for meals?—Forty minutes.

5246. Are the children brought in occasionally from their meals before the time?—Yes.

5247. By what means?—By the clock; sometimes the hand would have slipped down two or three minutes.

5248. Were the children whipped in sometimes to their work?—Yes, out of the mill-yard, the boys after they have gone out to play, the over-looker has got a strap, and gone out and strapped them in before their time, that they might come in and get on with their work.

5249. You have had the misfortune, from being a straight and healthful girl, to become very much otherwise in your person; do you know of any other girls that have become weak and deformed in like manner?—No.

5250. Do you know of any body that has been similarily injured in their health?—Yes, in their health, but not many deformed as I am.

5251. You are deformed in the shoulders?—Yes.

5252. It is very common to have weak ankles and crooked knees?— Yes, very common indeed.

5253. That is brought on by stopping the spindle?—Yes.

5254. Do you know anything of wet-spinning?—Yes, it is very uncomfortable; I have stood before the frame till I have been wet through to my skin; and in winter time, when we have gone home, our clothes have been frozen, and we have nearly caught our death of cold.

5255. Were you permitted to give up your labour at any time to suit your convenience and your health, and resume it again when you were more capable of it?—Yes, we have stopped at home one day or two days, just as we were situated in our health.

5256. If you had stopped away any length of time, should you have found a difficulty to keep your situation?—Yes, we should.

5257. Were the children constantly beaten to their labour, as you have described?—Yes.

5258. Where are you now?—In the poorhouse.

5259. Where?—At Hunslet.

5260. Do any of your former employers come to see you?—No.

5261. Did you ever receive any thing from them when you became afflicted?—When I was at home Mr. Walker made me a present of 1s. or 2s., but since I have left my work and gone to the poorhouse, they have not come nigh me.

5262. You are supported by the parish?—Yes.

5263. You are utterly incapable now of any exertion of that sort?—Yes.

5264. You were very willing to have worked as long as you were able, from your earliest age?—Yes.

5265. And to have supported your widowed mother as long as you could?—Yes.

5266. State what you think as to the circumstances in which you have been placed during all this time of labour, and what you have considered about it as to the hardship and cruelty of it.

[*The Witness was too much affected to answer the question.*]

THE INVESTIGATIONS of the Sadler Committee gave rise to the Factory Act of 1833 which mitigated somewhat the worst abuses of child labor.

3. THE ENGLISH FACTORY ACT OF 1833

SOURCE. Statutes of the United Kingdom, LXXIII, 985 f.:3–4, William IV, c. 103.

An act to regulate the labour of children and young persons in the mills and factories of the united kingdom. . . . no person under eighteen years of age shall be allowed to work in the night—that is to say, between the hours half-past eight o'clock in the evening and half-past five o'clock in the morning— . . . in or about any cotton, woolen, worsted, hemp, flax, tow, linen, or silk mill or factory. . . .

. . . no person under the age of eighteen years shall be employed in any such mill or factory . . . more than twelve hours in any one day, nor more than sixty-nine hours in any one week. . . . there shall be allowed in the course of every day not less than one and a half hours for meals. . . .

. . . it shall not be lawful for any person whatsoever to employ in any factory or mill as aforesaid, except in mills for the manufacture of silk, any child who shall not have completed his or her ninth year of age.

. . . it shall not be lawful for any person whosoever to employ, keep, or allow to remain in any factory or mill as aforesaid for a longer time than forty-eight hours in any one week, nor for a longer time than nine hours in any one day . . . , any child who shall not have completed his or her eleventh year of age; or, after the expiration of eighteen months from the passing of this act, any child who shall not have completed his or her twelfth year of age; or, after the expiration of thirty months from the passing of this act, any child who shall not have completed his or her thirteenth year of age. Provided, nevertheless, that, in mills for the manufacture of silk, children under the age of thirteen years shall be allowed to work ten hours in any one day.

. . . all children and young persons whose hours of work are regulated and limited by this act shall be entitled to the following holidays, *viz.*: on Christmas Day and Good Friday, the entire day; and not fewer than eight half-days besides in every year. . . .

And whereas, by an act . . . passed in the forty-second year of . . . George III[1], it was . . . provided that the justices of the peace . . . should appoint yearly two persons . . . to be visitors of . . . mills or factories . . . ; and whereas it appears that the provisions . . . were not duly carried into execution . . . : . . . it shall be lawful for his majesty by warrant under his sign-manual to appoint during his majesty's pleasure four persons to be inspectors of factories and places where the labour of children and young persons under eighteen years of age is employed. . . . And such inspectors or any of them are hereby empowered to enter any factory or mill, and any school attached or belonging thereto at all times and seasons, by day or by night, when such mills or factories are at work; and, having so entered, to examine therein the children and any other person or persons employed therein, and to make inquiry respecting their condition, employment, and education. And such inspectors, or any of them, are hereby empowered to take or call to their aid in such examination and inquiry such persons as they may choose, and to summon and require any person upon the spot or elsewhere to give evidence upon such examinations and inquiry. . . .

. . . every child hereinbefore restricted to the performance of forty-eight hours of labour in any one week shall, so long as such child shall be within the said restricted age, attend some school. . . .

---

[1] The Factory Act of 1802.

And whereas it is expedient that the proceedings, rules, orders, and regulations of the several inspectors appointed under this act should be as nearly alike as is practicable under all circumstances: therefore such inspectors are hereby required, within three months next after they shall have commenced the execution of their several duties and powers under this act, and twice at least in every year afterwards, to meet and confer together respecting their several proceedings, rules, orders, regulations, duties, and powers under this act, and at such meeting to make their proceedings, rules, orders, and regulations as uniform as is expedient.

LIFE IN THE NEW INDUSTRIAL CITIES remained grim and dehumanized, as is evident from the surgeon John Robertson's description of sanitary conditions in Manchester in 1840.

4. THE CONDITION OF MANCHESTER, 1840: A DESCRIPTION BY JOHN ROBERTSON, SURGEON

SOURCE. A. E. Bland, P. A. Brown, and R. H. Tawney, eds., *English Economic History: Select Documents*, London: G. Bell & Sons, 1925, pp. 519–521. Reprinted by permission of G. Bell & Sons, Ltd., London.

Until twelve years ago there was no paving and sewering Act in any of the townships; even in the township of Manchester, containing in the year 1831 upwards of 142,000 inhabitants, this was the case; and the disgraceful condition of the streets and sewers on the invasion of the cholera you have no doubt learned from Dr. Kay's able and valuable pamphlet. At the present time the paving of the streets proceeds rapidly in every direction, and great attention is given to the drains. Upon the whole, it is gratifying to bear testimony to the zeal of the authorities in carrying on the salutary improvements, especially when it is known that no street can be paved and sewered without the consent of the owners of property, unless a certain large proportion of the land on either side is built upon. Owing to this cause several important streets remain to this hour disgraceful nuisances.

Manchester has no Building Act, and hence, with the exception of certain central streets, over which the Police Act gives the Commissioners power, each proprietor builds as he pleases. New cottages, with or without cellars, huddled together row behind row, may be seen springing up in many parts, but especially in the township of Manchester, where the land is higher in price than the land for cottage sites in other townships is. With such proceedings as these the authorities cannot interfere. A cottage row may be badly drained, the streets may be full of pits, brimful of stagnant water, the receptacle of dead cats and dogs, yet no one may find fault. The number of cellar residences, you have probably learned from the papers published by the Manchester Statistical Society, is very great in all quarters of the town; and even in Hulme, a large portion of which consists of cottages recently erected, the same practice is continued. That it is an evil must be obvious on the slightest consideration, for how can a hole underground of from 12 to 15 feet square admit of ventilation so as to fit it for a human habitation?

We have no authorized inspector of dwellings and streets. If an epidemic disease were to invade, as happened in 1832, the authorities would probably order inspection, as they did on that occasion, but it would be merely by general permission, not of right.

So long as this and other great manufacturing towns were multiplying and extending their branches of manufacture and were prosperous, every fresh addition of operatives found employment, good wages, and plenty of food; and so long as the families of working people are well fed, it is certain they maintain their health in a surprising manner, even in cellars and other close dwellings. Now, however, the case is different. Food is dear, labour scarce, and wages in many branches very low; consequently, as might be expected, disease and death are making unusual havoc. In the years 1833, 1834, 1835, and 1836 (years of prosperity), the number of fever cases admitted into the Manchester House of Recovery amounted only to 1,685, or 421 per annum; while in the two pinching years, 1838 and 1839, the number admitted was 2,414, or 1,207 per annum. It is in such a depressed state of the manufacturing districts as at present exists that unpaved and badly sewered streets, narrow alleys, close, unventilated courts and cellars, exhibit their malign influence in augmenting the sufferings which that greatest of all physical evils, want of sufficient food, inflicts on young and old in large towns, but especially on the young.

Manchester has no public park or other grounds where the population can walk and breathe the fresh air. New streets are rapidly extending in every direction, and so great already is the expanse of the town, that those who live in the more populous quarters can seldom hope to see the green face of nature. . . . In this respect Manchester is disgracefully defective; more so, perhaps, than any other town in the empire. Every advantage of this nature has been sacrificed to the getting of money in the shape of ground-rents.

B. The Theoretical Response: The "Dismal Science"

THE GRIMNESS OF LIFE in industrial England was very nearly matched by the grimness of economic thought. In 1789 there appeared two important works in the laissez-faire *tradition:* A Manual of Political Economy *by the English utilitarian philosopher Jeremy Bentham (1748–1832), and* An Essay on the Principle of Population *by the English economist Thomas Robert Malthus (1766–1834). The Introduction to Bentham's work is a concise statement of the principle of governmental noninterference and an epitome of the viewpoint of the Classical or Liberal school of economics.*

1. JEREMY BENTHAM, FROM *A MANUAL OF POLITICAL ECONOMY*

SOURCE. *The Works of Jeremy Bentham,* Edinburgh: William Tait, 1843, III, pp. 33–34.

Political Economy is at once a *science* and an *art*. The value of the science has for its efficient cause and measure, its subserviency to the art.

According to the principle of utility in every branch of the art of legislation, the object or end in view should be the production of the maximum of happiness in a given time in the community in question.

In the instance of this branch of the art, the object or end in view should be the production of that maximum of happiness, in so far as this more general end is promoted by the production of the maximum of wealth and the maximum of population.

The practical questions, therefore, are—How far the measures respectively suggested by these two branches of the common end agree?—how far they differ, and which requires the preference?—how far the end in view is best promoted by individuals acting for themselves? and in what cases these ends may be best promoted by the hands of government?

Those cases in which, and those measures or operations by which, the end is promoted by individuals acting for themselves, and without any special interference exercised with this special view on the part of government, beyond the distribution made and maintained, and the protection afforded by the civil and penal branches of the law, may be said to arise *sponte acta*.

What the legislator and the minister of the interior have it in their power to do towards increase either of wealth or population, is as nothing in comparison with what is done of course, and without thinking of it, by the judge, and his assistant the minister of police.

The cases in which, and the measures by which, the common end may be promoted by the hands of government, may be termed *agenda*.

With the view of causing an increase to take place in the mass of national wealth, or with a view to increase of the means either of subsistence or enjoyment, without some special reason, the general rule is, that nothing ought to be done or attempted by government. The motto, or watchword of government, on these occasions, ought to be—*Be quiet*.

For this quietism there are two main reasons:—1. Generally speaking, any interference for this purpose on the part of government is *needless*. The wealth of the whole community is composed of the wealth of the several individuals belonging to it taken together. But to increase his particular portion is, generally speaking, among the constant objects of each individual's exertions and care. Generally speaking, there is no one who knows what is for your interest, so well as yourself—no one who is disposed with so much ardour and constancy to pursue it.

2. Generally speaking, it is moreover likely to be pernicious, viz. by being unconducive, or even obstructive, with reference to the attainment of the end in view. Each individual bestowing more time and attention upon the means of preserving and increasing his portion of wealth, than is or can be bestowed by government, is likely to take a more effectual course than what, in his instance and on his behalf, would be taken by government.

It is, moreover, universally and constantly pernicious in another way, by the restraint or constraint imposed on the free agency of the individual. Pain is the general concomitant of the sense of such restraint, wherever it is experienced.

Without being productive of such coercion, and thereby of such pain —in such a way more or less direct—more or less perceptible, with this or any other view, the interposition of government can hardly take place. If the coercion be not applied to the very individual whose conduct is endeavoured to be made immediately subservient to this purpose, it is at any rate applied to others—indeed, to the whole community taken together.

In coercive measures, so called, it is only to the individual that the coercion is applied. In the case of measures of encouragement, the field of coercion is vastly more extensive. Encouragements are grants of money or money's worth, applied in some shape or other to this purpose. But for this, any more than any other purpose, money is not raised but by taxes, and taxes are the produce of coercive laws applied to the most coercive purpose.

This would not be the less true, though the individual pieces of money thus applied happened to come from a source which had not been fed by any such means. In all communities, by far the greatest share of the money disposed of by government being supplied by taxes, whether this or that particular portion of money so applied, be supplied from that particular source, makes no sort of difference.

To estimate the good expected from the application of any particular mass of government money, compare it always with the mischief produced by the extraction of an equal sum of money by the most burthensome species of tax; since, by forbearing to make application of that sum of money, you might forbear levying the amount of that same sum of money by that tax, and thereby forbear imposing the mass of burthen that results from it.

MALTHUS' ESSAY made a deep impact on subsequent economic thought. It cast a shadow on Enlightenment optimism by arguing that population growth always tended to exceed increases in food production and that general prosperity was a will-o'-the-wisp.

2. THOMAS MALTHUS, FROM *AN ESSAY ON THE PRINCIPLE OF POPULATION AS IT AFFECTS THE FUTURE IMPROVEMENT OF SOCIETY*

SOURCE. Thomas Malthus, *An Essay on the Principle of Population as it Affects the Future Improvement of Society,* London: 1798, reprinted 1926, pp. 1–17.

The great and unlooked-for discoveries that have taken place of late years in natural philosophy; the increasing diffusion of general knowledge from the extension of the art of printing; the ardent and unshackled spirit of inquiry that prevails throughout the lettered, and even unlettered, world; the new and extraordinary lights that have been thrown on political subjects, which dazzle and astonish the understanding: and particularly that tremendous phenomenon in the political horizon, the French Revolution, which, like a blazing comet, seems destined either to inspire with fresh life and vigour, or to scorch up and destroy the thinking inhabitants of the earth, have all concurred to lead able men into the opinion, that we are touching upon a period big with the most important changes, changes that would in some measure be decisive of the future fate of mankind.

It has been said, that the great question is now at issue, whether man shall henceforth start forwards with accelerated velocity towards illimitable, and hitherto unconceived improvement; or be condemned to a perpetual oscillation between happiness and misery, and after every effort remain still at an immeasurable distance from the wished-for goal.

Yet, anxiously as every friend of mankind must look forwards to the termination of this painful suspense; and, eagerly as the inquiring mind would hail every ray of light that might assist its view into futurity, it is much to be lamented, that the writers on each side of this momentous question still keep far aloof from each other. Their mutual arguments do not meet with a candid examination. The question is not brought to rest on fewer points; and even in theory scarcely seems to be approaching to a decision.

The advocate for the present order of things, is apt to treat the sect of speculative philosophers, either as a set of artful and designing knaves, who preach up ardent benevolence, and draw captivating pictures of a happier state of society, only the better to enable them to destroy the present establishments, and to forward their own deep-laid schemes of ambition: or, as wild and madheaded enthusiasts, whose silly speculations, and absurd paradoxes, are not worthy the attention of any reasonable man.

The advocate for the perfectibility of man, and of society, retorts on the defender of establishments a more than equal contempt. He brands him as the slave of the most miserable and narrow prejudices; or, as the defender of the abuses of civil society, only because he profits by them. He paints him either as a character who prostitutes his understanding to his interest; or as one whose powers of mind are not of a size to grasp anything great and noble; who cannot see above five yards before him; and who must therefore be utterly unable to take in the views of the enlightened benefactor of mankind.

In this unamicable contest, the cause of truth cannot but suffer. The really good arguments on each side of the question are not allowed to have their proper weight. Each pursues his own theory, little solicitous to correct, or improve it, by an attention to what is advanced by his opponents.

The friend of the present order of things condemns all political speculations in the gross. He will not even condescend to examine the grounds from which the perfectibility of society is inferred. Much less will he give himself the trouble in a fair and candid manner to attempt an exposition of their fallacy.

The speculative philosopher equally offends against the cause of truth. With eyes fixed on a happier state of society, the blessings of which he paints in the most captivating colours, he allows himself to indulge in the most bitter invectives against every present establishment, without applying his talents to consider the best and safest means of removing abuses, and without seeming to be aware of the tremendous obstacles that threaten, even in theory, to oppose the progress of man towards perfection.

It is an acknowledged truth in philosophy, that a just theory will always be confirmed by experiment. Yet so much friction, and so many minute circumstances occur in practice, which it is next to impossible for the most enlarged and penetrating mind to foresee, that on few subjects can any theory be pronounced just, that has not stood the test of experience. But an untried theory cannot be advanced as probable, must less as just, till all the arguments against it have been maturely weighed, and clearly and consistently refuted.

I have read some of the speculations on the perfectibility of man and of society with great pleasure. I have been warmed and delighted with the enchanting picture which they hold forth. I ardently wish for such happy improvements. But I see great, and, to my understanding, unconquerable difficulties in the way to them. These difficulties it is my present purpose to state; declaring, at the same time, that so far from exulting in them, as a cause of triumphing over the friends of innovation, nothing would give me greater pleasure than to see them completely removed.

The most important argument that I shall adduce is certainly not new. The principles on which it depends have been explained in part by Hume, and more at large by Dr. Adam Smith. It has been advanced and applied to the present subject, though not with its proper weight, or in the most forcible point of view, by Mr. Wallace: and it may probably have been stated by many writers that I have never met with. I should certainly, therefore, not think of advancing it again, though I mean to place it in a point of view in some degree different from any that I have hitherto seen, if it had ever been fairly and satisfactorily answered.

The cause of this neglect on the part of the advocates for the perfectibility of mankind is not easily accounted for. I cannot doubt the talents of such men as Godwin and Condorcet. I am unwilling to doubt their candour. To my understanding, and probably to that of most others, the difficulty appears insurmountable. Yet these men of acknowledged ability and penetration, scarcely deign to notice it, and hold on their course in such speculations, with unabated ardour and undiminished confidence. I have certainly no right to say that they purposely shut their eyes to such arguments. I ought rather to doubt the validity of them, when neglected by such men, however forcibly their truth may strike my own mind. Yet in this respect it must be acknowledged that we are all of us too prone to err. If I saw a glass of wine repeatedly presented to a man, and he took no notice of it, I should be apt to think that he was blind or uncivil. A juster philosophy might teach me rather to think that my eyes deceived me, and that the offer was not really what I conceived it to be.

In entering upon the argument I must premise that I put out of the question, at present, all mere conjectures; that is, all suppositions, the probable realization of which cannot be inferred upon any just philosophical grounds. A writer may tell me that he thinks man will ultimately become an ostrich. I cannot properly contradict him. But before he can expect to bring any reasonable person over to his opinion, he ought to show that the necks of mankind have been gradually elongating; that the lips have grown harder, and more prominent; that the legs and feet are daily altering their shape; and that the hair is beginning to change into stubs of feathers. And till the probability of so wonderful a conversion can be shown, it is surely lost time and lost eloquence to expatiate on the happiness of man in such a state; to describe his powers, both of running and flying; to paint him in a condition where all narrow luxuries would be contemned; where he would be employed, only in collecting the necessaries of life; and where, consequently, each man's share of labour would be light, and his portion of leisure ample.

I think I may fairly make two postulata.

First, That food is necessary to the existence of man.

Secondly, That the passion between the sexes is necessary, and will remain nearly in its present state.

These two laws, ever since we have had any knowledge of mankind, appear to have been fixed laws of our nature; and, as we have not hitherto seen any alteration in them, we have no right to conclude that they will ever cease to be what they are now, without an immediate act of power in that Being who first arranged the system of the universe; and for the advantage of his creatures, still executes, according to fixed laws, all its various operations.

I do not know that any writer has supposed that on this earth man will ultimately be able to live without food. But Mr. Godwin has conjectured that the passion between the sexes may in time be extinguished. As, however, he calls this part of his work, a deviation into the land of conjecture, I will not dwell longer upon it at present, than to say, that the best arguments for the perfectibility of man are drawn from a contemplation of the great progress that he has already made from the savage state, and the difficulty of saying where he is to stop. But towards the extinction of the passion between the sexes, no progress whatever has hitherto been made. It appears to exist in as much force at present as it did two thousand, or four thousand years ago. There are individual exceptions now as there always have been. But, as these exceptions do not appear to increase in number, it would surely be a very unphilosophical mode of arguing, to infer merely from the existence of an exception, that the exception would, in time, become the rule, and the rule the exception.

Assuming, then, my postulata as granted, I say, that the power of population is indefinitely greater than the power in the earth to produce subsistence for man.

Population, when unchecked, increases in a geometrical ratio. Subsistence only increases in an arithmetical ratio. A slight acquaintance with numbers will show the immensity of the first power in comparison of the second.

By that law our nature which makes food necessary to the life of man, the effects of these two unequal powers must be kept equal.

This implies a strong and constantly operating check on population from the difficulty of subsistence. This difficulty must fall some where; and must necessarily be severely felt by a large portion of mankind.

Through the animal and vegetable kingdoms, nature has scattered the seeds of life abroad with the most profuse and liberal hand. She has been comparatively sparing in the room, and the nourishment necessarily to rear them. The germs of existence contained in this spot of earth, with ample food, and ample room to expand it, would fill millions of worlds in the course of a few thousand years. Necessity, that imperious, all-pervading law of nature, restrains them within the prescribed bounds. The race of plants, and the race of animals shrink under this great restrictive law. And the race of man cannot, by any efforts of reason, escape from it. Among plants and animals its effects are waste of seed, sickness, and premature death. Among mankind, misery and vice. The former, misery, is an absolutely necessary consequence of it. Vice is a highly probable consequence, and we therefore see it abundantly prevail; but it ought not, perhaps, to be called an absolutely necessary consequence. The ordeal of virtue is to resist all temptation to evil.

This natural inequality of the two powers of population, and of production in the earth, and that great law of our nature which must constantly keep their effects equal, form the great difficulty that to me appears insurmountable in the way to perfectibility of society. All other arguments are of slight and subordinate consideration in comparison of this. I see no way by which man can escape from the weight of this law which pervades all animated nature. No fancied equality, no agrarian regulations in their utmost extent, could remove the pressure of it even for a single century. And it appears, therefore to be decisive against the possible existence of a society, all the members of which should live in ease, happiness, and comparative leisure; and feel no anxiety about providing the means of subsistence for themselves and families.

Consequently, if the premises are just, the argument is conclusive against the perfectibility of the mass of mankind.

I have thus sketched the general outline of the argument; but I will examine it more particularly; and I think it will be found that experience, the true source and foundation of all knowledge, invariably confirms its truth.

DAVID RICARDO (1772–1823), in his great work The Principles of Political Economy and Taxation *(1817), developed some of the implications of the Malthusian doctrine into a definitive and closely reasoned system. At his hands, Classical economics was subjected to iron laws. Wages were bound to the level of subsistence by the inflexible pressures of supply and demand on the one hand and population growth on the other. The economic system of Ricardo was "dismal" indeed.*

3. DAVID RICARDO, "ON WAGES" FROM *THE PRINCIPLES OF POLITICAL ECONOMY AND TAXATION*

SOURCE. David Ricardo, *The Principles of Political Economy and Taxation*, London: J. M. Dent & Sons, 1911, pp. 52–56 and 61–63. Everyman's Library Edition. Reprinted by permission of J. M. Dent & Sons Ltd. and E. P. Dutton & Co., Inc.

Labour, like all other things which are purchased and sold, and which may be increased or diminished in quantity, has its natural and its market price. The natural price of labour is that price whis is necessary to enable the labourers, one with another, to subsist and to perpetuate their race, without either increase or diminution.

The power of the labourer to support himself, and the family which may be necessary to keep up the number of labourers, does not depend on the quantity of money which he may receive for wages, but on the quantity of food, necessaries, and conveniences become essential to him from habit which that money will purchase. The natural price of labour, therefore, depends on the price of the food, necessaries, and conveniences required for the support of the labourer and his family. With a rise in the price of food and necessaries, the natural price of labour will rise; with the fall in their price, the natural price of labour will fall.

With the progress of society the natural price of labour has always a tendency to rise, because one of the principal commodities by which its natural price is regulated has a tendency to become dearer from the greater difficulty of producing it. As, however, the improvements in agriculture, the discovery of new markets, whence provisions may be imported, may for a time counteract the tendency to a rise in the price of necessaries, and may even occasion their natural price to fall, so will the same causes produce the correspondent effects on the natural price of labour.

The natural price of all commodities, excepting raw produce and labour, has a tendency to fall in the progress of wealth and population; for though, on one hand, they are enhanced in real value, from the rise in the natural price of the raw material of which they are made, this is more than counterbalanced by the improvements in machinery, by the better division and distribution of labour, and by the increasing skill, both in science and art, of the producers.

The market price of labour is the price which is really paid for it, from the natural operation of the proportion of the supply to the demand: labour is dear when it is scarce and cheap when it is plentiful. However much the market price of labour may deviate from its natural price, it has, like commodities, a tendency to conform to it.

It is when the market price of labour exceeds its natural price that the condition of the labourer is flourishing and happy, that he has it in his power to command a greater proportion of the necessaries and enjoyments of life, and therefore to rear a healthy and numerous family. When, however, by the encouragement which high wages give to the increase of population, the number of labourers is increased, wages again fall to their natural price, and indeed from a reaction sometimes fall below it.

When the market price of labour is below its natural price, the condition of the labourers is most wretched: then poverty deprives them of those comforts which custom renders absolute necessaries. It is only after their privations have reduced their number, or the demand for labour has increased, that the market price of labour will rise to its natural price, and that the labourer will have the moderate comforts which the natural rate of wages will afford.

Notwithstanding the tendency of wages to conform to their natural rate, their market rate may, in an improving society, for an indefinite period, be constantly above it; for no sooner may the impulse which an increased capital gives to a new demand for labour be obeyed, than another increase of capital may produce the same effect; and thus, if the increase of capital be gradual and constant, the demand for labour may give a continued stimulus to an increase of people.

Capital is that part of the wealth of a country which is employed in production, and consists of food, clothing, tools, raw materials, machinery, etc., necessary to give effect to labour.

Capital may increase in quantity at the same time that its value rises. An addition may be made to the food and clothing of a country at the same time that more labour may be required to produce the additional quantity than before; in that case not only the quantity but the value of capital will rise.

Or capital may increase without its value increasing, and even while its value is actually diminishing; not only may an addition be made to the food and clothing of a country, but the addition may be made by the aid of machinery, without any increase, and even with an absolute diminution in the proportional quantity of labour required to produce them. The quantity of capital may increase, while neither the whole together, nor any part of it singly, will have a greater value than before, but may actually have a less.

In the first case, the natural price of labour, which always depends on the price of food, clothing, and other necessaries, will rise; in the second, it will remain stationary or fall; but in both cases the market rate of wages will rise, for in proportion to the increase of capital will be the increase in the demand for labour; in proportion to the work to be done will be the demand for those who are to do it.

In both cases, too, the market price of labour will rise above its natural price; and in both cases it will have a tendency to conform to its natural price, but in the first case this agreement will be most speedily effected. The situation of the labourer will be improved, but not much improved; for the increased price of food and necessaries will absorb a large portion of his increased wages; consequently a small supply of labour, or a trifling increase in the population, will soon reduce the market price to the then increased natural price of labour.

In the second case, the condition of the labourer will be very greatly improved; he will receive increased money wages without having to pay any increased price, and perhaps even a diminished price for the commodities which he and his family consume; and it will not be till after a great addition has been made to the population that the market price of labour will again sink to its then low and reduced natural price.

Thus, then, with every improvement of society, with every increase in its capital, the market wages of labour will rise; but the permanence of their rise will depend on the question whether the natural price of labour has also risen; and this again will depend on the rise in the natural price of those necessaries on which the wages of labour are expended.

It is not to be understood that the natural price of labour, estimated even in food and necessaries, is absolutely fixed and constant. It varies at different times in the same country, and very materially differs in different countries.[1] It essentially depends on the habits and customs of the people. An English labourer would consider his wages under their natural rate, and too scanty to support a family, if they enabled him to purchase no other food than potatoes, and to live in no better habitation than a mud

---

[1] "The shelter and the clothing which are indispensable in one country may be no way necessary in another; and a labourer in Hindostan may continue to work with perfect vigour, though receiving, as his natural wages, only such a supply of covering as would be insufficient to preserve a labourer in Russia from perishing. Even in countries situated in the same climate, different habits of living will often occasion variations in the natural price of labour as considerable as those which are produced by natural causes."
—P. 68. *An Essay on the External Corn Trade*, by R. Torrens, Esq.

The whole of this subject is most ably illustrated by Colonel Torrens.

cabin; yet these moderate demands of nature are often deemed sufficient in countries where "man's life is cheap" and his wants easily satisfied. Many of the conveniences now enjoyed in an English cottage would have been thought luxuries at an earlier period of our history.

From manufactured commodities always falling and raw produce always rising, with the progress of society, such a disproportion in their relative value is at length created, that in rich countries as labourer, by the sacrifice of a very small quantity only of his food, is able to provide liberally for all his other wants.

Independently of the variations in the value of money, which necessarily affect money wages, but which we have here supposed to have no operation, as we have considered money to be uniformly of the same value, it appears then that wages are subject to a rise or fall from two causes:—

First, the supply and demand of labourers.

Secondly, the price of the commodities on which the wages of labour are expended.

In different stages of society, the accumulation of capital, or of the means of employing labour, is more or less rapid, and must in all cases depend on the productive powers of labour. The productive powers of labour are generally greatest when there is an abundance of fertile land: at such periods accumulation is often so rapid that labourers cannot be supplied with the same rapidity as capital.

It has been calculated that under favourable circumstances population may be doubled in twenty-five years; but under the same favourable circumstances the whole capital of a country might possibly be doubled in a shorter period. In that case, wages during the whole period would have a tendency to rise, because the demand for labour would increase still faster than the supply.

In new settlements, where the arts and knowledge of countries far advanced in refinement are introduced, it is probable that capital has a tendency to increase faster than mankind; and if the deficiency of labourers were not supplied by more populous countries, this tendency would very much raise the price of labour. In proportion as these countries become populous, and land of a worse quality is taken into cultivation, the tendency to an increase of capital diminishes; for the surplus produce remaining, after satisfying the wants of the existing population, must necessarily be in proportion to the facility of production, viz. to the smaller number of persons employed in production. Although, then, it is probable that, under the most favourable circumstances, the power of production is still greater than that of population, it will not long continue so; for the land being limited in quantity, and differing in quality, with every increased portion of capital employed on it there will be a decreased rate of production, whilst the power of population continues always the same.

In those countries where there is abundance of fertile land, but where, from the ignorance, indolence, and barbarism of the inhabitants, they are exposed to all the evils of want and famine, and where it has been said that population presses against the means of subsistence, a very different remedy should be applied from that which is necessary in long settled countries, where, from the diminishing rate of the supply of raw produce, all the evils of a crowded population are experienced. In the one case, the evil proceeds from bad government, from the insecurity of property, and from a want of education in all ranks of the people. To be made happier they require only to be better governed and instructed, as the augmentation of capital, beyond the augmentation of people, would be the inevitable result. No increase in the population can be too great, as the powers of production are still greater. In the other case, the population increases faster than the funds required for its support. Every exertion of industry, unless accompanied by a diminished rate of increase in the population, will add to the evil, for production cannot keep pace with it.

With a population pressing against the means of subsistence, the only remedies are either a reduction of people or a more rapid accumulation of capital. In rich countries, where all the fertile land is already cultivated, the latter remedy is neither very practicable nor very desirable, because its effort would be, if pushed very far, to render all classes equally poor. . . .

These, then, are the laws by which wages are regulated, and by which the happiness of far the greatest part of every community is governed. Like all other contracts, wages should be left to the fair and free competition of the market, and should never be controlled by the interference of the legislature.

The clear and direct tendency of the poor laws is in direct opposition to these obvious principles: it is not, as the legislature benevolently intended, to amend the condition of the poor, but to deteriorate the condition of both poor and rich; instead of making the poor rich, they are calculated to make the rich poor; and whilst the present laws are in force, it is quite in the natural order of things that the fund for the maintenance of the poor should progressively increase till it has absorbed all the net revenue of the country, or at least so much of it as the state shall leave to us, after satisfying its own never-failing demands for the public expenditure.

This pernicious tendency of these laws is no longer a mystery, since it has been fully developed by the able hand of Mr. Malthus; and every friend to the poor must ardently wish for their abolition. Unfortunately, however, they have been so long established, and the habits of the poor have been so formed upon their operation, that to eradicate them with safety from our political system requires the most cautious and skilful management. It is agreed by all who are most friendly to a repeal of these laws that, if it be desirable to prevent the most overwhelming distress to those for whose benefit they were erroneously enacted, their abolition should be effected by the most gradual steps.

It is a truth which admits not a doubt that the comforts and well-being of the poor cannot be permanently secured without some regard on their part, or some effort on the part of the legislature, to regulate the increase of their numbers, and to render less frequent among them early and improvident marriages. The operation of the system of poor laws has been directly contrary to this. They have rendered restraint superfluous, and have invited imprudence, by offering it a portion of the wages of prudence and industry.

The nature of the evil points out the remedy. By gradually contracting the sphere of the poor laws; by impressing on the poor the value of independence, by teaching them that they must look not to systematic or casual charity, but to their own exertions for support, that prudence and forethought are neither unnecessary nor unprofitable virtues, we shall by degrees approach a sounder and more healthful state.

No scheme for the amendment of the poor laws merits the least attention which has not their abolition for its ultimate object; and he is the best friend of the poor, and to the cause of humanity, who can point out how this end can be attained with the most security, and at the same time with the least violence. It is not by raising in any manner different from the present the fund from which the poor are supported that the evil can be mitigated. It would not only be no improvement, but it would be an aggravation of the distress which we wish to see removed, if the fund were increased in amount or were levied according to some late proposals, as a general fund from the country at large. The present mode of its collection and application has served to mitigate its pernicious effects. Each parish raises a separate fund for the support of its own poor. Hence it becomes an object of more interest and more practicability to keep the rates low than if one general fund were raised for the relief of the poor of the whole kingdom. A parish is much more interested in an economical collection of the rate, and a sparing distribution of relief, when the whole saving will be for its own benefit, than if hundreds of other parishes were to partake of it.

It is to this cause that we must ascribe the fact of the poor laws not having yet absorbed all the net revenue of the country; it is to the rigour with which they are applied that we are indebted for their not having become overwhelmingly oppressive. If by law every human being wanting support could be sure to obtain it, and obtain it in such a degree as to make life tolerably comfortable, theory would lead us to expect that all other taxes together would be light compared with the single one of poor rates. The principle of gravitation is not more certain than the tendency of such laws to change wealth and power into misery and weakness; to call away the exertions of labour from every object, except that of providing mere subsistence; to confound all intellectual distinction; to busy the mind continually in supplying the body's wants; until at last all classes should be infected with the plague of universal poverty. Happily these laws have been in operation during a period of progressive prosperity, when the funds for the maintenance of labour have regularly increased, and when an increase of population would be naturally called for. But if our progress should become more slow; if we should attain the stationary state, from which I trust we are yet far distant, then will the pernicious nature of these laws become more manifest and alarming; and then, too, will their removal be obstructed by many additional difficulties.

Part II

THE GROWTH
OF SOCIALISM AND COMMUNISM

A. Nineteenth-Century Marxism and Its Variants

THE CLASSICAL SUMMARY of Communist doctrine and the call to revolution are to be found in The Communist Manifesto *(1848), written in Paris by Karl Marx and his disciple Friedrich Engels. In the extensive excerpts included here appear the basic Marxist doctrines of dialectical materialism, class struggle as the key dynamic force in history, and the inevitable victory of the proletariat. The immense impact of this document on its own and all subsequent generations goes without saying. It remains today the fundamental statement of the Communist ideology.*

1. KARL MARX AND FRIEDRICH ENGELS, FROM *THE COMMUNIST MANIFESTO*

SOURCE. Karl Marx and Friedrich Engels, *The Communist Manifesto,* Samuel Moore, tr., New York: Socialist Labor Party, 1888.

A spectre is haunting Europe—the spectre of Communism. All the powers of old Europe have entered into a holy alliance to exorcise this spectre; Pope and Czar, Metternich and Guizot, French Radicals and German police-spies.

Where is the party in opposition that has not been decried as communistic by its opponents in power? Where the Opposition that has not hurled back the branding reproach of Communism, against the more advanced opposition parties, as well as against its reactionary adversaries?

Two things result from this fact.

1. Communism is already acknowledged by all European Powers to be itself a Power.

2. It is high time that Communists should openly, in the face of the whole world, publish their views, their aims, their tendencies, and meet this nursery tale of the Spectre of Communism with a Manifesto of the party itself.

To this end, Communists of various nationalities have assembled in London, and sketched the following manifesto, to be published in the English, French, German, Italian, Flemish and Danish languages.

The history of all hitherto existing society is the history of class struggles.

Freeman and slave, patrician and plebian, lord and serf, guildmaster and journeyman, in a word, oppressor and oppressed, stood in constant opposition to one another, carried on an uninterrupted, now hidden, now open fight, a fight that each time ended, either in a revolutionary re-constitution of society at large, or in the common ruin of the contending classes.

In the earlier epochs of history, we find almost everywhere a complicated arrangement of society into various orders, a manifold graduation of social rank. In ancient Rome we have patricians, knights, plebians, slaves; in the Middle Ages, feudal lords, vassals, guildmasters, journeymen, apprentices, serfs; in almost all of these classes, again, subordinate gradations.

The modern bourgeois society that has sprouted from the ruins of feudal society, has not done away with class antagonisms. It has but established new classes, new conditions of oppression, new forms of struggle in place of the old ones.

Our epoch, the epoch of the bourgeoisie, possesses, however, this distinctive feature: it has simplified the class antagonisms. Society as a whole is more and more splitting up into two great hostile camps, into two great classes directly facing each other: Bourgeoisie and Proletariat.

From the serfs of the Middle Ages sprang the chartered burghers of the earliest towns. From these burgesses the first elements of the bourgeoisie were developed.

The discovery of America, the rounding of the Cape, opened up fresh ground for the rising bourgeoisie. The East-Indian and Chinese markets, the colonization of America, trade with the colonies, the increase in the means of exchange and in commodities generally, gave to commerce, to navigation, to industry, an impulse never before known, and thereby, to the revolutionary element in the tottering feudal society, a rapid development.

The feudal system of industry, under which industrial production was monopolized by close guilds, now no longer sufficed for the growing wants of the new markets. The manufacturing system took its place. The guildmasters were pushed on one side by the manufacturing middle-class; division of labor between the different corporate guilds vanished in the face of division of labor in each single workshop.

Meantime the markets kept growing, the demand, ever rising. Even manufacture no longer sufficed. Thereupon, steam and machinery revolutionized industrial production. The place of manufacture was taken by the giant, Modern Industry, the place of the industrial middle-class, by industrial millionaires, the leaders of whole industrial armies, the modern bourgeois.

Modern industry has established the world-market, for which the discovery of America paved the way. This market has given an immense development to commerce, to navigation, to communication by land. This development has, in its turn, reacted on the extension of industry; and in proportion as industry, commerce, navigation, railways extended, in the same proportion the bourgeoisie developed, increased its capital, and pushed into the background every class handed down from the Middle Ages.

We see, therefore, how the modern bourgeoisie is itself the product of a long course of development, of a series of revolutions in the modes of production and of exchange.

Each step in the development of the bourgeoisie was accompanied by a corresponding political advance of that class. An oppressed class under the sway of the feudal nobility, an armed and self-governing association in the medieval commune, here independent urban republic (as in Italy and Germany), there taxable "third estate" of the monarchy (as in France), afterwards, in the period of manufacture proper, serving either the semi-feudal or the absolute monarchy as a counterpoise against the nobility, and, in fact, corner stone of the great monarchies in general, the bourgeoisie has at last, since the establishment of Modern Industry and of the world-market, conquered for itself, in the modern representative State, exclusive political sway. The executive of the modern State is but a committee for managing the common affairs of the whole bourgeoisie.

The bourgeoisie, historically, has played a most revolutionary part.

The bourgeoisie, wherever it has got the upper hand, has put an end to all feudal, patriarchal, idyllic relations. It has pitilessly torn asunder the motley feudal ties that bound man to his "natural superiors," and has left remaining no other nexus between man and man than naked self-interest, than callous "cash payment." It has drowned the most heavenly ecstasies of religious fervor, of chivalrous enthusiasm, of philistine sentimentalism, in the icy water of egotistical calculation. It has resolved personal worth into exchange value, and in place of the numberless indefeasible chartered freedoms, has set up that single, unconscionable freedom—Free Trade. In one word, for exploitation, veiled by religious and political illusions, it has substituted naked, shameless, direct, brutal exploitation.

The bourgeoisie has stripped of its halo every occupation hitherto honored and looked up to with reverent awe. It has converted the physician, the lawyer, the priest, the poet, the man of science, into its paid wage-laborers.

The bourgeoisie has torn away from the family its sentimental veil, and has reduced the family relation to a mere money relation.

The bourgeoisie has disclosed how it came to pass that the brutal display of vigor in the Middle Ages, which Reactionists so much admire, found its fitting complement in the most slothful indolence. It has been the first to show what man's activity can bring about. It has accomplished wonders far surpassing Egyptian pyramids, Roman aqueducts, and Gothic cathedrals; it has conducted expeditions that put in the shade all former Exoduses of nations and crusades.

The bourgeoisie cannot exist without constantly revolutionizing the instruments of production, and thereby the relations of production, and with them the whole relations of society. Conservation of the old modes of production in unaltered form, was, on the contrary, the first condition of existence for all earlier industrial classes. Constant revolutionizing of production, uninterrupted disturbance of all social conditions, everlasting uncertainty and agitation distinguish the bourgeois epoch from all earlier ones. All fixed, fast-frozen relations, with their train of ancient and venerable prejudices and opinions, are swept away, all new-formed ones become antiquated before they can ossify. All that is solid melts into air, all that is holy is profaned, and man is at last compelled to face with sober senses, his real conditions of life, and his relations with his kind.

The need of a constantly expanding market for its products chases the bourgeoisie over the whole surface of the globe. It must nestle everywhere, establish connections everywhere.

The bourgeoisie has through its exploitation of the world-market given a cosmopolitan character to production and consumption in every country. To the great chagrin of Reactionists, it has drawn from under the feet of industry the national ground on which it stood. All old-established national industries have been destroyed or are daily being destroyed. They are dislodged by new industries, whose introduction becomes a life and death question for all civilized nations, by industries that no longer work up indigenous raw material, but raw material drawn from the remotest zones; industries whose products are consumed, not only at home, but in every quarter of the globe. In place of the old wants, satisfied by the productions of the country, we find new wants, requiring for their satisfaction the products of distant lands and climes. In place of the old local and national seclusion and self-sufficiency, we have intercourse in every direction, universal inter-dependence of nations. And as in material, so also in intellectual production. The intellectual creations of individual nations become common property. National one-sidedness and narrow-mindedness become more and more impossible, and from the numerous national and local literatures there arises a world-literature.

The bourgeoisie, by the rapid improvement of all instruments of production, by the immensely facilitated means of communication, draws all, even the most barbarian, nations into civilization. The cheap prices of its commodities are the heavy artillery with which it batters down all Chinese walls, with which it forces barbarians' intensely obstinate hatred of foreigners to capitulate. It compels all nations, on pain of extinction, to adopt the bourgeois mode of production; it compels them to introduce what it calls civilization into their midst, i.e., to become bourgeois themselves. In a word, it creates a world after its own image.

The bourgeoisie has subjected the country to the rule of the towns. It has created enormous cities, has greatly increased the urban population as compared with the rural, and has thus rescued a considerable part of the population from the idiocy of rural life. Just as it has made the country dependent on the towns, so it has made barbarian and semi-barbarian countries dependent on the civilized ones, nations of peasants on nations of bourgeois, the East on the West.

The bourgeoisie keeps more and more doing away with the scattered state of the population, of the means of production, and of property. It has agglomerated population, centralized means of production, and has concentrated property in a few hands. The necessary consequence of this was political centralization. Independent, or but loosely connected provinces, with separate interests, laws, governments, and systems of taxation, became lumped together in one nation, with one government, one code of laws, one national class-interest, one frontier and one customs-tariff.

The bourgeoisie, during its rule of scarce one hundred years, has created more massive and more colossal productive forces than have all preceding generations together. Subjection of Nature's forces to man, machinery, application of chemistry to industry and agriculture, steam-navigation, railways, electric telegraphs, clearing of whole continents for cultivation, canalization of rivers, whole populations conjured out of the ground—what earlier century had even a presentiment that such productive forces slumbered in the lap of social labor?

We see then: the means of production and of exchange on whose foundation the bourgeoisie built itself up, were generated in feudal society. At a certain stage in the development of these means of production and of exchange, the conditions under which feudal society produced and exchanged, the feudal organization of agriculture and manufacturing industry, in one word, the feudal relations of property became no longer compatible with the already developed productive forces; they became so many fetters. They had to burst asunder; they were burst asunder.

Into their places stepped free competition, accompanied by a social and political constitution adapted to it, and by the economical and political sway of the bourgeois class.

A similar movement is going on before our own eyes. Modern bourgeois society with its relations of production, of exchange and of property, a society that has conjured up such gigantic means of production and of exchange, is like the sorcerer, who is no longer able to control the powers of the nether world whom he has called up by his spells. For many a decade past the history of industry and commerce is but the history of the revolt of modern productive forces against modern conditions of production, against the property relations that are the conditions for the existence of the bourgeoisie and of its rule. It is enough to mention the commercial crises that by their periodical return put on its trial, each time more threateningly, the existence of the entire bourgeois society. In these crises a great part not only of the existing products, but also of the previously created productive forces, are periodically destroyed. In these crises there breaks out an epidemic that, in all earlier epochs, would have seemed an absurdity—the epidemic of over-production. Society suddenly finds itself put back into a state of momentary barbarism; it appears as if a famine, a universal war of devastation had cut off the supply of every means of subsistence; industry and commerce seem to be destroyed; and why? Because there is too much civilization, too much means of subsistence, too much industry, too much commerce. The productive forces at the disposal of society no longer tend to further the development of the conditions of bourgeois property; on the contrary, they have become too powerful for these conditions, by which they are fettered, and so soon as they overcome these fetters, they bring disorder into the whole of bourgeois society, endanger the existence of bourgeois property. The conditions of bourgeois society are too narrow to comprise the wealth created by them. And how does the bourgeoisie get over these crises? On the one hand by enforced destruction of a mass of productive forces; on the other, by the conquest of new markets, and by the more thorough exploitation of the old ones. That is to say, by paving the way for more extensive and more destructive crises, and by diminishing the means whereby crises are prevented.

The weapons with which the bourgeoisie felled feudalism to the ground are now turned against the bourgeoisie itself.

But not only has the bourgeoisie forged the weapons that bring death to itself; it has also called into existence the men who are to wield those weapons—the modern working-class—the proletarians.

In proportion as the bourgeoisie, i.e., capital, is developed, in the same proportion is the proletariat, the modern working-class, developed, a class of laborers, who live only so long as they find work, and who find work only so long as their labor increases capital. These laborers, who must sell themselves piecemeal, are a commodity, like every other article of commerce, and are consequently exposed to all the vicissitudes of competition, to all the fluctuations of the market.

Owing to the extensive use of machinery and to division of labor, the work of the proletarians has lost all individual character, and, consequently, all charm for the workman. He becomes an appendage of the machine, and it is only the most simple, most monotonous, and most easily acquired knack that is required of him. Hence, the cost of production of a workman is restricted, almost entirely, to the means of subsistence that he requires for his maintenance, and for the propagation of his race. But the price of a commodity, and also of labor, is equal to its cost of production. In proportion, therefore, as the repulsiveness of the work increases, the wage decreases. Nay more, in proportion as the use of machinery and division of labor increases, in the same proportion the burden of toil also increases, whether by prolongation of the working hours, by increase of the work enacted in a given time, or by increased speed of the machinery, etc.

Modern industry has converted the little workshop of the patriarchal master into the great factory of the industrial capitalist. Masses of laborers, crowded into the factory, are organized like soldiers. As privates of the industrial army they are placed under the command of a perfect hierarchy of officers and sergeants. Not only are they the slaves of the bourgeois class, and of the bourgeois State, they are daily and hourly enslaved by the machine, by the over-looker, and, above all, by the individual bourgeois manufacturer himself. The more openly despotism proclaims gain to be its end and aim, the more petty, the more hateful and the more embittering it is.

The less the skill and exertion or strength implied in manual labor, in other words, the more modern industry becomes developed, the more is the labor of men superseded by that of women. Differences of age and sex have no longer any distinctive social validity for the working class. All are instruments of labor, more or less expensive to use, according to their age and sex.

No sooner is the exploitation of the laborer by the manufacturer, so far at an end, that he receives his wages in cash, than he is set upon by the other portions of the bourgeoisie, the landlord, the shopkeeper, the pawnbroker, etc.

The lower strata of the middle class—the small tradespeople, shopkeepers, and retired tradesmen generally, the handicraftsmen and peasants—all these sink gradually into the proletariat, partly because their diminutive capital does not suffice for the scale on which Modern Industry is carried on, and is swamped in the competition with the large capitalists, partly because their specialized skill is rendered worthless by new methods of production. Thus the proletariat is recruited from all classes of the population.

The proletariat goes through various stages of development. With its birth begins its struggle with the bourgeoisie. At first the contest is carried on by individual laborers, then by the workpeople of a factory, then by the operatives of one trade, in one locality, against the individual bourgeois who directly exploits them. They direct their attacks not against the bourgeois conditions of production, but against the instruments of production themselves; they destroy imported wares that compete with their labor, they smash to pieces machinery, they set factories ablaze, they seek to restore by force the vanished status of the workman of the Middle Ages.

At this stage the laborers still form an incoherent mass scattered over the whole country, and broken up by their mutual competition. If anywhere they unite to form more compact bodies, this is not yet the consequence of their own active union, but of the union of the bourgeoisie, which class, in order to attain its own political ends, is compelled to set the whole proletariat in motion, and is moreover yet, for a time, able to do so. At this stage, therefore, the proletarians do not fight their enemies, but the enemies of their enemies, the remnants of absolute monarchy, the landowners, the non-industrial bourgeois, the petty bourgeoisie. Thus the whole historical movement is concentrated in the hands of the bourgeoisie; every victory so obtained is a victory for the bourgeoisie.

But with the development of industry the proletariat not only increases in number, it becomes concentrated in greater masses, its strength grows, and it feels that strength more. The various interests and conditions of life within the ranks of the proletariat are more and more equalized, in proportion as machinery obliterates all distinctions of labor, and nearly everywhere reduces wages to the same low level. The growing competition among the bourgeois, and the resulting commercial crises, make the wages of the workers ever more fluctuating. The unceasing improvement of machinery, every more rapidly developing, makes their livelihood more and more precarious; the collisions between individual workmen and individual bourgeois take more and more the character of collisions between two classes. Thereupon the workers begin to form combinations (Trades' Unions) against the bourgeois; they club together in order to keep up the rate of wages; they found permanent associations in order to make provision beforehand for these occasional revolts. Here and there the contest breaks out into riots.

Now and then the workers are victorious, but only for a time. The real fruit of their battles lies, not in the immediate result, but in the ever expanding union of the workers. This union is helped on by the improved means of communication that are created by modern industry, and that place the workers of different localities in contact with one another. It was just this contact that was needed to centralize the numerous local struggles, all of the same character, into one national struggle between classes. But every class struggle is a political struggle. And that union, to attain which the burghers of the Middle Ages, with their miserable highways, required centuries, the modern proletarians, thanks to railways, achieve in a few years.

This organization of the proletarians into a class, and consequently into a political party, is continually being upset again by the competition between the workers themselves. But it ever rises up again, stronger, firmer, mightier. It compels legislative recognition of particular interests of the workers, by taking advantage of the divisions among the bourgeoisie itself. Thus the ten-hour bill in England was carried.

Altogether collisions between the classes of the old society further, in many ways, the course of development of the proletariat. The bourgeoisie finds itself involved in a constant battle. At first with the aristocracy; later on, with those portions of the bourgeoisie itself, whose interests have become antagonistic to the progress of industry; at all times, with the bourgeoisie of foreign countries. In all these battles it sees itself compelled to appeal to the proletariat, to ask for its help, and thus, to drag it into the political arena. The bourgeoisie itself, therefore, supplies the proletariat with its own elements of political and general education, in other words, it furnishes the proletariat with weapons for fighting the bourgeoisie.

Further, as we have already seen, entire sections of the ruling classes are, by the advance of industry, precipitated into the proletariat, or are at least threatened in their conditions of existence. These also supply the proletariat with fresh elements of enlightenment and progress.

Finally, in times when the class-struggle nears the decisive hour, the process of dissolution going on within the ruling class, in fact, within the whole range of old society, assumes such a violent, glaring character, that a small section of the ruling class cuts itself adrift, and joins the revolutionary class, the class that holds the future in its hands. Just as, therefore, at an earlier period, a section of the nobility went over to the bourgeoisie, so now a portion of the bourgeoisie goes over to the proletariat, and in particular, a portion of the bourgeois ideologists, who have raised themselves to the level of comprehending theoretically the historical movements as a whole.

Of all the classes that stand face to face with the bourgeoisie today, the proletariat alone is a really revolutionary class. The other classes decay and finally disappear in the face of modern industry; the proletariat is its special and essential product.

The lower middle class, the small manufacturer, the shopkeeper, the artisan, the peasant, all these fight against the bourgeoisie, to save from extinction their existence as fractions of the middle class. They are, therefore, not revolutionary, but conservative. Nay more, they are reactionary, for they try to roll back the wheel of history. If by chance they are revolutionary, they are so, only in view of their impending transfer into the proletariat, they thus defend not their present, but their future interests, they desert their own standpoint to place themselves at that of the proletariat.

The "dangerous class," the social scum, that passively rotting mass thrown off by the lowest layers of old society, may, here and there, be swept into the movement by a proletarian revolution; its conditions of life, however, prepare it far more for the part of a bribed tool of reactionary intrigue.

In the conditions of the proletariat, those of old society at large are already virtually swamped. The proletarian is without property; his relation to his wife and children has no longer anything in common with the bourgeois family-relations; modern industrial labor, modern subjection to capital, the same in England as in France, in America as in Germany, has stripped him of every trace of national character. Law, morality, religion, are to him so many bourgeois prejudices, behind which lurk in ambush just as many bourgeois interests.

All the preceding classes that got the upper hand, sought to fortify their already acquired status by subjecting society at large to their conditions of appropriation. The proletarians cannot become masters of the productive forces of society, except by abolishing their own previous mode of appropriation, and thereby also every other previous mode of appropriation. They have nothing of their own to secure and to fortify; their mission is to destroy all previous securities for, and insurances of, individual property.

All previous historical movements were movements of minorities, or in the interest of minorities. The proletarian movement is the self-conscious, independent movement of the immense majority, in the interest of the immense majority. The proletariat, the lowest stratum of our present society, cannot stir, cannot raise itself up, without the whole superincumbent strata of official society being sprung into the air.

Though not in substance, yet in form, the struggle of the proletariat with the bourgeoisie is at first a national struggle. The proletariat of each country must, of course, first of all settle matters with its own bourgeoisie.

In depicting the most general phases of the development of the proletariat, we traced the more or less veiled civil war, raging within existing society, up to the point where that war breaks out into open revolution, and where the violent overthrow of the bourgeoisie lays the foundation for the sway of the proletariat.

Hitherto, every form of society has been based, as we have already seen, on the antagonism of oppressing and oppressed classes. But in order to oppress a class, certain conditions must be assured to it under which it can, at least, continue its slavish existence. The serf, in the period of serfdom, raised himself to membership in the commune, just as the petty bourgeois, under the yoke of feudal absolutism, managed to develop into a bourgeois. The modern laborer, on the contrary, instead of rising with the progress of industry, sinks deeper and deeper below the conditions of existence of his own class. He becomes a pauper, and pauperism develops more rapidly than population and wealth. And here is becomes evident, that the bourgeoisie is unfit any longer to be the ruling class in society, and to impose its conditions of existence upon society as an overriding law. It is unfit to rule, because it is incompetent to assure an existence to its slave within his slavery, because it cannot help letting him sink into such a state that it has to feed him, instead of being fed by him. Society can no longer live under this bourgeoisie, in other words, its existence is no longer compatible with society.

The essential condition for the existence, and for the sway of the bourgeois class, is the formation and augmentation of capital; the condition for capital is wage-labor. Wage-labor rests exclusively on competition between the laborers. The advance of industry, whose involuntary promoter is the bourgeoisie, replaces the isolation of the laborers, due to competition, by their revolutionary combination, due to association. The development of Modern Industry, therefore, cuts from under its feet the very foundation on which the bourgeoisie produces and appropriates products. What the bourgeoisie therefore produces, above all, are its own gravediggers. Its fall and the victory of the proletariat are equally inevitable.

In what relation do the Communists stand to the proletarians as a whole?

The Communists do not form a separate party opposed to other working class parties.

They have no interests separate and apart from those of the proletariat as a whole.

They do not set up any sectarian principles of their own, by which to shape and mould the proletarian movement.

The Communists are distinguished from the other working class parties by this only: 1. In the national struggles of the proletarians of the different countries, they point out and bring to the front the common interests of the entire proletariat independently of all nationality. 2. In the various stages of development which the struggle of the working class against the bourgeoisie has to pass through, they always and everywhere represent the interests of the movement as a whole.

The Communists, therefore, are on the one hand, practically, the most advanced and resolute section of the working class parties of every country, that section which pushes forward all others; on the other hand, theoretically, they have over the great mass of the proletariat the advantage of clearly understanding the line of march, the conditions, and the ultimate general results of the proletarian movement.

The immediate aim of the Communists is the same as that of all the other proletarian parties: formation of the proletariat into a class, overthrow of the bourgeois supremacy, conquest of political power by the proletariat.

The theoretical conclusions of the Communists are in no way based on ideas or principles that have been invented, or discovered, by this or that would-be universal reformer.

They merely express, in general terms, actual relations springing from an existing class struggle, from a historical movement going on under our very eyes. The abolition of existing property relations is not at all a distinctive feature of Communism.

All property relations in the past have continually been subject to historical change consequent upon the change in historical conditions.

The French Revolution, for example, abolished feudal property in favor of bourgeois property.

The distinguishing feature of Communism is not the abolition of property generally, but the abolition of bourgeois property. But modern bourgeois private property is the final and most complete expression of the system of producing and appropriating products, that is based on class antagonism, on the exploitation of the many by the few.

In this sense, the theory of the Communists may be summed up in the single sentence: Abolition of private property.

We Communists have been reproached with the desire of abolishing the right of personally acquiring property as the fruit of a man's own labor, which property is alleged to be the ground work of all personal freedom, activity and independence.

Hard-won, self-acquired, self-earned property! Do you mean the property of the petty artisan and of the small peasant, a form of property that preceded the bourgeois form? There is no need to abolish that; the development of industry has to a great extent already destroyed it, and is still destroying it daily.

Or do you mean modern bourgeois private property?

But does wage-labor create any property for the laborer? Not a bit. It creates capital, i.e., that kind of property which exploits wage-labor, and which cannot increase except upon condition of getting a new supply of wage-labor for fresh exploitation. Property, in its present form, is based on the antagonism of capital and wage-labor. Let us examine both sides of this antagonism.

To be a capitalist, is to have not only a purely personal, but a social status in production. Capital is a collective product, and only by the united action of many members, nay, in the last resort, only by the united action of all members of society, can it be set in motion.

Capital is therefore not a personal, it is a social power.

When, therefore, capital is converted into common property, into the property of all members of society, personal property is not thereby transformed into social property. It is only the social character of the property that is changed. It loses its class-character.

Let us now take wage-labor.

The average price of wage-labor is the minimum wage, i.e., that quantum of the means of subsistence, which is absolutely requisite to keep the laborer in bare existence as a laborer. What, therefore, the wage-laborer appropriates by means of his labor, merely suffices to prolong and reproduce a bare existence. We by no means intend to abolish this personal appropriation of the products of labor, an appropriation that is made for the maintenance and reproduction of human life, and that leaves no surplus wherewith to command the labor of others. All that we want to do away with is the miserable character of this appropriation, under which the laborer lives merely to increase capital, and is allowed to live only in so far as the interest of the ruling class requires it.

In bourgeois society, living labor is but a means to increase accumulated labor. In communist society, accumulated labor is a means to widen, to enrich, to promote the existence of the laborer.

In bourgeois society, therefore, the past dominates the present; in communist society, the present dominates the past. In bourgeois society capital is independent and has individuality, while the living person is dependent and has no individuality.

And the abolition of this state of things is called by the bourgeois, abolition of individuality and freedom! And rightly so. The abolition of bourgeois individuality, bourgeois independence, and bourgeois freedom is undoubtedly aimed at.

By freedom is meant, under the present bourgeois conditions of production, free trade, free selling and buying.

But if selling and buying disappears, free selling and buying disappears also. This talk about free selling and buying, and all the other "brave words" of our bourgeoisie about freedom in general, have a meaning, if any, only in contrast with restricted selling and buying, with the fettered traders of the Middle Ages, but have no meaning when opposed to the Communistic abolition of buying and selling, of the bourgeois conditions of production, and of the bourgeoisie itself.

You are horrified at our intending to do away with private property. But in your existing society, private property is already done away with for nine-tenths of the population; its existence for the few is solely due to its non-existence in the hands of those nine-tenths. You reproach us, therefore, with intending to do away with a form of property, the necessary condition for whose existence is, the non-existence of any property for the immense majority of society.

In one word, you reproach us with intending to do away with your property. Precisely so; that is just what we intend.

From the moment when labor can no longer be converted into capital, money, or rent, into a social power capable of being monopolized, i.e., from the moment when individual property can no longer be transformed into bourgeois property, into capital, from that moment, you say, individuality vanishes.

You must, therefore, confess that by "individual" you mean no other person than the bourgeois, than the middle-class owner of property. This person must, indeed, be swept out of the way, and made impossible.

Communism deprives no man of the power to appropriate the products of society: all that it does is to deprive him of the power to subjugate the labor of others by means of such appropriation.

It has been objected, that upon the abolition of private property all work will cease, and universal laziness will overtake us.

According to this, bourgeois society ought long ago to have gone to the dogs through sheer idleness; for those of its members who work, acquire nothing, and those who acquire anything, do not work. The whole of this objection is but another expression of the tautology: that there can no longer be any wage-labor when there is no longer any capital.

All objections urged against the Communistic mode of producing and appropriating material products, have, in the same way, been urged against the Communistic modes of producing and appropriating intellectual products. Just as, to the bourgeois, the disappearance of class property is the disappearance of production itself, so the disappearance of class culture is to him identical with the disappearance of all culture.

That culture, the loss of which he laments, is, for the enormous majority, a mere training to act as a machine.

But don't wrangle with us so long as you apply, to our intended abolition of bourgeois property, the standard of your bourgeois notions of freedom, culture, law, etc. Your very ideas are but the outgrowth of the conditions of your bourgeois production and bourgeois property, just as your jurisprudence is but the will of your class made into a law for all, a will, whose essential character and direction are determined by the economic conditions of existence of your class.

The selfish misconception that induces you to transform into eternal laws of nature and of reason, the social forms springing from your present mode of production and form of property—historical relations that rise and disappear in the progress of production—this misconception you share with every ruling class that has preceded you. What you see clearly in the case of ancient property, what you admit in the case of feudal property, you are of course forbidden to admit in the case of your own bourgeois form of property.

Abolition of the family! Even the most radical flare up at this infamous proposal of the Communists.

On what foundation is the present family, the bourgeois family, based? On capital, on private gain. In its completely developed form this family exists only among the bourgeoisie. But this state of things finds its complement in the practical absence of the family among the proletarians, and in public prostitution.

The bourgeois family will vanish as a matter of course when its complement vanishes, and both will vanish with the vanishing of capital.

Do you charge us with wanting to stop the exploitation of children by their parents? To this crime we plead guilty.

But, you will say, we destroy the most hallowed of relations, when we replace home education by social.

And your education! Is not that also social, and determined by the social conditions under which you educate, by the intervention, direct or indirect, of society by means of schools, etc? The Communists have not invented the intervention of society in education; they do but seek to alter the character of that intervention, and to rescue education from the influence of the ruling class.

The bourgeois clap-trap about the family and education, about the hallowed co-relation of parent and child, becomes all the more disgusting, the more, by the action of Modern Industry, all family ties among the proletarians are torn asunder, and their children transformed into simple articles of commerce and instruments of labor.

But you Communists would introduce community of women, screams the whole bourgeoisie in chorus.

The bourgeois sees in his wife a mere instrument of production. He hears that the instruments of production are to be exploited in common, and, naturally, can come to no other conclusion, than that the lot of being common to all will likewise fall to the women.

He has not even a suspicion that the real point aimed at is to do away with the status of women as mere instruments of production.

For the rest, nothing is more ridiculous than the virtuous indignation of our bourgeois at the community of women which, they pretend, is to be openly and officially established by the Communists. The Communists have no need to introduce community of women; it has existed almost from time immemorial.

Our bourgeois, not content with having the wives and daughters of their proletarians at their disposal, not to speak of common prostitutes, take the greatest pleasure in seducing each other's wives.

Bourgeois marriage is in reality a system of wives in common and thus, at the most, what the Communists might possibly be reproached with, is that they desire to introduce, in substitution for a hypocritically concealed, an openly legalized community of women. For the rest, it is self-evident, that the abolition of the present system of production must bring with it the abolition of the community of women springing from that system, i.e., of prostitution both public and private.

The Communists are further reproached with desiring to abolish countries and nationalities.

The working men have no country. We cannot take from them what they have not got. Since the proletariat must first of all acquire political supremacy, must rise to be the leading class of the nation, must constitute itself the nation, it is, so far, itself national, though not in the bourgeois sense of the word.

National differences, and antagonisms between peoples, are daily more and more vanishing, owing to the development of the bourgeoisie, to freedom of commerce, to the world-market, to uniformity in the mode of production and in the conditions of life corresponding thereto.

The supremacy of the proletariat will cause them to vanish still faster. United action, of the leading civilized countries at least, is one of the first conditions for the emancipation of the proletariat.

In proportion as the exploitation of one individual by another is put an end to, the exploitation of one nation by another will also be put an end to. In proportion as the antagonism between classes within the nation vanishes, the hostility of one nation to another will come to an end.

The charges against Communism made from a religious, a philosophical, and generally, from an ideological standpoint, are not deserving of serious examination.

Does it require deep intuition to comprehend that man's ideas, views, and conceptions, in one word, man's consciousness, changes with every change in the conditions of his material existence, in his social relations and in his social life?

What else does the history of ideas prove, than that intellectual production changes in character in proportion as material production is changed? The ruling ideas of each age have ever been the ideas of its ruling class.

When people speak of ideas that revolutionize society, they do but express the fact, that within the old society, the elements of a new one have been created, and that the dissolution of the old ideas keeps even pace with the dissolution of the old conditions of existence.

When the ancient world was in its last throes, the ancient religions were overcome by Christianity. When Christian ideas succumbed in the 18th century to rationalist ideas, feudal society fought its death-battle with the then revolutionary bourgeoisie. The ideas of religious liberty and freedom of conscience, merely gave expression to the sway of free competition within the domain of knowledge.

"Undoubtedly," it will be said, "religious, moral, philosophical and juridical ideas have been modified in the course of historical development. But religion, morality, philosophy, political science, and law, constantly survived this change.

"There are, besides, eternal truths, such as Freedom, Justice, etc., that are common to all states of society. But Communism abolishes eternal truths, it abolishes all religion, and all morality, instead of constituting them on a new basis; it therefore acts in contradiction to all past historical experience."

What does this accusation reduce itself to? The history of all past society has consisted in the development of class antagonisms, antagonisms that assume different forms at different epochs.

But whatever form they may have taken, one fact is common to all past ages, viz., the exploitation of one part of society by the other. No wonder, then, that the social consciousness of past ages, despite all the multiplicity and variety it displays, moves within certain common forms, or general ideas, which cannot completely vanish except with the total disappearance of class antagonisms.

The Communist revolution is the most radical rupture with traditional property-relations; no wonder that its development involves the most radical rupture with traditional ideas.

But let us have done with the bourgeois objections to Communism.

We have seen above, that the first step in the revolution by the working class, is to raise the proletariat to the position of ruling class, to win the battle of democracy.

The proletariat will use its political supremacy, to wrest, by degrees, all capital from the bourgeoisie, to centralize all instruments of production in the hands of the State, i.e., of the proletariat organized as the ruling class; and to increase the total of productive forces as rapidly as possible.

Of course, in the beginning, this cannot be effected except by means of despotic inroads on the rights of property, and on the conditions of bourgeois production; by means of measures, therefore, which appear economically insufficient and untenable, but which, in the course of the movement, outstrip themselves, necessitate further inroads upon the old social order, and are unavoidable as a means of entirely revolutionizing the mode of production.

These measures will of course be different in different countries.

Nevertheless in the most advanced countries the following will be pretty generally applicable:

1. Abolition of property in land and application of all rents of land to public purposes.

2. A heavy progressive or graduated income tax.

3. Abolition of all right of inheritance.

4. Confiscation of the property of all emigrants and rebels.

5. Centralization of credit in the hands of the state, by means of a national bank with State capital and an exclusive monopoly.

6. Centralization of the means of communication and transport in the hands of the State.

7. Extension of factories and instruments of production owned by the State; the bringing into cultivation of waste lands, and the improvement of the soil generally in accordance with a common plan.

8. Equal liability of all to labor. Establishment of industrial armies, especially for agriculture.

9. Combination of agriculture with manufacturing industries; gradual abolition of the distinction between town and country, by a more equable distribution of population over the country.

10. Free education for all children in public schools. Abolition of children's factory labor in its present form. Combination of education with industrial production, etc., etc.

When, in the course of development, class distinctions have disappeared, and all production has been concentrated in the hands of a vast association of the whole nation, the public power will lose its political character. Political power, properly so called, is merely the organized power of one class for oppressing another. If the proletariat during its contest with the bourgeoisie is compelled, by the force of circumstances, to organize itself as a class, if, by means of a revolution, it makes itself the ruling class, and, as such, sweeps away by force the old conditions of production, then it will, along with these conditions, have swept away the conditions for the existence of class antagonisms, and of classes generally, and will thereby have abolished its own supremacy as a class.

In place of the old bourgeois society, with its classes and class antagonisms, we shall have an association, in which the free development of each is the condition for the free development of all. . . .

The Communists turn their attention chiefly to Germany, because that country is on the eve of a bourgeois revolution, that is bound to be carried out under more advanced conditions of European civilization, and with a more developed proletariat, than that of England was in the seventeenth, and of France in the eighteenth century, and because the bourgeois revolution in Germany will be but the prelude to an immediately following proletarian revolution.

In short, the Communists everywhere support every revolutionary movement against the existing social and political order of things.

In all these movements they bring to the front, as the leading question in each, the property question, no matter what its degree of development at the time.

Finally, they labor everywhere for the union and agreement of the democratic parties of all countries.

The Communists disdain to conceal their views and aims. They openly declare that their ends can be attained only by the forcible overthrow of all existing social conditions. Let the ruling classes tremble at a Communistic revolution. The proletarians have nothing to lose but their chains. They have a world to win.

Working men of all countries, unite!

IN THE DECADES following the publication of The Communist Manifesto, *Socialist and Communist theory reflected profoundly the Marxist influence yet remained split into a number of different camps. In general, the differences centered around the question of whether Socialism would be achieved gradually through peaceful constitutional processes or by means of violent revolution. The English Fabian Society, which arose in the late nineteenth century and included such luminaries as H. G. Wells, George Bernard Shaw, and Sidney and Beatrice Webb, was a relatively restrained, middle-class movement whose devotion to gradualism and legality is clearly illustrated in an official statement the Fabians issued in 1896.*

2. FABIAN SOCIALISM: AIMS AND METHODS, 1896

SOURCE. *Full Report of the Proceedings of the International Workers' Congress, July and August, 1896*, London: 1896, pp. 45–49.

The object of the Fabian Society is to persuade the English people to make their political constitution thoroughly democratic and to socialise their industries sufficiently to make the livelihood of the people entirely independent of private Capitalism.

The Fabian Society endeavours to pursue its Socialist and Democratic objects with complete singleness of aim. For example:

It does not ask the English people to join the Fabian Society.

It does not propose that the practical steps towards Social-Democracy should be carried out by itself, or by any other specially organised Socialist society or party.

It brings all the pressure and persuasion in its power to bear, not on the imaginary forces of the future, but on the existing forces of to-day, caring nothing by what name any party calls itself, or what principles, Socialist or other, it professes, but having regard solely to the tendency of its actions, supporting those which make for Socialism and Democracy, and opposing those which are reactionary. . . .

The Fabian Society does not claim to be the people of England, or even the Socialist party, and therefore does not seek direct political representation by putting forward Fabian candidates at elections. But it loses no opportunity of influencing elections and inducing constituencies to select Socialists as their candidates. No person, however, can obtain the support of the Fabian Society, or escape its opposition, by merely repeating a few shibboleths. . . .

The Fabian Society is perfectly constitutional in its attitude, and its methods are those usual in political life in England.

The Fabian Society accepts the conditions imposed on it by human nature and by the national character and political circumstances of the English people. It sympathises with the ordinary man's preference for gradual, peaceful changes, to revolution, conflict with the army and police, and martyrdom. It recognises the fact that Social-Democracy is not the whole of the working-class programme, and that every separate measure towards the socialisation of industry will have to compete for precedence with numbers of other reforms. It therefore does not believe that the moment will ever come when the whole of Socialism will be staked on the issue of a single General Election or a single Bill in the House of Commons as between the proletariat on one side and the proprietariat on the other. Each instalment of Social-Democracy will only be a measure among other measures, and will have to be kept to the front by an energetic Fabian section of the working-class party. . . .

Socialism, as understood by the Fabian Society, means the organisation and conduct of the necessary industries of the country and the appropriation of all forms of economic rent of land and capital, by the nation as a whole, through the co-ordinate agency of the most suitable public authorities. . . .

The Fabian Society strenuously maintains its freedom of thought and speech with regard to the errors of Socialist authors, economists, leaders, and parties, no less than to those of its opponents. It insists on the necessity of maintaining as critical an attitude towards Marx and Lassalle, some of whose views must by this time be discarded as erroneous or obsolete, as these eminent Socialists themselves maintained towards their predecessors. . . .

In view of the fact that the Socialist movement has been hitherto inspired, instructed, led, and suffered for by members of the middle class or "bourgeoisie," the Fabian Society, though not at all surprised to find these middle-class leaders attacking with much bitterness the narrow social ideals current in their own class, protests against the absurdity of Socialists representing the very class from which Socialism has sprung as specially hostile to it. The Fabian Society has no romantic illusions as to the freedom of the proletariat from these same narrow ideals. Like all other Socialist societies, it can only educate the people in Socialism by making them conversant with the conclusions of the most enlightened members of the middle classes and their pupils. The Fabian Society therefore cannot reasonably use the words "bourgeois" or "middle class" as terms of reproach, more especially as it would thereby condemn a large proportion of its own members.

The Fabian Society endeavours to rouse social compunction by making the public conscious of the evil condition of society under the present system. This it does by the collection and publication of authentic and impartial statistical tracts, compiled, not from the works of Socialists, but from official sources. The first volume of Karl Marx's "Das Kapital," which contains an immense mass of carefully verified facts concerning modern capitalistic civilisation, and practically nothing at all about Socialism, is probably the most successful propagandist work ever published. The Fabian Society, in its endeavours to continue the work of Marx in this direction, has found that the guesses made by Socialists at the condition of the people almost invariably flatter the existing system instead of, as might be suspected, exaggerating its evils. The Fabian Society therefore concluded that in the natural philosophy of Socialism, light is a more important factor than heat. . . .

The Fabian Society does not put Socialism forward as a panacea for all the ills of human society, but only for those produced by defective organisation of industry and radically bad distribution of wealth.

The Fabian Society, by steadfastly refusing to sacrifice the interests of Socialism either to the mistakes of Socialists on the one hand, or the political convenience of the established political parties on the other, has been violently denounced from both sides, the Liberal and Socialist newspapers often vying with one another in their efforts to discredit the Fabian Society. The only compliments which the Fabian Society receives or expects from non-Fabian Socialists, are the applications for advice, speakers, and money, which are invariably made to it in all emergencies, and to which it always responds to the best of its ability.

CLOSER TO the Marxist tradition was the revisionist theory of Eduard Bernstein. This German evolutionary socialist summarized and defended his basic ideas in his letter of October 1898 to the German Social Democratic Party.

3. REVISIONIST MARXISM: EDUARD BERNSTEIN, FROM A LETTER TO THE GERMAN SOCIAL DEMOCRATIC PARTY, 1898

SOURCE. Eduard Bernstein, *Evolutionary Socialism*, New York: Schocken Books, 1961, preface to 1899 edition. Reprinted by permission of Schocken Books, Inc.

I set myself against the notion that we have to expect shortly a collapse of the bourgeois economy, and that social democracy should be induced by the prospect of such an imminent, great, social catastrophe to adapt its tactics to that assumption. That I maintain most emphatically.

The adherents of this theory of a catastrophe, base it especially on the conclusions of the *Communist Manifesto*. This is a mistake in every respect.

The theory which the *Communist Manifesto* sets forth of the evolution of modern society was correct as far as it characterised the general tendencies of that evolution. But it was mistaken in several special deductions, above all in the estimate of the *time* the evolution would take. The last has been unreservedly acknowledged by Friedrich Engels, the joint author with Marx of the *Manifesto*, in his preface to the *Class War in France*. But it is evident that if social evolution takes a much greater period of time than was assumed, it must also take upon itself *forms* and lead to forms that were not foreseen and could not be foreseen then.

Social conditions have not developed to such an acute opposition of things and classes as is depicted in the *Manifesto*. It is not only useless, it is the greatest folly to attempt to conceal this from ourselves. The number of members of the possessing classes is to-day not smaller but larger. The enormous increase of social wealth is not accompanied by a decreasing number of large capitalists but by an increasing number of capitalists of all degrees. The middle classes change their character but they do not disappear from the social scale.

The concentration in productive industry is not being accomplished even to day in all its departments with equal thoroughness and at an equal rate. In a great many branches of production it certainly justifies the forecasts of the socialist critic of society; but in other branches it lags even to-day behind them. The process of concentration in agriculture proceeds still more slowly. Trade statistics shown an extraordinarily elaborated graduation of enterpirses in regard to size. No rung of the ladder is disappearing from it. The significant changes in the inner structure of these enterprises and their inter-relationship cannot do away with this fact.

In all advanced countries we see the privileges of the capitalist bourgeoisie yielding step by step to democratic organisations. Under the influence of this, and driven by the movement of the working classes which is daily becoming stronger, a social reaction has set in against the exploiting tendencies of capital, a counteraction which, although it still proceeds timidly and feebly, yet does exist, and is always drawing more departments of economic life under its influence. Factory legislation, the democratising of local government, and the extension of its area of work, the freeing of trade unions and systems of co-operative trading from legal restrictions, the consideration of standard conditions of labour in the work undertaken by public authorities—all these characterise this phase of the evolution.

But the more the political organisations of modern nations are democratised the more the needs and opportunities of great political catastrophes are diminished. He who holds firmly to the catastrophic theory of evolution must, with all his power, withstand and hinder the evolution described above, which, indeed, the logical defenders of that theory formerly did. But is the conquest of political power by the proletariat simply to be by a political catastrophe? Is it to be the appropriation and utilisation of the power of the State by the proletariat exclusively against the whole nonproletarian world? . . .

No one has questioned the necessity for the working classes to gain the control of government. The point at issue is between the theory of a social cataclysm and the question whether with the given social development in Germany and the present advanced state of its working classes in the towns and the country, a sudden catastrophe would be desirable in the interest of the social democracy. I have denied it and deny it again, because in my judgment a greater security for lasting success lies in a steady advance than in the possibilities offered by a catastrophic crash.

And as I am firmly convinced that important periods in the development of nations cannot be leapt over I lay the greatest value on the next tasks of social democracy, on the struggle for the political rights of the working man, on the political activity of working men in town and country for the interests of their class, as well as on the work of the industrial organisation of the workers.

In this sense I wrote the sentence that the movement means everything for me and that what is *usually* called "the final aim of socialism" is nothing; and in this sense I write it down again to-day. Even if the word "usually" had not shown that the proposition was only to be understood conditionally, it was obvious that it *could* not express indifference concerning the final carrying out of socialist principles, but only indifference—or, as it would be better expressed, carelessness—as to the form of the final arrangement of things. I have at no time had an excessive interest in the future, beyond general principles; I have not been able to read to the end any picture of the future. My thoughts and efforts are concerned with the duties of the present and the nearest future, and I only busy myself with the perspectives beyond so far as they give me a line of conduct for suitable action now.

The conquest of political power by the working classes, the expropriation of capitalists, are no ends in themselves but only means for the accomplishment of certain aims and endeavours. As such they are demands in the programme of social democracy and are not attacked by me. Nothing can be said beforehand as to the circumstances of their accomplishment; we can only fight for their realisation. But the conquest of political power necessitates the possession of political *rights;* and the most important problem of tactics which German social democracy has at the present time to solve, appears to me to be to devise the best ways for the extension of the political and economic rights of the German working classes.

B. Communism in the Early Twentieth Century

THE EVOLUTIONARY MARXISM of Bernstein and others came under heavy attack by the strict Marxist Vladimir I. Lenin, the architect of the Communist Revolution in Russia. In his State and Revolution (1917), Lenin reasserted the traditional Marxist insistence on violent revolution. Both Bernstein and Lenin appealed to the authority of Marx and Engels in much the way that disputing Christians might cite passages from Scripture against one another.

1. LENIN, FROM *STATE AND REVOLUTION*, 1917

SOURCE. V. I. Lenin, *State and Revolution,* New York: International Publishers, New York, 1932, pp. 7–10, 12–13, 15–17, 69–75. Reprinted by permission of International Publishers Co., Inc.

What is now happening to Marx's doctrine has, in the course of history, often happened to the doctrines of other revolutionary thinkers and leaders of oppressed classes struggling for emancipation. During the lifetime of great revolutionaries, the oppressing classes have visited relentless persecution on them and received their teaching with the most savage hostility, the most furious hatred, the most ruthless campaign of lies and slanders. After their death, attempts are made to turn them into harmless icons, canonise them, and surround their *names* with a certain halo for the "consolation" of the oppressed classes and with the object of duping them, while at the same time emasculating and vulgarising the *real essence* of their revolutionary theories and blunting their revolutionary edge. At the present time, the bourgeoisie and the opportunists within the labour movement are co-operating in this work of adulterating Marxism. They omit, obliterate, and distort the revolutionary side of its teaching, its revolutionary soul. . . .

In such circumstances, the distortion of Marxism being so widespread, it is our first task to *resuscitate* the real teachings of Marx on the state. For this purpose it will be necessary to quote at length from the works of Marx and Engels themselves. . . .

Let us begin with the most popular of Engels' works, *Der Ursprung der Familie, des Privateigentums und des Staats,* the sixth edition of which was published in Stuttgart as far back as 1894. We must translate the quotations from the German originals, as the Russian translations, although very numerous, are for the most part either incomplete or very unsatisfactory.

Summarising his historical analysis Engels says:

The state is therefore by no means a power imposed on society from the outside; just as little is it "the reality of the moral idea," "the image and reality of reason," as Hegel asserted. Rather, it is a product of society at a certain stage of development; it is the admission that this society has become entangled in an insoluble contradiction with itself, that it is cleft into irreconcilable antagonisms which it is powerless to dispel. But in order that these antagonisms, classes with conflicting economic interests, may not consume themselves and society in sterile struggle, a power apparently standing above society becomes necessary, whose purpose is to moderate the conflict and keep it within the bounds of "order"; and this power arising out of society, but placing itself above it, and increasingly separating itself from it, is the state.

Here we have, expressed in all its clearness, the basic idea of Marxism on the question of the historical rôle and meaning of the state. The state is the product and the manifestation of the *irreconcilability* of class antagonisms. The state arises when, where, and to the extent that the class antagonisms *cannot* be objectively reconciled. And, conversely, the existence of the state proves that the class antagonisms *are* irreconcilable.

It is precisely on this most important and fundamental point that distortions of Marxism arise along two main lines.

On the one hand, the bourgeois, and particularly the petty-bourgeois, ideologists, compelled under the pressure of indisputable historical facts to admit that the state only exists where there are class antagonisms and the class struggle, "correct" Marx in such a way as to make it appear that the state is an organ for *reconciling* the classes. According to Marx, the state could neither arise nor maintain itself if a reconciliation of classes were possible. But with the petty-bourgeois and philistine professors and publicists, the state—and this frequently on the strength of benevolent references to Marx!—becomes a conciliator of the classes. According to Marx, the state is an organ of class *domination,* an organ of *oppression* of one class by another; its aim is the creation of "order" which legalises and perpetuates this oppression by moderating the collisions between the classes. But in the opinion of the petty-bourgeois politicians, order means reconciliation of the classes, and not oppression of one class by another; to moderate collisions does not mean, they say, to deprive the oppressed classes of certain definite means and methods of struggle for overthrowing the oppressors, but to practice reconciliation. . . .

Engels develops the conception of that "power" which is termed the state—a power arising from society, but placing itself above it and becoming more and more separated from it. What does this power mainly consist of? It consists of special bodies of armed men who have at their disposal prisons, etc.

We are justified in speaking of special bodies of armed men, because the public power peculiar to every state is not "absolutely identical" with the armed population, with its "self-acting armed organisation." . . .

For the maintenance of a special public force standing above society, taxes and state loans are needed.

Having at their disposal the public force and the right to exact taxes, the officials now stand as organs of society *above* society. The free, voluntary respect which was accorded to the organs of the gentilic form of government does not satisfy them, even if they could have it. . . .

Special laws are enacted regarding the sanctity and the inviolability of the officials. "The shabbiest police servant . . . has more authority" than the representative of the clan, but even the head of the military power of a civilised state "may well envy the least among the chiefs of the clan the unconstrained and uncontested respect which is paid to him." . . .

Engels' words regarding the "withering away" of the state enjoy such popularity, they are so often quoted, and they show so clearly the essence of the usual adulteration by means of which Marxism is made to look like opportunism, that we must dwell on them in detail. Let us quote the whole passage from which they are taken.

The proletariat seizes state power, and then transforms the means of production into state property. But in doing this, it puts an end to itself as the proletariat, it puts an end to all class differences and class antagonisms, it puts an end also to the state as the state. Former society, moving in class antagonisms, had need of the state, that is, or organisation of the exploiting class at each period for the maintenance of its external conditions of production; therefore, in particular, for the forcible holding down of the exploited class in the conditions of oppression (slavery, bondage or serfdom, wage-labour) determined by the existing mode of production. The state was the official representative of society as a whole, its embodiment in a visible corporate body; but it was this only in so far as it was the state of that class which itself, in its epoch, represented society as a whole: in ancient times, the state of the slave-owning citizens; in the Middle Ages, of the feudal nobility; in our epoch, of the bourgeoisie. When ultimately it becomes really representative of society as a whole, it makes itself superfluous. As soon as there is no longer any class of society to be held in subjection; as soon as, along with class domination and the struggle for individual existence based on the former anarchy of production, the collisions and excesses arising from these have also been abolished, there is nothing more to be repressed, and a special repressive force, a state, is no longer necessary. The first act in which the state really comes forward as the representative of society as a whole—the seizure of the means of production in the name of society—is at the same time its last independent act as a state. The interference of a state power in social relations becomes superfluous in one sphere after another, and then

becomes dormant of itself. Government over persons is replaced by the administration of things and the direction of the processes of production. The state is
not "abolished," *it withers away.* It is from this standpoint that we must appraise
the phrase "people's free state"—both its justification at times for agitational
purposes, and its ultimate scientific inadequacy—and also the demand of the
so-called Anarchists that the state should be abolished overnight.

Without fear of committing an error, it may be said that of this argument by Engels so singularly rich in ideas, only one point has become
an integral part of Socialist thought among modern Socialist parties,
namely, that, unlike the Anarchist doctrine of the "abolition" of the state,
according to Marx the state "withers away." To emasculate Marxism in
such a manner is to reduce it to opportunism, for such an "interpretation" only leaves the hazy conception of a slow, even, gradual change,
free from leaps and storms, free from revolution. The current popular
conception, if one may say so, of the "withering away" of the state undoubtedly means a slurring over, if not a negation, of revolution.

Yet, such an "interpretation" is the crudest distortion of Marxism,
which is advantageous only to the bourgeoisie; in point of theory, it is
based on a disregard for the most important circumstances and considerations pointed out in the very passage summarising Engels' ideas, which
we have just quoted in full.

In the first place, Engels at the very outset of his argument says that,
in assuming state power, the proletariat by that very act "puts an end
to the state as the state." One is "not accustomed" to reflect on what this
really means. Generally, it is either ignored altogether, or it is considered
as a piece of "Hegelian weakness" on Engels' part. As a matter of fact,
however, these words express succinctly the experience of one of the
greatest proletarian revolutions—the Paris Commune of 1871, of which
we shall speak in greater detail in its proper place. As a matter of fact,
Engels speaks here of the destruction of the bourgeois state by the proletarian revolution, while the words about its withering away refer to
the remains of *proletarian* statehood *after* the Socialist revolution. The
bourgeois state does not "wither away," according to Engels, but is "put
an end to" by the proletariat in the course of the revolution. What withers
away after the revolution is the proletarian state or semi-state.

Secondly, the state is a "special repressive force." This splendid and
extremely profound definition of Engels' is given by him here with complete lucidity. It follows from this that the "special repressive force" of
the bourgeoisie for the suppression of the proletariat, of the millions of
workers by a handful of the rich, must be replaced by a "special repressive force" of the proletariat for the suppression of the bourgeoisie (the
dictatorship of the proletariat). It is just this that constitutes the "act" of

"the seizure of the means of production in the name of society." And it is obvious that such a substitution of one (proletarian) "special repressive force" for another (bourgeois) "special repressive force" can in no way take place in the form of a "withering away."

Thirdly, as to the "withering away" or, more expressively and colourfully, as to the state "becoming dormant," Engels refers quite clearly and definitely to the period *after* "the seizure of the means of production [by the state] in the name of society," that is *after* the Socialist revolution. We all know that the political form of the "state" at that time is complete democracy. . . . The bourgeois state can only be "put an end to" by a revolution. The state in general, *i.e.*, most complete democracy, can only "wither away." . . .

The whole theory of Marx is an application of the theory of evolution —in its most consistent, complete, well considered and fruitful form—to modern capitalism. It was natural for Marx to raise the question of applying this theory both to the *coming* collapse of capitalism and to the *future* evolution of *future* Communism.

On the basis of what *data* can the future evolution of future Communism be considered?

On the basis of the fact that *it has its origin* in capitalism, that it develops historically from capitalism, that it is the result of the action of a social force to which capitalism *has given birth*. There is no shadow of an attempt on Marx's part to conjure up a Utopia, to make idle guesses about that which cannot be known. Marx treats the question of Communism in the same way as a naturalist would treat the question of the evolution of, say, a new biological species, if he knew that such and such was its origin, and such and such the direction in which it changed. . . .

The first fact that has been established with complete exactness by the whole theory of evolution, by science as a whole—a fact which the Utopians forgot, and which is forgotten by the present-day opportunists who are afraid of the Socialist revolution—is that, historically, there must undoubtedly be a special stage or epoch of *transition* from capitalism to Communism.

Between capitalist and Communist society—Marx continues—lies the period of the revolutionary transformation of the former into the latter. To this also corresponds a political transition period, in which the state can be no other than *the revolutionary dictatorship of the proletariat*.

This conclusion Marx bases on an analysis of the rôle played by the proletariat in modern capitalist society, on the data concerning the evolution of this society, and on the irreconcilability of the opposing interests of the proletariat and the bourgeoisie.

Earlier the question was put thus: to attain its emancipation, the proletariat must overthrow the bourgeoisie, conquer political power and establish its own revolutionary dictatorship.

Now the question is put somewhat differently: the transition from capitalist society, developing towards Communism, towards a Communist society, is impossible without a "political transition period," and the state in this period can only be the revolutionary dictatorship of the proletariat.

What, then, is the relation of this dictatorship to democracy?

We have seen that the *Communist Manifesto* simply places side by side the two ideas: the "transformation of the proletariat into the ruling class" and the "establishment of democracy." On the basis of all that has been said above, one can define more exactly how democracy changes in the transition from capitalism to Communism.

In capitalist society, under the conditions most favourable to its development, we have more or less complete democracy in the democratic republic. But this democracy is always bound by the narrow framework of capitalist exploitation, and consequently always remains, in reality, a democracy for the minority, only for the possessing classes, only for the rich. Freedom in capitalist society always remains just about the same as it was in the ancient Greek republics: freedom for the slave-owners. The modern wage-slaves, owing to the conditions of capitalist exploitation, are so much crushed by want and poverty that "democracy is nothing to them," "politics is nothing to them"; that, in the ordinary peaceful course of events, the majority of the population is debarred from participating in social and political life.

The correctness of this statement is perhaps most clearly proved by Germany, just because in this state constitutional legality lasted and remained stable for a remarkably long time—for nearly half a century (1871–1914)—and because Social-Democracy in Germany during that time was able to achieve far more than in other countries in "utilising legality," and was able to organise into a political party a larger proportion of the working class than anywhere else in the world.

What, then, is this largest proportion of politically conscious and active wage-slaves that has so far been observed in capitalist society? One million members of the Social-Democratic Party—out of fifteen million wage-workers! Three million organised in trade unions—out of fifteen millions!

Democracy for an insignificant minority, democracy for the rich—that is the democracy of capitalist society. If we look more closely into the mechanism of capitalist democracy, everywhere, both in the "petty"— so-called petty—details of the suffrage (residential qualification, exclusion of women, etc.), and in the technique of the representative institutions, in the actual obstacles to the right of assembly (public buildings are not for "beggars"!), in the purely capitalist organisation of the daily press, etc., etc.—on all sides we see restriction after restriction upon democracy. These restrictions, exceptions, exclusions, obstacles for the poor, seem slight, especially in the eyes of one who has himself never known want and has never been in close contact with the oppressed classes in their mass life (and nine-tenths, if not ninety-nine hundredths, of the bourgeois publicists and politicians are of this class), but in their sum total these restrictions exclude and squeeze out the poor from politics and from an active share in democracy.

Marx splendidly grasped this *essence* of capitalist democracy, when, in analysing the experience of the Commune, he said that the oppressed were allowed, once every few years, to decide which particular representatives of the oppressing class should be in parliament to represent and repress them!

But from this capitalist democracy—inevitably narrow, subtly rejecting the poor, and therefore hypocritical and false to the core—progress does not march onward, simply, smoothly and directly, to "greater and greater democracy," as the liberal professors and petty-bourgeois opportunists would have us believe. No, progress marches onward, *i.e.*, towards Communism, through the dictatorship of the proletariat; it cannot do otherwise, for there is no one else and no other way to *break the resistance* of the capitalist exploiters.

But the dictatorship of the proletariat—*i.e.*, the organisation of the vanguard of the oppressed as the ruling class for the purpose of crushing the oppressors—cannot produce merely an expansion of democracy. *Together* with an immense expansion of democracy which *for the first time* becomes democracy for the poor, democracy for the people, and not democracy for the rich folk, the dictatorship of the proletariat produces a series of restrictions of liberty in the case of the oppressors, the exploiters, the capitalists. We must crush them in order to free humanity from wage-slavery; their resistance must be broken by force; it is clear that where there is suppression there is also violence, there is no liberty, no democracy.

Engels expressed this splendidly in his letter to Bebel when he said, as the reader will remember, that "as long as the proletariat still *needs* the state, it needs it not in the interests of freedom, but for the purpose of crushing its antagonists; and as soon as it becomes possible to speak of freedom, then the state, as such, ceases to exist."

Democracy for the vast majority of the people, and suppression by force, *i.e.*, exclusion from democracy, of the exploiters and oppressors of the people—this is the modification of democracy during the *transition* from capitalism to Communism.

Only in Communist society, when the resistance of the capitalists has been completely broken, when the capitalists have disappeared, when there are no classes (*i.e.*, there is no difference between the members of society in their relation to the social means of production), *only then* "the state ceases to exist," and "*it becomes possible to speak of freedom.*" Only then a really full democracy, a democracy without any exceptions, will be possible and will be realised. And only then will democracy itself begin to *wither away* due to the simple fact that, freed from capitalist slavery, from the untold horrors, savagery, absurdities and infamies of capitalist exploitation, people will gradually *become accustomed* to the observance of the elementary rules of social life that have been known for centuries and repeated for thousands of years in all school books; they will become accustomed to observing them without force, without compulsion, without subordination, without the *special apparatus* for compulsion which is called the state.

The expression "the state *withers away*," is very well chosen, for it indicates both the gradual and the elemental nature of the process. Only habit can, and undoubtedly will, have such an effect; for we see around us millions of times how readily people get accustomed to observe the necessary rules of life in common, if there is no exploitation, if there is nothing that causes indignation, that calls forth protest and revolt and has to be *suppressed*.

Thus, in capitalist society, we have a democracy that is curtailed, poor, false; a democracy only for the rich, for the minority. The dictatorship of the proletariat, the period of transition to Communism, will, for the first time, produce democracy for the people, for the majority, side by side with the necessary suppression of the minority—the exploiters. Communism alone is capable of giving a really complete democracy, and the more complete it is the more quickly will it become unnecessary and wither away of itself.

In other words: under capitalism we have a state in the proper sense of the word, that is, special machinery for the suppression of one class by another, and of the majority by the minority at that. Naturally, for the successful discharge of such a task as the systematic suppression by the exploiting minority of the exploited majority, the greatest ferocity and savagery of suppression are required, seas of blood are required, through which mankind is marching in slavery, serfdom, and wage-labour.

Again, during the *transition* from capitalism to Communism, suppression is *still* necessary; but it is the suppression of the minority of exploiters by the majority of exploited. A special apparatus, special machinery for suppression, the "state," is *still* necessary, but this is now a transitional state, no longer a state in the usual sense, for the suppression of the minority of exploiters, by the majority of the wage slaves *of yesterday,* is a matter comparatively so easy, simple and natural that it will cost far less bloodshed than the suppression of the risings of slaves, serfs or wage labourers, and will cost mankind far less. This is compatible with the diffusion of democracy among such an overwhelming majority of the population, that the need for *special machinery* of suppression will begin to disappear. The exploiters are, naturally, unable to suppress the people without a most complex machinery for performing this task; but *the people* can suppress the exploiters even with very simple "machinery," almost without any "machinery," without any special apparatus, by the simple *organisation of the armed masses* (such as the Soviets of Workers' and Soldiers' Deputies, we may remark, anticipating a little).

Finally, only Communism renders the state absolutely unnecessary, for there is *no one* to be suppressed—"no one" in the sense of a *class,* in the sense of a systematic struggle with a definite section of the population. We are not Utopians, and we do not in the least deny the possibility and inevitability of excesses on the part of *individual persons,* nor the need to suppress *such* excesses. But, in the first place, no special machinery, no special apparatus of repression is needed for this; this will be done by the armed people itself, as simply and as readily as any crowd of civilised people, even in modern society, parts a pair of combatants or does not allow a woman to be outraged. And, secondly, we know that the fundamental social cause of excesses which consist in violating the rules of social life is the exploitation of the masses, their want and their poverty. With the removal of this chief cause, excesses will inevitably begin to *"wither away."* We do not know how quickly and in what succession, but we know that they will wither away. With their withering away, the state will also *wither away.*

THE MARXIST VISION of class struggle and cruel capitalist oppression of the proletariat was powerfully expressed in the art of the Mexican painter José Clemente Orozco (1883–1949). Shown here is his Victims *from a mural cycle painted in 1936 at the University of Guadalajara.*

2. JOSÉ CLEMENTE OROZCO, *VICTIMS*, 1936

Liberalism and Nationalism in the Nineteenth Century

THE forces of liberalism and nationalism, released into Europe in the age of the French Revolution and Napoleon, exerted a powerful influence on the politics of the nineteenth century. They underlay the Revolutions of 1830 and 1848 and expressed themselves in demands for democratic constitutions, widened suffrage, social reform measures, and movements for national independence in Germany, Italy, and the Balkans. In England, the growth of liberalism gave rise to the extension of voting privileges in the Reform Bills of 1832, 1867, and 1884. The liberal philosophy was lucidly presented in the writings of John Stuart Mill. In France, the Revolutions of 1830 and 1848 were followed by an imperial revival under Napoleon III which in turn gave way to the founding of the Third Republic (1870's), with a Chamber of Deputies elected on the basis of universal suffrage, but an undemocratic Senate and an unusually strong executive. Liberalism even made an impact in imperial Russia when, in 1861, Czar Alexander II abolished serfdom.

In Italy liberalism and nationalism worked together toward the goal of national unification. In the 1860's the constitutional monarchy of Piedmont, directed by its astute minister Count Cavour, became the ruling element of a united Italy. Liberalism was also a factor in early efforts to unify Germany, but it gave way to the "blood and iron" nationalism of Bismarck, the conservative Prussian chancellor, who by clever diplomacy and a calculated use of force made Prussia the nucleus of a new German Empire. Once German unification had been achieved, Bismarck sought to consolidate his gains by pursuing a policy of peace in Europe and protecting German security through a complex series of treaties with other powers. The Franco-Prussian War (1870–1871), which had been the final stroke of Bismarck's unification policy, left France defeated and hungering for revenge, and Bismarck sought to isolate France by entering into defensive alliances with Austria, Italy, and Russia.

The nineteenth century closed with republicanism or constitutional monarchy in the ascendance throughout western and central Europe. But social revolutionary unrest was never far from the surface, and the fierce nationalism that had unified Italy and Germany and secured the independence of several Balkan states tended to intensify national rivalries to an ominous degree. These rivalries, heightened by a sense of unquestioning devotion to the fatherland, led finally to the cataclysmic world wars of the twentieth century.

Part I

THE VICISSITUDES
OF LIBERALISM IN ENGLAND
AND FRANCE

A. England

THE REFORM ACT OF 1832, an indirect product of the revolutionary spirit of 1830, was aimed at revising the anachronistic "rotten borough" system and equalizing the suffrage. Its goals were persuasively set forth by Lord John Russell when he introduced the measure to Parliament on March 1, 1831.

1. LORD JOHN RUSSELL INTRODUCES THE REFORM BILL OF 1832 BEFORE PARLIAMENT, 1831

SOURCE. *Parliamentary Debates*, Third Series, II, 1061 f.

Lord John Russell: . . . The measure I have now to bring forward is a measure, not of mine, but of the government in whose name I appear— the deliberate measure of a whole cabinet, unanimous upon this subject and resolved to place their measure before this house in redemption of their pledge to their sovereign, the parliament, and to their country. . . .

It will not be necessary on this occasion that I should go over the arguments which have been so often urged in favour of parliamentary reform; but it is due to the question that I should state shortly the chief points of the general argument on which the reformers rest their claim. Looking at the question then as a question of right, the ancient statutes of Edward I contain the germ and vital principle of our political constitution. The 25th of Edward I, c. 6, declares in the name of the king that "for no business from henceforth we should take such manner of aids, tasks, nor prises, but by the common assent of the realm and for the common profit thereof, saving the ancient aids and prises due and accustomed." The 34th Edward I, commonly called the Statute de Tallagio Concedendo, provides "that no tallage or aid shall be taken or levied by us or our heirs in our realm without the good will and assent of archbishops, bishops, earls, barons, knights, burgesses, and other freemen of the land." . . .

To revert again for a moment to ancient times, the assent of the commonalty of the land, thus declared necessary for the grant of any aid or tax, was collected from their representatives consisting of two knights from each country, from each city two citizens, and from every borough two burgesses. For 250 years the constant number of boroughs so sending their representatives was about 120. Some thirty or forty others occasionally exercised or discontinued that practice or privilege, as they rose or fell in wealth and importance. How this construction of the house of commons underwent various changes, till the principle on which it was founded was lost sight of, I will not now detain the house by explaining. There can be no doubt, however, that at the beginning of the period I have alluded to the house of commons did represent the people of England. No man of common sense pretends that this assembly now represents the commonalty or people of England. If it be a question of right, therefore, right is in favour of reform.

Let us now look at the question as one of reason. Allow me to imagine, for a moment, a stranger from some distant country, who should arrive in England to examine our institutions. . . . He would have been told that the proudest boast of this celebrated country was its political freedom. If, in addition to this, he had heard that once in six years this country, so wise, so renowned, so free, chose its representatives to sit in the great council where all the ministerial affairs were discussed and determined, he would not be a little curious to see the process by which so important and solemn an operation was effected. What then would be his surprise if he were taken by his guide, whom he had asked to conduct him to one of the places of election, to a green mound and told that this green mound sent two members to parliament, or to be taken to a stone wall with three niches in it and told that these three niches sent two members to parliament; or, if he were shown a green park with many signs of flourishing vegetable life, but none of human habitation, and told that this green park sent two members to parliament! But his surprise would increase to astonishment if he were carried into the north of England, where he would see large flourishing towns, full of trade and activity, containing vast magazines of wealth and manufactures, and were told that these places had no representatives in the assembly which was said to represent the people. Suppose him, after all, for I will not disguise any part of the case—suppose him to ask for a specimen of popular election, and to be carried for that purpose to Liverpool; his surprise would be turned into disgust at the gross venality and corruption which he would find to pervade the electors. After seeing all this, would he not wonder that a nation which had made such progress in every kind of knowledge, and which valued itself for its freedom, should permit so absurd and defective a system of representation any longer to prevail? But whenever arguments of this kind have been urged, it has been replied—and Mr. Canning placed his opposition to reform on this ground—"We agree that the house of commons is not, in fact, sent here by the people; we agree that, in point of reason, the system by which it is sent is full of anomaly and, absurdity; but government is a matter of experience, and so long as the people are satisfied with the actual working of the house of commons, it would be unwise to embark in theoretical change." Of this argument, I confess, I always felt the weight, and so long as the people did not answer the appeals of the friends of reform, it was indeed an argument not to be resisted. But what is the case at this moment? The whole people call loudly for reform. . . .

I arrive at last at the objections which may be made to the plan we propose. I shall be told, in the first place, that we overturn the institutions of our ancestors. I maintain that, in departing from the letter, we preserve the spirit of those institutions. Our opponents say our ancestors gave Old Sarum representatives; therefore we should give Old Sarum representatives. We say our ancestors gave Old Sarum representatives because it *was* a large town; therefore we give representatives to Manchester, which *is* a large town. . . . It has been asserted also, if a reform were to be effected, that many men of great talents, who now get into this house for close boroughs, would not be able to procure seats. I have never entertained any apprehensions of the sort, for I believe that no reform that can be introduced will have the effect of preventing wealth, probity, learning, and wit from having their proper influence upon elections. . . . It may be said, too, that one great and injurious effect of the measures I propose will be to destroy the power and privileges of the aristocracy. This I deny. . . . Wherever the aristocracy reside, receiving large incomes, performing important duties, relieving the poor by charity, and evincing private worth and public virtue, it is not in human nature that they should not possess a great influence upon public opinion and have an equal weight in electing persons to serve their country in parliament. Though such persons may not have the direct nomination of members under this bill, I contend that they will have as much influence as they ought to have. But if by aristocracy those persons are meant who do not live among the people, who know nothing of the people, and who care nothing for them—who seek honours without merit, places without duty, and pensions without service—for such an aristocracy I have no sympathy. . . .

To establish the constitution on a firm basis, you must show that you are determined not to be the representatives of a small class or of a particular interest, but to form a body who, representing the people, springing from the people, and sympathizing with the people, can fairly call on the people to support the future burdens of the country. . . . I conclude, sir, by moving for leave to bring in a bill for amending the state of the representation in England and Wales.

THE REFORM ACT corrected a number of abuses in the electoral system, in particular the gross underrepresentation of the new industrial cities. But high property qualifications prevented workers themselves from voting, and the suffrage arrangements of 1832 could therefore hardly be described as democratic.

2. THE REFORM ACT OF 1832

SOURCE. Statutes of the United Kingdom, LXXII, 154 f. 2 William IV, c. 45.

An act to amend the representation of the people in England and Wales. Whereas it is expedient to take effectual measures for correcting divers abuses that have long prevailed in the choice of members to serve in the commons house of parliament; to deprive many inconsiderable places of the right of returning members; to grant such privilege to large, populous, and wealthy towns; to increase the number of knights of the shire; to extend the elective franchise to many of his majesty's subjects who have not heretofore enjoyed the same; and to diminish the expense of elections: be it therefore enacted . . . that each of the boroughs enumerated in the schedule marked A to this act annexed . . . shall, from and after the end of this present parliament, cease to return any member or members to serve in parliament.

And be it enacted that each of the boroughs enumerated in the schedule marked B . . . shall . . . return one member and no more to serve in parliament.

And be it enacted that each of the places named in the schedule marked C . . . shall for the purpose of this act be a borough, and shall . . . return two members to serve in parliament.

And be it enacted that each of the places named in the schedule marked D . . . shall for the purposes of this act be a borough, and shall . . . return one member to serve in parliament. . . .

And be it enacted that in all future parliaments there shall be six knights of the shire, instead of four, to serve for the county of York . . . ;

and . . . that in all future parliaments there shall be four knights of the shire, instead of two, to serve for the county of Lincoln. . . .

And be it enacted . . . that in all future parliaments there shall be four knights of the shire, instead of two, to serve for each of the . . . counties [enumerated in the schedule marked F] . . . ; and . . . that in all future parliaments there shall be three knights of the shire, instead of two, to serve for each of the counties enumerated in the schedule marked F2 . . . , and two knights of the shire, instead of one, to serve for each of the counties of Carmarthen, Denbigh, and Glamorgan. . . .

And be it enacted that every male person of full age and not subject to any legal incapacity who shall be seised at law or in equity of any lands or tenements of copyhold, or any other tenure whatever except freehold, for his own life or for the life of another or for any lives whatsoever . . . , of the clear yearly value of not less than £10 . . . shall be entitled to vote in the election of a knight or knights of the shire . . . for the county . . . in which such lands or tenements shall be respectively situate.

And be it enacted that every male person of full age and not subject to any legal incapacity who shall be entitled, either as lessee or assignee, to any lands or tenements . . . for the unexpired residue . . . of any term originally created for a period of not less than sixty years . . . of the clear yearly value of not less than £10 . . . , or for the unexpired residue . . . of any term originally created for a period of not less than twenty years . . . of the clear yearly value of not less than £50 . . . , or who shall occupy as tenant any lands or tenements for which he shall be *bona fide* liable to a yearly rent of not less than £50, shall be entitled to vote in the election of a knight or knights of the shire to serve in any future parliament for the county . . . in which such lands . . . shall be respectively situate. . . . And be it enacted that, notwithstanding anything hereinbefore contained, no person shall be entitled to vote in the election of a knight or knights of the shire to serve in any future parliament unless he shall have been duly registered according to the provisions hereinafter contained. . . .

And be it enacted that, in every city or borough which shall return a member or members to serve in any future parliament, every male person of full age and not subject to any legal incapacity who shall occupy within such city or borough . . . , as owner or tenant, any house, warehouse, counting-house, shop, or other building . . . of the clear yearly value of not less than £10 shall, if duly registered according to the provisions hereinafter contained, be entitled to vote in the election of a member or members to serve in any future parliament for such city or borough. Provided always that no such person shall be registered . . .

unless he shall have occupied such premises . . . for twelve calendar months . . . ; nor unless such person . . . shall have been rated in respect of such premises to all rates for the relief of the poor . . . made during the time of such his occupation . . . ; nor unless such person shall have paid . . . all the poor's rates and assessed taxes which shall have become payable from him in respect of such premises. . . .

And be it enacted that every person who would have been entitled to vote in the election of a member or members to serve in any future parliament for any city or borough, not included in the schedule marked A . . . , either as a burgess or freeman . . . , if this act had not been passed, shall be entitled to vote in such election, provided such person shall be duly registered. . . .

And be it enacted that . . . all booths erected for the convenience of taking polls shall be erected at the joint and equal expense of the several candidates . . . ; that the expense to be incurred for the booth or booths to be erected at the principal place of election for any county . . . or division of a county . . . shall not exceed the sum of £40 . . . ; and that the expense to be incurred for any booth or booths to be erected for any parish, district, or part of any city or borough shall not exceed the sum of £25. . . .

Provided always . . . that nothing in this act contained shall . . . in any wise affect the election of members to serve in parliament for the universities of Oxford or Cambridge.

A RADICAL WORKERS' MOVEMENT known as Chartism was inspired by the revolutionary fervor of 1848 to present to Parliament a petition known as the People's Charter. In this document the Chartists proposed a number of democratic reforms including universal suffrage and the secret ballot. Rejected at the time, the Chartists' demands were in later years gradually incorporated into the English constitution.

3. DEMANDS OF THE CHARTISTS, 1848

SOURCE. William Lovett, *Life and Struggles of William Lovett*, New York: 1920, II, pp. 456–467.

EQUAL REPRESENTATION

That the United Kingdom be divided into 200 electoral districts; dividing, as nearly as possible, an equal number of inhabitants; and that each district do send a representative to Parliament.

UNIVERSAL SUFFRAGE

That every person producing proof of his being 21 years of age, to the clerk of the parish in which he has resided six months, shall be entitled to have his name registered as a voter. That the time for registering in each year be from the 1st of January to the 1st of March.

ANNUAL PARLIAMENTS

That a general election do take place on the 24th of June in each year, and that each vacancy be filled up a fortnight after it occurs. That the hours for voting be from six o'clock in the morning till six o'clock in the evening.

NO PROPERTY QUALIFICATIONS

That there shall be no property qualification for members; but on a requisition, signed by 200 voters, in favour of any candidate being presented to the clerk of the parish in which they reside, such candidate shall be put in nomination. And the list of all the candidates nominated throughout the district shall be stuck on the church door in every parish, to enable voters to judge of their qualification.

VOTE BY BALLOT

That each voter must vote in the parish in which he resides. That each parish provide as many balloting boxes as there are candidates proposed in the district; and that a temporary place be fitted up in each parish church for the purpose of *secret voting*. And, on the day of election, as each voter passes orderly on to the ballot, he shall have given to him, by the officer in attendance, a balloting ball, which he shall drop into the box of his favourite candidate. At the close of the day the votes shall be counted, by the proper officers, and the numbers stuck on the church doors. The following day the clerk of the district and two examiners shall collect the votes of all the parishes throughout the district, and cause the name of the successful candidate to be posted in every parish of the district.

SITTINGS AND PAYMENTS TO MEMBERS

That the members do take their seats in Parliament on the first Monday in October next after their election, and continue their sittings every day (Sundays excepted) till the business of the sitting is terminated, but not later than the 1st of September. They shall meet every day (during the Session) for business at 10 o'clock in the morning, and adjourn at 4. And every member shall be paid quarterly out of the public treasury £400 a year. That all electoral officers shall be elected by universal suffrage.

AT THE INTELLECTUAL LEVEL, nineteenth-century English liberalism was cogently defended by John Stuart Mill (1806–1873) in his well-known work On Liberty *(1859) (4), and in his* Considerations on Representative Government *(1861) (5). Like Bentham and Ricardo, Mill was inclined to the view of the less government the better. He argued that a man should be free to do whatever he wished so long as he did not infringe on the liberty of others.*

4. JOHN STUART MILL FROM *ON LIBERTY*, 1859

SOURCE. John Stuart Mill, *Utilitarianism, Liberty, and Representative Government*, A. D. Lindsay, ed., London: J. M. Dent & Sons, 1910, pp. 65–67. Everyman's Library Edition. Reprinted by permission of J. M. Dent & Sons, Ltd. and E. P. Dutton & Co., Inc.

The subject of this Essay is not the so-called Liberty of the Will, so unfortunately opposed to the misnamed doctrine of Philosophical Necessity; but Civil, or Social Liberty: the nature and limits of the power which can be legitimately exercised by society over the individual. A question seldom stated, and hardly ever discussed, in general terms, but which profoundly influences the practical controversies of the age by its latent presence, and is likely soon to make itself recognised as the vital question of the future. It is so far from being new, that, in a certain sense, it has divided mankind, almost from the remotest ages; but in the stage of progress into which the more civilised portions of the species have now entered, it presents itself under new conditions, and requires a different and more fundamental treatment.

The struggle between Liberty and Authority is the most conspicuous feature in the portions of history with which we are earliest familiar, particularly in that of Greece, Rome, and England. But in old times this contest was between subjects, or some classes of subjects, and the Government. By liberty, was meant protection against the tyranny of the political rulers. The rulers were conceived (except in some of the popular governments of Greece) as in a necessarily antagonistic position to the people whom they ruled. They consisted of a governing One, or a governing tribe or caste, who derived their authority from inheritance or conquest, who, at all events, did not hold it at the pleasure of the governed, and whose supremacy men did not venture, perhaps did not desire, to contest, whatever precautions might be taken against its oppressive exercise. Their power was regarded as necessary, but also as highly dangerous; as a weapon which they would attempt to use against their subjects, no less than against external enemies. To prevent the weaker members of the community from being preyed upon by innumerable vultures, it was needful that there should be an animal of prey stronger than the rest, commissioned to keep them down. But as the king of the vultures would be no less bent upon preying on the flock than any of the minor harpies, it was indispensable to be in a perpetual attitude of defence against his beak and claws. The aim, therefore, of patriots was to set limits to the power which the ruler should be suffered to exercise over the community; and this limitation was what they meant by liberty. It was attempted in two ways. First, by obtaining a recognition of certain immunities, called political liberties or rights, which it was to be regarded as a breach of duty in the ruler to infringe, and which if he did infringe, specific resistance, or general rebellion, was held to be justifiable. A second, and generally a later expedient, was the establishment of constitutional checks, by which the consent of the community, or of a body of some sort, supposed to represent its interests, was made a necessary condition to some of the more important acts of the governing power. To the first of these modes of limitation, the ruling power, in most European countries, was compelled, more or less, to submit. It was not so with the second; and, to attain this, or when already in some degree possessed, to attain it more completely, became everywhere the principal object of the lovers of liberty. And so long as mankind were content to combat one enemy by another, and to be ruled by a master, on condition of being guaranteed more or less efficaciously against his tyranny, they did not carry their aspirations beyond this point.

A time, however, came, in the progress of human affairs, when men ceased to think it a necessity of nature that their governors should be an independent power, opposed in interest to themselves. It appeared to them much better that the various magistrates of the State should be their tenants or delegates, revocable at their pleasure. In that way alone, it seemed, could they have complete security that the powers of government would never be abused to their disadvantage. By degrees this new demand for elective and temporary rulers became the prominent object of the exertions of the popular party, wherever any such party existed; and superseded, to a considerable extent, the previous efforts to limit the power of rulers. As the struggle proceeded for making the ruling power emanate from the periodical choice of the ruled, some persons began to think that too much importance had been attached to the limitation of the power itself. *That* (it might seem) was a resource against rulers whose interests were habitually opposed to those of the people. What was now wanted was, that the rulers should be identified with the people; that their interest and will should be the interest and will of the nation. The nation did not need to be protected against its own will. There was no fear of its tyrannising over itself. Let the rulers be effectually responsible to it, promptly removable by it, and it could afford to trust them with power of which it could itself dictate the use to be made. Their power was but the nation's own power, concentrated, and in a form convenient for exercise. This mode of thought, or rather perhaps of feeling, was common among the last generation of European liberalism, in the Continental section of which it still apparently predominates. Those who admit any limit to what a government may do, except in the case of such governments as they think ought not to exist, stand out as brilliant exceptions among the political thinkers of the Continent. A similar tone of sentiment might by this time have been prevalent in our own country, if the circumstances which for a time encouraged it, had continued unaltered.

But, in political and philosophical theories, as well as in persons, success discloses faults and infirmities which failure might have concealed from observation. The notion, that the people have no need to limit their power over themselves, might seem axiomatic, when popular government was a thing only dreamed about, or read of as having existed at some distant period of the past. Neither was that notion necessarily disturbed by such temporary aberrations as those of the French Revolution, the worst of which were the work of a usurping few, and which, in any case, belonged, not to the permanent working of popular institutions, but to a sudden and convulsive outbreak against monarchical and aristocratic despotism. In time, however, a democratic republic came to occupy a large portion of the earth's surface, and made itself felt as one of the most powerful members of the community of nations; and elective and responsible government became subject to the observations and criticisms which wait upon a great existing fact. It was now perceived that such phrases as "self-government," and "the power of the people over themselves," do not express the true state of the case. The "people" who exercise the power are not always the same people with those over whom it is exercised; and the "self-government" spoken of is not the government of each by himself, but of each by all the rest. The will of the people, moreover, practically means the will of the most numerous or the most active *part* of the people; the majority, or those who succeed in making themselves accepted as the majority; the people, consequently *may* desire to oppress a part of their number; and precautions are as much needed against this as against any other abuse of power. The limitation, therefore, of the power of government over individuals loses none of its importance when the holders of power are regularly accountable to the community, that is, to the strongest party therein. This view of things, recommending itself equally to the intelligence of thinkers and to the inclination of those important classes in European society to whose real or supposed interests democracy is adverse, has had no difficulty in establishing itself; and in political speculations "the tyranny of the majority" is now generally included among the evils against which society requires to be on its guard.

Like other tyrannies, the tyranny of the majority was at first, and is still vulgarly, held in dread, chiefly as operating through the acts of the public authorities. But reflecting persons perceived that when society is itself the tyrant—society collectively over the separate individuals who compose it —its means of tyrannising are not restricted to the acts which it may do by the hands of its political functionaries. Society can and does execute its own mandates: and if it issues wrong mandates instead of right, or any mandates at all in things with which it ought not to meddle, it practises a social tyranny more formidable than many kinds of political oppression, since, though not usually upheld by such extreme penalties, it leaves fewer means of escape, penetrating much more deeply into the details of life, and enslaving the soul itself. Protection, therefore, against the tyranny of the magistrate is not enough: there needs protection also against the tyranny of the prevailing opinion and feeling; against the tendency of society to impose, by other means than civil penalties, its own ideas and practices as rules of conduct on those who dissent from them; to fetter the development, and, if possible, prevent the formation, of any individuality not in harmony with its ways, and compels all characters to fashion themselves upon the model of its own. There is a limit to the legitimate interference of collective opinion with individual independence: and to find that limit, and maintain it against encroachment, is as indispensable to a good condition of human affairs, as protection against political despotism.

But though this proposition is not likely to be contested in general terms, the practical question, where to place the limit—how to make the fitting adjustment between individual independence and social control— is a subject on which nearly everything remains to be done. All that makes existence valuable to any one, depends on the enforcement of restraints upon the actions of other people. Some rules of conduct, therefore, must be imposed, by law in the first place, and by opinion on many things which are not fit subjects for the operation of law. What these rules should be is the principal question in human affairs; but if we except a few of the most obvious cases, it is one of those which least progress has been made in resolving. No two ages, and scarcely any two countries, have decided it alike; and the decision of one age or country is a wonder to another. Yet the people of any given age and country no more suspect any difficulty in it, than if it were a subject on which mankind had always been agreed. The rules which obtain among themselves appear to them self-evident and self-justifying. This all but universal illusion is one of the examples of the magical influence of custom, which is not only, as the proverb says, a second nature, but is continually mistaken for the first. The effect of custom, in preventing any misgiving respecting the rules of conduct which mankind impose on one another, is all the more complete because the subject is one on which it is not generally considered necessary that reasons should be given, either by one person to others or by each to himself. People are accustomed to believe, and have been encouraged in the belief by some who aspire to the character of philosophers, that their feelings, on subjects of this nature, are better than reasons, and render reasons unnecessary. The practical principle which guides them to their opinions on the regulation of human conduct, is the feeling in each person's mind that everybody should be required to act as he, and those with whom he sympathises, would like them to act. No one, indeed, acknowledges to himself that his standard of judgment is his own liking; but an opinion on a point of conduct, not supported by reasons, can only count as one person's preference; and if the reasons, when given, are a mere appeal to a similar preference felt by other people, it is still only many people's liking instead of one. To an ordinary man, however, his own preference, thus supported, is not only a perfectly satisfactory reason, but the only one he generally has for any of his notions of morality, taste, or propriety, which are not expressly written in his religious creed; and his chief guide in the interpretation even of that. Men's opinions, accordingly, on what is laudable or blamable, are affected by all the multifarious causes which influence their wishes in regard to the conduct of others, and which are as numerous as those which determine their wishes on any other subject. Sometimes their reason—at other times their prejudices or superstitions: often their social affections, not seldom their antisocial ones, their envy or jealousy, their arrogance or contemptuousness: but most commonly their desires or fears for themselves—their legitimate or illegitimate self-interest. Wherever there is an ascendant class, a large portion of the morality of the country emanates from its class interests, and its feelings of class superiority. The morality between Spartans and Helots, between planters and negroes, between princes and subjects, between nobles and roturiers, between men and women, has been for the most part the creation of these class interests and feelings: and the sentiments thus generated react in turn upon the moral feelings of the members of the ascendant class, in their relations among themselves. Where, on the other hand, a class, formerly ascendant, has lost its ascendancy, or where its ascendancy is unpopular, the prevailing moral sentiments frequently bear the impress of an impatient dislike of superiority. Another grand determining principle of the rules of conduct, both in act and forbearance, which have been enforced by law or opinion, has been the servility of mankind towards the supposed preferences or aversions of their temporal masters or of their gods. This servility, though essentially selfish, is not hypocrisy; it gives rise to perfectly genuine sentiments of abhorrence; it made men burn magicians and heretics. Among so many baser influences, the general and obvious interests of society have of course had a share, and a large one, in the direction of the moral sentiments: less, however, as a matter of reason, and on their own account, than as a consequence of the sympathies and antipathies which grew out of them: and sympathies and antipathies which had little or nothing to do with the interests of society, have made themselves felt in the establishment of moralities with quite as great force.

The likings and dislikings of society, or of some powerful portion of it, are thus the main thing which has practically determined the rules laid down for general observance, under the penalties of law or opinion. And in general, those who have been in advance of society in thought and feeling, have left this condition of things unassailed in principle, however they may have come into conflict with it in some of its details. They have occupied themselves rather in inquiring what things society ought to like or dislike, than in questioning whether its likings or dislikings should be a law to individuals. They preferred endeavouring to alter the feelings of mankind on the particular points on which they were themselves heretical, rather than make common cause in defence of freedom, with heretics generally. The only case in which the higher ground has been taken on principle and maintained with consistency, by any but an individual here and there, is that of religious belief: a case instructive in many ways, and not least so as forming a most striking instance of the fallibility of what is called the moral sense: for the *odium theologicum*, in a sincere bigot, is one of the most unequivocal cases of moral feeling. Those who first broke the yoke of what called itself the Universal Church, were in general as little willing to permit difference of religious opinion as that church itself. But when the heat of the conflict was over, without giving a complete victory to any party, and each church or sect was reduced to limit its hopes to retaining possession of the ground it already occupied; minorities, seeing that they had no chance of becoming majorities, were under the necessity of pleading to those whom they could not convert, for permission to differ. It is accordingly on this battle field, almost solely, that the rights of the individual against society have been asserted on broad grounds of principle, and the claim of society to exercise authority over dissentients openly controverted. The great writers to whom the world owes what religious liberty it possesses, have mostly asserted freedom of conscience as an indefeasible right, and denied absolutely that a human being is accountable to others for his religious belief. Yet so natural to mankind is intolerance in whatever they really care about, that religious freedom has hardly anywhere been practically realised, except where religious indifference, which dislikes to have its peace disturbed by theological quarrels, has added its weight to the scale. In the minds of almost all religious persons, even in the most tolerant countries, the duty of toleration is admitted with tacit reserves. One person will bear with dissent in matters of church government, but not of dogma; another can tolerate everybody, short of a Papist or a Unitarian; another every one who believes in revealed religion; a few extend their charity a little further, but stop at the belief in a God and in a future state. Wherever the sentiment of the majority is still genuine and intense, it is found to have abated little of its claim to be obeyed.

In England, from the peculiar circumstances of our political history, though the yoke of opinion is perhaps heavier, that of law is lighter, than in most other countries of Europe; and there is considerable jealousy of direct interference, by the legislative or the executive power, with private conduct; not so much from any just regard for the independence of the individual, as from the still subsisting habit of looking on the government as representing an opposite interest to the public. The majority have not yet learnt to feel the power of the government their power, or its opinions their opinions. When they do so, individual liberty will probably be as much exposed to invasion from the government, as it already is from public opinion. But, as yet, there is a considerable amount of feeling ready to be called forth against any attempt of the law to control individuals in things in which they have not hitherto been accustomed to be controlled by it; and this with very little discrimination as to whether the matter is, or is not, within the legitimate sphere of legal control; insomuch that the feeling, highly salutary on the whole, is perhaps quite as often misplaced as well grounded in the particular instances of its application. There is, in fact, no recognised principle by which the propriety or impropriety of government interference is customarily tested. People decide according to their personal preferences. Some, whenever they see any good to be done, or evil to be remedied, would willingly instigate the government to undertake the business; while others prefer to bear almost any amount of social evil, rather than add one to the departments of human interests amenable to governmental control. And men range themselves on one or the other side in any particular case, according to this general direction of their sentiments; or according to the degree of interest which they feel in the particular thing which it is proposed that the government should do, or according to the belief they entertain that the government would, or would not, do it in the manner they prefer; but very rarely on account of any opinion to which they consistently adhere, as to what things are fit to be done by a government. And it seems to me that in consequence of this absence of rule or principle, one side is at present as often wrong as the other; the interference of government is, with about equal frequency, improperly invoked and improperly condemned.

The object of this Essay is to assert one very simple principle, as entitled to govern absolutely the dealings of society with the individual in the way of compulsion and control, whether the means used be physical force in the form of legal penalties, or the moral coercion of public opinion. That principle is, that the sole end for which mankind are warranted, individually or collectively, in interfering with the liberty of action of any of their number, is self-protection. That the only purpose for which power can be rightfully exercised over any member of a civilised community, against his will, is to prevent harm to others. His own good, either physical or moral, is not a sufficient warrant. He cannot rightfully be compelled to do or forbear because it will be better for him to do so, because it will make him happier, because, in the opinions of others, to do so would be wise, or even right. These are good reasons for remonstrating with him, or reasoning with him, or persuading him, or entreating him, but not for compelling him, or visiting him with any evil in case he do otherwise. To justify that, the conduct from which it is desired to deter him must be calculated to produce evil to some one else. The only part of the conduct of any one, for which he is amenable to society, is that which concerns others. In the part which merely concerns himself, his independence is, of right, absolute. Over himself, over his own body and mind, the individual is sovereign.

It is, perhaps, hardly necessary to say that this doctrine is meant to apply only to human beings in the maturity of their faculties. We are not speaking of children, or of young persons below the age which the law may fix as that of manhood or womanhood. Those who are still in a state to require being taken care of by others, must be protected against their own actions as well as against external injury. For the same reason, we may leave out of consideration those backward states of society in which the race itself may be considered as in its nonage. The early difficulties in the way of spontaneous progress are so great, that there is seldom any choice of means for overcoming them; and a ruler full of the spirit of improvement is warranted in the use of any expedients that will attain an end, perhaps otherwise unattainable. Despotism is a legitimate mode of government in dealing with barbarians, provided the end be their improvement, and the means justified by actually effecting that end. Liberty, as a principle, has no application to any state of things anterior to the time when mankind have become capable of being improved by free and equal discussion. Until then, there is nothing for them but implicit obedience to an Akbar or a Charlemagne, if they are so fortunate as to find one. But as soon as mankind have attained the capacity of being guided to their own improvement by conviction or persuasion (a period long since reached in all nations with whom we need here concern ourselves), compulsion, either in the direct form or in that of pains and penalties for non-compliance, is no longer admissible as a means to their own good, and justifiable only for the security of others.

It is proper to state that I forego any advantage which could be derived to my argument from the idea of abstract right, as a thing independent of utility. I regard utility as the ultimate appeal on all ethical questions; but it must be utility in the largest sense, grounded on the permanent interests of a man as a progressive being. Those interests, I contend, authorise the subjection of individual spontaneity to external control, only in respect to those actions of each, which concern the interest of other people. If any one does an act hurtful to others, there is a *prima facie* case for punishing him, by law, or, where legal penalties are not safely applicable, by general disapprobation. There are also many positive acts for the benefit of others, which he may rightfully be compelled to perform; such as to give evidence in a court of justice; to bear his fair share in the common defence, or in any other joint work necessary to the interest of the society of which he enjoys the protection; and to perform certain acts of individual beneficence, such as saving a fellow-creature's life, or interposing to protect the defenceless against ill-usage, things which whenever it is obviously a man's duty to do, he may rightfully be made responsible to society for not doing. A person may cause evil to others not only by his actions but by his inaction, and in either case he is justly accountable to them for the injury. The latter case, it is true, requires a much more cautious exercise of compulsion than the former. To make any one answerable for doing evil to others is the rule; to make him answerable for not preventing evil is, comparatively speaking, the exception. Yet there are many cases clear enough and grave enough to justify that exception. In all things which regard the external relations of the individual, he is *de jure* amenable to those whose interests are concerned, and, if need be, to society as their protector. There are often good reasons for not holding him to the responsibility; but these reasons must arise from the special expediencies of the case: either because it is a kind of case in which he is on the whole likely to act better, when left to his own discretion, than when controlled in any way in which society have it in their power to control him; or because the attempt to exercise control would produce other evils, greater than those which it would prevent. When such reasons as these preclude the enforcement of responsibility, the conscience of the agent himself should step into the vacant judgment seat, and protect those interests of others which have no external protection; judging himself all the more ridgidly, because the case does not admit of his being made accountable to the judgment of his fellow-creatures.

But there is a sphere of action in which society, as distinguished from the individual, has, if any, only an indirect interest; comprehending all that portion of a person's life and conduct which affects only himself, or if it also affects others, only with their free, voluntary, and undeceived consent and participation. When I say only himself, I mean directly, and in the first instance; for whatever affects himself, may affect others through himself; and the objection which may be grounded on this contingency, will receive consideration in the sequel. This, then, is the appropriate region of human liberty. It comprises, first, the inward domain of consciousness; demanding liberty of conscience in the most comprehensive sense; liberty of thought and feeling; absolute freedom of opinion and sentiment on all subjects, practical or speculative, scientific, moral, or theological. The liberty of expressing and publishing opinions may seem to fall under a different principle, since it belongs to that part of the conduct of an individual which concerns other people; but, being almost of as much importance as the liberty of thought itself, and resting in great part on the same reasons, is practically inseparable from it. Secondly, the principle requires liberty of tastes and pursuits; of framing the plan of our life to suit our own character; of doing as we like, subject to such consequences as may follow: without impediment from our fellow-creatures, so long as what we do does not harm them, even though they should think our conduct foolish, perverse, or wrong. Thirdly, from this liberty of each individual, follows the liberty, within the same limits, of combination among individuals; freedom to unite, for any purpose not involving harm to others: the persons combining being supposed to be of full age, and not forced or deceived.

No society in which these liberties are not, on the whole, respected, is free, whatever may be its form of government; and none is completely free in which they do not exist absolute and unqualified. The only freedom which deserves the name, is that of pursuing our own good in our own way, so long as we do not attempt to deprive others of theirs, or impede their efforts to obtain it. Each is the proper guardian of his own health, whether bodily, *or* mental and spiritual. Mankind are greater gainers by suffering each other to live as seems good to themselves, than by compelling each to live as seems good to the rest.

Though this doctrine is anything but new, and, to some persons, may have the air of a truism, there is no doctrine which stands more directly opposed to the general tendency of existing opinion and practice. Society has expended fully as much effort in the attempt (according to its lights) to compel people to conform to its notions of personal as of social excellence. The ancient commonwealths thought themselves entitled to practise, and the ancient philosophers countenanced, the regulation of every part of private conduct by public authority, on the ground that the State had a deep interest in the whole bodily and mental discipline of every one of its citizens; a mode of thinking which may have been admissible in small republics surrounded by powerful enemies, in constant peril of being subverted by foreign attack or internal commotion, and to which even a short interval of relaxed energy and self-command might so easily be fatal that they could not afford to wait for the salutary permanent effects of freedom. In the modern world, the greater size of political communities, and, above all, the separation between spiritual and temporal authority (which placed the direction of men's consciences in other hands than those which controlled their worldly affairs), prevented so great an interference by law in the details of private life; but the engines of moral repression have been wielded more strenuously against divergence from the reigning opinion in self-regarding, than even in social matters; religion, the most powerful of the elements which have entered into the formation of moral feeling, having almost always been governed either by the ambition of a hierarchy, seeking control over every department of human conduct, or by the spirit of Puritanism. And some of those modern reformers who have placed themselves in strongest opposition to the religions of the past, have been noway behind either churches or sects in their assertion of the right of spiritual domination: M. Comte, in particular, whose social system, as unfolded in his *Système de Politique Positive,* aims at establishing (though by moral more than by legal appliances) a despotism of society over the individual, surpassing anything contemplated in the political ideal of the most rigid disciplinarian among the ancient philosophers.

Apart from the peculiar tenets of individual thinkers, there is also in the world at large an increasing inclination to stretch unduly the powers of society over the individual, both by the force of opinion and even by that of legislation; and as the tendency of all the changes taking place in the world is to strengthen society, and diminish the power of the individual, this encroachment is not one of the evils which tend spontaneously to disappear, but, on the contrary, to grow more and more formidable. The disposition of mankind, whether as rulers or as fellow-citizens, to impose their own opinions and inclinations as a rule of conduct on others, is so energetically supported by some of the best and by some of the worst feelings incident to human nature, that it is hardly ever kept under restraint by anything but want of power; and as the power is not declining, but growing, unless a strong barrier of moral conviction can be raised against the mischief, we must expect, in the present circumstances of the world, to see it increase.

It will be convenient for the argument, if, instead of at once entering upon the general thesis, we confine ourselves in the first instance to a single branch of it, on which the principle here stated is, if not fully, yet to a certain point, recognised by the current opinions. This one branch is the Liberty of Thought: from which it is impossible to separate the cognate liberty of speaking and of writing. Although these liberties, to some considerable amount, form part of the political morality of all countries which profess religious toleration and free institutions, the grounds, both philosophical and practical, on which they rest, are perhaps not so familiar to the general mind, nor so thoroughly appreciated by many even of the leaders of opinion, as might have been expected. Those grounds, when rightly understood, are of much wider application than to only one division of the subject, and a thorough consideration of this part of the question will be found the best introduction to the remainder. Those to whom nothing which I am about to say will be new, may therefore, I hope, excuse me, if on a subject which for now three centuries has been so often discussed, I venture on one discussion more.

5. JOHN STUART MILL, FROM *CONSIDERATIONS ON REPRESENTATIVE GOVERNMENT,* 1861

SOURCE. John Stuart Mill, *Representative Government,* 1861, A. D. Lindsay, ed., London: J. M. Dent & Sons, 1910, pp. 208–211. Everyman's Library Edition. Reprinted by permission of J. M. Dent & Sons, Ltd. and E. P. Dutton & Co., Inc.

. . . The ideally best form of government, it is scarcely necessary to say, does not mean one which is practicable or eligible in all states of civilisation, but the one which, in the circumstances in which it is practicable and eligible, is attended with the greatest amount of beneficial consequences, immediate and prospective. A completely popular government is the only polity which can make out any claim to this character. It is pre-eminent in both the departments between which the excellence of a political constitution is divided. It is both more favourable to present good government, and promotes a better and higher form of national character, than any other polity whatsoever.

Its superiority in reference to present well-being rests upon two principles, of as universal truth and applicability as any general propositions which can be laid down respecting human affairs. The first is, that the rights and interests of every or any person are only secure from being disregarded when the person interested is himself able, and habitually disposed, to stand up for them. The second is, that the general prosperity attains a greater height, and is more widely diffused, in proportion to the amount and variety of the personal energies enlisted in promoting it.

Putting these two propositions into a shape more special to their present application; human beings are only secure from evil at the hands of others in proportion as they have the power of being, and are, self-*pro-*

tecting; and they only achieve a high degree of success in their struggle with Nature in proportion as they are self-*dependent,* relying on what they themselves can do, either separately or in concert, rather than on what others do for them.

The former proposition—that each is the only safe guardian of his own rights and interests—is one of those elementary maxims of prudence, which every person, capable of conducting his own affairs, implicitly acts upon, wherever he himself is interested. Many, indeed, have a great dislike to it as a political doctrine, and are fond of holding it up to obloquy, as a doctrine of universal selfishness. To which we may answer, that whenever it ceases to be true that mankind, as a rule, prefer themselves to others, and those nearest to them to those more remote, from that moment Communism is not only practicable, but the only defensible form of society; and will, when that time arrives, be assuredly carried into effect. For my own part, not believing in universal selfishness, I have no difficulty in admitting that Communism would even now be practicable among the *élite* of mankind, and may become so among the rest. But as this opinion is anything but popular with those defenders of existing institutions who find fault with the doctrine of the general predominance of self-interest, I am inclined to think they do in reality believe that most men consider themselves before other people. It is not, however, necessary to affirm even thus much in order to support the claim of all to participate in the sovereign power. We need not suppose that when power resides in an exclusive class, that class will knowingly and deliberately sacrifice the other classes to themselves: it suffices that, in the absence of its natural defenders, the interest of the excluded is always in danger of being overlooked; and, when looked at, is seen with very different eyes from those of the persons whom it directly concerns. In this country, for example, what are called the working classes may be considered as excluded from all direct participation in the government. I do not believe that the classes who do participate in it have in general any intention of sacrificing the working classes to themselves. They once had that intention; witness the persevering attempts so long made to keep down wages by law. But in the present day their ordinary disposition is the very opposite: they willingly make considerable sacrifices, especially of their pecuniary interest, for the benefit of the working classes, and err rather by too lavish and indiscriminating beneficence; nor do I believe that any rulers in history have been actuated by a more sincere desire to do their duty towards the poorer portion of their countrymen. Yet does Parliament, or almost any of the members composing it, ever for an instant look at any question with the eyes of a working man? When a subject arises in which the labourers as such have an interest, is it regarded from any point of view but that of the employers of labour? I do not say that the working men's view of these questions is in general nearer to the truth than the other: but it is sometimes quite as near; and in any case it ought to be respectfully listened to, instead of being, as it is, not merely turned away from, but ignored. On the question of strikes, for instance, it is doubtful if there is so much as one among the leading members of either House who is not firmly convinced that the reason of the matter is unqualifiedly on the side of the masters, and that the men's view of it is simply absurd. Those who have studied the question know well how far this is from being the case; and in how different, and how infinitely less superficial a manner the point would have to be argued, if the classes who strike were able to make themselves heard in Parliament.

It is an adherent condition of human affairs that no intention, however sincere, of protecting the interests of others can make it safe or salutary to tie up their own hands. Still more obviously true is it, that by their own hands only can any positive and durable improvement of their circumstances in life be worked out. Through the joint influence of these two principles, all free communities have both been more exempt from social injustice and crime, and have attained more brilliant prosperity, than any others, or than they themselves after they lost their freedom. Contrast the free states of the world, while their freedom lasted, with the contemporary subjects of monarchical or oligarchical despotism: the Greek cities with the Persian satrapies; the Italian republics and the free towns of Flanders and Germany, with the feudal monarchies of Europe; Switzerland, Holland, and England, with Austria or anterevolutionary France. Their superior prosperity was too obvious ever to have been gainsaid: while their superiority in good government and social relations is proved by the prosperity, and is manifest besides in every page of history. If we compare, not one age with another, but the different governments which co-existed in the same age, no amount of disorder which exaggeration itself can pretend to have existed amidst the publicity of the free states can be compared for a moment with the contemptuous trampling upon the mass of the people which pervaded the whole life of the monarchical countries, or the disgusting individual tyranny which was of more than daily occurrence under the systems of plunder which they called fiscal arrangements, and in the secrecy of their frightful courts of justice.

It must be acknowledged that the benefits of freedom, so far as they have hitherto been enjoyed, were obtained by the extension of its privileges to a part only of the community; and that a government in which they are extended impartially to all is a desideratum still unrealised. But though every approach to this has an independent value, and in many cases more than an approach could not, in the existing state of general improvement, be made, the participation of all in these benefits is the ideally perfect conception of free government. In proportion as any, no matter who, are excluded from it, the interests of the excluded are left without the guarantee accorded to the rest, and they themselves have less scope and encouragement than they might otherwise have to that exertion of their energies for the good of themselves and of the community, to which the general prosperity is always proportioned. . . .

OUR DOCUMENTS ON ENGLISH LIBERALISM conclude with the Reform Acts (literally, the Representation of the People Acts) of 1867 (6) and 1884 (7) which radically extended the suffrage by adding to the electorate most of the urban and rural working classes. By 1884 the election of the House of Commons had been put on a democratic basis.

6. THE REFORM ACT OF 1867

SOURCE. *Public General Statutes*, II, 1082 f.: 30–31 Victoria, c. 102.

An act further to amend the laws relating to the representation of the people in England and Wales. . . . Be it enacted . . . as follows:—

Every man shall, in and after the year 1868, be entitled to be registered as a voter and, when registered, to vote for a member or members to serve in parliament for a borough, who is qualified as follows: that is to say, (1) is of full age, and not subject to any legal incapacity; and (2) is on the last day of July in any year and has during . . . the preceding twelve calendar months been an inhabitant occupier, as owner or tenant, of any dwelling-house within the borough; and (3) has during the time of such occupation been rated as an ordinary occupier in respect of the premises so occupied by him within the borough to all rates, if any, made for the relief of the poor in respect of such premises; and (4) has, on or before the twentieth day of July in the same year, *bona fide* paid an equal amount in the pound to that payable by other ordinary occupiers in respect of all poor rates that have become payable by him in respect of the said premises up to the preceding fifth day of January. Provided, that no man shall under this section be entitled to be registered as a voter by reason of his being a joint occupier of any dwelling-house.

Every man shall, in and after the year 1868, be entitled to be registered as a voter and, when registered, to vote for a member or members to serve in parliament for a borough, who is qualified as follows: that is to say, (1) is of full age and not subject to any legal incapacity; and (2) as a lodger has occupied in the same borough separately and as sole tenant for the twelve months preceding the last day of July in any year the same lodgings, such lodgings being part of one and the same dwelling-house, and of a clear yearly value, if let unfurnished, of £10 or upwards; and (3) has resided in such lodgings during the twelve months immediately preceding the last day of July, and has claimed to be registered as a voter at the next ensuing registration of voters.

Every man shall, in and after the year 1868, be entitled to be registered as a voter and, when registered, to vote for a member or members to serve in parliament for a county, who is qualified as follows. . . .

From and after the end of this present parliament, no borough which had a less population than 10,000 at the census of 1861 shall return more than one member to serve in parliament. . . .

In all future parliaments the university of London shall return one member to serve in parliament. Every man whose name is for the time being on the register of graduates constituting the convocation of the university of London shall, if of full age and not subject to any legal incapacity, be entitled to vote in the election of a member to serve in any future parliament for the said university. . . .

Whereas great inconveniences may arise from the enactments now in force limiting the duration of the parliament in being at the demise of the crown: be it therefore enacted that the parliament in being at any future demise of the crown shall not be determined or dissolved by such demise, but shall continue so long as it would have continued but for such demise, unless it should be sooner prorogued or dissolved by the crown—anything in the act passed in the sixth year of her late majesty Queen Anne . . . in any way notwithstanding.

7. THE REFORM ACT OF 1884

SOURCE. *Public General Statutes,* XXI, 3 f.: 48 Victoria, c. 3.

An act to amend the law relating to the representation of the people of the united kingdom. Be it enacted . . . as follows:—

A uniform household franchise and a uniform lodger franchise at elections shall be established in all counties and boroughs throughout the united kingdom, and every man possessed of a household qualification or a lodger qualification shall, if the qualifying premises be situate in a county in England or Scotland, be entitled to be registered as a voter and when registered to vote at an election for such county; and if the qualifying premises be situate in a county or borough in Ireland, be entitled to be registered as a voter and when registered to vote at an election for such county or borough. . . .

Every man occupying any land or tenement in a county or borough in the united kingdom of a clear yearly value of not less than £10 shall be entitled to be registered as a voter and when registered to vote at an election for such county or borough in respect of such occupation subject to the like conditions respectively as a man is, at the passing of this act, entitled to be registered as a voter and to vote at an election for such county in respect of the county occupation franchise, and at an election for such borough in respect of the borough occupation franchise.

In this act the expression "a household qualification" means, as respects England and Ireland, the qualification enacted by the third section of the Representation of the People Act, 1867.

B. France

THE IMPORTANT SCHOLAR ERNEST RENAN (1823–1892), in his Recollections of My Youth, *expresses a cautiously optimistic view of French liberalism and its effect on science and the intellectual in society.*

1. ERNEST RENAN, FROM THE PREFACE TO RECOLLECTIONS OF MY YOUTH

SOURCE. Ernest Renan, *Recollections of My Youth,* Mme. Renan, rev., C. B. Pitman, tr., London: Chapman and Hall, 1883, Preface. Reprinted by permission of Chapman and Hall, Ltd.

The one object in life is the development of the mind, and the first condition for the development of the mind is that it should have liberty. The worst social state from this point of view is the theocratic state, like Islam or the ancient Pontifical state, in which dogma reigns supreme. Nations with an exclusive state religion, like Spain, are not much better off. Nations in which a religion of the majority is recognized are also exposed to serious drawbacks. In behalf of the real or assumed beliefs of the greatest number, the state considers itself bound to impose upon thought terms which thought cannot accept. The belief or the opinion of the one side should not be a fetter upon the other side. As long as the masses were believers, that is to say, as long as the same sentiments were almost universally professed by a people, freedom of research and discussion were impossible. A colossal weight of stupidity pressed down upon the human mind. The terrible catastrophe of the Middle Ages, that break of a thousand years in the history of civilization, is due less to the barbarians than to the triumph of the dogmatic spirit among the masses.

This is a state of things which is coming to an end in our time, and we must not be surprised if some disturbance ensues. There are no longer masses who believe; a great number of the people decline to recognize the supernatural, and the day is not far distant when beliefs of this kind will die out altogether in the masses, just as the belief in familiar spirits and ghosts have disappeared. Even if, as is probable, we are to have a temporary Catholic reaction, the people will not revert to the Church. Religion has become once and for all a matter of personal taste. Now beliefs are only dangerous when they represent something like unanimity or an unquestionable majority. When they are merely individual, there is not a word to be said against them, and it is our duty to treat them with the respect which they do not always exhibit for their adversaries, when they feel that they have force at their back.

There can be no denying that it will take time for the liberty, which is the aim and object of human society, to take root in France as it has in America. French democracy has several essential principles to acquire, before it can become a liberal régime. It will be above all things necessary that we should have laws as to associations, charitable foundations, and the right of legacy, analogous to those which are in force in England and America. Supposing this progress to be effected (if it is utopian to count upon it in France, it is not so for the rest of Europe, in which the aspirations for English liberty become every day more intense), we should really not have much cause to look regretfully upon the favours conferred by the *ancien régime* upon things of the mind.

I quite think that if democratic ideas were to secure a definitive triumph, science and scientific teaching would soon find the modest subsidies now accorded them cut off. This is an eventuality which would have to be accepted as philosophically as may be. The free foundations would take the place of the state institutes, the slight drawbacks being more than compensated for by the advantage of having no longer to make to the supposed prejudices of the majority concessions which the state exacted in return for its pittance. The waste of power in state institutes is enormous. Private foundations would not be exposed to nearly so much waste. It is true that spurious science would, in these conditions, flourish side by side with real science, enjoying the same privileges, and that there would be no official criterion, as there still is to a certain extent now, to distinguish the one from the other. But this criterion becomes every day less reliable. Reason has to submit to the indignity of taking second place behind those who have a loud voice, and who speak with a tone of command. The plaudits and favour of the public will, for a long time to come, be at the service of what is false. But the true has great power, when it is free; the true endures; the false is ever changing and decays. Thus it is that the true, though only understood by a select few, always rises to the surface, and in the end prevails.

In short, it is very possible that the American-like social condition towards which we are advancing, independently of any particular form of government, will not be more intolerable for persons of intelligence than the better guaranteed social conditions which we have already been subject to. We may at least hope that vulgarity will not yet a while persecute freedom of mind. Descartes, living in the brilliant seventeenth century, was nowhere so well off as at Amsterdam, because, as "everyone was engaged in trade there," no one paid any heed to him. It may be that general vulgarity will one day be the condition of happiness, for the worst American vulgarity would not send Giordano Bruno to the stake or persecute Galileo. . . . liberty is like truth; scarcely anyone loves it on its own account, and yet, owing to the impossibility of extremes, one always comes back to it.

AT THE POLITICAL LEVEL, liberalism in France underwent bewildering vicissitudes during the nineteenth century. The liberal rebellion of 1830 resulted in the disappointingly conservative July monarchy. The Second Republic, established in 1848, was compromised later in the same year by the election of Louis Napoleon to the presidency. The republic was demolished in 1852 by Louis Napoleon's coup d'état and the restoration of the Empire. Dissolving the recalcitrant Assembly, Louis issued on December 2, 1851, a proclamation calling for a plebiscite on his proposal to assume sweeping executive powers. The electorate approved the proposal, and the era of the Second Empire began, with Louis as Emperor Napoleon III.

2. LOUIS NAPOLEON'S PROCLAMATION TO THE PEOPLE, 1851

SOURCE. F. M. Anderson, ed., *The Constitutions and Other Select Documents Illustrative of the History of France,* Minneapolis: H. W. Wilson Co., 1904, pp. 539–540. Reprinted by permission of Dr. Gaylord W. Anderson.

Frenchmen!

The present situation cannot last much longer. Each day that passes increases the dangers of the country. The Assembly, which ought to be the firmest support of order, has become a centre of conspiracies. The patriotism of three hundred of its members was not able to arrest its fatal tendencies. Instead of making laws in the general interest, it forges weapons for civil war; it makes an attack upon the authority that I hold directly from the people; it encourages all the evil passions; it puts in jeopardy the repose of France: I have dissolved it, and I make the whole people judge between it and me.

The Constitution, as you know, was made with the purpose of weakening in advance the power that you were about to confer upon me. Six million votes were a striking protest against it, nevertheless I faithfully observed it. Provocations, calumnies, outrages, have found me unmoved. But now that the fundamental compact is no longer respected even by those who incessantly invoke it, and the men who have already destroyed two monarchies wish to bind my hands, in order to overthrow the Republic, it is my duty to defeat their wicked designs and to save the country by invoking the solemn judgment of the only sovereign that I recognize in France, the people.

I make, therefore, a loyal appeal to the whole nation, and I say to you: If you wish to continue this state of uneasiness which degrades us and makes uncertain our future, choose another in my place, for I no longer wish an authority which is powerless to do good, makes me responsible for acts I cannot prevent, and chains me to the helm when I see the vessel speeding toward the abyss.

If, on the contrary, you still have confidence in me, give me the means to accomplish the great mission that I hold from you.

This mission consists in bringing to a close the era of revolutions by satisfying the legitimate wants of the people and by protecting them against subversive passions. It consists, especially, in creating institutions that may survive men and that may be at length foundations upon which something durable can be established.

Persuaded that the instability of authority and the preponderance of a single Assembly are permanent causes of trouble and discord, I submit to you the following fundamental bases of a Constitution which the Assemblies will develop later.

1st. A responsible chief selected for ten years;

2d. Ministers dependent upon the executive power alone;

3d. A Council of State composed of the most distinguished men to prepare the laws and to discuss them before the legislative body;

4th. A legislative body to discuss and vote the laws, elected by universal suffrage without *scrutin de liste* which falsifies the election;

5th. A second assembly, composed of all the illustrious persons of the country, predominant authority, guardian of the fundamental compact and of the public liberties.

This system, created by the First Consul at the beginning of the century, has already given to France repose and prosperity; it will guarantee them to her again.

Such is my profound conviction. If you share it, declare the fact by your votes. If, on the contrary, you prefer a government without force, monarchical or republican, borrowed from I know not what past or from what chimerical future, reply in the negative.

Thus, therefore, for the first time since 1804, you will vote with knowledge of the case, knowing well for whom and for what.

If I do not obtain a majority of your votes I shall then bring about the meeting of a new Assembly, and I shall resign to it the mandate that I have received from you.

But if you believe that the cause of which my name is the symbol, that is, France regenerated by the revolution of '89 and organized by the Emperor, is always yours, proclaim it by sanctioning the powers that I ask of you.

Then France and Europe will be preserved from anarchy, obstacles will be removed, rivalries will have disappeared, for all will respect, in the decision of the people, the decree of Providence.

(*signed*)   LOUIS NAPOLEON

FRENCH DEFEATS in the Franco-Prussian War resulted in the fall of Louis Napoleon in 1870. Paris underwent a long and bitter siege by the Prussian army. The provisional French government, located first at Bordeaux and later at Versailles, recognized that the military position was hopeless and entered into an armistice with Prussia. The Parisians, feeling that they had been betrayed by the government, declared their independence and asserted their status as a free commune. At a time when monarchist sentiment was growing in France, the Paris Commune was dominated by republicanism of an increasingly radical sort. The political aims of the Communards are set forth in the Declaration of the Paris Commune to the French People, April 19, 1871. In May the Commune was crushed by the military force of the Versailles government, but the deep antagonisms which it caused divided France for years to come.

3. DECLARATION OF THE PARIS COMMUNE, 1871

SOURCE. F. M. Anderson, ed., *The Constitutions and Other Select Documents Illustrative of the History of France*, Minneapolis: H. W. Wilson Co., 1904, pp. 609–612. Reprinted by permission of Dr. Gaylord W. Anderson.

In the painful and terrible conflict which once again imposes upon Paris the horrors of siege and bombardment, which causes French blood to flow, which causes our brothers, our wives, and our children to perish, sinking before shells and grape shot, it is necessary that public opinion should not be divided and that the national conscience should not be troubled.

It is necessary that Paris and the whole country should know what is the nature, the reason, and the aim of the Revolution which is accomplished. It is necessary, in fine, that the responsibility for the sorrows, the sufferings and the misfortunes of which we are the victims should return upon those who, after having betrayed France and delivered Paris to the foreigner, are seeking with a blind and cruel obstinacy the ruin of the capital, in order to conceal in the disaster to the Republic and to Liberty the double testimony to their treason and their crime.

It is the duty of the Commune to ascertain and assert the aspirations and the views of the population of Paris, to state precisely the character of the movement of March 18, misunderstood, unknown and calumniated by the politicians who sit at Versailles.

Once again Paris labors and suffers for all France, for which by her conflicts and sacrifices she prepares intellectual, moral, administrative and economic regeneration, glory and prosperity.

What does she ask for?

The recognition and consolidation of the Republic, the only form of government compatible with the rights of the people and the regular and free development of society;

The absolute autonomy of the Commune extended to all the localities in France, and insuring to each the integrity of its rights and to every Frenchman the full exercise of his faculties and aptitudes, as man, citizen and worker;

The autonomy of the Commune shall have for its limits only the equal right of autonomy for all the other communes adhering to the contract, the association of which must insure French unity.

The rights inherent in the Commune are:

The voting of the communal budget, receipts and expenditures; the determination and partition of taxation; the management of the local services; the organization of its magistrature, the internal police and education; the administration of the property belonging to the Commune;

The choice by election or competition, with responsibility and the permanent right of control and of removal, of the communal magistrates and functionaries of all sorts;

The absolute guarantee of personal liberty, of liberty of conscience and liberty of labor;

The permanent participation of the citizens in communal affairs by the free expression of their ideas and the free defence of their interests; guarantees to be given for these expressions by the Commune, which alone is to be charged with the supervision and assuring of the free and just exercise of the right of meeting and of publicity;

The organization of urban defence and of the National Guard, which elects its leaders and alone watches over the maintenance of order within the city.

Paris wishes for nothing more in the way of local guarantees, on condition, well understood, of finding in the grand central administration, the delegation of the federated communes, the realization and the practice of the same principles.

But, in favor of its autonomy and profiting from its liberty of action, Paris reserves to herself to effect for herself, as she may think proper, the administrative and economic reforms which her population demand; to create suitable institutions to develop and promote education, production, exchange and credit; to universalize power and property, according to the necessities of the moment and the opinion of those interested and the data furnished by experience.

Our enemies deceive themselves or deceive the country when they accuse Paris of wishing to impose its will or its supremacy upon the remainder of the nation and of designing a dictatorship which would be a veritable attack upon the independence and sovereignty of the other communes.

They deceive themselves or deceive the country when they accuse Paris of seeking the destruction of French unity, established by the Revolution amid the acclamations of our fathers flocking to the Fête of the Federation from all points of old France.

Unity such as has been imposed on us up to this day by the Empire, the Monarchy and Parliamentarism is only despotic, unintelligent, arbitrary and onerous centralization.

Political unity such as Paris wishes is the voluntary association of all the local initiatives, the free and spontaneous cooperation of all the individual energies in view of a common purpose, the welfare, the liberty and the security of all.

The Communal Revolution, begun by the popular initiative of March 18, inaugurates a new political era, experimental, positive, and scientific.

It is the end of the old governmental and clerical world, of militarism, officialism, exploitation, stock jobbing, monopolies, and privileges, to which the proletariate owes its servitude and the fatherland its misfortunes and its disasters.

Let this beloved and splendid fatherland, imposed upon by falsehoods and calumnies, reassure itself then!

The struggle brought on between Paris and Versailles is one of those which cannot be terminated by illusory compromises; the issue of it cannot be doubtful. Victory, pursued with an indomitable energy by the National Guard, will remain with the idea and the right.

We appeal, therefore, to France!

Informed that Paris in arms possesses as much of calmness as of bravery; that it preserves order with as much energy as enthusiasm; that it sacrifices itself with as much reason as heroism; and that it has armed itself only out of devotion to the liberty and glory of all; let France cause this bloody conflict to cease!

It is for France to disarm Versailles by the solemn expression of her irresistible will.

Summoned to profit from our conquests, let her declare herself identified with our efforts; let her be our ally in this conflict which can end only by the triumph of the communal idea or the ruin of Paris!

As for ourselves, citizens of Paris, we have the mission of accomplishing the modern revolution, the greatest and the most fruitful of all those which have illuminated history.

It is our duty to struggle and to conquer!

THE COMMUNE OF PARIS.

Paris, April 19, 1871.

THE THIRD REPUBLIC, which developed in the aftermath of the Franco-Prussian War, took shape gradually in an atmosphere of bitter division between monarchists and republicans. The Rivet Law (August 31, 1871) defined the power of the president in such a way as to insure a strict subordination of executive authority to that of the National Assembly.

4. THE BIRTH PANGS OF THE THIRD REPUBLIC: THE RIVET LAW, 1871

SOURCE. F. M. Anderson, ed., *The Constitutions and Other Select Documents Illustrative of the History of France,* Minneapolis: H. W. Wilson Co., 1904, p. 605. Reprinted by permission of Dr. Gaylord W. Anderson.

1. The Head of the Executive Power shall take the title of *President of the French Republic* and shall continue to exercise, under the authority of the National Assembly, as long as it shall not have terminated its labors, the functions which were delegated to him by the decree of February 17, 1871.

2. The President of the Republic promulgates the laws as soon as they are transmitted to him by the president of the National Assembly.

He secures and supervises the execution of the laws.

He resides at the place where the National Assembly sits.

He is heard by the National Assembly whenever he believes it necessary and after he has informed the president of the National Assembly of his wish.

He appoints and dismisses the ministers. The council of ministers and the ministers are responsible to the Assembly.

Each of the acts of the President of the Republic must be countersigned by a minister.

3. The President of the Republic is responsible to the Assembly.

THE FIRST PRESIDENT, Louis Adolphe Thiers, was an elder statesman who had once supported Louis-Philippe. Thiers had by now become a republican, and his hostility to the monarchist sentiment that prevailed in the Assembly resulted in his resignation in 1873. He explained his preference for republicanism over monarchism in a letter of 1877.

5. THE BIRTH PANGS OF THE THIRD REPUBLIC: LOUIS THIERS ON REPUBLIC AND MONARCHY, 1877

SOURCE. François le Goff, *The Life of Louis Adolphe Thiers*, T. Stanton, tr.

. . . at Bordeaux we, who served the Republic, were formerly monarchists. This, however, was not true of all. But we were demanded; we did not step forward without being called, and we took office purely through goodwill, because our presence re-assured the alarmed nation. And at last we were convinced of the necessity of the Republic. I wish the Republic many similar servitors, and from whatever quarter they may come, they will always be welcomed if they are honestly determined to help on the common cause, which, if it succeed, will be a blessing and not a detriment to France.

The question, therefore, raised by the proceeding of May 16th, may be summed up as follows: Is the Republic needed, and, if so, should it be firmly established by men who wish its success? Herein lies the whole question at issue.

Now, I ask every honest man, to whatever party he may belong, if the Count de Chambord could be placed on the throne with the opinions that he professes and with the flag that he unfurls, or if it is hoped that he may some day be acceptable after he has modified his views? We respect him too much to believe it. I will say nothing of the Orleans princes, who wish to be mentioned only after the Count de Chambord, according to their hereditary rank; but I ask if the country is ready to receive the Prince Imperial, who, though innocent of the misfortunes of France, suggests them so keenly, that the nation still shudders at the bare mention of his name? Nobody dare answer me yes; and, in fact, all the friends of these candidates postpone, until a future time, the day when their claims may be put forward. The truth of this statement is seen in the fact that they make no move, though the greatest indulgence has been shown all the monarchical parties.

Now, until this day—more or less distant—arrives, what will France do? France will wait until her future masters are ready: until one is brought over to other ways of thinking, until another has made an advance in his right of succession, and until a third has finished his education. In the meanwhile everything will be in suspense, commerce, industry, finances, State affairs. How can business men be asked to engage in great industrial enterprises, and financiers to negotiate loans, when the future threatens fresh political troubles? And how can foreign Cabinets be expected to strengthen their relations and form alliances with us, when French policy is liable to be directed by new chiefs and influenced by new ideas? Dare anybody ask such sacrifices of a great nation, that Europe has admired in its prosperity and also in its misfortunes, on seeing it restored once more, on seeing it revive again, displaying a rare wisdom in the midst of provocations, which it endures with such *sang-froid* and calm firmness?

Some men who, because they call themselves monarchists, believe that they know the secrets of the crowned heads, pretend that their reign is desired, and that then France will regain its prestige and alliances. But we would say to these men who think they understand Europe, but who, in reality, know nothing about it, and attribute to it their own ignorance and prejudices, that Europe looks with pity on their pretensions and hopes, and blames them for having got their country into the present trouble, instead of giving it the only form of government possible to-day. This Europe was formerly under absolute princes, but, recognizing the march of time, it is now ruled by constitutional princes, and is satisfied with the change. Europe understands that France, after the fall of three dynasties, has gone over to the Republic, which, during the last six years, has lifted the country out of the abyss into which the monarchists precipitated it. Europe has seen our military prestige destroyed and a new prestige take its place, that of the inexhaustible vitality of a prostrate country, suddenly rising up and furnishing the world an unheard of example of resources of every kind, so that France, even after Wörth, Sedan and Metz, has shown herself to be great still. It was under the Monarchy that she fell, but under the Republic that she arose again. And once more on the road to prosperity, it was the monarchists again that threw obstacles in the way of her reconstruction. If it be the esteem of Europe that is sought, listen to Europe, hearken to its opinion!

For this it is, that we persistently ask if there be any other alternative than the following: Either the Monarchy, which is impossible, because there are three claimants and but one throne; or the Republic, difficult to establish without doubt, not because of itself, but because of the opposition of the monarchical parties, and, nevertheless, possible, for it is supported by an immense majority of the people.

It is the duty, therefore, of this immense majority of the people to consult together, to unite and to vote against those who resist the establishment of the only government possible. The Monarchy to-day, after the three revolutions that have overthrown it, is immediate civil war, if it be established now; and if put off for two years, or three years, the civil war is only postponed until that epoch. The Republic is an equitable participation of all the children of France in the government of their country, according to their abilities, their importance, and their callings.

AN ATTEMPT TO RESTORE the Bourbon monarchy having failed, the Assembly arrived at a compromise law in November, 1873, which was opposed by extreme republicans and extreme monarchists alike. This measure—the Law of the Septennate—conferred the presidency for seven years on the avowed royalist Marshal MacMahon, and granted him wide executive authority; France was to be a republic headed by a monarchist.

6. THE BIRTH PANGS OF THE THIRD REPUBLIC: THE LAW OF THE SEPTENNATE, 1873

SOURCE. F. M. Anderson, ed., *The Constitutions and Other Select Documents Illustrative of the History of France*, Minneapolis: H. W. Wilson Co., 1904, p. 630. Reprinted by permission of Dr. Gaylord W. Anderson.

1. The executive power is entrusted for seven years to Marshal de MacMahon, Duke of Magenta, dating from the promulgation of the present law; this power shall continue to be exercised with the title of

President of the Republic and under the existing conditions until the modifications which may be effected therein by the constitutional laws.

2. Within the three days which shall follow the promulgation of the present law, a commission of thirty members shall be selected, in public and by *scrutin de liste,* for the examination of constitutional laws.

Part II

UNIFICATION
AND EMANCIPATION

A. Italy

THE LIBERAL IDEALISM of the Italian unification movement emerges vividly from the essay "To the Italians" by the Italian patriot Giuseppe Mazzini (1805–1872).

1. GIUSEPPE MAZZINI, FROM "TO THE ITALIANS"

SOURCE. Giuseppe Mazzini, *The Duties of Man, and Other Essays*, Bolton King, ed., Thomas Okey, tr., London: J. M. Dent and Co., 1894, pp. 159–161, 165–167, 172–176. Everyman's Library Edition. Reprinted by permission of J. M. Dent & Sons, Ltd. and E. P. Dutton & Co., Inc.

It is high time to leave a policy of expedients, of opportunism, of entanglements and crooked ways, of parliamentary hypocrisy, concealment, and compromise, that characterises the languid life of worn-out nations, and return to the virgin, loyal, simple, logical policy that derives directly from a moral standard, that is the consequence of a ruling *principle*, that has always inaugurated the young life of peoples that are called to high destinies.

The first condition of this life, is the solemn declaration, made with the unanimous and free consent of our greatest in wisdom and virtue, that Italy, feeling the times to be ripe, rises with one spontaneous impulse, in the name of the Duty and Right inherent in a people, to constitute itself a Nation of free and equal brothers, and demand that rank which by right belongs to it among the Nations that are already formed. The next condition, is the declaration of the body of religious, moral, and political *principles* in which the Italian people believes at the present day, of the common ideal to which it is striving, of the *special* mission that distinguishes it from other peoples, and to which it intends to consecrate itself for its own benefit and for the benefit of Humanity. And the final condition, is to determine the methods to be employed, and the men to whom

374

the country should delegate the function of developing the national conception of life, and the application of its practical consequences to the manifold branches of social activity.

Without this, a *country* may exist, stumbling along from insurrection to insurrection, from revolution to revolution; but there cannot exist a NATION.

And these three conditions can only be fulfilled by a NATIONAL CONTRACT, dictated in Rome by a constituent assembly elected by direct or indirect suffrage, and by all the citizens that Italy contains.

The National Contract is the inauguration, the baptism of the nation. It is the *initiative* that determines the normal life, the successive and peaceful development of the forces and faculties of the country. Without that initiative, which gives life to the exercise of the vote, and directs it to the common *ideal* under the guidance of a *principle* and a *moral* doctrine, even popular suffrage is at the mercy of arbitrary influence, or the passions of the day, or the false suggestions of ambitious agitators. Plebiscites taken under circumstances like these, the perverted and unenlightened expression of mere brute numbers, have, within the space of a few years, led, and will lead again, to a republic, a limited monarchy, and the despotism of a Bonaparte. Until a people is educated to uniformity and brotherhood, the initiative determines in every place and time the character of the solemn acts to which the masses are called.

Everyone knows what is the form of government that we believe to be the logical deduction from the principles in which we believe, and from the national Italian tradition: we define it as *the development and application of a Nation's ideal, duly entrusted by the chosen of the Country to men of recognised capacity and proven virtue.* . . .

Our party is faithful to the ideal of our country's Traditions, but ready to harmonise them with the Traditions of Humanity and the inspirations of conscience; it is tolerant and moral, and it must therefore now confute, without attacking or misconstruing motives. We need not fear that we are forging weapons for the enemy, if we declare the religions of the world to be successive expressions of a series of ages that have educated the human race; if we recognise the religious faculty as eternal in the human soul, eternal, too, the bond between heaven and earth. We can admire in Gregory VII the gigantic energy of will, the sublime moral effort that could not be realised with the instrument that Christianity could lend, and, at the same time, in the name of the progress we have made, declare the Papacy to be for ever dead. We can recognise the Mission which Aristocracy and Monarchy had for other peoples in the past, and yet proclaim, for all of us, the duty and the right to outstrip those worn-out forms. We may, without denying the reverence due to Authority—for that is the real object of all our efforts—claim the task of attacking every

Authority that is not based on two conditions—the free and enlightened consent of the governed, and the power of directing the national life and making it fruitful.

We believe in God.

In a providential Law given by Him to life.

In a Law, not of the *Atonement,* not of the *Fall,* and *Redemption* by the *grace* of past or present mediators between God and *man,* but of PROGRESS, unlimited Progress, founded on, and measured by, our works.

In the *Unity* of Life, misunderstood, as we believe, by the Philosophy of the last two centuries.

In the *Unity* of the Law through both the manifestations of Life, *collective* and *individual.*

In the immortality of the *Ego,* which is nothing but the application of the Law of PROGRESS, revealed beyond doubt now and for every by Historical Tradition, by Science, by the aspirations of the soul, to the Life that is manifested in the individual.

In Liberty, by which alone exists responsibility, the consciousness and price of *progress.*

In the successive and increasing *association* of all human faculties and powers, as the sole normal means of *progress,* at once collective and individual.

In the *Unity* of the human race, and in the moral *equality* of all the children of God, without distinction of sex, colour, or condition, to be forfeited by *crime* alone.

And hence we believe in the holy, inexorable, dominating idea of DUTY, the sole standard of Life. *Duty* that embraces in each one, according to the sphere in which he moves and the means that he possesses, Family, Fatherland, Humanity. Family the altar of the Fatherland; Fatherland the sanctuary of Humanity; Humanity a part of the Universe, and a temple built to God, who created the Universe, that it might draw near to Him. *Duty,* that bids us promote the progress of others that our own may be effected, and of ourselves that it may profit that of others. *Duty,* without which no *right* exists, that creates the virtue of self-sacrifice, in truth the only pure virtue, holy and mighty in power, the noblest jewel that crowns and hallows the human soul. . . .

The problem that is agitating the world is not the rejection of authority, for without authority, moral anarchy, and therefore sooner or later material anarchy, are inevitable. It is the rejection of all lifeless authority which is founded on the mere fact of its existence in the past, or on privileges of birth, riches, or aught else, and maintained without the free discussion and assent of the citizens, and closed to all progress in the future. It is not the rejection of liberty, whose absence makes tyranny inevitable. It is the restoration of the idea contained in that word to its true meaning—*the power to choose, according to our tendencies, capacity, and circumstances, the means to be employed to reach the end.* It is the rejection of that liberty which is an *end* to itself, and which abandons society and the mission of humanity to the caprice of the impulses and passions of individuals. *Authority* and *Liberty,* conceived as we state them, are equally sacred to us, and should be reconciled in every question awaiting settlement. *All things in Liberty and for Association;* this is the republican formula. Liberty and Association, Conscience and Tradition, Individual and Nation, the *"I"* and the *"We"* are inseparable elements of human nature, all of them essential to its orderly development. Only in order to co-ordinate them and direct them to a purpose, some point of union is required which is *superior* to all. Hence practical necessity leads us inevitably back to the high principles that we enunciated in theory in an earlier part of our work.

Sovereignty exists neither in the *"I"* nor the *"We";* it exists in God, the source of Life; in the PROGRESS that defines life; in the Moral Law that defines Duty.

In other terms, Sovereignty is in the IDEAL.

We are all called to do its work.

The knowledge of the *ideal* is given to us—so far as it is understood by the age in which we live—by our intelligence when it is inspired by the love of Good, and proceeds from the Tradition of Humanity to question its own *conscience,* and reconciles these two sole criteria of Truth.

But the knowledge of the *ideal* needs an *interpreter* who may forthwith indicate the means that may best attain to it, and direct its application to the various branches of activity. And as this *interpreter* must embrace within itself the *"I"* and the *"We,"* Authority and Liberty, State and Individual; and as, moreover, it must be *progressive,* it cannot be a man or any order of men selected by chance, or by the prerogative of a privilege unprogressive by its very nature, or birth, or riches, or aught else. Given the principles contained in the contract of faith and brotherhood, this interpreter can only be the People, the Nation.

God and the People. These are the only two terms that survive the analysis of the elements which the Schools have given as the foundation of the social communion. Rome knows by what paths of self-sacrifice, civil virtue, and glory, the banner that bore these two solemn words inscribed upon it, awakened in 1849 the love of Italy for her.

And here for the present we may stop. The Italian Mission is therefore:—

The Unity of the Nation, in its *material* aspect, by the reconquest of the Trentino, of Istria and of Nice; in its *moral* aspect, by National Education, accompanied by the free and protected Instruction of every heterodox doctrine.

Unity of defence, or the *Nation armed*.

Unity of the Contract and every Institution that represents the civil, political, and economic progress of all Italians.

Steady activity of the legislative power; and the administration of the institutions that concern the national progress, to be entrusted, not to the executive power, but to Commissions by delegation from the legislative.

Communal liberty to be decreed so far as regards the special progress of the various localities.

Suppression of all offices intended at the present day to represent an undue influence of the Government over the different local districts.

Division of powers to be a consequence, not of an illogical distribution of *sovereignty*, but of the different functions of government.

A smaller number of State employees and a more equal payment for their services.

Abolition of political oaths.

Universal Suffrage as the beginning of political education.

Legislation tending to advance the intellectual and economic progress of those classes that need it most; and the nation to encourage industrial, agricultural, and labour associations, founded on certain general conditions, and of proven morality and capacity.

Special attention to be given to the uncultivated lands of Italy, to the vast unhealthy zones, to neglected communal property, and to the creation on them of a new class of small proprietors.

A general system of taxation so as to free life—that is, the necessaries of life—from all burdens, and so as to fall proportionately on superfluities, and avoid excessive expenses of collection.

Abolition of all impediments to the free circulation of produce within and without the country.

An economic system based on the saving of all useless expenditure and on the progressive increase of production.

Recognition of every debt contracted by the Nation in the past.

Simplification of the transfer of land.

Abolition of monopolies.

Responsibility of every public servant.

International policy to be governed by the moral *principle* that rules the Nation.

Alliances to be based on uniformity of tendencies and objects.

Especial favour to be shown to every movement that may fraternise Italy with the elements of future or growing Nationalities, with the Greek, Roumanian, or Slave populations, who are destined to solve the problem of Eastern Europe.

These, with many others, are but the consequences of the great *principles* we have enunciated, and will be developed in our Publication; and, if the Italians will help us with their effective assistance, a more popular explanation will be given in a paper which we will add, dedicated specially to the Working Classes.

MAZZINI'S DISCIPLE, Giuseppe Garibaldi (1807–1882), a flamboyant adventurer, organized in 1860 a volunteer force to conquer Sicily and southern Italy. Encouraged by Piedmont, which was then in the process of unifying northern Italy, and expressing his support for the Piedmontese King Victor Emmanuel, Garibaldi issued a ringing appeal to the Italian people on the eve of his arrival in Sicily. The response was enthusiastic, and Garibaldi was able very quickly to conquer Sicily and Naples.

2. GIUSEPPE GARIBALDI'S PROCLAMATION ON THE LIBERATION OF SICILY

SOURCE. "Public Documents," *The Annual Register, 1860,* London: 1861, pp. 281–282.

Italians!—The Sicilians are fighting against the enemies of Italy, and for Italy. It is the duty of every Italian to succour them with words, money, and arms, and, above all, in person.

The misfortunes of Italy arise from the indifference of one province to the fate of the others.

The redemption of Italy began from the moment that men of the same land ran to help their distressed brothers.

Left to themselves, the brave Sicilians will have to fight, not only the mercenaries of the Bourbon, but also those of Austria and the Priest of Rome.

Let the inhabitants of the free provinces lift their voices in behalf of their struggling brethren, and impel their brave youth to the conflict.

Let the Marches, Umbria, Sabina, Rome, the Neapolitan, rise to divide the forces of our enemies.

Where the cities suffice not for the insurrection, let them send bands of their bravest into the country.

The brave man finds an arm everywhere. Listen not to the voice of cowards, but arm, and let us fight for our brethren, who will fight for us to-morrow.

A band of those who fought with me the country's battles marches with me to the fight. Good and generous, they will fight for their country to the last drop of their blood, nor ask for other reward than a clear conscience.

"Italy and Victor Emmanuel!" they cried, on passing the Ticino. "Italy and Victor Emmanuel!" shall re-echo in the blazing caves of Mongibello.

At this cry, thundering from the great rock of Italy to the Tarpeian, the rotton Throne of tyranny shall crumble, and, as one man, the brave descendants of Vespro shall rise.

To arms! Let me put an end, once for all, to the miseries of so many centuries. Prove to the world that it is no lie that Roman generations inhabited this land.

(*Signed*)   G. GARIBALDI

B. Germany

JOHANN GOTTLIEB FICHTE (1792–1814) delivered a series of "Addresses to the German Nation" in Berlin in 1807–1808 which served as a significant source for later German nationalism. The eighth of these addresses, "The People and the Fatherland," is given here.

1. JOHANN GOTTLIEB FICHTE, "THE PEOPLE AND THE FATHERLAND" FROM *ADDRESSES TO THE GERMAN NATION*, 1807–1808

SOURCE. Guy Carleton Lee, ed., *The World's Orators*, New York: G. P. Putnam's Sons, 1900, V, pp. 177–182, 190–193, 195–201. Reprinted by permission of G. P. Putnam's Sons.

Let me make this clear by a simple example. Where is there a man of high mind and noble sentiments who does not desire that in his children and his children's children his own life may be repeated in a nobler and higher scale, that after his death his life may continue on this earth, only ennobled and perfected; who does not long to leave in the minds of those who remain behind him the spirit, the sense, the morality, which perhaps in his case was shocked by perversity and ruin, to rescue these from mortality and leave them as his best treasure to the future world; to strengthen the religious, animate the slothful, and raise the depressed? Where is there a man of high mind and noble sentiments who does not desire by his thought and actions to plant a seed to aid the endlessly increasing perfection of his race, to cast into the time something new, something that as yet has never been, that it may become an unfailing spring of new creation, that so he may pay for his place on earth and the short span of life granted to him with that which is of eternal permanence, so that although he be solitary and unknown to history—for the thirst for fame is an empty vanity—he may leave in his own conscience and faith a public monument to mark the fact that he has been? Where is there a man of high mind and noble sentiments, I ask, but desires this? Only according to the needs of those who are habitually thus minded should this world be regarded and ordered; only on their account is there any world at all. They are the kernel of the world, while they who are otherwise minded are mere parts of a transitory world, so long as they think that only for their sakes the world exists and that it must accommodate itself to them, until all have become as they are.

What is there of proof to fill this demand, this faith of the noble-minded in the imperishability, the eternity of his works? Surely it can be found only in an order of things which is itself eternal, and which may be regarded as able to take unto itself the eternal. Such an order there is. Though it may not be comprehended under one concept, yet it is certainly present. It is the peculiar spiritual nature, the human environment from which a man himself springs, with all his power of thinking and acting and with his faith in the eternity thereof. It is the people, the nation from which he descends and under which he has been trained and has grown to be that which he now is. . . .

This then is the meaning of the word *a people,* taken in a higher sense and regarded from the standpoint of a spiritual world, namely: that whole body of men living together in society, reproducing themselves from themselves both physically and spiritually, which whole body stands together under certain special laws of the development of the divine part thereof. The participation in these special laws is that which in the eternal world, and therefore in the transitory world as well, unites this mass into a natural and homogeneous whole. This law itself can, in respect to its contents, be well comprehended as a whole, as we have apprehended it in the case of the Germans as a principal race or people; in many of its future determinations it can still further be comprehended through a consideration of the appearance of such a people; but it can never be understood by any one who remains unconsciously under the law, although its existence may be clearly perceived. . . . This law determines and completes what has been called the national character of a people, namely, that law of the development of the original and divine. It is clear from this last consideration, that men who have hitherto described foreign lands do not at all believe in their originality and their continued development, but merely in an unending circulation of apparent life, and by their faith these peoples become according to their faith, but in the higher sense are no people, and since they are not that in reality, they are quite unable to have a national character.

The belief of the noble-minded in the eternal continuance of his activity, even on this earth, is founded, accordingly, on the hope of the eternal continuance of the people from whom he has himself sprung, and of the distinctive character of that people according to that hidden law, without any mixing with, or deprivation by, anything foreign to it or any not belonging to the fulness of that law. This distinctive character is the eternal, to which he trusts the eternity of himself and his continued activity; it is the eternal order in which he places that in himself which is eternal; he must desire its continuance, because it is his only means of deliverance, whereby the short span of his moral life may be prolonged to an enduring life. . . .

In this faith our oldest common ancestors, the original people of the new culture, the Teutons, called Germans by the Romans, set themselves bravely in opposition to the overwhelming worldwide rule of the Romans. Did they not see with their own eyes the finest blossom of the Roman provinces beside them, the finer enjoyment in the same, together with laws, courts of justice, lictors' staves and axes in superabundance? Were not the Romans ready and generous enough to let them share in all these benefits? Did they not see proof of the famous Roman clemency in the case of several of their own princes, who allowed themselves to think that war against such benefactors of the human race was rebellion? For the compliant were decorated with the title of king and rewarded with posts of importance as leaders in the Roman army, with Roman sacrificial wreaths; and when they were expelled by their countrymen, the Romans furnished them with a refuge and support in their colonies. Had they no appreciation of the advantages of Roman culture, for better organization of their armies, for example, in which even Arminius himself did not refuse to learn the art of war? It cannot be charged against them that in any one of these respects they were ignorant. Their descendants have appropriated that culture, as soon as they could do so without the loss of their own freedom, and as far as it was possible without loss of their distinctive character. Wherefore, then, have they fought for so many generations in bloody wars which have been repeatedly renewed with undiminished fury? A Roman writer represents their leaders as asking if anything else remained for them but to maintain their freedom or to die before they became slaves. Freedom was their possession, that they might remain Germans, that they might continue to settle their own affairs independently and originally and in their own way, and at the same time to advance their culture and to plant the same independence in the hearts of their posterity. Slavery was what they called all the benefits which the Romans offered them, because through them they would become other than Germans, they would have to become semi-Romans. It was perfectly clear, they assumed, that every man, rather than become this, would die, and that a true German could wish to live only to be and to remain a German, and to have his sons the same.

They have not all died; they have not seen slavery; they have bequeathed freedom to their children. To their constant resistance the
whole new world owes that it is as it is. Had the Romans succeeded in
subjugating them also, and, as the Romans everywhere did, destroying
them as a nation, the entire development of the human race would have
taken a different direction, and it cannot be thought a better one. We who
are the nearest heirs of their land, their language, and their sentiments,
owe to them that we are still Germans, that the stream of original and
independent life still bears us on; to them we owe that we have since
then become a nation; to them, if now perhaps it is not at an end with us
and the last drops of blood inherited from them are not dried in our
veins, we owe all that which we have become. To them, even the other
tribes, who have become to us aliens but through them our brethren,
owe their existence; when they conquered eternal Rome, there were no
others of all those peoples present; at that time was won for them the
possibility of their future origin. . . .

From all this it follows that the State, as a mere control of the human
life as it advances in customary and peaceful course, is not that which
is primary and existent for its own sake, but is merely a means for that
higher purpose, the eternally, uniformly progressive development of
the purely human in the nation; that it is only the image and the love of
this eternal progress, which shall in the quiet flow of time mould the
higher ideas in the conduct of the State, and which, when the independence of the people is in danger, is alone able to save it. Among the
Germans, amid whom as an original people this love of the fatherland
was possible, and, as one who knew firmly believed, thus far has also
been actual, this could so far with a high degree of confidence count upon
the security of its most important affairs. As in the case of the Greeks in
old time, so here in the case of the Germans the State and the nation were
separated from each other, and each was presented for itself, the former
in the various distinct German kingdoms and principalities, the latter
visibly in the imperial union, and invisibly, not according to a written
constitution but a fundamental law living in the hearts and minds of all,
in a multitude of customs and institutions. As far as the German tongue
was spoken, so far could every one upon whom the light dawned within
that radius regard himself in a twofold aspect as a citizen: on account of
his birthplace, to whose care he was first committed, and on account of
the entire common fatherland of the German nation. It was permitted
each one to obtain for himself over the entire surface of the fatherland
that culture which had the greatest affinity with his spirit, or that field of
work which was most appropriate to him, and his talent did not grow in
its place as a tree grows, but it was permitted him to seek it. Whoever,
by the direction which his education took, was estranged from his imme-

diate surroundings, easily found acceptance elsewhere, found new friends in place of those whom he had lost, found time and leisure to explain himself more particularly, and perhaps to win to himself those who had been estranged and so to unite the whole once more. No German prince has ever been able to compel his subjects to remain among the mountains and rivers where he rules, or to regard themselves as bound to the surface of the earth. A truth which might not be expressed in one place, might be expressed in another, in which place on the contrary those truths were forbidden which were allowed in the first region; and therefore, in spite of all the one-sidedness and narrow-mindedness of the various States, there was to be found in Germany, taken as a whole, the highest freedom of investigation and instruction ever possessed by a people, and the highest culture was, and everywhere remains, the result of the mutual action of the citizens of the German States, and this higher culture came gradually in this form to the vast multitude of the people also, so that it forthwith continued in the whole to educate itself by itself. This essential pledge of the continuance of a German nation detracts in no respect from any German soul who stands at the helm of the government; and although in respect to some original decisions have occurred, as has been thought, otherwise than as the higher German love of fatherland must wish, nevertheless the affairs of the State have at least not been handled directly contrary to what has been desired; no one has been tempted to undermine that love, to exterminate it and to bring a contrary love in its place.

If now, perhaps, the original guidance, not only of the higher culture but of the national power, which should be used as an end only for that and for its continuance, for it is the employment of German wealth and German blood, should be turned in another direction on account of the willingness of the German heart, what would necessarily follow? Here is the point where it is especially necessary that we should not be willing to be deceived in our own affairs, and be courageous enough to see the truth and to confess it; and it is, as far as I know, still allowed us to speak with one another in the German tongue of the fatherland, or at least to sigh; and, believe me, we would not do well if we, on our part, anticipated such a prohibition and clasped the shackles of timidity upon the courage of some who have, no doubt, already thought of the danger.

Picture to yourselves the new power as kind and benevolent as you will, make it as good as God, will you be able to attribute to it divine reason? Let it wish in all seriousness the highest happiness and prosperity of all; will that prosperity which it will be able to comprehend be the German prosperity? I hope then that the main point which I have today presented to you may be well understood by you; I hope that there are many here who have thought and felt that I merely express clearly and in words that which they have already felt in their hearts; I hope these words may stand in the same way toward them.

But several Germans before me have also said very nearly the same things, and the same sentiments, though obscure, have been at the foundation of that striving, always well maintained, against a merely mechanical arrangement and conception of the State. And now I call upon all who are acquainted with the recent foreign literature, to show me what modern sage, poet, or legislator of the same has ever shown thoughts like these, regarding the human race as eternally progressing, and describing all its activity in time as steps in that progress; whether any one, even in that point of time when men have risen to the boldest political conceptions, has ever demanded of the State more than the absence of inequality or internal peace and external national fame, and, where it is at the very best, domestic happiness. If this is their highest, as must follow from what has been pointed out, they will ascribe to us no higher necessities and no higher demands in life, and, assuming in them benevolent sentiments towards us and absence of all selfishness and all desire to be more than we are, they will believe that we have been well cared for, if we find all which they regard as alone desirable; but that for which alone the nobler of us live has been obliterated from public life, and the people, which has always shown itself sensitive to the suggestions of the nobler, and which one might for the majority hope to raise to the rank of nobility, so far as it is treated as those nobler men would treat it, has been degraded from its rank, dishonored, obliterated from the list of things, in as far as it is merged in what is lower.

He in whom there remains in life and strength those higher demands of life, together with a feeling for divine justice, feels himself led with deep reluctance back to those first days of Christianity, to those men to whom it was said, "Ye shall not resist evil, but if one shall smite thee on thy right cheek, turn to him the other also, and if any one will take away thy coat, let him have thy cloak also"; rightfully quoting the last saying, for so long as he sees a cloak on thee, he will contrive some way in which he can take it from thee; when thou art entirely naked thou wilt escape his notice and be let alone by him. Even his higher sense, which honors him, makes the earth for him a hell and a despair; he wishes that he had never been born, that his eyes may close forever before the glance of day and the sooner the better; unending mourning encompasses his days even to the grave; for him who is dear to him he can wish no better gift than a stupid, satiated sense, that with little pain he may approach an eternal life beyond the grave.

These orations have attempted, by the only means remaining after others have been tried in vain, to prevent this annihilation of every noble action that may in the future arise among us, and this degradation of our entire nation. They have attempted to implant in your minds the deep and immovable foundations of the true and almighty love of the fatherland, in the conception of our nation as eternal and the people as citizens of our own eternity through the education of all hearts and minds.

THERE FOLLOW THREE EXCERPTS from the Reflections and Reminiscences *of Otto von Bismarck (1815–1898) in which the retired statesman reflects on his political attitudes as a youth, relates the arguments he used to win King William I's support for his policy of "blood and iron," and expresses himself on the subject of nationalism* versus *dynasticism in Germany.*

2. OTTO VON BISMARCK, FROM *REFLECTIONS AND REMINISCENCES*

SOURCE. *Bismarck, The Man and The Statesman,* A. J. Butler, tr., New York: Harper Bros., 1899, I, pp. 1–3, 312–316, and 320–326. Reprinted by permission of Harper & Row, Publishers.

POLITICAL VIEWS AS A YOUTH

I left school at Easter 1832, a normal product of our state system of education; a Pantheist, and, if not a Republican, at least with the persuasion that the Republic was the most rational form of government; reflecting too upon the causes which could decide millions of men permanently to obey *one man,* when all the while I was hearing from group up people much bitter or contemptuous criticism of their rulers. Moreover, I had brought away with me 'German-National' impressions from Plamann's preparatory school, conducted on Jahn's drill-system, in which I lived from my sixth to my twelfth year. These impressions remained in the stage of theoretical reflections, and were not strong enough to extirpate my innate Prussian monarchical sentiments. My historical sympathies remained on the side of authority. To my childish ideas of justice Harmodius and Aristogeiton, as well as Brutus, were criminals, and Tell a rebel and murderer. Every German prince who resisted the Emperor before the Thirty Years' war rouse my ire; but from the Great Elector onwards I was partisan enough to take an anti-imperial view, and to find it natural that things should have been in readiness for the Seven Years' war. Yet the German-National feeling remained so strong in me that, at the beginning of my University life, I at once entered into relations with *Burschenschaft,* or group of students which made the promotion of a national sentiment its aim. But after personal intimacy with its members, I disliked their refusal to 'give satisfaction,' as well as their want of breeding in externals and of acquaintance with the forms and manners of good society; and a still closer acquaintance bred an aversion to the extravagance of their political views, based upon a lack of either culture or knowledge of the conditions of life which historical causes had brought into existence, and which I, with my seventeen years, had had more opportunities of observing than most of these students, for the most part older than myself. Their ideas gave me the impression of an association between Utopian theories and defective breeding. Nevertheless, I retained my own private National sentiments, and my belief that in the near future events would lead to German unity; in fact, I made a bet with my American friend Coffin that this aim would be attained in twenty years.

In my first half-year at Göttingen occurred the Hambach festival[1] (May 27, 1832), the 'festal ode' of which still remains in my memory; in my third the Frankfort outbreak[2] (April 3, 1833). These manifestations revolted me. Mob interference with political authority conflicted with my Prussian schooling, and I returned to Berlin with less liberal opinions than when I quitted it. . . .

BISMARCK WINS OVER WILLIAM I

In the beginning of October [1862] I went as far as Jüterbogk to meet the King, who had been at Baden-Baden for September 30, his wife's birthday, and waited for him in the still unfinished railway station, filled with third-class travellers and workmen, seated in the dark on an overturned wheelbarrow. My object in taking this opportunity for an interview was to set his Majesty at rest about a speech made by me in the Budget Commission on September 30, which had aroused some excitement, and which, though not taken down in shorthand, had still been reproduced with tolerable accuracy in the newspapers.

For people who were less embittered and blinded by ambition, I had indicated plainly enough the direction in which I was going. Prussia— such was the point of my speech—as a glance at the map will show, could no longer wear unaided on its long narrow figure the panoply which Germany required for its security; that must be equally distributed over all German peoples. We should get no nearer the goal by speeches,

[1] [A gathering of, it is said, 30,000 at the Castle of Hambach in the Palatinate; where speeches were made in favour of Germany, unity, and the Republic.]

[2] [An attempt made by a handful of students and peasants to blow up the Federal Diet in revenge for some Press regulations passed by it. They stormed the guard house, but were then suppressed.]

associations, decisions of majorities; we should be unable to avoid a serious contest, a contest which could only be settled by blood and iron. In order to secure our success in this, the deputies must place the greatest possible weight of blood and iron in the hands of the King of Prussia, in order that according to his judgment he might throw it into one scale or the other. I had already given expression to the same idea in the House of Deputies in 1849, in answer to Schramm on the occasion of an amnesty debate.

Roon, who was present, expressed his dissatisfaction with my remarks on our way home, and said, among other things, that he did not regard these 'witty digressions' as advantageous for our cause. For my part, I was torn between the desire of winning over members to an energetic national policy, and the danger of inspiring the King, whose own disposition was cautious, and shrank from violent measures, with mistrust in me and my intentions. My object in going to meet him at Jüterbogk was to counteract betimes the probable effect of press criticisms.

I had some difficulty in discovering from the curt answers of the officials the carriage in the ordinary train, in which the King was seated by himself in an ordinary first-class carriage. The after-effect of his intercourse with his wife was an obvious depression, and when I begged for permission to narrate the events which had occurred during his absence, he interrupted me with the words: 'I can perfectly well see where all this will end. Over there, in front of the Opera House, under my windows, they will cut off your head, and mine a little while afterwards.'

I guessed, and it was afterwards confirmed by witnesses, that during his week's stay at Baden his mind had been worked upon with variations on the theme of Polignac, Strafford, and Lewis XVI. When he was silent, I answered with the short remark, 'Et après, Sire.' 'Après, indeed; we shall be dead,' answered the King. 'Yes,' I continued, 'then we shall be dead; but we must all die sooner or later, and can we perish more honourably? I, fighting for my King's cause, and your Majesty sealing with your own blood your rights as King by the grace of God; whether on the scaffold or the battlefield, makes no difference to the glory of sacrificing life and limb for the rights assigned to you by the grace of God. Your Majesty must not think of Lewis XVI; he lived and died in a condition of mental weakness, and does not present a heroic figure in history. Charles I, on the other hand, will always remain a noble historical character, for after drawing his sword for his rights and losing the battle, he did not hesitate to confirm his royal intent with his blood. Your Majesty is bound to fight, you cannot capitulate; you must, even at the risk of bodily danger, go forth to meet any attempt at coercion.'

As I continued to speak in this sense, the King grew more and more animated, and began to assume the part of an officer fighting for kingdom and fatherland. In presence of external and personal danger he possessed a rare and absolutely natural fearlessness, whether on the field of battle or in the face of attempts on his life; his attitude in any external danger was elevating and inspiring. The ideal type of the Prussian officer who goes to meet certain death in the service with the simple words, 'At your orders,' but who, if he has to act on his own responsibility, dreads the criticism of his superior officer or of the world more than death, even to the extent of allowing his energy and correct judgment to be impaired by the fear of blame and reproof—this type was developed in him to the highest degree. Hitherto, on his journey, he had only asked himself whether, under the superior criticism of his wife and public opinion in Prussia, he would be able to keep steadfast on the road on which he was entering with me. The influence of our conversation in the dark railway compartment counteracted this sufficiently to make him regard the part which the situation forced upon him more from the standpoint of the officer. He felt as though he had been touched in his military honour, and was in the position of an officer who has orders to hold a certain position to the death, no matter whether he perishes in the task or not. This set him on a course of thought which was quite familiar to him; and in a few minutes he was restored to the confidence which he had lost at Baden, and even recovered his cheerfulness. To give up his life for King and Fatherland was the duty of an officer; still more that of a King, as the first officer in the land. As soon as he regarded his position from the point of view of military honour, it had no more terror for him than the command to defend what might prove a desperate position would have for any ordinary Prussian officer. This raised him above the anxiety about the criticism which public opinion, history, and his wife might pass on his political tactics. He fully entered into the part of the first officer in the Prussian monarchy, for whom death in the service would be an honourable conclusion to the task assigned him. The correctness of my judgment was confirmed by the fact that the King, whom I had found at Jüterbogk weary, depressed, and discouraged, had, even before we arrived at Berlin, developed a cheerful, I might almost say joyous and combative disposition, which was plainly evident to the ministers and officials who received him on his arrival. . . .

NATIONALISM AND DYNASTICISM IN GERMANY

In order that German patriotism should be active and effective, it needs as a rule to hang on the peg of dependence upon a dynasty; independent of dynasty it rarely comes to the rising point, though in theory it daily does so, in parliament, in the press, in public meeting; in practice the German needs either attachment to a dynasty or the goad of anger, hurrying him into action: the latter phenomenon, however, by its own nature is not permanent. It is as a Prussian, a Hanoverian, a Wurtemberger, a Bavarian or a Hessian, rather than as a German, that he is disposed to give unequivocal proof of patriotism; and in the lower orders and the parliamentary groups it will be long before it is otherwise. We cannot say that the Hanoverian, Hessian, and other dynasties were at any special pains to win the affections of their subjects; but nevertheless the German patriotism of their subjects is essentially conditioned by their attachment to the dynasty after which they call themselves. It is not differences of stock, but dynastic relations upon which in their origin the centrifugal elements repose. It is not attachment to Swabian, Lower Saxon, Thuringian, or other particular stock that counts for most, but the dynastic incorporation with the people of some severed portion of a ruling princely family, as in the instances of Brunswick, Brabant, and Wittelsbach dynasties. The cohesion of the kingdom of Bavaria does not rest merely on the Bajuvarian stock as it is found in South Bavaria and in Austria: the Swabian of Augsburg, the Alleman of the Palatinate, the Frank of the Main, though of widely different blood, call themselves Bavarians with as much satisfaction as does the Old-Bavarian at Munich or Landshut, and for no other reason than that they have been connected with the latter for three generations through the common dynasty. It is to dynastic influences that those stocks which present the most marked characteristics, as the Low-German, the *Platt-Deutsch*, the Saxon, owe their greater depth and distinctness of differentiation. The German's love of Fatherland has need of a prince on whom it can concentrate its attachment. Suppose that all the German dynasties were suddenly deposed; there would then be no likelihood that the German national sentiment would suffice to hold all Germans together from the point of view of international law amid the friction of European politics, even in the form of federated Hanse towns and imperial village communes. The Germans would fall a prey to more closely welded nations if they once lost the tie which resides in the princes' sense of community of rank.

History shows that in Germany the Prussian stock is that of which the individual character is most strongly stamped, and yet no one could decisively answer the question whether, supposing the Hohenzollern dynasty and all its rightful successors to have passed away, the political cohesion of Prussia would survive. Is it quite certain that the eastern and the western divisions, that Pomeranians and Hanoverians, natives of Holstein and Silesia, of Aachen and Königsberg, would then continue as they now are, bound together in the indisruptible unity of the Prussian state? Or Bavaria—if the Wittelbach dynasty were to vanish and leave not a trace behind, would Bavaria continue to hold together in isolated unity? Some dynasties have many memories which are not exactly of the kind to inspire attachment in the heterogeneous fragments out of which their states have, as a matter of history, been formed. Schleswig-Holstein has absolutely no dynastic memories, least of all any opposed to the House of Gottorp, and yet the prospect of the possible formation there of a small, independent, brand-new little court with ministers, court-marshals, and orders, in which the life of a petty state should be sustained at the cost of what Austria and Prussia would manage in the *Bund,* called forth very strong particularist movements in the Elbe duchies. The Grand Duchy of Baden has hardly a dynastic memory since the time of the Margrave Ludwig before Belgrade; the rapid growth of this little principality under French protection in the confederation of the Rhine, the court life of the last princes of the old line, the matrimonial alliance with the Beauharnais house, the Caspar Hauser story, the revolutionary proceedings of 1832, the banishment of the Grand Duke Leopold, the citizens' patron, the banishment of the reigning house in 1849, have not been able to break the power which subservience to dynasty has in that country, and Baden in 1866 fought against Prussia and the German idea because constrained thereto by the dynastic interests of the reigning house.

The other nations of Europe have need of no such go-between for their patriotism and national sentiment. Poles, Hungarians, Italians, Spaniards, Frenchmen would under any or without any dynasty preserve their homogeneous national unity. The Teutonic stocks of the north, the Swedes and the Danes, have shown themselves pretty free from dynastic sentiment; and in England, though external respect for the Crown is demanded by good society, and the formal maintenance of monarchy is held expedient by all parties that have hitherto had any share in government, I do not anticipate the disruption of the nation, or that such sentiments as were common in the time of the Jacobites would attain to any practical form, if in the course of its historical development the British people should come to deem a change of dynasty or the transition to a republican form of government necessary or expedient. The preponderance of dynastic attachment, and the use of a dynasty as the indispensable cement to hold together a definite portion of the nation calling itself by the name of the dynasty is a specific peculiarity of the German Empire. The particular nationalities, which among us have shaped themselves on the bases of dynastic family and possession, include in most cases heterogeneous elements, whose cohesion rests neither on identity of stock nor on similarity of historical development, but exclusively on the fact of some (in most cases questionable) acquisition by the dynasty whether by the right of the strong, or hereditary succession by affinity or compact of inheritance, or by some reversionary grant obtained from the imperial Court as the price of a vote.

Whatever may be the origin of this factitious union of particularist elements, its result is that the individual German readily obeys the command of a dynasty to harry with fire and sword, and with his own hands to slaughter his German neighbours and kinsfolk as a result of quarrels unintelligible to himself. To examine whether this characteristic be capable of rational justification is not the problem of a German statesman, so long as it is strongly enough pronounced for him to reckon upon it. The difficulty of either abolishing or ignoring it, or making any advance in theory towards unity without regard to this practical limitation, has often proved fatal to the champions of unity; conspicuously so in the advantage taken of the favourable circumstances in the national movements of 1848–50. The attachment of the modern Guelf party to the old dynasty I fully understand, and to that party perhaps I should myself have belonged had I been born an Old-Hanoverian. But in that case I should never have been able to escape the influence of the national German sentiment, or be surprised if the *vis majeure* of the collective nationality were relentlessly to annul my liege-loyalty and personal predilection. How to fall with a good grace! solicitude to solve that problem accords in politics—and not merely in German politics—with other and better justified aspirations; and the Elector of Brunswick's inability to achieve this result impairs in some degree the sympathy which the loyalty of her vassals inspires in me. In the German national sentiment I see the preponderant force always elicited by the struggle with particularism; for particularism—Prussian particularism too—came into being only by resistance to the collective German community, to Emperor and Empire, in revolt from both, leaning first on papal, then on French, in all cases on foreign support, all alike damaging and dangerous to the German community. In regard to the policy of the Guelfic efforts, their earliest historical landmark, the revolt of Henry the Lion before the battle of Legnano, the desertion of Emperor and Empire in the crisis of a most severe and perilous struggle, is for all time decisive.

Dynastic interests are justified in Germany so far as they fit in with the common national imperial interests: the two may very well go hand in hand; and a duke loyal to the Empire in the old sense is in certain circumstances more serviceable to the community than would be direct relations between the Emperor and the duke's vassals. So far, however, as dynastic interests threaten us once more with national disintegration and impotence, they must be reduced to their proper measure.

The German people and its national life cannot be portioned out as private possessions of princely houses. It has always been clear to me that this reflection applies to the electoral house of Brandenburg as well as to the Bavarian, the Guelf, or other houses; I should have been weaponless against the Brandenburg princely house, if in dealing with it I had needed to reinforce my German national feeling by rupture and resistance; in the predestination of history, however, it so fell out that my courtier-talents sufficed to gain the King, and with him by consequence his army, for the national cause. I have had perhaps harder battles to fight against Prussian particularism than against the particularism of the other German states and dynasties, and my relation to the Emperor William I as his born subject made these battles all the harder for me. Yet in the end, despite the strongly dynastic policy of the Emperor, but thanks to his national policy which, dynastically justified, became ever stronger in critical moments, I always succeeded in gaining his countenance for the German side of our development, and that too when a more dynastic and particularist policy prevailed on all other hands.

BISMARCK'S EFFORTS TO INSURE European peace and isolate France are exemplified in the Triple Alliance of May 20, 1882, between Germany, Austria-Hungary, and Italy (3) and in the Reinsurance Treaty with Russia (June 18, 1887) (4). Bismarck feared the possibility of an alliance between France and Russia which might put Germany in a vise, and by means of the Reinsurance Treaty he sought to prevent it. Russia and Austria were engaged in a bitter rivalry over hegemony in the Balkans, but Bismarck was determined to enter into treaty agreements with each of the two powers. Both the Triple Alliance and the Reinsurance Treaty were closely guarded state secrets, and Austria remained unaware of Bismarck's diplomatic promiscuity.

3. THE TRIPLE ALLIANCE, 1882

SOURCE. Alfred F. Pribam, ed., *The Secret Treaties of Austria-Hungary, 1879–1914,* A. C. Coolidge, tr., Cambridge, Mass.: Harvard University Press, 1920, I, pp. 65–69. Reprinted by permission of the Harvard University Press.

ARTICLE 1. The High Contracting Parties mutually promise peace and friendship, and will enter into no alliance or engagement directed against any one of their States.

The engage to proceed to an exchange of ideas on political and economic questions of a general nature which may arise, and they further promise one another mutual support within the limits of their own interests.

ARTICLE 2. In case Italy, without direct provocation on her part, should be attacked by France for any reason whatsoever, the two other Contracting Parties shall be bound to lend help and assistance with all their forces to the Party attacked.

This same obligation shall devolve upon Italy in case of any aggression without direct provocation by France against Germany.

ARTICLE 3. If one, or two, of the High Contracting Parties, without direct provocation on their part, should chance to be attacked and to be engaged in a war with two or more Great Powers nonsignatory to the present Treaty, the *casus foederis* will arise simultaneously for all the High Contracting Parties.

ARTICLE 4. In case a Great Power nonsignatory to the present Treaty should threaten the security of the states of one of the High Contracting Parties, and the threatened Party should find itself forced on that account to make war against it, the two others bind themselves to observe towards their Ally a benevolent neutrality. Each of them reserves to itself, in this case, the right to take part in the war, if it should see fit, to make common cause with its Ally.

ARTICLE 5. If the peace of any of the High Contracting Parties should chance to be threatened under the circumstances foreseen by the preceding Articles, the High Contracting Parties shall take counsel together in ample time as to the military measures to be taken with a view to eventual coöperation.

They engage henceforward, in all cases of common participation in a war, to conclude neither armistice, nor peace, nor treaty, except by common agreement among themselves.

ARTICLE 6. The High Contracting Parties mutually promise secrecy as to the contents and existence of the present Treaty.

ARTICLE 7. The present Treaty shall remain in force during the space of five years, dating from the day of the exchange of ratifications.

ARTICLE 8. The ratifications of the present Treaty shall be exchanged at Vienna within three weeks, or sooner if may be.

In witness whereof the respective Plenipotentiaries have signed the present Treaty and have affixed thereto the seal of their arms.

Done at Vienna, the twentieth day of the month of May of the year one thousand eight hundred and eighty-two.

(L.S.) KÁLNOKY
(L.S.) H. VII OF REUSS
(L.S.) C. ROBILANT

4. THE REINSURANCE TREATY, 1887

SOURCE. Alfred F. Pribam, ed., *The Secret Treaties of Austria-Hungary, 1879–1914*, A. C. Coolidge, tr., Cambridge, Mass.: Harvard University Press, 1920, I, pp. 275–281. Reprinted by permission of the Harvard University Press.

The Imperial Courts of Germany and of Russia, animated by an equal desire to strengthen the general peace by an understanding destined to assure the defensive position of their respective States, have resolved to confirm the agreement established between them by a special arrangement, in view of the expiration on June 15/27, 1887, of the validity of the secret Treaty and Protocol, signed in 1881 and renewed in 1884 by the three courts of Germany, Russia, and Austria-Hungary.

To this end the two Courts have named as Plenipotentiaries:

His Majesty the Emperor of Germany, King of Prussia, the Sieur Herbert Count Bismarck-Schoenhausen, His Secretary of State in the Department of Foreign Affairs;

His Majesty the Emperor of All the Russians, the Sieur Paul Count Schouvaloff, His Ambassador Extraordinary and Plenipotentiary to His Majesty the Emperor of Germany, King of Prussia, who, being furnished with full powers, which have been found in good and due form, have agreed upon the following articles:

ARTICLE 1. In case one of the High Contracting Parties should find itself at war with a third Great Power, the other would maintain a benevolent neutrality towards it, and would devote its efforts to the localization of the conflict. This provision would not apply to a war against Austria or France in case this war should result from an attack directed against one of these two latter Powers by one of the High Contracting Parties.

ARTICLE 2. Germany recognizes the rights historically acquired by Russia in the Balkan Peninsula, and particularly the legitimacy of her preponderant and decisive influence in Bulgaria and in Eastern Rumelia. The two Courts engage to admit no modification of the territorial status quo of the said peninsula without a previous agreement between them, and to oppose, as occasion arises, every attempt to disturb this status quo or to modify it without their consent.

ARTICLE 3. The two Courts recognize the European and mutually obligatory character of the principle of the closing of the Straits of the Bosporus and of the Dardanelles, founded on international law, confirmed by treaties, and summed up in the declaration of the second Plenipotentiary of Russia at the session of July 12 of the Congress of Berlin (Protocol 19).

They will take care in common that Turkey shall make no exception to this rule in favor of the interests of any Government whatsoever, by lending to warlike operations of a belligerent power the portion of its Empire constituted by the Straits. In case of infringement, or to prevent it if such infringement should be in prospect, the two Courts will inform Turkey that they would regard her, in that event, as putting herself in a state of war towards the injured Party, and as depriving herself thenceforth of the benefits of the security assured to her territorial status quo by the Treaty of Berlin.

ARTICLE 4. The present Treaty shall remain in force for the space of three years, dating from the day of the exchange of ratifications.

ARTICLE 5. The High Contracting Parties mutually promise secrecy as to the contents and the existence of the present Treaty and of the Protocol annexed thereto.

ARTICLE 6. The present Treaty shall be ratified and ratifications shall be exchanged at Berlin within a period of a fortnight, or sooner it may be.

In witness whereof the respective Plenipotentiaries have signed the present Treaty and have affixed thereto the seal of their arms.

Done at Berlin, the eighteenth day of the month of June, one thousand eight hundred and eighty-seven.

(L.S.) COUNT BISMARCK
(L.S.) COUNT PAUL SCHOUVALOFF

ADDITIONAL PROTOCOL. BERLIN, JUNE 18, 1887

In order to complete the stipulations of Articles 2 and 3 of the secret Treaty concluded on this same date, the two Courts have come to an agreement upon the following points:

1. Germany, as in the past, will lend her assistance to Russia in order to reëstablish a regular and legal government in Bulgaria. She promises in no case to give her consent to the restoration of the Prince of Battenberg.

2. In case His Majesty the Emperor of Russia should find himself under the necessity of assuming the task of defending the entrance of the Black Sea in order to safeguard the interests of Russia, Germany engages to accord her benevolent neutrality and her moral and diplomatic support to the measures which His Majesty may deem it necessary to take to guard the key of His Empire.

3. The present Protocol forms an integral part of the secret Treaty signed on this day at Berlin, and shall have the same force and validity.

In witness whereof the respective Plenipotentiaries have signed it and have affixed thereto the seal of their arms.

Done at Berlin, the eighteenth day of the month of June, one thousand eight hundred and eighty-seven.

COUNT BISMARCK

COUNT PAUL SCHOUVALOFF

C. Russia

LIBERALISM AND NATIONALISM accomplished far less in Russia than in central and western Europe. As the nineteenth century closed, the authority of the Czar remained unlimited by any legislature or constitution. Russia continued to be a largely agrarian state, and a middle class was slow in developing. Nevertheless, western ideas were percolating beneath the surface and were to erupt into revolution in 1905 and 1917. Meanwhile, Czar Alexander II (reigned 1855–1881) had undertaken a series of cautious and long-overdue reforms, the most far-reaching of which was his Imperial Ukase emancipating the Russian serfs (March 3, 1861). By his decree some 23,000,000 peasants were freed from servitude.

1. CZAR ALEXANDER II'S DECREE EMANCIPATING THE RUSSIAN SERFS, 1861

SOURCE. *Annual Register, 1861*, pp. 207–212, *passim.*

By the grace of God, we, Alexander II, Emperor and Autocrat of all the Russias, King of Poland, Grand Duke of Finland, etc., to all our faithful subjects, make known:

Called by Divine Providence and by the sacred right of inheritance to the throne of our ancestors, we took a vow in our innermost heart to respond to the mission which is intrusted to us as to surround with our affection and our Imperial solicitude all our faithful subjects of every rank and of every condition, from the warrior, who nobly bears arms for the defence of the country to the humble artisan devoted to the works of industry; from the official in the career of the high offices of the State to the laborer whose plough furrows the soil.

In considering the various classes and conditions of which the State is composed we came to the conviction that the legislation of the empire having wisely provided for the organization of the upper and middle classes and having defined with precision their obligations, their rights, and their privileges, has not attained the same degree of efficiency as regards the peasants attached to the soil, thus designated because either from ancient laws or from custom they have been hereditarily subjected to the authority of the proprietors, on whom it was incumbent at the same time to provide for their welfare. The rights of the proprietors have been hitherto very extended and very imperfectly defined by the law, which has been supplied by tradition, custom, and the good pleasure of the proprietors. . . .

These facts had already attracted the notice of our predecessors of glorious memory, and they had taken measures for improving the conditions of the peasants; but among those measures some were not stringent enough, insomuch that they remained subordinate to the spontaneous initiative of such proprietors who showed themselves animated with liberal intentions; and others, called forth by peculiar circumstances, have been restricted to certain localities or simply adopted as an experiment. It was thus that Alexander I published the regulation for the free cultivators, and that the late Emperor Nicholas, our beloved father, promulgated that one which concerns the peasants bound by contract. In the Western Governments regulations called "inventaires" had fixed the territorial allotments due to the peasants, as well as the amount of their rent dues; but all these reforms have only been applied in a very restricted manner.

We thus came to the conviction that the work of a serious improvement of the condition of the peasants was a sacred inheritance bequeathed to us by our ancestors, a mission which, in the course of events, Divine Providence called upon us to fulfil.

We have commenced this work by an expression of our Imperial confidence towards the nobility of Russia, which has given us so many proofs of its devotion to the Throne, and of its constant readiness to make sacrifices for the welfare of the country.

It is to the nobles themselves, conformable to their own wishes, that we have reserved the task of drawing up the propositions for the new organization of the peasants—propositions which make it incumbent upon them to limit their rights over the peasants, and to accept the onus of a reform which could not be accomplished without some material losses. Our confidence has not been deceived. We have seen the nobles assembled in committees in the districts, through the medium of their confidential agents, making the voluntary sacrifice of their rights as regards the personal servitude of the peasants. These committees, after having collected the necessary data, have formulated their propositions concerning the new organization of the peasants attached to the soil in their relations with the proprietors. . . .

In virtue of the new dispositions above mentioned, the peasants attached to the soil will be invested within a term fixed by the law with all the rights of free cultivators.

The proprietors retaining their rights of property on all the land belonging to them, grant to the peasants for a fixed regulated rental the full enjoyment of their close; and, moreover, to assure their livelihood and to guarantee the fulfilment of their obligations towards the Government, the quantity of arable land is fixed by the said dispositions, as well as other rural appurtenances.

But, in the enjoyment of these territorial allotments, the peasants are obliged, in return, to acquit the rentals fixed by the same dispositions to the profit of the proprietors. In this state, which must be a transitory one, the peasants shall be designated as "temporary bound."

At the same time, they are granted the right of purchasing their close, and, with the consent of the proprietors, they may acquire in full property the arable lands and other appurtenances which are allotted to them as a permanent holding. By the acquisition in full property of the quantity of land fixed, the peasants are free from their obligations towards the proprietors for land thus purchased, and they enter definitely into the condition of free peasants—landholders. . . .

And now, pious and faithful people, make upon the forehead the sacred sign of the cross, and join thy prayers to ours to call down the blessing of the Most High upon thy first free labors, the sure pledge of thy personal well-being and of the public prosperity.

Given at St. Petersburg, the 19th day of February (March 3), of the year of Grace 1861, and the seventh of our reign.

ALEXANDER

The Mind of the
Later Nineteenth Century

EVOLUTION was a basic concept in nineteenth-century thought. Romantics and economists, political theorists and scientists, tended to think of the world as an organism rather than as a machine. Karl Marx conceived of history in evolutionary terms, as a process of change brought on by class conflict. Romantic novelists and poets felt a deep kinship with the medieval past out of which their culture and institutions had developed. And a similar consciousness of the evolutionary connection between past and present is to be found among conservatives of the Burkean tradition. It was in science, however, that the idea of evolution found its most direct and fruitful expression.

Charles Darwin was by no means the first scientist to formulate a theory of evolution. His real contribution was to buttress the theory with firm observational evidence and to provide it with a simple naturalistic explanation—the doctrine of natural selection. Darwinism quickly became a center of explosive controversy. Many Christians regarded it as subversive to their Faith and opposed it vigorously. Some Darwinians attempted to use Darwin's notion of the survival of the fittest to justify the inequalities of the capitalist economic system and the exploitation of backward peoples. Others opposed this ruthless doctrine of social Darwinism with the argument that "survival of the fittest" implied struggle *between species,* not among members of the *same* species.

The German philosopher Friedrich Nietzsche was an evolutionist, too, but he rejected the passivity of Darwin's natural selection in favor of an evolutionary doctrine in which man ennobled himself through his own strivings. Bourgeois mediocrity, mass vulgarity, Christian humility—these were the barriers which man had overcome in order to advance toward his heroic destiny.

The art of the later nineteenth century moved beyond Romanticism into newer forms of expression: the uncompromising realism of Courbet, the poetic subjectivity of the Impressionists, and the increasingly bold distortions of Cézanne and Van Gogh, who sacrificed photographic representationalism for the sake of structural unity and fidelity to the personal vision. The evolution of later nineteenth-century art is marked by a restless dissatisfaction with traditional forms and a search for new and better means by which the artist might communicate his perceptions of the natural world. And more and more, the objective portrayal of a subject gave way to the artist's subjective reaction to it.

Part I

SCIENCE AND PHILOSOPHY

A. Darwinism

THE PUBLICATION OF DARWIN'S The Origin of Species *in 1859 was an event of notable importance in European intellectual history. The excerpts included here are taken from Darwin's own summary of his theory.*

1. CHARLES DARWIN, FROM *THE ORIGIN OF SPECIES,* 1859

SOURCE. Charles Darwin, *The Origin of Species,* 6th ed., New York: D. Appleton & Company, 1892, II, pp. 267–268, 270–282, 287–306. Reprinted by permission of Appleton-Century-Crofts.

Nothing at first can appear more difficult to believe than that the more complex organs and instincts have been perfected, not by means superior to, though analogous with, human reason, but by the accumulation of innumerable slight variations, each good for the individual possessor. Nevertheless, this difficulty, though appearing to our imagination insuperably great cannot be considered real if we admit the following propositions, namely, that all parts of the organisation and instincts offer, at least, individual differences—that there is a struggle for existence leading to the preservation of profitable deviations of structure or instinct—and, lastly, that gradations in the state of perfection of each organ may have existed, each good of its kind. The truth of these propositions cannot, I think, be disputed.

It is, no doubt, extremely difficult even to conjecture by what gradations many structures have been perfected, more especially amongst broken and failing groups of organic beings, which have suffered much extinction; but we see so many strange gradations in nature, that we ought to be extremely cautious in saying that any organ or instinct, or any whole structure, could not have arrived at its present state by many graduated steps. There are, it must be admitted, cases of special difficulty opposed to the theory of natural selection; . . . but I have attempted to show how these difficulties can be mastered. . . .

Turning to geographical distribution, the difficulties encountered on the theory of descent with modification are serious enough. All the individuals of the same species, and all the species of the same genus, or even higher group, are descended from common parents; and therefore, in however distant and isolated parts of the world they may now be found, they must in the course of successive generations have travelled from some one point to all the others. We are often wholly unable even to conjecture how this could have been effected. Yet, as we have reason to believe that some species have retained the same specific form for very long periods of time, immensely long as measured by years, too much stress ought not to be laid on the occasional wide diffusion of the same species; for during very long periods there will always have been a good chance for wide migration by many means. A broken or interrupted range may often be accounted for by the extinction of the species in the intermediate regions. It cannot be denied that we are as yet very ignorant as to the full extent of the various climatal and geographical changes which have affected the earth during modern periods; and such changes will often have facilitated migration. As an example, I have attempted to show how potent has been the influence of the Glacial period on the distribution of the same and of allied species throughout the world. We are as yet profoundly ignorant of the many occasional means of transport. With respect to distinct species of the same genus inhabiting distant and isolated regions, as the process of modification has necessarily been slow, all the means of migration will have been possible during a very long period; and consequently the difficulty of the wide diffusion of the species of the same genus is in some degree lessened.

As according to the theory of natural selection an interminable number of intermediate forms must have existed, linking together all the species in each group by gradations as fine as are our existing varieties, it may be asked, Why do we not see these linking forms all around us? Why are not all organic beings blended together in an inextricable chaos? With respect to existing forms, we should remember that we have no right to expect (excepting in rare cases) to discover *directly* connecting links between them, but only between each and some extinct and supplanted form. Even on a wide area, which has during a long period remained continuous, and of which the climatic and other conditions of life change insensibly in proceeding from a district occupied by one species into another district occupied by a closely allied species, we have no just right to expect often to find intermediate varieties in the intermediate zones. For we have reason to believe that only a few species of a genus ever undergo change; the other species becoming utterly extinct and leaving no modified progeny. Of the species which do change, only a few within the same country change at the same time; and all modifications are slowly effected. I have also shown that the intermediate varieties which probably at first existed in the intermediate zones, would be liable to be supplanted by the allied forms on either hand; for the latter, from existing in greater numbers, would generally be modified and improved at a quicker rate than the intermediate varieties, which existed in lesser numbers; so that the intermediate varieties would, in the long run, be supplanted and exterminated.

On this doctrine of the extermination of an infinitude of connecting links, between the living and extinct inhabitants of the world, and at each successive period between the extinct and still older species, why is not every geological formation charged with such links? Why does not every collection of fossil remains afford plain evidence of the gradation and mutation of the forms of life? Although geological research has undoubtedly revealed the former existence of many links, bringing numerous forms of life much closer together, it does not yield the infinitely many fine gradations between past and present species required on the theory; and this is the most obvious of the many objections which may be urged against it. Why, again, do whole groups of allied species appear, though this appearance is often false, to have come in suddenly on the successive geological stages? Although we now know that organic beings appeared on this globe, at a period incalculably remote, long before the lowest bed of the Cambrian system was deposited, why do we not find beneath this system great piles of strata stored with the remains of the progenitors of the Cambrian fossils? For on the theory, such strata must somewhere have been deposited at these ancient and utterly unknown epochs of the world's history.

I can answer these questions and objections only on the supposition that the geological record is far more imperfect than most geologists believe. The number of specimens in all our museums is absolutely as nothing compared with the countless generations of countless species which have certainly existed. The parent-form of any two or more species would not be in all its characters directly intermediate between its modified offspring, any more than the rock-pigeon is directly intermediate in crop and tail between its descendants, the pouter and fantail pigeons. We should not be able to recognise a species as the parent of another and modified species, if we were to examine the two ever so closely, unless we possessed most of the intermediate links; and owing to the imperfection of the geological record, we have no just right to expect to find so many links. If two or three, or even more linking forms were discovered, they would simply be ranked by many naturalists as so many new species, more especially if found in different geological sub-stages, let their differences be ever so slight. Numerous existing doubtful forms could be named which are probably varieties; but who will pretend that in future ages so many fossil links will be discovered, that naturalists will be able to decide whether or not these doubtful forms ought to be called varieties? Only a small portion of the world has been geologically explored. Only organic beings of certain classes can be preserved in a fossil condition, at least in any great number. Many species when once formed never undergo any further change but become extinct without leaving modified descendants; and the periods, during which species have undergone modification, though long as measured by years, have probably been short in comparison with the periods during which they retained the same form. It is the dominant and widely ranging species which vary most frequently and vary most, and varieties are often at first local—both causes rendering the discovery of intermediate links in any one formation less likely. Local varieties will not spread into other and distant regions until they are considerably modified and improved; and when they have spread, and are discovered in a geological formation, they appear as if suddenly created there, and will be simply classed as new species. Most formations have been intermittent in their accumulation; and their duration has probably been shorter than the average duration of specific forms. Successive formations are in most cases separated from each other by blank intervals of time of great length; for fossiliferous formations thick enough to resist future degradation can as a general rule be accumulated only where much sediment is deposited on the subsiding bed of the sea. During the alternate periods of elevation and of stationary level the record will generally be blank. During these latter periods there will probably be more variability in the forms of life; during periods of subsidence, more extinction.

With respect to the absence of strata rich in fossils beneath the Cambrian formation, I can recur only to the hypothesis given in the tenth chapter; namely, that though our continents and oceans have endured for an enormous period in nearly their present relative positions, we have no reason to assume that this has always been the case; consequently formations much older than any now known may lie buried beneath the great oceans. With respect to the lapse of time not having been sufficient since our planet was consolidated for the assumed amount of organic change, and this objection, as urged by Sir William Thompson, is probably one of the gravest as yet advanced, I can only say, firstly, that we do not know at what rate species change as measured by years, and secondly, that many philosophers are not as yet willing to admit that we know enough of the constitution of the universe and of the interior of our globe to speculate with safety on its past duration.

That the geological record is imperfect all will admit; but that it is imperfect to the degree required by our theory, few will be inclined to admit. If we look to long enough intervals of time, geology plainly declares that species have all changed; and they have changed in the manner required by the theory, for they have changed slowly and in a graduated manner. We clearly see this in the fossil remains from consecutive formations invariably being much more closely related to each other, than are the fossils from widely separated formations.

Such is the sum of the several chief objections and difficulties which may be justly urged against the theory; and I have now briefly recapitulated the answers and explanations which, as far as I can see, may be given. I have felt these difficulties far too heavily during many years to doubt their weight. But it deserves especial notice that the more important objections relate to questions on which we are confessedly ignorant; nor do we know how ignorant we are. We do not know all the possible transitional gradations between the simplest and the most perfect organs; it cannot be pretended that we know all the varied means of Distribution during the long lapse of years, or that we know how imperfect is the Geological Record. Serious as these several objections are, in my judgment they are by no means sufficient to overthrow the theory of descent with subsequent modification.

Now let us turn to the other side of the argument. Under domestication we see much variability, caused, or at least excited, by changed conditions of life; but often in so obscure a manner, that we are tempted to consider the variations as spontaneous. Variability is governed by many complex laws,—by correlated growth, compensation, the increased use and disuse of parts, and the definite action of the surrounding conditions. There is much difficulty in ascertaining how largely our domestic productions have been modified; but we may safely infer that the amount has been large, and that modifications can be inherited for long periods. As long as the conditions of life remain the same, we have reason to believe that a modification, which has already been inherited for many generations, may continue to be inherited for an almost infinite number of generations. On the other hand, we have evidence that variability when it has once come into play, does not cease under domestication for a very long period; nor do we know that it ever ceases, for new varieties are still occasionally produced by our oldest domesticated productions.

Variability is not actually caused by man; he only unintentionally exposes organic beings to new conditions of life, and then nature acts on the organisation and causes it to vary. But man can and does select the variations given to him by nature, and thus accumulates them in any desired manner. He thus adapts animals and plants for his own benefit or pleasure. He may do this methodically, or he may do it unconsciously by preserving the individuals most useful or pleasing to him without any intention of altering the breed. It is certain that he can largely influence the character of a breed by selecting, in each successive generation, individual differences so slight as to be inappreciable except by an educated eye. This unconscious process of selection has been the great agency in the formation of the most distinct and useful domestic breeds. That many breeds produced by man have to a large extent the character of natural species, is shown by the inextricable doubts whether many of them are varieties or aboriginally distinct species.

There is no reason why the principles which have acted so efficiently under domestication should not have acted under nature. In the survival of favoured individuals and races, during the constantly-recurrent struggle for Existence, we see a powerful and ever-acting form of Selection. The struggle for existence inevitably follows from the high geometrical ratio of increase which is common to all organic beings. This high rate of increase is proved by calculation,—by the rapid increase of many animals and plants during a succession of peculiar seasons, and when naturalised in new countries. More individuals are born than can possible survive. A grain in the balance may determine which individuals shall live and which shall die,—which variety or species shall increase in number, and which shall decrease, or finally become extinct. As the individuals of the same species come in all respects into the closest competition with each other, the struggle will generally be most severe between them; it will be almost equally severe between the varieties of the same species, and next in severity between the species of the same genus. On the other hand the struggle will often be severe between beings remote in the scale of nature. The slightest advantage in certain individuals, at any age or during any season, over those with which they come into competition, or better adaptation in however slight a degree to the surrounding physical conditions, will, in the long run, turn the balance.

With animals having separated sexes, there will be in most cases a struggle between the males for the possession of the females. The most vigorous males, or those which have most successfully struggled with their conditions of life, will generally leave most progeny. But success will often depend on the males having special weapons, or means of defence, or charms; and a slight advantage will lead to victory.

As geology plainly proclaims that each land has undergone great physical changes, we might have expected to find that organic beings have varied under nature, in the same way as they have varied under domestication. And if there has been any variability under nature, it would be an unaccountable fact if natural selection had not come into play. It has often been asserted, but the assertion is incapable of proof, that the amount of variation under nature is a strictly limited quantity. Man, though acting on external characters alone and often capriciously, can produce within a short period a great result by adding up mere individual differences in his domestic productions; and every one admits that species present individual differences. But, besides such differences, all naturalists admit that natural varieties exist, which are considered sufficiently distinct to be worthy of record in systematic works. No one has drawn any clear distinction between individual differences and slight varieties; or between more plainly marked varieties and sub-species, and species. On separate continents, and on different parts of the same continent when divided by barriers of any kind, and on outlying islands, what a multitude of forms exist, which some experienced naturalists rank as varieties, others as geographical races or sub-species, and others as distinct, though closely allied species!

If then, animals and plants do vary, let it be ever so slightly or slowly, why should not variations or individual differences, which are in any way beneficial, be preserved and accumulated through natural selection, or the survival of the fittest? If man can by patience select variations useful to him, why, under changing and complex conditions of life, should not variations useful to nature's living products often arise, and be preserved or selected? What limit can be put to this power, acting during long ages and rigidly scrutinising the whole constitution, structure, and habits of each creature,—favouring the good and rejecting the bad? I can see no limit to this power, in slowly and beautifully adapting each form to the most complex relations of life. The theory of natural selection, even if we look no farther than this, seems to be in the highest degree probable. I have already recapitulated, as fairly as I could, the opposed difficulties and objections: now let us turn to the special facts and arguments in favour of the theory.

On the view that species are only strongly marked and permanent varieties, and that each species first existed as a variety, we can see why it is that no line of demarcation can be drawn between species, commonly supposed to have been produced by special acts of creation, and varieties which are acknowledged to have been produced by secondary laws. On this same view we can understand how it is that in a region where many species of a genus have been produced, and where they now flourish, these same species should present many varieties; for where the manufactory of species has been active, we might expect, as a general rule, to find it still in action; and this is the case if varieties be incipient species. Moreover, the species of the larger genera, which afford the greater number of varieties or incipient species, retain to a certain degree the character of varieties; for they differ from each other by a less amount of difference than do the species of smaller genera. The closely allied species also of the larger genera apparently have restricted ranges, and in their affinities they are clustered in little groups round other species—in both respects resembling varieties. These are strange relations on the view that each species was independently created, but are intelligible if each existed first as a variety.

As each species tends by its geometrical rate of reproduction to increase inordinately in number; and as the modified descendants of each species will be enabled to increase by as much as they become more diversified in habits and structure, so as to be able to seize on many and widely different places in the economy of nature, there will be a constant tendency in natural selection to preserve the most divergent offspring of any one species. Hence, during a long-continued course of modification, the slight differences characteristic of varieties of the same species, tend to be augmented into the greater differences characteristic of the species of the same genus. New and improved varieties will inevitably supplant and exterminate the older, less improved, and intermediate varieties; and thus species are rendered to a large extent defined and distinct objects. Dominant species belonging to the larger groups within each class tend to give birth to new and dominant forms; so that each large group tends to become still larger, and at the same time more divergent in character. But as all groups cannot thus go on increasing in size, for the world would not hold them, the more dominant groups beat the less dominant. This tendency in the large groups to go on increasing in size and diverging in character, together with the inevitable contingency of much extinction, explains the arrangement of all the forms of life in groups subordinate to groups, all within a few great classes, which has prevailed throughout all time. This grand fact of the grouping of all organic beings under what is called the Natural System, is utterly inexplicable on the theory of creation.

As natural selection acts solely by accumulating slight, successive, favourable variations, it can produce no great or sudden modifications; it can act only by short and slow steps. . . . We can see why throughout nature the same general end is gained by an almost infinite diversity of means, for every peculiarity when once acquired is long inherited, and structures already modified in many different ways have to be adapted for the same general purpose. We can, in short, see why nature is prodigal in variety, though niggard in innovation. But why this should be a law of nature if each species has been independently created no man can explain. . . .

If we admit that the geological record is imperfect to an extreme degree, then the facts, which the record does give, strongly support the theory of descent with modification. New species have come on the stage slowly and at successive intervals; and the amount of change, after equal intervals of time, is widely different in different groups. The extinction of species and of whole groups of species, which has played so conspicuous a part in the history of the organic world, almost inevitably follows from the principle of natural selection; for old forms are supplanted by new and improved forms. Neither single species nor groups of species reappear when the chain of ordinary generation is once broken. The gradual diffusion of dominant forms, with the slow modification of their descendants, causes the forms of life, after long intervals of time, to appear as if they had changed simultaneously throughout the world. The fact of the fossil remains of each formation being in some degree intermediate in character between the fossils in the formations above and below, is simply explained by their intermediate position in the chain of descent. The grand fact that all extinct beings can be classed with all recent beings, naturally follows from the living and the extinct being the offspring of common parents. As species have generally diverged in character during their long course of descent and modification, we can understand why it is that the more ancient forms, or early progenitors of each group, so often occupy a position in some degree intermediate between existing groups. Recent forms are generally looked upon as being, on the whole, higher in the scale of organisation than ancient forms; and they must be higher, in so far as the later and more improved forms have conquered the older and less improved forms in the struggle for life; they have also generally had their organs more specialised for different functions. This fact is perfectly compatible with numerous beings still retaining simple and but little improved structures, fitted for simple conditions of life; it is likewise compatible with some forms having retrograded in organisation, by having become at each stage of descent better fitted for new and degraded habits of life. Lastly, the wonderful law of the long endurance of allied forms on the same continent,—of marsupials in Australia, of edentata in America, and other such cases,—is intelligible, for within the same country the existing and the extinct will be closely allied by descent.

Looking to geographical distribution, if we admit that there has been during the long course of ages much migration from one part of the world to another, owing to former climatal and geographical changes and to the many occasional and unknown means of dispersal, then we can understand, on the theory of descent with modification, most of the great leading facts in Distribution. We can see why there should be so striking a parallelism in the distribution of organic beings throughout space, and in their geological succession throughout time; for in both cases the beings have been connected by the bond of ordinary generation, and the means of modification have been the same. We see the full meaning of the wonderful fact, which has struck every traveller, namely, that on the same continent, under the most diverse conditions, under heat and cold, on mountain and lowland, on deserts and marshes, most of the inhabitants within each great class are plainly related; for they are the descendants of the same progenitors and early colonists. . . .

The fact, as we have seen, that all past and present organic beings can be arranged within a few great classes, in groups subordinate to groups, and with the extinct groups often falling in between the recent groups, is intelligible on the theory of natural selection with its contingencies of extinction and divergence of character. On these same principles we see how it is, that the mutual affinities of the forms within each class are so complex and circuitous. We see why certain characters are far more serviceable than others for classification;—why adaptive characters, though of paramount importance to the beings, are of hardly any importance in classification; why characters derived from rudimentary parts, though of no service to the beings, are often of high classificatory value; and why embryological characters are often the most valuable of all. The real affinities of all organic beings, in contradistinction to their adaptive resemblances, are due to inheritance or community of descent. The Natural System is a genealogical arrangement, with the acquired grades of difference, marked by the terms, varieties, species, genera, families, &c.; and we have to discover the lines of descent by the most permanent characters whatever they may be and of however slight vital importance.

The similar framework of bones in the hand of a man, wing of a bat, fin of the porpoise, and leg of the horse,—the same number of vertebrae forming the neck of the giraffe and of the elephant,—and innumerable other such facts, at once explain themselves on the theory of descent with slow and slight successive modifications. The similarity of pattern in the wing and in the leg of a bat, though used for such different purpose,—in the jaws and legs of a crab,—in the petals, stamens, and pistils of a flower, is likewise, to a large extent, intelligible on the view of the gradual modification of parts or organs, which were aboriginally alike in an early progenitor in each of these classes. On the principle of successive variations not always supervening at an early age, and being inherited at a corresponding not early period of life, we clearly see why the embryos of mammals, birds, reptiles, and fishes should be so closely similar, and so unlike the adult forms. We may cease marvelling at the embryo of an air-breathing mammal or bird having branchial slits and arteries running in loops, like those of a fish which has to breathe the air dissolved in water by the aid of well-developed branchiae.

Disuse, aided sometimes by natural selection, will often have reduced organs when rendered useless under changed habits or conditions of life; and we can understand on this view the meaning of rudimentary organs. But disuse and selection will generally act on each creature, when it has come to maturity and has to play its full part in the struggle for existence, and will thus have little power on an organ during early life; hence the organ will not be reduced or rendered rudimentary at this early age. The calf, for instance, has inherited teeth, which never cut through the gums of the upper jaw, from an early progenitor having well-developed teeth; and we may believe, that the teeth in the mature animal were formerly reduced by disuse, owing to the tongue and palate, or lips, having become excellently fitted through natural selection to browse without their aid; whereas in the calf, the teeth have been left unaffected, and on the principle of inheritance at corresponding ages have been inherited from a remote period to the present day. On the view of each organism with all its separate parts having been specially created, how utterly inexplicable is it that organs bearing the plain stamp of inutility, such as the teeth in the embryonic calf or the shrivelled wings under the soldered wing-covers of many beetles, should so frequently occur. Nature may be said to have taken pains to reveal her scheme of modification, by means of rudimentary organs, of embryological and homologous structures, but we are too blind to understand her meaning.

I have now recapitulated the facts and considerations which have thoroughly convinced me that species have been modified, during a long course of descent. This has been effected chiefly through the natural selection of numerous successive, slight, favourable variations; aided in an important manner by the inherited effects of the use and disuse of parts; and in an unimportant manner, that is in relation to adaptive structures, whether past or present, by the direct action of external conditions, and by variations which seem to us in our ignorance to arise spontaneously. It appears that I formerly underrated the frequency and value of these latter forms of variation, as leading to permanent modifications of structure independently of natural selection. But as my conclusions have lately been much misrepresented, and it has been stated that I attribute the modification of species exclusively to natural selection, I may be permitted to remark that in the first edition of this work, and subsequently, I placed in a most conspicuous position—namely, at the close of the Introduction—the following words: "I am convinced that natural selection has been the main but not the exclusive means of modification." This has been of no avail. Great is the power of steady misrepresentation; but the history of science shows that fortunately this power does not long endure.

It can hardly be supposed that a false theory would explain, in so satisfactory a manner as does the theory of natural selection, the several large classes of facts above specified. It has recently been objected that this is an unsafe method of arguing; but it is a method used in judging of the common events of life, and has often been used by the greatest natural philosophers. The undulatory theory of light has thus been arrived at; and the belief in the revolution of the earth on its own axis was until lately supported by hardly any direct evidence. It is no valid objection that science as yet throws no light on the far higher problem of the essence or origin of life. Who can explain what is the essence of the attraction of gravity? No one now objects to following out the results consequent on this unknown element of attraction; notwithstanding that Leibnitz formerly accused Newton of introducing "occult qualities and miracles into philosophy."

I see no good reason why the views given in this volume should shock the religious feelings of any one. It is satisfactory, as showing how transient such impressions are, to remember that the greatest discovery ever made by man, namely, the law of the attraction of gravity, was also attacked by Leibnitz, "as subversive of natural, and inferentially of revealed, religion." A celebrated author and divine has written to me that "he has gradually learnt to see that it is just as noble a conception of the Deity to believe that He created a few original forms capable of self-development into other and needful forms, as to believe that He required a fresh act of creation to supply the voids caused by the action of His laws."

Why, it may be asked, until recently did nearly all the most eminent living naturalists and geologists disbelieve in the mutability of species. It cannot be asserted that organic beings in a state of nature are subject to no variation; it cannot be proved that the amount of variation in the course of long ages is a limited quantity; no clear distinction has been, or can be, drawn between species and well-marked varieties. It cannot be maintained that species when intercrossed are invariably sterile, and varieties invariably fertile; or that sterility is a special endowment and sign of creation. The belief that species were immutable productions was almost unavoidable as long as the history of the world was thought to be of short duration; and now that we have acquired some idea of the lapse of time, we are too apt to assume, without proof, that the geological record is so perfect that it would have afforded us plain evidence of the mutation of species, if they had undergone mutation.

But the chief cause of our natural unwillingness to admit that one species has given birth to other and distinct species, is that we are always slow in admitting great changes of which we do not see the steps. The difficulty is the same as that felt by so many geologists, when Lyell first insisted that long lines of inland cliffs had been formed, and great valleys excavated, by the agencies which we see still at work. The mind cannot possibly grasp the full meaning of the term of even a million years; it cannot add up and perceive the full effects of many slight variations, accumulated during an almost infinite number of generations.

Although I am fully convinced of the truth of the views given in this volume under the form of an abstract, I by no means expect to convince experienced naturalists whose minds are stocked with a multitude of facts all viewed, during a long course of years, from a point of view directly oppposite to mine. It is so easy to hide our ignorance under such expressions as the "plan of creation," "unity of design," &c., and to think that we give an explanation when we only re-state a fact. Any one whose disposition leads him to attach more weight to unexplained difficulties than to the explanation of a certain number of facts will certainly reject the theory. A few naturalists, endowed with much flexibility of mind, and who have already begun to doubt the immutability of species, may be influenced by this volume; but I look with confidence to the future,—to young and rising naturalists, who will be able to view both sides of the question with impartiality. Whoever is led to believe that species are mutable will do good service by conscientiously expressing his conviction; for thus only can the load of prejudice by which this subject is overwhelmed be removed.

Several eminent naturalists have of late published their belief that a multitude of reputed species in each genus are not real species; but that other species are real, that is, have been independently created. This seems to me a strange conclusion to arrive at. They admit that a multitude of forms, which till lately they themselves thought were special creations, and which are still thus looked at by the majority of naturalists, and which consequently have all the external characteristic features of true species,—they admit that these have been produced by variation, but they refuse to extend the same view to other and slightly different forms. Nevertheless they do not pretend that they can define, or even conjecture, which are the created forms of life, and which are those produced by secondary laws. They admit variation as a *vera causa* in one case, they arbitrarily reject it in another, without assigning any distinction in the two cases. The day will come when this will be given as a curious illustration of the blindness of preconceived opinion. These authors seem no more startled at a miraculous act of creation than at an ordinary birth. But do they really believe that at innumerable periods in the earth's history certain elemental atoms have been commanded suddenly to flash into living tissues? Do they believe that at each supposed act of creation one individual or many were produced? Were all the infinitely numerous kinds of animals and plants created as eggs or seed, or as full grown? and in the case of mammals, were they created bearing the false marks of nourishment from the mother's womb? Undoubtedly some of these same questions cannot be answered by those who believe in the appearance or creation of only a few forms of life, or of some one form alone. It has been maintained by several authors that it is as easy to believe in the creation of a million beings as of one; but Maupertuis' philosophical axiom "of least action" leads the mind more willingly to admit the smaller number; and certainly we ought not to believe that innumerable beings within each great class have been created with plain, but deceptive, marks of descent from a single parent.

As a record of a former state of things, I have retained in the foregoing paragraphs, and elsewhere, several sentences which imply that naturalists believe in the separate creation of each species; and I have been much censured for having thus expressed myself. But undoubtedly this was the general belief when the first edition of the present work appeared. I formerly spoke to very many naturalists on the subject of evolution, and never once met with any sympathetic agreement. It is probable that some did them believe in evolution, but they were either silent, or expressed themselves so ambiguously that it was not easy to understand their meaning. Now things are wholly changed, and almost every naturalist admits the great principle of evolution. There are, however, some who still think that species have suddenly given birth, through quite unexplained means, to new and totally different forms: but, as I have attempted to show, weighty evidence can be opposed to the admission of great and abrupt modifications. Under a scientific point of view, and as leading to further investigation, but little advantage is gained by believing that new forms are suddenly developed in an inexplicable manner from old and widely different forms, over the old belief in the creation of species from the dust of the earth.

It may be asked how far I extend the doctrine of the modification of species. The question is difficult to answer, because the more distinct the forms are which we consider, by so much the arguments in favour of community of descent become fewer in number and less in force. But some arguments of the greatest weight extend very far. All the members of whole classes are connected together by a chain of affinities, and all can be classed on the same principle, in groups subordinate to groups. Fossil remains sometimes tend to fill up very wide intervals between existing orders.

Organs in a rudimentary condition plainly show that an early progenitor had the organ in a fully developed condition; and this in some cases implies an enormous amount of modification in the descendants. Throughout whole classes various structures are formed on the same pattern, and at a very early age of embryos closely resemble each other. Therefore I cannot doubt that the theory of descent with modification embraces all the members of the same great class or kingdom. I believe that animals are descended from at most only four or five progenitors, and plants from an equal or lesser number.

Analogy would lead me one step farther, namely, to the belief that all animals and plants are descended from some one prototype. But analogy may be a deceitful guide. Nevertheless all living things have much in common, in their chemical composition, their cellular structure, their laws of growth, and their liability to injurious influences. We see this even in so trifling a fact as that the same poison often similarly affects plants and animals; or that the poison secreted by the gall-fly produces monstrous growths on the wild rose or oak-tree. With all organic beings, excepting perhaps some of the very lowest, sexual reproduction seems to be essentially similar. With all, as far as is at present known, the germinal vesicle is the same; so that all organisms start from a common origin. If we look even to the two main divisions—namely, to the animal and vegetable kingdoms—certain low forms are so far intermediate in character that naturalists have disputed to which kingdom they should be referred. As Professor Asa Gray has remarked, "the spores and other reproductive bodies of many of the lower algae may claim to have first a characteristically animal, and then an unequivocally vegetable existence." Therefore, on the principle of natural selection with divergence of character, it does not seem incredible that, from some such low and intermediate form, both animals and plants may have been developed; and, if we admit this, we must likewise admit that all the organic beings which have ever lived on this earth may be descended from some one primordial form. But this inference is chiefly grounded on analogy, and it is immaterial whether or not it be accepted. No doubt it is possible, as Mr. G. H. Lewes has urged, that at the first commencement of life many different forms were evolved; but if so, we may conclude that only a very few have left modified descendants. For, as I have recently remarked in regard to the members of each great kingdom, such as the Vertebrata, Articulata, &c., we have distinct evidence in their embryological, homologous, and rudimentary structures, that within each kingdom all the members are descended from a single progenitor.

When the views advanced by me in this volume, and by Mr. Wallace, or when analogous views on the origin of species are generally admitted, we can dimly foresee that there will be a considerable revolution in natural history. Systematists will be able to pursue their labours as at present; but they will not be incessantly haunted by the shadowy doubt whether this or that form be a true species. This, I feel sure and I speak after experience, will be no slight relief. The endless disputes whether or not some fifty species of British brambles are good species will cease. Systematists will have only to decide (not that this will be easy) whether any form be sufficiently constant and distinct from other forms, to be capable of definition; and if definable, whether the differences be sufficiently important to deserve a specific name. This latter point will become a far more essential consideration than it is at present; for differences, however slight, between any two forms, if not blended by intermediate gradations, are looked at by most naturalists as sufficient to raise both forms to the rank of species.

Hereafter we shall be compelled to acknowledge that the only distinction between species and well-marked varieties is, that the latter are known, or believed, to be connected at the present day by intermediate gradations whereas species were formerly thus connected. Hence, without rejecting the consideration of the present existence of intermediate gradations between any two forms, we shall be led to weigh more carefully and to value higher the actual amount of difference between them. It is quite possible that forms now generally acknowledged to be merely varieties may hereafter be thought worthy of specific names; and in this case scientific and common language will come into accordance. In short, we shall have to treat species in the same manner as those naturalists treat genera, who admit that genera are merely artificial combinations made for convenience. This may not be a cheering prospect; but we shall at least be freed from the vain search for the undiscovered and undiscoverable essence of the term species.

The other and more general departments of natural history will rise greatly in interest. The terms used by naturalists, of affinity, relationship, community of type, paternity, morphology, adaptive characters, rudimentary and aborted organs, &c., will cease to be metaphorical, and will have a plain signification. When we no longer look at an organic being as a savage looks at a ship, as something wholly beyond his comprehension; when we regard every production of nature as one which has had a long history; when we contemplate every complex structure and instinct as the summing up of many contrivances, each useful to the possessor, in the same way as any great mechanical invention is the summing up of the labour, the experience, the reason, and even the blunders of numerous workmen; when we thus view each organic being, how far more interesting—I speak from experience—does the study of natural history become!

A grand and almost untrodden field of inquiry will be opened, on the causes and laws of variation, on correlation, on the effects of use and disuse, on the direct action of external conditions, and so forth. The study of domestic productions will rise immensely in value. A new variety raised by man will be a more important and interesting subject for study than one more species added to the infinitude of already recorded species. Our classifications will come to be, as far as they can be so made, genealogies; and will then truly give what may be called the plan of creation. The rules for classifying will no doubt become simpler when we have a definite object in view. We possess no pedigrees or armorial bearings; and we have to discover and trace the many diverging lines of descent in our natural genealogies, by characters of any kind which have long been inherited. Rudimentary organs will speak infallibly with respect to the nature of long-lost structures. Species and groups of species which are called aberrant, and which may fancifully be called living fossils, will aid us in forming a picture of the ancient forms of life. Embryology will often reveal to us the structure, in some degree obscured, of the proto-types of each great class.

When we can feel assured that all the individuals of the same species, and all the closely allied species of most genera, have within a not very remote period descended from one parent, and have migrated from some one birth-place; and when we better know the many means of migration, then, by the light which geology now throws, and will continue to throw, on former changes of climate and of the level of the land, we shall surely be enabled to trace in an admirable manner the former migrations of the inhabitants of the whole world. Even at present, by comparing the differences between the inhabitants of the sea on the opposite sides of a continent, and the nature of the various inhabitants on that continent in relation to their apparent means of immigration, some light can be thrown on ancient geography.

The noble science of Geology loses glory from the extreme imperfection of the record. The crust of the earth with its imbedded remains must not be looked at as a well-filled museum, but as a poor collection made at hazard and at rare intervals. The accumulation of each great fossiliferous formation will be recognised as having depended on an unusual concurrence of favourable circumstances, and the blank intervals between the successive stages as having been of vast duration. But we shall be able to gauge with some security the duration of these intervals by a comparison of the preceding and succeeding organic forms. We must be cautious in attempting to correlate as strictly contemporaneous two formations, which do not include many identical species, by the general succession of the forms of life. As species are produced and exterminated by slowly acting and still existing causes, and not by miraculous acts of creation; and as the most important of all causes of organic change is one which is almost independent of altered and perhaps suddenly altered physical conditions, namely, the mutual relation of organism to organism,—the improvement of one organism entailing the improvement or the extermination of others; it follows, that the amount of organic change in the fossils of consecutive formations probably serves as a fair measure of the relative, though not actual lapse of time. A number of species, however, keeping in a body might remain for a long period unchanged, whilst within the same period several of these species by migrating into new countries and coming into competition with foreign associates, might become modified; so that we must not overrate the accuracy of organic change as a measure of time.

In the future I see open fields for far more important researches. Psychology will be securely based on the foundation already well laid by Mr. Herbert Spencer, that of the necessary acquirement of each mental power and capacity by gradation. Much light will be thrown on the origin of man and his history.

Authors of the highest eminence seem to be fully satisfied with the view that each species has been independently created. To my mind it accords better with what we know of the laws impressed on matter by the Creator, that the production and extinction of the past and present inhabitants of the world should have been due to secondary causes, like those determining the birth and death of the individual. When I view all beings not as special creations, but as the lineal descendants of some few beings which lived long before the first bed of the Cambrian system was deposited, they seem to me to become ennobled. Judging from the past, we may safely infer that not one living species will transmit its unaltered likeness to a distant futurity. And of the species now living very few will transmit progeny of any kind to a far distant futurity; for the manner in which all organic beings are grouped, shows that the greater number of species in each genus, and all the species in many genera, have left no descendants, but have become utterly extinct. We can so far take a prophetic glance into futurity as to foretell that it will be the common and widely-spread species, belonging to the larger and dominant groups within each class, which will ultimately prevail and procreate new and dominant species. As all the living forms of life are the lineal descendants of those which lived long before the Cambrian epoch, we may feel certain that the ordinary succession by generation has never once been broken, and that no cataclysm has desolated the whole world. Hence we may look with some confidence to a secure future of great length. And as natural selection works solely by and for the good of each being, all corporeal and mental endowments will tend to progress towards perfection.

It is interesting to contemplate a tangled bank, clothed with many plants of many kinds, with birds singing on the bushes, with various insections flitting about, and with worms crawling through the damp earth, and to reflect that these elaborately constructed forms, so different from each other, and dependent upon each other in so complex a manner, have all been produced by laws acting around us. These laws, taken in the largest sense, being Growth with Reproduction; Inheritance which is almost implied by reproduction; Variability from the indirect and direct action of the conditions of life, and from use and disuse: a Ratio of Increase so high as to lead to a Struggle for Life, and as a consequence to

Natural Selection, entailing Divergence of Character and the Extinction of less-improved forms. Thus, from the war of nature, from famine and death, the most exalted object which we are capable of conceiving, namely, the production of the higher animals, directly follows. There is grandeur in this view of life, with its several powers, having been originally breathed by the Creator into a few forms or into one; and that, whilst this planet has gone cycling on according to the fixed law of gravity, from so simple a beginning endless forms most beautiful and most wonderful have been, and are being evolved.

IN HERBERT SPENCER'S Social Statics and Man Versus the State (1884) Darwinian evolution is given a political-economic dimension and is used to support a policy of strict laissez-faire. Spencer argued that the struggle between the fit and unfit, which dominates the world of nature, must not be thwarted in human society by social welfare measures. In the long run, the protection of the unfit will ruin the human race.

2. SOCIAL DARWINISM: HERBERT SPENCER, "POOR LAWS" AND "THE COMING SLAVERY," 1884

SOURCE. Herbert Spencer, *Social Statics and Man Versus the State*, New York: D. Appleton & Co., 1892, pp. 149–154, 302–303, 321–323, 327–333. Reprinted by permission of Appleton-Century-Crofts.

POOR LAWS

Pervading all Nature we may see at work a stern discipline which is a little cruel that it may be very kind. That state of universal warfare maintained throughout the lower creation, to the great perplexity of many worthy people, is at bottom the most merciful provision which the circumstances admit of. It is much better that the ruminant animal, when deprived by age of the vigour which made its existence a pleasure, should be killed by some beast of prey, than that it should linger out a life made painful by infirmities, and eventually die of starvation. By the destruction of all such, not only is existence ended before it becomes burdensome, but room is made for a younger generation capable of the fullest enjoyment; and, moreover, out of the very act of substitution happiness is derived for a tribe of predatory creatures. Note, further, that their carnivorous enemies not only remove from herbivorous herds individuals past their prime, but also weed out the sickly, the malformed, and the least fleet or powerful. By the aid of which purifying process, as well as by the fighting so universal in the pairing season, all vitiation of the race through the multiplication of its inferior samples is prevented; and the maintenance of a constitution completely adapted to surrounding conditions, and therefore most productive of happiness, is ensured.

The development of the higher creation is a progress towards a form of being, capable of a happiness undiminished by these drawbacks. It is in the human race that the consummation is to be accomplished. Civilization is the last stage of its accomplishment. And the ideal man is the man in whom all the conditions to that accomplishment are fulfilled. Meanwhile, the well-being of existing humanity and the unfolding of it into this ultimate perfection, are both secured by that same beneficial though severe discipline, to which the animate creation at large is subject. It seems hard that an unskilfulness which with all his efforts he cannot overcome, should entail hunger upon the artizan. It seems hard that a labourer incapacitated by sickness from competing with his stronger fellows, should have to bear the resulting privations. It seems hard that widows and orphans should be left to struggle for life or death. Nevertheless, when regarded not separately but in connexion with the interests of universal humanity, these harsh fatalities are seen to be full of beneficence—the same beneficence which brings to early graves the children of diseased parents, and singles out the intemperate and the debilitated as the victims of an epidemic.

There are many very amiable people who have not the nerve to look this matter fairly in the face. Disabled as they are by their sympathies with present suffering, from duly regarding ultimate consequences, they pursue a course which is injudicious, and in the end even cruel. We do not consider it true kindness in a mother to gratify her child with sweetmeats that are likely to make it ill. We should think it a very foolish sort of benevolence which led a surgeon to let his patient's disease progress to a fatal issue, rather than inflict pain by an operation. Similarly, we must call those spurious philanthropists who, to prevent present misery, would entail greater misery on future generations. That rigorous necessity which, when allowed to operate, becomes so sharp a spur to the lazy and so strong a bridle to the random, these paupers' friends would repeal, because of the wailings it here and there produces. Blind to the fact that under the natural order of things society is constantly excreting its unhealthy, imbecile, slow, vacillating, faithless members, these unthinking, though well-meaning, men advocate an interference which not only stops the purifying process, but even increases the vitiation—absolutely encourages the multiplication of the reckless and incompetent by offering them an unfailing provision, and *dis*courages the multiplication of the competent and provident by heightening the difficulty of maintaining a family. And thus, in their eagerness to prevent the salutary sufferings that surround us, these sigh-wise and groan-foolish people bequeath to posterity a continually increasing curse.

Returning again to the highest point of view, we find that there is a second and still more injurious mode in which law-enforced charity checks the process of adaptation. To become fit for the social state, man has not only to lose his savageness but he has to acquire the capacities needful for civilized life. Power of application must be developed; such modification of the intellect as shall qualify it for its new tasks must take place; and, above all, there must be gained the ability to sacrifice a small immediate gratification for a future great one. The state of transition will of course be an unhappy state. Misery inevitably results from incongruity between constitution and conditions. Humanity is being pressed against the inexorable necessities of its new position—is being moulded into harmony with them, and has to bear the resulting happiness as best it can. The process *must* be undergone and the sufferings *must* be endured. No power on Earth, no cunningly-devised laws of statesmen, no world-rectifying schemes of the humane, no communist panaceas, no reforms that men ever did broach or ever will broach, can diminish them one jot. Intensified they may be, and are; and in preventing their intensification the philanthropic will find ample scope for exertion. But there is bound up with the change a *normal* amount of suffering, which cannot be lessened without altering the very laws of life. Every attempt at mitigation of this eventuates in exacerbation of it. All that a poor-law or any kindred institution can do, is to partially suspend the transition—to take off for a time, from certain members of society, the painful pressure which is effecting their transformation. At best this is merely to postpone what must ultimately be borne. But it is more than this: it is to undo what has already been done. For the circumstances to which adaptation is taking place cannot be superseded without causing a retrogression; and as the whole process must some time or other be passed through, the lost ground must be gone over again, and the attendant pain borne afresh.

At first sight these considerations seem conclusive against *all* relief to the poor—voluntary as well as compulsory; and it is no doubt true that they imply a condemnation of whatever private charity enables the recipients to elude the necessities of our social existence. With this condemnation, however, no rational man will quarrel. That careless squandering of pence which has fostered into perfection a system of organized begging—which has made skilful mendicancy more profitable than ordinary manual labour—which induces the simulation of diseases and deformities—which has called into existence warehouses for the sale and hire of impostor's dresses—which has given to pity-inspiring babes a market value of 9*d.* per day—the unthinking benevolence which has generated all this, cannot but be disapproved by every one. Now it is only against this injudicious charity that the foregoing argument tells. To that charity which may be described as helping men to help themselves, it makes no objection—countenances it rather. And in helping men to help themselves, there remains abundant scope for the exercise of a people's sympathies. Accidents will still supply victims on whom generosity may be legitimately expended. Men thrown off the track by unforeseen events, men who have failed for want of knowledge inaccessible to them, men ruined by the dishonesty of others, and men in whom hope long delayed has made the heart sick, may, with advantage to all parties, be assisted. Even the prodigal, after severe hardships has branded his memory with the unbending conditions of social life to which he must submit, may properly have another trial afforded him. And, although by these ameliorations the process of adaptation must be remotely interfered with, yet, in the majority of cases, it will not be so much retarded in one direction as it will be advanced in another.

Objectionable as we find a poor-law to be, even under the supposition that it does what it is intended to do—diminish present suffering—how shall we regard it on finding that in reality it does no such thing—cannot do any such thing? Yet, paradoxical as the assertion looks, this is absolutely the fact. Let but the observer cease to contemplate so fixedly one side of the phenomenon—pauperism and its relief, and begin to examine the other side—rates and the *ultimate* contributors of them, and he will discover that to suppose the sum-total of distress diminishable by act-of-parliament bounty is a delusion.

Here, at any specified period, is a given quantity of food and things exchangeable for food, in the hands or at the command of the middle and upper classes. A certain portion of this food is needed by these classes themselves, and is consumed by them at the same rate, or very near it, be there scarcity or abundance. Whatever variation occurs in the sum-total of food and its equivalents, must therefore affect the remaining portion, not used by these classes for personal sustenance. This remaining portion is paid by them to the people in return for their labour, which is partly expended in the production of a further supply of necessaries, and partly in the production of luxuries. Hence, by how much this portion is deficient, by so much must the people come short. A re-distribution by legislative or other agency cannot make that sufficient for them which was previously insufficient. It can do nothing but change the parties by whom the insufficiency is felt. If it gives enough to some who else would not have enough, it must inevitably reduce certain others to the condition of not having enough.

THE COMING SLAVERY

The kinship of pity to love is shown among other ways in this, that it idealizes its object. Sympathy with one in suffering suppresses, for the time being, remembrance of his transgressions. The feeling which vents itself in "poor fellow!" on seeing one in agony, excludes the thought of "bad fellow," which might at another time arise. Naturally, then, if the wretched are unknown or but vaguely known, all the demerits they may have are ignored; and thus it happens that when the miseries of the poor are dilated upon, they are thought of as the miseries of the deserving poor, instead of being thought of as the miseries of the undeserving poor, which in large measure they should be. Those whose hardships are set forth in pamphlets and proclaimed in sermons and speeches which echo throughout society, are assumed to be all worthy souls, grievously wronged; and none of them are thought of as bearing the penalties of their misdeeds.

On hailing a cab in a London street, it is surprising how frequently the door is officiously opened by one who expects to get something for his trouble. The surprise lessens after counting the many loungers about tavern-doors, or after observing the quickness with which a street-performance, or procession, draws from neighbouring slums and stable-yards a group of idlers. Seeing how numerous they are in every small area, it becomes manifest that tens of thousands of such swarm through London. "They have no work," you say. Say rather that they either refuse work or quickly turn themselves out of it. They are simply good-for-nothings, who in one way or other live on the good-for-somethings—vagrants and sots, criminals and those on the way to crime, youths who are burdens on hard-worked parents, men who appropriate the wages of their wives, fellows who share the gains of prostitutes; and then, less visible and less numerous, there is a corresponding class of women.

Is it natural that happiness should be the lot of such? or is it natural that they should bring unhappiness on themselves and those connected with them? Is it not manifest that there must exist in our midst an immense amount of misery which is a normal result of misconduct, and ought not to be dissociated from it? There is a notion, always more or less prevalent and just now vociferously expressed, that all social suffering is removable, and that it is the duty of somebody or other to remove it. Both these beliefs are false. To separate pain from ill-doing is to fight against the constitution of things, and will be followed by far more pain. Saving men from the natural penalties of dissolute living, eventually necessitates the infliction of artificial penalties in solitary cells, on tread-wheels, and by the lash. I suppose a dictum on which the current creed and the creed of science are at one, may be considered to have as high an authority as can be found. Well, the command "if any would not work neither should he eat," is simply a Christian enunciation of that universal law of Nature under which life has reached its present height—the law that a creature not energetic enough to maintain itself must die: the sole difference being that the law which in the one case is to be artificially enforced, is, in the other case, a natural necessity. And yet this particular tenet of their religion which science so manifestly justifies, is the one which Christians seem least inclined to accept. The current assumption is that there should be no suffering, and that society is to blame for that which exists. . . .

. . . Influences of various kinds conspire to increase corporate action and decrease individual action. And the change is being on all sides aided by schemers, each of whom thinks only of his pet plan and not at all of the general reorganization which his plan, joined with others such, are working out. It is said that the French Revolution devoured its own children. Here, an analogous catastrophe seems not unlikely. The numerous socialistic changes made by Act of Parliament, joined with the numerous others presently to be made, will by-and-by be all merged in State-socialism—swallowed in the vast wave which they have little by little raised.

"But why is this change described as 'the coming slavery'?" is a question which many will still ask. The reply is simple. All socialism involves slavery.

What is essential to the idea of a slave? We primarily think of him as one who is owned by another. To be more than nominal, however, the ownership must be shown by control of the slave's actions—a control which is habitually for the benefit of the controller. That which fundamentally distinguishes the slave is that he labours under coercion to satisfy another's desires. The relation admits of sundry gradations. Remembering that originally the slave is a prisoner whose life is at the mercy of his captor, it suffices here to note that there is a harsh form of slavery in which, treated as an animal, he has to expend his entire effort for his owner's advantage. Under a system less harsh, though occupied chiefly in working for his owner, he is allowed a short time in which to work for himself, and some ground on which to grow extra food. A further amelioration gives him power to sell the produce of his plot and keep the proceeds. Then we come to the still more moderated form which commonly arises where, having been a free man working on his own land, conquest turns him into what we distinguish as a serf; and he has to give to his owner each year a fixed amount of labour or produce, or both: retaining the rest himself. Finally, in some cases, as in Russia before serfdom was abolished, he is allowed to leave his owner's estate and work or trade for himself elsewhere, under the condition that he shall pay an annual sum. What is it which, in these cases, leads us to qualify our conception of the slavery as more or less severe? Evidently the greater or smaller extent to which effort is compulsorily expended for the benefit of another instead of for self-benefit. If all the slave's labour is for his owner the slavery is heavy, and if but little it is light. Take now a further step. Suppose an owner dies, and his estate with its slaves comes into the hands of trustees; or suppose the estate and everything on it to be bought by a company; is the condition of the slave any the better if the amount of his compulsory labour remains the same? Suppose that for a company we substitute the community; does it make any difference to the slave if the time he has to work for others is as great, and the time left for himself is as small, as before? The essential question is—How much is he compelled to labour for other benefit than his own, and how much can he labour for his own benefit? The degree of his slavery varies according to the ratio between that which he is forced to yield up and that which he is allowed to retain; and it matters not whether his master is a single person or a society. If, without option, he has to labour for the society, and receives from the general stock such portion as the society awards him, he becomes a slave to the society. . . .

Evidently then, the changes made, the changes in progress, and the changes urged, will carry us not only towards State-ownership of land and dwellings and means of communication, all to be administered and worked by State-agents, but towards State-usurpation of all industries: the private forms of which, disadvantaged more and more in competition with the State, which can arrange everything for its own convenience, will more and more die away; just as many voluntary schools have, in presence of Board-schools. And so will be brought about the desired ideal of the socialists.

And now when there has been compassed this desired ideal, which "practical" politicians are helping socialists to reach, and which is so tempting on that bright side which socialists contemplate, what must be the accompanying shady side which they do not contemplate? It is a matter of common remark, often made when a marriage is impending, that those possessed by strong hopes habitually dwell on the promised pleasures and think nothing of the accompanying pains. A further exemplification of this truth is supplied by these political enthusiasts and fanatical revolutionists. Impressed with the miseries existing under our present social arrangements, and not regarding these miseries as caused by the ill-working of a human nature but partially adapted to the social state, they imagine them to be forthwith curable by this or that rearrangement. Yet, even did their plans succeed it could only be by substituting one kind of evil for another. A little deliberate thought would show that under their proposed arrangements, their liberties must be surrendered in proportion as their material welfares were cared for.

For no form of co-operation, small or great, can be carried on without regulation, and an implied submission to the regulating agencies. Even one of their own organizations for effecting social changes yields them proof. It is compelled to have its councils, its local and general officers, its authoritative leaders, who must be obeyed under penalty of confusion and failure. And the experience of those who are loudest in their advocacy of a new social order under the paternal control of a Government, shows that even in private voluntarily-formed societies, the power of the regulative organization becomes great, if not irresistible: often, indeed, causing grumbling and restiveness among those controlled. Trades-unions which carry on a kind of industrial war in defence of workers' interests *versus* employers' interests, find that subordination almost military in its strictness is needful to secure efficient action; for divided councils prove fatal to success. And even in bodies of co-operators, formed for carrying on manufacturing or distributing businesses, and not needing that obedience to leaders which is required where the aims are offensive or defensive, it is still found that the administrative agency gains such supremacy that there arise complaints about "the tyranny of organization." Judge then what must happen when, instead of relatively small combinations, to which men may belong or not as they please, we have a national combination in which each citizen finds himself incorporated, and from which he cannot separate himself without leaving the country. Judge what must under such conditions become the despotism of a graduated and centralized officialism, holding in its hands the resources of the community, and having behind it whatever amount of force it finds requisite to carry out its decrees and maintain what it calls order. Well may Prince Bismarck display leanings towards State-socialism.

And then after recognizing, as they must if they think out their scheme, the power possessed by the regulative agency in the new social system so temptingly pictured, let its advocates ask themselves to what end this power must be used. Not dwelling exclusively, as they habitually do, on the material well-being and the mental gratifications to be provided for them by a beneficent administration, let them dwell a little on the price to be paid. The officials cannot create the needful supplies: they can but distribute among individuals that which the individuals have joined to produce. If the public agency is required to provide for them, it must reciprocally require them to furnish the means. There cannot be, as under our existing system, agreement between employer and employed—this the scheme excludes. There must in place of it be command by local authorities over workers, and aceptance by the workers of that which the authorities assign to them. And this, indeed, is the arrangement distinctly, but as it would seem inadvertently, pointed to by the members of the Democratic Federation. For they propose that production should be carried on by "agricultural and industrial *armies* under State-control": apparently not remembering that armies pre-suppose grades of officers, by whom obedience would have to be insisted upon; since otherwise neither order nor efficient work could be ensured. So that each would stand toward the governing agency in the relation of slave to master.

"But the governing agency would be a master which he and others made and kept constantly in check; and one which therefore would not control him or others more than was needful for the benefit of each and all."

To which reply the first rejoinder is that, even if so, each member of the community as an individual would be a slave to the community as a whole. Such a relation has habitually existed in militant communities, even under quasi-popular forms of government. In ancient Greece the accepted principle was that the citizen belonged neither to himself nor to his family, but belonged to his city—the city being with the Greek equivalent to the community. And this doctrine, proper to a state of constant warfare, is a doctrine which socialism unawares re-introduces into a state intended to be purely industrial. The services of each will belong to the aggregate of all; and for these services, such returns will be given as the authorities think proper. So that even if the administration is of the beneficent kind intended to be secured, slavery, however mild, must be the outcome of the arrangement.

A second rejoinder is that the administration will presently become not of the intended kind, and that the slavery will not be mild. The socialist speculation is vitiated by an assumption like that which vitiates the speculations of the "practical" politician. It is assumed that officialism will work as it is intended to work, which it never does. The machinery of Communism, like existing social machinery, has to be framed out of existing human nature; and the defects of existing human nature will generate in the one the same evils as in the other. The love of power, the selfishness, the injustice, the untruthfulness, which often in comparatively short times bring private organizations to disaster, will inevitably, where their effects accumulate from generation to generation, work evils far greater and less remediable; since, vast and complex and possessed of all the resources, the administrative organization once developed and consolidated, must become irresistible. And if there needs proof that the periodic exercise of electoral power would fail to prevent this, it suffices to instance the French Government, which, purely popular in origin, and subject at short intervals to popular judgment, nevertheless tramples on the freedom of citizens to an extent which the English delegates to the late Trades Unions Congress say "is a disgrace to, and an anomaly in, a Republican nation."

The final result would be a revival of despotism. A disciplined army of civil officials, like an army of military officials, gives supreme power to its head—a power which has often led to usurpation, as in mediæval Europe and still more in Japan—nay, has thus so led among our neighbours, within our own times. The recent confessions of M. de Maupas have shown how readily a constitutional head, elected and trusted by the whole people, may, with the aid of a few unscrupulous confederates, paralyze the representative body and make himself autocrat. That those who rose to power in a socialistic organization would not scruple to carry out their aims at all costs, we have good reason for concluding. When we find that shareholders who, sometimes gaining but often losing, have made that railway-system by which national prosperity has been so greatly increased, are spoken of by the council of the Democratic Federation as having "laid hands" on the means of communication, we may infer that those who directed a socialistic administration might interpret with extreme perversity the claims of individuals and classes under their control. And when, further, we find members of this same council urging that the State should take possession of the railways, "with or without compensation," we may suspect that the heads of the ideal society desired, would be but little deterred by considerations of equity from pursuing whatever policy they thought needful: a policy which would always be one identified with their own supremacy. It would need but a war with an adjacent society, or some internal discontent demanding forcible suppression, to at once transform a socialistic administration into a grinding tyranny like that of ancient Peru; under which the mass of the people, controlled by grades of officials, and leading lives that were inspected out-of-doors and in-doors, laboured for the support of the organization which regulated them, and were left with but a bare subsistence for themselves. And then would be completely revived, under a different form, that *régime* of status—that system of compulsory co-operation, the decaying tradition of which is represented by the old Toryism, and towards which the new Toryism is carrying us back.

"But we shall be on our guard against all that—we shall take precautions to ward off such disasters," will doubtless say the enthusiasts. Be they "practical" politicians with their new regulative measures, or communists with their schemes for re-organizing labour their reply is ever the same;—"It is true that plans of kindred nature have, from unforeseen causes or adverse accidents, or the misdeeds of those concerned, been brought to failure; but this time we shall profit by past experiences and succeed." There seems no getting people to accept the truth, which nevertheless is conspicuous enough, that the welfare of a society and the justice of its arrangements are at bottom dependent on the characters of its members; and that improvement in neither can take place without that improvement in character which results from carrying on peaceful industry under the restraints imposed by an orderly social life. The belief, not only of the socialists but also of those so-called Liberals who are diligently preparing the way for them, is that by due skill an ill-working humanity may be framed into well-working institutions. It is a delusion. The defective natures of citizens will show themselves in the bad acting of whatever social structure they are arranged into. There is no political alchemy by which you can get golden conduct out of leaden instincts.

PETER KROPOTKIN, a Russian prince turned scientist and revolutionary, took a very different stand in his work Mutual Aid *(1902). Kropotkin maintained that love, not life-and-death competition, characterized the relationships between members of a single species throughout most of the animal kingdom.*

3. DARWINISM AND LOVE: PETER KROPOTKIN, FROM *MUTUAL AID, A FACTOR OF EVOLUTION,* 1902

SOURCE. Peter Kropotkin, *Mutual Aid, a Factor of Evolution,* London: William Heinemann, 1902, pp. 1–3. Reprinted by permission of William Heinemann Ltd.

Two aspects of animal life impressed me most during the journeys which I made in my youth in Eastern Siberia and Northern Manchuria. One of them was the extreme severity of the struggle for existence which most species of animals have to carry on against an inclement Nature; the enormous destruction of life which periodically results from natural agencies; and the consequent paucity of life over the vast territory which fell under my observation. And the other was, that even in those few spots where animal life teemed in abundance, I failed to find—although I was eagerly looking for it—that bitter struggle for the means of existence, *among animals belonging to the same species,* which was considered by most Darwinists (though not always by Darwin himself) as the dominant characteristic of struggle for life, and the main factor of evolution.

The terrible snow-storms which sweep over the northern portion of Eurasia in the later part of the winter, and the glazed frost that often follows them; the frosts and the snow-storms which return every year in the second half of May, when the trees are already in full blossom and insect life swarms everywhere; the early frosts and, occasionally, the heavy snowfalls in July and August, which suddenly destroy myriads of insects, as well as the second broods of the birds in the prairies; the torrential rains, due to the monsoons, which fall in more temperate regions in August and September—resulting in inundations on a scale which is only known in America and in Eastern Asia, and swamping, on the plateaus, areas as wide as European States; and finally, the heavy snowfalls, early in October, which eventually render a territory as large as France and Germany, absolutely impracticable for ruminants, and destroy them by the thousand—these were the conditions under which I saw animal life struggling in Northern Asia. They made me realize at an early date the overwhelming importance in Nature of what Darwin described as "the natural checks to over-multiplication," in comparison to the struggle between individuals of the same species for the means of subsistence, which may go on here and there, to some limited extent, but never attains the importance of the former. Paucity of life, under-population—not over-population—being the distinctive feature of that immense part of the globe which we name Northern Asia, I conceived since then serious doubts—which subsequent study has only confirmed—as to the reality of that fearful competition for food and life within each species, which was an article of faith with most Darwinists, and, consequently, as to the dominant part which this sort of competition was supposed to play in the evolution of new species.

On the other hand, wherever I saw animal life in abundance, as, for instance, on the lakes where scores of species and millions of individuals came together to rear their progeny; in the colonies of rodents; in the migrations of birds which took place at that time on a truly American scale along the Usuri; and especially in a migration of fallow-deer which I witnessed on the Amur, and during which scores of thousands of these intelligent animals came together from an immense territory, flying before the coming deep snow, in order to cross the Amur where it is narrowest—in all these scenes of animal life which passed before my eyes, I saw Mutual Aid and Mutual Support carried on to an extent which made me suspect in it a feature of the greatest importance for the maintenance of life, the preservation of each species, and its further evolution.

And finally, I saw among the semi-wild cattle and horses in Transbaikalia, among the wild ruminants everywhere, the squirrels, and so on,

that when animals have to struggle against scarcity of food, in consequence of one of the above-mentioned causes, the whole of that portion
of the species which is affected by the calamity, comes out of the ordeal
so much impoverished in vigour and health, that *no progressive evolution
of the species can be based upon such periods of keen competition.*

Consequently, when my attention was drawn, later on, to the relations
between Darwinism and Sociology, I could agree with none of the works
and pamphlets that had been written upon this important subject. They
all endeavoured to prove that Man, owing to his higher intelligence and
knowledge, *may* mitigate the harshness of the struggle for life between
men; but they all recognized at the same time that the struggle for the
means of existence, of every animal against all its congeners, and of every
man against all other men, was "a law of Nature." This view, however,
I could not accept, because I was persuaded that to admit a pitiless inner
war for life within each species, and to see in that war a condition of
progress was to admit something which not only had not yet been
proved, but also lacked confirmation from direct observation.

On the contrary, a lecture "On the Law of Mutual Aid," which was
delivered at a Russian Congress of Naturalists, in January 1880, by the
well-known zoologist, Professor Kessler, the then Dean of the St. Petersburg University, struck me as throwing a new light on the whole subject. Kessler's idea was that besides the *law of Mutual Struggle* there is
in Nature *the law of Mutual Aid,* which, for the success of the struggle
for life, and especially for the progressive evolution of the species, is
far more important than the law of mutual contest. This suggestion—
which was, in reality, nothing but a further development of the ideas
expressed by Darwin himself in *The Descent of Man*—seemed to me so
correct and of so great an importance, that since I became acquainted
with it (in 1883) I began to collect materials for further developing the
idea, which Kessler had only cursorily sketched in his lecture, but had
not lived to develop.

B. Man as Hero

FRIEDRICH NIETZSCHE (1844–1900) scorned timidity, mediocrity, and abjectness, and put his hope in the man of fearless intelligence and boldness of spirit—the superman who was beyond good and evil. These views are stated with characteristic flair in Nietzsche's The Genealogy of Morals *(1887) from which the following excerpt is taken.*

1. FRIEDRICH NIETZSCHE, FROM THE GENEALOGY OF MORALS, 1887

SOURCE. Friedrich Nietzsche, *The Genealogy of Morals*, William A. Haussmann and John Gray, trs., London: T. Fisher Unwin, 1889. Reprinted by permission of Ernest Benn Ltd.

It is impossible not to recognise at the core of all these aristocratic races the beast of prey; the magnificent *blonde brute*, avidly rampant for spoil and victory; this hidden core needed an outlet from time to time, the beast must get loose again, must return into the wilderness—the Roman, Arabic, German, and Japanese nobility, the Homeric heroes, the Scandinavian Vikings, are all alike in this need. It is the aristocratic races who have left the idea "Barbarian" on all the tracks in which they have marched; nay, a consciousness of this very barbarianism, and even a pride in it, manifests itself even in their highest civilisation (for example, when Pericles says to his Athenians in that celebrated funeral oration, "Our audacity has forced a way over every land and sea, rearing everywhere imperishable memorials of itself for *good* and for *evil*"). This audacity of aristocratic races, mad, absurd, and spasmodic as may be its expression; the incalculable and fantastic nature of their enterprises,— Pericles sets in special relief and glory the *rhathumia* of the Athenians, their nonchalance and contempt for safety, body, life, and comfort, their awful joy and intense delight in all destruction, in all the ecstasies of victory and cruelty,—all these features become crystallised, for those who suffered thereby in the picture of the "barbarian," of the "evil enemy," perhaps of the "Goth" and of the "Vandal." The profound, icy mistrust which the German provokes, as soon as he arrives at power,—even at the present time,—is always still an aftermath of that inextinguishable horror with which for whole centuries Europe has regarded the wrath of the blonde Teuton beast (although between the old Germans and ourselves there exists scarcely a psychological, let alone a physical, relationship). I have once called attention to the embarrassment of Hesiod, when he conceived the series of social ages, and endeavoured to express them in gold, silver, and bronze. He could only dispose of the contradiction, with which he was confronted, by the Homeric world, an age magnificent indeed, but at the same time so awful and so violent, by making two ages out of one, which he henceforth placed one behind the other—first, the age of the heroes and demigods, as that world had remained in the memories of the aristocratic families, who found therein their own ancestors; secondly, the bronze age, as that corresponding age appeared to the descendants of the oppressed, spoiled, ill-treated, exiled, enslaved; namely, as an age of bronze, as I have said, hard, cold, terrible, without feelings and without conscience, crushing everything, and bespattering everything with blood. Granted the truth of the theory now believed to be true, that the very *essence of all civilisation* is to *train* out of man, the beast of prey, a tame and civilised animal, a domesticated animal, it follows indubitably that we must regard as the real *tools of civilisation* all those instincts of reaction and resentment, by the help of which the aristocratic races, together with their ideals, were finally degraded and overpowered; though that has not yet come to be synonymous with saying that the bearers of those tools also *represented* the civilisation. It is rather the contrary that is not only probable—nay, it is *palpable* to-day; these bearers of vindictive instincts that have to be bottled up, these descendants of all European and non-European slavery, especially of the pre-Aryan population—these people, I say, represent the *decline* of humanity! These "tools of civilisation" are a disgrace to humanity, and constitute in reality more of an argument against civilisation, more of a reason why civilisation should be suspected. One may be perfectly justified in being always afraid of the blonde beast that lies at the core of all aristocratic races, and in being on one's guard: but who would not a hundred times prefer to be afraid, when one at the same time admires, than to be immune from fear, at the cost of being perpetually obsessed with the loathsome spectacle of the distorted, the dwarfed, the stunted, the envenomed? And is that not our fate? What produces to-day our repulsion towards "man"?—for we *suffer* from "man," there is no doubt about it. It is not fear; it is rather that we have nothing more to fear from men; it is that the worm "man" is in the foreground and pullulates; it is that the "tame man," the wretched mediocre and unedifying creature, has learnt to consider himself a goal and a pinnacle, an inner meaning, an historic principle, a "higher man"; yes, it is that he has a certain right so to consider himself, in so far as he feels that in contrast to that excess of deformity, disease, exhaustion, and effeteness whose odour is beginning to pollute present-day Europe, he at any rate has achieved a relative success, he at any rate still says "yes" to life.

I cannot refrain at this juncture from uttering a sigh and one last hope. What is it precisely which I find intolerable? That which I alone cannot get rid of, which makes me choke and faint? Bad air! Bad air! That something misbegotten comes near me; that I must inhale the odour of the entrails of a misbegotten soul!—That excepted, what can one not endure in the way of need, privation, bad weather, sickness, toil, solitude? In point of fact, one manages to get over everything, born as one is to a burrowing and battling existence; one always returns once again to the light, one always lives again one's golden hour of victory—and then one stands as one was born, unbreakable, tense, ready for something more difficult, for something more distant, like a bow stretched but the tauter by every strain. But from time to time do ye grant me—assuming that "beyond good and evil" there are goddesses who can grant—one glimpse, grant me but one glimpse only, of something perfect, fully realised, happy, mighty, triumphant, or something that still gives cause for fear! A glimpse of a man that justifies the existence of man, a glimpse of an incarnate human happiness that realises and redeems, for the sake of which one may hold fast to *the belief in man!* For the position is this: in the dwarfing and levelling of the European man lurks *our* greatest peril, for it is this outlook which fatigues—we see to-day nothing which wishes to be greater, we surmise that the process is always still backwards, still backwards towards something more attenuated, more inoffensive, more cunning, more comfortable, more mediocre, more indifferent, more Chinese, more Christian—man, there is no doubt about it, grows always "better"—the destiny of Europe lies even in this—that in losing the fear of man, we have also lost the hope in man, yea, the will to be man. The sight of man now fatigues.—What is present-day Nihilism if it is not *that?* —We are tired of *man.*

But let us come back to it; the problem of *another* origin of the good— of the good, as the resentful man has thought it out—demands its solution. It is not surprising that the lambs should bear a grudge against the great birds of prey, but that is no reason for blaming the great birds of prey for taking the little lambs. And when the lambs say among themselves, "Those birds of prey are evil, and he who is as far removed from being a bird of prey, who is rather its opposite, a lamb,—is he not good?" then there is nothing to cavil at in the setting up of this ideal, though it may also be that the birds of prey will regard it a little sneeringly, and perchance say to themselves, "*We* bear no grudge against them, these good lambs, we even like them: nothing is tastier than a tender lamb." To require of strength that it should *not* express itself as strength, that it should not be a wish to overpower, a wish to overthrow, a wish to become master, a thirst for enemies and antagonisms and triumphs, is just as absurd as to require of weakness that it should express itself as strength. A quantum of force is just such a quantum of movement, will, action—rather it is nothing else than just those very phenomena of moving, willing, acting, and can only appear otherwise in the misleading errors of language (and the fundamental fallacies of reason which have become petrified therein), which understands, and understands wrongly, all working as conditioned by a worker, by a "subject." And just exactly as the people separate the lightning from its flash, and interpret the latter as a thing done, as the working of a subject which is called lightning, so also does the popular morality separate strength from the expression of strength, as though behind the strong man there existed some indifferent neutral *substratum*, which enjoyed a *caprice and option* as to whether or not it should express strength. But there is no such *substratum*, there is no "being" behind doing, working, becoming; "the doer" is a mere appanage to the action. The action is everything. In point of fact, the people duplicate the doing, when they make the lightning lighten, that is a "doing-doing"; they make the same phenomenon first a cause, and then, secondly, the effect of that cause. The scientists fail to improve matters when they say, "Force moves, force causes," and so on. Our whole science is still, in spite of all its coldness, of all its freedom from passion, a dupe of the tricks of language, and has never succeeded in getting rid of that superstitious changeling "the subject" (the atom, to give another instance, is such a changeling, just as the Kantian "Thing-in-itself"). What wonder, if the suppressed and stealthily simmering passions of revenge and hatred exploit for their own advantage their belief, and indeed hold no belief with a more steadfast enthusiasm than this— "that the strong has the *option* of being weak, and the bird of prey of being a lamb." Thereby do they win for themselves the right of attributing to the birds of prey the *responsibility* for being birds of prey: when the oppressed, downtrodden, and overpowered say to themselves with the vindictive guile of weakness, "Let us be otherwise than the evil, namely, good! and good is every one who does not oppress, who hurts no one, who does not attack, who does not pay back, who hands over revenge to God, who holds himself, as we do, in hiding; who goes out of the way of evil, and demands, in short, little from life; like ourselves the patient, the meek, the just,"—yet all this, in its cold and unprejudiced interpretation, means nothing more than "once for all, the weak are weak; it is good to do *nothing for which we are not strong enough*"; but this dismal state of affairs, this prudence of the lowest order, which even insects possess (which in a great danger are fain to sham death so as to avoid doing "too much"), has, thanks to the counterfeiting and self-deception of weakness, come to masquerade in the pomp of an ascetic, mute, and expectant virtue, just as though the *very* weakness of the weak—that is, forsooth, its *being*, its working, its whole unique inevitable inseparable reality—were a voluntary result, something wished, chosen, a deed, an act of *merit*. This kind of man finds the belief in a neutral, free-choosing "subject" *necessary* from an instinct of self-preservation, of self-assertion, in which every lie is fain to sanctify itself. The subject (or, to use popular language, the *soul*) has perhaps proved itself the best dogma in the world simply because it rendered possible to the horde of mortal, weak, and oppressed individuals of every kind, that most sublime specimen of self-deception, the interpretation of weakness as freedom, of being this, or being that, as *merit*.

Will any one look a little into—right into—the mystery of how *ideals* are *manufactured* in this world? Who has the courage to do it? Come!

Here we have a vista opened into these grimy workshops. Wait just a moment, dear Mr. Inquisitive and Foolhardy; your eye must first grow accustomed to this false changing light—Yes! Enough! Now speak! What is happening below down yonder? Speak out! Tell what you see, man of the most dangerous curiosity—for now *I* am the listener.

"I see nothing, I hear the more. It is a cautious, spiteful, gentle whispering and muttering together in all the corners and crannies. It seems to me that they are lying; a sugary softness adheres to every sound. Weakness is turned to *merit*, there is no doubt about it—it is just as you say."

Further!

"And the impotence which requites not, is turned to 'goodness,' craven baseness to meekness, submission to those whom one hates, to obedience (namely, obedience to one of whom they say that he ordered this submission—they call him God). The inoffensive character of the weak, the very cowardice in which he is rich, his standing at the door, his forced necessity of waiting, gain here fine names, such as 'patience,' which is also called 'virtue'; not being able to avenge one's self, is called not wishing to avenge one's self, perhaps even forgiveness (for *they* know not what they do—we alone know what they do). They also talk of the 'love of their enemies' and sweat thereby."

Further!

"They are miserable, there is no doubt about it, all these whisperers and counterfeiters in the corners, although they try to get warm by crouching close to each other, but they tell me that their misery is a favour and distinction given to them by God, just as one beats the dogs one likes best; that perhaps this misery is also a preparation, a probation, a training; that perhaps it is still more something which will one day be compensated and paid back with a tremendous interest in gold, nay in happiness. This they call 'Blessedness.' "

Further!

"They are now giving me to understand, that not only are they better men than the mighty, the lords of the earth, whose spittle they have got to lick (*not* out of fear, not at all out of fear! But because God ordains that one should honour all authority)—not only are they better men, but that they also have a 'better time,' at any rate, will one day have a 'better time.' But enough! Enough! I can endure it no longer. Bad air! Bad air! These workshops *where ideals are manufactured*—verily they reek with the crassest lies."

Nay. Just one minute! You are saying nothing about the masterpieces of these virtuosos of black magic, who can produce whiteness, milk, and innocence out of any black you like: have you not noticed what a pitch of refinement is attained by their *chef d'œuvre*, their most audacious, subtle, ingenious, and lying artist-trick? Take care! These cellar-beasts, full of revenge and hate—what do they make, forsooth, out of their revenge and hate? Do you hear these words? Would you suspect, if you trusted only their words, that you are among men of resentment and nothing else?

"I understand, I prick my ears up again (ah! ah! ah! and I hold my nose). Now do I hear for the first time that which they have said so often: 'We good, *we are the righteous*'—what they demand they call not revenge but 'the triumph of *righteousness*'; what they hate is not their enemy, no, they hate 'unrighteousness,' 'godlessness'; what they believe in and hope is not the hope of revenge, the intoxication of sweet revenge (—"sweeter than honey," did Homer call it?), but the victory of God, of the *righteous God* over the 'godless'; what is left for them to love in this world is not their brothers in hate, but their 'brothers in love,' as they say, all the good and righteous on the earth."

And how do they name that which serves them as a solace against all the troubles of life—their phantasmagoria of their anticipated future blessedness?

"How? Do I hear right? They call it 'the last judgment,' the advent of *their* kingdom, 'the kingdom of God'—but *in the meanwhile* they live 'in faith,' 'in love,' 'in hope.'"

Enough! Enough!

Part II

ART

A. Realism

TOWARD THE MIDDLE of the nineteenth century a reaction began to set in against the artistic values of Romanticism. Gustave Courbet (1819–1877), a socialist and a renegade Romantic, became convinced that the emotional and imaginative emphasis of Romanticism was in fact a flight from reality. Courbet turned to a sober, matter-of-fact exposition of ordinary subjects, seeking through artistic understatement to portray the heroism of real life. His Stone Breakers *(1849) is a moving expression of the realist point of view.*

1. GUSTAVE COURBET, *THE STONE BREAKERS*, 1849

B. Impressionism

THE COMING OF IMPRESSIONISM in the 1860's and 1870's marks an important new departure in the history of art—a shift in emphasis from the outside world to the artist's own particular vision of it. Perhaps it was the advent of photography that drove painters to strive for a radically unphotographic style in order to assert the integrity and uniqueness of their art. However this may be, the painter's canvas was no longer a "window" to the outside world but a surface on which the artist worked with brush strokes and color to depict his own vision. Later Impressionists turned increasingly to the portrayal of subjects under particular conditions of light and atmosphere—a city shrouded by fog, or the reflection of sunlight on a rippling pool. The style is typified in Fishermen on the Seine *by Claude Monet (1840–1926) (1) and* The Road in the Woods *by Alfred Sisley (1839–1899) (2).*

1. CLAUDE MONET, *FISHERMEN ON THE SEINE*

2. ALFRED SISLEY, *THE ROAD IN THE WOODS*

C. Post-Impressionism

POST-IMPRESSIONISM, which became important in the 1880's, was hardly a style at all. Rather it is a label that is applied to the work of a group of highly individual artists such as Cézanne, Van Gogh, Seurat, and Gauguin, who learned from the Impressionists and went beyond them, each in his own way. In Paul Cézanne (1839–1906) in particular, the emphasis on treating the canvas as a colored surface rather than a window is carried well beyond the limits of the Impressionists. Cézanne was deeply interested in the structure of his compositions, and was willing to sacrifice photographic accuracy in order to achieve formal unity. This quality is evident in his Large Bathers *(1), in which the figures and the trees are so placed as to create a triangular form for the painting as a whole. His* Mont Sainte-Victoire *(1904–1906) (2) illustrates the solidity of his artistic conception, which contrasts sharply with the Impressionist emphasis on fluidity and change.*

1. PAUL CÉZANNE, *THE LARGE BATHERS*, 1898–1905

2. PAUL CÉZANNE, *MONT SAINTE-VICTOIRE*

THE DUTCH ARTIST Vincent Van Gogh (1853–1890) transcended Impressionist values in quite a different way. He developed a bold, free style and filled his canvases with movement and luminous color. His Wheat Field and Cypress Trees *(1889) (3), and* The Starry Night *(1889) (4), both illustrate his exciting and intensely personal vision.*

3. VINCENT VAN GOGH, *WHEAT FIELD AND CYPRESS TREES*, 1889

4. VINCENT VAN GOGH, *THE STARRY NIGHT*, 1889

Part III

INTELLECTUAL ATTITUDES TOWARD IMPERIALISM

A. Divine Mission

THE UPSURGE OF IMPERIALISM in the later nineteenth and early twentieth centuries won the support of a number of writers who justified colonial expansion on the basis of nationalism, social Darwinism, and notions of ethnic superiority. Darwin's concept of the survival of the fittest underwent its own curious evolution; it was adapted to justify such concepts as white supremacy, Nordic superiority, and the manifest destiny of the Anglo-Saxon race. Typical of this trend are the crude racial ideas to be found in Our Country (1885) *by the American clergyman Josiah Strong (1847–1916).*

1. JOSIAH STRONG, FROM *OUR COUNTRY*, 1885

SOURCE. Josiah Strong, *Our Country*, New York: The Baker and Taylor Publishing Company for The American Home Missionary Society, 1885, pp. 159–160, 165–168, 174–178.

Every race which has deeply impressed itself on the human family has been the representative of some great idea—one or more—which has given direction to the nation's life and form to its civilization. Among the Egyptians this seminal idea was life, among the Persians it was light, among the Hebrews it was purity, among the Greeks it was beauty, among the Romans it was law. The Anglo-Saxon is the representative of two great ideas, which are closely related. One of them is that of civil liberty. Nearly all of the civil liberty in the world is enjoyed by Anglo-Saxons: the English, the British colonists, and the people of the United States. To some, like the Swiss, it is permitted by the sufferance of their neighbors; others, like the French, have experimented with it; but, in modern times, the peoples whose love of liberty has won it, and whose genius for self-government has preserved it, have been Anglo-Saxons. The noblest races have always been lovers of liberty. That love ran strong in early German blood, and has profoundly influenced the institutions of all the branches of the great German family; but it was left for the Anglo-Saxon branch fully to recognize the right of the individual to himself, and formally to declare it the foundation stone of government.

The other great idea of which the Anglo-Saxon is the exponent is that of a pure *spiritual* Christianity. It was no accident that the great reformation of the sixteenth century originated among a Teutonic, rather than a Latin people. It was the fire of liberty burning in the Saxon heart that flamed up against the absolutism of the Pope. Speaking roughly, the peoples of Europe which are Celtic are Catholic, and those which are Teutonic are Protestant; and where the Teutonic race was purest, there Protestantism spread with the greatest rapidity. . . .

. . . North America is to be the great home of the Anglo-Saxon, the principal seat of his power, the center of his life and influence. Not only does it constitute seven-elevenths of his possessions, but his empire is unsevered, while the remaining four-elevenths are fragmentary and scattered over the earth. Australia will have a great population; but its disadvantages, as compared with North America, are too manifest to need mention. Our continent has room and resources and climate, it lies in the pathway of the nations, it belongs to the zone of power, and already, among Anglo-Saxons, do we lead in population and wealth. . . . America is to have the great preponderance of numbers and of wealth, and by the logic of events will follow the scepter of controlling influence. This will be but the consummation of a movement as old as civilization—a result to which men have looked forward for centuries. John Adams records that nothing was "more ancient in his memory than the observation that arts, sciences and empire had traveled westward. . . .

But we are to have not only the larger portion of the Anglo-Saxon race for generations to come, we may reasonably expect to develop the highest type of Anglo-Saxon civilization. If human progress follows a law of development, if

Time's noblest offspring is the last,

our civilization should be the noblest; for we are

The heirs of all the ages in the foremost files of time,

and not only do we occupy the latitude of power, but *our land is the last to be occupied in that latitude.* There is no other virgin soil in the North Temperate Zone. If the consummation of human progress is not to be looked for here, if there is yet to flower a higher civilization, where is the soil that is to produce it? . . .

. . . God, with infinite wisdom and skill, is training the Anglo-Saxon race for an hour sure to come in the world's future. Heretofore there has always been in the history of the world a comparatively unoccupied land westward, into which the crowded countries of the East have poured their surplus populations. But the widening waves of migration, which millenniums ago rolled east and west from the valley of the Euphrates meet to-day on our Pacific coast. There are no more new worlds. . . . The time is coming when the pressure of population on the means of subsistence will be felt here as it is now felt in Europe and Asia. Then will the world enter upon a new stage of its history—*the final competition of races, for which the Anglo-Saxon is being schooled.* Long before the thousand millions are here, the mighty *centrifugal* tendency, inherent in this stock and strengthened in the United States, will assert itself. Then this race of unequaled energy, with all the majesty of numbers and the might of wealth behind it—the representative, let us hope, of the largest liberty, the purest Christianity, the highest civilization—having developed peculiarly aggressive traits calculated to impress its institutions upon mankind, will spread itself over the earth. If I read not amiss, this powerful race will move down upon Mexico, down upon Central and South America, out upon the islands of the sea, over upon Africa and beyond. And can any one doubt that the result of this competition of races will be the "survival of the fittest"? "Any people," says Dr. Bushnell, "that is physiologically advanced in culture, though it be only in a degree beyond another which is mingled with it on strictly equal terms, is sure to live down and finally live out its inferior. Nothing can save the inferior race but a ready and pliant assimilation. Whether the feebler and more abject races are going to be regenerated and raised up, is already very much of a question. What if it should be God's plan to people the world with better and finer material? Certain it is, whatever expectations we may indulge, that there is a tremendous overbearing surge of power in the Christian nations, which, if the others are not speedily raised to some vastly higher capacity, will inevitably submerge and bury them forever. These great populations of Christendom—what are they doing, but throwing out their colonies on every side, and populating themselves, if I may so speak, into the possession of all countries and climes?" To this result no war of extermination is needful; the contest is not one of arms, but of vitality and of civilization. "At the present day," says Mr. Darwin, "civilized nations are everywhere supplanting barbarous nations. . . ."

Some of the stronger races, doubtless, may be able to preserve their integrity; but, in order to compete with the Anglo-Saxon, they will probably be forced to adopt his methods and instruments, his civilization and his religion. . . . The contact of Christian with heathen nations is awaking the latter to new life. Old superstitions are loosening their grasp. The dead crust of fossil faiths is being shattered by the movements of life underneath. In Catholic countries, Catholicism is losing its influence over educated minds, and in some cases the masses have already lost all faith in it. Thus, while on this continent God is training the Anglo-Saxon race for its mission, a complemental work has been in progress in the great world beyond. God has two hands. Not only is he preparing in our civilization the die with which to stamp the nations, but . . . he is preparing mankind to receive our impress.

Is there room for reasonable doubt that this race, unless devitalized by alcohol and tobacco, is destined to dispossess many weaker races, assimilate others, and mold the remainder, until, in a very true and important sense, it has Anglo-Saxonized mankind?

RUDYARD KIPLING, in his "The White Man's Burden" (1899), wrote of the hard mission of the white race to uplift its "new-caught, sullen peoples."

2. RUDYARD KIPLING, "THE WHITE MAN'S BURDEN," 1899

Take up the White Man's burden—
    Send forth the best ye breed—
Go bind your sons to exile
    To serve your captives' need;
To wait in heavy harness
    On fluttered folk and wild—
Your new-caught, sullen peoples,
    Half devil and half child.

Take up the White Man's burden—
    In patience to abide,
To veil the threat of terror
    And check the show of pride;
By open speech and simple,
    An hundred times made plain,
To seek another's profit,
    And work another's gain.

Take up the White Man's burden—
    The savage wars of peace—
Fill full the mouth of Famine
    And bid the sickness cease;
And when your goal is nearest
    The end for others sought,
Watch Sloth and heathen Folly
    Bring all your hope to nought.

Take up the White Man's burden—
  No tawdry rule of kings,
But toil of serf and sweeper—
  The tale of common things.
The ports ye shall not enter,
  The roads ye shall not tread,
Go make them with your living,
  And mark them with your dead!

Take up the White Man's burden—
  And reap his old reward:
The blame of those ye better,
  The hate of those ye guard—
The cry of hosts ye humour
  (Ah, slowly!) toward the light:—
'Why brought ye us from bondage,
  'Our loved Egyptian night?'

Take up the White Man's burden—
  Ye dare not stoop to less—
Nor call too loud on Freedom
  To cloak your weariness;
By all ye cry or whisper,
  By all ye leave or do,
The silent, sullen peoples
  Shall weigh your Gods and you.

Take up the White Man's burden—
  Have done with childish days—
The lightly proffered laurel,
  The easy, ungrudged praise.
Comes now, to search your manhood
  Through all the thankless years,
Cold-edged with dear-bought wisdom,
  The judgment of your peers!

B. Exploitation

MANY OF STRONG'S AND KIPLING'S *contemporaries opposed colonialism, and none more vigorously than Lenin. In his* Imperialism: the Highest Stage of Capitalism *(1916), he pictured it as the evil product of monopolistic greed and the last phase in the decline of the capitalist system.*

1. LENIN, FROM *IMPERIALISM: THE HIGHEST STAGE OF CAPITALISM*

SOURCE. V. I. Lenin, *Imperialism: The Highest Stage of Capitalism,* New York: International Publishers, 1939, pp. 109–111, 123–124, 126–127. Reprinted by permission of International Publishers Co., Inc.

The enormous dimensions of finance capital concentrated in a few hands and creating an extremely extensive and close network of ties and relationships which subordinate not only the small and medium, but also even the very small capitalists and small masters, on the one hand, and the intense struggle waged against other national state groups of financiers for the division of the world and domination over other countries, on the other hand, cause the wholesale transition of the possessing classes to the side of imperialism. The signs of the times are a "general" enthusiasm regarding its prospects, a passionate defence of imperialism, and every possible embellishment of its real nature. The imperialist ideology also penetrates the working class. There is no Chinese Wall between it and the other classes. The leaders of the so-called "Social-Democratic" Party of Germany are today justly called "social-imperialists," that is, socialists in words and imperialists in deeds; but as early as 1902, Hobson noted the existence of "Fabian imperialists" who belonged to the opportunist Fabian Society in England.

Bourgeois scholars and publicists usually come out in defence of imperialism in a somewhat veiled form, and obscure its complete domination and its profound roots; they strive to concentrate attention on partial and secondary details and do their very best to distract attention from the main issue by means of ridiculous schemes for "reform," such as police supervision of the trusts and banks, etc. Less frequently, cynical and frank imperialists speak out and are bold enough to admit the absurdity of the idea of reforming the fundamental features of imperialism. . . .

The question as to whether it is possible to reform the basis of imperialism, whether to go forward to the accentuation and deepening of the antagonisms which it engenders, or backwards, towards allaying these antagonisms, is a fundamental question in the critique of imperialism. As a consequence of the fact that the political features of imperialism are reaction all along the line, and increased national oppression, resulting from the oppression of the financial oligarchy and the elimination of free competition, a petty-bourgeois—democratic opposition has been rising against imperialism in almost all imperialist countries since the beginning of the twentieth century. . . .

In the United States, the imperialist war waged against Spain in 1898 stirred up the opposition of the "anti-imperialists," the last of the Mohicans of bourgeois democracy. They declared this war to be "criminal"; they denounced the annexation of foreign territories as being a violation of the Constitution, and denounced the "Jingo treachery" by means of which Aguinaldo, leader of the native Filipinos, was deceived (the Americans promised him the independence of his country, but later they landed troops and annexed it). They quoted the words of Lincoln:

"When the white man governs himself, that is self-government; but when he governs himself and also governs another man, that is more than self-government—that is despotism."

But while all this criticism shrank from recognising the indissoluble bond between imperialism and the trusts, and, therefore, between imperialism and the very foundations of capitalism; while it shrank from joining up with the forces engendered by large-scale capitalism and its development—it remained a "pious wish." . . .

We have seen that the economic quintessence of imperialism is monopoly capitalism. This very fact determines its place in history, for monopoly that grew up on the basis of free competition, and precisely out of free competition, is the transition from the capitalist system to a higher social-economic order. We must take special note of the four principal forms of monopoly, or the four principal manifestations of monopoly capitalism, which are characteristic of the epoch under review.

Firstly, monopoly arose out of the concentration of production at a very advanced stage of development. This refers to the monopolist capitalist combines, cartels, syndicates and trusts. We have seen the important part that these play in modern economic life. At the beginning of the twentieth century, monopolies acquired complete supremacy in the advanced countries. And although the first steps towards the formation of the cartels were first taken by countries enjoying the protection of high tariffs (Germany, America), Great Britain, with her system of free trade, was not far behind in revealing the same basic phenomenon, namely, the birth of monopoly out of the concentration of production.

Secondly, monopolies have accelerated the capture of the most important sources of raw materials, especially for the coal and iron industries, which are the basic and most highly cartelised industries in capitalist society. The monopoly of the most important sources of raw materials has enormously increased the power of big capital, and has sharpened the antagonism between cartelised and non-cartelised industry.

Thirdly, monopoly has sprung from the banks. The banks have developed from modest intermediary enterprises into the monopolists of finance capital. Some three or five of the biggest banks in each of the foremost capitalist countries have achieved the "personal union" of industrial and bank capital, and have concentrated in their hands the disposal of thousands upon thousands of millions which form the greater part of the capital and income of entire countries. A financial oligarchy, which throws a close net of relations of dependence over all the economic and political institutions of contemporary bourgeois society without exception —such is the most striking manifestation of this monopoly.

Fourthly, monopoly has grown out of colonial policy. To the numerous "old" motives of colonial policy, finance capital has added the struggle for the sources of raw materials, for the export of capital, for "spheres of influence," *i.e.*, for spheres for profitable deals, concessions, monopolist profits and so on; in fine, for economic territory in general. When the colonies of the European powers in Africa, for instance, comprised only one-tenth of that territory (as was the case in 1876), colonial policy was able to develop by methods other than those of monopoly—by the "free grabbing" of territories, so to speak. But when nine-tenths of Africa had been seized (approximately by 1900), when the whole world had been divided up, there was inevitably ushered in a period of colonial monopoly and, consequently, a period of particularly intense struggle for the division and the redivision of the world.

The extent to which monopolist capital has intensified all the contradictions of capitalism is generally known. It is sufficient to mention the high cost of living and the oppression of the cartels. This intensification of contradictions constitutes the most powerful driving force of the transitional period of history, which began from the time of the definite victory of world finance capital.

Monopolies, oligarchy, the striving for domination instead of the striving for liberty, the exploitation of an increasing number of small or weak nations by an extremely small group of the richest or most powerful nations—all these have given birth to those distinctive characteristics of imperialism which compel us to define it as parasitic or decaying capitalism. . . .

The receipt of high monopoly profits by the capitalists in one of the numerous branches of industry, in one of numerous countries, etc., makes it economically possible for them to corrupt certain sections of the working class, and for a time a fairly considerable minority, and win them to the side of the bourgeoisie of a given industry or nation against all the others. The intensification of antagonisms between imperialist nations for the division of the world increases this striving. And so there is created that bond between imperialism and opportunism, which revealed itself first and most clearly in England, owing to the fact that certain features of imperialist development were observable there much earlier than in other countries. . . .

From all that has been said . . . on the economic nature of imperialism, it follows that we must define it as capitalism in transition, or, more precisely, as moribund capitalism. It is very instructive in this respect to note that the bourgeois economists, in describing modern capitalism, frequently employ terms like "interlocking," "absence of isolation," etc.; "in conformity with their functions and course of development," banks are "not purely private business enterprises; they are more and more outgrowing the sphere of purely private business regulation." And this very Riesser, who uttered the words just quoted, declares with all seriousness that the "prophecy" of the Marxists concerning "socialisation" has "not come true"!

What then does this word "interlocking" express? It merely expresses the most striking feature of the process going on before our eyes. It shows that the observer counts the separate trees, but cannot see the wood. It slavishly copies the superficial, the fortuitous, the chaotic. It reveals the observer as one who is overwhelmed by the mass of raw material and is utterly incapable of appreciating its meaning and importance. Ownership of shares and relations between owners of private property "interlock in a haphazard way." But the underlying factor of this interlocking, its very base, is the changing social relations of production. When a big enterprise assumes gigantic proportions, and, on the basis of exact computation of mass data, organises according to plan the supply of primary raw materials to the extent of two-thirds, or three-fourths of all that is necessary for tens of millions of people; when the raw materials are transported to the most suitable place of production, sometimes hundreds or thousands of miles away, in a systematic and organised manner; when a single centre directs all the successive stages of work right up to the manufacture of numerous varieties of finished articles; when these products are distributed according to a single plan among tens and hundreds of millions of consumers (as in the case of the distribution of oil in America and Germany by the American "oil trust") —then it becomes evident that we have socialisation of production, and not mere "interlocking"; that private economic relations and private property relations constitute a shell which is no longer suitable for its contents, a shell which must inevitably begin to decay if its destruction be delayed by artificial means; a shell which may continue in a state of decay for a fairly long period (particularly if the cure of the opportunist abscess is protracted), but which will inevitably be removed.

World War I and the Rise of Totalitarianism

THE outbreak of World War I was a product of several causes: the intensification of national rivalries which expressed itself in arms races and in the polarization of Europe into two mutually hostile alliance systems; a continuing struggle over colonies and spheres of influence in Asia and Africa; and most particularly, the contest between Austria-Hungary and Russia for hegemony in the Balkans, where, in the course of the previous century, a number of newly independent states had broken loose from the crumbling Ottoman Empire. Austria-Hungary was particularly sensitive on the matter of Balkan nationalism, for the movement was generating unrest among the Slavic peoples within her own territories. Russia, conscious of her Slavic heritage and anxious to use it to her own political advantage, encouraged Balkan nationalism while Austria-Hungary opposed it.

The Slavic state of Serbia, fiercely independent and hopeful of becoming the nucleus of a unified Balkan nation, was a constant threat to the internal security of Austria-Hungary. When a Serbian terrorist assassinated Archduke Francis Ferdinand, heir to the Austro-Hungarian throne, at Sarajevo on June 28, 1914 a crisis was provoked that led directly to World War I. Austria retaliated for the assassination by issuing an ultimatum to Serbia containing demands that no independent nation could honorably accept. In the days immediately following, as a consequence of the two alliance systems, the great powers entered the conflict one after another. Russia came to Serbia's defense, Germany joined Austria, France and England joined Russia, most of the smaller European states took one side or the other, and by mid-August Europe was in a state of general war.

World War I was a momentous historical catastrophe. It dragged on for months and years, taking a fearful toll of European manhood and resources. American intervention in 1917 tipped the scales against the Central Powers, and in September 1918 the German government asked for an armistice on the basis of the moderate peace proposals—the Fourteen Points—of President Woodrow Wilson. The armistice was concluded in November but the ultimate settlement —the Treaty of Versailles—imposed a series of unexpectedly harsh penalties on Germany and Austria. The Austro-Hungarian kingdom was broken up into its component parts, and Germany was stripped of extensive territories, "permanently" demilitarized, and saddled with a heavy indemnity.

The war had wrought a profound transformation in European politics. Crowns fell in Russia, Austria, and Germany. Russia became Europe's first Communist state; Austria and Germany became republics. The European economy was badly shaken, and European optimism gave way to disillusionment. The economic and political turbulence of the postwar years provoked the rise of authoritarian dictatorships first in Italy, later in Germany. Right-wing totalitarianism under Mussolini in Fascist Italy and Hitler in Nazi Germany, and left-wing totalitarianism in Soviet Russia, came increasingly to threaten the security of Europe's democracies. Hitler in particular, playing on the themes of anti-Semitism and the "betrayal" at Versailles, re-armed Germany and pursued a policy of systematic aggression against neighboring states. Throughout Europe and the world, so it seemed, the nineteenth-century wave of democratic liberalism was giving way to a new wave of nationalist and Communist dictatorship.

Part I

WORLD WAR I

A. The Coming of War

THE AUSTRO-HUNGARIAN ULTIMATUM to Serbia, July 23, 1914, following upon the assassination at Sarajevo, is perhaps the key document in the outbreak of World War I. The assassin was a member of a Serbian secret society rather than a direct agent of the Serbian government, but Serbian officials had been aware of the plot, and the government cannot be regarded as innocent. To Austria, the assassination provided a priceless opportunity to humble and humiliate her small but troublesome neighbor, and that was precisely the purpose of the ultimatum. Austria did not expect Serbia to accept it, and Serbian rejection would provide Austria with an excuse for war. Austria banked on the hope that such a war would not spread—that Russia would not come to Serbia's defense. Serbia's response to the ultimatum was conciliatory, but she rejected the demand that Austrian agents be allowed to enter Serbia to join with Serbian officials in the investigation of the assassination. This demand was clearly an affront to Serbia's sovereignty. On July 28, Austria-Hungary declared war against Serbia, and within two weeks the major powers of Europe were at war.

1. THE AUSTRO-HUNGARIAN ULTIMATUM TO SERBIA, 1914

SOURCE. Max Montgelas and Walter Schuckling, eds., *Outbreak of the World War: Documents Collected by Karl Kautsky*, New York: Carnegie Endowment for International Peace, 1924, Supplement I, pp. 603–606. Reprinted by permission of the Carnegie Endowment for International Peace.

Vienna, July 22, 1914

Your Excellency will present the following note to the Royal Government on the afternoon of Thursday, July 23:

On the 31st of March, 1909, the Royal Serbian Minister at the Court of Vienna made, in the name of his Government, the following declaration to the Imperial and Royal Government:

Serbia recognizes that her rights were not affected by the state of affairs created in Bosnia, and states that she will accordingly accommodate herself to the decisions to be reached by the Powers in connection with Article 25 of the Treaty of Berlin. Serbia, in accepting the advice of the Great Powers, binds herself to desist from the attitude of protest and opposition which she has assumed with regard to the annexation since October last, and she furthermore binds herself to alter the tendency of her present policy toward Austria-Hungary, and to live on the footing of friendly and neighborly relations with the latter in the future.

Now the history of the past few years, and particularly the painful events of the 28th of June, have proved the existence of a subversive movement in Serbia, whose object it is to separate certain portions of its territory from the Austro-Hungarian Monarchy. This movement, which came into being under the very eyes of the Serbian Government, subsequently found expression outside of the territory of the Kingdom in acts of terrorism, in a number of attempts at assassination, and in murders.

Far from fulfilling the formal obligations contained in its declaration of the 31st of March, 1909, the Royal Serbian Government has done nothing to suppress this movement. It has tolerated the criminal activities of the various unions and associations directed against the Monarchy, the unchecked utterances of the press, the glorification of the authors of assassinations, the participation of officers and officials in subversive intrigues; it has tolerated an unhealthy propaganda in its public instruction; and it has tolerated, finally, every manifestation which could betray the people of Serbia into hatred of the Monarchy and contempt for its institutions.

This toleration of which the Royal Serbian Government was guilty, was still in evidence at that moment when the events of the twenty-eighth of June exhibited to the whole world the dreadful consequences of such tolerance.

It is clear from the statements and confessions of the criminal authors of the assassination of the twenty-eighth of June, that the murder at Sarajevo was conceived at Belgrade, that the murderers received the weapons and the bombs with which they were equipped from Serbian officers and officials who belonged to the *Narodna Odbrana,* and, finally, that the dispatch of the criminals and of their weapons to Bosnia was arranged and effected under the conduct of Serbian frontier authorities.

The results brought out by the inquiry no longer permit the Imperial and Royal Government to maintain the attitude of patient tolerance which it has observed for years toward those agitations which center at Belgrade and are spread thence into the territories of the Monarchy. Instead, these results impose upon the Imperial and Royal Government the obligation to put an end to those intrigues, which constitute a standing menace to the peace of the Monarchy.

In order to attain this end, the Imperial and Royal Government finds itself compelled to demand that the Serbian Government give official assurance that it will condemn the propaganda directed against Austria-Hungary, that is to say, the whole body of the efforts whose ultimate object it is to separate from the Monarchy territories that belong to it; and that it will obligate itself to suppress with all the means at its command this criminal and terroristic propaganda.

In order to give these assurances a character of solemnity, the Royal Serbian Government will publish on the first page of its official organ of July 26/13, the following declaration:

"The Royal Serbian Government condemns the propaganda directed against Austria-Hungary, that is to say, the whole body of the efforts whose ultimate object it is to separate from the Austro-Hungarian Monarchy territories that belong to it, and it most sincerely regrets the dreadful consequences of these criminal transactions.

"The Royal Serbian Government regrets that Serbian officers and officials should have taken part in the above-mentioned propaganda and thus have endangered the friendly and neighborly relations, to the cultivation of which the Royal Government had most solemnly pledged itself by its declarations of March 31, 1909.

"The Royal Government, which disapproves and repels every idea and every attempt to interfere in the destinies of the population of whatever portion of Austria-Hungary, regards it as its duty most expressly to call attention of the officers, officials and the whole population of the kingdom to the fact that for the future it will proceed with the utmost rigor against any persons who shall become guilty of any such activities, activities to prevent and to suppress which, the Government will bend every effort."

This declaration shall be brought to the attention of the Royal army simultaneously by an order of the day from His Majesty the King, and by publication in the official organ of the army.

The Royal Serbian Government will furthermore pledge itself:

1. to suppress every publication which shall incite to hatred and contempt of the Monarchy, and the general tendency of which shall be directed against the territorial integrity of the latter;

2. to proceed at once to the dissolution of the *Narodna Odbrana,* to confiscate all of its means of propaganda, and in the same manner to proceed against the other unions and associations in Serbia which occupy themselves with propaganda against Austria-Hungary; the Royal Government will take such measures as are necessary to make sure that the dissolved associations may not continue their activities under other names or in other forms;

3. to eliminate without delay from public instruction in Serbia, every-thing, whether connected with the teaching corps or with the methods of teaching, that serves or may serve to nourish the propaganda against Austria-Hungary;

4. to remove from the military and administrative service in general all officers and officials who have been guilty of carrying on the propa-ganda against Austria-Hungary, whose names the Imperial and Royal Government reserves the right to make known to the Royal Government when communicating the material evidence now in its possession;

5. to agree to the coöperation in Serbia of the organs of the Imperial and Royal Government in the suppression of the subversive movement directed against the integrity of the Monarchy;

6. to institute a judicial inquiry against every participant in the con-spiracy of the twenty-eighth of June who may be found in Serbian terri-tory; the organs of the Imperial and Royal Government delegated for this purpose will take part in the proceedings held for this purpose;

7. to undertake with all haste the arrest of Major Voislav Tankositch and of one Milan Ciganovitch, a Serbian official, who have been compro-mised by the results of the inquiry;

8. by efficient measures to prevent the participation of Serbian authori-ties in the smuggling of weapons and explosives across the frontier; to dismiss from the service and to punish severely those members of the Frontier Service at Schabats and Losnitza who assisted the authors of the crime of Sarajevo to cross the frontier;

9. to make explanations to the Imperial and Royal Government con-cerning the unjustifiable utterances of high Serbian functionaries in Serbia and abroad, who, without regard for their official position, have not hesitated to express themselves in a manner hostile toward Austria-Hungary since the assassination of the twenty-eighth of June;

10. to inform the Imperial and Royal Government without delay of the execution of the measures comprised in the foregoing points.

The Imperial and Royal Government awaits the reply of the Royal Government by Saturday, the twenty-fifth instant, at 6 p.m., at the latest.

THE BRILLIANT GERMAN PAINTER George Grosz, in his Fit for Active Service *and similar works, bitterly satirized Prussian militarism.*

2. GEORGE GROSZ, *FIT FOR ACTIVE SERVICE*, 1918

B. The Making of Peace

IN 1918 GERMANY, exhausted by war, agreed to enter the armistice negotiations and was obliged to accept a harsh series of Armistice Demands (November 10, 1918) (1), and the final peace settlement—the Treaty of Versailles (June 28, 1919) (2)—was harsher still. The signing of the Treaty was deliberately scheduled to coincide with the fifth anniversary of Sarajevo, and the place of the signing—the Hall of Mirrors in the Versailles Palace—was chosen because it was the setting where the now-defunct German Empire had been proclaimed after the Franco-Prussian War. The clauses of the Treaty, no less than the circumstances of its signing, were calculated to humble Germany.

1. THE ARMISTICE DEMANDS, 1918

SOURCE. Louis Snyder, ed., *Fifty Major Documents of The Twentieth Century,* Anvil #5, Princeton: D. Van Nostrand Co., Inc. 1955, pp. 29–30. From Official German Government release, *Kreuz-Zeitung,* November 11, 1918. Copyright 1955, D. Van Nostrand Co., Inc., Princeton, N. J. Reprinted by permission of D. Van Nostrand Co., Inc.

1. Effective six hours after signing.

2. Immediate clearing of Belgium, France, Alsace-Lorraine, to be concluded within 14 days. Any troops remaining in these areas to be interned or taken as prisoners of war.

3. Surrender 5000 cannon (chiefly heavy), 30,000 machine guns, 3000 trench mortars, 2000 planes.

4. Evacuation of the left bank of the Rhine, Mayence, Coblence, Cologne, occupied by the enemy to a radius of 30 kilometers deep.

5. On the right bank of the Rhine a neutral zone from 30 to 40 kilometers deep, evacuation within 11 days.

6. Nothing to be removed from the territory on the left bank of the Rhine, all factories, railroads, etc. to be left intact.

7. Surrender of 5000 locomotives, 150,000 railway coaches, 10,000 trucks.

8. Maintenance of enemy occupation troops through Germany.

9. In the East all troops to withdraw behind the boundaries of August 1, 1914, fixed time not given.

10. Renunciation of the Treaties of Brest-Litovsk and Bucharest.

11. Unconditional surrender of East Africa.

12. Return of the property of the Belgian Bank, Russian and Rumanian gold.

13. Return of prisoners of war without reciprocity.

14. Surrender of 160 U-boats, 8 light cruisers, 6 Dread-noughts; the rest of the fleet to be disarmed and controlled by the Allies in neutral or Allied harbors.

15. Assurance of free trade through the Cattegat Sound; clearance of mine-fields and occupation of all forts and batteries, through which transit could be hindered.

16. The blockade remains in effect. All German ships to be captured.

17. All limitations by Germany on neutral shipping to be removed.

18. Armistice lasts 30 days.

2. EXTRACTS FROM THE TREATY OF VERSAILLES, 1919

SOURCE. United States, 66th Congress, 1st Session, Senate Document No. 49, *Treaty of Peace with Germany*, Washington, 1919.

ARTICLE 31. Germany, recognizing that the Treaties of April 19, 1839, which established the status of Belgium before the war, no longer conform to the requirements of the situation, consents to the abrogation of the said treaties and undertakes immediately to recognize and to observe whatever conventions may be entered into by the Principal Allied and Associated Powers, or by any of them, in concert with the Governments of Belgium and of the Netherlands, to replace the said Treaties of 1839. If her formal adhesion should be required to such conventions or to any of their stipulations, Germany undertakes immediately to give it. . . .

ARTICLE 42. Germany is forbidden to maintain or construct any fortifications either on the left bank of the Rhine or on the right bank to the west of a line drawn 50 kilometres to the East of the Rhine.

ARTICLE 43. In the area defined above the maintenance and the assembly of armed forces, either permanently or temporarily, and military manœuvres of any kind, as well as the upkeep of all permanent works for mobilization, are in the same way forbidden.

ARTICLE 44. In case Germany violates in any manner whatever the provisions of Articles 42 and 43, she shall be regarded as committing a hostile act against the Powers signatory of the present Treaty and as calculated to disturb the peace of the world.

ARTICLE 45. As compensation for the destruction of the coal-mines in the north of France and as part payment towards the total reparation due from Germany for the damage resulting from the war, Germany cedes to France in full and absolute possession, with exclusive rights of exploitation, unencumbered and free from all debts and charges of any kind, the coal-mines situated in the Saar Basin as defined in Article 48. . . .

ARTICLE 49. Germany renounces in favour of the League of Nations, in the capacity of trustee, the government of the territory defined above.

ARTICLE 50. The stipulations under which the cession of the mines in the Saar Basin shall be carried out, together with the measures intended to guarantee the rights and the well-being of the inhabitants and the government of the territory, as well as the conditions in accordance with which the plebiscite hereinbefore provided for is to be made, are laid down in the Annex hereto. This Annex shall be considered as an integral part of the present Treaty, and Germany declares her adherence to it.

ARTICLE 51. The territories which were ceded to Germany in accordance with the Preliminaries of Peace signed at Versailles on February 26, 1871, and the Treaty of Frankfurt of May 10, 1871, are restored to French sovereignty as from the date of the Armistice of November 11, 1918.

The provisions of the Treaties establishing the delimitation of the frontiers before 1871 shall be restored. . . .

ARTICLE 80. Germany acknowledges and will respect strictly the independence of Austria, within the frontiers which may be fixed in a Treaty between that State and the Principal Allied and Associated Powers; she agrees that this independence shall be inalienable, except with the consent of the Council of the League of Nations.

ARTICLE 81. Germany, in conformity with the action already taken by the Allied and Associated Powers, recognizes the complete independence of the Czecho-Slovak State which will include the autonomous territory of the Ruthenians to the south of the Carpathians. Germany hereby recognizes the frontiers of this State as determined by the Principal Allied and Associated Powers and the other interested States. . . .

ARTICLE 87. Germany, in conformity with the action already taken by the Allied and Associated Powers, recognizes the complete independence of Poland, and renounces in her favour all rights and title over the territory [of Poland].

The boundaries of Poland not laid down in the present Treaty will be subsequently determined by the Principal Allied and Associated Powers.

A Commission consisting of seven members, five of whom shall be nominated by the Principal Allied and Associated Powers, one by Germany and one by Poland, shall be constituted fifteen days after the coming into force of the present Treaty to delimit on the spot the frontier line between Poland and Germany.

The decisions of the Commission will be taken by a majority of votes and shall be binding upon the parties concerned.

ARTICLE 88. In the portion of Upper Silesia included within the boundaries described below, the inhabitants will be called upon to indicate by a vote whether they wish to be attached to Germany or to Poland. . . .

ARTICLE 99. Germany renounces in favour of the Principal Allied and Associated Powers all rights and title over the territories included between the Baltic, the north-eastern frontier of East Prussia as defined in Article 28 of Part II (Boundaries of Germany) of the present Treaty and the former frontier between Germany and Russia.

Germany undertakes to accept the settlement made by the Principal Allied and Associated Powers in regard to these territories, particularly in so far as concerns the nationality of the inhabitants. . . .

ARTICLE 102. The Principal Allied and Associated Powers undertake to establish the town of Danzig, together with the rest of the territory described in Article 100, as a Free City. It will be placed under the protection of the League of Nations. . . .

ARTICLE 119. Germany renounces in favour of the Principal Allied and Associated Powers all her rights and titles over her oversea possessions. . . .

ARTICLE 141. Germany renounces all rights, titles and privileges conferred on her by the General Act of Algeciras of April 7, 1906, and by the Franco-German Agreements of February 9, 1909, and November 4, 1911. All treaties, agreements, arrangements and contracts concluded by her with the Sherifian Empire are regarded as abrogated as from August 3, 1914.

In no case can Germany take advantage of these instruments and she undertakes not to intervene in any way in negotiations relating to Morocco which may take place between France and the other Powers. . . .

ARTICLE 156. Germany renounces, in favour of Japan, all her rights, title and privileges—particularly those concerning the territory of Kiao-chow, railways, mines and submarine cables—which she acquired in virtue of the Treaty concluded by her with China on March 6, 1898, and of all other arrangements relative to the Province of Shantung.

All German rights in the Tsingtao-Tsinanfu Railway, including its branch lines, together with its subsidiary property of all kinds, stations, shops, fixed and rolling stock, mines, plant and material for the exploitation of the mines, are and remain acquired by Japan, together with all rights and privileges attaching thereto.

The German State submarine cables from Tsingtao to Shanghai and from Tsingtao to Chefoo, with all the rights, privileges and properties attaching thereto, are similarly acquired by Japan, free and clear of all charges and encumbrances. . . .

ARTICLE 159. The German military forces shall be demobilized and reduced as prescribed hereinafter.

ARTICLE 160. By a date which must not be later than March 31, 1920, the German Army must not comprise more than seven divisions of infantry and three divisions of cavalry.

After that date the total number of effectives in the Army of the States constituting Germany must not exceed one hundred thousand men, including officers and establishments of depots. The Army shall be devoted exclusively to the maintenance of order within the territory and to the control of the frontiers.

The total effective strength of officers, including the personnel of staffs, whatever their composition, must not exceed four thousand.

. . . The Great German General Staff and all similar organizations shall be dissolved and may not be reconstituted in any form. . . .

ARTICLE 179. All fortified works, fortresses and field works situated in German territory to the west of a line drawn fifty kilometres to the east of the Rhine shall be disarmed and dismantled. . . .

ARTICLE 181. After the expiration of a period of two months from the coming into force of the present Treaty the German naval forces in commission must not exceed:

6 battleships of the *Deutschland* or *Lothringen* type,

6 light cruisers,

12 destroyers,

12 torpedo boats,

or an equal number of ships constructed to replace them as provided in Article 190.

No submarines are to be included.

All other warships, except where there is provision to the contrary in the present Treaty, must be placed in reserve or devoted to commercial purposes. . . .

ARTICLE 198. The armed forces of Germany must not include any military or naval air forces. . . .

ARTICLE 231. The Allied and Associated Governments affirm and Germany accepts the responsibility of Germany and her allies for causing all the loss and damage to which the Allied and Associated Governments and their nationals have been subjected as a consequence of the war imposed upon them by the aggression of Germany and her allies.

ARTICLE 232. The Allied and Associated Governments recognize that the resources of Germany are not adequate, after taking into account permanent diminutions of such resources which will result from other provisions of the present Treaty, to make complete reparation for all such loss and damage.

The Allied and Associated Governments, however, require, and Germany undertakes, that she will make compensation for all damage done to the civilian population of the Allied and Associated Powers and to their property during the period of the belligerency of each as an Allied or Associated Power against Germany by such aggression by land, by sea and from the air, and in general all damage as defined in Annex I hereto.

ARTICLE 233. The amount of the above damage for which compensation is to be made by Germany shall be determined by an Inter-Allied Commission, to be called the *Reparation Commission* and constituted in the form and with the powers set forth hereunder and in Annexes II to VII inclusive hereto.

This Commission shall consider the claims and give to the German Government a just opportunity to be heard.

The findings of the Commission as to the amount of damage defined as above shall be concluded and notified to the German Government on or before May 1, 1921, as representing the extent of that Government's obligations.

ARTICLE 234. The Reparation Commissions shall after May 1, 1921, from time to time, consider the resources and capacity of Germany, and, after giving her representatives a just opportunity to be heard, shall have discretion to extend the date, and to modify the form of payments, such as are to be provided for in accordance with Article 233; but not to cancel any part, except with the specific authority of the several Governments represented upon the Commission. . . .

ARTICLE 428. As a guarantee for the execution of the present Treaty by Germany, the German territory situated to the west of the Rhine, together with the bridgeheads, will be occupied by Allied and Associated troops for a period of fifteen years from the coming into force of the present Treaty. . . .

ARTICLE 431. If before the expiration of the period of fifteen years Germany complies with all the undertakings resulting from the present Treaty, the occupying forces will be withdrawn immediately.

Part II

TOTALITARIANISM

A. Communism

THE RISE OF THE BOLSHEVIKS to power in Russia in the October Revolution of 1917 marked the establishment of the first Communist state. We have already encountered the Communist philosophy in an earlier section (Section Eleven, II) and have seen how Lenin developed his interpretation of Communist ideology on strict Marxist lines (Section Eleven, II, B, 1; compare Section Thirteen, III, B, 1). At the Second Congress of the Third Communist International, Moscow, 1920, Lenin set forth the revolutionary programme of international Communism in uncompromising terms.

1. LENIN ON THE COMMUNIST PROGRAMME, 2ND CONGRESS OF THE THIRD COMMUNIST INTERNATIONAL, MOSCOW, 1920

SOURCE. V. I. Lenin, *Collected Works*, English ed., Moscow, Vol. IX.

1. A characteristic feature of the present moment in the development of the international Communist movement is the fact that in all the capitalist countries the best representatives of the revolutionary proletariat have completely understood the fundamental principles of the Communist International, namely, the dictatorship of the proletariat and the power of the Soviets; and with a loyal enthusiasm have placed themselves on the side of the Communist International. A still more important and great step forward is the unlimited sympathy with these principles manifested by the wider masses not only of the proletariat of the towns, but also by the advanced portion of the agrarian workers.

On the other hand two mistakes or weaknesses in the extraordinarily rapidly increasing international Communist movement have shown themselves. One very serious weakness directly dangerous to the success of the cause of the liberation of the proletariat consists in the fact that some of the old leaders and old parties of the Second International—partly half-unconsciously yielding to the wishes and pressures of the masses, partly consciously deceiving them in order to preserve their former role of agents and supporters of the bourgeoisie inside the Labor movement—are declaring their conditional or even unconditional affiliation to the Third International, while remaining, in relality, in the whole practice of their party and political work, on the level of the Second International. Such a state of things is absolutely inadmissible, because it demoralizes the masses, hinders the development of a strong Communist Party, and lowers their respect for the Third International by threatening repetition of such betrayals as that of the Hungarian Social-Democrats, who had rapidly assumed the disguise of Communists. The second much less important mistake, which is, for the most part, a malady inherent in the party growth of the movement, is the tendency to be extremely "left," which leads to an erroneous valuation of the role and duties of the party in respect to the class and to the mass, and of the obligation of the revolutionary Communists to work in the bourgeois parliaments and reactionary labor unions.

The duty of the Communists is not to gloss over any of the weaknesses of their movement, but to criticize them openly, in order to get rid of them promptly and radically. To this end it is necessary, 1) to establish concretely, especially on the basis of the already acquired practical experience, the meaning of the term: "Dictatorship of the Proletariat" and "Soviet Power," and, 2) to point out what could and should be in all countries the immediate and systematic preparatory work to realizing these formulas; and, 3) to indicate the ways and means of curing our movement of its defects.

2. The victory of Socialism over Capitalism—as the first step to Communism—demands the accomplishment of the three following tasks by the proletariat, as the only really revolutionary class:

The first step is to lay low the exploiters, and above all the bourgeoisie as their chief economic and political representative; to defeat them completely; to crush their resistance; to render impossible any attempts on their part to reimpose the yoke of capitalism and wage-slavery.

The second is to inspire and lead in the footsteps of the revolutionary advance guard of the proletariat, its Communist party—not only the whole proletariat or the great majority, but the entire mass of workers and those exploited by capital; to enlighten, organize, instruct, and discipline them during the course of the bold and mercilessly firm struggle against the exploiters; to wrench this enormous majority of the population in all the capitalist countries out of their state of dependence on the bourgeoisies; to instill in them, through practical experience, confidence in the leading role of the proletariat and its revolutionary advance guard. The third is to neutralize or render harmless the inevitable fluctuations between the bourgeoisie and the proletariat, between bourgeois democracy and Soviet Power, on the part of that rather numerous class in all advanced countries—although constituting a minority of the population—the small owners and proprietors in agriculture, industry, commerce, and the corresponding layers of intellectuals, employees, and so on.

The first and second tasks are independent ones, demanding each of them their special methods of action in respect to the exploiters and to the exploited. The third task results from the two first, demanding only a skilful, timely, supple combination of the methods of the first and second kind, depending on the concrete circumstances of each separate case of fluctuation.

3. Under the circumstances which have been created in the whole world, and especially in the most advanced, most powerful, most enlightened and freest capitalist countries by militarist imperialism—oppression of colonies and weaker nations, the universal imperialist slaughter, the "peace" of Versailles—to admit the idea of a voluntary submission of the capitalists to the will of the majority of the exploited, of a peaceful, reformist passage to Socialism, is not only to give proof of an extreme petty bourgeois stupidity, but it is a direct deception of the workmen, a disguisal of capitalist wage-slavery, a concealment of the truth. This truth is that the bourgeoisie, the most enlightened and democratic portion of the bourgeoisie, is even now not stopping at deceit and crime, at the slaughter of millions of workmen and peasants, in order to retain the right of private ownership over the means of production. Only a violent defeat of the bourgeoisie, the confiscation of its property, the annihilation of the entire bourgeois governmental apparatus, parliamentary, judicial, military, bureaucratic, administrative, municipal, etc., even the individual exile or internment of the most stubborn and dangerous exploiters, the establishment of a strict control over them for the repression of all inevitable attempts at resistance and restoration of capitalist slavery—only such measures will be able to guarantee the complete submission of the whole class of exploiters.

On the other hand, it is the same disguising of capitalism and bourgeois democracy, the same deceiving of the workmen, when the old parties and old leaders of the Second International admit the idea that the majority of the workers and exploited will be able to acquire a clear Socialist consciousness, firm Socialist convictions and character under the conditions of capitalist enslavement, under the yoke of the bourgeoisie, which assumes an endless variety of forms—the more refined and at the same time the more cruel and pitiless, the more cultured the given capitalist nation. In reality it is only when the advance guard of the proletariat, supported by the whole class as the only revolutionary one, or a majority of the same, will have overthrown the exploiters, crushed them, freed all the exploited from their position of slaves, improved their conditions of life immediately at the expense of the expropriated capitalists—only after that, and during the very course of the acute class struggle, it will be possible to bring about the enlightenment, education and organization of the wildest masses of workers and exploited around the proletariat, under its influence and direction; to cure them of their egotism, their non-solidarity, their vices and weaknesses engendered by private ownership, and to transform them into free workers.

4. For victory over capitalism a correct correlation between the leading Communist Party—the revolutionary class, the proletariat—and the masses, i.e., the whole mass of workers and exploited, is essential. If the Communist Party is really the advance guard of the revolutionary class, if it includes the best representatives of the class, if it consists of perfectly conscious and loyal Communists, enlightened by experience gained in the stubborn revolutionary struggle—if it can be bound indissolubly with the entire life of its class, and through the latter with the whole mass of the exploited, and if it can inspire full confidence in this class and this mass, only then is it capable of leading the proletariat in the pitiless, decisive, and final struggle against all the forces of capitalism. On the other hand, only under the leadership of such a Party will the proletariat be able to employ all the forces of its revolutionary onslaught, nullifying the inevitable apathy and partial resistance of the insignificant minority of the demoralized labor aristocracy, the old trade-union and guild leaders, etc. Only then will the proletariat be able to display its power which is immeasurably greater than its share in the population, by reason of the economic organization of capitalist society itself. Lastly, only when practically freed from the yoke of the bourgeoisie and the bourgeois governing apparatus, only after acquiring the possibility of freely (from all capitalist exploitation) organizing into its own Soviets, will the mass— i.e., the total of all the workers and exploited—employ for the first time in history all the initiative and energy of tens of millions of people, formerly crushed by capitalism. Only when the Soviets will become the only State apparatus, will effectual participation in the administration be realized for the entire mass of the exploited, who, even under the most cultured and free bourgeois democracy, remain practically excluded from participation in the administration. Only in the Soviets does the mass really begin to study, not out of books, but out of its own practical experience, the work of Socialist construction, the creation of a new social discipline, a free union of free workers.

6. The conquest of political power by the proletariat does not put a stop to its class struggle against the bourgeoisie; on the contrary, it makes

the struggle especially broad, acute, and pitiless. All the groups, parties, leaders of the Labor movement, fully or partially on the side of reformism, the "center," and so on, turn inevitably, during the most acute periods of the struggle, either to the side of the bourgeoisie or to that of the wavering ones, and the most dangerous are added to the number of the unreliable friends of the vanquished proletariat. Therefore the preparation of the dictatorship of the proletariat demands not only an increased struggle against all reformists and "centrist" tendencies, but a modification of the nature of this struggle.

The struggle should not be limited to an explanation of the fallacy of such tendencies, but it should stubbornly and mercilessly denounce any leader in the Labor movement who may be manifesting such tendencies, otherwise the proletariat will not know whom it must trust in the most decisive struggle against the bourgeoisie. The struggle is such, that the slightest hesitation or weakness in the denunciation of those who show themselves to be reformists or "centrists," means a direct increase of the danger that the power of the proletariat may be overthrown by the bourgeoisie, which will on the morrow utilize in favor of the counter-revolution all that which to short-sighted people appears only as a "theoretical difference of opinion" to-day.

7. In particular one cannot stop at the usual doctrinaire refutation of all "collaboration" between the proletariat and the bourgeoisie:

The simple defense of "liberty and equality," under the condition of preserving the right of private ownership of the means of production, becomes transformed under the conditions of the dictatorship of the proletariat—which will never be able to suppress completely all private ownership—into a "collaboration" with the bourgeoisie, which undermines directly the power of the working class. The dictatorship of the proletariat means the strengthening and defense, by means of the ruling power of the State, of the "non-liberty" of the exploiter to continue his work of oppression and exploitation, the "inequality" of the proprietor (i.e., of the person who has taken for himself personally the means of production created by public labor and the proletariat). That which before the victory of the proletariat seems but a theoretical difference of opinion on the question of "democracy," becomes inevitably on the morrow of the victory, a question which can only be decided by force of arms. Consequently, without a radical modification of the whole nature of the struggle against the "centrists" and "defenders of democracy," even a preliminary preparation of the mass for the realization of a dictatorship of the proletariat is impossible.

8. The dictatorship of the proletariat is the most decisive and revolutionary form of class struggle between the proletariat and the bourgeoi-

sie. Such a struggle can be successful only when the revolutionary advance guard of the proletariat leads the majority. The preparation of the dictatorship of the proletariat demands, therefore, not only the elucidation of the bourgeois nature of all reformism, all defense of "democracy," with the preservation of the right to the ownership of the means of production; not only the denunciation of such tendencies, which in practice mean the defense of the bourgeoisie inside the Labor movement— but it demands also the replacing of the old leaders by Communists in all kinds of proletarian organizations, not only political, but industrial, co-operative, educational, etc. The more lasting, complete, and solid the rule of the bourgeois democracy has been in any country, the more has it been possible for the bourgeoisie to appoint as labor leaders men who have been educated by it, imbued with its views and prejudices and very frequently directly or indirectly bribed by it. It is necessary to remove all these representatives of the Labor aristocracy, all such "bourgeois" workmen, from their posts and replace them by even inexperienced workers, so long as these are in unity with the exploited masses, and enjoy the latter's confidence in the struggle against the exploiters. The dictatorship of the proletariat will demand the appointment of such inexperienced workmen to the most responsible State functions, otherwise the rule of the Labor government will be powerless and it will not have the support of the masses.

9. The dictatorship of the proletariat is the most complete realization of a leadership over all workers and exploited, who have been oppressed, beaten down, crushed, intimidated, dispersed, deceived by the class of capitalists, on the part of the only class prepared for such a leading role by the whole history of capitalism. Therefore the preparation of the dictatorship of the proletariat must begin immediately and in all places by means of the following methods among others:

In every organization, union, association—beginning with the proletarian ones at first, and afterwards in all those of the non-proletarian workers and exploited masses (political, professional, military, co-operative, educational, sporting, etc., etc.) must be formed groups or nuclei of Communists—mostly open ones, but also secret ones which become necessary in each case when the arrest or exile of their members or the dispersal of their organization is threatened; and these nuclei, in close contact with one another and with the central Party, exchanging experiences, carrying on the work of propaganda, campaign, organization, adapting themselves to all the branches of social life, to all the various forms and subdivisions of the working masses, must systematically train themselves, the Party, the class, and the masses by such multiform work.

At the same time it is most important to work out practically the necessary methods on the one hand in respect to the "leaders" or responsible representatives, who are very frequently hopelessly infected with petty bourgeois and imperialist prejudices; on the other hand, in respect to the masses, who, especially after the imperialist slaughter, are mostly inclined to listen to and accept the doctrine of the necessity of leadership of the proletariat as the only way out of capitalistic enslavement. The masses must be approached with patience and caution, and with an understanding of the peculiarities, the special psychology of each layer, each profession of these masses.

10. In particular one of the groups or nuclei of the Communists deserves the exclusive attention and care of the party, namely, the parliamentary faction, i.e., the group of members of the Party who are members of bourgeois representative institutions. . . . from this very tribune, the Communists must carry on their work of propaganda, agitation, organization, explaining to the masses why the dissolution of the bourgeois parliament (Constituent Assembly) by the national Congress of Soviets was a legitimate proceeding at the time in Russia (as it will be in all countries in due time). . . .

11. One of the chief causes of difficulty in the revolutionary Labor movement in the advanced capitalist countries lies in the fact that owing to colonial dominions and super-dividends of a financial capital, etc., capital has been able to attract a comparatively more solid and broader group of a small minority of the labor aristocracy. The latter enjoy better conditions of pay and are most of all impregnated with the spirit of professional narrow-mindedness, bourgeois and imperialist prejudices. This is the true social "support" of the Second International reformists and centrists, and at the present moment almost the chief social support of the bourgeoisie.

Not even preliminary preparation of the proletariat for the overthrow of the bourgeoisie is possible without an immediate, systematic, widely organized and open struggle against the group which undoubtedly—as experience has already proved—will furnish plenty of men for the White Guards of the bourgeoisie after the victory of the proletariat. All the parties adhering to the Third International must at all costs put into practice the mottoes: "deeper into the masses," "in closer contact with the masses," understanding by the word "masses" the entire mass of workers and those exploited by capitalism, especially the less organized and enlightened. . . .

12. For all countries, even for most free "legal" and "peaceful" ones in the sense of a lesser acuteness in the class struggle, the period has arrived, when it has become absolutely necessary for every Communist party to join systematically lawful and unlawful work, lawful and unlawful organization. . . . It is especially necessary to carry on unlawful work in the army, navy, and police, as, after the imperialist slaughter, all the gov-

ernments in the world are becoming afraid of the national armies, open to all peasants and workingmen, and they are setting up in secret all kinds of select military organizations recruited from the bourgeoisie and especially provided with improved technical equipment.

On the other hand, it is also necessary, in all cases without exception, not to limit oneself to unlawful work, but to carry on also lawful work overcoming all difficulties, founding a lawful press and lawful organizations under the most diverse, and in case of need, frequently changing names.

ONE OF THE CHARACTERISTICS of twentieth-century politics is the tendency for governments, whether liberal or totalitarian, to describe themselves as "democratic." This approach is clearly evident in a Soviet document of November 28, 1936, asserting the democracy of Stalin's 1936 Constitution of the USSR. Russia nevertheless remained a single-party state whose elections and legislative bodies were firmly controlled by the Communist hierarchy and whose people were kept under the surveillance of the secret police.

2. "DEMOCRACY" IN THE 1936 CONSTITUTION OF THE USSR

SOURCE. *International Press Correspondence,* English edition, November 28, 1936, p. 139.

Finally, there is one group of critics [who] charge that the draft makes no change in the existing position in the U.S.S.R., that it leaves the dictatorship of the working class intact, does not provide for the freedom of political parties and preserves the present leading position of the Communist Party in the U.S.S.R. At the same time, this group of critics believes that the absence of freedom for parties in the U.S.S.R. is an indication of the violation of fundamental principles of democracy.

I must admit that the Draft New Constitution really does leave in force the regime of the dictatorship of the working class and also leaves unchanged the present leading position of the Communist Party in the U.S.S.R.

If our venerable critics regard this as a shortcoming of the Draft Constitution, this can only be regretted. We Bolsheviks, however, consider this as a merit of the Draft Constitution. As for the freedom of various political parties, we here adhere to somewhat different views. A party is part of a class, its vanguard section. Several parties, and consequently freedom of parties, can only exist in a society, where there are antagonistic classes whose interests are hostile and irreconcilable, where there are, say, capitalists and workers, landlords and peasants, kulaks and poor peasants, and so on. But in the U.S.S.R. there are no longer such classes as capitalists, landlords, kulaks and so on. There are only two classes in the U.S.S.R., workers and peasants, whose interests are not only not antagonistic, but on the contrary, are amicable. Consequently, in the U.S.S.R. there is no ground for the existence of several parties, not therefore, for the existence of freedom for such parties.

In the U.S.S.R. there are grounds for only one party, the Communist Party. In the U.S.S.R. only one party can exist, the Communist Party, a party which boldly defends the interests of workers and peasants to the very end. And there can hardly be any doubts about the fact that it defends the interests of these classes not so badly.

They talk about democracy, but what is democracy? Democracy in capitalist countries where there are antagonistic classes is, in the last analysis, democracy for the strong, democracy for a propertied minority. Democracy in the U.S.S.R., on the other hand, is democracy for the toilers, is democracy for all. But from this it follows that the principles of democracy are violated, not by the draft of a new Constitution of the U.S.S.R., but by bourgeois constitutions. This is why I think that the Constitution of the U.S.S.R. is the only thoroughly democratic Constitution in the world.

B. Fascism

BENITO MUSSOLINI (1883–1945) rose to power in Italy in 1922. His right-wing ideology was vague and incoherent, based on the cloudy concept of "national rebirth" and on a fervent hostility to leftist radicalism. In an article in the Enciclopaedia Italiana *(1932), Mussolini clarified Fascist doctrine and presented in a somewhat more systematic form his notions of activism, militarism, and ultra-nationalism.*

1. BENITO MUSSOLINI, "THE POLITICAL AND SOCIAL DOCTRINE OF FASCISM," 1932

SOURCE. Benito Mussolini in *International Conciliation*, No. 306, January 1935, pp. 5–17. Reprinted by permission of the Carnegie Endowment for International Peace.

When, in the now distant March of 1919, I summoned a meeting at Milan through the columns of the *Popolo d'Italia* of the surviving members of the Interventionist Party who had themselves been in action, and who had followed me since the creation of the Fascist Revolutionary Party (which took place in the January of 1915), I had no specific doctrinal attitude in mind. I had a living experience of one doctrine only— that of Socialism, from 1903–4 to the winter of 1914—that is to say, about a decade: and from Socialism itself, even though I had taken part in the movement first as a member of the rank and file and then later as a leader, yet I had no experience of its doctrine in practice. My own doctrine, even in this period, had always been a doctrine of action. A unanimous, universally accepted theory of Socialism did not exist after 1905, when the revisionist movement began in Germany under the leadership of Bernstein, while under pressure of the tendencies of the time, a Left Revolutionary movement also appeared, which though never getting further than talk in Italy, in Russian Socialistic circles laid the foundations of Bolshevism. Reformation, Revolution, Centralization—already the echoes of these terms are spent—while in the great stream of Fascism are to be found ideas which began with Sorel, Péguy, with Lagardelle in the "Mouvement Socialiste," and with the Italian trade union movement which throughout the period of 1904–14 was sounding a new note in Italian Socialist circles (already weakened by the betrayal of Giolitti) through Olivetti's *Pagine Libre*, Orano's *La Lupa*, and Enrico Leone's *Divenire Sociale*.

After the War, in 1919, Socialism was already dead as a doctrine: it existed only as hatred. There remained to it only one possibility of action, especially in Italy, reprisals against those who had desired the War and who must now be made to "expiate" its results. The *Popolo d'Italia* was then given the subtitle of "The newspaper of ex-servicemen and producers," and the word "producers" was already the expression of a mental attitude. Fascism was not the nursling of a doctrine worked out beforehand with detailed elaboration; it was born of the need for action and it was itself from the beginning practical rather than theoretical; it was not merely another political party but, even in the first two years, in opposition to all political parties as such, and itself a living movement. The name which I then gave to the organization fixed its character. And yet, if one were to re-read, in the now dusty columns of that date, the report of the meeting in which the *Fasci Italiani di combattimento* were constituted, one would there find no ordered expression of doctrine, but a series of aphorisms, anticipations, and aspirations which, when refined by time from the original ore, were destined after some years to develop into an ordered series of doctrinal concepts, forming the Fascists' political doctrine—different from all others either of the past or the present day.

"If the bourgeoisie," I said then, "think that they will find lightning-conductors in us, they are the more deceived. . . . We want to accustom the working-class to real and effectual leadership, and also to convince them that it is no easy thing to direct an industry or a commercial enterprise successfully. . . . When the succession to the seat of government is open, we must not be unwilling to fight for it. We must make haste; when the present regime breaks down, we must be ready at once to take its place. It is we who have the right to the succession, because it was we who forced the country into the War, and led her to victory. The present method of political representation cannot suffice, we must have a representation direct from the individuals concerned. It may be objected against this program that it is a return to the conception of the corporation, but that is no matter. . . .

Now is it not a singular thing that even on this first day in the Piazza San Sepolcro that word "corporation" arose, which later, in the course of the Revolution, came to express one of the creations of social legislation at the very foundation of the regime?

The years which preceded the March to Rome were years of great difficulty, during which the necessity for action did not permit of research or any complete elaboration of doctrine. The battle had to be fought in the towns and villages. There was much discussion, but—what was more important and more sacred—men died. They knew how to die. Doctrine, beautifully defined and carefully elucidated, with headlines and paragraphs, might be lacking; but there was to take its place something more decisive—Faith. Even so, anyone who can recall the events of the time through the aid of books, articles, votes of congresses, and speeches of great and minor importance—anyone who knows how to research and weigh evidence—will find that the fundamentals of doctrine were cast during the years of conflict. It was precisely in those years that Fascist thought armed itself, was refined, and began the great task of organization. The problem of the relation between the individual citizen and the State; the allied problems of authority and liberty; political and social problems as well as those specifically national—a solution was being sought for all these while at the same time the struggle against Liberalism, Democracy, Socialism, and the Masonic bodies was being carried on, contemporaneously with the "punitive expedition." But, since there was inevitably some lack of system, the adversaries of Fascism have disingenuously denied that it had any capacity to produce a doctrine of its own, though that doctrine was growing and taking shape under their very eyes, even though tumultuously; first, as happens to all ideas in their beginnings, in the aspect of a violent and dogmatic negation, and then in the aspect of positive construction which has found its realization in the laws and institutions of the regime as enacted successively in the years 1926, 1927, and 1928.

Fascism is now a completely individual thing, not only as a regime, but as a doctrine. And this means that today Fascism, exercising its critical sense upon itself and upon others, has formed its own distinct and peculiar point of view, to which it can refer and upon which, therefore, it can act in the face of all problems, practical or intellectual, which confront the world.

And above all, Fascism, the more it considers and observes the future and the development of humanity quite apart from political considerations of the moment, believes neither in the possibility nor the utility of perpetual peace. It thus repudiates the doctrine of Pacifism—born of a renunciation of the struggle and an act of cowardice in the face of sacrifice. War alone brings up to its highest tension all human energy and puts the stamp of nobility upon the peoples who have the courage to meet it. All other trials are substitutes, which never really put men into the position where they have to make the great decision—the alternative of life or death. Thus a doctrine which is founded upon this harmful postulate of peace is hostile to Fascism. And thus hostile to the spirit of Fascism, though accepted for what use they can be in dealing with particular political situations, are all the international leagues and societies which, as history will show, can be scattered to the winds when once strong national feeling is aroused by any motive—sentimental, ideal, or practical. This anti-pacifist spirit is carried by Fascism even into the life of the individual; the proud motto of the Squadrista, "*Me ne frego*" (I do not fear), written on the bandage of the would, is an act of philosophy not only stoic, the summary of a doctrine not only political—it is the education to combat, the acceptance of the risks which combat implies, and a new way of life for Italy. Thus the Fascist accepts life and loves it, knowing nothing of and despising suicide: he rather conceives of life as duty and struggle and conquest, life which should be high and full, lived for oneself, but above all for others—those who are at hand and those who are far distant, contemporaries, and those who will come after.

This "demographic" policy of the regime is the result of the above premise. Thus the Fascist loves in actual fact his neighbor, but this "neighbor" is not merely a vague and undefined concept, this love for one's neighbor puts no obstacle in the way of necessary educational severity, and still less to differentiation of status and to physical distance. Fascism repudiates any universal embrace, and in order to live worthily in the community of civilized peoples watches its contemporaries with vigilant eyes, takes good note of their state of mind and, in the changing trend of their interests, does not allow itself to be deceived by temporary and fallacious appearances.

Such a conception of life makes Fascism the complete opposite of that doctrine, the base of the so-called scientific and Marxian Socialism, the materialist conception of history; according to which the history of human civilization can be explained simply through the conflict of interests among the various social groups and by the change and development in the means and instruments of production. That the changes in the economic field—new discoveries of raw materials, new methods of working them, and the inventions of science—have their importance no one can deny; but that these factors are sufficient to explain the history of humanity excluding all others is an absurd delusion. Fascism, now and always, believes in holiness and in heroism; that is to say, in actions influenced by no economic motive, direct or indirect. And if the economic conception of history be denied, according to which theory men are no more than puppets, carried to and fro by the waves of chance, while the real directing forces are quite out of their control, it follows that the existence of an unchangeable and unchanging class war is also denied—the natural progeny of the economic conception of history. And above all Fascism denies that class war can be the preponderant force in the transformation of society. These two fundamental concepts of Socialism being thus refuted, nothing is left of it but the sentimental aspiration—as old as humanity itself—towards a social convention in which the sorrows and sufferings of the humblest shall be alleviated. But here again Fascism repudiates the conception of "economic" happiness, to be realized by Socialism and, as it were, at a given moment in economic evolution to assure to everyone the maximum of well-being. Fascism denies the materialist conception of happiness as a possibility, and abandons it to its inventors, the economists of the first half of the nineteenth century: that is to say, Fascism denies the validty of the equation, wellbeing = happiness, which would reduce men to the level of animals, caring for one thing only—to be fat and well-fed—and would thus degrade humanity to a purely physical existence.

After Socialism, Fascism combats the whole complex system of democratic ideology, and repudiates it, whether in its theoretical premises or in its practical application. Fascism denies that the majority, by the simple fact that it is a majority, can direct human society; it denies that numbers alone can govern by means of a periodical consultation, and it affirms the immutable, beneficial, and fruitful inequality of mankind, which can never be permanently leveled through the mere operation of a mechanical process such as universal suffrage. The democratic regime may be defined as from time to time giving the people the illusion of sovereignty, while the real effective sovereignty lies in the hands of other concealed and irresponsible forces. Democracy is a regime nominally without a king, but it is ruled by many kings—more absolute, tyrannical, and ruinous than one sole king, even though a tyrant. This explains why Fascism, having first in 1922 (for reasons of expediency) assumed an attitude tending towards republicanism, renounced this point of view before the March to Rome; being convinced that the question of political form is not today of prime importance, and after having studied the examples of monarchies and republics past and present reached the conclusion that monarchy or republicanism are not to be judged, as it were, by an absolute standard; but that they represent forms in which the evolution—political, historical, traditional, or psychological—of a particular country has expressed itself.

Fascism has taken up an attitude of complete opposition to the doctrines of Liberalism, both in the political field and the field of economics. There should be no undue exaggeration (simply with the object of immediate success in controversy) of the importance of Liberalism in the last century, nor should what was but one among many theories which appeared in that period be put forward as a religion for humanity for all time, present and to come. Liberalism only flourished for half a century. It was born in 1830 in reaction against the Holy Alliance, which had been formed with the object of diverting the destinies of Europe back to the period before 1789, and the highest point of its success was the year 1848, when even Pius IX was a Liberal. Immediately after that date it began to decay, for if the year 1848 was a year of light and hope, the following year, 1849, was a year of darkness and tragedy. The Republic of Rome was dealt a mortal blow by a sister republic—that of France—and in the same year Marx launched the gospel of the Socialist religion, the famous *Communist Manifesto*. In 1851 Napoleon III carried out his far from liberal *coup d'état* and reigned in France until 1870, when he was deposed by a popular movement as the consequence of a military defeat which must be counted as one of the most decisive in history. The victor was Bismarck, who knew nothing of the religion of liberty, or the prophets by which that faith was revealed. And it is symptomatic that such a highly civilized people as the Germans were completely ignorant of the religion of liberty during the whole of the nineteenth century. It was nothing but a parenthesis, represented by that body which has been called "The ridiculous Parliament of Frankfort," which lasted only for a short period. Germany attained her national unity quite outside the doctrines of Liberalism

—a doctrine which seems entirely foreign to the German mind, a mind essentially monarchic—while Liberalism is the logical and, indeed, historical forerunner of anarchy. The stages in the achievement of German unity are the three wars of '64, '66, and '70, which were guided by such "Liberals" as Von Moltke and Bismarck. As for Italian unity, its debt to Liberalism is completely inferior in contrast to that which it owes to the work of Mazzini and Garibaldi, who were not Liberals. Had it not been for the intervention of the anti-Liberal Bismarck at Sadowa and Sedan it is very probable that we should never have gained the province of Venice in '66, or been able to enter Rome in '70. From 1870 to 1914 a period began during which even the very high priests of the religion themselves had to recognize the gathering twilight of their faith—defeated as it was by the decadence of literature and atavism in practice—that is to say, Nationalism, Futurism, Fascism. The era of Liberalism, after having accumulated an infinity of Gordian knots, tried to untie them in the slaughter of the World War—and never has any religion demanded of its votaries such a monstrous sacrifice. Perhaps the Liberal Gods were athirst for Blood? But now, today, the Liberal faith must shut the doors of its deserted temples, deserted because the peoples of the world realize that its worship—agnostic in the field of economics and indifferent in the field of politics and morals—well lead, as it has already led, to certain ruin. In addition to this, let it be pointed out that all the political hopes of the present day are anti-Liberal, and it is therefore supremely ridiculous to try to classify this sole creed as outside the judgment of history, as though history were a hunting ground reserved for the professors of Liberalism alone—as though Liberalism weer the final unalterable verdict of civilization.

But the Fascist negation of Socialism, Democracy, and Liberalism must not be taken to mean that Fascism desires to lead the world back to the state of affairs before 1789, the date which seems to be indicated as the opening year of the succeeding semi-Liberal century: we do not desire to turn back; Fascism has not chosen De Maistre for its high-priest. Absolute monarchy has been and can never return, any more than blind acceptance of ecclesiastical authority.

So, too, the privileges of the feudal system "have been," and the division of society into castes impenetrable from outside, and with no intercommunication among themselves: the Fascist conception of authority has nothing to do with such a polity. A party which entirely governs a nation is a fact entirely new to history, there are no possible references or parallels. Fascism uses in its construction whatever elements in the Liberal, Social, or Democratic doctrines still have a living value; it maintains what may be called the certainties which we owe to history, but it rejects all the rest—that is to say, the conception that there can be any doctrine of unquestioned efficacy for all times and all peoples. Given that the nineteenth century was the century of Socialism, Liberalism, and Democracy: political doctrines pass, but humanity remains; and it may rather be expected that this will be a century of Fascism. For if the nineteenth century was the century of individualism (Liberalism always signifying individualism) it may be expected that this will be the century of collectivism, and hence the century of the State. It is a perfectly logical deduction that a new doctrine can utilize all the still vital elements of previous doctrines.

No doctrine has ever been born completely new, completely defined and owing nothing to the past; no doctrine can boast a character of complete originality; it must always derive, if only historically, from the doctrines which have preceded it and develop into further doctrines which will follow. Thus the scientific Socialism of Marx is the heir of the Utopian Socialism of Fourier, of the Owens and of Saint-Simon; thus again the Liberalism of the eighteenth century is linked with all the advanced thought of the seventeenth century, and thus the doctrines of Democracy are the heirs of the Encyclopedists. Every doctrine tends to direct human activity towards a determined objective; but the action of men also reacts upon the doctrine, transform it, adapts it to new needs, or supersedes it with something else. A doctrine then must be no mere exercise in words, but a living act; and thus the value of Fascism lies in the fact that it is veined with pragmatism, but at the same time has a will to exist and a will to power, a firm front in face of the reality of "violence."

The foundation of Fascism is the conception of the State, its character, its duty, and its aim. Fascism conceives of the State as an absolute, in comparison with which all individuals or groups are relative, only to be conceived of in their relation to the State. The conception of the Liberal State is not that of a directing force, guiding the play and development, both material and spiritual, of a collective body, but merely a force limited to the function of recording results: on the other hand, the Fascist State is itself conscious, and has itself a will and a personality—thus it may be called the "ethic" State. In 1929, at the first five-yearly assembly of the Fascist regime, I said:

"For us Fascists, the State is not merely a guardian, preoccupied solely with the duty of assuring the personal safety of the citizens; nor is it an organization with purely material aims, such as to guarantee a certain level of well-being and peaceful conditions of life; for a mere council of administration would be sufficient to realize such objects. Nor is it a purely political creation, divorced from all contact with the complex material reality which makes up the life of the individual and the life of the people as a whole. The State, as conceived of and as created by Fascism, is a spiritual and moral fact in itself, since its political, juridical, and economic organization of the nation is a concrete thing: and such an organization must be in its origins and development a manifestation of the spirit. The State is the guarantor of security both internal and external, but it is also the custodian and transmitter of the spirit of the people, as it has grown up through the centuries in language, in customs, and in faith. And the State is not only a living reality of the present, it is also linked with the past and above all with the future, and thus transcending the brief limits of individual life, it represents the immanent spirit of the nation. The forms in which States express themselves may change, but the necessity for such forms is eternal. It is the State which educates its citizens in civic virtue, gives them a consciousness of their mission and welds them into unity; harmonizing their various interests through justice, and transmitting to future generations the mental conquests of science, of art, of law and the solidarity of humanity. It leads men from primitive tribal life to the highest expression of human power which is Empire; it links up through the centuries the names of those of its members who have died for its existence and in obedience to its laws, it holds up the memory of the leaders who have increased its territory and the geniuses who have illuminated it with glory as an example to be followed by future generations. When the conception of the State declines, and disunifying and centrifugal tendencies prevail, whether of individuals or of particular groups, the nations where such phenomena appear are in their decline."

From 1929 until today, evolution, both political and economic, has everywhere gone to prove the validity of these doctrinal premises. Of such gigantic importance is the State. It is the force which alone can provide a solution to the dramatic contradictions of capitalism. . . . Fascism desires the State to be a strong and organic body, at the same time reposing upon broad and popular support. The Fascist State has drawn into itself even the economic activities of the nation, and, through the corporative social and educational institutions created by it, its influence reaches every aspect of the national life and includes, framed in their respective organizations, all the political, economic and spiritual forces of the nation. A State which reposes upon the support of millions of individuals who recognize its authority, are continually conscious of its power and are ready at once to serve it, is not the old tyrannical State of the medieval lord nor has it anything in common with the absolute governments either before or after 1789. The individual in the Fascist State is not annulled but rather multiplied, just in the same way that a soldier in a regiment is not diminished but rather increased by the number of his comrades. The Fascist State organizes the nation, but leaves a sufficient margin of liberty to the individual; the latter is deprived of all useless and possibly harmful freedom, but retains what is essential; the deciding power in this question cannot be the individual, but the State alone.

The Fascist State is not indifferent to the fact of religion in general, or to that particular and positive faith which is Italian Catholicism. The State professes no theology, but a morality, and in the Fascist State religion is considered as one of the deepest manifestations of the spirit of man; thus it is not only respected but defended and protected. The Fascist State has never tried to create its own God, as at one moment Robespierre and the wildest extremists of the Convention tried to do; nor does it vainly seek to obliterate religion from the hearts of men as does Bolshevism; Fascism respects the God of the ascetics, the saints and heroes, and equally, God, as He is perceived and worshipped by simple people.

The Fascist State is an embodied will to power and government; the Roman tradition is here an ideal of force in action. According to Fascism, government is not so much a thing to be expressed in territorial or military terms as in terms of morality and the spirit. It must be thought of as an empire—that is to say, a nation which directly or indirectly rules other nations, without the need for conquering a single square yard of territory. For Fascism, the growth of empire, that is to say the expansion of the nation, is an essential manifestation of vitality, and its opposite a sign of decadence. Peoples which are rising, or rising again after a period of decadence, are always imperialist: any renunciation is a sign of decay and of death.

Fascism is the doctrine best adapted to represent the tendencies and the aspirations of a people, like the people of Italy, who are rising again after many centuries of abasement and foreign servitude. But empire demands discipline, the co-ordination of all forces and a deeply felt sense of duty and sacrifice: this fact explains many aspects of the practical working of the regime, the character of many forces in the State, and the necessarily severe measures which must be taken against those who would oppose this spontaneous and inevitable movement of Italy in the twentieth century, and would oppose it by recalling the outworn ideology of the nineteenth century—repudiated wheresoever there has been the courage to undertake great experiments of social and political transformation: for never before has the nation stood more in need of authority, of direction, and of order. If every age has its own characteristic doctrine, there are a thousand signs which point to Fascism as the characteristic doctrine of our time. For if a doctrine must be a living thing, this is proved by the fact that Fascism has created a living faith; and that this faith is very powerful in the minds of men, is demonstrated by those who have suffered and died for it.

Fascism has henceforth in the world the universality of all those doctrines which, in realizing themselves, have represented a stage in the history of the human spirit.

C. Nazism

*NAZISM, AN IDEOLOGICAL BLOOD-BROTHER TO FASCISM, was
the political philosophy of Hitler's National Socialist Party which was itself
an outgrowth of the earlier German Workers' Party. On February 25, 1920,
the German Workers' Party issued a 25-point program which anticipated later
Hitlerian views on anti-Semitism, anti-Bolshevism, and the unjustness of the
Versailles settlement.*

1. THE PROGRAM OF THE NATIONAL SOCIALIST GERMAN WORKERS' PARTY, FEBRUARY 25, 1920

SOURCE. The Program of the National Socialist Workers' Party, Munich, 1920.

The program of the German Workers' Party is limited as to period. The
leaders have no intention, once the aims announced in it have been
achieved, of setting up fresh ones, merely in order to increase the discontent of the masses artificially and so ensure the continued existence of
the party.

1. We demand the union of all Germans to form a Great Germany on
the basis of the right of self-determination of nations.

2. We demand equality of rights for the German people in its dealings
with other nations, and abolition of the Peace Treaties of Versailles and
Saint-Germain.

3. We demand land and territory [colonies] for the nourishment of our
people and for settling our surplus population.

4. None but members of the nation [*Volksgenossen*] may be citizens
of the State. None but those of German blood, whatever their creed, may
be members of the nation. No Jew, therefore, may be a member of the
nation.

5. Any one who is not a citizen of the State may live in Germany only
as a guest and must be subject to laws for aliens.

6. The right of voting for the leaders and laws of the State is to be
enjoyed by the citizen of the State alone. We demand therefore that all

official appointments, of whatever kind, whether in the Reich, in the Länder, or in the smaller localities, shall be granted to citizens of the State alone.

We oppose the corrupting custom of Parliament of filling posts merely with a view of party considerations, and without reference to character or capability.

7. We demand that the State shall make it its first duty to promote the industry and livelihood of citizens of the State. If it is not possible to nourish the entire population of the State, foreign nationals [non-citizens] must be excluded from the Reich.

8. All further non-German immigration must be prevented. We demand that all non-Germans who entered Germany subsequent to August 2nd, 1914, shall be compelled forthwith to depart from the Reich.

9. All citizens of the State shall be equal as regards rights and duties.

10. It must be the first duty of each citizen of the State to work with his mind or with his body. The activities of the individual may not clash with the interests of the whole, but must proceed within the frame of the community and be for the general good.

We demand therefore:

11. Abolition of all incomes unearned by work.

12. In view of the enormous sacrifice of life and property demanded of a nation by every war, personal enrichment due to a war must be regarded as a crime against the nation. We demand therefore ruthless confiscation of all war gains.

13. We demand nationalization of all businesses which have been up to the present formed into companies [trusts].

14. We demand that all the profits from wholesale trade shall be shared out.

15. We demand extensive development of provision for old age.

16. We demand creation and maintenance of a healthy middle class, immediate communalization of department stores, and their lease at a cheap rate to small traders, and extreme consideration for all small purveyors to the State, district authorities, and smaller localities.

17. We demand land reform suitable to our national requirements, passing of a law for confiscation without compensation of land for common purposes; abolition of interest on land loans, and prevention of all speculation in land.

18. We demand a ruthless struggle against those whose activities are injurious to the common interest. Common criminals against the nation, usurers, profiteers, etc., must be punished with death, whatever their creed or race.

19. We demand that the Roman Law, which serves the materialistic world order, shall be replaced by a German legal system.

20. With the aim of opening to every capable and industrious German the possibility of higher education and of thus obtaining advancement, the State must consider a thorough reconstruction of our national system of education. The curriculum of all educational establishments must be brought into line with the requirements of practical life. Comprehension of the State idea [civic training] must be the school objective, beginning with the first dawn of understanding in the pupil. We demand development of the gifted children of poor parents, whatever their class or occupation, at the expense of the State.

21. The State must see to raising the standard of health in the nation by protecting mothers and infants, prohibiting child labor, increasing bodily efficiency by obligatory gymnastics and sports laid down by law, and by extensive support of clubs engaged in the bodily development of the young.

22. We demand abolition of a paid army, and formation of a national army.

23. We demand legal warfare against conscious political lying and its dissemination in the press. In order to facilitate creation of a German national press we demand:

(a) that all editors and their co-workers on newspapers employing the German language must be members of the nation;

(b) that special permission from the State shall be necessary before non-German newspapers may appear. These must not be printed in the German language;

(c) that non-Germans shall be prohibited by law from participation financially in or influencing German newspapers, and that the penalty for contravention of the law shall be suppression of any such newspaper and immediate deportation of the non-German concerned in it.

It must be forbidden to publish papers which do not conduce to the national welfare. We demand legal prosecution of all tendencies in art and literature of a kind likely to disintegrate our life as a nation, and the suppression of institutions which militate against the requirements above mentioned.

24. We demand liberty for all religious denominations in the State, so far as they are not a danger to, and do not militate against the moral feelings of, the German race.

The party, as such, stands for positive Christianity, but does not bind itself in the matter of creed to any particular confession. It combats the Jewish-materialist spirit within us and without us and is convinced that our nation can only achieve permanent health from within on the principle:

25. That all the foregoing may be realized, we demand the creation of a strong central power of the State. Unquestioned authority of the

politically centralized Parliament over the entire Reich and its organizations; and formation of Chambers for classes and occupations for the purpose of carrying out the general laws promulgated by the Reich in the various states of the confederation.

The leaders of the party swear to go straight forward—if necessary to sacrifice their lives—in securing fulfilment of the foregoing points.

NAZI THOUGHT IS FURTHER DEVELOPED in a speech by Adolf Hitler, who assumed political control in Germany in 1933 and established the "Third Reich." At Nuremberg on September 1, 1933, Hitler stressed the dangers of Bolshevism, the ineptitude of liberal democracy, and the virility and popular basis of National Socialism.

2. SEPTEMBER 1, 1933: CHANCELLOR HITLER COMPARES MARXISM, LIBERALISM, AND NATIONAL SOCIALISM

SOURCE. Adolph Hitler, *My New Order*, Raoul de Roussy de Sales, ed., New York: Reynal and Hitchcock, 1941, pp. 191–197. Reprinted by permission of Harcourt, Brace & World, Inc.

When in the year 1919 the National Socialist Movement came into being in order to create a new Reich in place of the Marxist-democratic Republic, such an enterprise seemed hopeless and foolish. Above all, the caviling intellectuals with their superficial historical education had no more than a pitying smile for such an undertaking. Most of them very well knew that Germany would fall on evil times. The greater part of the so-called intelligentsia understood very well that the rules of the November Republic were either too evil or too incompetent to lead our people. But they did not recognize that this new regime could not be overcome by those forces which for fifty years have steadily retreated before the attacks of Marxism, finally, in the hour of greatest emergency, to capitulate miserably. Perhaps part of the reason for this was that the political leaders of the nation were aging, outdated. They could not or would not recognize the time necessary for the restoration of the strength of a nation.

Strength cannot be found in an organization which has none. It was therefore an error when in 1919 and 1920 the men who recognized the distress of the Fatherland thought that a change in the leadership of the bourgeois parties would suddenly give them the strength to annihilate the inner enemy . . .

When one has glorified a false democracy for seventy years, one cannot attempt a dictatorship in the seventy-first year. It leads to ridiculous experiments.

With few exceptions, age destroys the mental as well as the physical powers of generation. Because each man wishes to see for himself the growth and the fruits of his struggle, he seeks for easier, that is, quicker ways to transform his ideas into realities. The rootless intellectual, lacking all understanding of organic development, tries to evade the law of growth by hasty experiments. Nationalism, on the other hand, was ready from the very first to undertake the long and painful task of building up anew the structure which would later destroy Marxism. But because this way was not understood by the superficial intelligence of our politicalized bourgeoisie, the new Movement could at first develop only among those groups who were not miseducated, who were uncomplicated and therefore closer to nature.

What the intellect of the intellectual could not see was grasped immediately by the soul, the heart, the instinct of this simple, primitive, but healthy man. It is another one of the tasks of the future to re-establish the unity between feeling and intellect; that is, to educate an unspoiled generation which will perceive with clear understanding the eternal law of development and at the same time will consciously return to the primitive instinct.

National Socialism directed its appeal for the formation of a new Movement to the broad masses of the people. Its first task was to inspire by suggestion those few whom it had first won over with the belief that they would one day be the saviors of their Fatherland. This problem of educating men to believe and have faith in themselves was as necessary as it was difficult. Men who socially and economically belonged to subordinate, and frequently oppressed groups, had to be given the political conviction that some day they would represent the leadership of the nation.

While the former leaders of the bourgeois world talked about "quiet progress" and declaimed profound treatises at tea parties, National Socialism began its march into the heart of the people. We held hundreds of thousands of demonstrations. A hundred and a hundred thousand times our speakers spoke in meeting halls, in small, smoky taverns, and in great sports arenas. And each demonstration not only won us new adherents, but above all made the others firm in their belief and filled them by suggestion with the kind of self-confidence without which success is not possible. The others talked about democracy and kept away from the people. National Socialism talked about authority, but it fought and wrestled with the people as no movement in Germany had ever done.

For all time to come this city shall be the place where our Movement will hold its Party Congress, for it was here that for the first time we proclaimed the new will of Germany. . . .

The National Socialist Revolution has overthrown the republic of treason and perjury, and in its place has created once more a Reich of honor, loyalty, and decency. It is our great good fortune that we did not have to bring about this Revolution as leaders of the "historic minority" against the majority of the German nation. We rejoice that at the end of our struggle but before the final turn in our destiny, the overwhelming majority of the German people had already declared itself for our principles. Thus it was possible to accomplish one of the greatest revolutions in history with hardly any bloodshed. As a result of the splendid organization of the movement which brought about this Revolution, at no moment did we lose control of it.

Aside from the Fascist Revolution in Italy, no similar historic action is comparable in discipline and order with the National Socialist uprising. It is particularly pleasing that today the great majority of the German people stand loyal and united behind the new regime. . . .

Our perilous political situation was accompanied by a no less dangerous economic situation. The rapid decline of the past winter seemed to be leading to a complete collapse. The great historian, Mommsen, once characterized the Jews in the life of nations as a "ferment of decomposition." In Germany this decomposition had already made great progress. National Socialism opposed with fierce resoluteness this creeping "decline of the West," because we were convinced that those inner values which are natural to the civilized nations of Europe, and to our own German nation in particular, had not yet been completely destroyed. . . .

As sole possessor of State power, the Party must recognize that it bears the entire responsibility for the course of German history. The work of education which the Movement must carry on is tremendous. For it is not enough to organize the State in accordance with pacific principles; it is necessary to educate the people inwardly. Only if the people has an intimate sympathy with the principles and methods which inspire and move the organization of its State, will there grow up a living organism instead of a dead, because purely formal and mechanistic, organization.

Among the tasks we face, the most important is the question of eliminating unemployment. The danger in unemployment is not only a material one. It is neither logical, nor moral, nor just, to continue taking away from those who are able to work a part of the fruits of their industry in order to maintain those unable to work—no matter for what reasons they are unable. It is more logical to distribute the work itself instead of distributing wages. No one has a moral right to demand that others should work for him so that he will not have to work himself. Each has a right to demand that the political organization of his nation, the State, find ways and means to give work to all.

We are following paths for which there is hardly any model in history. It is thus at any time possible that one or another measure that we take today may prove unworkable. It is thus all the more necessary to put a stop to that carping criticism which tends only towards disintegration. It is no matter whether a thousand critics live or die, what does matter is whether a people shall be conquered and ruined and in consequence as a community lose its life. All those who since November, 1918, through their mad or criminal action hurled our people into their present misfortunes, those who proclaimed such phrases as "Freedom," "Brotherliness," and "Equality," as the *leit-motiv* of their action—they do not share today the fate and the sufferings of the victims of their policy! Millions of our German fellow-countrymen through them have been given over to the hardest stress imaginable. Need, misery, hunger, do violence to their existence. Those who misled them indeed enjoy abroad the freedom to slander their own people for foreign gold, the liberty to deliver them up to the hatred of their neighbors: they would, if they could, see them attacked and shot down, defenseless, on the battlefield. . . .

The rise and the astonishing final victory of the National Socialist Movement would never have happened if the Party had ever formulated the principle that in our ranks everyone can do as he likes. This watchword of democratic freedom led only to insecurity, indiscipline, and at length to the downfall and destruction of all authority. Our opponents' objection that we, too, once made use of these rights, will not hold water; for we made use of an unreasonable right, which was part and parcel of an unreasonable system, in order to overthrow the unreason of this system. No fruit falls which is not ripe for falling. When old Germany fell, it betrayed its inner weakness, just as the November Republic has revealed its weakness to everyone by now.

By its political education, therefore, the Party will have to fortify the mind of the German people against any tendency to regression. While we deny the parliamentary-democratic principle, we champion most definitely the right of the people itself to determine its own life. In the parliamentary system we do not recognize any true expression of the will of the people, but we see in it a perversion, if not a violation, of that will. The will of a people to maintain its existence appears first and in its most useful form in its best brains.

The greater the tasks with which we are faced, the greater must be the authority of those who must accomplish these tasks. It is important that the self-assurance of the leaders of the whole organization in their decisions should arouse in the members and followers of the Party an untroubled confidence. For the people will justifiably never understand it if they are suddenly asked to discuss problems which their leaders cannot cope with. It is conceivable that even wise men should not in questions of special difficulty be able to reach complete clarity. But it means a capitulation of all leadership if it hands over precisely those questions to public discussion and allows the public to state its views. For the leaders thereby imply that the masses have more judgment than they themselves have. This cannot be the attitude of the National Socialist party. The Party must be convinced that it will be able to cope with all problems, that because it has chosen its human material in living struggle, its leaders are politically the most competent men in Germany.

Our Party must follow the same law that it wishes to see the masses of the nation follow. It must, therefore, constantly educate itself to recognize authority, to submit voluntarily to the highest discipline, so that it will be able to educate the followers of the Party to do the same. And in doing this the Party must be hard and logical. . . .

Power and the brutal application of power can accomplish much. But in the long run no state of affairs is secure unless it is firmly rooted in logic. Above all: The National Socialist Movement must profess its faith in that heroism which is content to face all opposition and every trial rather than for a moment to be false to the principles which it has recognized to be right. The Movement must be filled with one fear alone—the fear lest the time should ever come when it could be charged with dishonesty or thoughtlessness.

To save a nation one must think heroically. But the heroic thinker must always be willing to renounce the approval of his contemporaries where truth is at stake.

May the very manner of this demonstration renew our understanding that the Government of the nation must never harden into a purely bureaucratic machine; it must ever remain a living leadership, a leadership which does not view the people as an object of its activity, but which lives within the people, feels with the people and fights for the people. Forms and organizations can pass, but what does and must remain is the living substance of flesh and blood. All of us desire that the German people shall remain forever upon this earth, and we believe that by our struggle we are but carrying out the will of the Creator, who imbued all creatures with the instinct for self-preservation. Long live our nation. Long live the National Socialist party!

THE RADICAL AUTHORITARIANISM of the National Socialist Party is illustrated by excerpts from the Nazi Party Organization Book (1940) dealing with the duties of party members.

3. THE NATIONAL SOCIALIST COMMANDMENTS, 1940

SOURCE. *National Socialism*, Washington: U. S. Government Printing Office, 1943, p. 195.

The National Socialist commandments:

The Führer is always right!

Never go against discipline!

Don't waste your time in idle chatter or in self-satisfying criticism, but take hold and do your work!

Be proud but not arrogant!

Let the program be your dogma. It demands of you the greatest devotion to the movement.

You are a representative of the party; control your bearing and your manner accordingly!

Let loyalty and unselfishness be your highest precepts!

Practice true comradeship and you will be a true socialist!

Treat your racial comrades as you wish to be treated by them!

In battle be hard and silent!

Spirit is not unruliness!

That which promotes the movement, Germany, and your people, is right!

If you act according to these commandments, you are a true soldier of your Führer.

THE UNPARALLELED BARBARISM of the Nazis was not fully compre-hended until the close of World War II, when Allied armies uncovered the full horror of the German concentration camps and testimony at the Nuremberg War Crimes Trials disclosed in detail the Nazi medical experiments and the mass murders of Jews. The next two documents require no further comment.

4. NAZI MEDICAL EXPERIMENTS: TESTIMONY OF DR. FRANZ BLAHA, A CZECHOSLOVAKIAN PRISONER

SOURCE. Nuremberg Document # 3249-PS.

From the middle of 1941 to the end of 1942 some 500 operations on healthy prisoners were performed [at Dachau]. These were for the instructions of the SS medical students and doctors and included operations on the stomach, gall bladder and throat. These were performed by students and doctors of only 2 years' training, although they were very dangerous and difficult. Ordinarily they would not have been done except by surgeons with at least 4 years' surgical practice. Many prisoners died on the operating table and many others from later complications. I performed autopsies on all of these bodies. The doctors who supervised these operations were Lang, Muermelstadt, Wolter, Ramsauer, and Kahr. Standartenführer Dr. Lolling frequently witnessed these operations.

During my time at Dachau I was familiar with many kinds of medical experiments carried on there on human victims. These persons were never volunteers but were forced to submit to such acts. Malaria experiments on about 1,200 people were conducted by Dr. Klaus Schilling between 1941 and 1945. Schilling was personally ordered by Himmler to conduct these experiments. The victims were either bitten by mosquitoes or given injections of malaria sporozoites taken from mosquitoes. Different kinds of treatment were applied including quinine, pyrifer, neosalvarsan, antipyrin, pyramidon, and a drug called 2516 Behring. I performed autopsies on the bodies of people who died from these malaria experiments. Thirty to 40 died from the malaria itself. Three hundred to four hundred died later from diseases which were fatal because of the physical condition resulting from the malaria attacks. In addition there were deaths resulting from poisoning due to overdoses of neosalvarsan and pyramidon. Dr. Schilling was present at my autopsies on the bodies of his patients.

In 1942 and 1943 experiments on human beings were conducted by Dr. Sigmund Rascher to determine the effects of changing air pressure. As many as 25 persons were put at one time into a specially constructed van in which pressure could be increased or decreased as required. The purpose was to find out the effects on human beings of high altitude and of rapid descents by parachute. Through a window in the van I have seen the people lying on the floor of the van. Most of the prisoners used died from these experiments, from internal hemorrhage of the lungs or brain. The survivors coughed blood when taken out. It was my job to take the bodies out and as soon as they were found to be dead to send the internal organs to Munich for study. About 400 to 500 prisoners were experimented on. The survivors were sent to invalid blocks and liquidated shortly after-wards. Only a few escaped.

Rascher also conducted experiments on the effect of cold water on human beings. This was done to find a way for reviving airmen who had fallen into the ocean. The subject was placed in ice cold water and kept there until he was unconscious. Blood was taken from his neck and tested each time his body temperature dropped one degree. This drop was determined by a rectal thermometer. Urine was also periodically tested. Some men stood it as long as 24 to 36 hours. The lowest body tempera-ture reached was 19 degrees centigrade, but most men died at 25 or 26 degrees. When the men were removed from the ice water attempts were made to revive them by artificial sunshine, with hot water, by electro-therapy, or by animal warmth. For this last experiment prostitutes were used and the body of the unconscious man was placed between the bodies of two women. Himmler was present at one such experiment. I could see him from one of the windows in the street between the blocks. I have personally been present at some of these cold water experiments when Rascher was absent, and I have seen notes and diagrams on them in Rascher's laboratory. About 300 persons were used in these experiments. The majority died. Of those who survived, many became mentally de-ranged. Those who did not die were sent to invalid blocks and were killed just as were the victims of the air pressure experiments. I know only two who survived, a Yugoslav and a Pole, both of whom are mental cases.

Liver puncture experiments were performed by Dr. Brachtl on healthy people and on people who had diseases of the stomach and gall bladder. For this purpose a needle was jabbed into the liver of a person and a small piece of the liver was extracted. No anaesthetic was used. The ex-periment is very painful and often had serious results, as the stomach or large blood vessels were often punctured, resulting in hemorrhage. Many persons died of these tests for which Polish, Russian, Czech, and German prisoners were employed. Altogether about 175 people were subjected to these experiments.

Phlegmone experiments were conducted by Dr. Schütz, Dr. Babor, Dr. Kieselwetter and Professor Lauer. Forty healthy men were used at a time, of which twenty were given intramuscular and twenty intravenous injections of pus from diseased persons. All treatment was forbidden for 3 days, by which time serious inflammation and in many cases general blood poisoning had occurred. Then each group was divided again into groups of 10. Half were given chemical treatment with liquid and special pills every 10 minutes for 24 hours. The remainder were treated with sulfanamide and surgery. In some cases all the limbs were amputated. My autopsy also showed that the chemical treatment had been harmful and had even caused perforations of the stomach wall. For these experiments Polish, Czech, and Dutch priests were ordinarily used. Pain was intense in such experiments. Most of the 600 to 800 persons who were used finally died. Most of the others became permanent invalids and were later killed.

In the fall of 1944 there were 60 to 80 persons who were subjected to salt water experiments. They were locked in a room and for 5 days were given nothing for food but salt water. During this time their urine, blood, and excrement were tested. None of these prisoners died, possibly because they received smuggled food from other prisoners. Hungarians and Gypsies were used for these experiments.

It was common practice to remove the skin from dead prisoners. I was commanded to do this on many occasions. Dr. Rascher and Dr. Wolter in particular asked for this human skin from human backs and chests. It was chemically treated and placed in the sun to dry. After that it was cut into various sizes for use as saddles, riding breeches, gloves, house slippers, and ladies' handbags. Tattooed skin was especially valued by SS men. Russians, Poles, and other inmates were used in this way, but it was forbidden to cut out the skin of a German. This skin had to be from healthy prisoners and free from defects. Sometimes we did not have enough bodies with good skin and Rascher would say, "All right, you will get the bodies." The next day we would receive 20 or 30 bodies of young people. They would have been shot in the neck or struck on the head so that the skin would be uninjured. Also we frequently got requests for the skulls or skeletons of prisoners. In those cases we boiled the skull or the body. Then the soft parts were removed and the bones were bleached and dried and reassembled. In the case of skulls it was important to have a good set of teeth. When we got an order for skulls from Oranienburg the SS men would say, "We will try to get you some with good teeth." So it was dangerous to have good skin or good teeth.

5. THE MASS MURDERS OF JEWS: TESTIMONY OF RUDOLF HOESS

SOURCE. Nuremberg Document # 3868-PS.

. . . I have been constantly associated with the administration of concentration camps since 1934, serving at Dachau until 1938; then as Adjutant in Sachsenhausen from 1938 to 1 May 1940, when I was appointed Commandant of Auschwitz. I commanded Auschwitz until 1 December 1943, and estimate that at least 2,500,000 victims were executed and exterminated there by gassing and burning, and at least another half million succumbed to starvation and disease making a total dead of about

3,000,000. This figure represents about 70 or 80 percent of all persons sent to Auschwitz as prisoners, the remainder having been selected and used for slave labor in the concentration camp industries; included among the executed and burned were approximately 20,000 Russian prisoners of war (previously screened out of prisoner-of-war cages by the Gestapo) who were delivered at Auschwitz in Wehrmacht transports operated by regular Wehrmacht officers and men. The remainder of the total number of victims included about 100,000 German Jews, and great numbers of citizens, mostly Jewish, from Holland, France, Belgium, Poland, Hungary, Czechoslovakia, Greece, or other countries. We executed about 400,000 Hungarian Jews alone at Auschwitz in the summer of 1944. . . .

The "final solution" of the Jewish question meant the complete extermination of all Jews in Europe. I was ordered to establish extermination facilities at Auschwitz in June 1941. At that time, there were already in the General Government three other extermination camps: Belzek, Treblinka, and Wolzek. These camps were under the Einsatzkommando of the Security Police and SD. I visited Treblinka to find out how they carried out their exterminations. The camp commandant at Treblinka told me that he had liquidated 80,000 in the course of one-half year. He was principally concerned with liquidating all the Jews from the Warsaw Ghetto. He used monoxide gas, and I did not think that his methods were very efficient. So when I set up the extermination building at Auschwitz, I used Cyklon B, which was a crystallized prussic acid which we dropped into the death chamber from a small opening. It took from 3 to 15 minutes to kill the people in the death chamber, depending upon climatic conditions. We knew when the people were dead because their screaming stopped. We usually waited about one-half hour before we opened the doors and removed the bodies. After the bodies were removed our special Kommandos took off the rings and extracted the gold from the teeth of the corpses. . . .

Another improvement we made over Treblinka was that we built our gas chamber to accommodate 2,000 people at one time whereas at Treblinka their gas chambers only accommodated 200 people each. The way we selected our victims was as follows: We had two SS doctors on duty at Auschwitz to examine the incoming transports of prisoners. The prisoners would be marched by one of the doctors who would make spot decisions as they walked by. Those who were fit for work were sent into the camp. Others were sent immediately to the extermination plants. Children of tender years were invariably exterminated since by reason of their youth they were unable to work. Still another improvement we made over Treblinka was that at Treblinka the victims almost always knew that they were to be exterminated and at Auschwitz we endeavored to fool the victims into thinking that they were to go through a delousing process. Of course, frequently they realized our true intentions and we sometimes had riots and difficulties due to that fact. Very frequently women would hide their children under the clothes, but of course when we found them we would send the children in to be exterminated. We were required to carry out these exterminations in secrecy but of course the foul and nauseating stench from the continuous burning of bodies permeated the entire area and all of the people living in the surrounding communities knew that exterminations were going on at Auschwitz.

World War II and the Postwar World

THE causes of World War II are tied to the events of World War I. The inter-war years were marked by a three-way ideological split between liberal democ-racy, Communism, and right-wing totalitarianism. Communist Russia was a child of World War I, and Fascist Italy and Nazi Germany were products of the economic and political chaos that followed it. Ultimately, World War II was brought about by the militant expansionism of the Axis powers—Italy, Japan, and in particular, Germany—and by the rather delayed response of the democ-racies and Russia to these aggressions.

Step by step, Hitler undid the provisions of the Versailles Treaty. Repeatedly affirming his peaceful intentions, he rearmed Germany, incorporated Austria into his Reich, and, in the Munich agreement of 1938, bluffed England and France into conceding him a portion of Czechoslovakia (the "Sudetenland") which was heavily German in population. Shortly thereafter he occupied the re-mainder of Czechoslovakia. In August, 1939, he startled the world by conclud-ing a Non-Aggression Pact with the Soviet Union, and a few days afterward, assured of Russian neutrality, he sent his armies into Poland. This last act prompted England and France to declare war.

In 1940 Germany conquered France, occupied much of western and central Europe, and staggered England with devastating air raids. But Hitler's invasion of Russia and the Japanese bombing of Pearl Harbor brought the two supreme powers of the mid-twentieth century into the struggle, and the combined efforts of the United States, the Soviet Union, and Great Britain resulted ultimately in the total defeat of the Axis powers.

Italy capitulated first, then Germany, and finally, in August, 1945, Japan was brought to her knees by the American atomic bomb. The month of August wit-nessed the end of World War II and the beginning of the atomic age. The Al-lied powers, in an effort to secure permanent peace through international co-operation, affixed their signatures to the United Nations Charter in June, 1945, and with the crushing of right-wing totalitarianism many people hoped for a new era of peace and civilized behavior among nations. Such hopes were thwarted by the continued commitment of the Soviet Union to world Commu-nist revolution. A new type of aggression, based on Soviet aid to "national liber-ation movements," provoked an ever-widening split between America and Rus-sia, and the high hopes of the immediate postwar world gave way to an era of Cold War. The new power struggle and ideological conflict were conducted under the constant threat of atomic annihilation and aggravated by a condition of worldwide instability caused by the distintegration of the old colonial system and the rise of ambitious newly independent states. Former colonial areas such as Korea, Cuba, and Vietnam now became settings for ominous confrontations between the two antagonistic power blocs. At the same time, a growing split between the United States and France, and between the Soviet Union and Communist China, betokened an end to the extreme polarization of power that characterized the postwar years. The political configurations of the present are becoming at once more complex and less predictable than those of the past.

Part I

WORLD WAR II

A. The Road to War

IN DIRECT VIOLATION of the Versailles Treaty, Hitler undertook a policy of German rearmament and at the same time took pains to assure the world of his peaceful intentions. In a speech delivered in Berlin on May 21, 1935, Hitler affirmed his dedication to peace.

1. HITLER'S THIRTEEN POINTS, 1935: AN AFFIRMATION OF HIS PEACEFUL INTENTIONS

SOURCE. Adolph Hitler, *My New Order*, Raoul de Roussy de Sales, ed., New York: Reynal and Hitchcock, 1941, pp. 327–333. Reprinted by permission of Harcourt, Brace & World, Inc.

. . . I hereby declare that the position of the German Government is as follows:

1. The German Government rejects the Geneva resolution of April 17. It was not Germany which unilaterally broke the Versailles Treaty. The Versailles Dictate was unilaterally broken, and thereby rendered invalid as regards the points at issue, by those Powers who could not decide to carry out in their turn the disarmament which was imposed on Germany and which should have followed in their case by virtue of the Treaty.

The new discrimination introduced at Geneva makes it impossible for the German Government to return to that institution until the preconditions for a real legal equality of all members has been established. For this purpose the German Government considers it necessary to make a clear separation between the Treaty of Versailles, which was based on a classification of the nations into victors and vanquished, and the League of Nations, which must be constituted on the basis of equal valuation and equality of rights for all the members.

This equality of rights must be extended to all functions and all property rights in international life.

2. The German Government, consequent on the failure of the other States to fulfill their disarmament obligations, has on its part renounced those articles of the Versailles Treaty which, because of the one-sided burden this laid on Germany contrary to the provisions of the Treaty, have constituted a discrimination against Germany for an unlimited period of time. It hereby most solemnly declares that these measures relate exclusively to the points which involve moral and material discrimination against the German people and of which notice has been given. The German Government will therefore unconditionally respect the articles concerning the mutual relations of the nations in other respects, including the territorial provisions, and those revisions which shall be rendered necessary in the course of time will be put into effect only by the method of peaceful understandings.

3. The German Government intends not to sign any treaty which seems to them incapable of fulfillment; but they will scrupulously maintain every treaty voluntarily signed, even though it was concluded before their accession to power and office. In particular they will uphold and fulfill all obligations arising out of the Locarno Treaty, so long as the other partners are on their side ready to stand by that Pact. In respecting the demilitarized zone the German Government considers its action as a contribution to the appeasement of Europe, which contribution is of an unheard-of hardness for a sovereign State. But it feels bound to point out that the continual increase of troops on the other side can in no way be regarded as a complement to these endeavors.

4. The German Government is ready at any time to participate in a system of collective co-operation for safeguarding European peace, but regards it necessary to recognize the law of perpetual evolution by keeping open the way to treaty revision. . . .

5. The German Government is of the opinion that the reconstruction of European collaboration cannot be achieved by the method of imposing conditions unilaterally. In view of the fact that the various interests involved are not always concordant, it believes it right to be content with a minimum instead of allowing this collaboration to break down on account of an unalterable maximum of demands. It has the further conviction that this understanding—with a great aim in view—can be brought about only step by step.

6. The German Government is ready in principle to conclude pacts of non-aggression with its neighbor States and to supplement these pacts with all provisions that aim at isolating the warmaker and localizing the area of the war. In particular it is ready to assume all consequent obligations regarding the supply of material and arms in peace or war where such obligations are also assumed and respected by all the partners.

7. The German Government is ready to supplement the Locarno Treaty with an air agreement and to enter upon discussions regarding this matter.

8. The German Government has announced the extent of the expansion of the new German Defence Force. Under no circumstances will it depart from this. It does not regard the fulfillment of its program in the air, on land, or at sea, as constituting a menace to any nation. It is ready at any time to limit its armaments to any degree that is also adopted by the other Powers.

The German Government has already spontaneously made known the definite limitations of its intentions, thereby giving the best evidence of its good will to avoid an unlimited armaments race. Its limitation of the German air armaments to parity with the individual Great Powers of the West makes it possible at any time to fix a maximum which Germany will be under a binding obligation to observe with the other nations. The limitation of the German Navy is placed at thirty-five per cent of the British Navy, and therewith still at fifteen per cent below the total tonnage of the French Navy. As the opinion has been expressed in various press commentaries that this demand is only a beginning and would increase, particularly with the possession of colonies, the German Government hereby makes the binding declaration: For Germany this demand is final and abiding.

Germany has not the intention or the necessity or the means to participate in any new naval rivalry. The German Government recognizes of itself the overpowering vital importance, and therewith the justification, of a dominating protection for the British Empire on the sea, precisely as we are resolved conversely to do all that is necessary for the protection of our continental existence and freedom. The German Government has the straightforward intention to find and maintain a relationship with the British people and State which will prevent for all time a repetition of the only struggle there has been between the two nations hitherto.

9. The German Government is ready to take an active part in all efforts which may lead to a practical limitation of boundless armaments. It regards a return to the former idea of the Geneva Red Cross Convention as the only possible way to achieve this. It believes that first there will be only the possibility of a gradual abolition and outlawry of weapons and methods of warfare which are essentially contrary to the Geneva Red Cross Convention, which is still valid. . . .

The German Government considers as erroneous and ineffective the idea of doing away with airplanes while leaving bombardment free. But they believe it possible to proscribe the use of certain arms as contrary to international law and to excommunicate those nations still using them from the community of mankind—its rights and its laws.

Here also they believe that gradual progress is the best way to success. For example, there might be prohibition of the dropping of gas, incendiary, and explosive bombs outside the real battle zone. This limitation could then be extended to complete international outlawry of all bombing. But so long as bombing as such is permitted, any limitation of the number of bombing planes is questionable in view of the possibility of rapid substitution.

Should bombing as such be branded as an illegal barbarity, the construction of bombing airplanes will soon be abandoned as superfluous and of no purpose. If, through the Geneva Red Cross Convention, it became possible as a matter of fact to prevent the killing of a defenseless wounded man or prisoner, then it ought to be equally possible to forbid, by an analogous convention, and finally to stop, the bombing of equally defenseless civil populations.

In such a fundamental way of dealing with the problem, Germany sees a greater reassurance and security for the nations than in all pacts of assistance and military conventions.

10. The German Government is ready to agree to any limitation which leads to abolition of the heaviest arms, especially suited for aggression. Such are, first, the heaviest artillery, and, secondly, the heaviest tanks. In view of the enormous fortifications on the French frontier such international abolition of the heaviest weapons of attack would *ipso facto* give France one hundred per cent security.

11. Germany declares herself ready to agree to any limitation whatsoever of the caliber strength of artillery, battleships, cruisers, and torpedo boats. In like manner, the German Government is ready to accept any international limitation of the size of warships. And finally it is ready to agree to the limitation of tonnage for submarines, or to their complete abolition in case of international agreement. And it gives the further assurance that it will agree to any international limitation or abolition of arms whatsoever for a uniform space of time.

12. The German Government is of the opinion that all attempts to bring about an alleviation of certain strained relations between individual States by means of international or multilateral agreements must be in vain until suitable measures are taken to prevent the poisoning of public opinion among the nations by irresponsible elements orally or in writing, through the theater or the cinema.

13. The German Government is ready at any time to reach an international agreement which shall effectively prevent all attempts at outside interference in the affairs of other States. It must demand, however, that such a settlement be internationally effective, and work out for the benefit of all States. As there is a danger that in countries where the Government

does not rest on the general confidence of the people, internal upheavals may all too easily be ascribed to external interference, it seems necessary that the conception of "interference" should be subjected to a precise international definition.

Members of the German Reichstag:

I have been at pains to give you a picture of the problems which confront us today. However great the difficulties and worries may be in individual questions, I consider that I owe it to my position as Füehrer and Chancellor of the Reich not to admit a single doubt as to the possibility of maintaining peace. The peoples wish for peace. It must be possible for the Governments to maintain it. I believe that the restoration of the German defense force will contribute to this peace. Not because we intend to increase it beyond all bounds, but because the simple fact of its existence has got rid of a dangerous vacuum in Europe. Germany does not intend to increase her armaments beyond all bounds. We have not got ten thousand bombing planes and we shall not build them. . . .

I cannot better conclude my speech of today to you, my fellow-fighters and trustees of the nation, than by repeating our confession of faith in peace. The nature of our new constitution makes it possible for us in Germany to put a stop to the machinations of war agitators. May the other nations too be able to give bold expression to their real inner longing for peace. Whoever lights the torch of war in Europe can wish for nothing but chaos. We, however, live in the firm conviction that in our time will be fulfilled, not the decline but the renaissance of the West. That Germany may make an imperishable contribution to this great work is our proud hope and our unshakable belief.

A FAR DIFFERENT and undoubtedly more accurate picture of Hitler's policy emerges from the Hossbach Notes. On November 5, 1937, Hitler met in secret conference with his Foreign Minister, his War Minister, and the Commanders-in-Chief of the Army, Navy, and Air Force. From the minutes of this conference, taken by Hitler's adjutant, Colonel Hossbach, there emerges a clear assertion of the Fuehrer's plans for military aggression in Europe.

2. THE HOSSBACH NOTES, 1937

SOURCE. Nuremberg Document # 386-PS.

The Fuehrer stated initially that the subject matter of today's conference was of such high importance, that its further detailed discussion would probably take place in Cabinet sessions. However, he, the Fuehrer, had decided NOT to discuss this matter in the larger circle of the Reich Cabinet, because of its importance. His subsequent statements were the result of detailed deliberations and of the experiences of his 4 and 1/2 years in Government; he desired to explain to those present his fundamental ideas on the possibilities and necessities of expanding our foreign policy and in the interests of a far-sighted policy he requested his statement be looked upon in the case of his death as his last will and testament.

The Fuehrer then stated:

The aim of the Germany policy is the security and preservation of the nation, and its propagation. This is, consequently, a problem of space.

The German nation is composed of 85 million people, which, because of the number of individuals and the compactness of habitation, form a homogeneous European racial body which cannot be found in any other country. On the other hand it justifies the demand for larger living space more than for any other nation. If no political body exists in space, corresponding to the German racial body, [this void] will represent the greatest danger to the preservation of the German nation at its present high level. An arrest of the deterioration of the German element in Austria and Czechoslovakia is just as little possible as the preservation of the present state in Germany itself. . . . The German future is therefore dependent exclusively on the solution of the need for living space. . . .

The question for Germany is where the greatest possible conquest could be made at lowest cost. . . .

The German question can be solved only by way of force, and this is never without risk. The battles of Frederick the Great for Silesia, and Bismarck's wars against Austria and France had been a tremendous risk and the speed of the Russian action in 1870 had prevented Austria from participating in the war. If we place the decision to apply force at the head of the following expositions, then we are left to reply to the questions "when" and "how."

BEGUILED BY HITLER'S SPEECHES and desperately anxious to avoid military conflict, England and France responded to German demands with a policy of appeasement. In the Munich Agreement of September 29, 1938, they submitted to German annexation of the Czechoslovakian Sudetenland which Hitler claimed on the basis that its population was heavily German.

3. THE MUNICH AGREEMENT, 1938

SOURCE. Great Britain, House of Commons, XXX (1937–38), *Accounts and Papers*, XV. Cmd. 5848, "Further Documents Respecting Czechoslovakia, Including the Agreement Concluded at Munich on September 29, 1938," Miscellaneous No. 8 (1938), pp. 3–4.

Germany, the United Kingdom, France, and Italy, taking into consideration the agreement, which has been already reached in principle for the cession to Germany of the Sudeten German territory, have agreed on the following terms and conditions governing the said cession and the measures consequent thereon, and by this agreement they each hold themselves responsible for the steps necessary to secure its fulfillment:

1. The evacuation will begin on the 1st October.

2. The United Kingdom, France, and Italy agree that the evacuation of the territory shall be completed by the 10th October, without any existing installations having been destroyed and that the Czechoslovak Government will be held responsible for carrying out the evacuation without damage to the said installations.

3. The conditions governing the evacuation will be laid down in detail by an international commission composed of representatives of Germany, the United Kingdom, France, Italy, and Czechoslovakia.

4. The occupation by stages of the predominantly German territory by German troops will begin on the 1st October. The four territories marked on the attached map will be occupied by German troops in the following order: the territory marked No. I on the 1st and 2nd of October, the territory marked No. II on the 2nd and 3rd of October, the territory marked No. III on the 3rd, 4th and 5th of October, the territory marked No. IV on the 6th and 7th of October. The remaining territory of preponderantly German character will be ascertained by the aforesaid international commission forthwith and be occupied by German troops by the 10th of October.

5. The international commission referred to in paragraph 3 will determine the territories in which a plebiscite is to be held. These territories will be occupied by international bodies until the plebiscite has been completed. The same commission will fix the conditions in which the

plebiscite is to be held, taking as a basis the conditions of the Saar plebiscite. The commission will also fix a date, not later than the end of November, on which the plebiscite will be held.

6. The final determination of the frontiers will be carried out by the international commission. This commission will also be entitled to recommend to the four Powers, Germany, the United Kingdom, France and Italy, in certain exceptional cases minor modifications in the strictly ethnographical determination of the zones which are to be transferred without plebiscite.

7. There will be a right of option into and out of the transferred territories, the option to be exercised within six months from the date of this agreement. A German-Czechoslovak commission shall determine the details of the option, consider ways of facilitating the transfer of population and settle questions of principle arising out of the said transfer.

8. The Czechoslovak Government will within a period of four weeks from the date of this agreement release from their military and police forces any Sudeten Germans who may wish to be released, and the Czechoslovak Government will within the same period release Sudeten German prisoners who are serving terms of imprisonment for political offences.

ADOLF HITLER
NEVILLE CHAMBERLAIN
ÉDOUARD DALADIER
BENITO MUSSOLINI

ON THE NEXT DAY, September 30, Prime Minister Neville Chamberlain announced to the British people in an airport speech that Hitler had reassured him personally of his peaceful intentions.

4. THE PERSONAL AGREEMENT BETWEEN HITLER AND CHAMBERLAIN, 1938

SOURCE. Neville Chamberlain, *In Search of Peace*, New York: G. P. Putnam's Sons, 1939, p. 200. Reprinted by permission of G. P. Putnam's Sons.

. . . This morning I had another talk with the German Chancellor, Herr Hitler, and here is a paper which bears his name upon it as well as mine. Some of you perhaps have already heard what it contains, but I would just like to read it to you.

We, the German Führer and Chancellor and the British Prime Minister, have had a further meeting today and are agreed in recognizing that the question of Anglo-German relations is of the first importance for the two countries and for Europe.

We regard the agreement signed last night and the Anglo-German Naval Agreement as symbolic of the desire of our two peoples never to go to war with one another again.

We are resolved that the method of consultation shall be the method adopted to deal with any other questions that may concern our two countries, and we are determined to continue our efforts to remove possible sources of difference and thus to assure the peace of Europe.

NEVERTHELESS, IN MARCH, 1939, German troops marched into Prague, and Czechoslovakia became a German protectorate. Hitler now began speaking ominously about Poland's persecution of its German inhabitants. The path to the conquest of Poland was cleared by a totally unexpected treaty of nonaggression between Germany and the Soviet Union (August 23, 1939) which in fact opened the way for aggression by both parties in Poland and the Baltic states.

5. THE RUSSO-GERMAN NONAGGRESSION PACT, 1939

SOURCE. R. G. Sontag and J. Beddie, eds., *Nazi-Soviet Relations, 1939–1941*, Washington, D. C.: U. S. Department of State, 1948, pp. 76 and 78.

ARTICLE I

Both High Contracting Parties obligate themselves to desist from any act of violence, any aggressive action, and any attack on each other, either individually or jointly with other powers. . . .

Secret Additional Protocol

On the occasion of the signature of the Nonaggression Pact between the German Reich and the Union of Socialist Soviet Republics the undersigned plenipotentiaries of each of the two parties discussed in strictly confidential conversations the question of the boundary of their respective spheres of influence in Eastern Europe. These conversations led to the following conclusions:

1. In the event of a territorial and political rearrangement in the areas belonging to the Baltic States (Finland, Estonia, Latvia, Lithuania), the northern boundary of Lithuania shall represent the boundary of the spheres of influence of Germany and the U.S.S.R. In this connection the interest of Lithuania in the Vilna area is recognized by each party.

2. In the event of a territorial and political rearrangement of the areas belonging to the Polish state the spheres of influence of Germany and the U.S.S.R. shall be bounded approximately by the line of the rivers Narew, Vistula, and San.

The question of whether the interests of both parties make desirable the maintenance of an independent Polish state and how such a state should be bounded can only be definitely determined in the course of further political developments.

In any event both Governments will resolve this question by means of a friendly agreement.

3. With regard to Southeastern Europe attention is called by the Soviet side to its interest in Bessarabia. The German side declares its complete political disinterestedness in these areas.

4. This protocol shall be treated by both parties as strictly secret.

Moscow, August 23, 1939.

For the Government
of the German Reich:
  V. Ribbentrop

Plenipotentiary of the
Government of the U.S.S.R.
  V. Molotov

THE COLD CYNICISM of the Russo-German pact drove many European and American Communists out of the Party. The fundamental dishonesty of Hitler's fervent anti-Bolshevik assertions is attested by the secret transcript of a conversation between the German Foreign Minister Ribbentrop and Joseph Stalin on the night following the signing of the Nonaggression Pact. With Hitler's invasion of Poland on September 1, and the declaration of war by Britain and France against Germany two days later, World War II began.

6. TRANSCRIPT OF A CONVERSATION BETWEEN RIBBENTROP AND STALIN, 1939

SOURCE: R. G. Sontag and J. Beddie, eds., *Nazi-Soviet Relations, 1939–1941*, Washington, D. C.: U. S. Department of State, 1948, pp. 72–75 and 76.

Memorandum of a Conversation Held on the Night of August 23rd to 24th, between the Reich Foreign Minister, on the One Hand, and Herr Stalin and the Chairman of the Council of People's Commissars Molotov, on the Other Hand.

VERY SECRET!

STATE SECRET

The following problems were discussed:

1) *Japan*:

The REICH FOREIGN MINISTER stated that the German-Japanese friendship was in no wise directed against the Soviet Union. We were, rather, in a position, owing to our good relations with Japan, to make an effective contribution to an adjustment of the differences between the Soviet Union and Japan. Should Herr Stalin and the Soviet Government desire it, the Reich Foreign Minister was prepared to work in this direction. He would use his influence with the Japanese Government accordingly and keep in touch with the Soviet representative in Berlin in this matter.

HERR STALIN replied that the Soviet Union indeed desired an improvement in its relations with Japan, but that there were limits to its patience with regard to Japanese provocations. If Japan desired war, it could have it. The Soviet Union was not afraid of it and was prepared for it. If Japan desired peace—so much the better! Herr Stalin considered the assistance of Germany in bringing about an improvement in Soviet-Japanese relations as useful, but he did not want the Japanese to get the impression that the initiative in this direction had been taken by the Soviet Union.

The REICH FOREIGN MINISTER assented to this and stressed the fact that his cooperation would mean merely the continuation of talks that he had for months been holding with the Japanese Ambassador in Berlin in the sense of an improvement in Soviet-Japanese relations. Accordingly, there would be no new initiative on the German side in this matter.

2) *Italy*:

HERR STALIN inquired of the Reich Foreign Minister as to Italian aims. Did not Italy have aspirations beyond the annexation of Albania—perhaps for Greek territory? Small, mountainous, and thinly populated Albania was, in his estimation, of no particular use to Italy.

The REICH FOREIGN MINISTER replied that Albania was important to Italy for strategic reasons. Moreover, Mussolini was a strong man who could not be intimidated.

This he had demonstrated in the Abyssinian conflict, in which Italy had asserted its aims by its own strength against a hostile coalition. Even Germany was not yet in a position at that time to give Italy appreciable support.

Mussolini welcomed warmly the restoration of friendly relations between Germany and the Soviet Union. He had expressed himself as gratified with the conclusion of the Nonaggression Pact.

3) *Turkey*:

HERR STALIN asked the Reich Foreign Minister what Germany thought about Turkey.

The REICH FOREIGN MINISTER expressed himself as follows in this matter: he had months ago declared to the Turkish Government that Germany desired friendly relations with Turkey. The Reich Foreign Minister had himself done everything to achieve this goal. The answer had been that Turkey became one of the first countries to join the encirclement pact against Germany and had not even considered it necessary to notify the Reich Government of the fact.

HERREN STALIN and MOLOTOV hereupon observed that the Soviet Union had also had a similar experience with the vacillating policy of the Turks.

The REICH FOREIGN MINISTER mentioned further that England had spent five million pounds in Turkey in order to disseminate propaganda against Germany.

HERR STALIN said that according to his information the amount which England had spent in buying Turkish politicians was considerably more than five million pounds.

4) *England*:

HERREN STALIN and MOLOTOV commented adversely on the British Military Mission in Moscow, which had never told the Soviet Government what it really wanted.

The REICH FOREIGN MINISTER stated in this connection that England had always been trying and was still trying to disrupt the development of good relations between Germany and the Soviet Union. England was weak and wanted to let others fight for its presumptuous claim to world domination.

HERR STALIN eagerly concurred and observed as follows: the British Army was weak; the British Navy no longer deserved its previous reputation. England's air arm was being increased, to be sure, but there was a lack of pilots. If England dominates the world in spite of this, this was due to the stupidity of the other countries that always let themselves be bluffed. It was ridiculous, for example, that a few hundred British should dominate India.

The REICH FOREIGN MINISTER concurred and informed Herr Stalin confidentially that England had recently put out a new feeler which was connected with certain allusions to 1914. It was a matter of a typically English, stupid maneuver. The Reich Foreign Minister had proposed to the Führer to inform the British that every hostile British act, in case of a German-Polish conflict, would be answered by a bombing attack on London.

HERR STALIN remarked that the feeler was evidently Chamberlain's letter to the Führer, which Ambassador Henderson delivered on August 23 at the Obersalzberg. Stalin further expressed the opinion that England, despite its weakness, would wage war craftily and stubbornly.

5) *France*:

HERR STALIN expressed the opinion that France, nevertheless, had an army worthy of consideration.

The REICH FOREIGN MINISTER, on his part, pointed out to Herren Stalin and Molotov the numerical inferiority of France. While Germany had available an annual class of more than 300,000 soldiers, France could muster only 150,000 recruits annually. The West Wall was five times as strong as the Maginot Line. If France attempted to wage war with Germany, she would certainly be conquered.

6) *Anti-Comintern Pact*:

The REICH FOREIGN MINISTER observed that the Anti-Comintern Pact was basically directed not against the Soviet Union but against the Western democracies. He knew, and was able to infer from the tone of the Russian press, that the Soviet Government fully recognized this fact.

HERR STALIN interposed that the Anti-Comintern Pact had in fact frightened principally the City of London and the small British merchants.

The REICH FOREIGN MINISTER concurred and remarked jokingly that Herr Stalin was surely less frightened by the Anti-Comintern Pact than the City of London and the small British merchants. What the German people thought of this matter is evident from a joke which had originated with the Berliners, well known for their wit and humor, and which had been going the rounds for several months, namely, "Stalin will yet join the Anti-Comintern Pact." . . .

9) When they took their leave, HERR STALIN addressed to the Reich Foreign Ministers words to this effect:

The Soviet Government takes the new Pact very seriously. He could guarantee on his word of honor that the Soviet Union would not betray its partner.

Moscow, August 24, 1939.   HENCKE

B. The War Years

THE RESOLUTION OF THE BRITISH was strengthened by the deter-mined policies and eloquent speeches of its wartime Prime Minister, Winston Churchill, who, on May 13, 1940, delivered his first and most memorable ad-dress to the House of Commons.

1. WINSTON CHURCHILL'S FIRST ADDRESS TO COMMONS, 1940

SOURCE. Great Britain, House of Commons, *Parliamentary Debates,* 5th Series, CCCLX, p. 1502.

. . . In this crisis I hope I may be pardoned if I do not address the House at any length today. I hope that any of my friends and colleagues, or former colleagues, who are affected by the political reconstruction, will make allowance, all allowance, for any lack of ceremony with which it has been necessary to act. I would say to the House, as I said to those who have joined this Government; "I have nothing to offer but blood, toil, tears and sweat."

We have before us an ordeal of the most grievous kind. We have before us many, many long months of struggle and of suffering. You ask, what is our policy? I will say: It is to wage war, by sea, land, and air, with all our might and with all the strength that God can give us: to wage war against a monstrous tyranny, never surpassed in the dark, lamentable catalogue of human crime. That is our policy. You ask, what is our aim? I can answer in one word: It is victory, victory at all costs, victory in spite of all terror, victory, however long and hard the road may be; for without victory there is no survival. Let that be realized; no survival for the British Empire; no survival for all that the British Empire has stood for, no sur-vival for the urge and impulse of the ages, that mankind will move for-ward towards its goal. But I take up my task with buoyancy and hope. I feel sure that our cause will not be suffered to fail among men. At this time I feel entitled to claim the aid of all, and I say, "Come, then, let us go forward together with our united strength."

ON SEPTEMBER 27, 1940, Germany, Italy, and Japan concluded a pact of alliance known as the Rome–Berlin–Tokyo Axis.

2. THE AXIS PACT, 1940

SOURCE. German Library of Information, *Facts in Review*, New York, 1941, II, p. 486.

The Governments of Germany, Italy, and Japan consider it the prerequisite of lasting peace that every nation in the world shall receive the space to which it is entitled. They have, therefore, decided to stand by and co-operate with one another in their efforts in Greater East Asia and the regions of Europe respectively. In doing this it is their prime purpose to establish and maintain a new order of things, calculated to promote the mutual prosperity and welfare of the peoples concerned.

It is, furthermore, the desire of the three Governments to extend co-operation to other nations . . . who are inclined to direct their efforts along lines similar to their own for the purpose of realizing their ultimate object, world peace.

Accordingly, the Governments of Germany, Italy and Japan have agreed as follows:

ARTICLE 1. Japan recognizes and respects the leadership of Germany and Italy in the establishment of a new order in Europe.

ARTICLE 2. Germany and Italy recognize and respect the leadership of Japan in the establishment of a new order in Greater East Asia.

ARTICLE 3. Germany, Italy and Japan agree to co-operate in their efforts on the aforesaid lines. They further undertake to assist one another with all political, economic and military means if one of the three Contracting Powers is attacked by a Power at present not involved in the European War or in the Chinese-Japanese conflict.

ARTICLE 4. With a view to implementing the present pact, joint technical commissions, the members of which are to be appointed by the governments of Germany, Italy, and Japan, will meet without delay.

ARTICLE 6. The present pact shall become valid immediately upon signature and shall remain in force ten years. . . .

Done in triplicate at Berlin, the 27th day of September, 1940, in the eighteenth year of the Fascist era, corresponding to the 27th day of the ninth month of the fifteenth year of Showa.

MEANWHILE THE UNITED STATES, although not yet formally a belligerent, was providing massive aid to Britain. On August 14, 1941, President Franklin D. Roosevelt and Prime Minister Churchill, meeting aboard a battleship in mid-ocean, issued an important declaration of common aims known as the Atlantic Charter which became a basis of Allied war goals.

3. THE ATLANTIC CHARTER, 1941

SOURCE. *Congressional Record*, LXXXVII, 77th Congress, 1st Session, p. 7217.

The President of the United States of America and the Prime Minister, Mr. Churchill, representing His Majesty's Government in the United Kingdom, being met together, deem it right to make known certain common principles in the national policies of their respective countries on which they base their hopes for a better future for the world.

First, their countries seek no aggrandizement, territorial or other;

Second, they desire to see no territorial changes that do not accord with the freely expressed wishes of the peoples concerned;

Third, they respect the right of all peoples to choose the form of government under which they will live; and they wish to see sovereign rights and self-government restored to those who have been forcibly deprived of them;

Fourth, they will endeavor, with due respect for their existing obligations, to further the enjoyment by all States, great or small, victor or vanquished, of access, on equal terms, to the trade and to the raw materials of the world which are needed for their economic prosperity;

Fifth, they desire to bring about the fullest collaboration between all nations in the economic field with the object of securing, for all, improved labor standards, economic adjustment and social security;

Sixth, after the final destruction of the Nazi tyranny, they hope to see established a peace which will afford all nations the means of dwelling in safety within their own boundaries, and which will afford assurance that all the men in all the lands may live out their lives in freedom from fear and want;

Seventh, such a peace should enable all men to traverse the high seas and oceans without hindrance;

Eighth, they believe that all of the nations of the world, for realistic as well as spiritual reasons, must come to the abandonment of the use of force. Since no future peace can be maintained if land, sea or air armaments continue to be employed by nations which threaten, or may threaten, aggression outside of their frontiers, they believe, pending the establishment of a wider and permanent system of general security, that the disarmament of such nations is essential. They will likewise aid and encourage all other practicable measures which will lighten for peaceloving peoples the crushing burden of armaments.

FRANKLIN D. ROOSEVELT
WINSTON S. CHURCHILL

WITH THE JAPANESE ATTACK on Pearl Harbor, America entered fully into the war. On December 8, 1941, President Roosevelt delivered a ringing war message to Congress, and the two Houses responded with a formal declaration of war against the Axis powers.

4. PRESIDENT FRANKLIN D. ROOSEVELT'S WAR MESSAGE TO CONGRESS, 1941

SOURCE. *World Almanac, 1942*, New York: N. Y. World Telegram, 1943, p. 44. Reprinted by permission of World Almanac.

Yesterday, December 7, 1941—A date which will live in infamy—the United States of America was suddenly and deliberately attacked by naval and air forces of the Empire of Japan.

The United States was at peace with that nation and, at the solicitation of Japan, was still in conversation with its Government and its Emperor looking toward the maintenance of peace in the Pacific.

Indeed, one hour after Japanese air squadrons had commenced bombing Oahu, the Japanese Ambassador to the United States and his colleague delivered to the Secretary of State a formal reply to a recent American message. While this reply stated that it seemed useless to continue the existing diplomatic negotiations, it contained no threat or hint of war or armed attack.

It will be recorded that the distance of Hawaii from Japan makes it obvious that the attack was deliberately planned many days or even weeks ago. During the intervening time, the Japanese Government has deliberately sought to deceive the United States by false statements and expressions of hope for continued peace.

The attack yesterday on the Hawaiian Islands has caused severe damage to American naval and military forces. Very many American lives have been lost. In addition, American ships have been reported torpedoed on the high seas between San Francisco and Honolulu.

Yesterday the Japanese Government also launched an attack against Malaya.

Last night Japanese forces attacked Hong Kong.

Last night Japanese forces attacked Guam.

Last night Japanese forces attacked the Philippine Islands.

Last night the Japanese attacked Wake Island.

This morning the Japanese attacked Midway Island.

Japan has, therefore, undertaken a surprise offensive extending throughout the Pacific area. The facts of yesterday speak for themselves. The people of the United States have already formed their opinions and well understand the implications to the very life and safety of our nation.

As Commander in Chief of the army and navy I have directed that all measures be taken for our defense.

Always will we remember the character of the onslaught against us.

No matter how long it may take us to overcome this premeditated invasion, the American people in their righteous might will win through the absolute victory.

I believe I interpret the will of the Congress and of the people when I assert that we will not only defend ourselves to the uttermost but will make very certain that this form of treachery shall never endanger us again.

Hostilities exist. There is no blinking at the fact that our people, our territory and our interests are in grave danger.

With confidence in our armed forces—with the unbounding determination of our people—we will gain the inevitable triumph—so help us God.

I ask that the Congress declare that since the unprovoked and dastardly attack by Japan on Sunday, December 7, a state of war has existed between the United States and the Japanese Empire.

FRANKLIN D. ROOSEVELT

SHORTLY BEFORE THE END of the war, Roosevelt, Churchill, and Stalin met at Yalta in the Crimea (February 4–11, 1945) in order to reach agreement on aspects of the coming postwar settlement. Stalin made territorial demands in violation of the Atlantic Charter, and Roosevelt and Churchill, anxious to obtain Russian participation in the war against Japan, bowed to Stalin's wishes.

5. THE JAPANESE AGREEMENT FROM THE YALTA TREATY, 1945

SOURCE. Department of State Press Release, No. 239, March 24, 1947.

The leaders of the three great powers—the Soviet Union, the United States of America, and Great Britain—have agreed that in two or three months after Germany has surrendered and the war in Europe has terminated, the Soviet Union shall enter into the war against Japan on the side of the Allies on condition that:

1. The *status quo* in Outer Mongolia (the Mongolian People's Republic) shall be preserved;

2. The former rights of Russia violated by the treacherous attack of Japan in 1904 shall be restored, viz.:

a. The southern part of Sakhalin as well as the islands adjacent to it shall be returned to the Soviet Union;

b. The commercial port of Dairen shall be internationalized, the preeminent interests of the Soviet Union in this port being safeguarded, and the lease of Port Arthur as a naval base of U.S.S.R. restored;

c. The Chinese Eastern Railroad and the South Manchurian Railroad, which provides an outlet to Dairen, shall be jointly operated by the establishment of a joint Soviet-Chinese company, it being understood that the preeminent interests of the Soviet Union shall be safeguarded and that China shall retain full sovereignty in Manchuria;

3. The Kurile Islands shall be handed over to the Soviet Union. It is understood that the agreement concerning Outer Mongolia and the ports and railroads referred to above will require concurrence of Generalissimo Chiang Kai-shek. The President [*Roosevelt*] will take measures in order to obtain this concurrence on advice from Marshal Stalin.

The heads of the three great powers have agreed that these claims of the Soviet Union shall be unquestionably fulfilled after Japan has been defeated.

For its part, the Soviet Union expresses its readiness to conclude with the National Government of China a pact of friendship and alliance between the U.S.S.R. and China in order to render assistance to China with its armed forces for the purpose of liberating China from the Japanese yoke.

JOSEPH V. STALIN
FRANKLIN D. ROOSEVELT
WINSTON S. CHURCHILL

AT A TIME WHEN the success of the atomic bomb was yet uncertain, it seemed to Roosevelt that Russian entry into the struggle with Japan would shorten the war considerably. Nevertheless, a number of postwar observers regarded the Yalta concessions as an unfortunate revival of appeasement. Two months after the defeat of Nazi Germany, the "Big Three" met again at Potsdam, with Stalin representing the Soviet Union and President Harry S. Truman now representing the United States. The new British Labour Prime Minister, Clement Attlee, replaced Winston Churchill midway through the conference. The Potsdam Declaration (August 2, 1945) dealt with the problems of German occupation and political and economic reconstitution.

6. THE POTSDAM DECLARATION, 1945

SOURCE. U. S. Department of State, *Bulletin*, XIII, No. 319, August 5, 1945, pp. 154–156.

The Allied Armies are in occupation of the whole of Germany and the German people have begun to atone for the terrible crimes committed under the leadership of those whom in the hour of their success, they openly approved and blindly obeyed.

Agreement has been reached at this conference on the political and economic principles of a co-ordinated Allied policy toward defeated Germany during the period of Allied control.

The purpose of this agreement is to carry out the Crimea [Yalta] Declaration on Germany. German militarism and Nazism will be extirpated and the Allies will take in agreement together, now and in the future, the other measures necessary to assure that Germany never again will threaten her neighbors or the peace of the world.

It is not the intention of the Allies to destroy or enslave the German people. It is the intention of the Allies that the German people be given the opportunity to prepare for the eventual reconstruction of their life on a democratic and peaceful basis. If their own efforts are steadily directed to this end, it will be possible for them in due course to take their place among the free and peaceful peoples of the world.

The text of the agreement is as follows:

1. In accordance with the agreement on control machinery in Germany, supreme authority in Germany is exercised on instructions from their respective governments, by the Commanders-in-Chief of the armed forces of the United States of America, the United Kingdom, the Union of Soviet Socialist Republics, and the French Republic, each in his own zone of occupation, and also jointly, in matters affecting Germany as a whole, in their capacity as members of the Control Council.

2. So far as practicable, there shall be uniformity of treatment of the German population throughout Germany.

3. The purposes of the occupation of Germany by which the Control Council shall be guided are:

(i) The complete disarmament and demilitarization of Germany and the elimination or control of all German industry that could be used for military production. To these ends:

(a) All German land, naval and air forces, the S.S., S.A., S.D., and Gestapo, with all their organizations, staffs and institutions, including the General Staff, the Officers' Corps, Reserve Corps, military schools, war veterans' organizations and all other military and quasi-military organizations, together with all clubs and associations which serve to keep alive the military tradition in Germany, shall be completely and finally abolished in such manner as permanently to prevent the revival or reorganization of German militarism and Nazism.

(b) All arms, ammunition and implements of war and all specialized facilities for their production shall be held at the disposal of the Allies or destroyed. The maintenance and production of all aircraft and all arms, ammunition and implements of war shall be prevented.

(ii) To convince the German people that they have suffered a total military defeat and that they cannot escape responsibility for what they have brought upon themselves, since their own ruthless warfare and the fanatical Nazi resistance have destroyed German economy and made chaos and suffering inevitable.

(iii) To destroy the National Socialist Party and its affiliated and supervised organizations, to dissolve all Nazi institutions, to ensure that they are not revived in any form, and to prevent all Nazi and militarist activity or propaganda.

(iv) To prepare for the eventual reconstruction of German political life on a democratic basis and for eventual peaceful cooperation in international life by Germany.

4. All Nazi laws which provided the basis of the Hitler regime or established discrimination on grounds of race, creed, or political opinion shall be abolished. No such discrimination, whether legal, administrative or otherwise, shall be tolerated.

5. War criminals and those who have participated in planning or carrying out Nazi enterprises involving or resulting in atrocities or war crimes shall be arrested and brought to judgment. Nazi leaders, influential Nazi supporters and high officials of Nazi organizations and institutions and any other persons dangerous to the occupation or its objectives shall be arrested and interned.

6. All members of the Nazi party who have been more than nominal participants in its activities and all other persons hostile to allied purposes shall be removed from public and semi-public office, and from positions of responsibility in important private undertakings. Such persons shall be replaced by persons who, by their political and moral qualities, are deemed capable of assisting in developing genuine democratic institutions in Germany.

7. German education shall be so controlled as completely to eliminate Nazi militarist doctrines and to make possible the successful development of democratic ideas.

8. The judicial system will be reorganized in accordance with the principles of democracy, of justice under law, and of equal rights for all citizens without distinction of race, nationality or religion.

9. The administration of affairs in Germany should be directed towards the decentralization of the political structure and the development of local responsibility. To this end:

(i) Local self-government shall be restored throughout Germany on democratic principles and in particular through elective councils as rapidly as is consistent with military security and the purposes of military occupation;

(ii) All democratic political parties with rights of assembly and of public discussion shall be allowed and encouraged throughout Germany;

(iii) Representative and elective principles shall be introduced into regional, provincial and state (land) administration as rapidly as may be justified by the successful application of these principles in local self-government;

(iv) For the time being no central German government shall be established. Notwithstanding this, however, certain essential central German administrative departments, headed by state secretaries, shall be established, particularly in the fields of finance, transport, communications, foreign trade and industry. Such departments will act under the direction of the Control Council.

10. Subject to the necessity for maintaining military security, freedom of speech, press and religion shall be permitted, and religious institutions shall be respected. Subject likewise to the maintenance of military security, the formation of free trade unions shall be permitted.

A FEW DAYS after the Potsdam Declaration the war with Japan came to an end with the dropping of atomic bombs on Hiroshima and Nagasaki. In a speech of August 6, President Truman announced America's first use of the awesome new weapon that was soon to hold the entire world in a precarious balance of terror.

7. PRESIDENT HARRY S. TRUMAN ANNOUNCES THE BOMBING OF HIROSHIMA, 1945

SOURCE. *The New York Times,* August 7, 1945, p. 4. Copyright 1945 by The New York Times Co. Reprinted by permission of *The New York Times.*

Sixteen hours ago an American airplane dropped one bomb on Hiroshima, an important Japanese Army base. That bomb had more power than 20,000 tons of TNT. . . .

The Japanese began the war from the air at Pearl Harbor. They have been repaid manyfold. And the end is not yet. With this bomb we have now added a new and revolutionary increase in destruction to supplement the growing power of our armed forces. In their present form these bombs are now in production and even more powerful forms are in development.

It is an atomic bomb. It is a harnessing of the basic power of the universe. The force from which the sun draws its powers has been loosed against those who brought war to the Far East.

Before 1939, it was the accepted belief of scientists that it was theoretically possible to release atomic energy. But no one knew any practical method of doing it. By 1942, however, we knew that the Germans were working feverishly to find a way to add atomic energy to the other engines of war with which they hoped to enslave the world. But they failed. We may be grateful to Providence that the Germans got the V-1's and the V-2's late and in limited quantities and even more grateful that they did not get the atomic bomb at all.

The battle of the laboratories held fateful risks for us as well as the battles of the air, land, and sea, and we have now won the battle of the laboratories as we have won the other battles.

Beginning in 1940. . . . American and British scientists working together . . . entered the race of discovery against the Germans. . . .

In the United States the laboratory work and the production plants, on which a substantial start had already been made, would be out of the reach of enemy bombing, while at the time Britain was exposed to constant air attack and was still threatened with the possibility of invasion.

For these reasons Prime Minister Churchill and President Roosevelt agreed that it would be wise to carry on the project here. We now have two great plants and many lesser works devoted to the production of atomic power. Employment during peak construction numbered 125,000. . . . Few know what they have been producing. . . . We have spent two billion dollars on the greatest scientific gamble in history—and won. . . .

We are now prepared to obliterate more rapidly and completely every productive enterprise the Japanese have above ground in any city. . . . Let there be no mistake; we shall completely destroy Japan's power to make war.

It was to spare the Japanese people from destruction that the ultimatum of July 26 was issued at Potsdam. Their leaders promptly rejected that ultimatum. If they do not now accept our terms they may expect a rain of ruin from the air, the like of which has never been seen on this earth. . . .

The fact that we can release atomic energy ushers in a new age in man's understanding of nature's forces. . . . It has never been the habit

of the scientists of this country or the policy of the Government to withhold from the world scientific knowledge. . . .

But under present circumstances it is not intended to divulge the ter-
minal processes of production of all the military applications pending
further examination of possible methods of protecting us and the rest of
the world from the danger of sudden destruction.

I shall recommend that the Congress of the United States consider
promptly the establishment of an appropriate commission to control the
production and use of atomic power.

Part II

THE POSTWAR WORLD

A. The Promise of Peace

WITH THE SIGNING of the United Nations Charter on June 26, 1945, the world took a new step in the direction of international cooperation and world government. The postwar career of the United Nations has been disappointing to many, for the development of the Cold War tended to weaken the peace-enforcing machinery of the Security Council. Nevertheless, the United Nations played a significant role in the Korean War, the Suez crisis, the Congo crisis, and other postwar conflicts.

1. EXCERPTS FROM THE UNITED NATIONS CHARTER, 1945

SOURCE. Reprinted by permission of The United Nations.

WE THE PEOPLES OF THE UNITED NATIONS DETERMINED

to save succeeding generations from the scourge of war, which twice in our lifetime has brought untold sorrow to mankind, and

to reaffirm faith in fundamental human rights, in the dignity and worth of the human person, in the equal rights of men and women and of nations large and small, and

to establish conditions under which justice and respect for the obligations arising from treaties and other sources of international law can be maintained, and

to promote social progress and better standards of life in larger freedom,

AND FOR THESE ENDS

to practice tolerance and live together in peace with one another as good neighbors, and

to unite our strength to maintain international peace and security, and

to ensure, by the acceptance of principles and the institution of methods, that armed force shall not be used, save in the common interest, and to employ international machinery for the promotion of the economic and social advancement of all peoples,

HAVE RESOLVED TO COMBINE OUR EFFORTS TO ACCOMPLISH THESE AIMS.

Accordingly, our respective Governments, through representatives assembled in the city of San Francisco, who have exhibited their full powers found to be in good and due form, have agreed to the present Charter of the United Nations and do hereby establish an international organization to be known as the United Nations.

Chapter 1. Purposes and Principles

ARTICLE 1

The Purposes of the United Nations are:

1. To maintain international peace and security, and to that end: to take effective collective measures for the prevention and removal of threats to the peace, and for the suppression of acts of aggression or other breaches of the peace, and to bring about by peaceful means, and in conformity with the principles of justice and international law, adjustment or settlement of international disputes or situations which might lead to a breach of the peace;

2. To develop friendly relations among nations based on respect for the principle of equal rights and self-determination of peoples, and to take other appropriate measures to strengthen universal peace;

3. To achieve international cooperation in solving international problems of an economic, social, cultural, or humanitarian character, and in promoting and encouraging respect for human rights and for fundamental freedoms for all without distinction as to race, sex, language, or religion; and

4. To be a center for harmonizing the actions of nations in the attainment of these common ends.

ARTICLE 2

The Organization and its Members, in pursuit of the Purposes stated in Article 1, shall act in accordance with the following Principles.

1. The Organization is based on the principle of the sovereign equality of all its Members.

2. All Members, in order to ensure to all of them the rights and benefits resulting from membership, shall fulfil in good faith the obligations assumed by them in accordance with the present Charter.

3. All Members shall settle their international disputes by peaceful means in such a manner that international peace and security, and justice, are not endangered.

4. All Members shall refrain in their international relations from the threat or use of force against the territorial integrity or political independence of any state, or in any other manner inconsistent with the Purposes of the United Nations.

5. All Members shall give the United Nations every assistance in any action it takes in accordance with the present Charter, and shall refrain from giving assistance to any state against which the United Nations is taking preventive or enforcement action.

6. The Organization shall ensure that states which are not Members of the United Nations act in accordance with these Principles so far as may be necessary for the maintenance of international peace and security.

7. Nothing contained in the present Charter shall authorize the United Nations to intervene in matters which are essentially within the domestic jurisdiction of any state or shall require the Members to submit such matters to settlement under the present Charter; but this principle shall not prejudice the application of enforcement measures under Chapter VII.

Chapter II. Membership

ARTICLE 3

The original Members of the United Nations shall be the states which, having participated in the United Nations Conference on International Organization at San Francisco, or having previously signed the Declaration by United Nations of January 1, 1942, sign the present Charter and ratify it in accordance with Article 110.

ARTICLE 4

1. Membership in the United Nations is open to all other peace-loving states which accept the obligations contained in the present Charter and, in the judgment of the Organization, are able and willing to carry out these obligations.

2. The admission of any such state to membership in the United Nations will be effected by a decision of the General Assembly upon the recommendation of the Security Council.

ARTICLE 5

A Member of the United Nations against which preventive or enforcement action has been taken by the Security Council may be suspended from the exercise of the rights and privileges of membership by the General Assembly upon the recommendation of the Security Council. The exercise of these rights and privileges may be restored by the Security Council.

ARTICLE 6

A Member of the United Nations which has persistently violated the Principles contained in the present Charter may be expelled from the Organization by the General Assembly upon the recommendation of the Security Council.

Chapter III. Organs

ARTICLE 7

1. There are established as the principal organs of the United Nations: a General Assembly, a Security Council, an Economic and Social Council, a Trusteeship Council, an International Court of Justice, and a Secretariat.

2. Such subsidiary organs as may be found necessary may be established in accordance with the present Charter.

ARTICLE 8

The United Nations shall place no restrictions on the eligibility of men and women to participate in any capacity and under conditions of equality in its principal and subsidiary organs.

Chapter IV. The General Assembly

Composition

ARTICLE 9

1. The General Assembly shall consist of all the Members of the United Nations.

2. Each Member shall have not more than five representatives in the General Assembly.

Functions and Powers

ARTICLE 10

The General Assembly may discuss any questions or any matters within the scope of the present Charter or relating to the powers and functions of any organs provided for in the present Charter, and, except as provided in Article 12, may make recommendations to the Members of the United Nations or to the Security Council or to both on any such questions or matters.

ARTICLE 11

1. The General Assembly may consider the general principles of co-operation in the maintenance of international peace and security, including the principles governing disarmament and the regulation of armaments, and may make recommendations with regard to such principles to the Members or to the Security Council or to both.

2. The General Assembly may discuss any questions relating to the maintenance of international peace and security brought before it by any Member of the United Nations, or by the Security Council, or by a state which is not a Member of the United Nations in accordance with Article 35, paragraph 2, and, except as provided in Article 12, may make recommendations with regard to any such question to the state or states concerned or to the Security Council or to both. Any such question on which action is necessary shall be referred to the Security Council by the General Assembly either before or after discussion.

3. The General Assembly may call the attention of the Security Council to situations which are likely to endanger international peace and security.

4. The powers of the General Assembly set forth in this Article shall not limit the general scope of Article 10. . . .

Voting

ARTICLE 18

1. Each member of the General Assembly shall have one vote.

2. Decisions of the General Assembly on important questions shall be made by a two-thirds majority of the members present and voting. These questions shall include: recommendations with respect to the maintenance of international peace and security, the election of the non-permanent members of the Security Council, the election of the members of the Economic and Social Council, the election of members of the Trusteeship Council in accordance with paragraph 1(c) of Article 86, the admission of new Members to the United Nations, the suspension of the rights and privileges of membership, the expulsion of Members, questions relating to the operation of the trusteeship system, and budgetary questions.

3. Decisions on other questions, including the determination of additional categories of questions to be decided by a two-thirds majority, shall be made by a majority of the members present and voting.

ARTICLE 19

A Member of the United Nations which is in arrears in the payment of its financial contributions to the Organization shall have no vote in the General Assembly if the amount of its arrears equals or exceeds the amount of the contributions due from it for the preceding two full years. The General Assembly may, nevertheless, permit such a Member to vote if it is satisfied that the failure to pay is due to conditions beyond the control of the Member. . . .

Chapter V. The Security Council

Composition

ARTICLE 23

1. The Security Council shall consist of eleven Members of the United Nations. The Republic of China, France, the Union of Soviet Socialist Republics, the United Kingdom of Great Britain and Northern Ireland, and the United States of America shall be permanent members of the Security Council. The General Assembly shall elect six other Members of the United Nations to be non-permanent members of the Security Council, due regard being specially paid, in the first instance to the contribution of Members of the United Nations to the maintenance of international peace and security and to the other purposes of the Organization, and also to equitable geographical distribution.

2. The non-permanent members of the Security Council shall be elected for a term of two years. In the first election of the non-permanent members, however, three shall be chosen for a term of one year. A retiring member shall not be eligible for re-election.

3. Each member of the Security Council shall have one representative.

Functions and Powers

ARTICLE 24

1. In order to ensure prompt and effective action by the United Nations, its Members confer on the Security Council primary responsibility for the maintenance of international peace and security, and agree that in carrying out its duties under this responsibility the Security Council acts on their behalf.

2. In discharging these duties the Security Council shall act in accordance with the Purposes and Principles of the United Nations. . . .

Voting

ARTICLE 27

1. Each member of the Security Council shall have one vote.

2. Decisions of the Security Council on procedural matters shall be made by an affirmative vote of seven members.

3. Decisions of the Security Council on all other matters shall be made by an affirmative vote of seven members including the concurring votes of the permanent members. . . .

Chapter VI. Pacific Settlement of Disputes

ARTICLE 33

1. The parties to any dispute, the continuance of which is likely to endanger the maintenance of international peace and security, shall, first of all, seek a solution by negotiation, enquiry, mediation, conciliation, arbitration, judicial settlement, resort to regional agencies or arrangements, or other peaceful means of their own choice.

2. The Security Council shall, when it deems necessary, call upon the parties to settle their dispute by such means.

ARTICLE 34

The Security Council may investigate any dispute, or any situation which might lead to international friction or give rise to a dispute, in order to determine whether the continuance of the dispute or situation is likely to endanger the maintenance of international peace and security.

ARTICLE 35

1. Any Member of the United Nations may bring any dispute, or any situation of the nature referred to in Article 34, to the attention of the Security Council or of the General Assembly.

2. A state which is not a Member of the United Nations may bring to the attention of the Security Council or of the General Assembly any dispute to which it is a party if it accepts in advance, for the purposes of the dispute, the obligations of pacific settlement provided in the present Charter. . . .

Chapter VII. Action with Respect to Threats to the Peace, Breaches of the Peace, and Acts of Aggression

ARTICLE 39

The Security Council shall determine the existence of any threat to the peace, breach of the peace, or act of aggression and shall make recommendations, or decide what measures shall be taken in accordance with Articles 41 and 42, to maintain or restore international peace and security.

ARTICLE 40

In order to prevent an aggravation of the situation, the Security Council may, before making the recommendations or deciding upon the measures provided for in Article 39, call upon the parties concerned to comply with such provisional measures as it deems necessary or desirable. Such provisional measures shall be without prejudice to the rights, claims, or position of the parties concerned. The Security Council shall duly take account of failure to comply with such provisional measures.

ARTICLE 41

The Security Council may decide what measures not involving the use of armed force are to be employed to give effect to its decisions, and it may call upon the Members of the United Nations to apply such measures. These may include complete or partial interruption of economic relations and of rail, sea, air, postal, telegraphic, radio, and other means of communication, and the severance of diplomatic relations.

ARTICLE 42

Should the Security Council consider that measures provided for in Article 41 would be inadequate or have proved to be inadequate, it may take such action by air, sea, or land forces as may be necessary to maintain or restore international peace and security. Such action may include demonstration, blockade, and other operations by air, sea, or land forces of Members of the United Nations.

ARTICLE 43

1. All Members of the United Nations, in order to contribute to the maintenance of international peace and security, undertake to make available to the Security Council, on its call and in accordance with a special agreement or agreements, armed forces, assistance, and facilities, including rights of passage, necessary for the purpose of maintaining international peace and security.

2. Such agreement or agreements shall govern the numbers and types of forces, their degree of readiness and general location, and the nature of the facilities and assistance to be provided. . . .

ARTICLE 51

Nothing in the present Charter shall impair the inherent right of individual or collective self-defense if an armed attack occurs against a Member of the United Nations, until the Security Council has taken measures necessary to maintain international peace and security. Measures taken by Members in the exercise of this right of self-defense shall be immediately reported to the Security Council and shall not in any way affect the authority and responsibility of the Security Council under the present Charter to take at any time such action as it deems necessary in order to maintain or restore international peace and security.

Chapter VIII. Regional Arrangements

ARTICLE 52

1. Nothing in the present Charter precludes the existence of regional arrangements or agencies for dealing with such matters relating to the maintenance of international peace and security as are appropriate for regional action, provided that such arrangements or agencies and their activities are consistent with the Purposes and Principles of the United Nations.

2. The Members of the United Nations entering into such arrangements or constituting such agencies shall make every effort to achieve pacific settlement of local disputes through such regional arrangements or by such regional agencies before referring them to the Security Council.

3. The Security Council shall encourage the development of pacific settlement of local disputes through such regional arrangements or by such regional agencies either on the initiative of the states concerned or by reference from the Security Council. . . .

ARTICLE 54

The Security Council shall at all times be kept fully informed of activities undertaken or in contemplation under regional arrangements or by regional agencies for the maintenance of international peace and security.

Chapter IX. International Economic and Social Cooperation

ARTICLE 55

With a view to the creation of conditions of stability and well-being which are necessary for peaceful and friendly relations among nations based on respect for the principle of equal rights and self-determination of peoples, the United Nations shall promote:

a. higher standards of living, full employment, and conditions of economic and social progress and development;

b. solutions of international economic, social, health, and related problems; and international cultural and educational cooperation; and

c. universal respect for, and observance of, human rights and fundamental freedoms for all without distinction as to race, sex, language, or religion. . . .

Chapter XIV. *The International Court of Justice*

ARTICLE 92

The International Court of Justice shall be the principal judicial organ of the United Nations. It shall function in accordance with the annexed Statute, which is based upon the Statute of the Permanent Court of International Justice and forms an integral part of the present Charter.

ARTICLE 93

1. All Members of the United Nations are *ipso facto* parties to the Statute of the International Court of Justice.

2. A state which is not a Member of the United Nations may become a party to the Statute of the International Court of Justice on condition to be determined in each case by the General Assembly upon the recommendation of the Security Council.

ARTICLE 94

1. Each Member of the United Nations undertakes to comply with the decision of the International Court of Justice in any case to which it is a party.

2. If any party to a case fails to perform the obligations incumbent upon it under a judgment rendered by the Court, the other party may have recourse to the Security Council, which may, if it deems necessary, make recommendations or decide upon measures to be taken to give effect to the judgment.

ARTICLE 95

Nothing in the present Charter shall prevent Members of the United Nations from entrusting the solution of their differences to other tribunals by virtue of agreements already in existence or which may be concluded in the future.

ARTICLE 96

1. The General Assembly or the Security Council may request the International Court of Justice to give an advisory opinion on any legal question.

2. Other organs of the United Nations and specialized agencies, which may at any time be so authorized by the General Assembly, may also request advisory opinions of the Court on legal questions arising within the scope of their activities.

Chapter XV. The Secretariat

ARTICLE 97

The Secretariat shall comprise a Secretary-General and such staff as the Organization may require. The Secretary-General shall be appointed by the General Assembly upon the recommendation of the Security Council. He shall be the chief administrative officer of the Organization.

ARTICLE 98

The Secretary-General shall act in that capacity in all meetings of the General Assembly, of the Security Council, of the Economic and Social Council, and of the Trusteeship Council, and shall perform such other functions as are entrusted to him by these organs. The Secretary-General shall make an annual report to the General Assembly on the work of the Organization.

ARTICLE 99

The Secretary-General may bring to the attention of the Security Council any matter which in his opinion may threaten the maintenance of international peace and security.

ARTICLE 100

1. In the performance of their duties the Secretary-General and the staff shall not seek or receive instructions from any government or from any other authority external to the Organization. They shall refrain from any action which might reflect on their position as international officials responsible only to the Organization.

2. Each Member of the United Nations undertakes to respect the exclusively international character of the responsibilities of the Secretary-General and the staff and not to seek to influence them in the discharge of their responsibilities.

THE TERRIFYING POTENTIAL of atomic weaponry prompted Bernard Baruch, speaking for the United States government, to present to the United Nations Atomic Energy Commission in June, 1946, a series of proposals for international atomic control. Russia, which had not yet developed the bomb, nevertheless rejected the proposals on the grounds of the inspection provisions and the absence of a veto power in the proposed new atomic authority.

2. THE BARUCH PROPOSALS ON ATOMIC CONTROL

SOURCE. U. S. Department of State, *The United States and the United Nations,* Report Series No. 7, Washington, D. C.: 1947, pp. 169–178.

My Fellow Members of the United Nations Atomic Energy Commission, and My Fellow Citizens of the World:

We are here to make a choice between the quick and the dead.

That is our business.

Behind the black portent of the new atomic age lies a hope which, seized upon with faith, can work our salvation. If we fail, then we have damned every man to be the slave of Fear. Let us not deceive ourselves: We must elect World Peace or World Destruction.

Science has torn from nature a secret so vast in its potentialities that our minds cower in fear from the terror it creates. Yet terror is not enough to inhibit the use of the atomic bomb. The terror created by weapons has never stopped man from employing them. For each new weapon a defense has been produced, in time. But now we face a condition in which adequate defense does not exist.

Science, which gave us this dread power, shows that it can be made a giant help to humanity, but science does *not* show us how to prevent its baleful use. So we have been appointed to obviate that peril by finding a meeting of the minds and hearts of our people. Only in the will of mankind lies the answer.

It is to express this will and make it effective that we have been assembled. We must provide the mechanisms to assure that atomic energy is used for peaceful purposes and preclude its use in war. To that end, we must provide immediate, swift, and sure punishment of those who violate the agreements that are reached by the nations. Penalization is essential if peace is to be more than a feverish interlude between wars. . . .

I now submit the following measures as representing the fundamental features of a plan which could give effect to certain of the conclusions which I have epitomized.

1. *General.* The Authority should set up a thorough plan for control of the field of atomic energy, through various forms of ownership, dominion, licenses, operation, inspection, research, and management by competent personnel. After this is provided for, there should be as little interference as may be with the economic plans and the present private, corporate, and state relationships in the several countries involved.

2. *Raw Materials.* The Authority should have as one of its earliest purposes to obtain and maintain complete and accurate information on world supplies of uranium and thorium and to bring them under its dominion. The precise pattern of control for various types of deposits of such materials will have to depend upon the geological, mining, refining, and economic facts involved in different situations.

The Authority should conduct continuous surveys so that it will have the most complete knowledge of the world geology of uranium and thorium. Only after all current information on world sources of uranium and thorium is known to us all can equitable plans be made for their production, refining, and distribution.

3. *Primary Production Plants.* The Authority should exercise complete managerial control of the production of fissionable materials. This means that it should control and operate all plants producing fissionable materials in dangerous quantities and must own and control the product of these plants.

4. *Atomic Explosives.* The Authority should be given sole and exclusive right to conduct research in the field of atomic explosives. Research activities in the field of atomic explosives are essential in order that the Authority may keep in the forefront of knowledge in the field of atomic energy and fulfil the objective of preventing illicit manufacture of bombs. Only by maintaining its position as the best-informed agency will the Authority be able to determine the line between intrinsically dangerous and non-dangerous activities.

5. *Strategic Distribution of Activities and Materials.* The activities entrusted to the Authority because they are intrinsically dangerous to security should be distributed throughout the world. Similarly, stockpiles of raw materials and fissionable materials should not be centralized.

6. *Non-dangerous Activities.* A function of the Authority should be promotion of the peacetime benefits of atomic energy.

Atomic research (except in explosives), the use of research reactors, the production of radioactive tracers by means of non-dangerous reactors, the use of such tracers, and to some extent the production of power should be open to nations and their citizens under reasonable licensing arrangements from the Authority. Denatured materials, whose use we know also requires suitable safeguards, should be furnished for such purposes by the Authority under lease or other arrangement. Denaturing seems to have been overestimated by the public as a safety measure.

7. *Definition of Dangerous and Non-dangerous Activities.* Although a reasonable dividing line can be drawn between dangerous and non-dangerous activities, it is not hard and fast. Provision should, therefore, be made to assure constant reexamination of the questions and to permit revision of the dividing line as changing conditions and new discoveries may require.

8. *Operations of Dangerous Activities.* Any plant dealing with uranium and thorium after it once reaches the potential of dangerous use must be not only subject to the most rigorous and competent inspection by the Authority, but its actual operation shall be under the management, supervision, and control of that authority.

9. *Inspection.* By assigning intrinsically dangerous activities exclusively to the Authority, the difficulties of inspection are reduced. If the Authority is the only agency which may lawfully conduct dangerous activities, then visible operation by others than the Authority will constitute an unambiguous danger signal. Inspection will also occur in connection with the licensing function of the Authority.

10. *Freedom of Access.* Adequate ingress and egress for all qualified representatives of the Authority must be assured. Many of the inspection activities of the Authority should grow out of, and be incidental to, its other functions. Important measures of inspection will be associated with the tight control of raw materials, for this is a keynote of the plan. The continuing activities of prospecting, survey, and research in relation to raw materials will be designed not only to serve the affirmative development functions of the authority but also to assure that no surreptitious operations are conducted in the raw-material field by nation or their citizens.

11. *Personnel.* The personnel of the Authority should be recruited on a basis of proven competence but also as far as possible on an international basis.

12. *Progress by Stages.* A primary step in the creation of the system of control is the setting forth, in comprehensive terms, of the functions, responsibilities, powers, and limitations of the Authority. Once a charter for the Authority has been adopted, the Authority and the system of control for which it will be responsible will require time to become fully organized and effective. The plan of control will, therefore, have to come into effect in successive stages. These should be specifically fixed in the charter or means should otherwise be set forth in the charter for transitions from one stage to another, as contemplated in the resolution of the United Nations Assembly which created this Commission.

13. *Disclosures.* In the deliberations of the United Nations Commission on Atomic Energy, the United States is prepared to make available the information essential to a reasonable understanding of the proposals which it advocates. Further disclosures must be dependent, in the interests of all, upon the effective ratification of the treaty. When the Authority is actually created, the United States will join the other nations in making available the further information essential to that organization for the performance of its functions. As the successive stages of international control are reached, the United States will be prepared to yield, to the extent required by each stage, national control of the activities in this field to the Authority.

14. *International Control.* There will be questions about the extent of control to be allowed to national bodies, when the Authority is established. Purely national authorities for control and development of atomic energy should to the extent necessary for the effective operation of the Authority be subordinate to it. This is neither an endorsement nor a disapproval of the creation of national authorities. The Commission should evolve a clear demarcation of the scope of duties and responsibities of such national authorities.

B. The Cold War: The American Response

THE WIDENING SPLIT between the United States and the Soviet Union, the slow pace of economic recovery in Western Europe, and the growth of Communism in the western European states were all factors underlying the American program of massive economic aid to Europe known as the Marshall Plan. Described by Secretary of State George C. Marshall in an address at Harvard University on June 5, 1947, it resulted in the spending of some four and a half billion dollars during its first year of operation. It was markedly successful in building European prosperity and curbing the spread of European Communism.

1. THE MARSHALL PLAN, 1947

SOURCE. *The New York Times,* June 6, 1947. Copyright 1947 by The New York Times Company. Reprinted by permission of *The New York Times.*

I need not tell you, gentlemen, that the world situation is very serious. That must be apparent to all intelligent people. I think one difficulty is that the problem is one of such enormous complexity that the very mass of facts presented to the public by press and radio make it exceedingly difficult for the man in the street to reach a clear appraisement of the situation. Furthermore, the people of this country are distant from the troubled areas of the earth and it is hard for them to comprehend the plight and consequent reactions on their governments in connection with our efforts to promote peace in the world.

In considering the requirements for the rehabilitation of Europe the physical loss of life, the visible destruction of cities, factories, mines and railroads was correctly estimated, but it has become obvious during recent months that this visible destruction was probably less serious than the dislocation of the entire fabric of European economy. For the past ten years conditions have been highly abnormal.

The feverish preparation for war and the more feverish maintenance of the war effort engulfed all aspects of national economies. Machinery has fallen into disrepair or is entirely obsolete. Under the arbitrary and destructive Nazi rule, virtually every possible enterprise was geared into the German war machine. Long-standing commercial ties, private institutions, banks, insurance companies and shipping companies disappeared, through loss of capital, absorption through nationalization or by simple destruction.

In many countries, confidence in the local currency has been severely shaken. The breakdown of the business structure of Europe during the war was complete. Recovery has been seriously retarded by the fact that two years after the close of hostilities a peace agreement with Germany and Austria has not been agreed upon. But even given a more prompt solution of these difficult problems, the rehabilitation of the economic structure of Europe quite evidently will require a much longer time and greater effort than had been foreseen.

There is a phase of this matter which is both interesting and serious. The farmer has always produced the foodstuffs to exchange with the city dweller for the other necessities of life. The division of labor is the basis of modern civilization. At the present time it is threatened with breakdown. The town and city industries are not producing adequate goods to exchange with the food-producing farmer. Raw materials and fuel are in short supply. Machinery is lacking or worn out.

The farmer or the peasant cannot find the goods for sale which he desires to purchase. So the sale of his farm produce for money which he cannot use, seems to him an unprofitable transaction. He, therefore, has withdrawn many fields from crop cultivation and is using them for grazing. He feeds more grain to stock and finds for himself and his family an ample supply of food, however short he may be on clothing and the other ordinary gadgets of civilization. Meanwhile, people in the cities are short of food and fuel. So the governments are forced to use their foreign money and credits to procure these necessities abroad. This process exhausts funds which are urgently needed for reconstruction. Thus a very serious situation is rapidly developing which bodes no good for the world. The modern system of the division of labor upon which the exchange of products is based is in danger of breaking down.

The truth of the matter is that Europe's requirements for the next three or four years of foreign food and other essential products—principally from America—are so much greater than her present ability to pay that she must have substantial additional help, or face economic, social and political deterioration of a very grave character.

The remedy lies in breaking the vicious circle and restoring the confidence of the European people in the economic future of their own countries and of Europe as a whole. The manufacturer and the farmer throughout wide areas must be able and willing to exchange their products for currencies, the continuing value of which is not open to question.

Aside from the demoralizing effect on the world at large and the possibilities of disturbances arising as a result of the desperation of the people concerned, the consequences to the economy of the United States should be apparent to all. It is logical that the United States should do whatever it is able to do to assist in the return of normal economic health to the world, without which there can be no political stability and no assured peace.

Our policy is directed not against any country or doctrine but against hunger, poverty, desperation and chaos. Its purpose should be the revival of a working economy in the world so as to permit the emergence of political and social conditions in which free institutions can exist. Such assistance, I am convinced, must not be on a piecemeal basis as various crises develop. Any assistance that this government may develop in the future should provide a cure rather than a mere palliative.

Any government that is willing to assist in the task of recovery will find full cooperation, I am sure, on the part of the United States Government. Any government which maneuvers to block the recovery of other countries cannot expect help from us. Furthermore, governments, political parties or groups which seek to perpetuate human misery in order to profit therefrom politically or otherwise will encounter the opposition of the United States.

It is already evident that, before the United States Government can proceed much further in its efforts to alleviate the situation and help start the European world on its way to recovery, there must be some agreement among the countries of Europe as to the requirements of the situation and the part those countries themselves will take in order to give proper effect to whatever action might be undertaken by this Government. It would be neither fitting nor efficacious for this Government to undertake to draw up unilaterally a program designed to place Europe on its feet economically. This is the business of the Europeans. The initiative, I think, must come from Europe. The role of this country should consist of friendly aid in the drafting of a European program and of later support of such a program so far as it may be practical for us to do so. The program should be a joint one, agreed to by a number, if not all European nations.

An essential part of any successful action on the part of the United States is an understanding on the part of the people of America of the character of the problem and the remedies to be applied. Political passion and prejudice should have no part. With foresight, and a willingness on the part of our people to face up to the vast responsibility which history has clearly placed upon our country, the difficulties I have outlined can and will be overcome.

AS A FURTHER STEP against Soviet expansion in Europe, a mutual defense alliance—the North Atlantic Treaty—was drawn up in the fall of 1948. On April 4, 1949, the Treaty was signed by Great Britain, France, The Netherlands, Belgium, Luxembourg, Canada, the United States, Norway, Denmark, Iceland, Italy, and Portugal. The North Atlantic Treaty Organization (NATO) became the chief international organ for coordinating the military defense of western Europe.

2. THE NORTH ATLANTIC TREATY, 1949

SOURCE. *The New York Times,* March 19, 1949. Copyright 1949 by The New York Times Co. Reprinted by permission of *The New York Times.*

PREAMBLE. The parties to this treaty reaffirm their faith in the purposes and principles of the Charter of the United Nations and their desire to live in peace with all peoples and all governments.

They are determined to safeguard the freedom, common heritage and civilization of their peoples, founded on the principles of democracy, individual liberty and the rule of law.

They seek to promote stability and well-being in the North Atlantic area.

They are resolved to unite their efforts for collective defense and for the preservation of peace and security.

They therefore agree to this North Atlantic Treaty:

ARTICLE 1. The parties undertake, as set forth in the Charter of the United Nations, to settle any international disputes in which they may be involved by peaceful means in such a manner that international peace and security, and justice, are not endangered, and to refrain in their international relations from the threat or use of force in any manner inconsistent with the purposes of the United Nations.

ARTICLE 2. The parties will contribute toward the further development of peaceful and friendly international relations by strengthening their free institutions, by bringing about a better understanding of the principles upon which these institutions are founded, and by promoting conditions of stability and well-being. They will seek to eliminate conflict in their international economic policies and will encourage economic collaboration between any or all of them.

ARTICLE 3. In order more effectively to achieve the objectives of this treaty, the parties, separately and jointly, by means of continuous and effective self-help and mutual aid, will maintain and develop their individual and collective capacity to resist armed attack.

ARTICLE 4. The parties will consult together whenever, in the opinion of any of them, the territorial integrity, political independence or security of any of the parties is threatened.

ARTICLE 5. The parties agree that an armed attack against one or more of them in Europe or North America shall be considered an attack against them all; and consequently they agree that, if such an armed attack occurs, each of them, in exercise of the right of individual or collective self-defense recognized by Article 51 of the Charter of the United Nations, will assist the party or parties so attacked by taking forthwith, individually and in concert with the other parties, such action as it deems necessary, including the use of armed force, to restore and maintain the security of the North Atlantic area.

Any such armed attack and all measures taken as a result thereof shall immediately be reported to the Security Council. Such measures shall be terminated when the Security Council has taken the measures necessary to restore and maintain international peace and security.

ARTICLE 6. For the purpose of Article 5 an armed attack on one or more of the parties is deemed to include an armed attack on the territory of any of the parties in Europe or North America, on the Algerian Departments of France, on the occupation forces of any party in Europe, on the islands under the jurisdiction of any party in the North Atlantic area north of the Tropic of Cancer or on the vessels or aircraft in this area of any of the parties.

ARTICLE 7. This treaty does not affect, and shall not be interpreted as affecting, in any way the rights and obligations under the Charter of the parties which are members of the United Nations, or the primary responsibility of the Security Council for the maintenance of international peace and security.

ARTICLE 8. Each party declares that none of the international engagements now in force between it and any other of the parties or any third state is in conflict with the provisions of this treaty, and undertakes not to enter into any international engagement in conflict with this treaty.

ARTICLE 9. The parties hereby establish a Council, on which each of them shall be represented, to consider matters concerning the implementation of this treaty. The Council shall be so organized as to be able to meet promptly at any time. The Council shall set up such subsidiary bodies as may be necessary; in particular it shall establish immediately a defense committee which shall recommend measures for the implementation of Articles 3 and 5.

ARTICLE 10. The parties may, by unanimous agreement, invite any other European state in a position to further the principles of this treaty and to contribute to the security of the North Atlantic area to accede to this treaty. Any state so invited may become a party to the treaty by depositing its instrument of accession with the Government of the United States of America. The Government of the United States of America will inform each of the parties of the deposit of each such instrument of accession.

ARTICLE 11. This treaty shall be ratified and its provisions carried out by the parties in accordance with their respective constitutional processes. The instruments of ratification shall be deposited as soon as possible with the Government of the United States of America, which will notify all the other signatories of each deposit. The treaty shall enter into force between the states which have ratified it as soon as the ratifications of the majority of the signatories, including the ratifications of Belgium, Canada, France, Luxembourg, the Netherlands, the United Kingdom and the United States, have been deposited and shall come into effect with respect to other states on the date of the deposit of their ratifications.

ARTICLE 12. After the treaty has been in force for ten years, or at any time thereafter, the parties shall, if any of them so requests, consult together for the purpose of reviewing the treaty, having regard for the factors then affecting peace and security in the North Atlantic area, including the development of universal as well as regional arrangements under the Charter of the United Nations for the maintenance of international peace and security.

ARTICLE 13. After the treaty has been in force for twenty years, any party may cease to be a party one year after its notice of denunciation has been given to the Government of the United States of America, which will inform the Governments of the other parties of the deposit of each notice of denunciation.

ARTICLE 14. This treaty, of which the English and French texts are equally authentic, shall be deposited in the archives of the Government of the United States of America. Duly certified copies thereof will be transmitted by that Government to the Governments of the other signatories.

IN WITNESS WHEREOF, the undersigned plenipotentiaries have signed this treaty.

C. The Hungarian Rebellion, November 1956

IN THE AUTUMN OF 1956, as the presidential campaign between Dwight D. Eisenhower and Adlai E. Stevenson was drawing to its conclusion, two major world crises broke out almost simultaneously: the invasion of Egypt by English, French, and Israeli forces in response to Egypt's earlier nationalization of the Suez Canal, and the rebellion against the Communist regime in Hungary. An anti-Communist Hungarian government, headed by Premier Imre Nagy, held power briefly, but the rebellion was quickly crushed by the tanks and troops of Soviet Russia. The final moments of the rebellion are dramatically captured in Premier Nagy's last message to the Hungarian people and the free world.

1. PREMIER IMRE NAGY'S FINAL MESSAGE

SOURCE. "United Nations Report of the Special Committee on the Problem of Hungary," *General Assembly Official Records*, 11th Session Supplement #18 A/3592.

This fight is the fight for freedom by the Hungarian people against the Russian intervention, and it is possible that I shall only be able to stay at my post for one or two hours. The whole world will see how the Russian armed forces, contrary to all treaties and conventions, are crushing the resistance of the Hungarian people. They will also see how they are kidnapping the Prime Minister of a country which is a Member of the United

Nations, taking him from the capital, and therefore it cannot be doubted at all that this is the most brutal form of intervention. I should like in these last moments to ask the leaders of the revolution, if they can, to leave the country. I ask that all that I have said in my broadcast, and what we have agreed on with the revolutionary leaders during meetings in Parliament, should be put in a memorandum, and the leaders should turn to all the peoples of the world for help and explain that today it is Hungary and tomorrow, or the day after tomorrow, it will be the turn of other countries because the imperialism of Moscow does not know borders, and is only trying to play for time.

ENGLAND, FRANCE, AND ISRAEL withdrew from Egypt on the strength of United Nations and world opposition, but appeals by the United Nations General Assembly for Russian withdrawal from Hungary were ignored. The rebellion was extinguished, but the ruthless policy of the Soviet Union dealt a serious blow to the prestige of world Communism and provoked numerous resignations from the Party.

2. TWO UNITED NATIONS RESOLUTIONS ON HUNGARY, NOVEMBER 4 AND 9, 1956

SOURCE. Resolutions 1004 and 1005 (ES II).

The General Assembly,

Considering that the United Nations is based on the principle of the sovereign equality of all its Members,

Recalling that the enjoyment of human rights and of fundamental freedom in Hungary was specifically guaranteed by the Peace Treaty between Hungary and the Allied and Associated Powers signed at Paris on 10 February 1947 and that the general principle of these rights and this freedom is affirmed for all peoples in the Charter of the United Nations,

Convinced that recent events in Hungary manifest clearly the desire of the Hungarian people to exercise and to enjoy fully their fundamental rights, freedom and independence,

Condemning the use of Soviet military forces to suppress the efforts of the Hungarian people to reassert their rights,

Noting moreover the declaration of 30 October 1956 by the Government of the Union of Soviet Socialist Republics of its avowed policy of nonintervention in the internal affairs of other States,

Noting the communication of 1 November 1956 (A/3251) of the Government of Hungary to the Secretary-General regarding demands made by that Government to the Government of the Union of Soviet Socialist Republics for the instant and immediate withdrawal of Soviet forces,

Noting further the communication of 2 November 1956 (S/3726) from the Government of Hungary to the Secretary-General asking the Security Council to instruct the Government of the Union of Soviet Socialist Republics and the Government of Hungary to start the negotiations immediately on withdrawal of Soviet forces,

Noting that the intervention of Soviet military forces in Hungary has resulted in grave loss of life and widespread bloodshed among the Hungarian people,

Taking note of the radio appeal of Prime Minister Imre Nagy of 4 November 1956,

1. *Calls upon* the Government of the Union of Soviet Socialist Republics to desist forthwith from all attack on the people of Hungary and from any form of intervention, in particular armed intervention, in the internal affairs of Hungary;

2. *Calls upon* the Union of Soviet Socialist Republics to cease the introduction of additional armed forces into Hungary and to withdraw all of its forces without delay from Hungarian territory;

3. *Affirms* the rights of the Hungarian people to a government responsive to its national aspirations and dedicated to its independence and well-being;

4. *Requests* the Secretary-General to investigate the situation caused by foreign intervention in Hungary, to observe the situation directly through representatives named by him, and to report thereon to the General Assembly at the earliest moment, and as soon as possible suggest methods to bring an end to the foreign intervention in Hungary in accordance with the principles of the Charter of the United Nations;

5. *Calls upon* the Government of Hungary and the Government of the Union of Soviet Socialist Republics to permit observers designated by the Secretary-General to enter the territory of Hungary, to travel freely therein, and to report their findings to the Secretary-General;

6. *Calls upon* all Members of the United Nations to co-operate with the Secretary-General and his representatives in the execution of his functions;

7. *Requests* the Secretary-General in consultation with the heads of appropriate specialized agencies to inquire, on an urgent basis, into the needs of the Hungarian people for food, medicine and other similar supplies, and to report to the General Assembly as soon as possible;

8. *Requests* all Members of the United Nations, and invites national

and international humanitarian organizations to co-operate in making available such supplies as may be required by the Hungarian people.

564th Plenary Meeting
4 November 1956.

The General Assembly,

Noting with deep concern that the provisions of its resolution 1004 (ES-II) of 4 November 1956 have not yet been carried out and that the violent repression by the Soviet forces of the efforts of the Hungarian people to achieve freedom and independence continues,

Convinced that the recent events in Hungary manifest clearly the desire of the Hungarian people to exercise and to enjoy fully their fundamental rights, freedom and independence,

Considering that foreign intervention in Hungary is an intolerable attempt to deny to the Hungarian people the exercise and the enjoyment of such rights, freedom and independence, and in particular to deny to the Hungarian people the right to a government freely elected and representing their national aspirations,

Considering that the repression undertaken by the Soviet forces in Hungary constitutes a violation of the Charter of the United Nations and of the Peace Treaty between Hungary and the Allied and Associated Powers,

Considering that the immediate withdrawal of the Soviet forces from Hungarian territory is necessary,

1. *Calls again* upon the Government of the Union of Soviet Socialist Republics to withdraw its forces from Hungary without any further delay;

2. *Considering* that free elections should be held in Hungary under United Nations auspices, as soon as law and order have been restored, to enable the people of Hungary to determine for themselves the form of government they wish to establish in their country;

3. *Reaffirms* its request to the Secretary-General to continue to investigate, through representatives named by him, the situation caused by foreign intervention in Hungary and to report at the earliest possible moment to the General Assembly;

4. *Requests* the Secretary-General to report in the shortest possible time to the General Assembly on compliance herewith.

571st Plenary Meeting
9 November 1956.

D. The New Face of Russian Communism

BY THE LATER 1950's signs of a slight thaw in the Cold War were begin-
ning to appear. Communist China held to the traditional position that war be-
tween the Communist states and their opponents was inevitable, but Premier
Nikita Khrushchev advanced the notion of peaceful coexistence, maintaining
that atomic war would be a catastrophe for all concerned and that the Commu-
nist victory could be achieved through peaceful economic competition with the
capitalist states. He expressed these views succinctly in an address to the Rou-
manian Communist Party in Bucharest on June 21, 1960.

1. PREMIER NIKITA KHRUSHCHEV UPDATES LENIN, 1960

SOURCE. Soviet Embassy, *Soviet News*, #4229, June 22, 1960.

Comrades, questions of international relations, questions of war and
peace, have always deeply concerned the mass of the people. That is natural. More than once in history the anti-national policy of the imperialists,
their desire for a redivision of the world, for the seizure of new colonies,
have subjected mankind to the horrors of devastating wars. But no matter
how terrible wars have been in the past, if the imperialist circles should
succeed in unleashing another world war, its calamities would be incom-
parably more terrible. For millions of people might burn in the conflagra-
tion of hydrogen explosions, and for some states a nuclear war would be
literally a catastrophe. That is why the Marxist-Leninist parties, in all
their activity, have always been consistent champions of a reasonable
peaceloving policy, of the prevention of another world war. . . .

This is a policy of coexistence, a policy of consolidating peace, easing
international tension and doing away with the cold war.

The thesis that in our time war is not inevitable has a direct bearing on
the policy of peaceful coexistence proclaimed at the 20th and 21st Congresses of our party. Lenin's propositions about imperialism remain in
force and are still a lodestar for us in our theory and practice. But it
should not be forgotten that Lenin's propositions on imperialism were
advanced and developed tens of years ago, when the world did not know
many things that are now decisive for historical development, for the
entire international situation.

Some of Lenin's propositions on imperialism date back to the period
when there was no Soviet Union, when the other socialist countries did
not exist.

The powerful Soviet Union, with its enormous economic and military potential, is now growing and gaining in strength; the great socialist camp, which now numbers over 1,000 million people, is growing and gaining in strength; the organisation and political consciousness of the working class have grown, and even in the capitalist countries it is actively fighting for peace. Such factors are in operation now as, for instance, the broad movement of peace champions; the number of countries coming out for peace among nations is increasing. It should also be pointed out that imperialism no longer has such a rear to fall back upon as the colonial system which it had formerly.

Besides, comrades, one cannot mechanically repeat now on this question what Vladimir Ilyich Lenin said many decades ago on imperialism, and go on asserting that imperialist wars are inevitable until socialism triumphs throughout the world. We are now living in such a period when the forces of socialism are increasingly growing and becoming stronger, where ever-broader masses of the working people are rallying behind the banner of Marxism-Leninism.

History will possibly witness such a time when capitalism is preserved only in a small number of states, maybe states for instance, as small as a button on a coat. Well? And even in such conditions would one have to look up in a book what Vladimir Ilyich Lenin quite correctly said for his time, would one just have to repeat that wars are inevitable since capitalist countries exist?

Of course, the essence of capitalism, of imperialism, does not change even if it is represented by small countries. It is common knowledge that a wolf is just as bloodthirsty a beast of prey as a lion or a tiger, although he is much weaker. That is why man fears less to meet a wolf than a tiger or a lion. Of course, small beasts of prey can also bite, essentially they are the same but they have different possibilities, they are not so strong and it is easier to render them harmless.

Therefore one cannot ignore the specific situation, the changes in the correlation of forces in the world and repeat what the great Lenin said in quite different historical conditions. If Lenin could rise from his grave he would take such people, as one says, to task and would teach them how one must understand the essence of the matter.

We live in a time when we have neither Marx, nor Engels, nor Lenin with us. If we act like children who, studying the alphabet, compile words from letters, we shall not go very far. Marx, Engels and Lenin created their immortal works which will not fade away in centuries. They indicated to mankind the road to communism. And we confidently follow this road. On the basis of the teaching of Marxism-Leninism we must think ourselves, profoundly study life, analyse the present situation and draw the conclusions which benefit the common cause of communism.

One must not only be able to read but also correctly understand what one has read and apply it in the specific conditions of the time in which we live, taking into consideration the existing situation, and the real balance of forces. A political leader acting in this manner shows that he not only can read but can also creatively apply the revolutionary teaching. If he does not do this, he resembles a man about whom people say: "He looks into a book, but sees nothing!"

All this gives grounds for saying with confidence that under present conditions war is not inevitable.

He who fails to understand this does not believe in the strength and creative abilities of the working class, underestimates the power of the socialist camp, does not believe in the great force of attraction of socialism, which has demonstrated its superiority over capitalism with the utmost clarity.

Is the possibility of the imperialists unleashing war under present conditions ruled out? We have said several times and we repeat once again: No, it is not. But . . . . the imperialists do not want to trigger off war in order to perish in it. . . . Therefore today even the stupid, frenzied representatives of the imperialist circles will think twice about our power before they start a military gamble. . . .

The U.S.S.R. pursued a policy of peace even when it stood alone, facing the powerful camp of imperialist states. We are also pursuing this policy now when the forces of peace are undoubtedly superior to the forces of war and aggression.

This position of ours stems from our firm belief in the stability of the socialist system, in our system. . . .

No world war is needed for the triumph of socialist ideas throughout the world. These ideas will get the upper hand in the peaceful competition between the countries of socialism and capitalism.

E. Cuba and Vietnam

DESPITE TALK OF PEACEFUL COEXISTENCE, military crises between the United States and the Communist powers continued to occur. In October, 1962, the world was brought to the brink of war by a strong American reaction to the Soviet policy of secretly introducing intermediate-range ballistic missiles into Communist Cuba. The United States position was set forth in a dramatic speech to the American people by President John F. Kennedy. As a consequence of the American stand, the Soviet Union withdrew its missiles from Cuba.

1. THE CUBA MISSILE CRISIS: PRESIDENT JOHN F. KENNEDY'S ADDRESS OF OCTOBER 22, 1962: "THE SOVIET THREAT TO THE AMERICAS"

SOURCE. Dept. of State Bulletin, Vol. XLVII, No. 1220, Nov. 12, 1962.

Good evening, my fellow citizens. This Government, as promised, has maintained the closest surveillance of the Soviet military buildup on the island of Cuba. Within the past week unmistakable evidence has established the fact that a series of offensive missile sites is now in preparation on that imprisoned island. The purpose of these bases can be none other than to provide a nuclear strike capability against the Western Hemisphere.

Upon receiving the first preliminary hard information of this nature last Tuesday morning [October 16] at 9:00 a.m., I directed that our surveillance be stepped up. And having now confirmed and completed our evaluation of the evidence and our decision on a course of action, this Government feels obliged to report this new crisis to you in fullest detail.

The characteristics of these new missile sites indicate two distinct types of installations. Several of them include medium-range ballistic missiles capable of carrying a nuclear warhead for a distance of more than 1,000 nautical miles. Each of these missiles, in short, is capable of striking Washington, D. C., the Panama Canal, Cape Canaveral, Mexico City, or any other city in the southeastern part of the United States, in Central America, or in the Caribbean area.

Additional sites not yet completed appear to be designed for intermediate-range ballistic missiles capable of traveling more than twice as far— and thus capable of striking most of the major cities in the Western Hemisphere, ranging as far north as Hudson Bay, Canada, and as far south as Lima, Peru. In addition, jet bombers, capable of carrying nuclear weapons, are now being uncrated and assembled in Cuba, while the necessary air bases are being prepared.

This urgent transformation of Cuba into an important strategic base— by the presence of these large, long-range, and clearly offensive weapons of sudden mass destruction—constitutes an explicit threat to the peace and security of all the Americas, in flagrant and deliberate defiance of the Rio Pact of 1947, the traditions of this nation and hemisphere, the Joint Resolution of the 87th Congress, the Charter of the United Nations, and my own public warnings to the Soviets on September 4 and 13.

This action also contradicts the repeated assurances of Soviet spokesmen, both publicly and privately delivered, that the arms buildup in Cuba would retain its original defensive character and that the Soviet

Union had no need or desire to station strategic missiles on the territory of any other nation.

The size of this undertaking makes clear that it has been planned for some months. Yet only last month, after I had made clear the distinction between any introduction of ground-to-ground missiles and the existence of defensive antiaircraft missiles, the Soviet Government publicly stated on September 11 that, and I quote, "The armaments and military equipment sent to Cuba are designed exclusively for defensive purposes," and, and I quote the Soviet Government, "There is no need for the Soviet Government to shift its weapons for a retaliatory blow to any other country, for instance Cuba," and that, and I quote the Government, "The Soviet Union has so powerful rockets to carry these nuclear warheads that there is no need to search for sites for them beyond the boundaries of the Soviet Union." That statement was false.

Only last Thursday, as evidence of this rapid offensive buildup was already in my hand, Soviet Foreign Minister Gromyko told me in my office that he was instructed to make it clear once again, as he said his Government had already done, that Soviet assistance to Cuba, and I quote, "pursued solely the purpose of contributing to the defense capabilities of Cuba," that, and I quote him, "training by Soviet specialists of Cuban nationals in handling defensive armaments was by no means offensive," and that "if it were otherwise," Mr. Gromyko went on, "the Soviet Government would never become involved in rendering such assistance." That statement also was false.

Neither the United States of America nor the world community of nations can tolerate deliberate deception and offensive threats on the part of any nation, large or small. We no longer live in a world where only the actual firing of weapons represents a sufficient challenge to a nation's security to constitute maximum peril. Nuclear weapons are so destructive and ballistic missiles are so swift that any substantially increased possibility of their use or any sudden change in their deployment may well be regarded as a definite threat to peace.

For many years both the Soviet Union and the United States, recognizing this fact, have deployed strategic nuclear weapons with great care, never upsetting the precarious *status quo* which insured that these weapons would not be used in the absence of some vital challenge. Our own strategic missiles have never been transferred to the territory of any other nation under a cloak of secrecy and deception; and our history, unlike that of the Soviets since the end of World War II, demonstrates that we have no desire to dominate or conquer any other nation or impose our system upon its people. Nevertheless, American citizens have become adjusted to living daily on the bull's eye of Soviet missiles located inside the

U.S.S.R. or in submarines.

In that sense missiles in Cuba add to an already clear and present danger—although it should be noted the nations of Latin America have never previously been subjected to a potential nuclear threat.

But this secret, swift, and extraordinary buildup of Communist missiles —in an area well known to have a special and historical relationship to the United States and the nations of the Western Hemisphere, in violation of Soviet assurances, and in defiance of American and hemispheric policy —this sudden, clandestine decision to station strategic weapons for the first time outside of Soviet soil—is a deliberately provocative and unjustified change in the *status quo* which cannot be accepted by this country if our courage and our commitments are ever to be trusted again by either friend or foe.

The 1930's taught us a clear lesson: Aggressive conduct, if allowed to grow unchecked and unchallenged, ultimately leads to war. This nation is opposed to war. We are also true to our word. Our unswerving objective, therefore, must be to prevent the use of these missiles against this or any other country and to secure their withdrawal or elimination from the Western Hemisphere.

Our policy has been one of patience and restraint, as befits a peaceful and powerful nation, which leads a worldwide alliance. We have been determined not to be diverted from our central concerns by mere irritants and fanatics. But now further action is required—and it is underway; and these actions may only be the beginning. We will not prematurely or unnecessarily risk the costs of worldwide nuclear war in which even the fruits of victory would be ashes in our mouth—but neither will we shrink from that risk at any time it must be faced.

Acting, therefore, in the defense of our own security and of the entire Western Hemisphere, and under the authority entrusted to me by the Constitution as endorsed by the resolution of the Congress, I have directed that the following *initial* steps be taken immediately:

First: To halt this offensive buildup, a strict quarantine on all offensive military equipment under shipment to Cuba is being initiated. All ships of any kind bound for Cuba from whatever nation or port will, if found to contain cargoes of offensive weapons, be turned back. This quarantine will be extended, if needed, to other types of cargo and carriers. We are not at this time, however, denying the necessities of life as the Soviets attempted to do in their Berlin blockade of 1948.

Second: I have directed the continued and increased close surveillance of Cuba and its military buildup. The Foreign Ministers of the OAS [Organization of American States] in their communique of October 3 rejected secrecy on such matters in this hemisphere. Should these offensive military preparations continue, thus increasing the threat to the hemisphere, further action will be justified. I have directed the Armed Forces to prepare for any eventualities; and I trust that, in the interest of both the Cuban people and the Soviet technicians at the sites, the hazards to all concerned of continuing this threat will be recognized.

Third: It shall be the policy of this nation to regard any nuclear missile launched from Cuba against any nation in the Western Hemisphere as an attack by the Soviet Union on the United States, requiring a full retaliatory response upon the Soviet Union.

Fourth: As a necessary military precaution I have reinforced our base at Guantanamo, evacuated today the dependents of our personnel there, and ordered additional military units to be on a standby alert basis.

Fifth: We are calling tonight for an immediate meeting of the Organ of Consultation, under the Organization of American States, to consider this threat to hemispheric security and to invoke articles 6 and 8 of the Rio Treaty in support of all necessary action. The United Nations Charter allows for regional security arrangements—and the nations of this hemisphere decided long ago against the military presence of outside powers. Our other allies around the world have also been alerted.

Sixth: Under the Charter of the United Nations, we are asking tonight that an emergency meeting of the Security Council be convoked without delay to take action against this latest Soviet threat to world peace. Our resolution will call for the prompt dismantling and withdrawal of all offensive weapons in Cuba, under the supervision of U.N. observers, before the quarantine can be lifted.

Seventh and finally: I call upon Chairman Khrushchev to halt and eliminate this clandestine, reckless, and provocative threat to world peace and to stable relations between our two nations. I call upon him further to abandon this course of world domination and to join in an historic effort to end the perilous arms race and transform the history of man. He has an opportunity now to move the world back from the abyss of destruction— by returning to his Government's own words that it had no need to station missiles outside its own territory, and withdrawing these weapons from Cuba—by refraining from any action which will widen or deepen the present crisis—and then by participating in a search for peaceful and permanent solutions.

This nation is prepared to present its case against the Soviet threat to peace, and our own proposals for a peaceful world, at any time and in any forum—in the OAS, in the United Nations, or in any other meeting that could be useful—without limiting our freedom of action.

We have in the past made strenuous efforts to limit the spread of nuclear weapons. We have proposed the elimination of all arms and military bases in a fair and effective disarmament treaty. We are prepared to discuss new proposals for the removal of tensions on both sides—including the possibilities of a genuinely independent Cuba, free to determine its own destiny. We have no wish to war with the Soviet Union, for we are a peaceful people who desire to live in peace with all other peoples.

But it is difficult to settle or even discuss these problems in an atmosphere of intimidation. That is why this latest Soviet threat—or any other threat which is made either independently or in response to our actions this week—must and will be met with determination. Any hostile move anywhere in the world against the safety and freedom of peoples to whom we are committed—including in particular the brave people of West Berlin—will be met by whatever action is needed.

Finally, I want to say a few words to the captive people of Cuba, to whom this speech is being directly carried by special radio facilities. I speak to you as a friend, as one who knows of your deep attachment to your fatherland, as one who shares your aspirations for liberty and justice for all. And I have watched and the American people have watched with deep sorrow how your nationalist revolution was betrayed and how your fatherland fell under foreign domination. Now your leaders are no longer Cuban leaders inspired by Cuban ideals. They are puppets and agents of an international conspiracy which has turned Cuba against your friends and neighbors in the Americas—and turned it into the first Latin American country to become a target for nuclear war, the first Latin American country to have these weapons on its soil.

These new weapons are not in your interest. They contribute nothing to your peace and well-being. They can only undermine it. But this country has no wish to cause you to suffer or to impose any system upon you. We know that your lives and land are being used as pawns by those who deny you freedom.

Many times in the past the Cuban people have risen to throw out tyrants who destroyed their liberty. And I have no doubt that most Cubans today look forward to the time when they will be truly free—free from foreign domination, free to choose their own leaders, free to select their own system, free to own their own land, free to speak and write and worship without fear or degradation. And then shall Cuba be welcomed back to the society of free nations and to the associations of this hemisphere.

My fellow citizens, let no one doubt that this is a difficult and dangerous effort on which we have set out. No one can foresee precisely what course it will take or what costs or casualties will be incurred. Many months of sacrifice and self-discipline lie ahead—months in which both our patience and our will will be tested, months in which many threats and denunciations will keep us aware of our dangers. But the greatest danger of all would be to do nothing.

The path we have chosen for the present is full of hazards, as all paths are; but it is the one most consistent with our character and courage as a nation and our commitments around the world. The cost of freedom is always high—but Americans have always paid it. And one path we shall never choose, and that is the path of surrender or submission.

Our goal is not the victory of might but the vindication of right—not peace at the expense of freedom, but both peace *and* freedom, here in this hemisphere and, we hope, around the world. God willing, that goal will be achieved.

A FAR MORE PROLONGED CONFLICT had meanwhile developed in Vietnam, formerly a part of French Indo-China, which was now divided into two states: Communist North Vietnam and non-Communist South Vietnam. The government of South Vietnam, backed vigorously by the United States, was having increasing difficulty in subduing a rebellion of South Vietnamese Communists known as the Viet Cong who were aided by the North Vietnamese. In the course of the year 1965, the United States adopted the policy of bombing North Vietnam and significantly increasing the number of American troops in South Vietnam. It was argued by some that this policy was needlessly bellicose and gravely endangered world peace. The response of the American government to these attacks was set forth by President Lyndon B. Johnson in a news conference of July 28, 1965.

2. THE VIETNAM CRISIS: FROM PRESIDENT LYNDON B. JOHNSON'S NEWS CONFERENCE, JULY 28, 1965

SOURCE. *Weekly Compilation of Presidential Documents*, Vol. I, No. 1, August 2, 1965.

My fellow Americans:

Not long ago I received a letter from a woman in the Midwest. She wrote:

Dear Mr. President:
In my humble way I am writing to you about the crisis in Viet-Nam. I have a son who is now in Viet-Nam. My husband served in World War II. Our country was at war, but now, this time, it is just something that I don't understand. Why?

Well, I have tried to answer that question dozens of times and more in practically every State in this Union. I have discussed it fully in Baltimore in April, in Washington in May, in San Francisco in June. Let me again, now, discuss it here in the East Room of the White House.

Why must young Americans, born into a land exultant with hope and with golden promise, toil and suffer and sometimes die in such a remote and distant place?

The answer, like the war itself, is not an easy one, but it echoes clearly from the painful lessons of half a century. Three times in my lifetime in two world wars and in Korea Americans have gone to far lands to fight for freedom. We have learned at a terrible and a brutal cost that retreat does not bring safety and weakness does not bring peace.

It is this lesson that has brought us to Viet-Nam. This is a different kind of war. There are no marching armies or solemn declarations. Some citizens of South Viet-Nam at times with understandable grievances have joined in the attack on their own government.

But we must not let this mask the central fact that this is really war. It is guided by North Viet-Nam and it is spurred by Communist China. Its goal is to conquer the South, to defeat American power, and to extend the Asiatic dominion of communism.

There are great stakes in the balance.

Most of the non-Communist nations of Asia cannot, by themselves and alone, resist the growing might and the grasping ambition of Asian communism.

Our power, therefore, is a very vital shield. If we are driven from the field in Viet-Nam, then no nation can ever again have the same confidence in American promise, or in American protection.

In each land the forces of independence would be considerably weakened and an Asia so threatened by Communist domination would certainly imperil the security of the United States itself.

We did not choose to be the guardians at the gate, but there is no one else.

Nor would surrender in Viet-Nam bring peace, because we learned from Hitler at Munich that success only feeds the appetite of aggression. The battle would be renewed in one country and then another country, bringing with it perhaps even larger and crueler conflict, as we have learned from the lessons of history.

Moreover, we are in Viet-Nam to fulfill one of the most solemn pledges of the American Nation. Three Presidents—President Eisenhower, President Kennedy, and your present President—over 11 years have committed themselves and have promised to help defend this small and valiant nation.

Strengthened by that promise, the people of South Viet-Nam have fought for many long years. Thousands of them have died. Thousands more have been crippled and scarred by war. We just cannot now dishonor our word, or abandon our commitment, or leave those who believed us and who trusted us to the terror and repression and murder that would follow.

This, then, my fellow Americans, is why we are in Viet-Nam.

What are our goals in that war-strained land?

First, we intend to convince the Communists that we cannot be defeated by force of arms or by superior power. They are not easily convinced. In recent months they have greatly increased their fighting forces and their attacks and the number of incidents.

I have asked the Commanding General, General Westmoreland, what more he needs to meet this mounting aggression. He has told me. We will meet his needs.

I have today ordered to Viet-Nam the Air Mobile Division and certain other forces which will raise our fighting strength from 75,000 to 125,000 men almost immediately. Additional forces will be needed later, and they will be sent as requested.

This will make it necessary to increase our active fighting forces by raising the monthly draft call from 17,000 over a period of time to 35,000 per month, and for us to step up our campaign for voluntary enlistments.

After this past week of deliberations, I have concluded that it is not essential to order Reserve units into service now. If that necessity should later be indicated, I will give the matter most careful consideration and I will give the country—you—an adequate notice before taking such action, but only after full preparations.

We have also discussed with the Government of South Viet-Nam lately, the steps that we will take to substantially increase their own effort, both on the battlefield and toward reform and progress in the villages. Ambassador Lodge is now formulating a new program to be tested upon his return to that area.

I have directed Secretary Rusk and Secretary McNamara to be available immediately to the Congress to review with these committees, the appropriate Congressional committees, what we plan to do in these areas. I have asked them to be able to answer the questions of any Member of Congress.

Secretary McNamara, in addition, will ask the Senate Appropriations Committee to add a limited amount to present legislation to help meet part of this new cost until a supplemental measure is ready and hearings can be held when the Congress assembles in January. In the meantime, we will use the authority contained in the present Defense appropriation bill under consideration to transfer funds in addition to the additional money that we will ask.

These steps, like our actions in the past, are carefully measured to do what must be done to bring an end to aggression and a peaceful settlement.

We do not want an expanding struggle with consequences that no one can perceive, nor will we bluster or bully or flaunt our power, but we will not surrender and we will not retreat.

For behind our American pledge lies the determination and resources, I believe, of all of the American Nation.

Second, once the Communists know, as we know, that a violent solution is impossible, then a peaceful solution is inevitable.

We are ready now, as we have always been, to move from the battlefield to the conference table. I have stated publicly and many times, again and again, America's willingness to begin unconditional discussions with any government at any place at any time. Fifteen efforts have been made to start these discussions with the help of 40 nations throughout the world, but there has been no answer.

But we are going to continue to persist, if persist we must, until death and desolation have led to the same conference table where others could now join us at a much smaller cost.

I have spoken many times of our objectives in Viet-Nam. So has the government of South Viet-Nam. Hanoi has set forth its own proposals. We are ready to discuss their proposals and our proposals and any proposals of any government whose people may be affected, for we fear the meeting room no more than we fear the battlefield.

In this pursuit we welcome and we ask for the concern and the assistance of any nation and all nations. If the United Nations and its officials or any one of its 114 members can by deed or word, private initiative or public action, bring us nearer an honorable peace, then they will have the support and the gratitude of the United States of America.

I have directed Ambassador Goldberg to go to New York today and to present immediately to Secretary General U Thant a letter from me requesting that all the resources, energy, and immense prestige of the United Nations be employed to find ways to halt aggression and to bring peace in Viet-Nam.

I made a similar request at San Francisco a few weeks ago, because we do not seek the destruction of any government, nor do we covet a foot of any territory. But we insist and we will always insist that the people of South Viet-Nam shall have the right of choice, the right to shape their own destiny in free elections in the South or throughout all Viet-Nam under international supervision, and they shall not have any government imposed upon them by force and terror so long as we can prevent it.

This was the purpose of the 1954 agreements which the Communists have now cruelly shattered. If the machinery of those agreements was tragically weak, its purposes still guide our action. As battle rages, we will continue as best we can to help the good people of South Viet-Nam enrich the condition of their life, to feed the hungry and to tend the sick, and teach the young, and shelter the homeless, and help the farmer to increase his crops, and the worker to find a job.

It is an ancient but still terrible irony that while many leaders of men create division in pursuit of grand ambitions, the children of man are really united in the simple elusive desire for a life of fruitful and rewarding toil.

As I said at Johns Hopkins in Baltimore, I hope that one day we can help all the people of Asia toward that desire. Eugene Black has made great progress since my appearance in Baltimore in that direction—not as the price of peace, for we are ready always to bear a more painful cost, but rather as a part of our obligations of justice toward our fellow man.

Let me also add now a personal note. I do not find it easy to send the flower of our youth, our finest young men, into battle. I have spoken to you today of the divisions and the forces and the battalions and the units, but I know them all, every one. I have seen them in a thousand streets, of a hundred towns, in every State in this Union—working and laughing and building, and filled with hope and life. I think I know, too, how their mothers weep and how their families sorrow.

This is the most agonizing and the most painful duty of your President.

There is something else, too. When I was young, poverty was so common that we didn't know it had a name. An education was something that you had to fight for, and water was really life itself. I have now been in public life 35 years, more than three decades, and in each of those 35 years I have seen good men, and wise leaders, struggle to bring the blessings of this land to all of our people.

And now I am the President. It is now my opportunity to help every child get an education, to help every Negro and every American citizen have an equal opportunity, to have every family get a decent home, and to help bring healing to the sick and dignity to the old.

As I have said before, that is what I have lived for, that is what I have wanted all my life since I was a little boy, and I do not want to see all those hopes and all those dreams of so many people for so many years now drowned in the wasteful ravages of cruel wars. I am going to do all I can do to see that that never happens.

But I also know, as a realistic public servant, that as long as there are men who hate and destroy, we must have the courage to resist, or we will see it all, all that we have built, all that we hope to build, all of our dreams for freedom—all, *all* will be swept away on the flood of conquest.

So, too, this shall not happen. We will stand in Viet-Nam.

QUESTIONS: THE WAR IN VIET-NAM

Q. Mr. President, in the light of the decisions on Viet-Nam which you have just announced, is the United States prepared with additional plans should North Viet-Nam escalate its military effort and how do you anticipate that the Chinese Communists will react to what you have announced today?

THE PRESIDENT. I do not want to speculate on the reactions of other people. This Nation is prepared, and will always be prepared, to protect its national interest.

Q. Mr. President, you have never talked about a timetable in connection with Viet-Nam. You have said, and you repeated today, that the United States will not be defeated, will not grow tired.

Donald Johnson, National Commander of the American Legion, went over to Viet-Nam in the spring and later called on you. He told White House reporters that he could imagine the war over there going on for 5, 6, or 7 years. Have you thought of that possibility, sir? And do you think the American people ought to think of that possibility?

THE PRESIDENT. Yes, I think the American people ought to understand that there is no quick solution to the problem that we face there. I would not want to prophesy or predict whether it would be a matter of months or years or decades. I do not know that we had any accurate timetable on how long it would take to bring victory in World War I. I don't think anyone really knew whether it would be 2 years or 4 years, or 6 years, to meet with success in World War II. I do think our cause is just. I do think our purposes and objectives are beyond any question.

I do believe that America will stand united behind her men that are there. I plan, as long as I am President, to see that our forces are strong enough to protect our national interest, our right hand constantly protecting that interest with our military, and that our diplomatic and political negotiations are constantly attempting to find some solution that would substitute words for bombs.

As I have said so many times, if anyone questions our good faith and will ask us to meet them to try to reason this matter out, they will find us at the appointed place at the appointed time, in the proper chair.

Q. Mr. President, there is now a representative of the Government of Ghana in Hanoi talking with the Foreign Minister of North Viet-Nam about the war in Viet-Nam. Do you see any indication of hope that something good will come of these talks?

THE PRESIDENT. We are always hopeful that every effort in that direction will meet with success. We welcome those efforts as we welcomed the Commonwealth proposal, as we welcomed Mr. Davies' visit, as we welcomed the Indian suggestion, as we have welcomed the efforts of the distinguished Prime Minister of Great Britain and others from time to time.

As I just said, I hope that every member of the United Nations that has any idea, any plan, any program, any suggestion, that they will not let them go unexplored.

Q. Mr. President, from what you have outlined as your program for now, it would seem that you feel that we can have guns and butter for the foreseeable future. Do you have any idea right now, though, that down the road a piece the American people may have to face the problem of guns or butter?

THE PRESIDENT. I have not the slightest doubt but whatever it is necessary to face, the American people will face. I think that all of us know that we are now in the 52nd month of the prosperity that has been unequaled in this Nation, and I see no reason for declaring a national emergency and I rejected that course of action earlier today when I made my decision.

I cannot foresee what next year or the following year or the following year will hold. I only know that the Americans will do whatever is necessary. At the moment we enjoy the good fortune of having an unparalleled period of prosperity with us, and this government is going to do all it can to see it continue.

Mr. Lisagor?

Q. Mr. President, can you tell us whether the missile sites in North Viet-Nam that were bombed yesterday were manned by Russians and whether or not the administration has a policy about Russian technicians in North Viet-Nam?

THE PRESIDENT. No, we have no information as to how they were manned. We cannot speak with any authority on that matter. We made the decision that we felt our national interests required, and as those problems present themselves we will face up to them.

Q. Mr. President, I wonder if you have had any communications from Chiang Kai-shek that he is ready to go to war with you?

THE PRESIDENT. We have communicated with most of the friendly nations of the world in the last few days and we have received from them responses that have been encouraging. I would not want to go into any individual response here, but I would say that I have indicated to all of the friendly nations what our problems were there, the decision that confronted us, and asked for their help and for their suggestions.

Mr. Roberts?

Q. Mr. President, given the Russian military involvement, or apparent involvement on the side of Hanoi on the one side, and the dialog which Mr. Harriman has been conducting for you on the other, as well as the disarmament talks in Geneva at the moment, could you tell us whether you believe this war, as you now call it, can be contained in this corner of Southeast Asia without involving a U.S.-Soviet confrontation?

THE PRESIDENT. We would hope very much that it could and we will do nothing to provoke that confrontation if we can avoid it. As you know, immediately after I assumed the Presidency I immediately sent messages to the Soviet Union. We have had frequent exchange of views by letter and by conversation with Mr. Gromyko and Mr. Dobrynin. We are doing nothing to provoke the Soviet Union. We are very happy that they agreed to resume the disarmament conference.

I went to some length to try to extend ourselves to make the proposals that I would hope would meet with acceptance of the peoples of the world. We would like to believe that there could be some success flow from this conference although we have not been too successful.

I know of nothing that we have in mind that should arouse the distrust or provoke any violence on the part of the Soviet Union.

Q. Mr. President, does the fact that you are sending additional forces to Viet-Nam imply any change in the existing policy of relying mainly on the South Vietnamese to carry out offensive operations and using American forces to guard American installations and to act as an emergency backup?

THE PRESIDENT. It does not imply any change in policy whatever. It does not imply any change of objective.

Q. Mr. President, would you like to see the United Nations now move formally as an organization to attempt to achieve a settlement in Viet-Nam?

THE PRESIDENT. I have made very clear in my San Francisco speech my hope that the Secretary General, under his wise leadership, would explore every possibility that might lead to a solution of this matter. In my letter to the Secretary General this morning, which Ambassador Goldberg will deliver later in the day, I reiterate my hopes and my desires and I urge upon him that he—if he agrees—that he undertake new efforts in this direction.

Ambassador Goldberg understands the challenge. We spent the weekend talking about the potentialities and the possibilities, our hopes and our dreams, and I believe that we will have an able advocate and a searching negotiator who, I would hope, would some day find success.

Mrs. Craig?

Q. Mr. President, what are the borders of your power to conduct a war? At what point might you have to ask Congress for a declaration?

THE PRESIDENT. I don't know. That would depend on the circumstances. I can't pinpoint the date on the calendar, or the hour of the day. I have to ask Congress for their judgments and for their decisions almost every hour of the day.

One of the principal duties of the office of President is to maintain constant consultation. I have talked to, I guess, more than 50 Members of Congress in the last 24 hours. I have submitted myself to their questions, and the Secretary of State and the Secretary of Defense will meet with them tomorrow if they are ready, to answer any questions that they may need.

Up to now, we have had ample authority, excellent cooperation, a united Congress behind us, and—as near as I could tell from my meetings last night with the leaders, and from my meetings today with the distinguished chairmen of the committees and the members of both parties— we all met as Americans, united and determined to stand as one.

Q. Mr. President, in this connection, however, last night one of the leading Governors of the Republicans said some rather strong things. Governor Hatfield of Oregon said the most recent escalation of action in Viet-Nam is moving all the people of the world closer to world war III, and we have no moral right to commit the world and especially our own people to world war III unilaterally or by the decision of a few experts.

This seemed to imply rather strong criticism of present policies. Do you care to express any reaction?

THE PRESIDENT. Yes. I don't interpret it that way. I think that there are dangers in escalation. I don't think I have any right to commit the whole world to world war III. I am doing everything I know how to avoid it. But retreat is not necessarily the best way to avoid it.

I have outlined to you what I think is the best policy. I would hope that Governor Hatfield and the other Governors, when they understand what we are doing, and when I have a chance to submit myself to their questioning and to counsel with them, would share my view.

I know they have the same concern for the American people and the people of the world as I do. I don't believe our objectives will be very different.

As a matter of fact, I asked the Governors if they could, to come here at the conclusion of their deliberations. I will have my plane go to Minneapolis tomorrow, and I believe 43 of the 48 have indicated a desire to come here.

I will give them all the information I can—confidential, secret, and otherwise—because I have great respect for them, their judgments, their opinions, and their leadership. It is going to be necessary in this effort.

I will also have the Secretary of State and Secretary of Defense review with them all their plans and answer any of their inquiries and we hope resolve any doubts they might have. Nancy?

Q. Mr. President, after the week of deliberations on Viet-Nam, how do you feel—in the context of your office? We always hear it is the loneliest in the world.

THE PRESIDENT. Nancy, I am sorry, but because of the cameras and microphones, I didn't get your question. Raise the microphone up where I can hear, and you camera boys give her a chance.

Q. Mr. President, I said, after the week of deliberations on Viet-Nam, how do you feel, personally, particularly in the context we always hear that your office is the loneliest in the world?

THE PRESIDENT. Well, I don't agree with that. I don't guess there is anyone in this country that has as much understanding and as much help, and as many experts, and as good advice, and many people of both parties trying to help them, as they are me. Of course I admit I need it more than anybody else.

Nancy, I haven't been lonely the last few days—I have had lots of callers.

Q. Mr. President, would you be willing to permit direct negotiations with the Viet Cong forces that are in South Viet-Nam?

THE PRESIDENT. We have stated time and time again that we would negotiate with any government, any place, any time. The Viet Cong would have no difficulty in being represented and having their views presented if Hanoi for a moment decides she wants to cease aggression. And I would not think that would be an insurmountable problem at all. I think that could be worked out. . . .

Reporter: Thank you, Mr. President.

BUT HOSTILITY TO President Johnson's policy continued in the United States and abroad. It is exemplified in a letter by W. H. Ferry of the Center for the Study of Democratic Institutions to the editor of the Santa Barbara News-Press, *August 5, 1965.*

3. A LETTER OF PROTEST AGAINST AMERICAN POLICY IN VIETNAM

SOURCE. *Santa Barbara News-Press*, August 5, 1965. Reprinted by permission of W. H. Ferry.

Editor, News-Press: A letter to President Lyndon B. Johnson: I am so ashamed and dismayed by the actions announced by you in the past several days that I am today withdrawing from the Democratic Party. Neither our honor nor security are involved in Vietnam. But your policies there have become more abhorrent and inhumane; and it is clear now that you intend not to diminish our reliance on violence but to increase it indefinitely. Therefore I must, after more than 30 years as a Democrat, get out. This is a weak way of expressing my total disagreement with programs that call themselves peace but are war. It is the only way I know of dissociating myself from actions that provoke disgust and apprehension all over the world.

Perhaps withdrawing from the Democratic Party is not much of a protest. However, I shall do my best to persuade others to do the same thing. I shall argue that you are taking us into World War III. Two world conflicts under Democratic leadership are enough for me, and should be enough for many other Democrats.

W. H. FERRY

The Contemporary Mind

THE twentieth century is an era of momentous scientific and technological revolutions—an epoch in which the "information explosion" has driven scholars into ever-narrowing fields of specialization and vastly increased the difficulties of the man who would wish to be both broadly and deeply educated. It is an age of widening schism between the sciences and humanities, of dramatic contrast between the mass affluence of some countries and the mass poverty of others, of striking contradiction between the wonders of technology and the vulgarities of mass culture.

Freudian psychology—a dominant theme in the twentieth century—has placed heavy emphasis on the dark, subconscious levels of the human mind, thereby tending to discredit the old belief that man is an essentially rational being. Yet in no other century has man's reason produced such spectacular triumphs. In the field of technology, rockets have been directed to the moon and the planets, and the older industrial revolution has given way to a new electronic revolution. Cybernetics has become basic to modern thought and modern life: remarkably sophisticated "thinking machines" have been used to plot economic trends, predict election results, calculate the orbits of rockets and artificial satellites, and automate factories. Automation, indeed, is in the process of transforming the economies of the advanced industrial states, vastly increasing the efficiency of production and at the same time sharply reducing the need for unskilled labor and aggravating the unemployment problem.

Notable progress has occurred in the sciences—in medicine, biology, and, in particular, the physical sciences. The fundamental theories of contemporary physics are beyond the grasp of all but a few. In astronomy, the concept has emerged of a vastly larger universe than the nineteenth century knew—a universe of countless immense galaxies all receding from one another.

Twentieth-century art has evolved in a bewildering variety of directions. In painting, the emphasis of the later nineteenth century was on the work of art itself rather than the outside world which it depicted. This trend has become increasingly pronounced in the present century, and the drift from objectivism to subjectivism has been carried to its ultimate degree in the work of abstract expressionists such as Jackson Pollock, who made no attempt whatever to represent the natural world but created paintings that were pure expressions of design and color. Sculptors, likewise, have made use of ever-increasing distortions of "objective" reality in order to communicate their own personal vision of things, and have sometimes devoted themselves to creating shapes, masses, and mobiles which represent no outside reality at all. In both painting and sculpture, however, representationalism (usually of a highly subjective sort) continues to hold the allegiance of most artists.

Twentieth-century architecture has shifted steadily toward a more severe, less cluttered style, culminating in the great slab-like concrete, steel, and glass buildings of the International Style designed by such artists as Ludwig Mies van der Rhoe. More recently, the International Style has tended to give way to structures characterized by greater fluidity and decorative beauty.

Man in the twentieth century, surrounded by technological marvels and an abstruse science, often living in huge, impersonal cities, has been haunted by a sense of lonelines, disorientation, and loss of identity. Many have turned to the contemporary philosophy of existentialism. Jean Paul Sartre, Albert Camus, and other existentialist writers have been deeply conscious of the alienation of modern man from his society and his world. They have suggested, as answers, an unreserved assertion of responsibility for the actions of all human beings, a new existential identification with humanity, a reaffirmation of man's freedom to make significant moral decisions, and an ultimate acceptance of the world despite its absurdity.

Part I

SCIENCE AND
SOCIAL SCIENCE

A. Man and Machine

SIGMUND FREUD (1865–1939) was the real founder of modern psychology. With his emphasis on the subconscious parts of the human mind—the id in particular—he demonstrated the irrational basis of many human actions. The Freudian vision of human irrationality has made a deep impact on the thoughts and attitudes of the twentieth century. Freud summarized some of the basic elements of his psychology in his book The Ego and the Id *(1927) from which a number of representative passages are extracted here.*

1. SIGMUND FREUD, FROM *THE EGO AND THE ID*

SOURCE. Sigmund Freud, "The Ego and the Id," from *The Standard Edition of the Complete Psychological Works of Sigmund Freud*, Volume XIX, translated from the German and edited by James Strachey, London: The Hogarth Press, 1961, pp. 13–18, 25–28, 50–52, 54–56, and 58–59. Copyright 1960 by James Strachey. Reprinted by permission of The Hogarth Press Ltd. and W. W. Norton & Company, Inc.

The division of the psychical into what is conscious and what is unconscious is the fundamental premise of psycho-analysis; and it alone makes it possible for psycho-analysis to understand the pathological processes in mental life, which are as common as they are important, and to find a place for them in the framework of science. To put it once more, in a different way: psycho-analysis cannot situate the essence of the psychical in consciousness, but is obliged to regard consciousness as a quality of the psychical, which may be present in addition to other qualities or may be absent.

If I could suppose that everyone interested in psychology would read this book, I should also be prepared to find that at this point some of my readers would already stop short and would go no further; for here we have the first shibboleth of psycho-analysis. To most people who have been educated in philosophy the idea of anything psychical which is not also conscious is so inconceivable that it seems to them absurd and refutable simply by logic. I believe this is only because they have never studied the relevant phenomena of hypnosis and dreams, which—quite apart from pathological manifestations—necessitate this view. Their psychology of consciousness is incapable of solving the problems of dreams and hypnosis.

'Being conscious' is in the first place a purely descriptive term, resting on perception of the most immediate and certain character. Experience goes on to show that a psychical element (for instance, an idea) is not as a rule conscious for a protracted length of time. On the contrary, a state of consciousness is characteristically very transitory; an idea that is conscious now is no longer so a moment later, although it can become so again under certain conditions that are easily brought about. In the interval the idea was—we do not know what. We can say that it was *latent*, and by this we mean that it was *capable of becoming conscious* at any time. Or, if we say that is was *unconscious*, we shall also be giving a correct description of it. Here 'unconscious' coincides with 'latent and capable of becoming conscious.' The philosophers would no doubt object: 'No, the term "unconscious" is not applicable here; so long as the idea was in a state of latency it was not anything psychical at all.' To contradict them at this point would lead to nothing more profitable than a verbal dispute.

But we have arrived at the term or concept of the unconscious along another path, by considering certain experiences in which mental *dynamics* play a part. We have found—that is, we have been obliged to assume—that very powerful mental processes or ideas exist (and here a quantitative or *economic* factor comes into question for the first time) which can produce all the effects in mental life that ordinary ideas do (including effects that can in their turn become conscious as ideas), though they themselves do not become conscious. It is unnecessary to repeat in detail here what has been explained so often before. It is enough to say that at this point psycho-analytic theory steps in and asserts that the reason why such ideas cannot become conscious is that a certain force opposes them, that otherwise they could become conscious, and that it would then be apparent how little they differ from other elements which are admittedly psychical. The fact that in the technique of psychoanalysis a means has been found by which the opposing force can be removed and the ideas in question made conscious renders this theory irrefutable. The state in which the ideas existed before being made conscious is called by us *repression*, and we assert that the force which instituted the repression and maintains it is perceived as *resistance* during the work of analysis.

Thus we obtain our concept of the unconscious from the theory of repression. The repressed is the prototype of the unconscious for us. We see, however, that we have two kinds of unconscious—the one which is latent but capable of becoming conscious, and the one which is repressed and which is not, in itself and without more ado, capable of becoming conscious. This piece of insight into psychical dynamics cannot fail to affect terminology and description. The latent, which is unconscious only descriptively, not in the dynamic sense, we call *preconscious;* we restrict the term *unconscious* to the dynamically unconscious repressed; so that now we have three terms, conscious (*Cs.*), preconscious (*Pcs.*), and unconscious (*Ucs.*), whose sense is no longer purely descriptive. The *Pcs.* is presumably a great deal closer to the *Cs.* than is the *Ucs.*, and since we have called the *Ucs.* psychical we shall with even less hesitation call the latent *Pcs.* psychical. But why do we not rather, instead of this, remain in agreement with the philosophers and, in a consistent way, distinguish the *Pcs.* as well as the *Ucs.* from the conscious psychical? The philosophers would then propose that the *Pcs.* and the *Ucs.* should be described as two species or stages of the 'psychoid,' and harmony would be established. But endless difficulties in exposition would follow; and the one important fact, that these two kinds of 'psychoid' coincide in almost every other respect with what is admittedly psychical, would be forced into the background in the interests of a prejudice dating from a period in which these psychoids, or the most important part of them, were still unknown.

We can now play about comfortably with our three terms, *Cs.*, *Pcs.*, and *Ucs.*, so long as we do not forget that in the descriptive sense there are two kinds of unconscious, but in the dynamic sense only one. For purposes of exposition this distinction can in some cases be ignored, but in others it is of course indispensable. At the same time, we have become more or less accustomed to this ambiguity of the unconscious and have managed pretty well with it. As far as I can see, it is impossible to avoid this ambiguity; the distinction between conscious and unconscious is in the last resort a question of perception, which must be answered 'yes' or 'no,' and the act of perception itself tells us nothing of the reason why a thing is or is not perceived. No one has a right to complain because the actual phenomenon expresses the dynamic factor ambiguously.

In the further course of psycho-analytic work, however, even these distinctions have proved to be inadequate and, for practical purposes, insufficient. This has become clear in more ways than one; but the decisive instance is as follows. We have formed the idea that in each individual there is a coherent organization of mental processes; and we call this his *ego.* It is to this ego that consciousness is attached; the ego controls the approaches to motility—that is, to the discharge of excitations into the external world; it is the mental agency which supervises all its own constituent processes, and which goes to sleep at night, though even then it exercises the censorship on dreams. From this ego proceed the repressions, too, by means of which it is sought to exclude certain trends in the mind not merely from consciousness but also from other forms of effectiveness and activity. In analysis these trends which have been shut out stand in opposition to the ego, and the analysis is faced with the task of removing the resistances which the ego displays against concerning itself with the repressed. Now we find during analysis that, when we put certain tasks before the patient, he gets into difficulties; his associations fail when they should be coming near the repressed. We then tell him that he is dominated by a resistance; but he is quite unaware of the fact, and, even if he guesses from his unpleasurable feelings that a resistance is now at work in him, he does not know what it is or how to describe it. Since, however, there can be no question but that this resistance emanates from his ego and belongs to it, we find ourselves in an unforeseen situation. We have come upon something in the ego itself which is also unconscious, which behaves exactly like the repressed—that is, which produces powerful effects without itself being conscious and which requires special work before it can be made conscious. From the point of view of analytic practice, the consequence of this discovery is that we land in endless obscurities and difficulties if we keep to our habitual forms of expression and try, for instance, to derive neuroses from a conflict between the conscious and the unconscious. We shall have to substitute for this antithesis another, taken from our insight into the structural conditions of the mind—the antithesis between the coherent ego and the repressed which is split off from it.

For our conception of the unconscious, however, the consequences of our discovery are even more important. Dynamic considerations caused us to make our first correction; our insight into the structure of the mind leads to the second. We recognize that the *Ucs.* does not coincide with the repressed; it is still true that all that is repressed is *Ucs.*, but not all that is *Ucs.* is repressed. A part of the ego, too—and Heaven knows how important a part—may be *Ucs.*, undoubtedly is *Ucs.* And this *Ucs.* belonging to the ego is not latent like the *Pcs.*; for if it were, it could not be activated without becoming *Cs.*, and the process of making it conscious would not encounter such great difficulties. When we find ourselves thus confronted by the necessity of postulating a third *Ucs.*, which is not repressed, we must admit that the characteristic of being unconscious begins to lose significance for us. It becomes a quality which can have many meanings, a quality which we are unable to make, as we should have hoped to do, the basis of far-reaching and inevitable conclusions. Nevertheless we must beware of ignoring this characteristic, for the property of being conscious or not is in the last resort our one beacon-light in the darkness of depth-psychology. . . .

. . . the ego seeks to bring the influence of the external world to bear upon the id and its tendencies, and endeavours to substitute the reality principle for the pleasure principle which reigns unrestrictedly in the id. For the ego, perception plays the part which in the id falls to instinct. The ego represents what may be called reason and common sense, in contrast to the id, which contains the passions. All this falls into line with popular distinctions which we are all familiar with; at the same time, however, it is only to be regarded as holding good on the average or 'ideally.'

The functional importance of the ego is manifested in the fact that normally control over the approaches to motility devolves upon it. Thus in its relation to the id it is like a man on horseback, who has to hold in check the superior strength of the horse; with this difference, that the rider tries to do so with his own strength while the ego uses borrowed forces. The analogy may be carried a little further. Often a rider, if he is not to be parted from his horse, is obliged to guide it where it wants to go; so in the same way the ego is in the habit of transforming the id's will into action as if it were its own. . . .

The relation of the ego to consciousness has been entered into repeatedly; yet there are some important facts in this connection which remain to be described here. Accustomed as we are to taking our social or ethical scale of values along with us wherever we go, we feel no surprise at hearing that the scene of the activities of the lower passions is in the unconscious; we expect, moreover, that the higher any mental function ranks in our scale of values the more easily it will find access to consciousness assured to it. Here, however, psycho-analytic experience disappoints us. On the one hand, we have evidence that even subtle and difficult intellectual operations which ordinarily require strenuous reflection can equally be carried out preconsciously and without coming into consciousness. Instances of this are quite incontestable; they may occur, for example, during the state of sleep, as is shown when someone finds, immediately after waking, that he knows the solution to a difficult mathematical or other problem with which he had been wrestling in vain the day before.

There is another phenomenon, however, which is far stranger. In our analyses we discover that there are people in whom the faculties of self-criticism and conscience—mental activities, that is, that rank as extremely high ones—are unconscious and unconsciously produce effects of the greatest importance; the example of resistance remaining unconscious during analysis is therefore by no means unique. But this new discovery, which compels us, in spite of our better critical judgement, to speak of an 'unconscious sense of guilt,' bewilders us far more than the other and sets us fresh problems, especially when we gradually come to see that in a great number of neuroses an unconscious sense of guilt of this kind plays a decisive economic part and puts the most powerful obstacles in the way of recovery. If we come back once more to our scale of values, we shall have to say that not only what is lowest but also what is highest in the ego can be unconscious. . . .

If the ego were merely the part of the id modified by the influence of the perceptual system, the representative in the mind of the real external world, we should have a simple state of things to deal with. But there is a further complication.

The considerations that led us to assume the existence of a grade in the ego, a differentiation within the ego, which may be called the 'ego ideal' or 'super-ego,' have been stated elsewhere. They still hold good. The fact that this part of the ego is less firmly connected with consciousness is the novelty which calls for explanation. . . .

An interpretation of the normal, conscious sense of guilt (conscience) presents no difficulties; it is based on the tension between the ego and the ego ideal and is the expression of a condemnation of the ego by its critical agency. The feelings of inferiority so well known in neurotics are presumably not far removed from it. In two very familiar maladies the sense of guilt is over-strongly conscious; in them the ego ideal displays particular severity and often rages against the ego in a cruel fashion. The attitude of the ego ideal in these two conditions, obsessional neurosis and melancholia, presents, alongside of this similarity, differences that are no less significant.

In certain forms of obsessional neurosis the sense of guilt is over-noisy but cannot justify itself to the ego. Consequently the patient's ego rebels against the imputation of guilt and seeks the physician's support in repudiating it. It would be folly to acquiesce in this, for to do so would have no effect. Analysis eventually shows that the super-ego is being influenced by processes that have remained unknown to the ego. It is possible to discover the repressed impulses which are really at the bottom of the sense of guilt. Thus in this case the super-ego knew more than the ego about the unconscious id.

In melancholia the impression that the super-ego has obtained a hold upon consciousness is even stronger. But here the ego ventures no objection; it admits its guilt and submits to the punishment. We understand the difference. In obsessional neurosis what were in question were objectionable impulses which remained outside the ego, while in melancholia the object to which the super-ego's wrath applies has been taken into the ego through identification.

It is certainly not clear why the sense of guilt reaches such an extraordinary strength in these two neurotic disorders; but the main problem presented in this state of affairs lies in another direction. We shall postpone discussion of it until we have dealt with the other cases in which the sense of guilt remains unconscious.

It is essentially in hysteria and in states of a hysterical type that this is found. Here the mechanism by which the sense of guilt remains unconscious is easy to discover. The hysterical ego fends off a distressing perception with which the criticisms of its super-ego threaten it . . . by an act of repression. It is the ego, therefore, that is responsible for the sense of guilt remaining unconscious. We know that as a rule the ego carries out repressions in the service and at the behest of its super-ego; but this is a case in which it has turned the same weapon against its harsh taskmaster. In obsessional neurosis, as we know, the phenomena of reaction-formation predominate; but here [in hysteria] the ego succeeds only in keeping at a distance the material to which the sense of guilt refers.

One may go further and venture the hypothesis that a great part of the sense of guilt must normally remain unconscious, because the origin of conscience is intimately connected with the Oedipus complex, which belongs to the unconscious. If anyone were inclined to put forward the paradoxical proposition that the normal man is not only far more immoral than he believes but also far more moral than he knows, psychoanalysis, on whose findings the first half of the assertion rests, would have no objection to raise against the second half.[1]

It was a surprise to find that an increase in this *Ucs.* sense of guilt can turn people into criminals. But it is undoubtedly a fact. In many criminals, especially youthful ones, it is possible to detect a very powerful sense of guilt which existed before the crime, and is therefore not its result but its motive. It is as if it was a relief to be able to fasten this unconscious sense of guilt on to something real and immediate. . . .

From the point of view of instinctual control, of morality, it may be said of the id that it is totally non-moral, of the ego that it strives to be moral, and of the super-ego that it can be super-moral and then become as cruel as only the id can be. It is remarkable that the more a man checks his aggressiveness towards the exterior the more severe—that is aggressive—he becomes in his ego ideal. The ordinary view sees the situation the other way round: the standard set up by the ego ideal seems to be the motive for the suppression of aggressiveness. The fact remains, however, as we have stated it: the more a man controls his aggressiveness, the more

[1] This proposition is only apparently a paradox; it simply states that human nature has a far greater extent, both for good and for evil, than it thinks it has—i.e. than its ego is aware of through conscious perception.

intense becomes his ideal's inclination to aggressiveness against his ego. It is like a displacement, a turning round upon his own ego. But even ordinary normal morality has a harshly restraining, cruelly prohibiting quality. It is from this, indeed, that the conception arises of a higher being who deals out punishment inexorably. . . .

Our ideas about the ego are beginning to clear, and its various relationships are gaining distinctness. We now see the ego in its strength and in its weaknesses. It is entrusted with important functions. By virtue of its relation to the perceptual system it gives mental processes an order in time and submits them to 'reality-testing.' By interposing the processes of thinking, it secures a postponement of motor discharges and controls the access to motility. This last power is, to be sure, a question more of form than of fact; in the matter of action the ego's position is like that of a constitutional monarch, without whose sanction no law can be passed but who hesitates long before imposing his veto on any measure put forward by Parliament. All the experiences of life that originate from without enrich the ego; the id, however, is its second external world, which it strives to bring into subjection to itself. . . . With the aid of the super-ego, in a manner that is still obscure to us, it draws upon the experiences of past ages stored in the id.

There are two paths by which the contents of the id can penetrate into the ego. The one is direct, the other leads by way of the ego ideal; which of these two paths they take may, for some mental activities, be of decisive importance. The ego develops from perceiving instincts to controlling them, from obeying instincts to inhibiting them. In this achievement a large share is taken by the ego ideal, which indeed is partly a reaction-formation against the instinctual process of the id. Psycho-analysis is an instrument to enable the ego to achieve a progressive conquest of the id.

From the other point of view, however, we see this same ego as a poor creature owing service to three masters and consequently menaced by three dangers: from the external world, from the libido of the id, and from the severity of the super-ego. Three kinds of anxiety correspond to these three dangers, since anxiety is the expression of a retreat from danger. As a frontier-creature, the ego tries to mediate between the world and the id, to make the id pliable to the world and, by means of its muscular activity, to make the world fall in with the wishes of the id. . . . it disguises the id's conflicts with reality and, if possible, its conflicts with the super-ego too. In its position midway between the id and reality, it only too often yields to the temptation to become sycophantic, opportunist and lying, like a politician who sees the truth but wants to keep his place in popular favour. . . .

We know that the fear of death makes its appearance under two conditions (which, moreover, are entirely analogous to situations in which other kinds of anxiety develop), namely, as a reaction to an external danger and as an internal process, as for instance in melancholia. Once again a neurotic manifestation may help us to understand a normal one.

The fear of death in melancholia only admits of one explanation: that the ego gives itself up because it feels itself hated and persecuted by the super-ego, instead of loved. To the ego, therefore, living means the same as being loved—being loved by the super-ego, which here again appears as the representative of the id. The super-ego fulfils the same function of protecting and saving that was fulfilled in earlier days by the father and later by Providence or Destiny. But, when the ego finds itself in an excessive real danger which it believes itself unable to overcome by its own strength, it is bound to draw the same conclusion. It sees itself deserted by all protecting forces and lets itself die. Here, moreover, is once again the same situation as that which underlay the first great anxiety-state of birth and the infantile anxiety of longing—the anxiety due to separation from the protecting mother.

These considerations make it possible to regard the fear of death, like the fear of conscience, as a development of the fear of castration. The great significance which the sense of guilt has in the neuroses makes it conceivable that common neurotic anxiety is reinforced in severe cases by the generating of anxiety between the ego and the super-ego (fear of castration, of conscience, of death).

The id, to which we finally come back, has no means of showing the ego either love or hate. It cannot say what it wants; it has achieved no unified will. Eros and the death instinct struggle within it; we have seen with what weapons the one group of instincts defends itself against the other. It would be possible to picture the id as under the domination of the mute but powerful death instincts, which desire to be at peace and (prompted by the pleasure principle) to put Eros, the mischief-maker, to rest; but perhaps that might be to undervalue the part played by Eros.

THE GREAT CYBERNETICIST Norbert Wiener (b. 1894) comments on the fundamental role of cybernetics in the modern world in "Cybernetics in History," from his book The Human Use of Human Beings: Cybernetics and Society *(1950).*

2. NORBERT WIENER, "CYBERNETICS IN HISTORY," FROM *THE HUMAN USE OF HUMAN BEINGS: CYBERNETICS AND SOCIETY*

SOURCE. Norbert Wiener, *The Human Use of Human Beings: Cybernetics and Society*, Boston: Houghton Mifflin Co., 1954, Doubleday Anchor edition, pp. 15–27. Copyright 1950, 1954 by Norbert Wiener. Reprinted by permission of the publisher, Houghton Mifflin Company.

Since the end of World War II, I have been working on the many ramifications of the theory of messages. Besides the electrical engineering theory of the transmission of messages, there is a larger field which includes not only the study of language but the study of messages as a means of controlling machinery and society, the development of computing machines and other such automata, certain reflections upon psychology and the nervous system, and a tentative new theory of scientific method. This larger theory of messages is a probabilistic theory, an intrinsic part of the movement that owes its origin to Willard Gibbs and which I have described in the introduction.

Until recently, there was no existing word for this complex of ideas, and in order to embrace the whole field by a single term, I felt constrained to invent one. Hence "Cybernetics," which I derived from the Greek word *kubernētēs*, or "steersman," the same Greek word from which we eventually derive our word "governor." Incidentally, I found later that the word had already been used by Ampère with reference to political science, and had been introduced in another context by a Polish scientist, both uses dating from the earlier part of the nineteenth century.

I wrote a more or less technical book entitled *Cybernetics* which was published in 1948. In response to a certain demand for me to make its ideas acceptable to the lay public, I published the first edition of *The Human Use of Human Beings* in 1950. Since then the subject has grown from a few ideas shared by Drs. Claude Shannon, Warren Weaver, and myself, into an established region of research. Therefore, I take this opportunity occasioned by the reprinting of my book to bring it up to date, and to remove certain defects and inconsequentialities in its original structure.

In giving the definition of Cybernetics in the original book, I classed communication and control together. Why did I do this? When I communicate with another person, I impart a message to him, and when he communicates back with me he returns a related message which contains information primarily accessible to him and not to me. When I control the actions of another person, I communicate a message to him, and although this message is in the imperative mood, the technique of communication does not differ from that of a message of fact. Furthermore, if my control is to be effective I must take cognizance of any messages from him which may indicate that the order is understood and has been obeyed.

It is the thesis of this book that society can only be understood through a study of the messages and the communication facilities which belong to it; and that in the future development of these messages and communication facilities, messages between man and machines, between machines and man, and between machine and machine, are destined to play an ever-increasing part.

When I give an order to a machine, the situation is not essentially different from that which arises when I give an order to a person. In other words, as far as my consciousness goes I am aware of the order that has gone out and of the signal of compliance that has come back. To me, personally, the fact that the signal in its intermediate stages has gone through a machine rather than through a person is irrelevant and does not in any case greatly change my relation to the signal. Thus the theory of control in engineering, whether human or animal or mechanical, is a chapter in the theory of messages.

Naturally there are detailed differences in messages and in problems of control, not only between a living organism and a machine, but within each narrower class of beings. It is the purpose of Cybernetics to develop a language and techniques that will enable us indeed to attack the problem of control and communication in general, but also to find the proper repertory of ideas and techniques to classify their particular manifestations under certain concepts.

The commands through which we exercise our control over our environment are a kind of information which we impart to it. Like any form of information, these commands are subject to disorganization in transit. They generally come through in less coherent fashion and certainly not more coherently than they were sent. In control and communication we are always fighting nature's tendency to degrade the organized and to destroy the meaningful; the tendency, as Gibbs has shown us, for entropy to increase.

Much of this book concerns the limits of communication within and among individuals. Man is immersed in a world which he perceives through his sense organs. Information that he receives is co-ordinated through his brain and nervous system until, after the proper process of storage, collation, and selection, it emerges through effector organs, generally his muscles. These in turn act on the external world, and also react on the central nervous system through receptor organs such as the end organs of kinaesthesia; and the information received by the kinaesthetic organs is combined with his already accumulated store of information to influence future action.

Information is a name for the content of what is exchanged with the outer world as we adjust to it, and make our adjustment felt upon it. The process of receiving and of using information is the process of our adjusting to the contingencies of the outer environment, and of our living effectively within that environment. The needs and the complexity of modern life make greater demands on this process of information than ever before, and our press, our museums, our scientific laboratories, our universities, our libraries and textbooks, are obliged to meet the needs of this process or fail in their purpose. To live effectively is to live with adequate information. Thus, communication and control belong to the essence of man's inner life, even as they belong to his life in society.

The place of the study of communication in the history of science is neither trivial, fortuitous, nor new. Even before Newton such problems were current in physics, especially in the work of Fermat, Huygens, and Leibnitz, each of whom shared an interest in physics whose focus was not mechanics but optics, the communication of visual images.

Fermat furthered the study of optics with his principle of minimization which says that over any sufficiently short part of its course, light follows the path which it takes the least time to traverse. Huygens developed the primitive form of what is now known as "Huygens' Principle" by saying that light spreads from a source by forming around that source something like a small sphere consisting of secondary sources which in turn propagate light just as the primary sources do. Leibnitz, in the meantime, saw the whole world as a collection of beings called "monads" whose activity consisted in the perception of one another on the basis of a pre-established harmony laid down by God, and it is fairly clear that he thought of this interaction largely in optical terms. Apart from this perception, the monads had no "windows," so that in his view all mechanical interaction really becomes nothing more than a subtle consequence of optical interaction.

A preoccupation with optics and with message, which is apparent in this part of Leibnitz's philosophy, runs through its whole texture. It plays a large part in two of his most original ideas: that of the *Characteristica Universalis,* or universal scientific language, and that of the *Calculus Ratiocinator,* or calculus of logic. This Calculus Ratiocinator, imperfect as it was, was the direct ancestor of modern mathematical logic.

Leibnitz, dominated by ideas of communication, is, in more than one way, the intellectual ancestor of the ideas of this book, for he was also interested in machine computation and in automata. My views in this book are very far from being Leibnitzian, but the problems with which I am concerned are most certainly Leibnitzian. Leibnitz's computing machines were only an offshoot of his interest in a computing language, a reasoning calculus which again was in his mind, merely an extension of his idea of a complete artificial language. Thus, even in his computing machine, Leibnitz's preoccupations were mostly linguistic and communicational.

Toward the middle of the last century, the work of Clerk Maxwell and of his precursor, Faraday, had attracted the attention of physicists once more to optics, the science of light, which was now regarded as a form of electricity that could be reduced to the mechanics of a curious, rigid, but invisible medium known as the ether, which, at the time, was supposed to permeate the atmosphere, interstellar space and all transparent materials. Clerk Maxwell's work on optics consisted in the mathematical development of ideas which had been previously expressed in a cogent but non-mathematical form by Faraday. The study of ether raised certain questions whose answers were obscure, as, for example, that of the motion of matter through the ether. The famous experiment of Michelson and Morley, in the nineties, was undertaken to resolve this problem, and it gave the entirely unexpected answer that there simply was no way to determine the motion of matter through the ether.

The first satisfactory solution to the problems aroused by this experiment was that of Lorentz, who pointed out that if the forces holding matter together were conceived as being themselves electrical or optical in nature, we should expect a negative result from the Michelson-Morley experiment. However, Einstein in 1905 translated these ideas of Lorentz into a form in which the unobservability of absolute motion was rather a postulate of physics than the result of any particular structure of matter. For our purposes, the important thing is that in Einstein's work, light and matter are on an equal basis, as they had been in the writings before Newton; without the Newtonian subordination of everything else to matter and mechanics.

In explaining his views, Einstein makes abundant use of the observer who may be at rest or may be moving. In his theory of relativity it is impossible to introduce the observer without also introducing the idea of message, and without, in fact, returning the emphasis of physics to a quasi-Leibnitzian state, whose tendency is once again optical. Einstein's theory of relativity and Gibbs' statistical mechanics are in sharp contrast, in that Einstein, like Newton, is still talking primarily in terms of an absolutely rigid dynamics not introducing the idea of probability. Gibbs' work, on the other hand, is probabilistic from the very start, yet both directions of work represent a shift in the point of view of physics in which the world as it actually exists is replaced in some sense or other by the world as it happens to be observed, and the old naïve realism of physics gives way to something on which Bishop Berkeley might have smiled with pleasure.

At this point it is appropriate for us to review certain notions pertaining to entropy which have already been presented in the introduction. As we have said, the idea of entropy represents several of the most important departures of Gibbsian mechanics from Newtonian mechanics. In Gibbs' view we have a physical quantity which belongs not to the outside world as such, but to certain sets of possible outside worlds, and therefore to the answer to certain specific questions which we can ask concerning the outside world. Physics now becomes not the discussion of an outside universe which may be regarded as the total answer to all the questions concerning it, but an account of the answers to much more limited questions. In fact, we are now no longer concerned with the study of all possible outgoing and incoming messages which we may send and receive, but with the theory of much more specific outgoing and incoming messages; and it involves a measurement of the no-longer infinite amount of information that they yield us.

Messages are themselves a form of pattern and organization. Indeed, it is possible to treat sets of messages as having an entropy like sets of states of the external world. Just as entropy is a measure of disorganization, the information carried by a set of messages is a measure of organization. In fact, it is possible to interpret the information carried by a message as essentially the negative of its entropy, and the negative logarithm of its probability. That is, the more probable the message, the less information it gives. Clichés, for example, are less illuminating than great poems.

I have already referred to Leibnitz's interest in automata, an interest incidentally shared by his contemporary, Pascal, who made real contributions to the development of what we now know as the desk adding-machine. Leibnitz saw in the concordance of the time given by clocks set at the same time, the model for the pre-established harmony of his monads. For the technique embodied in the automata of his time was that of the clockmaker. Let us consider the activity of the little figures which dance on the top of a music box. They move in accordance with a pattern, but it is a pattern which is set in advance, and in which the past activity of the figures has practically nothing to do with the pattern of their future activity. The probability that they will diverge from this pattern is nil. There is a message, indeed; but it goes from the machinery of the music box to the figures, and stops there. The figures themselves have no trace of communication with the outer world, except this one-way stage of communication with the pre-established mechanism of the music box. They are blind, deaf, and dumb, and cannot vary their activity in the least from the conventionalized pattern.

Contrast with them the behavior of man, or indeed of any moderately intelligent animal such as a kitten. I call to the kitten and it looks up. I have sent it a message which it has received by its sensory organs, and which it registers in action. The kitten is hungry and lets out a pitiful wail. This time it is the sender of a message. The kitten bats at a swinging spool. The spool swings to its left, and the kitten catches it with its left paw. This time messages of a very complicated nature are both sent and received within the kitten's own nervous system through certain nerve end-bodies in its joints, muscles, and tendons; and by means of nervous messages sent by these organs, the animal is aware of the actual position and tensions of its tissues. It is only through these organs that anything like a manual skill is possible.

I have contrasted the prearranged behavior of the little figures on the music box on the one hand, and the contingent behavior of human beings and animals on the other. But we must not suppose that the music box is typical of all machine behavior.

The older machines, and in particular the older attempts to produce automata, did in fact function on a closed clockwork basis. But modern automatic machines such as the controlled missile, the proximity fuse, the automatic door opener, the control apparatus for a chemical factory, and the rest of the modern armory of automatic machines which perform military or industrial functions, possess sense organs; that is, receptors for messages coming from the outside. These may be as simple as photo-electric cells which change electrically when a light falls on them, and which can tell light from dark, or as complicated as a television set. They may measure a tension by the change it produces in the conductivity of a wire exposed to it, or they may measure temperature by means of a thermocouple, which is an instrument consisting of two distinct metals in contact with one another through which a current flows when one of the points of contact is heated. Every instrument in the repertory of the scientific-instrument maker is a possible sense organ, and may be made to record its reading remotely through the intervention of appropriate electrical apparatus. Thus the machine which is conditioned by its relation to the external world, and by the things happening in the external world, is with us and has been with us for some time.

The machine which acts on the external world by means of messages is also familiar. The automatic photoelectric door opener is known to every person who has passed through the Pennsylvania Station in New York, and is used in many other buildings as well. When a message consisting of the interception of a beam of light is sent to the apparatus, this message actuates the door, and opens it so that the passenger may go through.

The steps between the actuation of a machine of this type by sense organs and its performance of a task may be as simple as in the case of the electric door; or it may be in fact of any desired degree of complexity within the limits of our engineering techniques. A complex action is one in which the data introduced, which we call the *input,* to obtain an effect on the outer world, which we call the *output,* may involve a large number of combinations. These are combinations, both of the data put in at the moment and of the records taken from the past stored data which we call the *memory.* These are recorded in the machine. The most complicated machines yet made which transform input data into output data are the high-speed electrical computing machines, of which I shall speak later in more detail. The determination of the mode of conduct of these machines is given through a special sort of input, which frequently consists of punched cards or tapes or of magnetized wires, and which determines the way in which the machine is going to act in one operation, as distinct from the way in which it might have acted in another. Because of the frequent use of punched or magnetic tape in the control, the data which are fed in, and which indicate the mode of operation of one of these machines for combining information, are called the *taping.*

I have said that man and the animal have a kinaesthetic sense, by which they keep a record of the position and tensions of their muscles. For any machine subject to a varied external environment to act effectively it is necessary that information concerning the results of its own action be furnished to it as part of the information on which it must continue to act. For example, if we are running an elevator, it is not enough to open the outside door because the orders we have given should make the elevator be at that door at the time we open it. It is important that the release for opening the door be dependent on the fact that the elevator is actually at the door; otherwise something might have detained it, and the passenger might step into the empty shaft. This control of a machine on the basis of its *actual* performance rather than its *expected* performance is known as *feedback,* and involves sensory members which are actuated by motor members and perform the function of *tell-tales* or *monitors*— that is, of elements which indicate a performance. It is the function of these mechanisms to control the mechanical tendency toward disorganization; in other words, to produce a temporary and local reversal of the normal direction of entropy.

I have just mentioned the elevator as an example of feedback. There are other cases where the importance of feedback is even more apparent. For example, a gun-pointer takes information from his instruments of observation, and conveys it to the gun, so that the latter will point in such a direction that the missile will pass through the moving target at a certain time. Now, the gun itself must be used under all conditions of weather. In some of these the grease is warm, and the gun swings easily and rapidly. Under other conditions the grease is frozen or mixed with sand, and the gun is slow to answer the orders given to it. If these orders are reinforced by an extra push given when the gun fails to respond easily to the orders and lags behind them, then the error of the gun-pointer will be decreased. To obtain a performance as uniform as possible, it is customary to put into the gun a control feedback element which reads the lag of the gun behind the position it should have according to the orders given it, and which uses this difference to give the gun an extra push.

It is true that precautions must be taken so that the push is not too hard, for if it is, the gun will swing past its proper position, and will have to be pulled back in a series of oscillations, which may well become wider and wider, and lead to a disastrous instability. If the feedback system is itself controlled—if, in other words, its own entropic tendencies are checked by still other controlling mechanisms—and kept within limits sufficiently stringent, this will not occur, and the existence of the feedback will increase the stability of performance of the gun. In other words, the performance will become less dependent on the frictional load; or what is the same thing, on the drag created by the stiffness of the grease.

Something very similar to this occurs in human action. If I pick up my cigar, I do not will to move any specific muscles. Indeed in many cases, I do not know what those muscles are. What I do is to turn into action a certain feedback mechanism; namely, a reflex in which the amount by which I have yet failed to pick up the cigar is turned into a new and increased order to the lagging muscles, whichever they may be. In this way, a fairly uniform voluntary command will enable the same task to be performed from widely varying initial positions, and irrespective of the decrease of contraction due to fatigue of the muscles. Similarly, when I drive a car, I do not follow out a series of commands dependent simply on a mental image of the road and the task I am doing. If I find the car swerving too much to the right, that causes me to pull it to the left. This depends on the actual performance of the car, and not simply on the road; and it allows me to drive with nearly equal efficiency a light Austin or a heavy truck, without having formed separate habits for the driving of the two. I shall have more to say about this in the chapter in this book on special machines, where we shall discuss the service that can be done to neuropathology by the study of machines with defects in performance similar to those occurring in the human mechanism.

It is my thesis that the physical functioning of the living individual and the operation of some of the newer communication machines are precisely parallel in their analogous attempts to control entropy through feedback. Both of them have sensory receptors as one stage in their cycle of operation: that is, in both of them there exists a special apparatus for collecting information from the outer world at low energy levels, and for making it available in the operation of the individual or of the machine. In both cases these external messages are not taken *neat,* but through the internal transforming powers of the apparatus, whether it be alive or dead. The information is then turned into a new form available for the further stages of performance. In both the animal and the machine this performance is made to be effective on the outer world. In both of them, their *performed* action on the outer world, and not merely their *intended* action, is reported back to the central regulatory apparatus. This complex of behavior is ignored by the average man, and in particular does not play the role that it should in our habitual analysis of society; for just as individual physical responses may be seen from this point of view, so may the organic responses of society itself. I do not mean that the sociologist is unaware of the existence and complex nature of communications in society, but until recently he has tended to overlook the extent to which they are the cement which binds its fabric together.

We have seen in this chapter the fundamental unity of a complex of ideas until recently had not been sufficiently associated with one another, namely, the contingent view of physics that Gibbs introduced as a modification of the traditional, Newtonian conventions, the Augustinian attitude toward order and conduct which is demanded by this view, and the theory of the message among men, machines, and in society as a sequence of events in time which, though it itself has a certain contingency, strives to hold back nature's tendency toward disorder by adjusting its parts to various purposive ends.

B. The Cosmos

PROFESSOR FRED HOYLE, one of the most imaginative of contemporary astronomers and cosmologists, explains in relatively simple terms in his Frontiers of Astronomy *(1955) the modern conception of the cosmos. His chapter "The Expanding Universe" deals with the galaxies and galaxian clusters, and their characteristic of receding from one another. He also touches on his "steady-state" theory of cosmology in which he proposes a process of continuous creation of matter. Hoyle's steady-state theory is an important cosmological hypothesis but is viewed skeptically by many astronomers and astrophysicists. It should be added that astronomical investigations subsequent to the publication of Hoyle's book, particularly those in the new field of radio astronomy, have added important new elements to the contemporary view of the universe.*

1. FRED HOYLE, "THE EXPANDING UNIVERSE," FROM *FRONTIERS OF ASTRONOMY*

SOURCE. Fred Hoyle, *Frontiers of Astronomy*, New York: Harper & Row, 1955, New American Library, 1957, pp. 270–284. Copyright 1955 by Fred Hoyle. Reprinted by permission of Harper & Row Publishers Inc. and Heinemann Educational Books Ltd.

The Universe is everything; both living and inanimate things; both atoms and galaxies; and if the spiritual exists as well as the material, of spiritual things also; and if there is a Heaven and a Hell, Heaven and Hell too; for by its very nature the Universe is the totality of all things.

There is a general impression abroad that the large scale aspects of the Universe are not very important to us in our daily lives—that if the Earth and Sun remained all else might be destroyed without causing us any serious inconvenience. Yet this view is very likely to prove wildly wrong. Present-day developments in cosmology are coming to suggest rather insistently that everyday conditions could not persist but for the distant parts of the Universe, that all our ideas of space and of geometry would become entirely invalid if the distant parts of the Universe were taken away. Our everyday experience even down to the smallest details seems to be so closely integrated to the grand scale features of the Universe that it is wellnigh impossible to contemplate the two being separated.

OLBERS' PARADOX

Let us start with an everyday question, one so trivial that probably few have ever bothered to ask it, and yet one that has the most profound connections with the distant parts of the Universe. This is a question first asked by Olbers in 1826, and recently revived by H. Bondi. Why is the sky dark at night? To appreciate the depth of this strange query suppose the Universe to be uniformly populated with clusters of galaxies. Draw a sphere with a large radius, anything you please, say 1,000 million parsecs. Then draw a series of larger spheres, all with the same centre, the difference in radius between one and the next being always the same, say 1,000 parsecs. The regions between successive spheres form the skins of an onion but of an infinite onion: they extend out indefinitely—however many spheres we draw, we can always draw one more. Now the volume of the successive skins increases proportionately to the square of the radius. Then since for a uniformly populated Universe the number of stars that fall in a particular skin must on the average be proportional to its volume, we see that the number of stars in successive skins increases as the square of the radius. But the intensity of the light that we receive from any individual star is proportional to the inverse of the square of its distance away from us—double the distance and we receive only a quarter of the light. So we have the following situation: each skin of the onion contains on the average a number of stars proportional to the square of its radius, while the intensity of radiation from each star—as measured by an observer at the centre of the system—is inversely proportional to the square of the radius. So the total intensity of the radiation received at the centre from all the stars of a particular skin does not depend at all on its radius—the increase in one factor simply cancels the decrease in the other. But since the number of skins can be made as large as we please, this means that the intensity of the light at the centre can also be made as large as we please—or at any rate large to the point where one star blocks out the light of another, and this does not arise until the whole sky becomes everywhere as bright as the disk of the Sun (taking the Sun to be a typical star). This requires the light and heat received from the Universe by the Earth to be about 6,000 million times greater than the intensity of full sunlight. Well, we don't receive this amount of radiation, otherwise we should be instantly burned up.

Obviously something has gone very wrong with the argument. The question is where? The immediate temptation is to doubt our starting assumption that the Universe is uniformly populated. The paradox would not arise if the material of the Universe were to exist in an isolated region of space, since in such a case the contributions of the skins could not be continued indefinitely. This was indeed the way that the scientists of the nineteenth century sought to escape from the dilemma. According to nineteenth-century views our Galaxy was to be regarded as isolated in space with nothing outside it. As late as the beginning of the present century a great controversy took place at an international conference of astronomers. On the one side, championed notably by R. A. Proctor, was the view that large numbers of galaxies exist outside our own, stretching away into the depths of space. On the other side, at that time the victorious side, the view was still expressed that the Universe consisted of our Galaxy only. Other galaxies were interpreted as local nebulosities lying within our own. The protagonists of this latter quite erroneous view based their case on a thoroughly wrong-headed argument, namely that no galaxies are observed in directions along the plane of the Milky Way. This was thought to prove the association of the galaxies with the Milky Way. But Proctor argued, just as we do today, that this apparent absence of galaxies is simply due to the absorbing effects of dust along the plane of the Galaxy. But the majority of astronomers in the first two decades of the present century could not accept this view for the reason that most of their researchers on the structure of our Galaxy had proceeded on the assumption that dust was not a serious obscuring agent. It was not until about 1925 that these views became discredited, and the suggestions of

Proctor became thoroughly vindicated. Notably as a result of the work of J. H. Oort and B. Lindblat it became realised that the structure of our Galaxy is radically different from what had formerly been thought, and that the older views were wholly in error due to the neglect of the obscuring effects of the interstellar dust particles. At about the same time it was established beyond question by E. P. Hubble that the galaxies are great independent star systems similar to our own and lying at enormous distances from us. In a few years Hubble took man's conception of the Universe from a localised region of a few thousand parsecs in dimensions out to unprecedented distances of hundreds of millions of parsecs; for not only did Hubble show that the galaxies are unquestionably great starsystems, as the Galaxy is, but he showed that out to distances of hundreds of millions of parsecs there is no evidence that we live in a purely localised aggregation of matter. The galaxies stretch away from us farther and farther into space and by the time they are lost to view (through faintness due to great distance) some 100 million or more of them are accounted for.

Since this decisive reorientation of man's outlook on the Universe—one of the most important scientific revolutions of thought of all time—no one has thought fit to suggest that the distribution of matter is localised in space. Rather has the opposite point of view come to gain general credence, that apart from local variations—the presence of a cluster of galaxies in one locality rather than in another, there are no marked spatial fluctuations in the distribution of matter on the large scale, that regardless of what the special position of the observer happens to be the Universe presents the same large scale aspects in the distribution of galaxies. It follows that Olbers' paradox is reinstated. It cannot be answered in the manner that scientists of the nineteenth and early twentieth centuries attempted to answer it.

A more sophisticated attempt to defeat Olbers' paradox depends on a time argument instead of a space argument. If all the stars of the Universe were younger than a definite age our former considerations would become invalid, since light from sufficiently distant skins of our onion would not yet have reached us. The process would have to be 'cut off' at a certain distance, the distance from which the transit time of light equalled the ages of the oldest stars. No light from still more distant skins could yet have arrived into our locality. This would invalidate our procedure of adding together equal contributions from as many skins as we please. Only a limited number could be reckoned as contributing to the light of the night sky.

Now we saw in Chapter 9 that the stars in our Galaxy are probably all younger than about 6,000 million years, and the similarity of the stars of neighboring galaxies with those of our own suggests that they too are probably not much older than about 6,000 million years. So there is a measure of observational support for the present line of escape from Olbers' paradox. What we are now saying is that the Universe, although not constructed in such a way that its material content is confined to a particular spatial locality (and indeed although it may be spacially unlimited) is limited in time.

But this is a view that we consider with some caution. There is a suspicious similarity between the nineteenth-century attempt to localise the material content of the Universe in space and the present suggestion of confining the existence of matter (or at any rate of stars) in time. In the case of spacial limitation the old views were supported by the finite spacial extension of our Galaxy. Now we are supporting the time limitation by the finite ages of the stars of our Galaxy. The two processes are logically similar in character and one of them having proved disastrously wrong we must be a little chary of accepting the other.

When the proposition is generalised from the statement that all stars are younger than a definite age to the proposition that the Universe is younger than a definite age I am inclined to be still more sceptical. What is implied by this view is that at a certain definite time in the past—say 6,000 million years ago, the laws of physics suddenly became applicable. Before this time physics was not applicable. After this time physics dominated the behaviour of the Universe. The transition between no-physics and all-physics was instantaneous.[1]

One has to be particularly cautious in accepting this sort of view because the human brain apparently possesses a kink in these matters that only too readily leads to serious mistakes. Europeans of the eighteenth century used to believe that the Universe came into being about 6,000 years ago! When this view was shown to be utterly wrong it was then said that the Universe was 20 million years old, then 100 million years, and so by a series of steps up to the 6,000 million years mentioned above.

Such arguments carry one no further, however, than the stage of suggestive speculation. But what does go further is a staggering discovery made by V. M. Slipher and by E. P. Hubble and M. Humason. If a singular origin of the Universe were the only escape from Olbers' paradox we should be well-nigh forced to accept it. But the discovery just alluded to provides an escape along entirely unexpected lines. The existence of such a very strange resolution of the paradox greatly increases my doubts of the correctness of a finite temporal origin of the Universe.

---

[1] Expressed in mathematical terminology, that the equations of physics possessed singularities about 6,000 million years ago, and that the equations cannot be continued through these singularities.

The Universe is expanding. This is the purport of these discoveries. It is important to say right at the outset that the expansion is on the large scale, not local. The distances in our own solar system are not expanding, nor are the distances in our Galaxy, nor the distances in the Local Group. But beyond the Local Group, beyond about half a million parsecs, expansion begins. The giant galaxy M 81 at a distance of 2,500,000 parsecs is moving away from us, its distance is increasing at about 80 miles per second. The galaxies of the Virgo cloud at a distance of perhaps 10 million parsecs are moving away from us at a speed of about 750 miles per second. The Corona cluster of galaxies is moving away from us at rather more than 13,000 miles per second, while the Hydra cluster at a distance of some 400 million parsecs is increasing its distance every second by a further 38,000 miles. It may be of interest to compute how much farther away the Hydra cluster is now than it was at the moment when you began to read this chapter.

THE RED-SHIFT

Now how is this known? In Chapter 13 we saw how motions towards or away from the observer can be determined by a study of the pitch of spectral lines emitted by a source of light. Our present sources are whole galaxies. It is thus found that all galaxies outside the Local Group are steadily moving away from us. Before examining Plate LVII, which illustrates these observations, we should notice that spectral lines can occur in two forms, as bright lines or as dark lines, the two cases being rather like the negative and positive of a photograph. When the atoms of a gas emit spectral lines the lines are bright. For example the lines emitted by a hot interstellar gas cloud are bright. When on the other hand light of all wavelengths without spectral lines is produced by a hot source—e.g. by the photosphere of a star, and when the light then passes through a comparatively cool cloud of gas, the cool gas often absorbs light at just the same characteristic wavelengths that it would emit if it were hot. In such a case the light that comes through the cool cloud is weakened at these characteristic wavelengths, which therefore appear as dark lines. The light from the Sun contains dark lines rather than bright lines, because the light from the photosphere passes through the slightly cooler material in the lower parts of the solar atmosphere. This is also the situation for most other stars. Dark lines are not of invariable occurrence, however. Very hot stars, stars very high on the main-sequence, emit bright lines. And some very cool stars also emit bright lines, as if particular patches on their otherwise cool surfaces become heated to comparatively high temperatures.

The relation of all this to the measurement of the red-shifts—the displacement of lines in the direction of decreasing wavelengths—is that because the great majority of stars show dark lines, the combined light of all the stars of a galaxy also shows dark lines. Several of the classic measurements by M. Humason are shown in Plate LVII, the lines employed being the H and K lines of calcium. In Plate LVII it is the somewhat hazy central band that represents the emission of the galaxy, wavelength increasing from left to right. The strong upper and lower lines were produced by terrestrial atoms. These were also photographed for comparison purposes.

The great discovery that galaxies far off are increasing their distances much more rapidly than the comparatively nearby galaxies is clearly shown by the examples given in Plate LVII. It may be noted that the distances marked in Plate LVII do not represent the original measurements of Hubble but have been modified to take account of more recent estimates to be discussed in the next chapter. The dependence of recessional velocities on the distances of the galaxies is shown in a more direct form in Fig. 64. The outstanding feature of this representation is the line that can be drawn through the observed results, showing that the expansion of the Universe takes place in a linear fashion—double the distance of a galaxy and the rate at which its distance is increasing also doubles. This result can be expressed in more precise form by saying that for every increase of a million parsecs in the distance the recessional speed increases by about 100 miles per second. A galaxy at 10 million parsecs has a recessional speed of about 1,000 miles per second; a galaxy at 100 million parsecs has a recessional speed of about 10,000 miles per second; a galaxy at 500 million parsecs has a recessional speed of about 50,000 miles per second.

The fastest rate of recession so far measured is close to 40,000 miles per second. Still more distant galaxies are so faint that it is difficult to measure their speeds because of a lack of light. There are good grounds, however, for the hope that by improved techniques it will eventually prove possible to extend the measurements to still more distant galaxies. If this becomes possible what will the result be? Almost I think without exception astronomers are prepared to predict that the rates of recession will continue to increase in accordance with the straight line of Fig. 64. This straight line is taken to represent a fundamental feature of the Universe. It has been generally accepted that the line can be extended indefinitely to distances as great as we please. Whether or not this extrapolation is really justified is something that needs urgent confirmation, but unfortunately a complete verification up to speeds comparable with that of light itself is probably beyond the power of observation. In conformity with general opinion we shall assume that the line of Fig. 64 can be extended indefinitely. Many of the arguments that will be used below would need serious alteration if this assumption should be found to be in error.

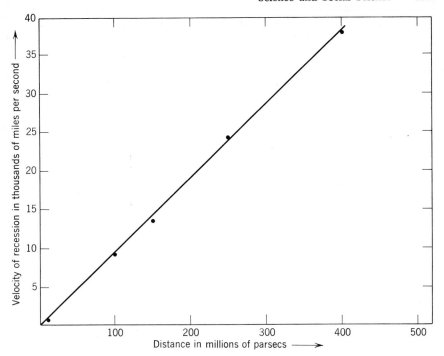

Fig. 64. The linear relation between distance and speed of recession (dots refer to actual observations).

The observed uniform expansion of the Universe out to distances of the order of 400 million parsecs occurs in all directions. Whatever the direction of observation the results are always the same. That apart from the galaxies of the Local Group the whole system of galaxies seems to be expanding away from us has suggested to many people that our Local Group must be at the centre of the Universe. But this idea is a logical *non sequitur*. Imagine a pudding containing raisins being steamed in an oven. Let the raisins represent the clusters of galaxies. Suppose that the raisins do not expand as the pudding cooks, but that the pudding itself swells steadily. Then in the swelling every raisin moves away from every other raisin: an observer attached to *any* raisin would see the others all receding away from him. Moreover, if the pudding were to swell uniformly (in such a way that its material remained of a uniform consistency) the raisins would have the linear property shown in Fig. 64—the greater the distance between two raisins the greater rate at which their distance apart increases—double the distance and the rate of increase also doubles.

Of course it can be said that pudding has a centre but we judge the centre of a pudding from the shape of its boundary. To give a parallel with the Universe we must imagine the pudding not possessing a boundary, but being an infinite pudding. The word 'infinite' should cause no conceptual difficulties. It simply means that however much of the pudding we consider there is always more of it.

OLBERS' PARADOX AGAIN

It is now necessary to relate all this back to Olbers' paradox. It will be recalled that Olbers' paradox arose from dividing space up by a series of spheres thereby forming a series of skins. It turned out that the contribution of the stars in a particular skin to the light received at the centre was always the same no matter what the radius of the skin happened to be. This property depended on the number of stars in a skin increasing with the radius of the skin in a way that just compensated for the weakening by increasing distance of the light received from each star. Now this cancellation no longer occurs when the clusters of galaxies are receding from each other. This is a most important and significant point. It turns out that expansion causes a further weakening of the light, an additional weakening that destroys the cancellation, and which completely resolves Olbers' paradox.

This further weakening of the light is very small for galaxies that are near to us, such as the galaxies of the Virgo cloud. But the effect becomes stronger as the distances increase. At the greatest distance to which redshift measurements have been made (the galaxies of the Hydra cluster at about 400 million parsecs) the weakening is to about ⅔ of the intensity that the light would have if no expansion were occurring. At the maximum distance of about 1,000 million parsecs to which the 200-inch telescope at Palomar Mt. can penetrate the light is weakened to about ⅓ of what it would be if no expansion were occurring. The situation becomes even more drastic at still greater distances (assuming the extrapolation of the line of Fig. 64). Indeed at a distance of about 2,000 million parsecs, where the rate of increase of the distance comes up to the speed of light itself, the light is weakened to nothing at all! No light emitted by the stars in a skin with a radius greater than about 2,000 million parsecs can ever reach us. There is an absolute cut-off at this distance. So our former argument that the number of contributing skins can be made as large as we please is no longer valid. Hence the amount of light received cannot be made extremely great and Olbers' paradox is resolved. Indeed the amount of light that we can receive can be worked out from the known distribution of galaxies. It turns out to be very small, much less than the sunlight scattered by the gases that lie within our own planetary system and which contributes to the glow of the night sky. The effect of the very distant galaxies on this glow is therefore very small. *The sky is dark at night because the Universe expands.* This is the unexpected resolution of the puzzle—so unexpected that it never occurred to the scientists of the nineteenth century. We started the present chapter by saying that every-day matter of fact observations are deeply related to the grand scale features of the Universe. Here we have an illustration of this statement.

At an earlier stage we considered the possibility of avoiding Olbers' paradox by assigning a definite origin in time to the Universe. Now that Olbers' paradox is resolved in a far subtler way it would be natural to discount entirely the idea of a singular origin were it not that the expansion of the Universe apparently gives support to it from an unexpected direction.

Expansion takes the clusters of galaxies apart from each other. Space is therefore (it seems) getting more and more empty as time goes on. Space must accordingly (it seems) have been more densely occupied in the past than it is today. Indeed if the Universe has always been expanding as it is at present, space must (it seems) have been jammed tight with matter not so very long ago.

Let us formulate the argument a little more precisely. Suppose we take the distance of a particular cluster of galaxies and divide by the rate at which its distance is increasing. Because of the linear property of Fig. 64 the result is essentially the same whatever cluster we elect to use for this purpose. The result is a period of time known as the Hubble constant—constant because it is the same for all clusters. Perhaps the best value consistent with all present-day knowledge is about 7,000 million years. The determination of this particular value will be discussed in the next chapter. Now let us imagine ourselves going backwards in time for 7,000 million years (not a fantastic piece of theorising; the Earth is some 4,000 million years old). Then if the clusters of galaxies have always had their present rates of recession the manner of derivation of Hubble's constant requires all the clusters of galaxies to have been jammed on top of each other at that time, giving a density of matter in space that rises inordinately high, indefinitely high, infinitely high. This state of affairs represents, according to the view of some astronomers, the singular start of the Universe. On this view such important features of the Universe as its expansion and its large scale uniformity of composition were impressed on the Universe at the start by the manner of creation. Creation could have occurred quite differently, matter might have been distributed lopsidedly without large scale uniformity, but it isn't because it wasn't created that way. Indeed the Universe might have been created in any of an infinity of other ways but it wasn't. It was created to have just the properties of expansion and of uniformity that we observe. If we ask why so, no answer can be given.

At the time of creation the density of material was very high, much higher than the density of water. As expansion proceeded the density became steadily less: it decreased to the density of water; then steadily down and down until it reached a millionth of the density of water; then steadily further down to a millionth millionth of the density of water; down and ever down to a million million millionth of the density of water; further down and still further down to a million million million millionth of the density of water; and so down to about a thousand million million million millionth of the density of water, when at long last something happened—the clusters of galaxies were formed, presumably as a result of some such process as was described in the previous chapter. Once the clusters of galaxies had condensed, the expansion continued by way of increasing the distances between the clusters, this being the stage of the proceedings that we now observe.

Let us see whether this argument is really an inescapable one. What are the alternative possibilities? One alternative is to deny that the Universe has always been expanding. This can be done in a consistent way by postulating that the real nature of gravitation differs from classical Newtonian ideas. Instead of requiring attraction always to occur between two particles as in the Newtonian theory it can be argued that attraction occurs only if the distance between two particles is not too great, otherwise attraction is replaced by repulsion. And if instead of considering just two particles we consider a whole cloud of matter the modified situation is that gravitation produces a condensation of the cloud only if its density is sufficiently high, otherwise a general repulsion and dispersal occur. The densities at which repulsive gravitation thus becomes operative are so low that there is no question of the ordinary attractive form of gravitation being appreciably modified in our solar system or in the Galaxy or in other galaxies.

Similar arguments can be applied to the Universe at large. If the average density in the Universe is less than a certain critical value (fixed by hypothesis) then the Universe will start to expand even if it is not expanding to begin with. If on the other hand the average density in the Universe is just equal to the critical value, the Universe remains static if it is initially static. But this state of balance is unstable—give the Universe a slight expansion and it continues to expand with ever increasing speed, give it a slight contraction and it contracts with ever increasing speed.

The object of thus altering the law of gravitation is to explain the observed expansion of the Universe without any need for an initially explosive state. On this view when we go back into the past the density of matter does not pile up indefinitely because the expansion was then slower than it is now; and sufficiently back in the past there was no expansion at all because the Universe started from the balanced state just described.

A special feature of this theory is that it provides a better way of forming galaxies. It can be shown that clusters of galaxies could condense in the balanced initial state. Although on the very large scale it must be supposed that some unknown cause disturbed the Universe in such a way as to set it off expanding instead of contracting, in local regions the reverse situation might have occurred—local regions might have started contracting instead of expanding, thereby forming clusters of galaxies. In the explosion theory the formation of clusters of galaxies has to be introduced as an *ad hoc* process that takes place for no good reason at just the stage where the density of matter falls to a thousand million million million millionth part of the density of water (or perhaps somewhat less than this). But in a theory with gravitation modified along the lines indicated above the origin of the clusters of galaxies is afforded a more natural explanation. A state of balance implies the possibility of the balance being tipped in localised regions towards contraction.

To end the present chapter a second flaw in the argument for a superdense singular explosive origin of the Universe will be discussed. Without any modification of gravitation of the sort contemplated above it is still incorrect to argue that expansion necessarily implies a superdense singular explosive origin of the Universe. This inference is not valid unless all the matter now in existence was also in existence in the past.

It is therefore important to examine the idea that many of the atoms now in existence were not in existence in the past, and that many of the atoms of the Universe that will be in existence in the future are not in existence today. This idea requires atoms to appear in the Universe continually instead of being created explosively at some definite time in the past. There is an important contrast here. An explosive creation of the Universe is not subject to analysis. It is something that must be impressed by way of an arbitrary fiat. In the case of a continuous origin of matter on the other hand the creation must obey a definite law, a law that has just the same sort of logical status as the laws of gravitation, of nuclear physics, of electricity and magnetism. This distinction is very important and is worth a rather more detailed exposition.

The laws of physics are expressed by mathematical equations. The symbols that appear in the equations are related either directly or indirectly to quantities that can be determined by observation. The logic of classical physics is very straightforward. If the observable quantities are known at one particular instant of time, the equations must enable us to determine their values at all other times. That is to say the laws of physics allow us to proceed from a known situation to a *prediction* of what is going to happen in the future. It is because of the ability to make correct predictions that physics has come to play such a dominant role in our modern civilisation. Past societies of men are referred to as the stone-age, the bronze-age, and the iron-age. The civilisation of the present day might perhaps most appropriately be termed the age of physics. In the past there has been no shortage of prophets and necromancers, but it is physics that has proved the first really reliable agent in human experience for the making of predictions.

Now what decides the laws of physics? What decides the form of the mathematical equations that refer to the phenomenon of gravitation for instance—the equations that determine how the planets move around the Sun? What decides the form of the mathematical equations that refer to the propagation of radio-waves? The answer to these questions is very simple—the success of the predictions that are made by the equations. The laws of physics are governed by a process of intellectual natural selection. When they make correct predictions they survive. When they make incorrect predictions they become extinct. Physicists then look for new laws that do not make incorrect predictions.

By now we are in a position to appreciate the difference between the two views on the origin of the material of the Universe. In the case of an explosive origin of the material, the origin is expressed by the starting conditions, not by the laws of physics themselves. In the case of a continuous origin there is no possibility of expressing the creation as a starting condition, since creation happens all the time. A continuous origin must therefore be expressed in terms of equations whose properties can be worked out by the processes of mathematics, and whose predictions can be confirmed or disproved. In one case the origin is assigned to an arbitrary fiat and no modification of the laws of physics is required. In the other case there is no arbitrary fiat but a modification of the laws of physics has to be made. The origin of matter thus becomes susceptible to treatment on a similar footing to the phenomena of gravitation, of electro-magnetism, and of the forces that bind the atomic nuclei together. We shall have more to say on the divergence between these two points of views in the last chapter. For the present it is sufficient to realise that a theory of the continuous origin of matter must face up to the challenging issue of determining a mathematical law that serves to control the creation of matter. Let it be said at once that no thoroughly satisfactory way of devising such a law has yet been found. All the attempts that have yet been made are clearly susceptible of improvement, and one can now be fairly sure of the direction that the improvements are likely to take. This again is an issue that we shall take up in the last chapter. For the present it is enough that imperfect as the equations no doubt are they are good enough to enable a number of very interesting results to be obtained.

The first is that the Universe must expand. The steady origin of matter forces the Universe to expand. The effect of the origin is to cause a stretching of space that takes the clusters of galaxies apart from each other. The stretching of space takes the part of the swelling of the pudding in the analogy we used above. The steady potentiality for new atoms to appear in space gives space active physical properties, it is no longer an inert something in which matter resides.

The origin of matter not only forces the Universe to expand but the rate of expansion is determined. If the Universe were expanding initially at some arbitrary rate, then the origin of matter causes the rate either to increase or to decrease according to the initial conditions until a definite value is reached, after which the rate is steadily maintained. The expansion rate so reached has the same value irrespective of the initial state of affairs, a value such that the average density of matter in space is maintained constant. The steady origin of matter in space does not therefore lead to space becoming fuller and fuller of material. Nor does the expansion of the Universe lead to space becoming more and more empty. The rate of expansion is forced to come into step so as to compensate exactly for the steady origin of material. It is the appearance of this remarkable balance as a *consequence* of the theory that gives one of the strongest reasons for regarding the continuous origin of matter as a serious possibility whose consequences demand just as careful consideration as those of the two other types of theory that were discussed above. It should be explained here that a somewhat different outlook on the whole problem of the continuous origin of matter has been put forward by Bondi and Gold. Bondi has described this in detail in a recent book *Cosmology*. The present development expresses my own outlook, which has been also influenced by the work of W. H. McCrea and by F. Pirani.

The maintenance of a constant average density of matter in space has led to the concept of the steady-state universe. Since the average density of matter in space is the same at all times, the present and the future should be just as good for the condensation of clusters of galaxies as the past was. So the theory suggests that clusters of galaxies should not only have formed in the past but should be forming at present and should go on forming in the future. This is in sharp distinction to the other two types of theory, which require all galaxies to have condensed about 6,000 million years ago. The steady-state theory suggests that although expansion leads to the distances between the centres of clusters of galaxies increasing, new clusters of galaxies condense at such a rate that the average number within a fairly large region of space remain effectively unaltered

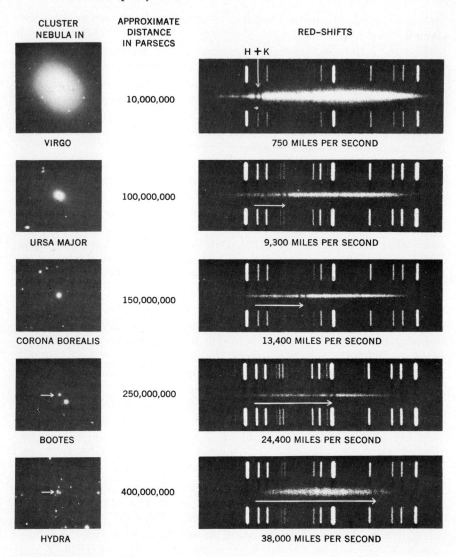

CLUSTER NEBULA IN	APPROXIMATE DISTANCE IN PARSECS	RED–SHIFTS
VIRGO	10,000,000	750 MILES PER SECOND
URSA MAJOR	100,000,000	9,300 MILES PER SECOND
CORONA BOREALIS	150,000,000	13,400 MILES PER SECOND
BOOTES	250,000,000	24,400 MILES PER SECOND
HYDRA	400,000,000	38,000 MILES PER SECOND

The red-shift effect. Observational evidence for the expansion of the Universe. One parsec equals 19,200,000,000,000 miles. (Photographs from the Mt. Wilson and Palomar Observatories.)

with time. In this way we arrive at a Universe in which the individuals—the clusters of galaxies—change and evolve with time but which itself does not change. The old queries about the beginning and end of the Universe are dealt with in a surprising manner—by saying that they are meaningless for the reason that the Universe did not have a beginning and it will not have an end. Every cluster of galaxies, every star, every atom had a beginning, but not the Universe itself. The Universe is something more than its parts, a perhaps unexpected conclusion.

ADVANCES IN SCIENCE have had interesting ramifications in the fields of literature and philosophy. One very direct effect has been the growth of a literature of science fiction, largely at the popular level. The disorientation of man, adrift in an awesome and incomprehensible universe, has been countered to a degree by a revival of interest in religion which has expressed itself in such forms as Catholic Neo-Thomism, Protestant Neo-Orthodoxy, and Christian existentialism. The next excerpt—from the novel Out of the Silent Planet *by C. S. Lewis (1898–1963)—is an interesting synthesis of contemporary Christian orthodoxy and science fiction of a rather high literary order. It is a story of a journey to Mars, known to its inhabitants as Malacandra. The central figure in the novel, the English philologist Ransom, was kidnapped by two English scientists, Weston and Devine, who carried him off to Mars in their private experimental rocket ship. They had planned to turn Ransom over to the Martian leader Oyarsa who, as they understood it, demanded a human hostage. But on Mars Ransom became separated from his two captors. He encountered various types of Martians, among whom were a race of innocent and agreeable creatures known as* hrossa. *Gradually he came to realize that all the inhabitants of Mars—or Malacandra—were in a state of innocence and that the leader Oyarsa was an angelic creature—a servant of God. He discovered that mankind alone, of all God's creatures, was in a fallen state and separated from communion with the deity. The earth was a citadel of greed, selfishness, and other forms of evil; it was the realm of the Devil—the "silent planet." Malacandra, and the rest of the universe, were unspoiled—were in a state of grace. In the excerpts given here, Ransom encounters his two former captors after a long separation and hardly recognizes them. Weston and Devine are now themselves captives of the Martian* hrossa *and are brought into the presence of Oyarsa. There follows a long discussion between Weston and Oyarsa in which C. S. Lewis engages in a ruthless satire of modern scientific humanism and suggests that man, in exploring the universe, would only defile it.*

2. C. S. LEWIS, FROM *OUT OF THE SILENT PLANET*

SOURCE. C. S. Lewis, *Out of the Silent Planet,* New York: Macmillan, 1943, pp. 135 and 144–152. Copyright 1943 by The Macmillan Company. Reprinted by permission of The Macmillan Company.

The light was behind them as they entered between the two farthest monoliths. They were much shorter than any animal he [Ransom] had yet seen on Malacandra, and he gathered that they were bipeds, though the lower limbs were so thick and sausage-like that he hesitated to call them legs. The bodies were a little narrower at the top than at the bottom so as to be very slightly pear-shaped, and the heads were neither round like those of *hrossa* nor long like those of *sorns,* but almost square. They stumped along on narrow, heavy-looking feet which they seemed to press into the ground with unnecessary violence. And now their faces were becoming visible as masses of lumped and puckered flesh of variegated colour fringed in some bristly, dark substance. . . . Suddenly, with an indescribable change of feeling, he realized that he was looking at men. The two prisoners were Weston and Devine and he, for one privileged moment, had seen the human form with almost Malacandrian eyes. . . .

The *hross* who headed this procession was a conscientious creature and began at once explaining itself in a rather troubled voice.

'I hope we have done right, Oyarsa,' it said. 'But we do not know. We dipped his head in the cold water seven times, but the seventh time something fell off it. We had thought it was the top of his head, but now we saw it was a covering made of the skin of some other creature. Then some said we had done your will with the seven dips, and others said not. In the end we dipped it seven times more. We hope that was right. The creature talked a lot between the dips, and most between the second seven, but we could not understand it.'

'You have done very well, Hnoo,' said Oyarsa. 'Stand away that I may see it, for now I will speak to it.'

The guards fell away on each side. Weston's usually pale face, under the bracing influence of the cold water, had assumed the colour of a ripe tomato, and his hair, which had naturally not been cut since he reached Malacandra, was plastered in straight, lank masses across his forehead. A good deal of water was still dripping over his nose and ears. His expression—unfortunately wasted on an audience ignorant of terrestrial physiognomy—was that of a brave man suffering in a great cause, and rather eager than reluctant to face the worst or even to provoke it. In explanation of his conduct it is only fair to remember that he had already that morning endured all the terrors of an expected martyrdom and all the anticlimax of fourteen compulsory cold douches. Devine, who knew his man, shouted out to Weston in English:

'Steady, Weston. These devils can split the atom or something pretty like it. Be careful what you say to them and and don't let's have any of your bloody nonsense.'

'Huh!' said Weston. 'So you've gone native too?'

'Be silent,' said the voice of Oyarsa. 'You, thick one, have told me nothing of yourself, so I will tell it to you. In your own world you have attained great wisdom concerning bodies and by this you have been able to make a ship that can cross the heaven; but in all other things you have the mind of an animal. When first you came here, I sent for you, meaning you nothing but honour. The darkness in your own mind filled you with fear. Because you thought I meant evil to you, you went as a beast goes against a beast of some other kind, and snared this Ransom. You would give him up to the evil you feared. To-day, seeing him here, to save your own life, you would have given him to me a second time, still thinking I meant him hurt. These are your dealings with your own kind. And what you intend to my people, I know. Already you have killed some. And you have come here to kill them all. To you it is nothing whether a creature is *hnau*[1] or not. At first I thought this was because you cared only whether a creature had a body like your own; but Ransom has that and you would kill him as lightly as any of my *hnau*. I did not know that the Bent One[2] had done so much in your world and still I do not understand it. If you were mine, I would unbody you even now. Do not think follies; by my hand Maleldil[3] does greater things than this, and I can unmake you even on the borders of your own world's air. But I do not yet resolve to do this. It is for you to speak. Let me see if there is anything in your mind besides fear and death and desire.'

Weston turned to Ransom. 'I see,' he said, 'that you have chosen the most momentous crisis in the history of the human race to betray it.' Then he turned in the direction of the voice.

'I know you kill us,' he said. 'Me not afraid. Others come, make it our world——'

But Devine had jumped to his feet, and interrupted him.

'No, no, Oyarsa,' he shouted. 'You no listen him. He very foolish man, he have dreams. We little people, only want pretty sun-bloods. You give us plenty sun-bloods, we go back into sky, you never see us no more. All done, see?'

'Silence,' said Oyarsa. There was an almost imperceptible change in the

[1] An intelligent creature possessed of a soul.

[2] The Evil One; the Devil.

[3] God.

light, if it could be called light, out of which the voice came, and Devine crumpled up and fell back on the ground. When he resumed his sitting position he was white and panting.

'Speak on,' said Oyarsa to Weston.

'Me no . . . no,' began Weston in Malacandrian and then broke off. 'I can't say what I want in their accursed language,' he said in English.

'Speak to Ransom and he shall turn it into our speech,' said Oyarsa.

Weston accepted the arrangement at once. He believed that the hour of his death was come and he was determined to utter the thing—almost the only thing outside his own science—which he had to say. He cleared his throat, almost he struck a gesture, and began:

'To you I may seem a vulgar robber, but I bear on my shoulders the destiny of the human race. Your tribal life with its stone-age weapons and bee-hive huts, its primitive coracles and elementary social structure, has nothing to compare with our civilization—with our science, medicine and law, our armies, our architecture, our commerce, and our transport system which is rapidly annihilating space and time. Our right to supersede you is the right of the higher over the lower. Life——'

'Half a moment,' said Ransom in English. 'That's about as much as I can manage at one go.' Then, turning to Oyarsa, he began translating as well as he could. The process was difficult and the result—which he felt to be rather unsatisfactory—was something like this:

'Among us, Oyarsa, there is a kind of *hnau* who will take other *hnau's* food and—and things, when they are not looking. He says he is not an ordinary one of that kind. He says what he does now will make very different things happen to those of our people who are not yet born. He says that, among you, *hnau* of one kindred all live together and the *hrossa* have spears like those we used a very long time ago and your huts are small and round and your boats small and light and like our old ones, and you have only one ruler. He says it is different with us. He says we know much. There is a thing happens in our world when the body of a living creature feels pains and becomes weak, and he says we sometimes know how to stop it. He says we have many bent people and we kill them or shut them in huts and that we have people for settling quarrels between the bent *hnau* about their huts and mates and things. He says we have many ways for the *hnau* of one land to kill those of another and some are trained to do it. He says we build very big and strong huts of stones and other things. . . . And he says we exchange many things among ourselves and can carry heavy weights very quickly a long way. Because of all this, he says it would not be the act of a bent *hnau* if our people killed all your people.'

As soon as Ransom had finished, Weston continued.

'Life is greater than any system of morality; her claims are absolute.

It is not by tribal taboos and copy-book maxims that she has pursued her relentless march from the amœba to man and from man to civilization.'

'He says,' began Ransom, 'that living creatures are stronger than the question whether an act is bent or good—no, that cannot be right—he says it is better to be alive and bent than to be dead—no—he says, he says—I cannot say what he says, Oyarsa, in your language. But he goes on to say that the only good thing is that there should be very many creatures alive. He says there were many other animals before the first men and the later ones were better than the earlier ones; but he says the animals were not born because of what is said to the young about bent and good action by their elders. And he says these animals did not feel any pity.'

'She——' began Weston.

'I'm sorry,' interrupted Ransom, 'but I've forgotten who She is.'

'Life, of course,' snapped Weston. 'She has ruthlessly broken down all obstacles and liquidated all failures and to-day in her highest form—civilized man—and in me as his representative, she presses forward to that interplanetary leap which will, perhaps, place her, for ever beyond the reach of death.'

'He says,' resumed Ransom, 'that these animals learned to do many difficult things, except those who could not; and those ones died and the other animals did not pity them. And he says the best animal now is the kind of man who makes the big huts and carries the heavy weights and does all the other things I told you about; and he is one of these and he says that if the others all knew what he was doing they would be pleased. He says that if he could kill you all and bring our people to live in Malacandra, then they might be able to go on living here after something had gone wrong with our world. And then if something went wrong with Malacandra they might go and kill all the *hnau* in another world. And then another—and so they would never die out.'

'It is in her right,' said Weston, 'the right, or, if you will, the might of Life herself, that I am prepared without flinching to plant the flag of man on the soil of Malacandra: to march on, step by step, superseding, where necessary, the lower forms of life that we find, claiming planet after planet, system after system, till our posterity—whatever strange form and yet unguessed mentality they have assumed—dwell in the universe wherever the universe is habitable.'

'He says,' translated Ransom, 'that because of this it would *not* be a bent action—or else, he says, it *would* be a possible action—for him to kill you all and bring us here. He says he would feel no pity. He is saying again that perhaps they would be able to keep moving from one world to another and wherever they came they would kill everyone. I think he is now talking about worlds that go round other suns. He wants the creatures born from us to be in as many places as they can. He says he does not know what kind of creatures they will be.'

'I may fall,' said Weston. 'But while I live I will not, with such a key in my hand, consent to close the gates of the future on my race. What lies in that future, beyond our present ken, passes imagination to conceive: it is enough for me that there is a Beyond.'

'He is saying,' Ransom translated, 'that he will not stop trying to do all this unless you kill him. And he says that though he doesn't know what will happen to the creatures sprung from us, he wants it to happen very much.'

Weston, who had now finished his statement, looked round instinctively for a chair to sink into. On Earth he usually sank into a chair as the applause began. Finding none—he was not the kind of man to sit on the ground like Devine—he folded his arm and stared with a certain dignity about him.

'It is well that I have heard you,' said Oyarsa. 'For though your mind is feebler, your will is less bent than I thought. It is not for yourself that you would do all this.'

'No,' said Weston proudly in Malacandrian. 'Me die. Man live.'

'Yet you know that these creatures would have to be made quite unlike you before they lived on other worlds.'

'Yes, yes. All new. No one know yet. Strange! Big!'

'Then it is not the shape of body that you love?'

'No. Me no care how they shaped.'

'One would think, then, that it is for the mind you care. But that cannot be, or you would love *hnau* wherever you met it.'

'No care for *hnau*. Care for man.'

'But if it is neither man's mind, which is as the mind of all other *hnau*— is not Maleldil maker of them all?—nor his body, which will change—if you care for neither of these, what do you mean by man?'

This had to be translated to Weston. When he understood it, he replied:

'Me care for man—care for our race—what man begets—' He had to ask Ransom the words for *race* and *beget*.

'Strange!' said Oyarsa. 'You do not love any one of your race—you would have let me kill Ransom. You do not love the mind of your race, nor the body. Any kind of creature will please you if only it is begotten by your kind as they now are. It seems to me, Thick One, that what you really love is no completed creature but the very seed itself: for that is all that is left.'

'Tell him,' said Weston when he had been made to understand this, 'that I don't pretend to be a metaphysician. I have not come here to chop logic. If he cannot understand—as apparently you can't either—anything so fundamental as a man's loyalty to humanity, I can't make him understand it.'

But Ransom was unable to translate this and the voice of Oyarsa continued:

'I see now how the lord of the silent world has bent you. There are laws that all *hnau* know, of pity and straight dealing and shame and the like, and one of these is the love of kindred. He has taught you to break all of them except this one, which is not one of the greatest laws; this one he has bent till it becomes folly and has set it up, thus bent, to be a little, blind Oyarsa in your brain. And now you can do nothing but obey it, though if we ask you why it is a law you can give no other reason for it than for all the other and greater laws which it drives you to disobey. Do you know why he has done this?'

'Me think no such person—me wise, new man—no believe all that old talk.'

'I will tell you. He has left you this one because a bent *hnau* can do more evil than a broken one. He has only bent you; but this Thin One who sits on the ground he has broken, for he has left him nothing but greed. He is now only a talking animal and in my world he could do no more evil than an animal. If he were mine I would unmake his body for the *hnau* in it is already dead. But if you were mine I would try to cure you. Tell me, Thick One, why did you come here?'

'Me tell you. Make man live all the time.'

'But are your wise men so ignorant as not to know that Malacandra is older than your own world and nearer its death? Most of it is dead already. My people live only in the *handramits*,[4] the heat and the water have been more and will be less. Soon now, very soon, I will end my world and give back my people to Maleldil.'

'Me know all that plenty. This only first try. Soon they go on another world.'

'But do you not know that all worlds will die?'

'Men go jump off each before it deads—on and on, see?'

'And when all are dead?'

Weston was silent. After a time Oyarsa spoke again.

'Do you not ask why my people, whose world is old, have not rather come to yours and taken it long ago?'

'Ho! Ho!' said Weston. 'You not know how.'

'You are wrong,' said Oyarsa. 'Many thousands of thousand years before this, when nothing yet lived on your world, the cold death was com-

[4] Deep valleys.

ing on my *harandra*.[5] Then I was in deep trouble, not chiefly for the death of my *hnau*—Maleldil does not make them long-livers—but for the things which the lord of your world, who was not yet bound, put into their minds. He would have made them as your people are now—wise enough to see the death of their kind approaching but not wise enough to endure it. Bent counsels would soon have risen among them. They were well able to have made sky-ships. By me Maleldil stopped them. Some I cured, some I unbodied——'

'And see what come!' interrupted Weston. 'You now very few—shut up in *handramits*—soon all die.'

'Yes,' said Oyarsa, 'but one thing we left behind us on the *harandra*: fear. And with fear, murder and rebellion. The weakest of my people does not fear death. It is the Bent One, the lord of your world, who wastes your lives and befouls them with flying from what you know will overtake you in the end. If you were subjects of Maleldil you would have peace.'

Weston writhed in the exasperation born of his desire to speak and his ignorance of the language.

'Trash! Defeatist trash!' he shouted at Oyarsa in English; then drawing himself up to his full height, he added in Malacandrian, 'You say your Maleldil let all go dead. Other one, Bent One, he fight, jump, live—not all talkee-talkee. Me no care Maleldil. Like Bent One better: me on his side.'

'But do you not see that he never will nor can,' began Oyarsa, and then broke off, as if recollecting himself. 'But I must learn more of your world from Ransom, and for that I need till night. I will not kill you, not even the Thin One, for you are out of my world. To-morrow you shall go hence again in your ship.'

[5] High plains.

Part II

ART

A. Painting

IN THE LATER NINETEENTH CENTURY, painters recoiled increasingly from photographic representationalism, rejected the notion of a painting as a window to the natural world, and concentrated increasingly on the aspects of design and color in the painting itself. These trends continued to develop during the twentieth century. For the sake of formal structure and the communication of the artists' personal perceptions and emotions, painters moved farther and farther from objective realism and engaged in increasingly bold distortions of their subjects. In the cubist style of Pablo Picasso and others, illustrated in highly developed form by Picasso's Three Musicians *(1921), the human form becomes merely a point of departure for the artist's fantastic imagination and boundless inventiveness (1). This characteristic is further developed in works such as Joan Miró's* Dutch Interior. *(2). The impression that these works convey is at once comic, grotesque, and tragic.*

621

1. PABLO PICASSO, *THREE MUSICIANS*, 1921

2. JOAN MIRO, *DUTCH INTERIOR*, 1928

THE QUALITY OF TRAGEDY takes priority in the works of the more con-servative Catholic artist Georges Rouault (1871–1958), whose early work in stained glass carries over in the heavy, dark outlines which he used in his paint-ings. His fundamental theme is that of passion—human and divine—and his paintings, whether of scriptural subjects or of prostitutes and clowns, are in-fused with his vision of the tragic corruption of humanity and the possibility of redemption through Christ. His Christ Mocked by the Soldiers *(1932), like so much of his own art and that of his contemporaries, is a powerful and deeply personal statement (1). In surrealist works such as René Magritte's* Castle of the Pyrenees *(1955), the imaginative reorganization of the natural order, evident in Picasso's* Three Musicians *and Miró's* Dutch Interior, *is brought to the point of pure fantasy (2).*

3. GEORGES ROUAULT, *CHRIST MOCKED BY THE SOLDIERS*, 1932

4. RENÉ MAGRITTE, *CASTLE OF THE PYRENEES*, 1955

THE ABSTRACT EXPRESSIONIST STYLE carried the trend toward sub-jectivity beyond the reordering of nature to the point of a total break with the outside world. The style is exemplified by the painting entitled Number One *(1948) by Jackson Pollock (1912–56). To the question, "What is it?" the abstract expressionist would answer, "It is a painting." The answer reflects the basic artistic trend of the past century.*

5. JACKSON POLLOCK, *NUMBER ONE,* 1948

ABSTRACT EXPRESSIONISM acquired great vogue in the middle decades of the twentieth century, but many painters continued to produce representa-tional paintings and retained the artist's traditional relationship with the out-side world. In the late 1950's several artists turned to an irreverent and witty new style known as pop art which emphasized imaginative presentations of the inanely ordinary. The face of an old bureau drawer might be mounted on a canvas, an American flag might be set in a frame, the artist might paint his own version of a commercial sign or highway marker.

6. POP ART: MARISOL, *THE FAMILY*, 1962

B. Sculpture

TWO EXAMPLES of twentieth-century sculpture are given here. Both reflect a tendency toward primitivism and the subordination of objective accuracy to inner meaning. Henry Moore's King and Queen *(1952–1953) are huge, faceless figures which give the impression of having been eroded by sea or wind (1). Jacques Lipchitz'* Figure *(1926–1930) possesses the Picasso-like quality of a wildly inventive reordering of the human form (2).*

1. HENRY MOORE, *KING AND QUEEN*, 1952–1953

2. JACQUES LIPCHITZ, *FIGURE*, 1926–1930

C. Architecture

PERHAPS THE LEADING EXPONENT of the severe International Style in modern architecture is Ludwig Mies van der Rohe (b. 1888). His Lake Shore Drive Apartment Houses, Chicago, 1950–1952, are characteristic masterpieces of the style that has dominated mid-twentieth-century architecture (1). As the Lake Shore Apartments were being constructed, a radically new architectural style was finding expression in Le Corbusier's church of Notre-Dame-du-Haut, erected in Ronchamp, France, between 1950 and 1955. Le Corbusier rejected the geometric purism of the International Style in favor of a flowing, organic quality akin to that of contemporary sculpture. His Notre-Dame-du-Haut is a significant landmark in the development of modern architecture—a structure which is serving as the inspiration for many of the more advanced architects of today (2). The work of the American architect, Edward Durell Stone is representative of a somewhat different kind of departure from the International Style. Stone has pioneered in a new trend away from the austerity of Mies van der Rohe and his followers toward a reassertion of decorative values and a search for beauty through tasteful ornamentation. His prize-winning United States Embassy at New Delhi (completed in 1959) is a graceful, placid, harmoniously balanced structure faced with a decorative screen, its outlines clearly defined by a cornice, its entrance strongly emphasized, its interior merging into an inner court. Stone was remarkably successful in adapting his own techniques and values to the traditional architectural style of India and thereby creating a work of art that is perfectly appropriate to its setting (3).

1. LUDWIG MIES VAN DER ROHE, LAKE SHORE DRIVE APARTMENT HOUSES, CHICAGO, 1950–1952

2. LE CORBUSIER, NOTRE-DAME-DU-HAUT,
   RONCHAMP, FRANCE, 1950–1955

3. EDWARD DURELL STONE, UNITED STATES EMBASSY,
   NEW DELHI, INDIA

Part III

THE HUMAN PREDICAMENT

A. Existentialism

JEAN PAUL SARTRE (born 1905) is perhaps the most widely known of the twentieth-century existentialists. In "Freedom and Responsibility," from his book Being and Nothingness, *Sartre presents some of his most important ethical ideas. Man is responsible for the world and for himself, Sartre argues, and man's responsibility is a necessary consequence of his freedom.*

1. JEAN PAUL SARTRE, "FREEDOM AND RESPONSIBILITY," FROM *BEING AND NOTHINGNESS*

SOURCE. Jean Paul Sartre, *Being and Nothingness,* Hazel E. Barnes, tr., reprinted in *Existentialism and Human Emotion,* New York: Philosophical Library, 1957, pp. 52–59. Copyright 1957 by Philosophical Library Co., Inc. Reprinted by permission of the Philosophical Library Co., Inc.

Although the considerations which are about to follow are of interest primarily to the ethicist, it may nevertheless be worthwhile after these descriptions and arguments to return to the freedom of the for-itself and to try to understand what the fact of this freedom represents for human destiny.

The essential consequence of our earlier remarks is that man being condemned to be free carries the weight of the whole world on his shoulders; he is responsible for the world and for himself as a way of being. We are taking the world "responsibility" in its ordinary sense as "consciousness (of) being the incontestable author of an event or of an object." In this sense the responsibility of the for-itself is overwhelming since he is the one by whom it happens that *there is* a world; since he is also the one who makes himself be, then whatever may be the situation in which he finds himself, the for-itself must wholly assume this situation with its peculiar coefficient of adversity, even though it be insupportable. He must assume the situation with the proud consciousness of being the author of it, for the very worst disadvantages or the worst threats which can endanger my person have meaning only in and through my project; and it is on the ground of the engagement which I am that they appear. It is therefore senseless to think of complaining since nothing foreign has decided what we feel, what we live, or what we are.

Furthermore this absolute responsibility is not resignation; it is simply the logical requirement of the consequences of our freedom. What happens to me happens through me, and I can neither affect myself with it nor revolt against it nor resign myself to it. Moreover everything which happens to me is *mine*. By this we must understand first of all that I am always equal to what happens to me *qua* man, for what happens to a man through other men and through himself can be only human. The most terrible situations of war, the worst tortures do not create a non-human state of things; there is no non-human situation. It is only through fear, flight, and recourse to magical types of conduct that I shall decide on the non-human, but this decision is human, and I shall carry the entire responsibility for it. But in addition the situation is *mine* because it is the image of my free choice of myself, and everything which it presents to me is *mine* in that this represents me and symbolizes me. Is it not I who decide the coefficient of adversity in things and even their unpredictability by deciding myself?

Thus there are no *accidents* in a life; a community event which suddenly bursts forth and involves me in it does not come from the outside. If I am mobilized in a war, this war is *my* war; it is in my image and I deserve it. I deserve it first because I could always get out of it by suicide or by desertion; these ultimate possibilities are those which must always be present for us when there is a question of envisaging a situation. For lack of getting out of it, I have *chosen* it. This can be due to inertia, to cowardice in the face of public opinion, or because I prefer certain other values to the value of the refusal to join in the war (the good opinion of my relatives, the honor of my family, *etc.*). Anyway you look at it, it is a matter of a choice. This choice will be repeated later on again and again without a break until the end of the war. Therefore we must agree with the statement by J. Romains, "In war there are no innocent victims." If therefore I have preferred war to death or to dishonor, everything takes place as if I bore the entire responsibility for this war. Of course others have declared it, and one might be tempted perhaps to consider me as a simple accomplice. But this notion of complicity has only a juridical sense, and it does not hold here. For it depended on me that for me and by me this war should not exist, and I have decided that it does exist. There was no compulsion here, for the compulsion could have got no hold on a freedom. I did not have any excuse; for as we have said repeatedly in this book, the peculiar character of human-reality is that it is without excuse. Therefore it remains for me only to lay claim to this war.

But in addition the war is *mine* because by the sole fact that it arises in a situation which I cause to be and that I can discover it there only by engaging myself for or against it, I can no longer distinguish at present the choice which I make of myself from the choice which I make of the war. To live this war is to choose myself through it and to choose it through my choice of myself. There can be no question of considering it as "four years of vacation" or as a "reprieve," as a "recess," the essential part of my responsibilities being elsewhere in my married, family, or professional life. In this war which I have chosen I choose myself from day to day, and I make it mine by making myself. If it is going to be four empty years, then it is I who bear the responsibility for this.

Finally, as we pointed out earlier, each person is an absolute choice of self from the standpoint of a world of knowledges and of techniques which this choice both assumes and illumines; each person is an absolute upsurge at an absolute date and is perfectly unthinkable at another date. It is therefore a waste of time to ask what I should have been if this war had not broken out, for I have chosen myself as one of the possible meanings of the epoch which imperceptibly led to war. I am not distinct from this same epoch; I could not be transported to another epoch without contradiction. Thus *I am* this war which restricts and limits and makes comprehensible the period which preceded it. In this sense we may define more precisely the responsibility of the for-itself if to the earlier quoted statement, "There are no innocent victims," we add the words, "We have the war we deserve." Thus, totally free, undistinguishable from the period for which I have chosen to be the meaning, as profoundly responsible for the war as if I had myself declared it, unable to live without integrating it in *my* situation, engaging myself in it wholly and stamping it with my seal, I must be without remorse or regrets as I am without excuse; for from the instant of my upsurge into being, I carry the weight of the world by myself alone without anything or any person being able to lighten it.

Yet this responsibility is of a very particular type. Someone will say, "I did not ask to be born." This is a naive way of throwing greater emphasis on our facticity. I am responsible for everything, in fact, except for my very responsibility, for I am not the foundation of my being. Therefore everything takes place as if I were compelled to be responsible. I am *abandoned* in the world, not in the sense that I might remain abandoned and passive in a hostile universe like a board floating on the water, but rather in the sense that I find myself suddenly alone and without help, engaged in a world for which I bear the whole responsibility without being able, whatever I do, to tear myself away from this responsibility for an instant. For I am responsible for my very desire of fleeing responsibilities. To make myself passive in the world, to refuse to act upon things and upon Others is still to choose myself, and suicide is one mode among others of being-in-the-world. Yet I find an absolute responsibility for the fact that my facticity (here the fact of my birth) is directly inapprehensible and even inconceivable, for this fact of my birth never appears as a brute fact but always across a projective reconstruction of my for-itself. I am ashamed of being born or I am astonished at it or I rejoice over it, or in attempting to get rid of my life I affirm that I live and I assume this life as bad. Thus in a certain sense I *choose* being born. This choice itself is integrally affected with facticity since I am not able not to choose, but this facticity in turn will appear only in so far as I surpass it toward my ends. Thus facticity is everywhere but inapprehensible; I never encounter anything except my responsibility. That is why I can not ask, "*Why* was I born?" or curse the day of my birth or declare that I did not ask to be born, for these various attitudes toward my birth—*i.e.*, toward the *fact* that I realize a presence in the world—are absolutely nothing else but ways of assuming this birth in full responsibility and of making it *mine*. Here again I encounter only myself and my projects so that finally my abandonment—*i.e.*, my facticity—consists simply in the fact that I am condemned to be wholly responsible for myself. I am the being which *is* in such a way that in its being its being is in question. And this "is" of my being *is* as present and inapprehensible.

Under these conditions since every event in the world can be revealed to me only as an *opportunity* (an opportunity made use of, lacked, neglected, *etc.*), or better yet since everything which happens to us can be considered as a *chance* (*i.e.*, can appear to us only as a way of realizing this being which is in question in our being) and since others as transcendences-transcended are themselves only *opportunities* and *chances*, the responsibility of the for-itself extends to the entire world as a peopled-world. It is precisely thus that the for-itself apprehends itself in anguish; that is, as a being which is neither the foundation of its own being nor of the Other's being nor of the in-itselfs which form the world, but a being which is compelled to decide the meaning of being—within it and everywhere outside of it. The one who realizes in anguish his condition as *being* thrown into a responsibility which extends to his very abandonment has no longer either remorse or regret or excuse; he is no longer anything but a freedom which perfectly reveals itself and whose being resides in this very revelation. But as we pointed out at the beginning of this work, most of the time we flee anguish in bad faith.

B. Love of Man and Praise of God

MANY PEOPLE REGARD Dylan Thomas (1914–1953) as the most exciting poet of the century. Thomas described himself in these words: "One: I am a Welshman; two: I am a drunkard; three: I am a lover of the human race, especially of women." All these things were true. But Dylan Thomas was also an intensely sensitive and self-aware individual, a consummate artist of the English language whose poems, although sometimes superficially obscure, are tightly packed with ideas and images. Like C. S. Lewis, Dylan Thomas was obsessed by the notion of man's fall from grace, and he was fond of evoking the innocence of childhood. The boundless imagination and remarkable descriptive powers of this inventive poet find full expression in his "Poem in October." Dylan Thomas' description of his own works captures an important element in the spirit of twentieth-century man: "These poems, with all their crudities, doubts, and confusions, are written for the love of Man and in praise of God, and I'd be a damn' fool if they weren't."

1. DYLAN THOMAS, "POEM IN OCTOBER"

SOURCE. Dylan Thomas, *Collected Poems*, Norwalk, Conn.: New Directions, 1957, pp. 113–115. Copyright 1953 by Dylan Thomas. Copyright 1957 by New Directions. Reprinted by permission of the publisher, New Directions Publishing Corp.

It was my thirtieth year to heaven
Woke to my hearing from harbour and neighbour wood
    And the mussel pooled and the heron
            Priested shore
        The morning beckon
With water praying and call of seagull and rook
And the knock of sailing boats on the net webbed wall
        Myself to set foot
            That second
In the still sleeping town and set forth.

My birthday began with the water-
Birds and the birds of the winged trees flying my name
    Above the farms and the white horses
            And I rose
        In rainy autumn
And walked abroad in a shower of all my days.

High tide and the heron dived when I took the road
        Over the border
          And the gates
Of the town closed as the town awoke.

     A springful of larks in a rolling
Cloud and the roadside bushes brimming with whistling
      Blackbirds and the sun of October
           Summery
       On the hill's shoulder,
Here were fond climates and sweet singers suddenly
Come in the morning where I wandered and listened
        To the rain wringing
          Wind blow cold
In the wood faraway under me.

     Pale rain over the dwindling harbour
And over the sea wet church the size of a snail
      With its horns through mist and the castle
          Brown as owls
       But all the gardens
Of spring and summer were blooming in the tall tales
Beyond the border and under the lark full cloud.
       There could I marvel
         My birthday
Away but the weather turned around.

     It turned away from the blithe country
And down the other air and the blue altered sky
      Streamed again a wonder of summer
         With apples
      Pears and red currants
And I saw in the turning so clearly a child's
Forgotten mornings when he walked with his mother
       Through the parables
        Of sun light
And the legends of the green chapels

     And the twice told fields of infancy
That his tears burned my cheeks and his heart moved in mine.
      These were the woods the river and sea
         Where a boy
       In the listening
Summertime of the dead whispered the truth of his joy

To the trees and the stones and the fish in the tide.
> And the mystery
> > Sang alive
> Still in the water and singingbirds.

> And there could I marvel my birthday
Away but the weather turned around. And the true
> Joy of the long dead child sang burning
> > In the sun.
> > It was my thirtieth
Year to heaven stood there then in the summer noon
Though the town below lay leaved with October blood.
> > O may my heart's truth
> > > Still be sung
> On this high hill in a year's turning.